# MY HERO ACADEMIA
## Ultra Analysis

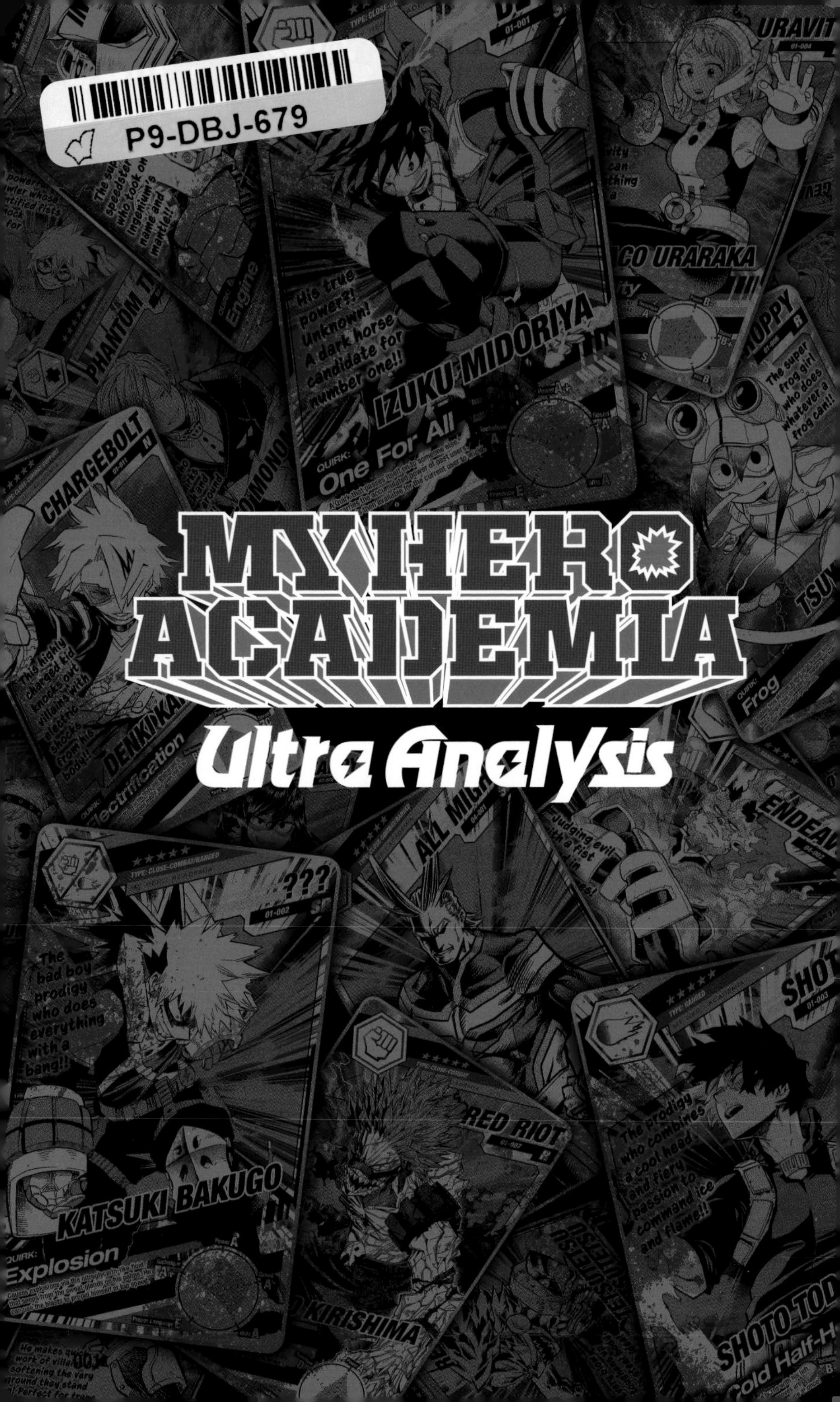

IZUKU MIDORIYA
His true powers?! Unknown! A dark horse candidate for number one!!
QUIRK: One For All
CHARGEBOLT
This highly charged kid knocks out villains with electric shocks from his body!!
DENKI KAMINARI
QUIRK: Electrification
The frog girl who does whatever a frog can!!
QUIRK: Frog
CO URARAKA
KATSUKI BAKUGO
The bad boy prodigy who does everything with a bang!!
QUIRK: Explosion
RED RIOT
KIRISHIMA
The prodigy who combines a cool head and fiery passion to command ice and flame!!
SHOTO TOD
Cold Half-H
ALL MIGHT
Judging evil with a fist
PHANTOM TH

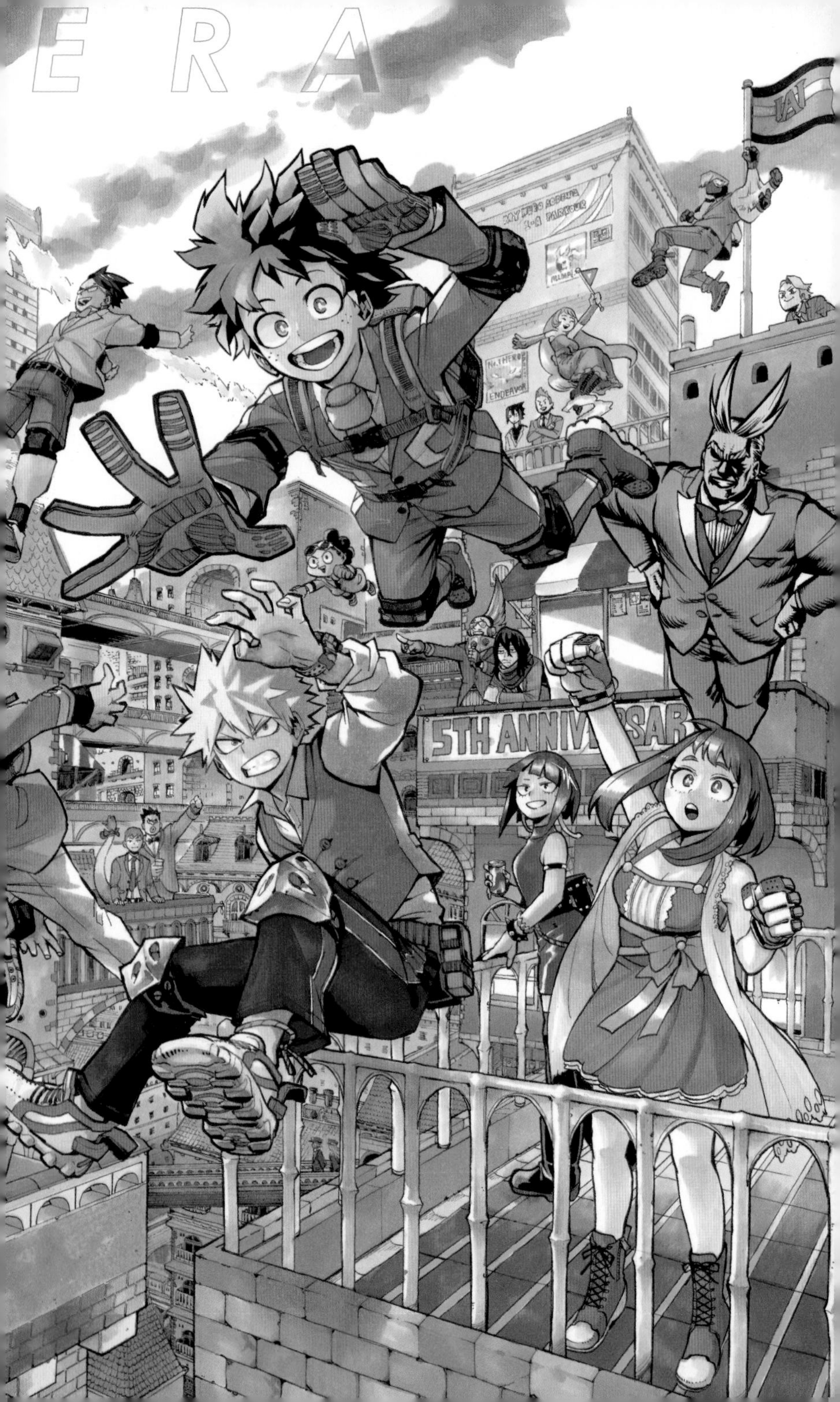
ERA
1-A PARKOUR
ENDEAVOR
5TH ANNIVERSAR

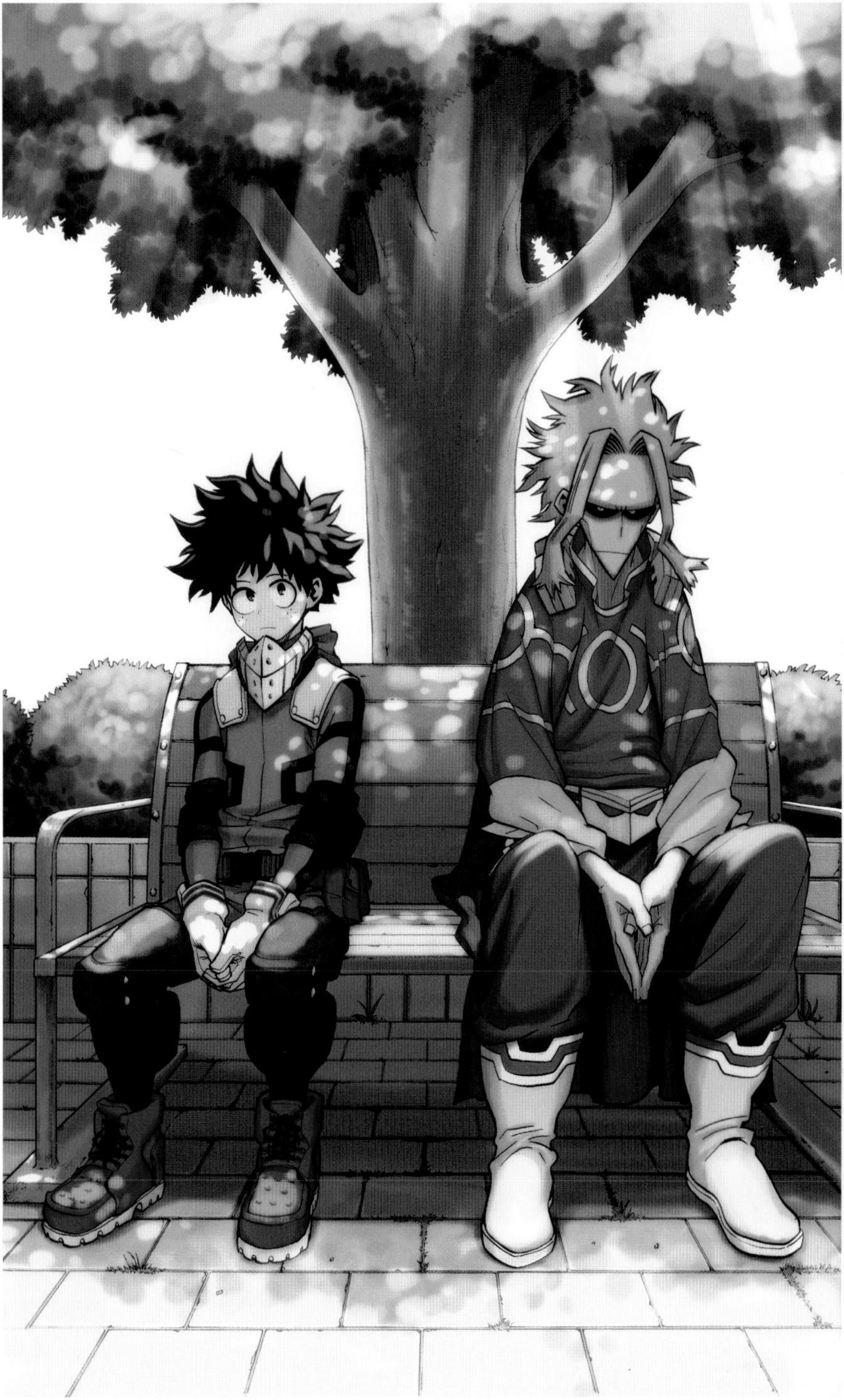

*Weekly Shonen Jump*, 2016, Issue 30, Title Page

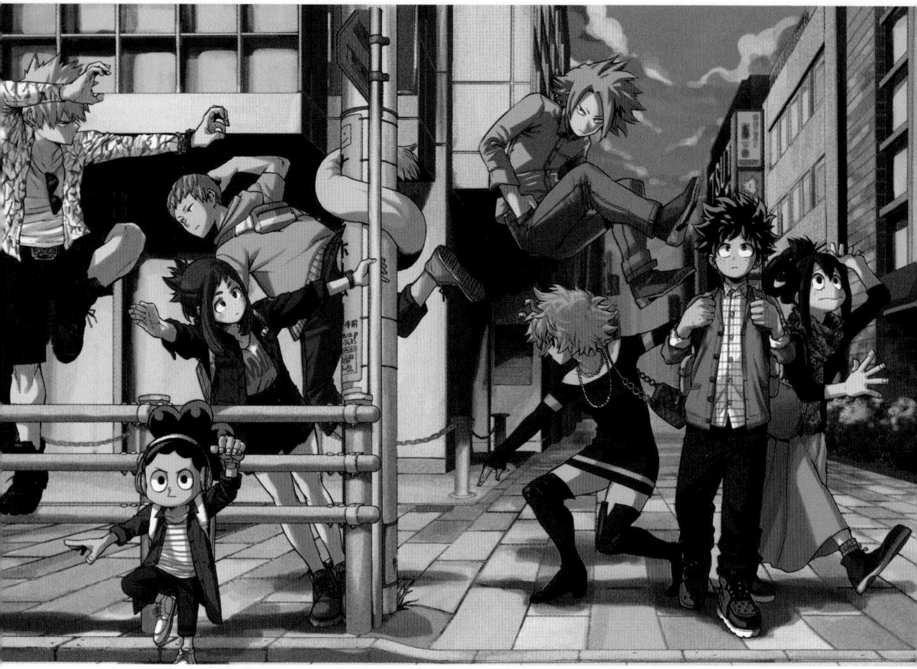

*Weekly Shonen Jump*, 2016, Issue 25, Title Spread

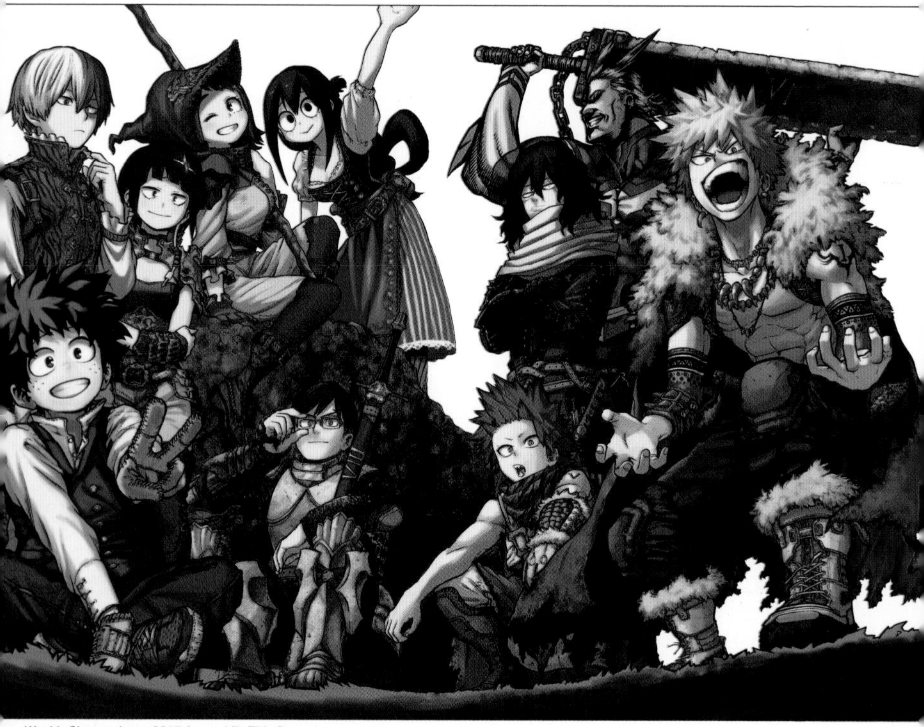

*Weekly Shonen Jump*, 2017, Issue 4/5, Title Spread

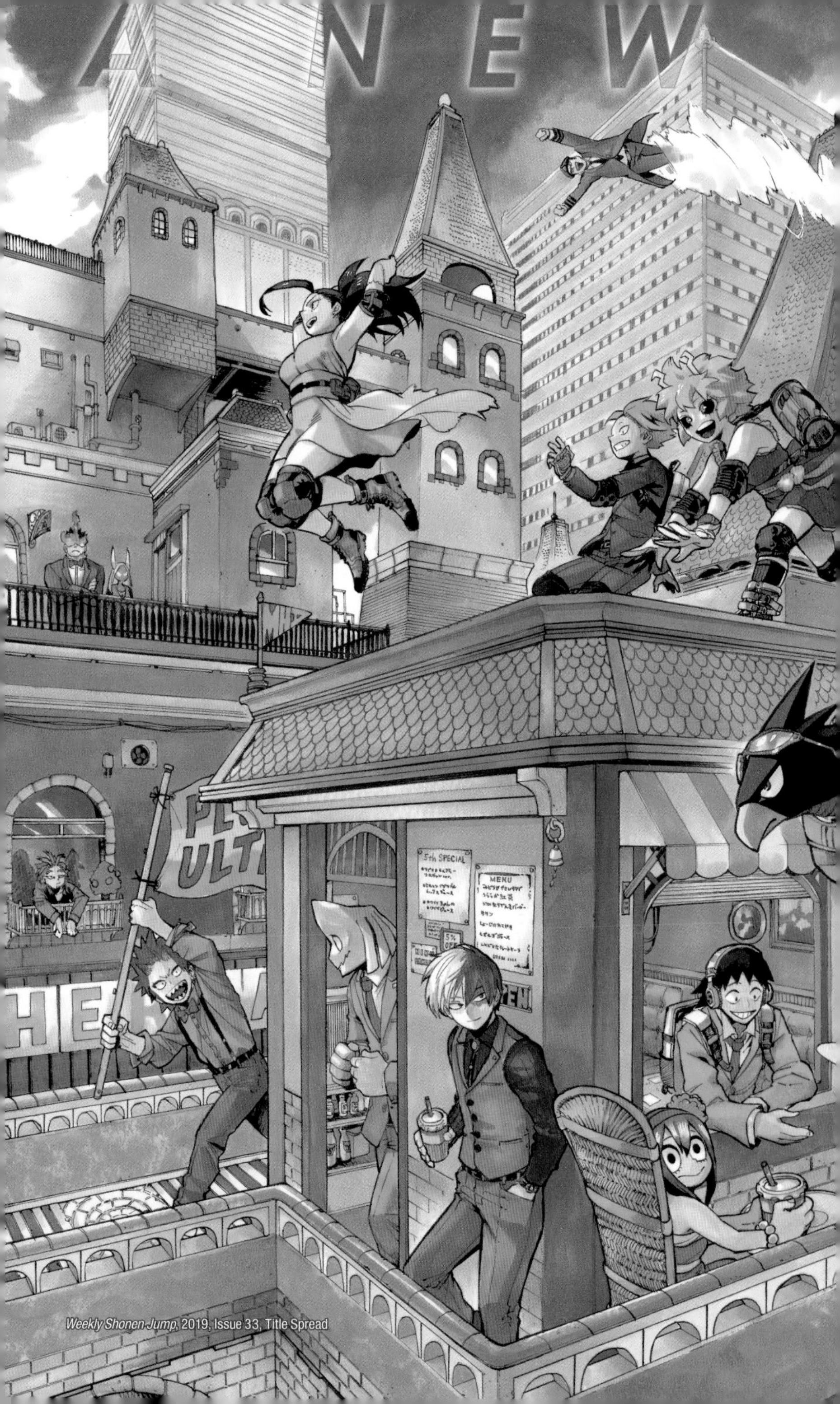
A NEW

*Weekly Shonen Jump*, 2019, Issue 33, Title Spread

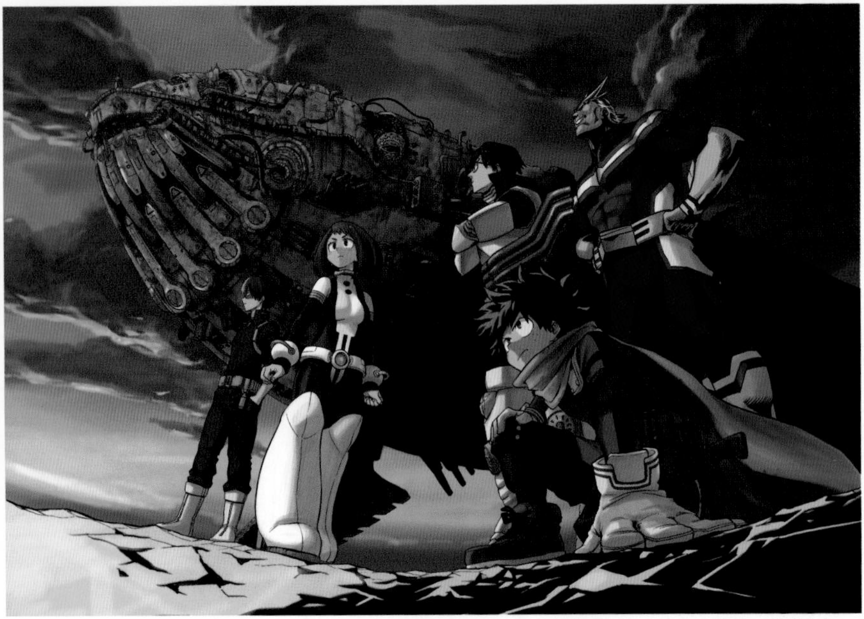

*Weekly Shonen Jump*, 2016, Issue 17, Title Spread

BONDS OF JUSTICE

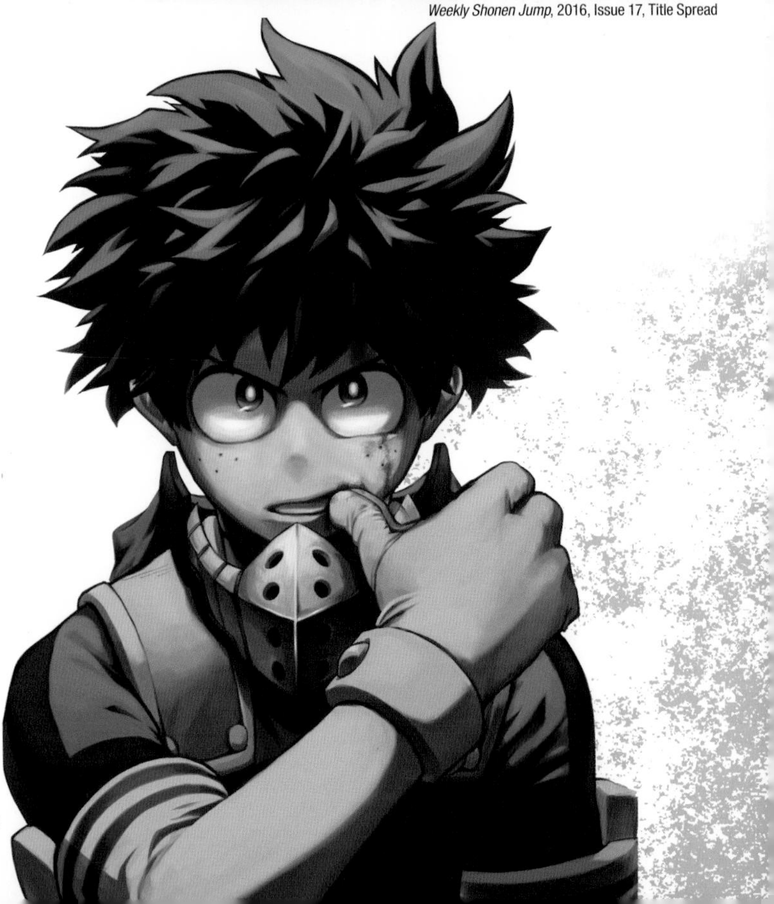

*GIGA*, 2016, Volume 3

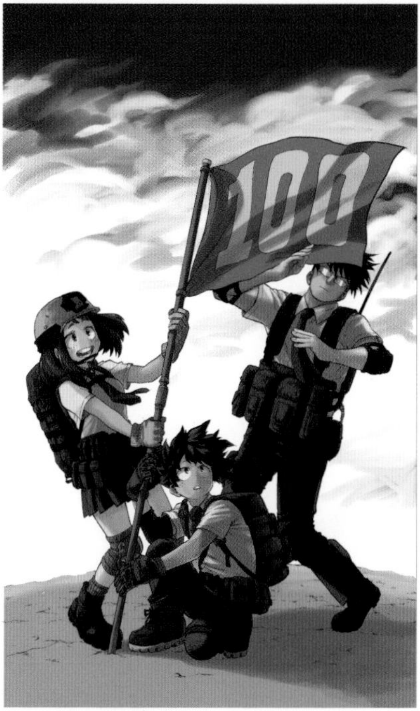
100

Weekly Shonen Jump, 2016
Issue 34, Title Page

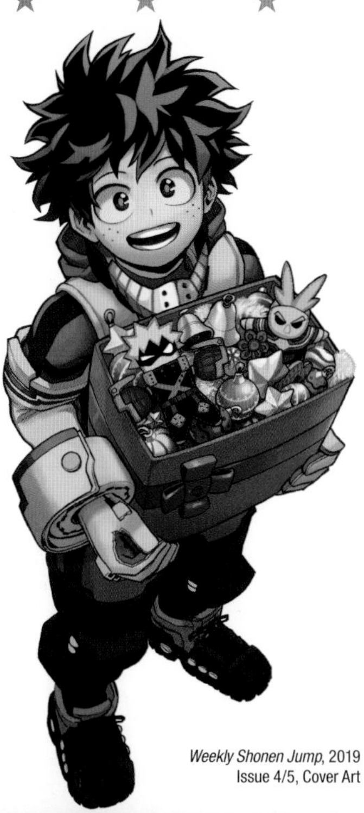

*Weekly Shonen Jump*, 2019
Issue 4/5, Cover Art

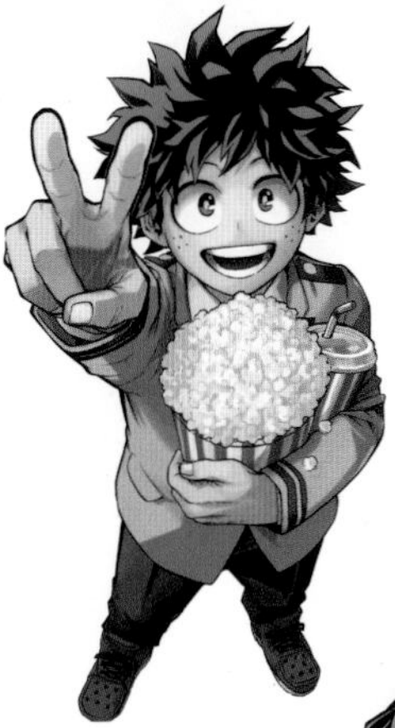

*Weekly Shonen Jump*, 2018
Issue 35, Cover Art

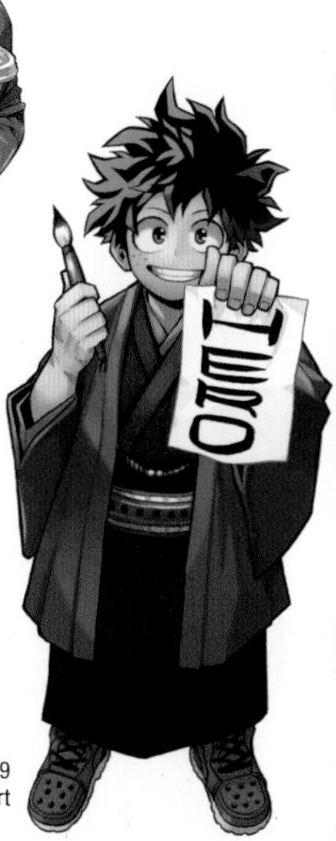
HERO

*Weekly Shonen Jump*, 2019
Issue 6/7, Cover Art

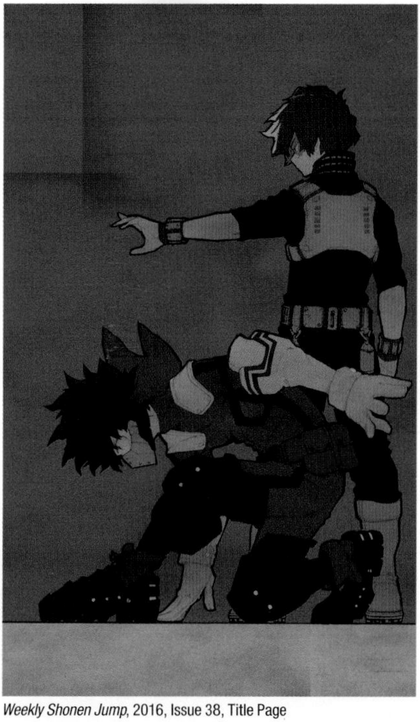

*Weekly Shonen Jump*, 2016, Issue 38, Title Page

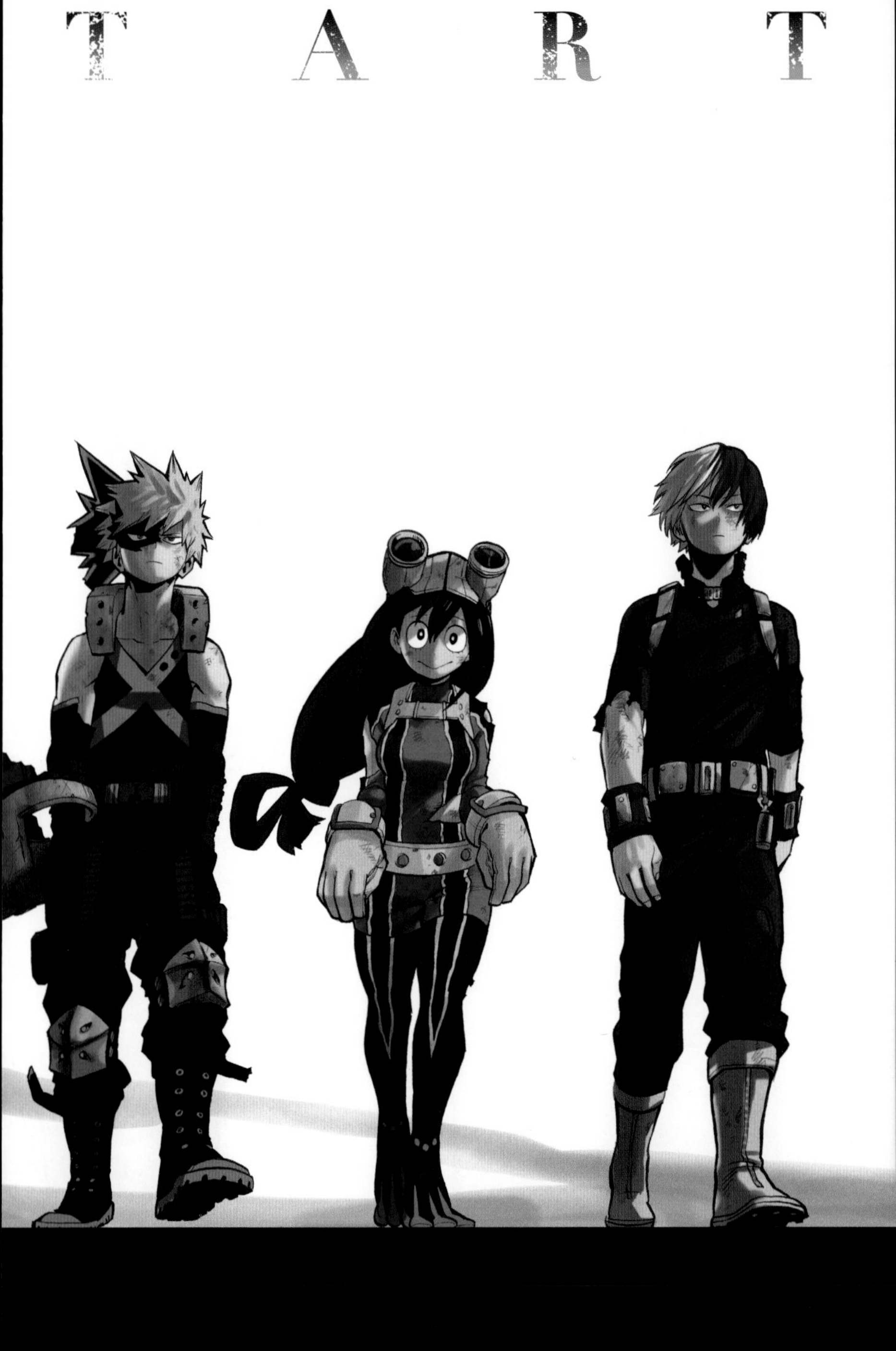
T A R T

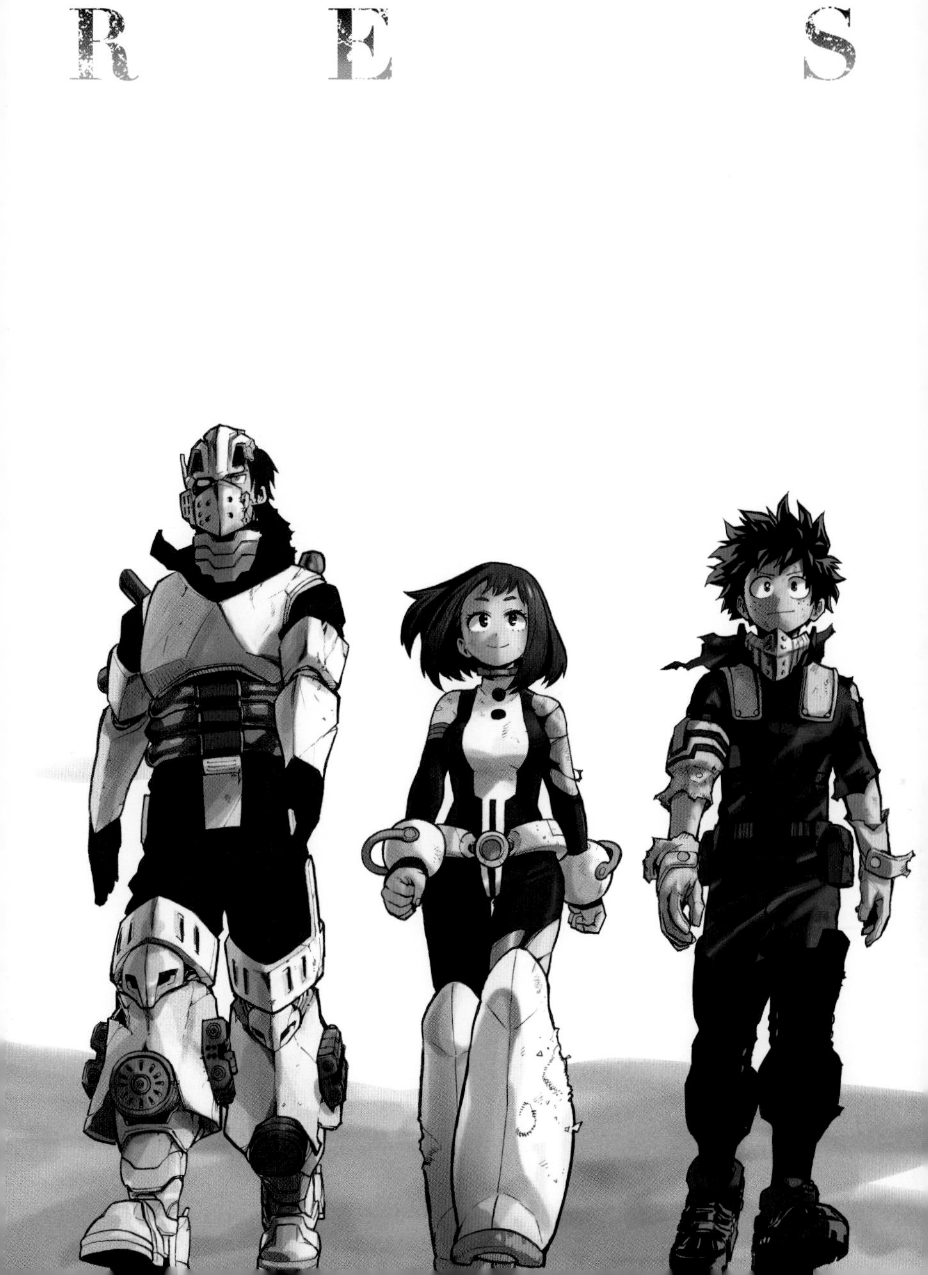
R E S

*Weekly Shonen Jump*, 2016
Issue 49, Title Page

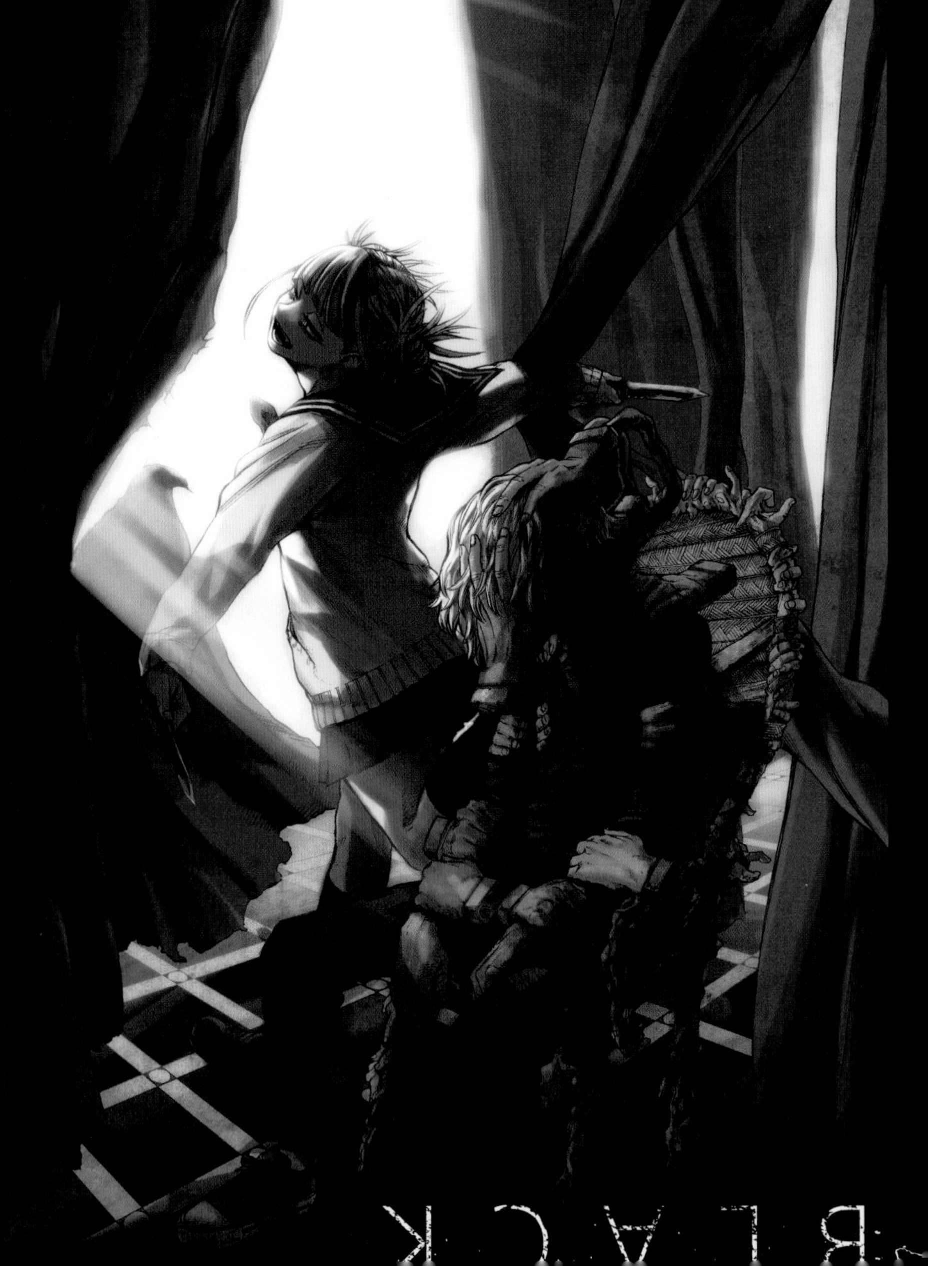
BLACK

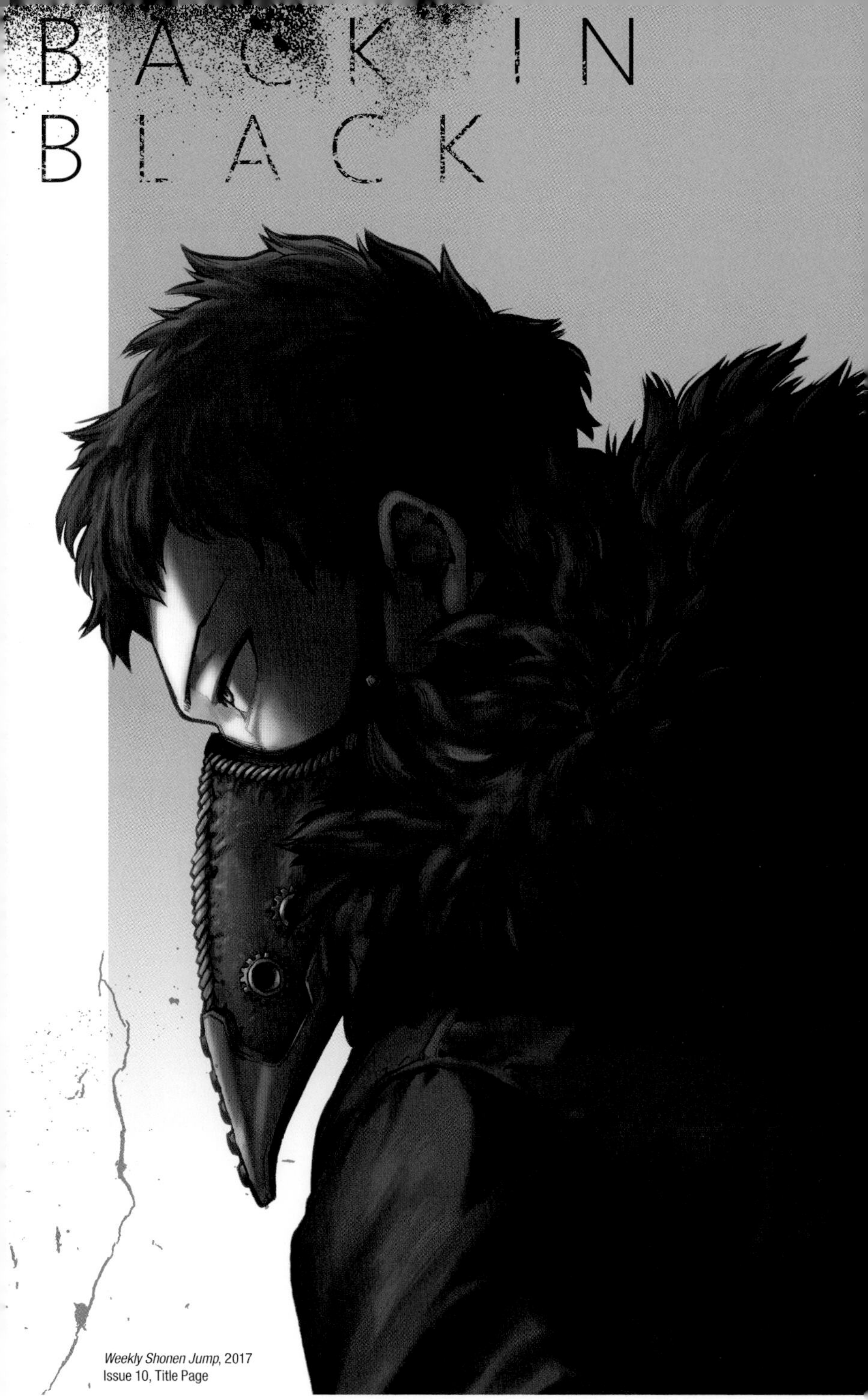
BACK IN
BLACK

*Weekly Shonen Jump*, 2017
Issue 10, Title Page

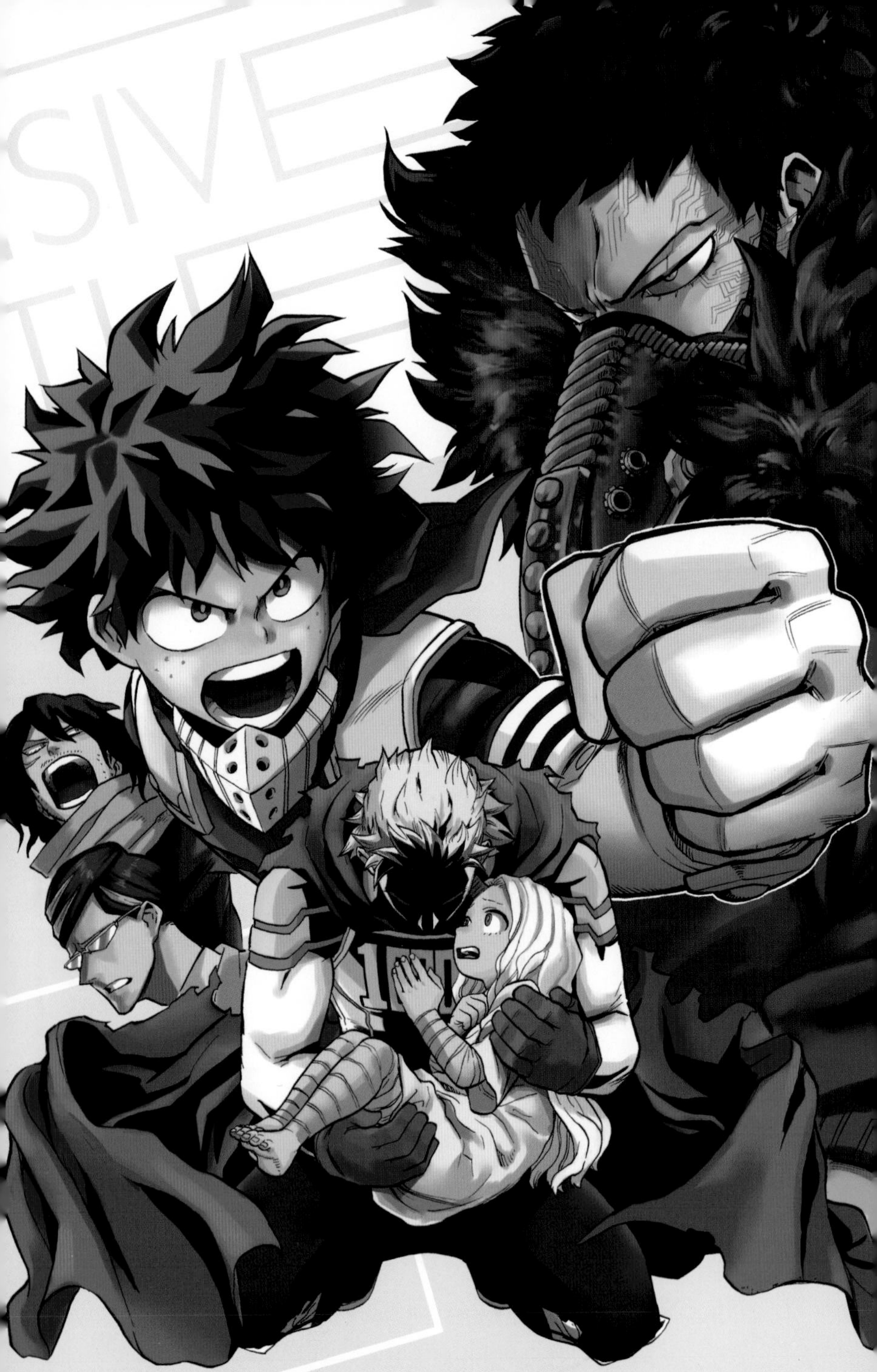

*Weekly Shonen Jump*, 2017, Issue 42, Title Page

*Weekly Shonen Jump*, 2017
Issue 18, Title Page

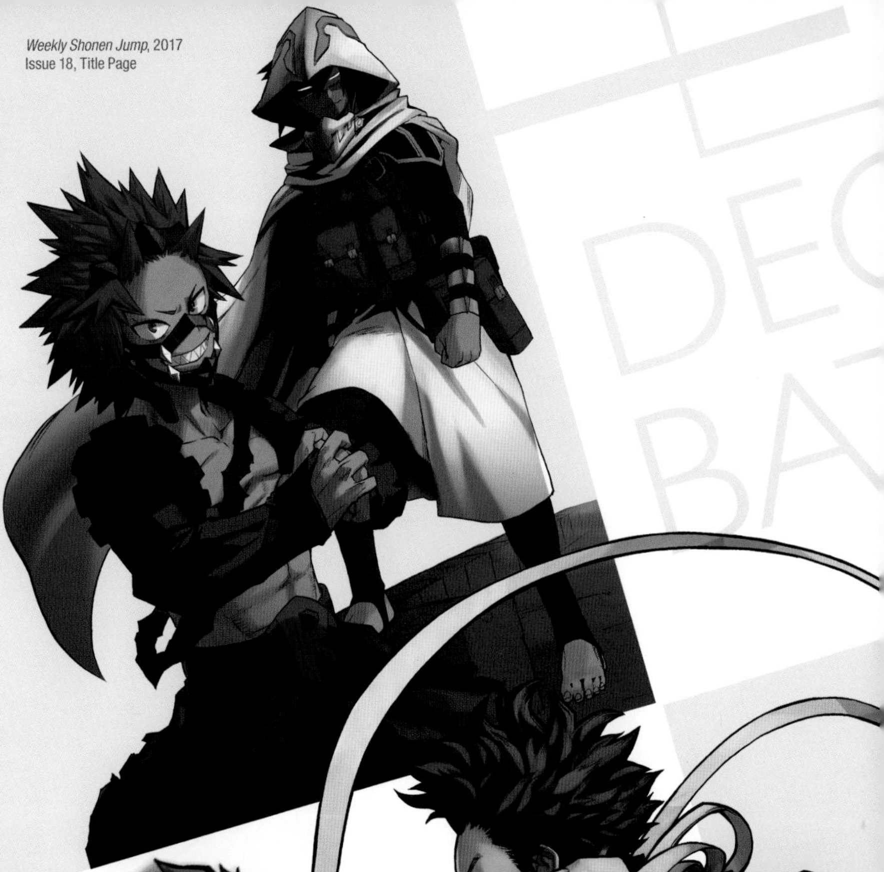

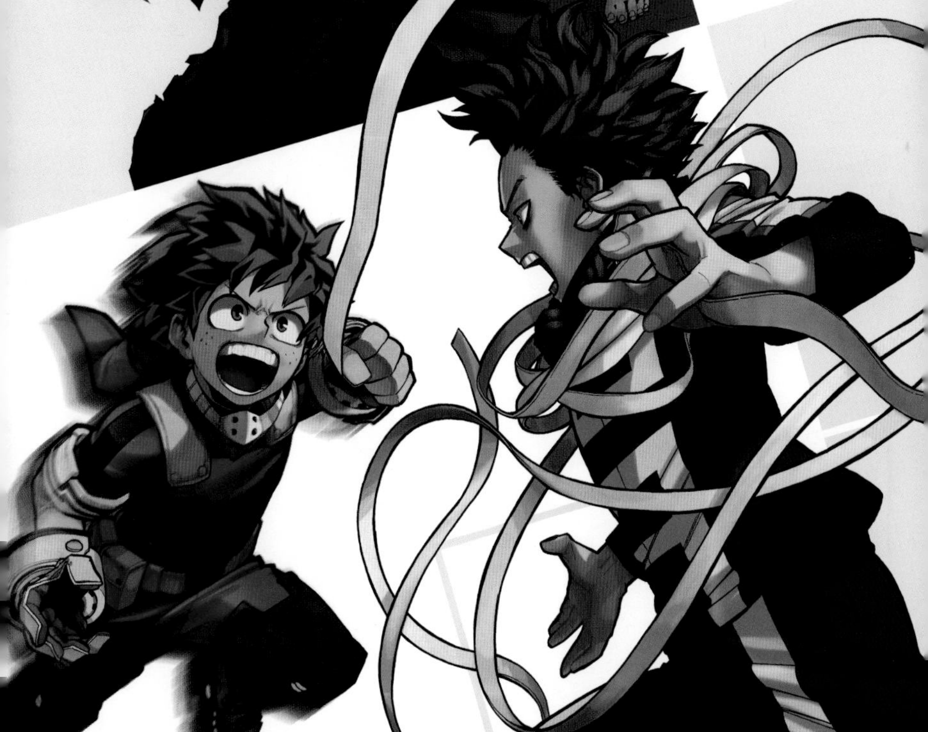

*Weekly Shonen Jump*, 2019, Issue 9, Cover Art

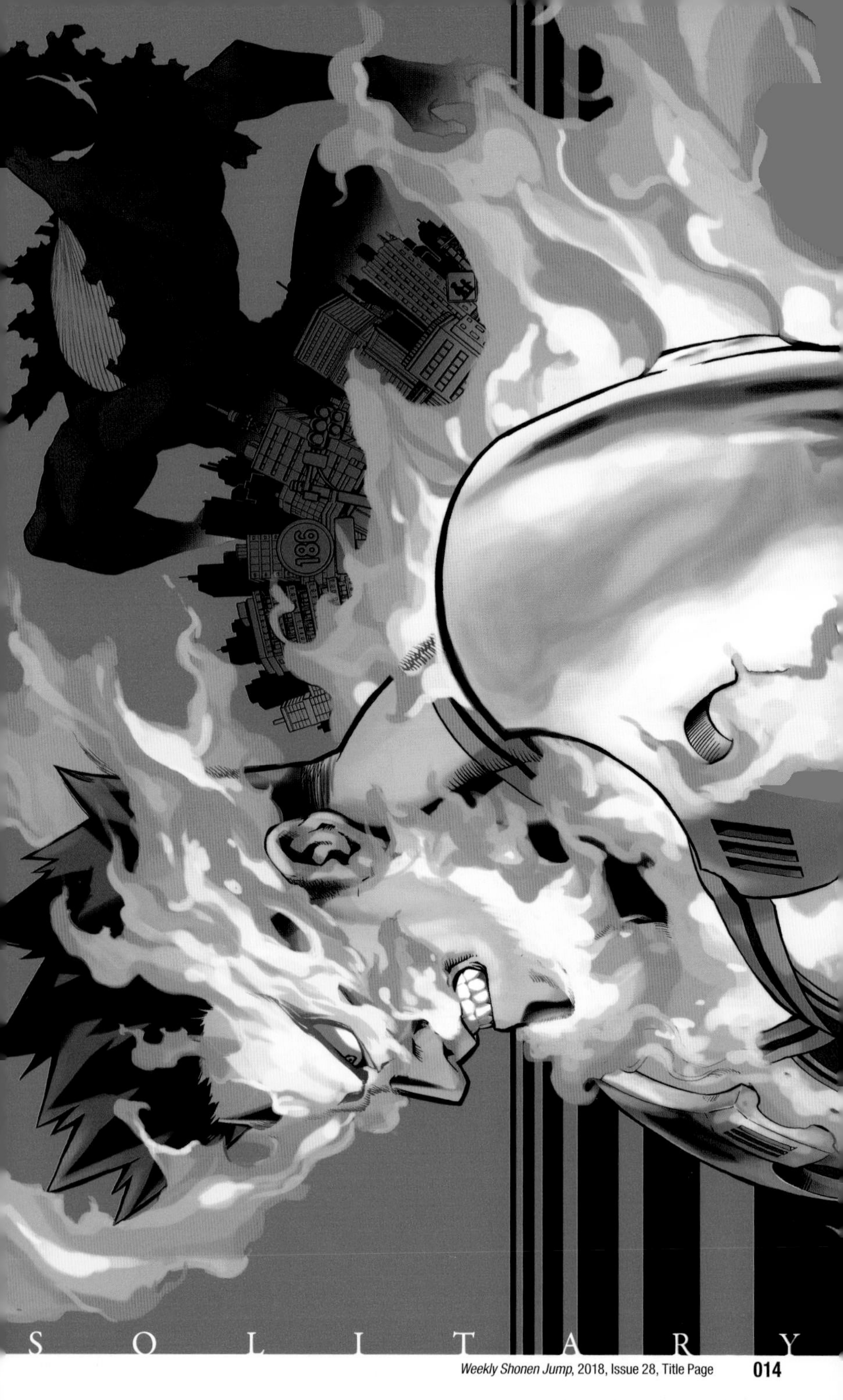
186
S O L I T A R Y

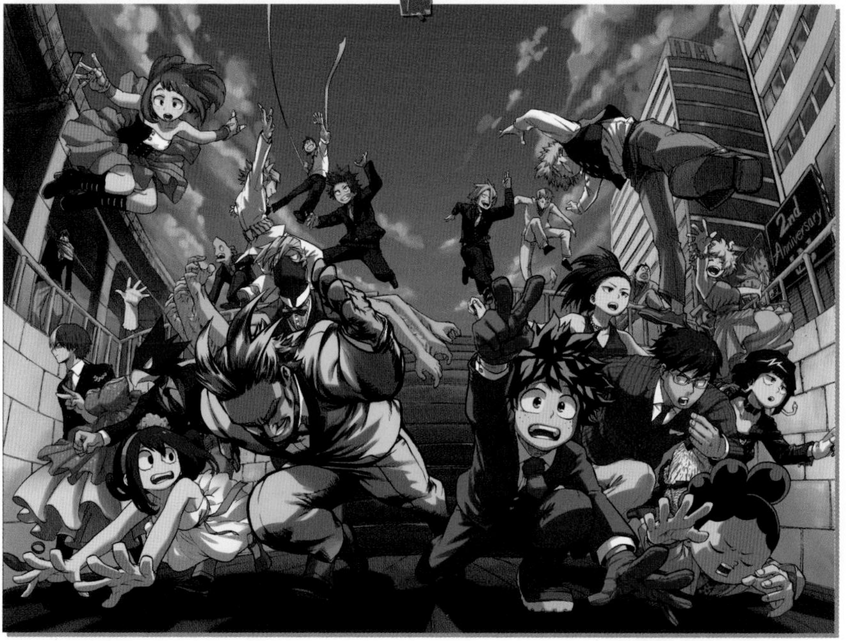
2nd Anniversary

*Weekly Shonen Jump*, 2016, Issue 41, Title Spread

# SCHOOL LIFE

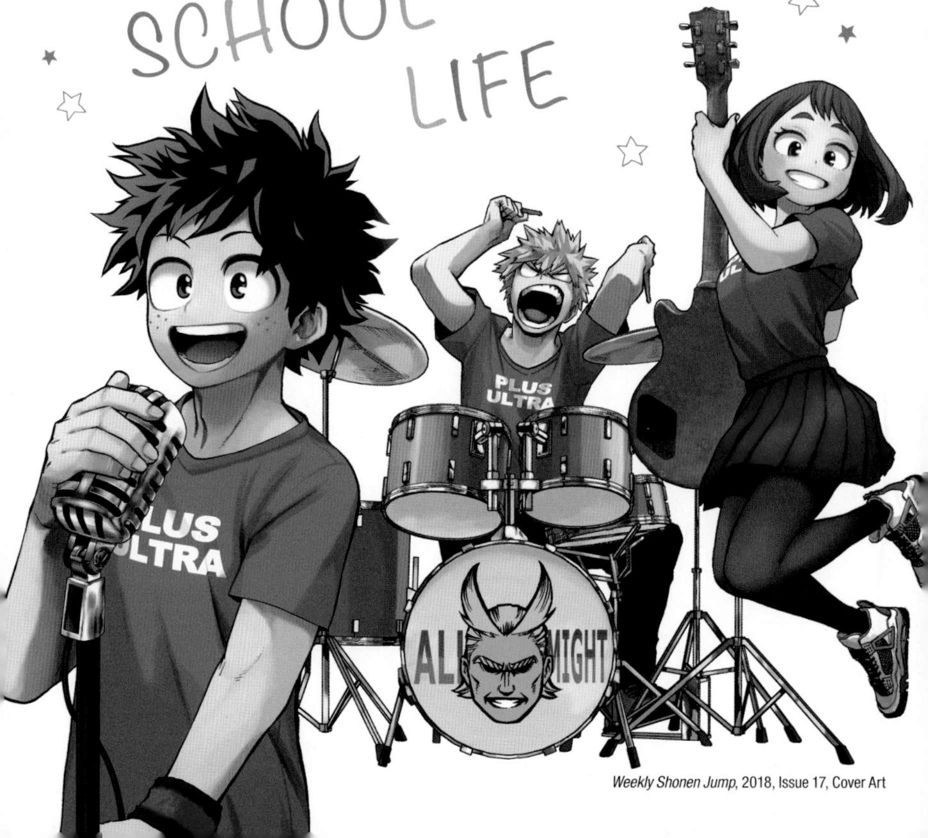
PLUS
ULTRA
PLUS
ULTRA
PLUS
ULTRA
AL
MIGHT

*Weekly Shonen Jump*, 2018, Issue 17, Cover Art

*Weekly Shonen Jump*, 2017
Issue 34, Title Spread

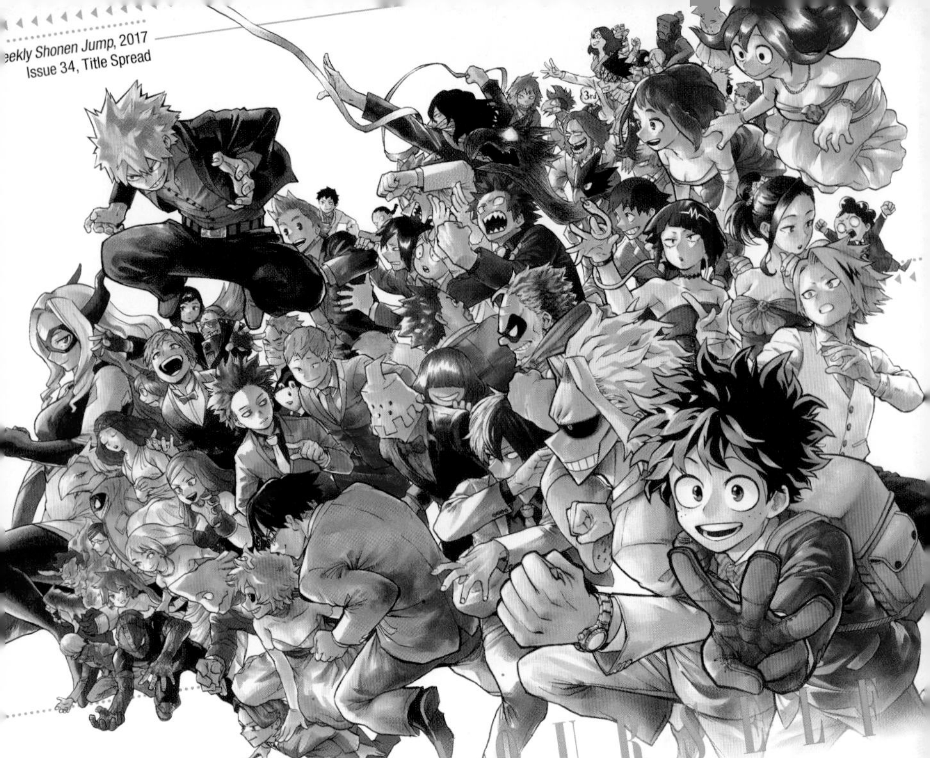

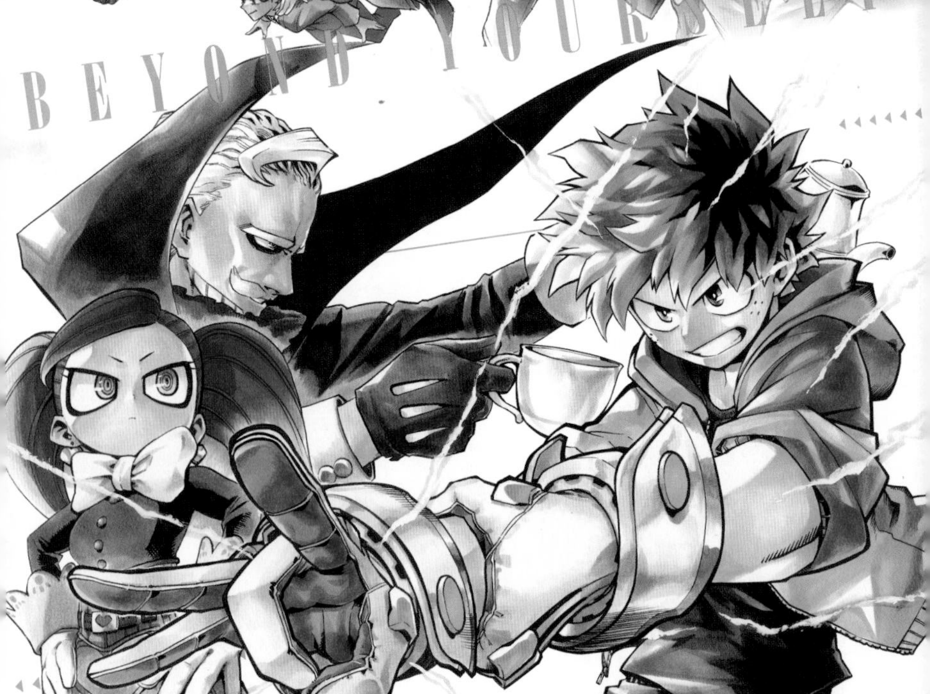
BEYOND YOURSELF

*Weekly Shonen Jump*, 2018, Issue 17, Title Spread

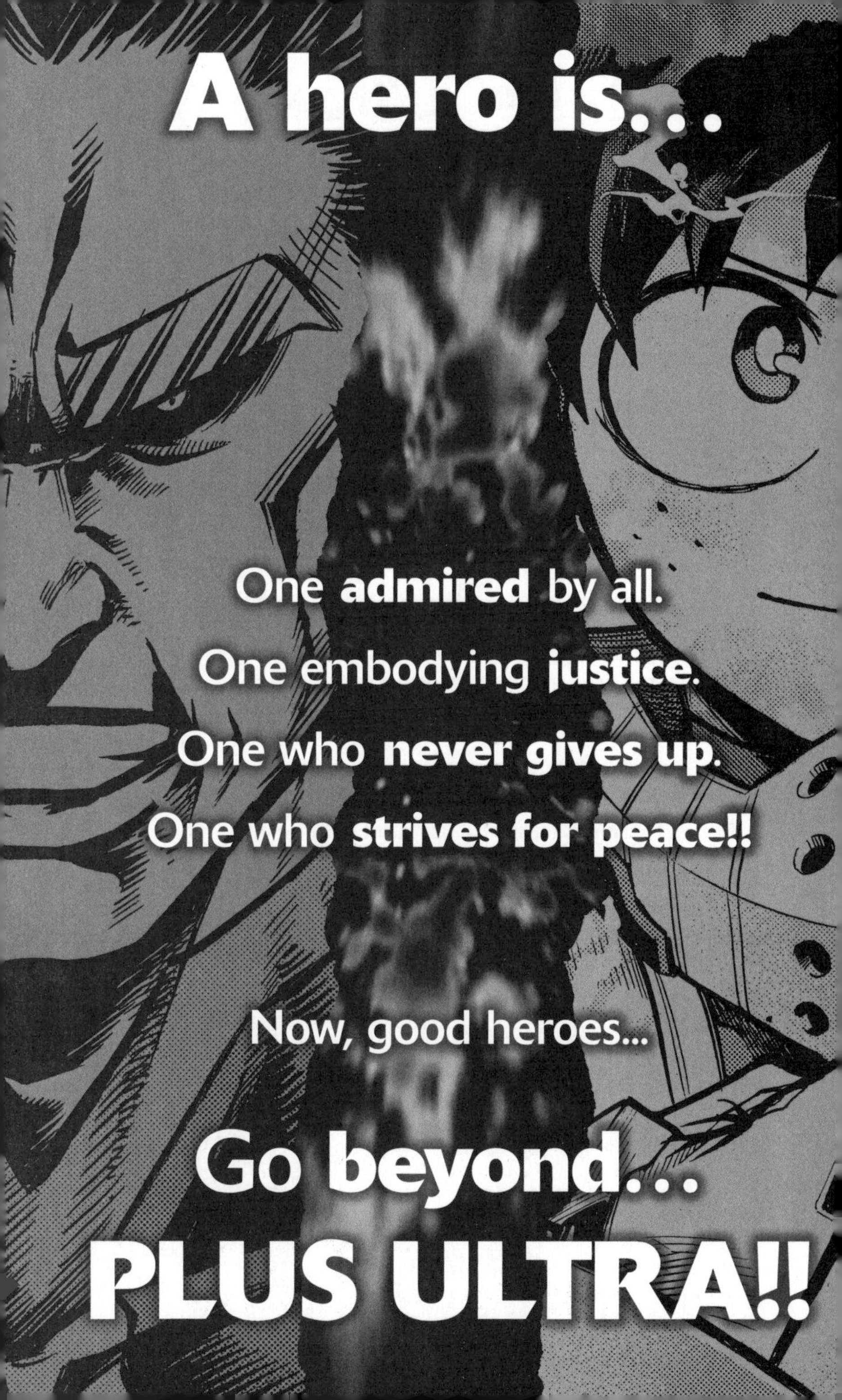
A hero is...
One admired by all.
One embodying justice.
One who never gives up.
One who strives for peace!!
Now, good heroes...
Go beyond...
PLUS ULTRA!!

# MY HERO ACADEMIA Ultra Analysis

CONTENTS



## How to Read the Hero Cards

In this book, you'll find Midoriya, All Might, and the whole gang represented in card form! Check out all their hero data at a glance!

1. **Hero Name**
2. **Real Name** (except pro heroes)
3. **Type**

CLOSE-COMBAT · RANGED · SUPPORT

4. **Quirk**
5. **Skill Parameter Chart**

DEKU
01-001
TYPE: CLOSE-COMBAT
His true power?! Unknown! A dark horse candidate for number one!!
IZUKU MIDORIYA
QUIRK:
One For All

# 1st EDITION

## NEW HEROES I

The students of class 1-A have undergone endless training and trials, and after a few encounters with villains, they've done plenty of growing. Learn about how their bodies and minds have gotten stronger via the explosive data in this section.

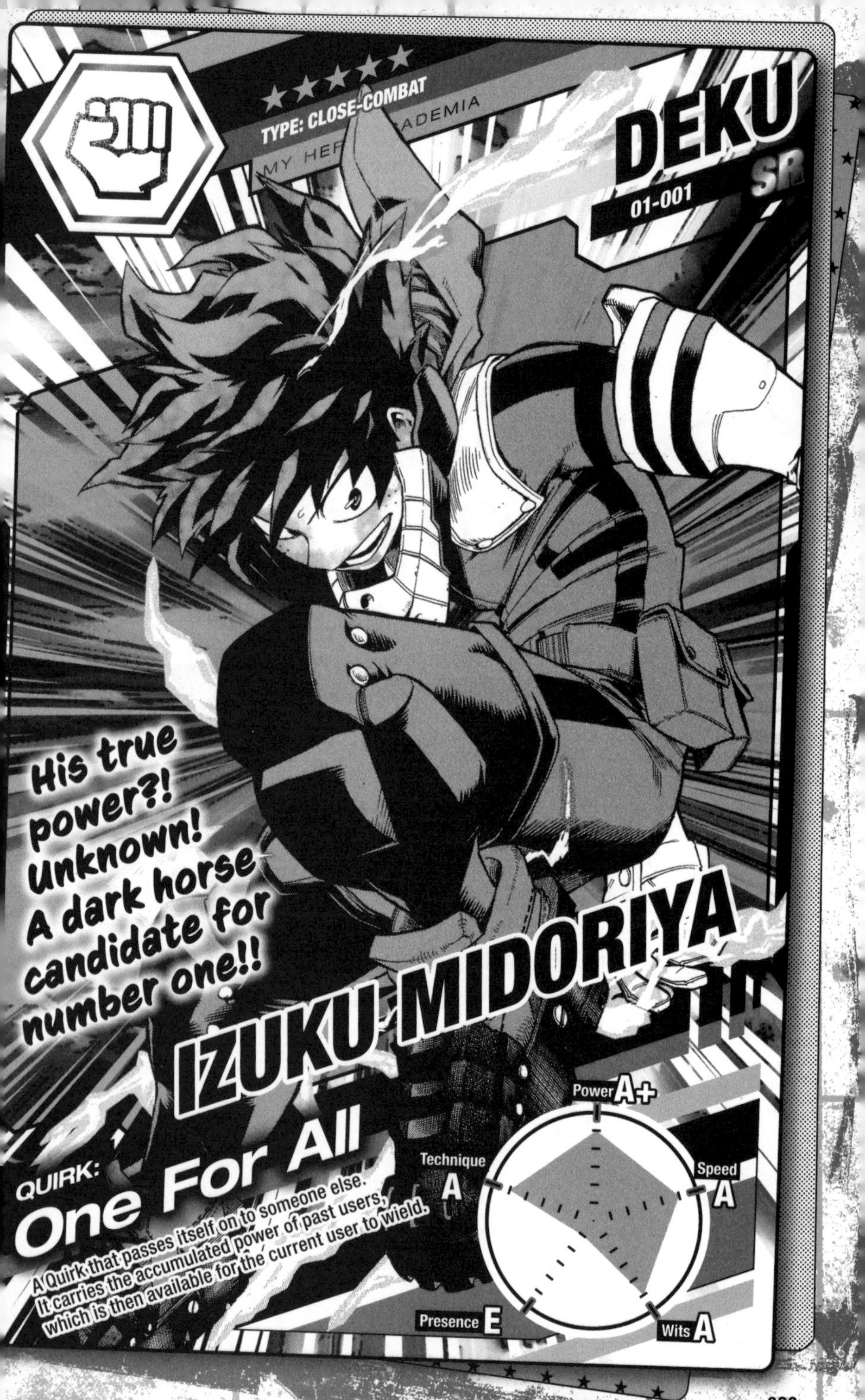
★★★★★
TYPE: CLOSE-COMBAT
MY HERO ACADEMIA
DEKU
SR
01-001
His true power?! Unknown! A dark horse candidate for number one!!
IZUKU MIDORIYA
QUIRK:
One For All
A Quirk that passes itself on to someone else. It carries the accumulated power of past users, which is then available for the current user to wield.
Power A+
Speed A
Wits A
Presence E
Technique A

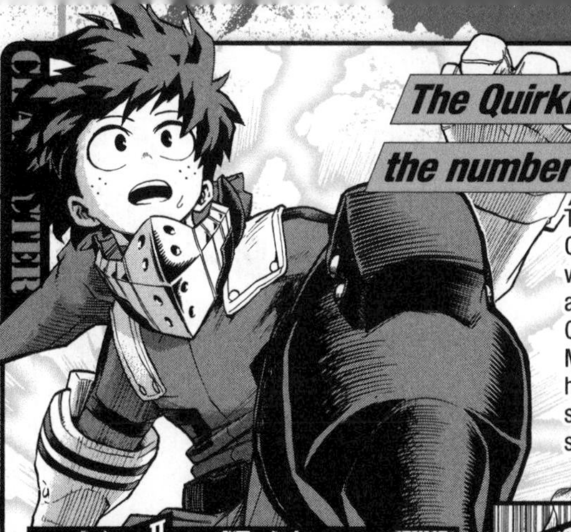

# The Quirkless boy who inherited the number one hero's mantle.

This hero fanboy wasn't born with a Quirk of his own, but a chance encounter with his idol, All Might, would forever alter Midoriya's fate. After inheriting a Quirk, he vowed to become a great hero. Midoriya treasures the thank-you letter he received from Kota—a boy he saved—and recently he received a similar precious letter from Eri.

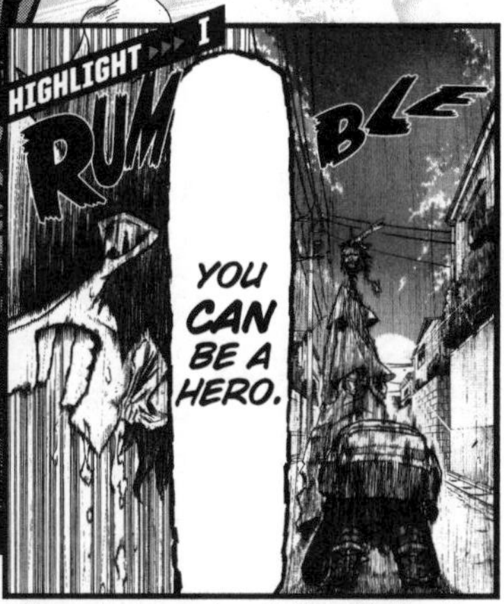
HIGHLIGHT I
RUMBLE
YOU CAN BE A HERO.

⬆ He received power from his idol, rekindling his dying dream.

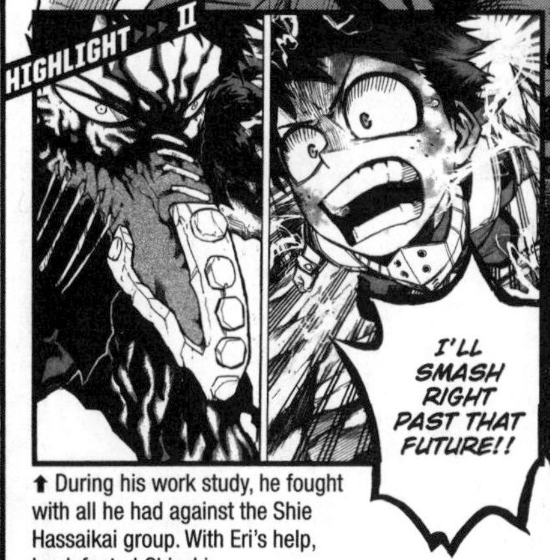
HIGHLIGHT II
I'LL SMASH RIGHT PAST THAT FUTURE!!

⬆ During his work study, he fought with all he had against the Shie Hassaikai group. With Eri's help, he defeated Chisaki.

## RELATIONSHIPS

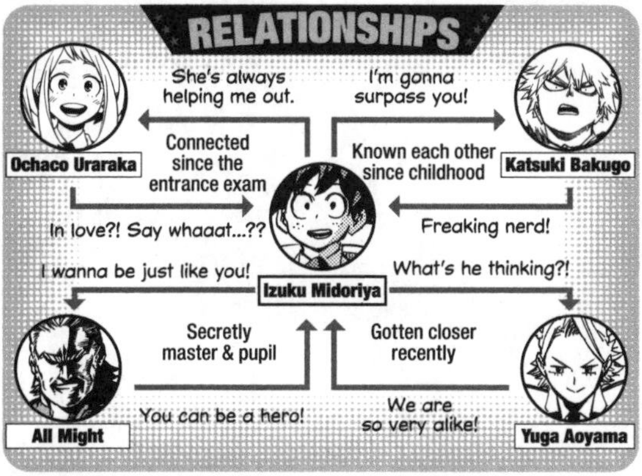
Ochaco Uraraka
She's always helping me out.
Connected since the entrance exam
In love?! Say whaaat...??
Katsuki Bakugo
I'm gonna surpass you!
Known each other since childhood
Freaking nerd!
Izuku Midoriya
I wanna be just like you!
Secretly master & pupil
You can be a hero!
All Might
What's he thinking?!
Gotten closer recently
We are so very alike!
Yuga Aoyama

## PROFILE

Name: **Izuku Midoriya**
Hero name: **Deku**
Quirk: **One For All**
Birthday: **July 15**
Height: **166 cm**
Blood type: **O**
Birthplace: **Around Shizuoka Prefecture**
Personality: **Get-it-done fanboy**
Ultimate moves: **Detroit Smash, Delaware Smash, Full Cowling, etc.**

- "You looked like you needed saving." (vol. 1, chap. 1)
- "Your power is your own!!" (vol. 5, chap. 39)
- "There are people who respected me for it! I gotta honor that! I wanna be the guy to show them all a bright future!" (vol. 20, chap. 180)

**Midoriya's Notable Quotables**

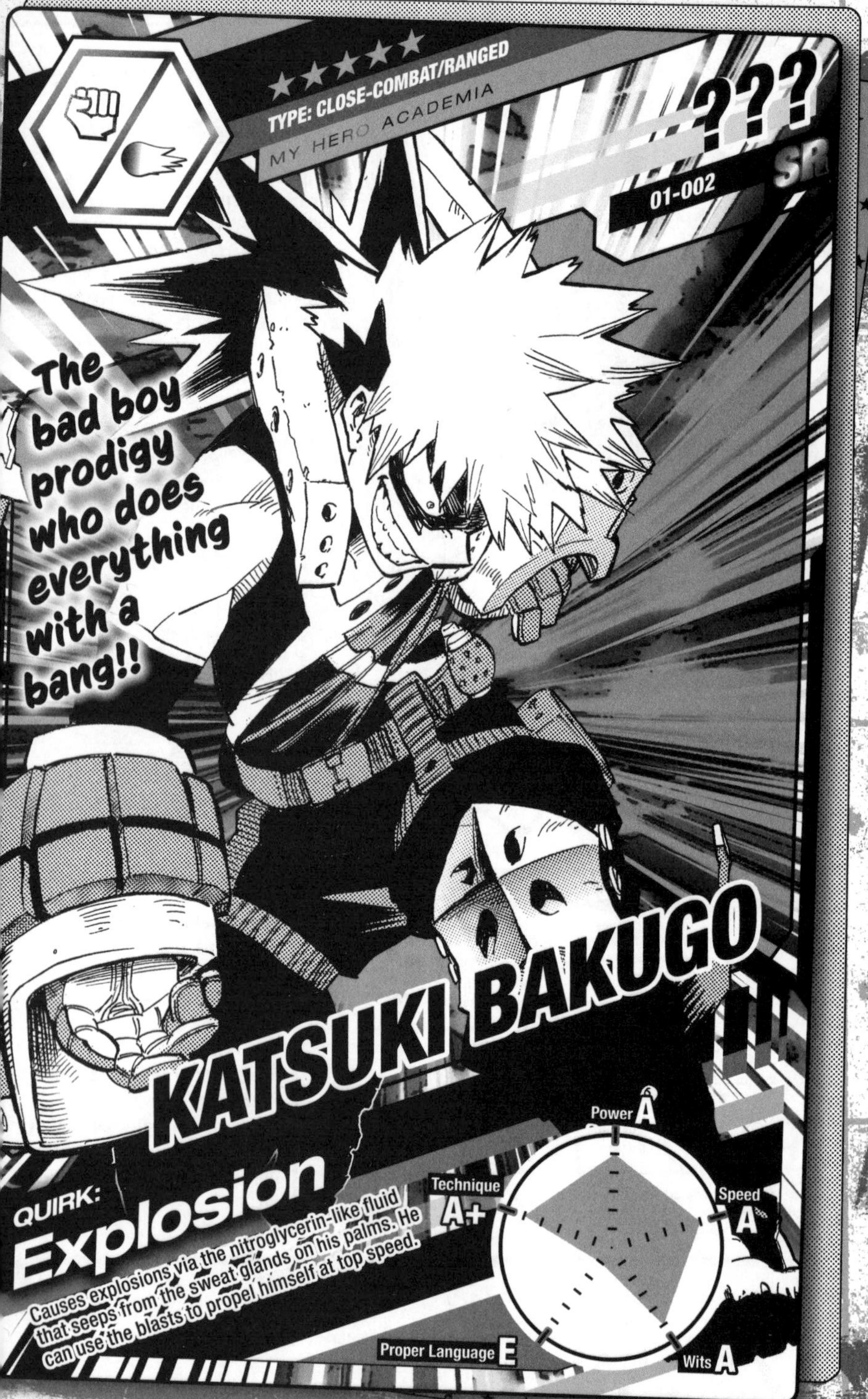
TYPE: CLOSE-COMBAT/RANGED
MY HERO ACADEMIA
???
SR
01-002
The bad boy prodigy who does everything with a bang!!
KATSUKI BAKUGO
QUIRK:
Explosion
Causes explosions via the nitroglycerin-like fluid that seeps from the sweat glands on his palms. He can use the blasts to propel himself at top speed.
Power A
Technique A+
Speed A
Wits A
Proper Language E

CHARACTER

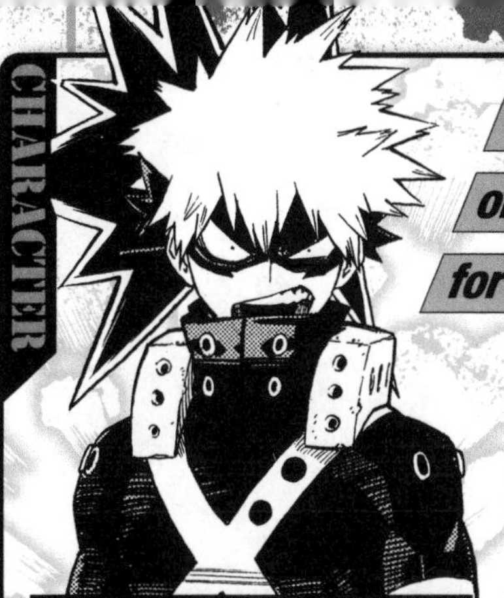

## This prodigy admires the number one hero, but can he use his talent for the sake of others?!

Bakugo once believed only in himself as he sought to become number one, but after getting kidnapped, being rescued, witnessing All Might's retirement, and learning the truth about Midoriya, his attitude has begun to shift. He's become capable of battling while actually minding his surroundings. When his parents text, he always replies with either "Shut up" or "Yeah, I know."

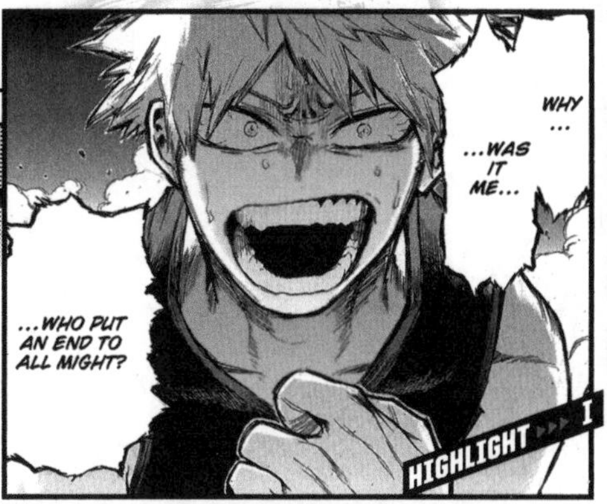

WHY...
...WAS IT ME...
...WHO PUT AN END TO ALL MIGHT?
HIGHLIGHT ▸▸▸ I


⬆ Plots by the League of Villains led to All Might's retirement, and the responsibility Bakugo feels is eating him up.

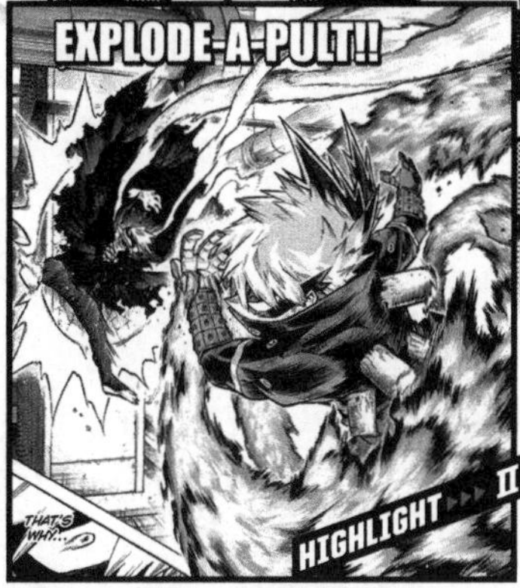

EXPLODE-A-PULT!!
THAT'S WHY...
HIGHLIGHT ▸▸▸ II


⬆ During training against class B, Bakugo defended his team with a trailblazing "save to win" style.

## PROFILE

Name: **Katsuki Bakugo**
Hero name: **Undecided**
Quirk: **Explosion**
Birthday: **April 20**
Height: **172 cm**
Blood type: **A**
Birthplace: **Around Shizuoka Prefecture**
Personality: **Abusive egotist**
Ultimate moves: **Howitzer Impact, Stun Grenade, Armor-Piercing Shot, AP Shot: Auto-Cannon, Explode-a-Pult**

## RELATIONSHIPS

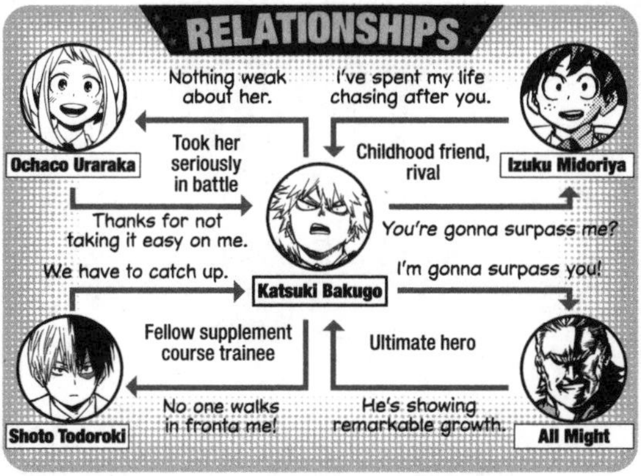

Ochaco Uraraka
Nothing weak about her.
Took her seriously in battle
Thanks for not taking it easy on me.
Izuku Midoriya
I've spent my life chasing after you.
Childhood friend, rival
You're gonna surpass me?
I'm gonna surpass you!
Katsuki Bakugo
Shoto Todoroki
We have to catch up.
Fellow supplement course trainee
No one walks in fronta me!
All Might
Ultimate hero
He's showing remarkable growth.


- "Not just first place, no. I'm taking the first to end all firsts!" (vol. 4, chap. 29)
- "If you keep looking down your nose at everyone, you're never gonna notice your own weaknesses." (vol. 18, chap. 166)
- "I made a pledge! I will achieve absolute victory, every time! We're taking this 4–0, no casualties! The strong don't settle for anything less!" (vol. 22, chap. 208)

Bakugo's Notable Quotables

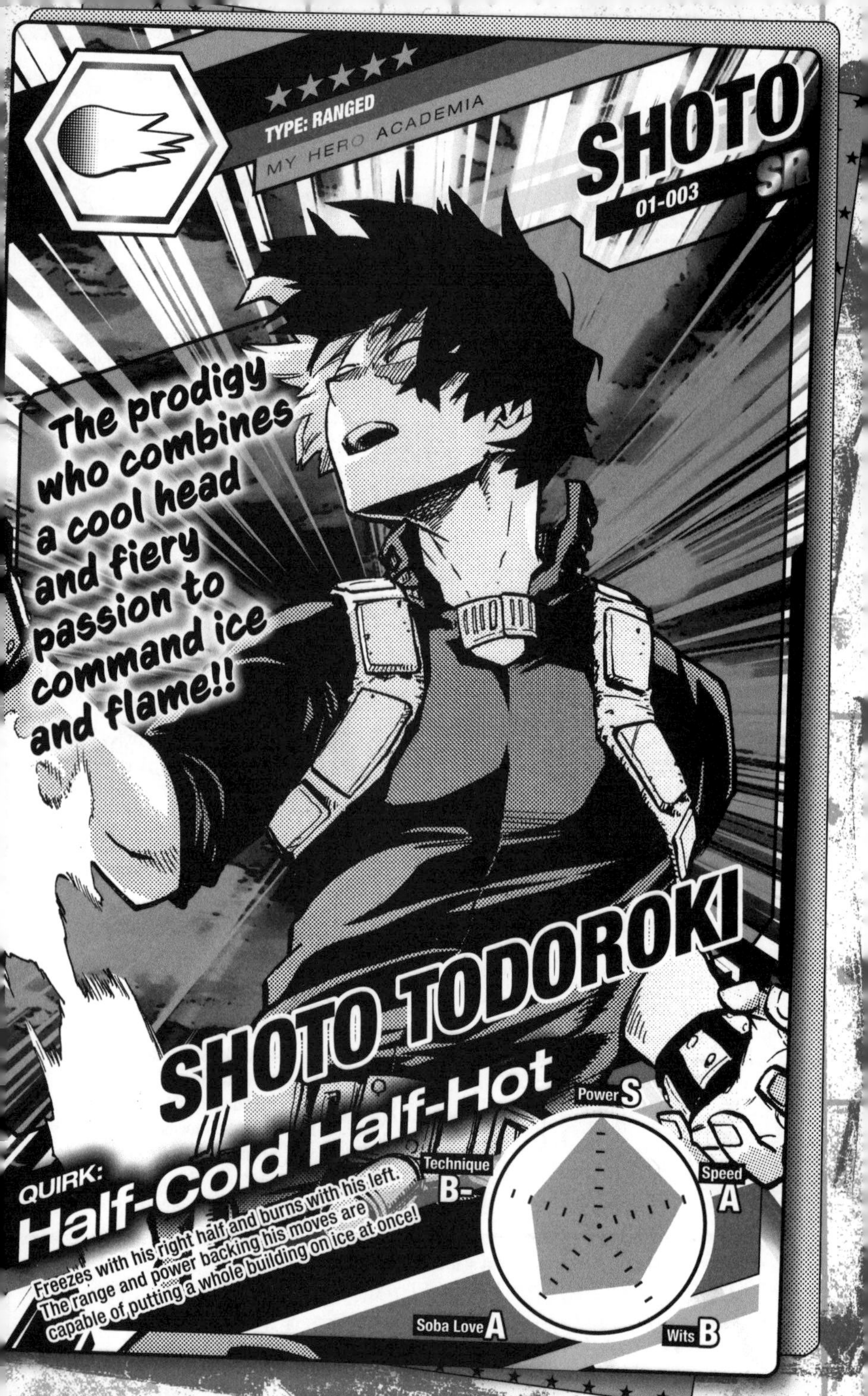

TYPE: RANGED
MY HERO ACADEMIA
SHOTO
SR
01-003
The prodigy who combines a cool head and fiery passion to command ice and flame!!
SHOTO TODOROKI
QUIRK:
Half-Cold Half-Hot
Freezes with his right half and burns with his left. The range and power backing his moves are capable of putting a whole building on ice at once!
Power S
Technique B-
Speed A
Soba Love A
Wits B

# Having accepted his father's flame, his strength grows to new heights.

Son of the current number one hero, Endeavor. Todoroki's battle against Midoriya unleashed the fiery half of the Quirk he inherited from his father, which he had been rejecting. When attacking with ice, he's capable of forming different shapes to some extent. Since the Sports Festival and the incident following the receipt of his provisional license, Todoroki has been gaining fans.

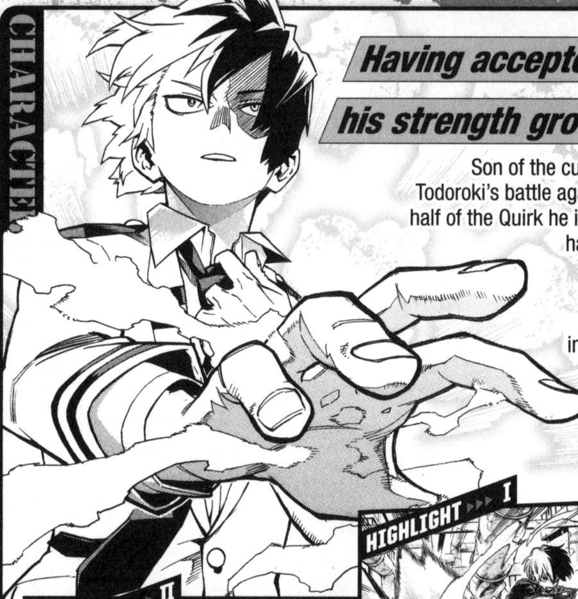

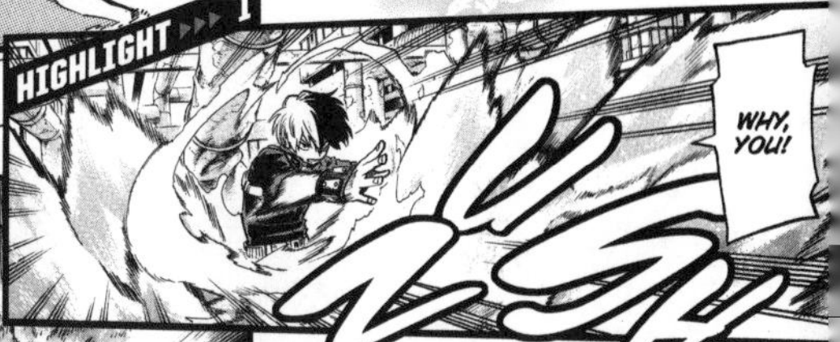
HIGHLIGHT ▸▸▸ I
WHY, YOU!
WHSH

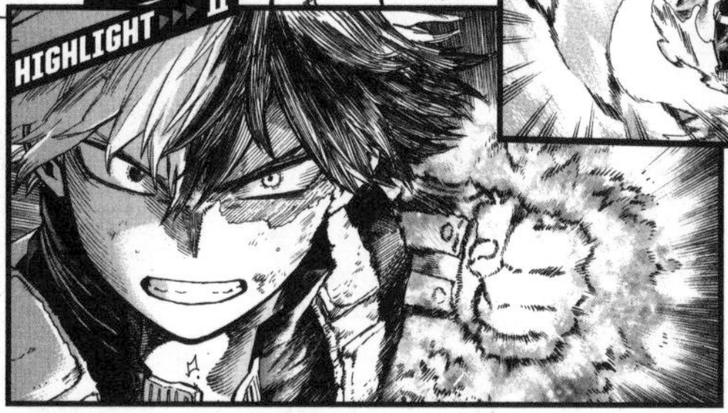
HIGHLIGHT ▸▸▸ II

⬆ Honenuki realized that Todoroki has a tendency to lead with his ice powers. He's more hesitant to use flames.

⬅ Part of Todoroki's Quirk is dangerous, and he'll have to master it to become the hero he wants to be.

## RELATIONSHIPS

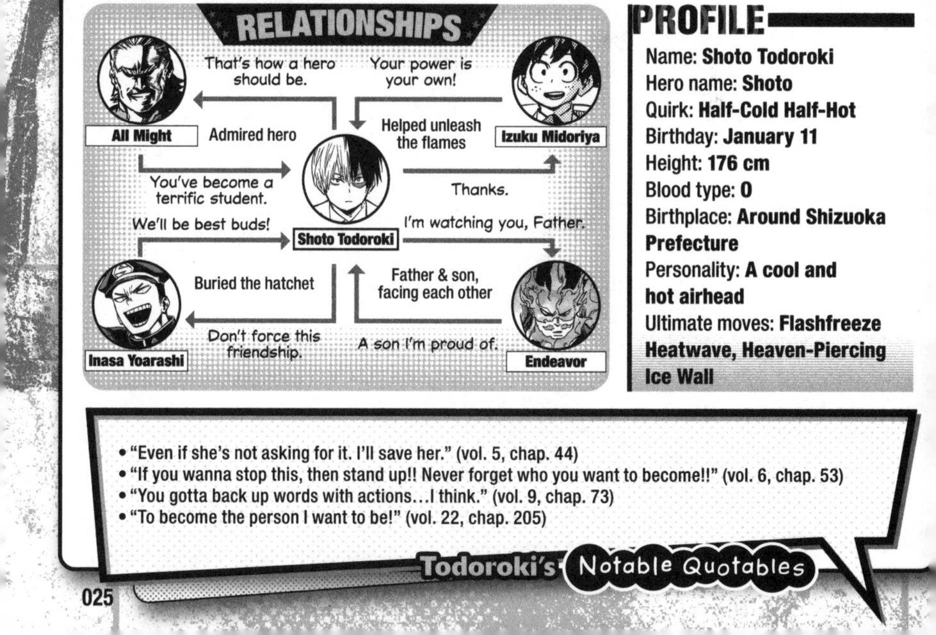
That's how a hero should be.
Your power is your own!
All Might
Admired hero
Helped unleash the flames
Izuku Midoriya
You've become a terrific student.
Thanks.
Shoto Todoroki
We'll be best buds!
I'm watching you, Father.
Buried the hatchet
Father & son, facing each other
Inasa Yoarashi
Don't force this friendship.
A son I'm proud of.
Endeavor

## PROFILE

Name: **Shoto Todoroki**
Hero name: **Shoto**
Quirk: **Half-Cold Half-Hot**
Birthday: **January 11**
Height: **176 cm**
Blood type: **O**
Birthplace: **Around Shizuoka Prefecture**
Personality: **A cool and hot airhead**
Ultimate moves: **Flashfreeze Heatwave, Heaven-Piercing Ice Wall**

- "Even if she's not asking for it. I'll save her." (vol. 5, chap. 44)
- "If you wanna stop this, then stand up!! Never forget who you want to become!!" (vol. 6, chap. 53)
- "You gotta back up words with actions…I think." (vol. 9, chap. 73)
- "To become the person I want to be!" (vol. 22, chap. 205)

**Todoroki's Notable Quotables**

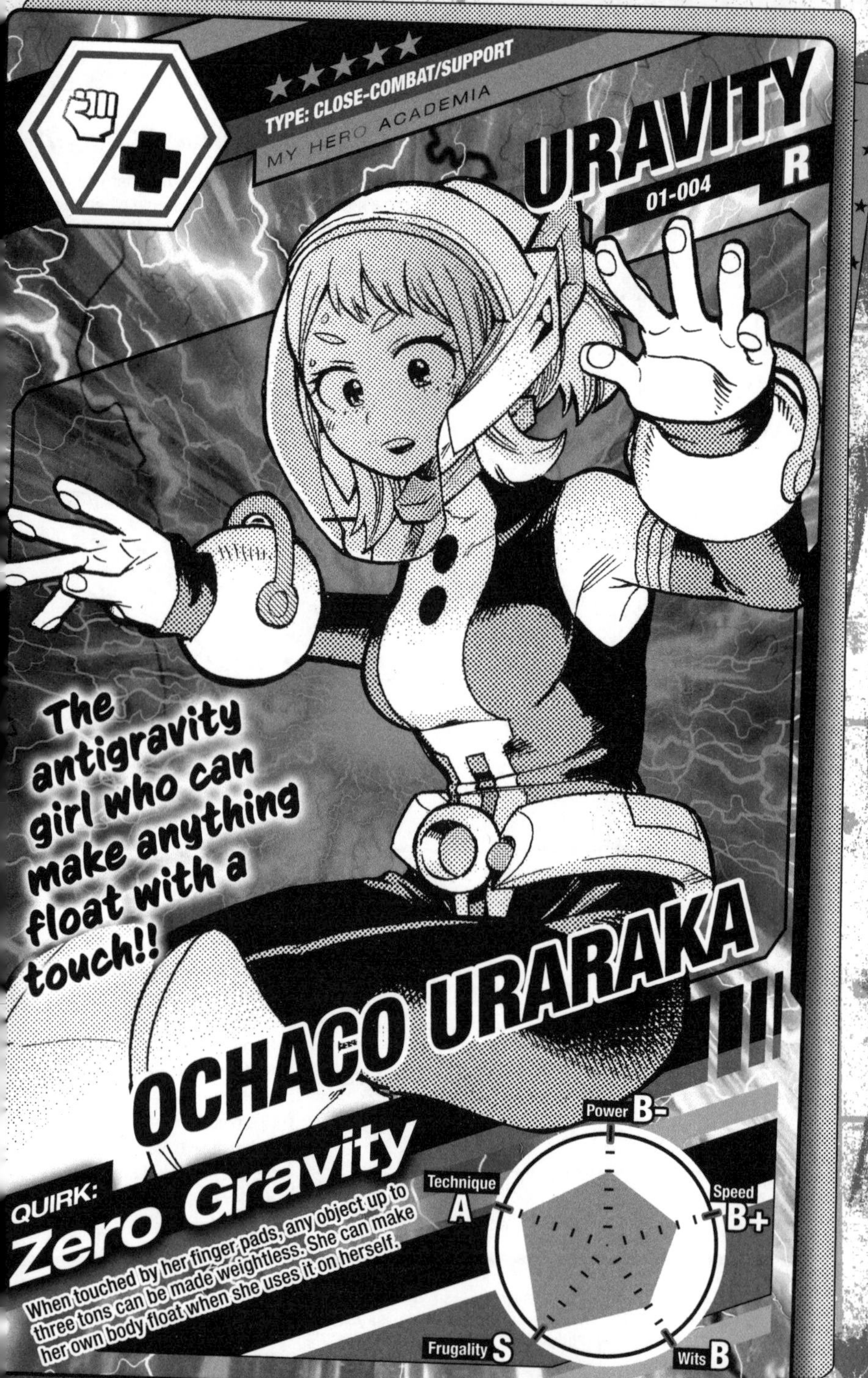
TYPE: CLOSE-COMBAT/SUPPORT
MY HERO ACADEMIA
URAVITY
R
01-004
The antigravity girl who can make anything float with a touch!!
OCHACO URARAKA
Power B-
Technique A
Speed B+
Frugality S
Wits B
QUIRK:
Zero Gravity
When touched by her finger pads, any object up to three tons can be made weightless. She can make her own body float when she uses it on herself.

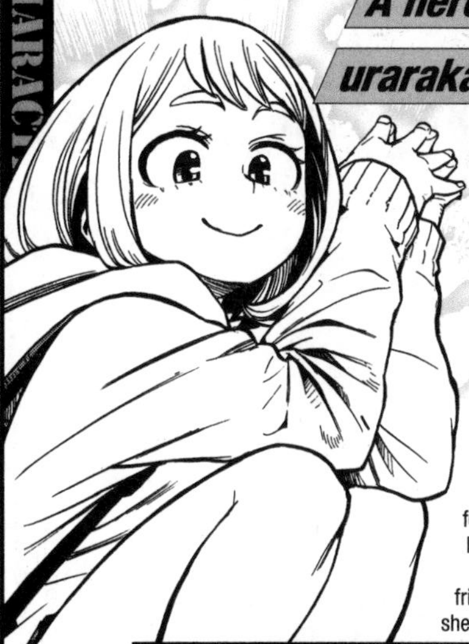

## A hero for her parents' sake, her uraraka smile hides her resolve.

Always upbeat and cheery, class A's Uraraka wants to become a hero in order to provide for her parents, who run a construction company. In battle, she's got plenty of guts. She greatly admires Midoriya, one of her most heroic friends. She recently submitted an application for a costume revision.

HIGHLIGHT ▸▸▸ I

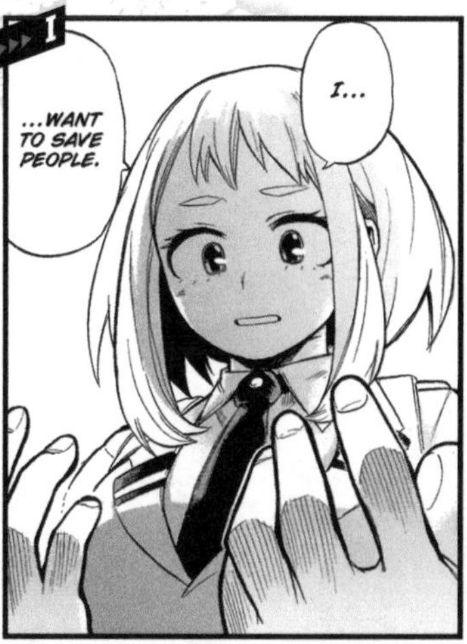
I...
...WANT TO SAVE PEOPLE.

⬆ Uraraka witnessed death firsthand during her work study under Ryukyu, resulting in some personal growth.

HIGHLIGHT ▸▸▸ II

⬇ Her feelings for Midoriya are locked up tight, but when her friends poke fun, she gets flustered.

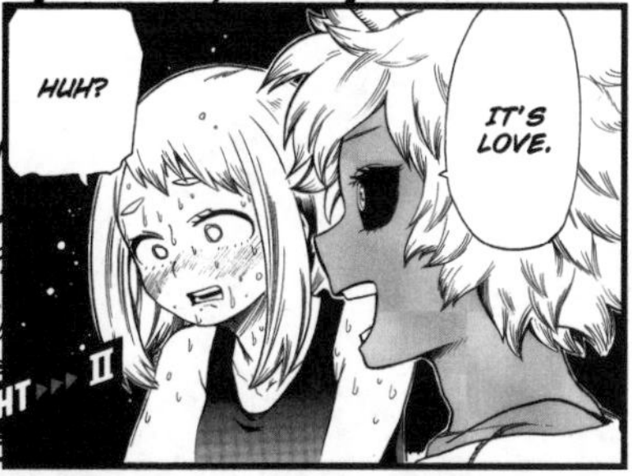
IT'S LOVE.
HUH?

## RELATIONSHIPS

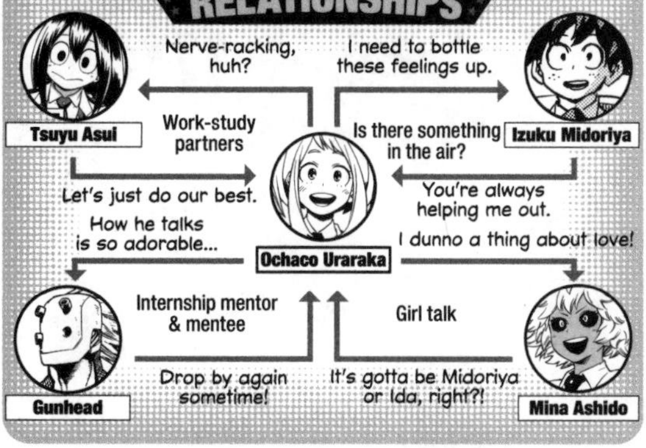
Tsuyu Asui
Nerve-racking, huh?
Work-study partners
Let's just do our best.
Izuku Midoriya
I need to bottle these feelings up.
Is there something in the air?
You're always helping me out.
Ochaco Uraraka
How he talks is so adorable...
I dunno a thing about love!
Gunhead
Internship mentor & mentee
Drop by again sometime!
Mina Ashido
Girl talk
It's gotta be Midoriya or Ida, right?!

## PROFILE

Name: **Ochaco Uraraka**
Hero name: **Uravity**
Quirk: **Zero Gravity**
Birthday: **December 27**
Height: **156 cm**
Blood type: **B**
Birthplace: **Mie Prefecture**
Personality: **Eternally uraraka**
Ultimate moves: **Comet Home Run, Meteor Shower, Gunhead Martial Arts**

- "But 'Deku,' well... It just screams, 'Do your best!!' I kinda like it." (vol. 1, chap. 7)
- "I'll see you in the finals!" (vol. 4, chap. 35)
- "So we're just supposed to do nothing?! There's no telling what the future holds!" (vol. 17, chap. 157)

Uraraka's Notable Quotables

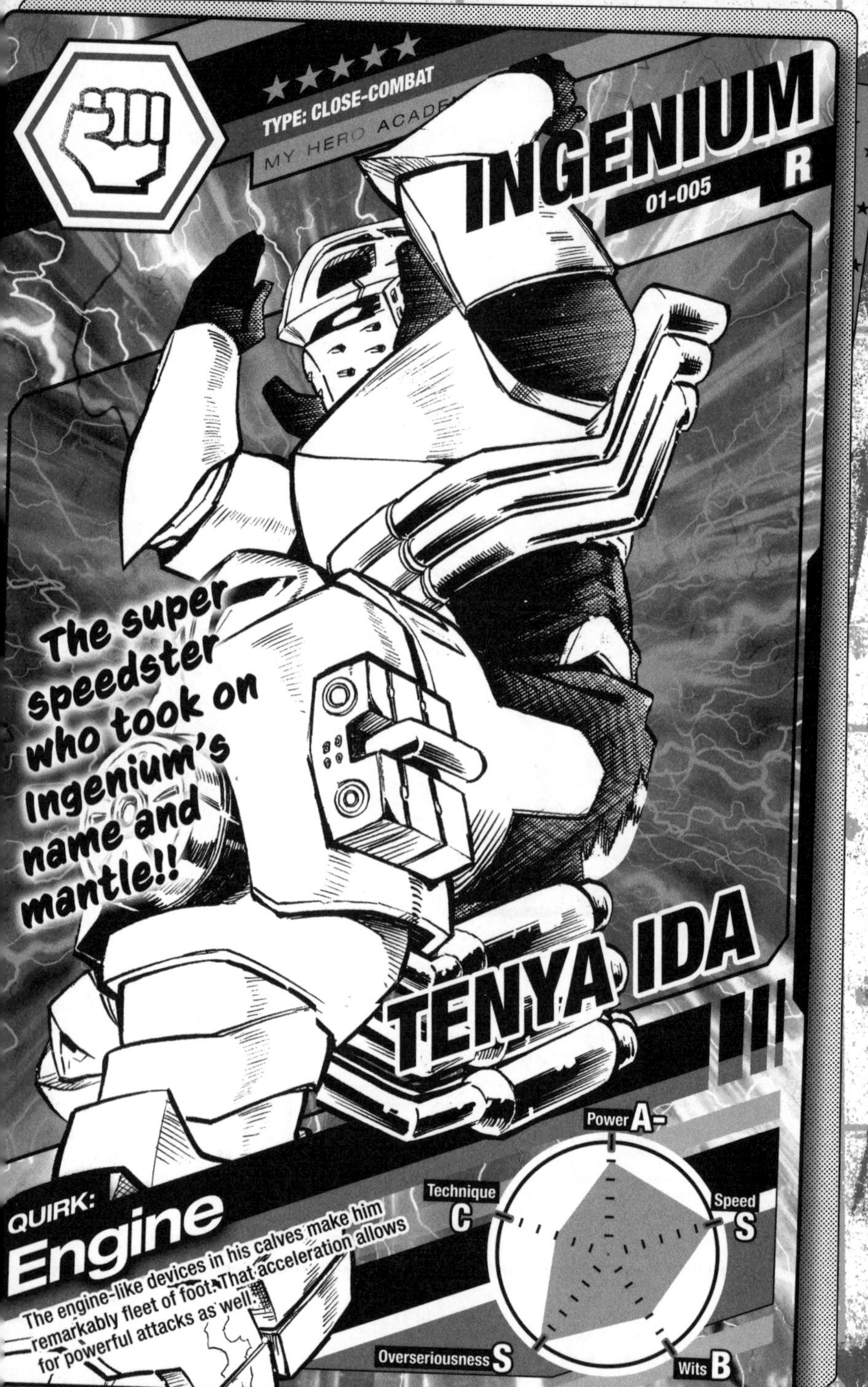
TYPE: CLOSE-COMBAT
INGENIUM
R
01-005
The super speedster who took on Ingenium's name and mantle!!
TENYA IDA
Power A-
Technique C
Speed S
Overseriousness S
Wits B
QUIRK:
Engine
The engine-like devices in his calves make him remarkably fleet of foot. That acceleration allows for powerful attacks as well.

# This by-the-book square aims to become a hero like his older brother.

Ida serves as class president and hopes to one day be a hero like his brother. He and Midoriya are close and, as fellow kickers, often exchange tips. He sometimes acts out of self-interest, but the events in Hosu City caused him to mature, making him more flexible. Recently, he started using the Recipro Turbo move.

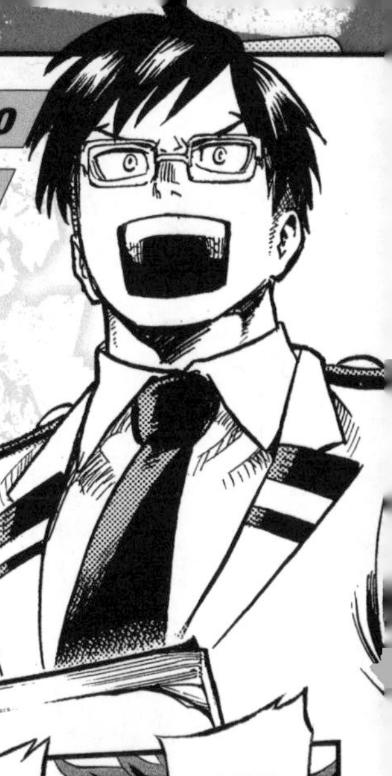

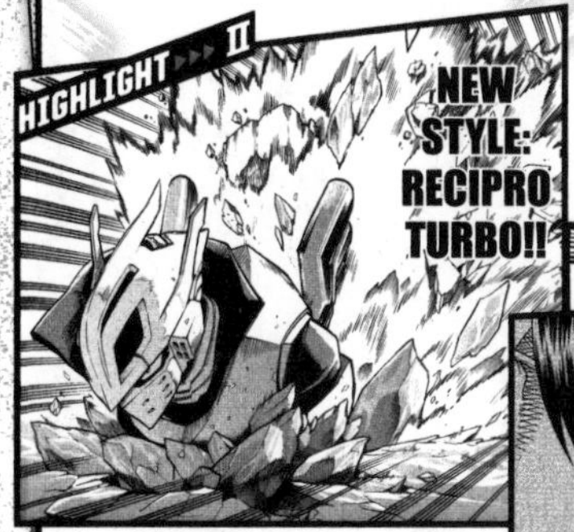
HIGHLIGHT ▸▸▸ II
NEW STYLE: RECIPRO TURBO!!

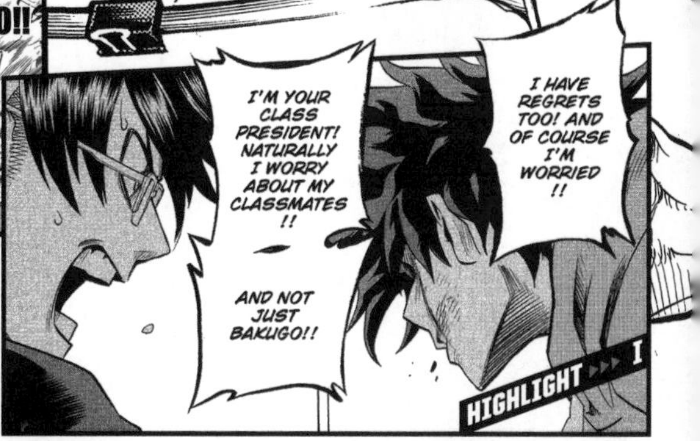
I HAVE REGRETS TOO! AND OF COURSE I'M WORRIED !!
I'M YOUR CLASS PRESIDENT! NATURALLY I WORRY ABOUT MY CLASSMATES !!
AND NOT JUST BAKUGO!!
HIGHLIGHT ▸▸▸ I

⬆ Ida's newest move, Recipro Turbo, allows him to move at top speed for ten whole minutes!!

➡ Ida feels grateful that Midoriya saved him, so he's adamant about not letting his friend stroll into danger!

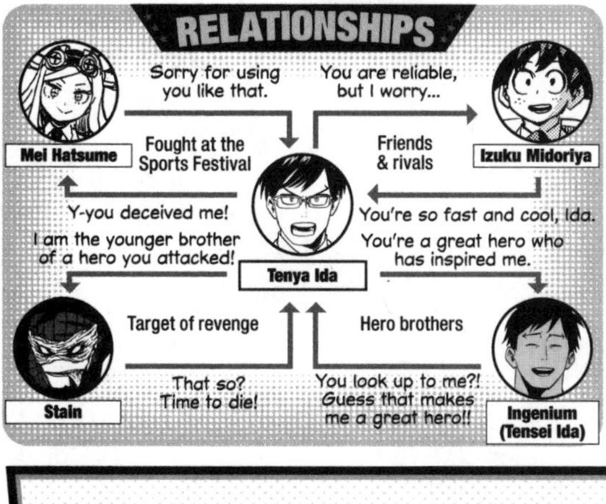
RELATIONSHIPS
Mei Hatsume
Sorry for using you like that.
Fought at the Sports Festival
Y-you deceived me!
Izuku Midoriya
You are reliable, but I worry...
Friends & rivals
You're so fast and cool, Ida.
Tenya Ida
Stain
I am the younger brother of a hero you attacked!
Target of revenge
That so? Time to die!
Ingenium (Tensei Ida)
You're a great hero who has inspired me.
Hero brothers
You look up to me?! Guess that makes me a great hero!!

## PROFILE

Name: **Tenya Ida**
Hero name: **Ingenium**
Quirk: **Engine**
Birthday: **August 22**
Height: **179 cm**
Blood type: **A**
Birthplace: **Tokyo**
Personality: **Class-presidential**
Ultimate moves: **Reciproburst, Recipro Extend, Recipro Turbo**

- "President of class 1-A, Tenya Ida!! Reporting for duty!!" (vol. 3, chap. 20)
- "I'm Ingenium. The hero who's going to take you down!!" (vol. 6, chap. 50)
- "This time, I'll be the one to protect you." (vol. 10, chap. 86)
- "I must once again show that I have the mettle to be my brother's successor!!" (vol. 22, chap. 202)

Ida's Notable Quotables

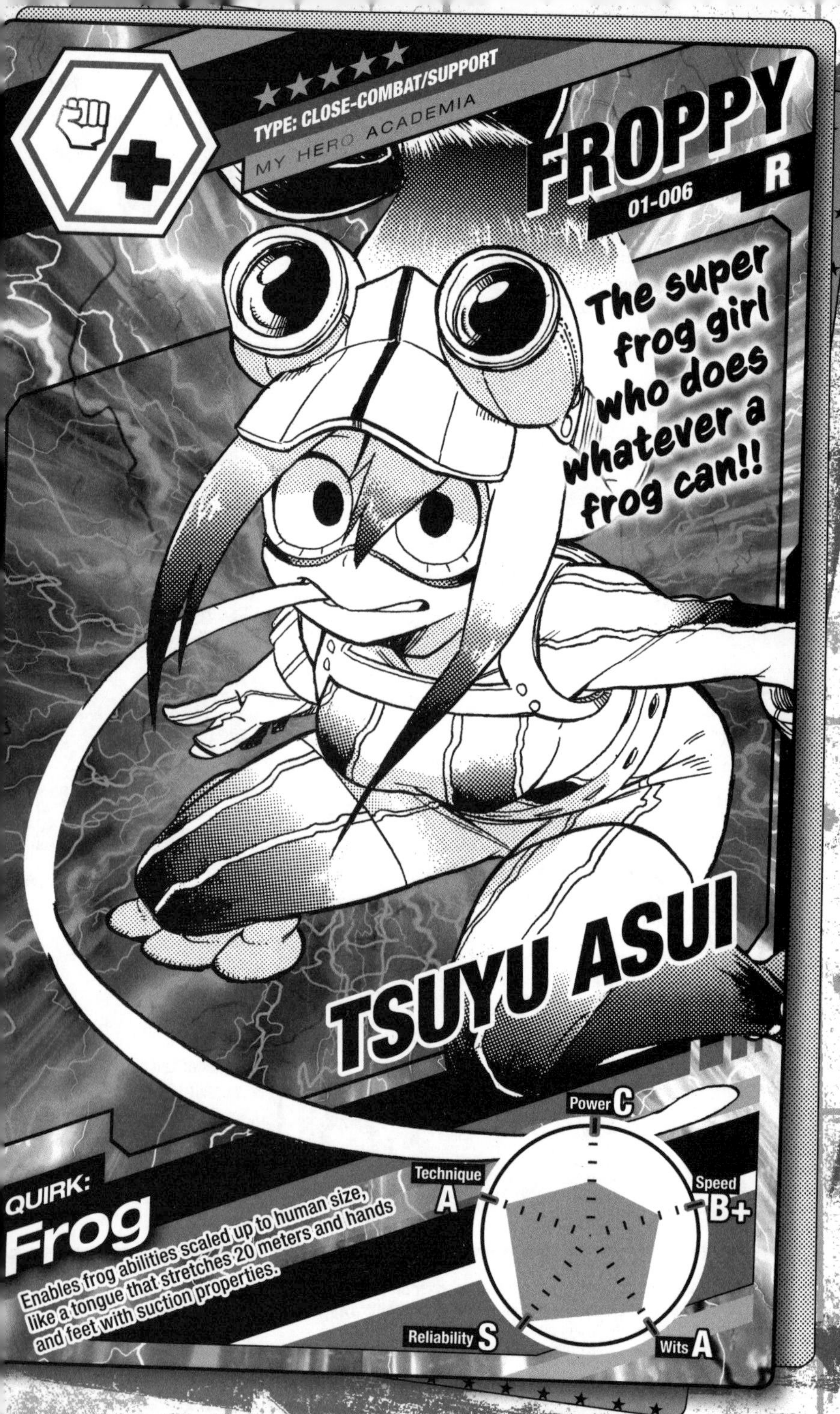
TYPE: CLOSE-COMBAT/SUPPORT
MY HERO ACADEMIA
FROPPY
R
01-006
The super frog girl who does whatever a frog can!!
TSUYU ASUI
Power C
Technique A
Speed B+
Reliability S
Wits A
QUIRK:
Frog
Enables frog abilities scaled up to human size, like a tongue that stretches 20 meters and hands and feet with suction properties.

## Her insight and judgment make her an emotional pillar.

A top-class student who excels in her studies and has impressive physical abilities and emotional maturity. With her trademark ribbits and poker face, it takes a lot to fluster Asui, and her insight and composure help her keep calm. Her parents' jobs have calmed down a little recently, so home life is good. Asui often video chats with her younger siblings to stay in touch.

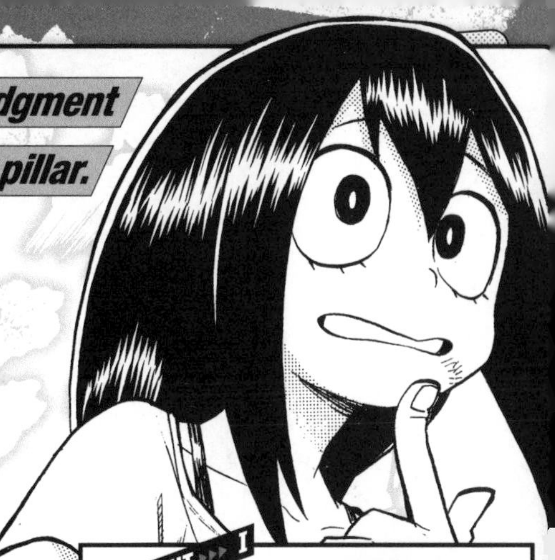

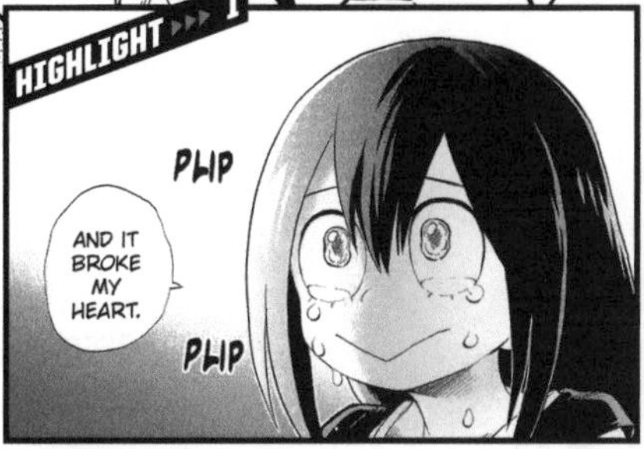
HIGHLIGHT ▸▸▸ I
PLIP
AND IT BROKE MY HEART.
PLIP

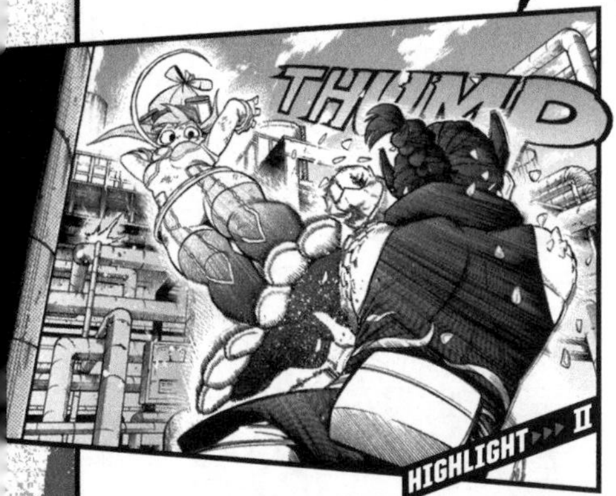
THUMP
HIGHLIGHT ▸▸▸ II

⬆ She seems aloof, but Asui has a sensitive side. She wept when explaining how conflicted she'd been about rescuing Bakugo.

⬅ Through intensive Quirk training, Asui learned to camouflage herself, so she can blend in with her surroundings!

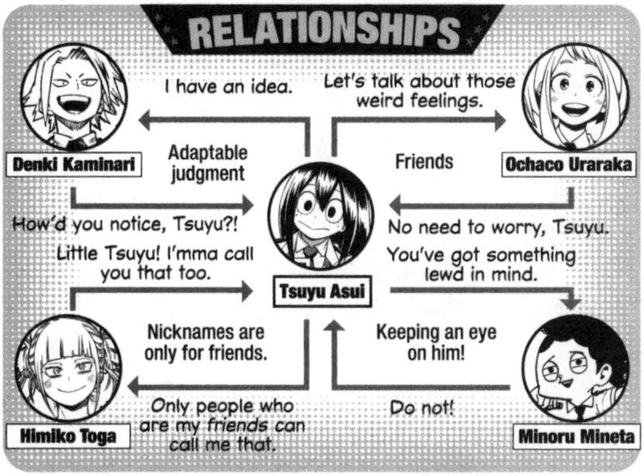
RELATIONSHIPS
Denki Kaminari
I have an idea.
Adaptable judgment
How'd you notice, Tsuyu?!
Little Tsuyu! I'mma call you that too.
Ochaco Uraraka
Let's talk about those weird feelings.
Friends
No need to worry, Tsuyu.
Tsuyu Asui
You've got something lewd in mind.
Himiko Toga
Nicknames are only for friends.
Only people who are my friends can call me that.
Minoru Mineta
Keeping an eye on him!
Do not!

## PROFILE

Name: **Tsuyu Asui**
Hero name: **Froppy**
Quirk: **Frog**
Birthday: **February 12**
Height: **150 cm**
Blood type: **B**
Birthplace: **Aichi Prefecture**
Personality: **Great friend and a composed lady**
Ultimate moves: **Camouflage, Froppy Hopper**

- "Just call me Tsuyu." (vol. 2, chap. 11)
- "But, Ida, we haven't known each other long enough to build any trust." (vol. 2, chap. 12)
- "Your Quirk resembles All Might's." (vol. 2, chap. 13)
- "We lost two. I wanted to win with the whole team intact." (vol. 21, chap. 198)

**Asui's Notable Quotables**

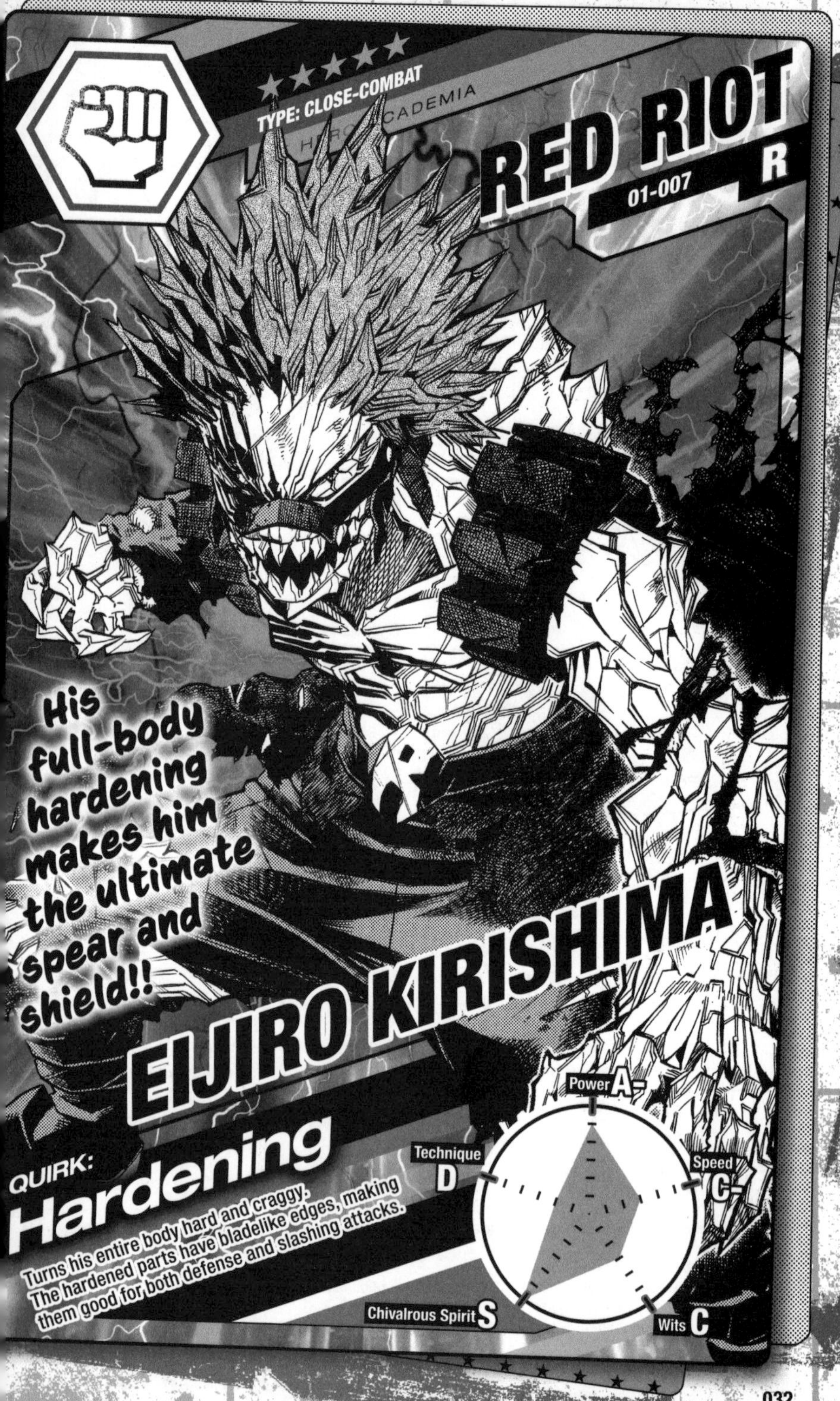

★★★★★★
TYPE: CLOSE-COMBAT
HERO ACADEMIA
RED RIOT
R
01-007
His full-body hardening makes him the ultimate spear and shield!!
EIJIRO KIRISHIMA
QUIRK:
Hardening
Turns his entire body hard and craggy. The hardened parts have bladelike edges, making them good for both defense and slashing attacks.
Power A-
Technique D
Speed C-
Chivalrous Spirit S
Wits C

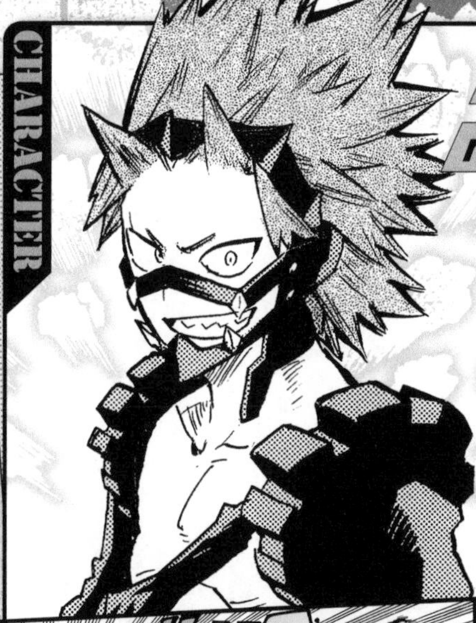
CHARACTER

# A chivalrous, hot-blooded du
# reflecting on his past weaknes

This energetic guy believes in chivalry. Kirishima suffered from an inferiority complex in middle school, but inspiration from his favorite hero—Crimson Riot—spurred him to part ways with that side of himself. As a display of his newfound resolve, Kirishima began dying his hair red after getting into U.A.! Every day, he uses a shampoo that helps the dye take hold, so his hair is red down to the roots.

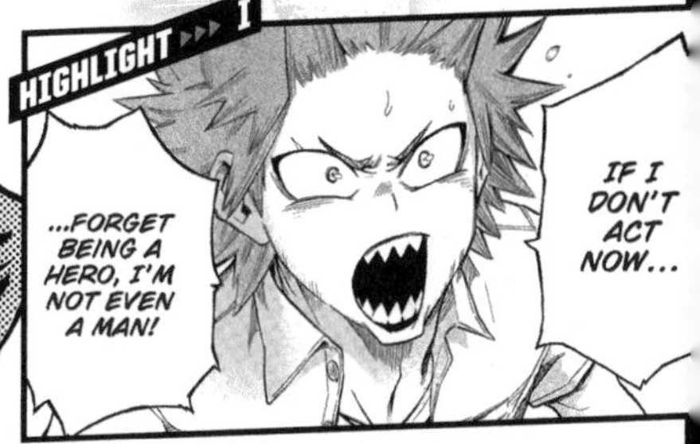
HIGHLIGHT ▸▸▸ I
IF I DON'T ACT NOW...
...FORGET BEING A HERO, I'M NOT EVEN A MAN!

⬆ Even All Might gave him props for his incredible strength of character and chivalrous spirit. He was the first to suggest rescuing Bakugo.

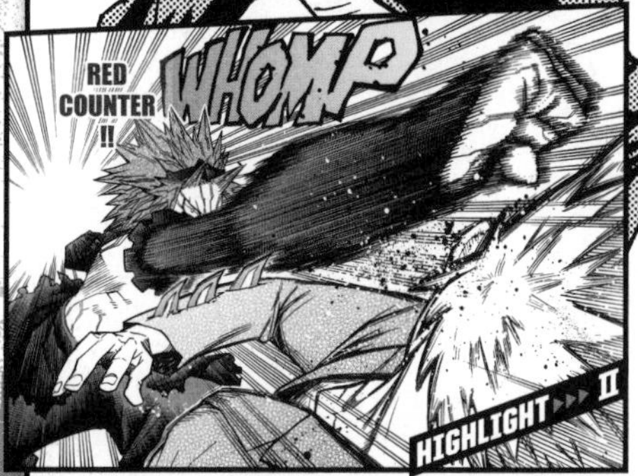
WHOMP
RED COUNTER !!
HIGHLIGHT ▸▸▸ II

⬅ Kirishima's Quirk gives him a big advantage in brawls, but the challenge is luring his opponent close enough to strike.

## RELATIONSHIPS

- Eijiro Kirishima → Fat Gum: I gotta protect you, Fat!
- Fat Gum → Eijiro Kirishima: Craggy meets squishy / Even villains respect you.
- Eijiro Kirishima → Katsuki Bakugo: I love how manly you are, dude!!
- Katsuki Bakugo → Eijiro Kirishima: Friends on even footing / You're an idiot, but I don't hate ya.
- Eijiro Kirishima → Tetsutetsu Tetsutetsu: You learned from my mistakes!
- Tetsutetsu Tetsutetsu → Eijiro Kirishima: Rock-hard friendship / We gotta face off again sometime soon.
- Eijiro Kirishima → Mina Ashido: Say bye to the old me!
- Mina Ashido → Eijiro Kirishima: Witness to the chivalrous awakening / You're still a bundle of nerves!

## PROFILE

Name: **Eijiro Kirishima**
Hero name: **Red Riot**
Quirk: **Hardening**
Birthday: **October 16**
Height: **170 cm**
Blood type: **O**
Birthplace: **Chiba Prefecture**
Personality: **Enthusiasm generator**
Ultimate moves: **Red Counter, Unbreakable, Red Gauntlet**

- "You gotta trust your pals! Be a man, Bakugo! You've convinced me!" (vol. 2, chap. 17)
- "Shooting someone and then getting scared and running away ain't manly!!" (vol. 15, chap. 133)
- "That's why I never wanna regret anything ever again!! I'll be...a hero who protects others." (vol. 16, chap. 145)
- "I'm just a pathetic guy who abandons people in danger. But no more!" (vol. 16, chap. 146)

**Kirishima's Notable Quotables**

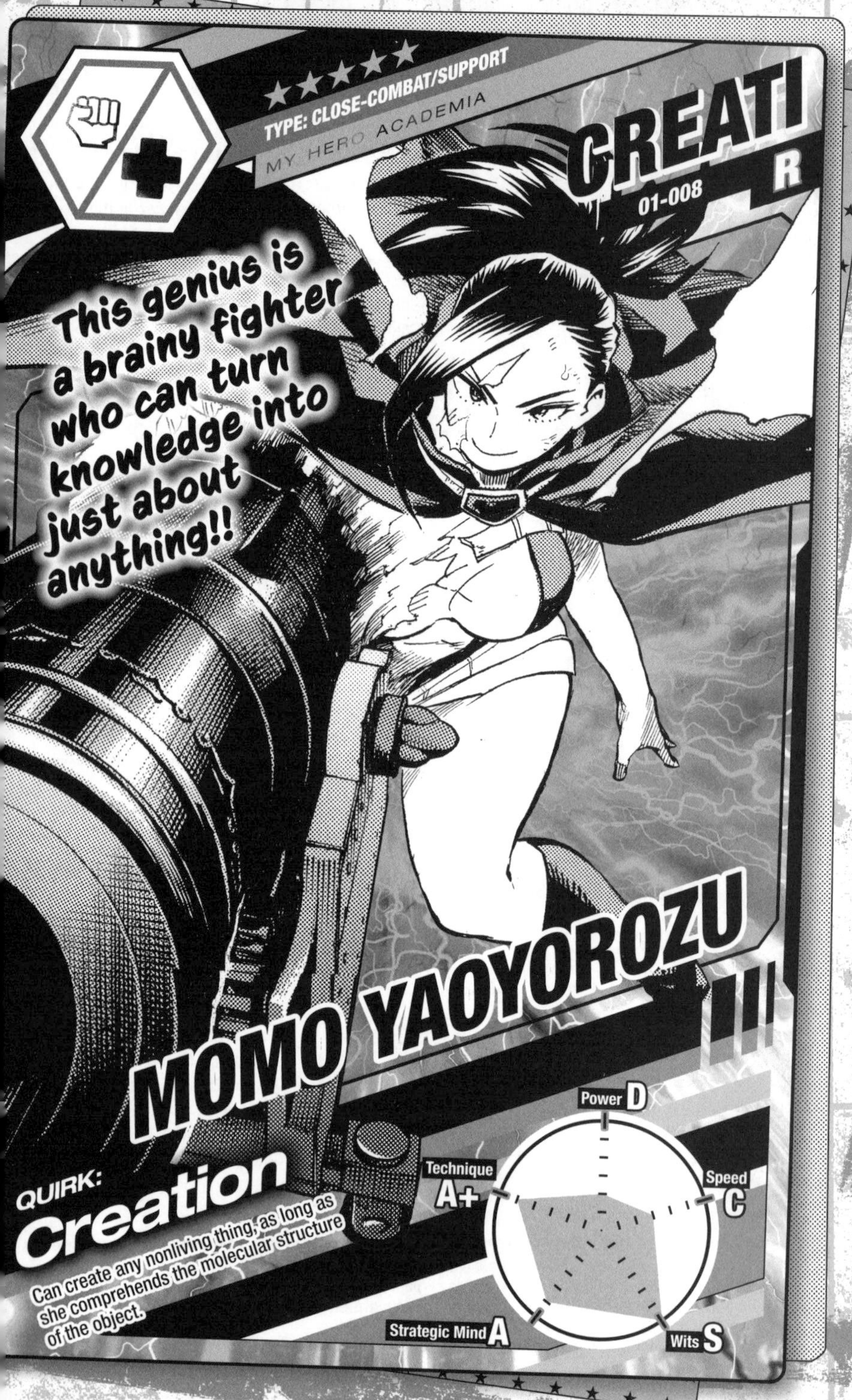

TYPE: CLOSE-COMBAT/SUPPORT
MY HERO ACADEMIA
CREATI
R
01-008
This genius is a brainy fighter who can turn knowledge into just about anything!!
MOMO YAOYOROZU
QUIRK:
Creation
Can create any nonliving thing, as long as she comprehends the molecular structure of the object.
Power D
Technique A+
Speed C
Strategic Mind A
Wits S

## A brilliant hotshot with leadership skills to boot!

This knowledgeable and cultured princess uses her unparalleled judgment and analytical skills to lead her classmates. She and Jiro started growing especially close after overcoming the U.S.J. training, and Jiro is the one who got Yaoyorozu listening to heavy metal.

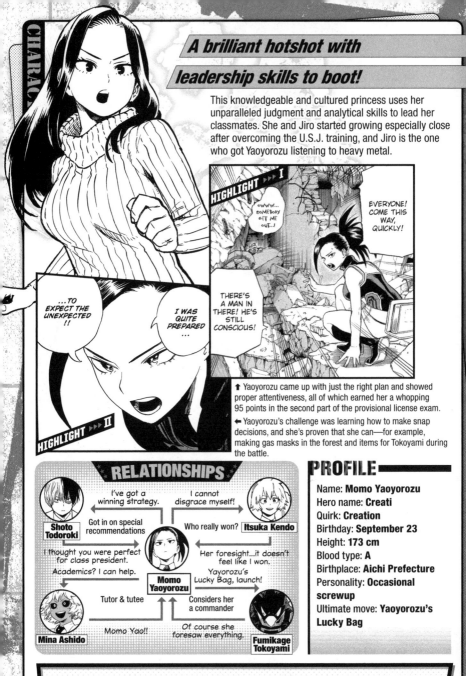

HIGHLIGHT ▸▸▸ I
EVERYONE! COME THIS WAY, QUICKLY!
OWWW... SOMEBODY GET ME OUT...!
THERE'S A MAN IN THERE! HE'S STILL CONSCIOUS!

I WAS QUITE PREPARED ...
...TO EXPECT THE UNEXPECTED !!
HIGHLIGHT ▸▸▸ II

⬆ Yaoyorozu came up with just the right plan and showed proper attentiveness, all of which earned her a whopping 95 points in the second part of the provisional license exam.

⬅ Yaoyorozu's challenge was learning how to make snap decisions, and she's proven that she can—for example, making gas masks in the forest and items for Tokoyami during the battle.

## RELATIONSHIPS

Shoto Todoroki
I've got a winning strategy.
Got in on special recommendations
I thought you were perfect for class president.
Itsuka Kendo
I cannot disgrace myself!
Who really won?
Her foresight...it doesn't feel like I won.
Momo Yaoyorozu
Academics? I can help.
Tutor & tutee
Momo Yao!!
Mina Ashido
Yayorozu's Lucky Bag, launch!
Considers her a commander
Of course she foresaw everything.
Fumikage Tokoyami

## PROFILE

Name: **Momo Yaoyorozu**
Hero name: **Creati**
Quirk: **Creation**
Birthday: **September 23**
Height: **173 cm**
Blood type: **A**
Birthplace: **Aichi Prefecture**
Personality: **Occasional screwup**
Ultimate move: **Yaoyorozu's Lucky Bag**

- "If we don't earnestly cheer each other on, we'll never be top heroes!" (vol. 2, chap. 11)
- "They're Russian matryoshka dolls." (vol. 8, chap. 63)
- "I have a plan in mind that's sure to lead us to victory against Aizawa Sensei!!" (vol. 8, chap. 63)
- "It takes quite a bit of time to create something so big." (vol. 22, chap. 201)

**Yaoyorozu's Notable Quotables**

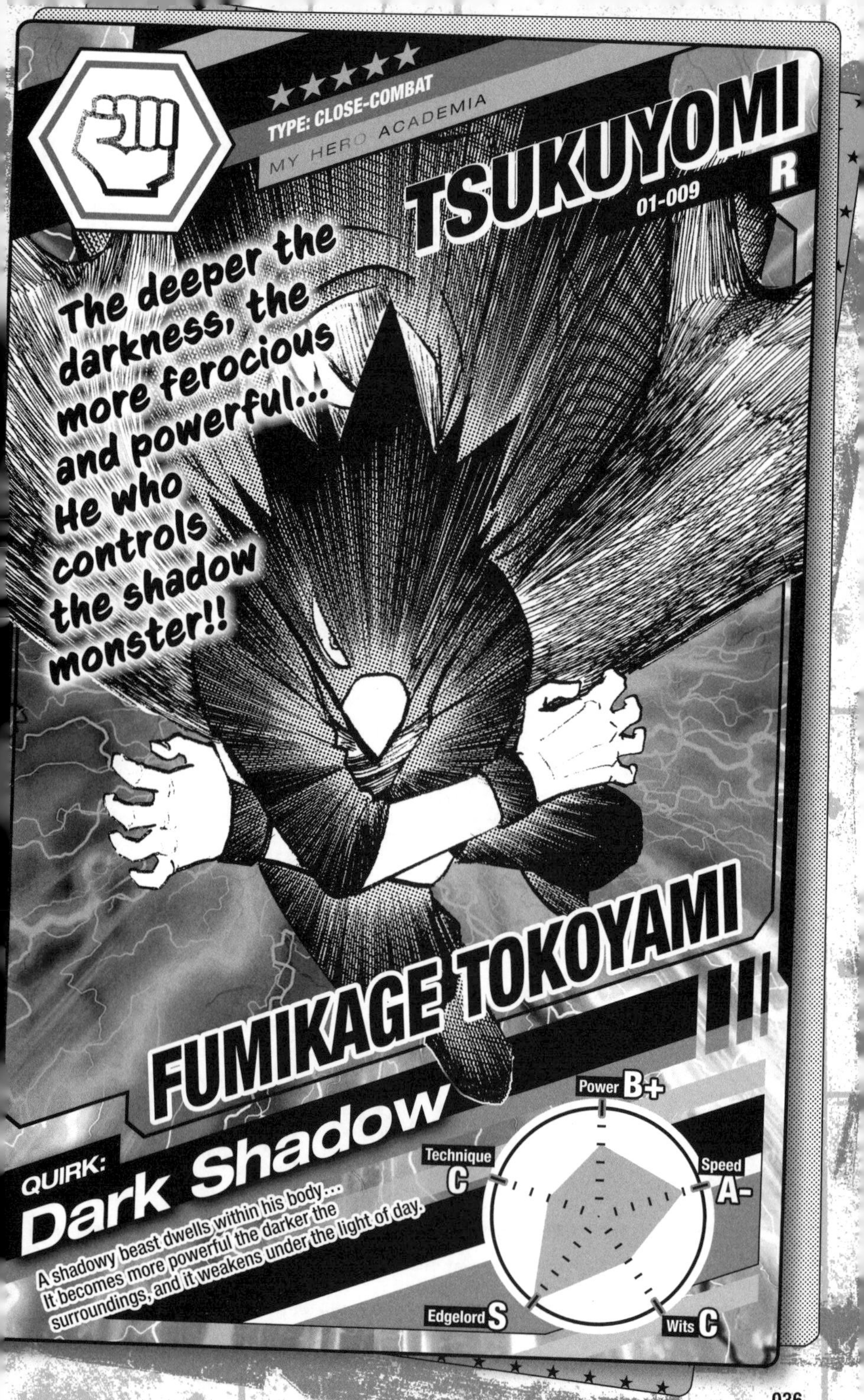
TYPE: CLOSE-COMBAT
MY HERO ACADEMIA
TSUKUYOMI
R
01-009
The deeper the darkness, the more ferocious and powerful... He who controls the shadow monster!!
FUMIKAGE TOKOYAMI
QUIRK:
Dark Shadow
A shadowy beast dwells within his body... It becomes more powerful the darker the surroundings, and it weakens under the light of day.
Power B+
Speed A-
Wits C
Edgelord S
Technique C

CHARACTER

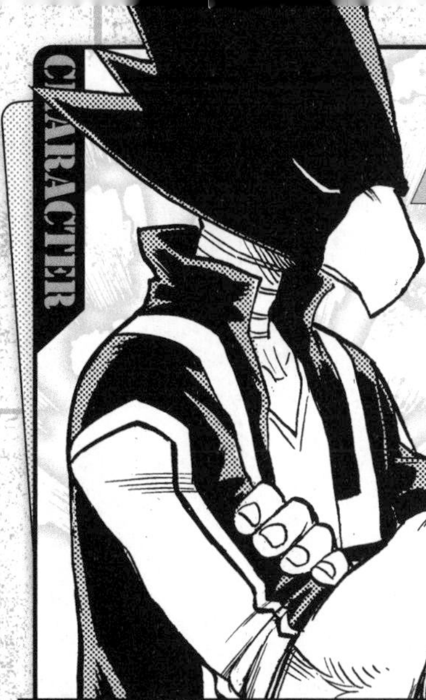

## Silent and skilled: the edgy dark hero.

His edgelord nature makes him talk kind of funny. Special training led Tokoyami to invent the Abyssal Black Body move, where he cloaks himself with Dark Shadow for more powerful abilities. According to him, that's a choker around his neck—not bandages. Tokoyami is heavily inspired by his favorite hero, Dark Crystal.

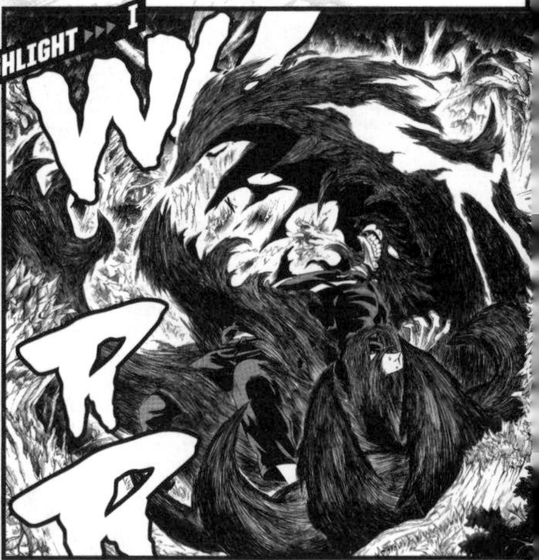
HIGHLIGHT ▸▸▸ I
WRR

↑ When Shoji was injured, Tokoyami's emotions took over and Dark Shadow went wild. Afterward, it was clear that he needed more control over his familiar…

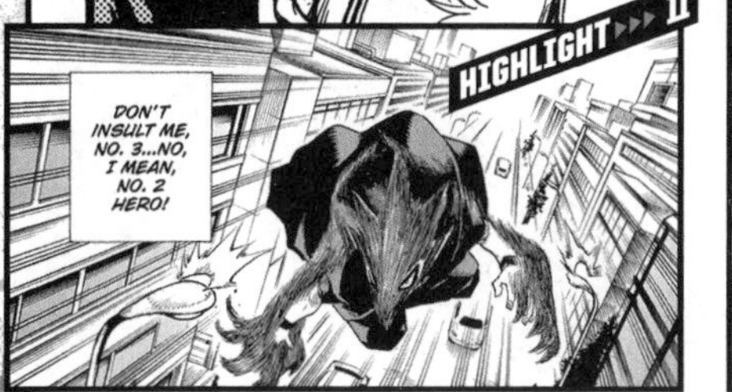
HIGHLIGHT ▸▸▸ II
DON'T INSULT ME, NO. 3...NO, I MEAN, NO. 2 HERO!

↑ Tokoyami did his work study under Hawks, the no. 3 hero at the time. That was when he learned to fly using Dark Shadow.

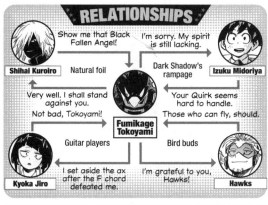

## RELATIONSHIPS

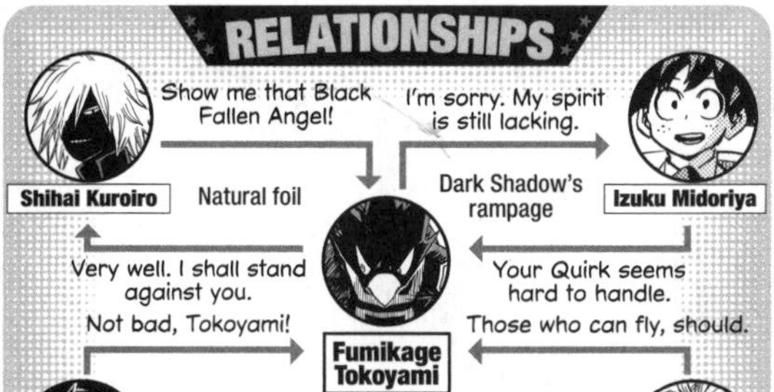
Shihai Kuroiro
Show me that Black Fallen Angel!
Natural foil
Very well. I shall stand against you.
Izuku Midoriya
I'm sorry. My spirit is still lacking.
Dark Shadow's rampage
Your Quirk seems hard to handle.
Fumikage Tokoyami
Not bad, Tokoyami!
Guitar players
I set aside the ax after the F chord defeated me.
Kyoka Jiro
Those who can fly, should.
Bird buds
I'm grateful to you, Hawks!
Hawks

## PROFILE

Name: **Fumikage Tokoyami**
Hero name: **Tsukuyomi**
Quirk: **Dark Shadow**
Birthday: **October 30**
Height: **158 cm**
Blood type: **AB**
Birthplace: **Shizuoka Prefecture**
Personality: **Calm and collected denizen of the abyss**
Ultimate moves: **Abyssal Black Body, Piercing Twilight Claws, Covert Black-Ops Arms, Dark Shadow: Black Fallen Angel, etc.**

- "The fate of those who are pursued… Make your choice, Midoriya!" (vol. 4, chap. 28)
- "Calm yourself…Dark…Shadow!!" (vol. 9, chap. 79)
- "I'm no dumb carrier pigeon." (vol. 21, chap. 199)
- "H-Hawks!! It's like we've become the wind!" (vol. 21, chap. 199)

**Tokoyami's Notable Quotables**

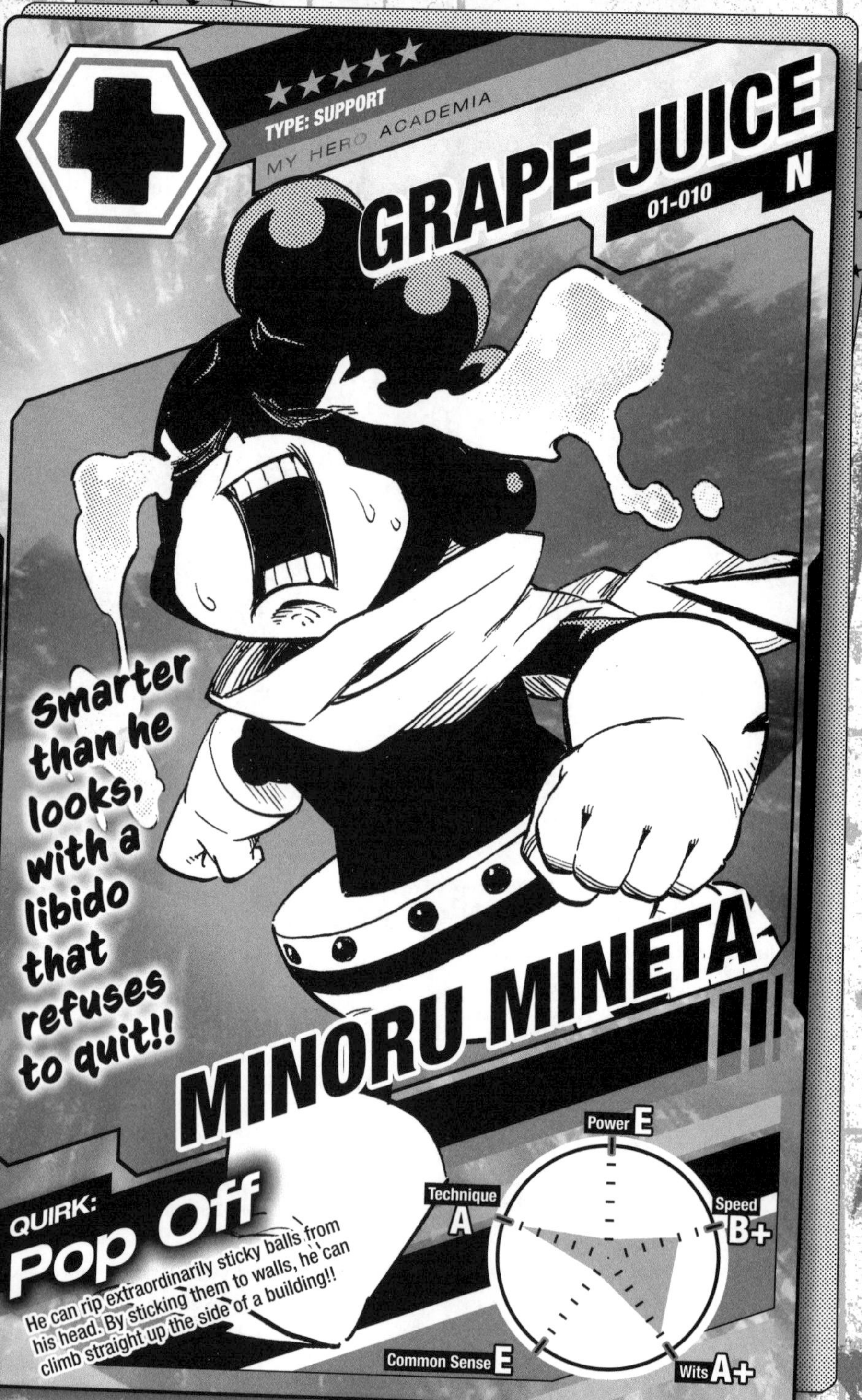
TYPE: SUPPORT
MY HERO ACADEMIA
GRAPE JUICE
N
01-010
Smarter than he looks, with a libido that refuses to quit!!
MINORU MINETA
QUIRK:
Pop Off
He can rip extraordinarily sticky balls from his head. By sticking them to walls, he can climb straight up the side of a building!!
Power E
Technique A
Speed B+
Common Sense E
Wits A+

CHARACTER

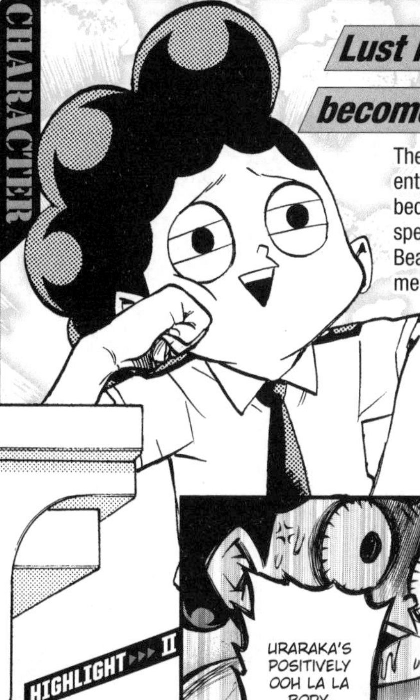

# Lust motivates him, and he seeks to become a hero as an in with the ladi

The number one perv of the Hero Course. Though entirely lacking in sex appeal, Mineta believes that becoming a hero will help him get lucky, so to speak. His new weapon (one of his few)—Mineta Beads—was inspired by something we won't mention in a book read by children!

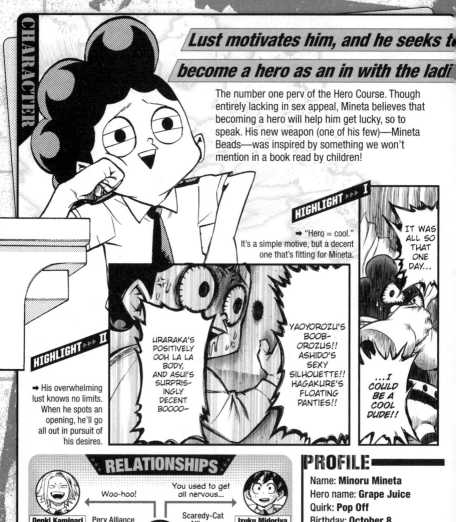

HIGHLIGHT ▸▸▸ I

➡ "Hero = cool." It's a simple motive, but a decent one that's fitting for Mineta.

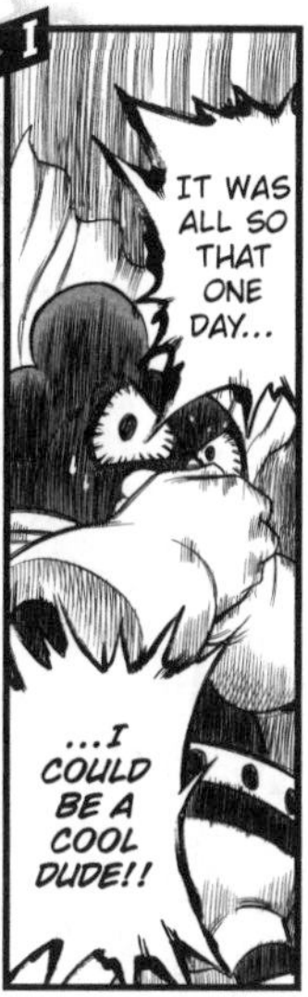
IT WAS ALL SO THAT ONE DAY...
...I COULD BE A COOL DUDE!!

HIGHLIGHT ▸▸▸ II

➡ His overwhelming lust knows no limits. When he spots an opening, he'll go all out in pursuit of his desires.

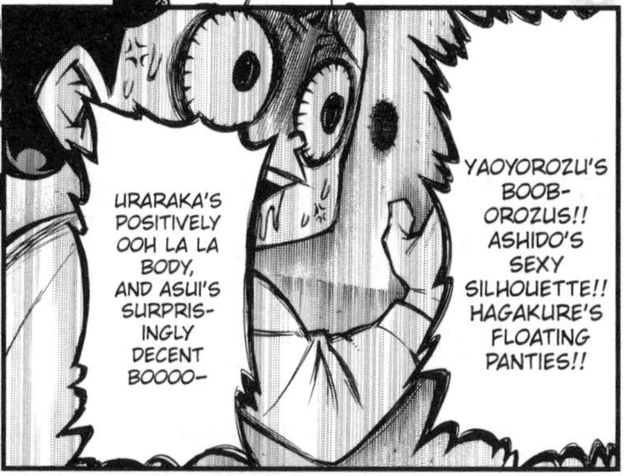
YAOYOROZU'S BOOB-OROZUS!! ASHIDO'S SEXY SILHOUETTE!! HAGAKURE'S FLOATING PANTIES!!
URARAKA'S POSITIVELY OOH LA LA BODY, AND ASUI'S SURPRIS-INGLY DECENT BOOOO-

## RELATIONSHIPS

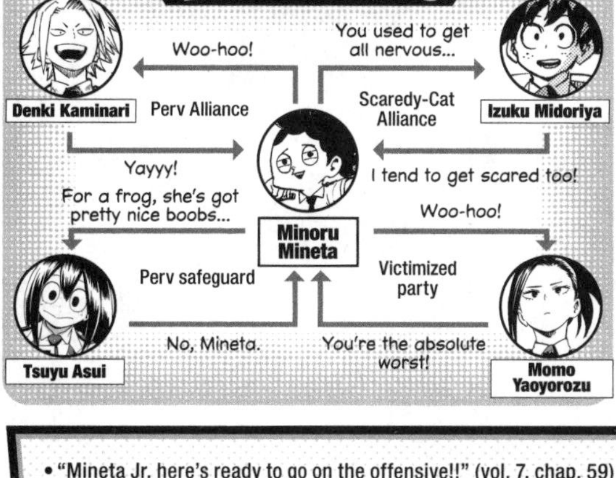
Denki Kaminari
Woo-hoo!
Perv Alliance
Yayyy!
Izuku Midoriya
You used to get all nervous...
Scaredy-Cat Alliance
I tend to get scared too!
Minoru Mineta
For a frog, she's got pretty nice boobs...
Perv safeguard
No, Mineta.
Tsuyu Asui
Woo-hoo!
Victimized party
You're the absolute worst!
Momo Yaoyorozu

## PROFILE

Name: **Minoru Mineta**
Hero name: **Grape Juice**
Quirk: **Pop Off**
Birthday: **October 8**
Height: **108 cm**
Blood type: **A**
Birthplace: **Kanagawa Prefecture**
Personality: **Perverted straight shooter**
Ultimate moves: **Grape Rush, Grape Buckler**

- "Mineta Jr. here's ready to go on the offensive!!" (vol. 7, chap. 59)
- "Just this one time, I'll let you have those boobs." (vol. 8, chap. 67)
- "Boy, did we misjudge you, you womanizing scum!!" (vol. 13, chap. 109)
- "I'm sold. I can't wait for this festival to start." (vol. 19, chap. 172)

Mineta's Notable Quotables

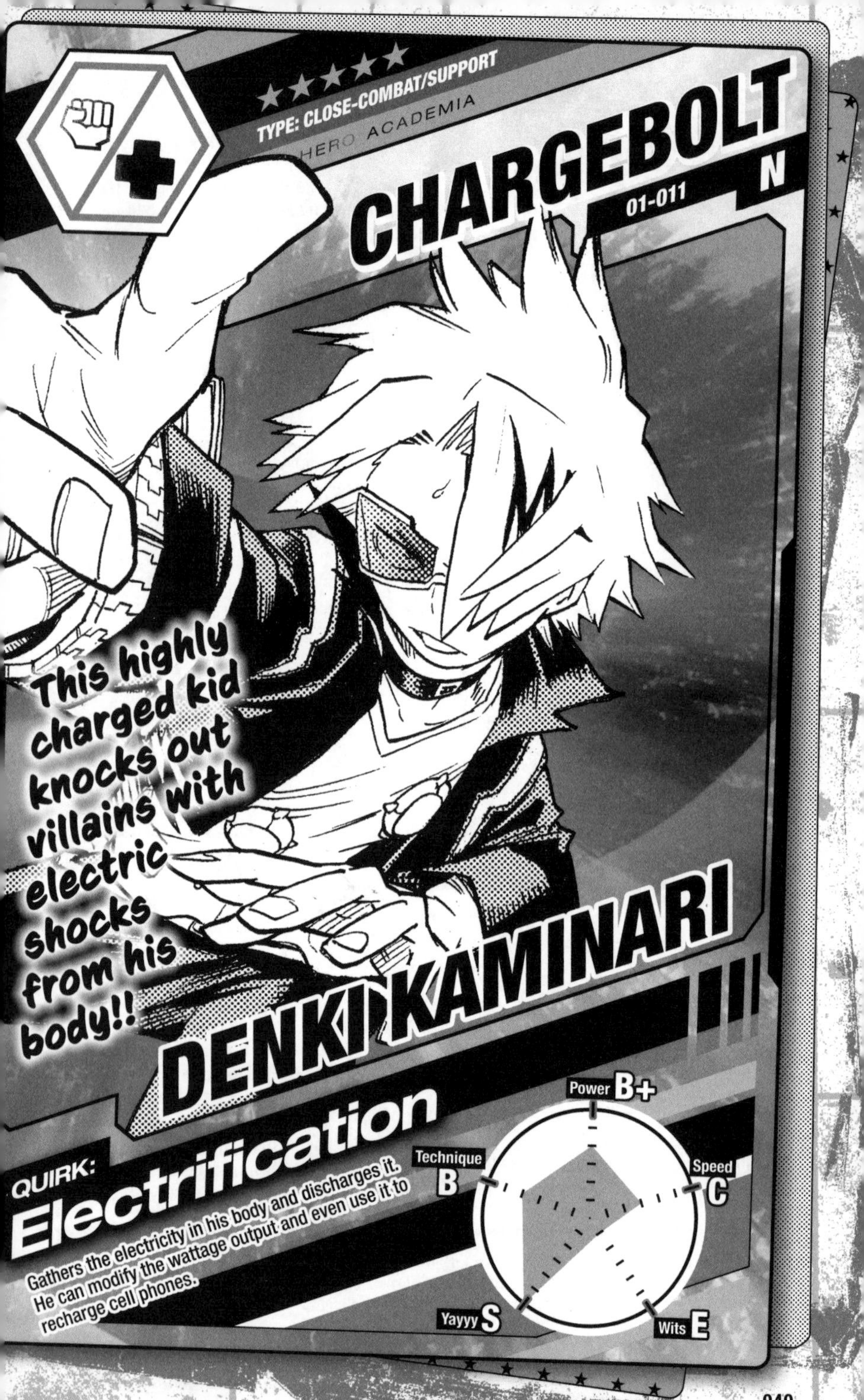
TYPE: CLOSE-COMBAT/SUPPORT
HERO ACADEMIA
CHARGEBOLT
01-011
N
This highly charged kid knocks out villains with electric shocks from his body!!
DENKI KAMINARI
QUIRK:
Electrification
Gathers the electricity in his body and discharges it. He can modify the wattage output and even use it to recharge cell phones.
Power B+
Technique B
Speed C
Yayyy S
Wits E

CHARACTER

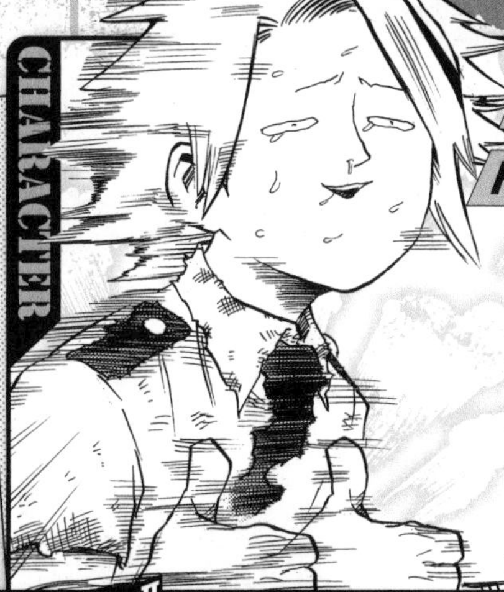

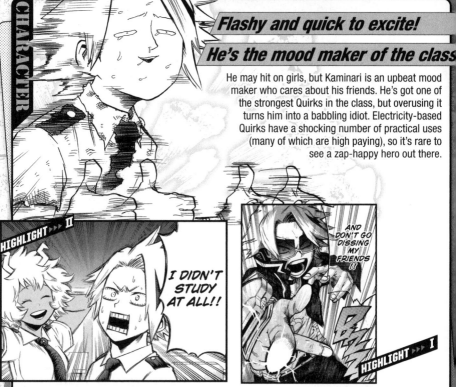

## *Flashy and quick to excite!*

## *He's the mood maker of the class*

He may hit on girls, but Kaminari is an upbeat mood maker who cares about his friends. He's got one of the strongest Quirks in the class, but overusing it turns him into a babbling idiot. Electricity-based Quirks have a shocking number of practical uses (many of which are high paying), so it's rare to see a zap-happy hero out there.

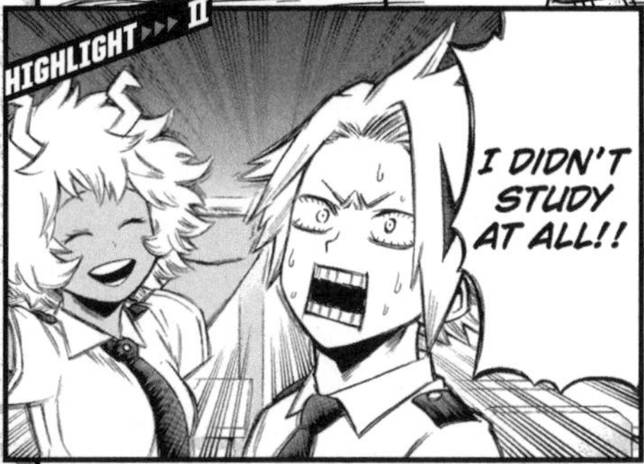

HIGHLIGHT ▸▸▸ II
I DIDN'T STUDY AT ALL!!


⬆ He barely holds it together academically. He got the lowest scores on the midterm exams, and then he and Ashido lost to Principal Nezu during the final exams and had to attend remedial lessons.

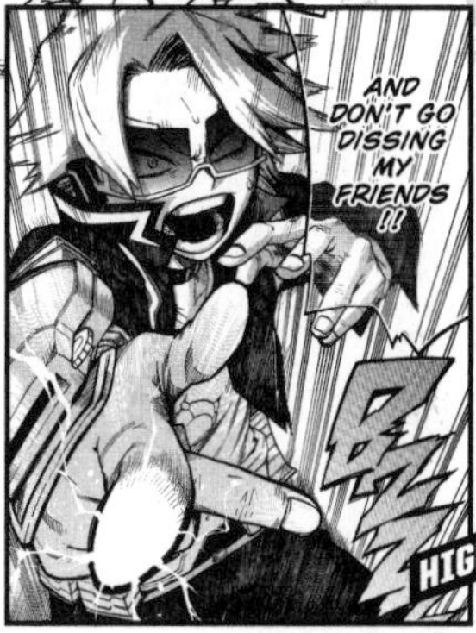

AND DON'T GO DISSING MY FRIENDS!!
BZZ
HIGHLIGHT ▸▸▸ I


⬆ During the provisional license exam, Kaminari was enraged when Shishikura insulted Bakugo and Kirishima. His passionate feelings translated into some powerful electric attacks!

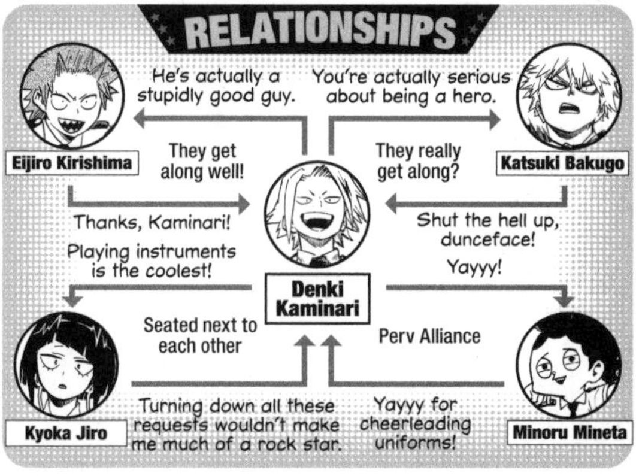

RELATIONSHIPS
Eijiro Kirishima
He's actually a stupidly good guy.
They get along well!
Thanks, Kaminari!
Katsuki Bakugo
You're actually serious about being a hero.
They really get along?
Shut the hell up, dunceface!
Denki Kaminari
Playing instruments is the coolest!
Kyoka Jiro
Seated next to each other
Turning down all these requests wouldn't make me much of a rock star.
Yayyy!
Perv Alliance
Yayyy for cheerleading uniforms!
Minoru Mineta


## PROFILE

Name: **Denki Kaminari**
Hero name: **Chargebolt**
Quirk: **Electrification**
Birthday: **June 29**
Height: **168 cm**
Blood type: **O**
Birthplace: **Saitama Prefecture**
Personality: **All flash, little substance**
Ultimate moves: **Indiscriminate Shock 1.3 Million Volts, Target Electo**

- "This match will probably be over in an instant." (vol. 4, chap. 35)
- "Don't think some half-baked intel is enough for you to know him… And don't go dissing my friends!!" (vol. 12, chap. 107)
- "You said you're not here to make friends, but I'm a fan already. You're cut out to be a hero, for sure." (vol. 21, chap. 196)

**Kaminari's Notable Quotables**

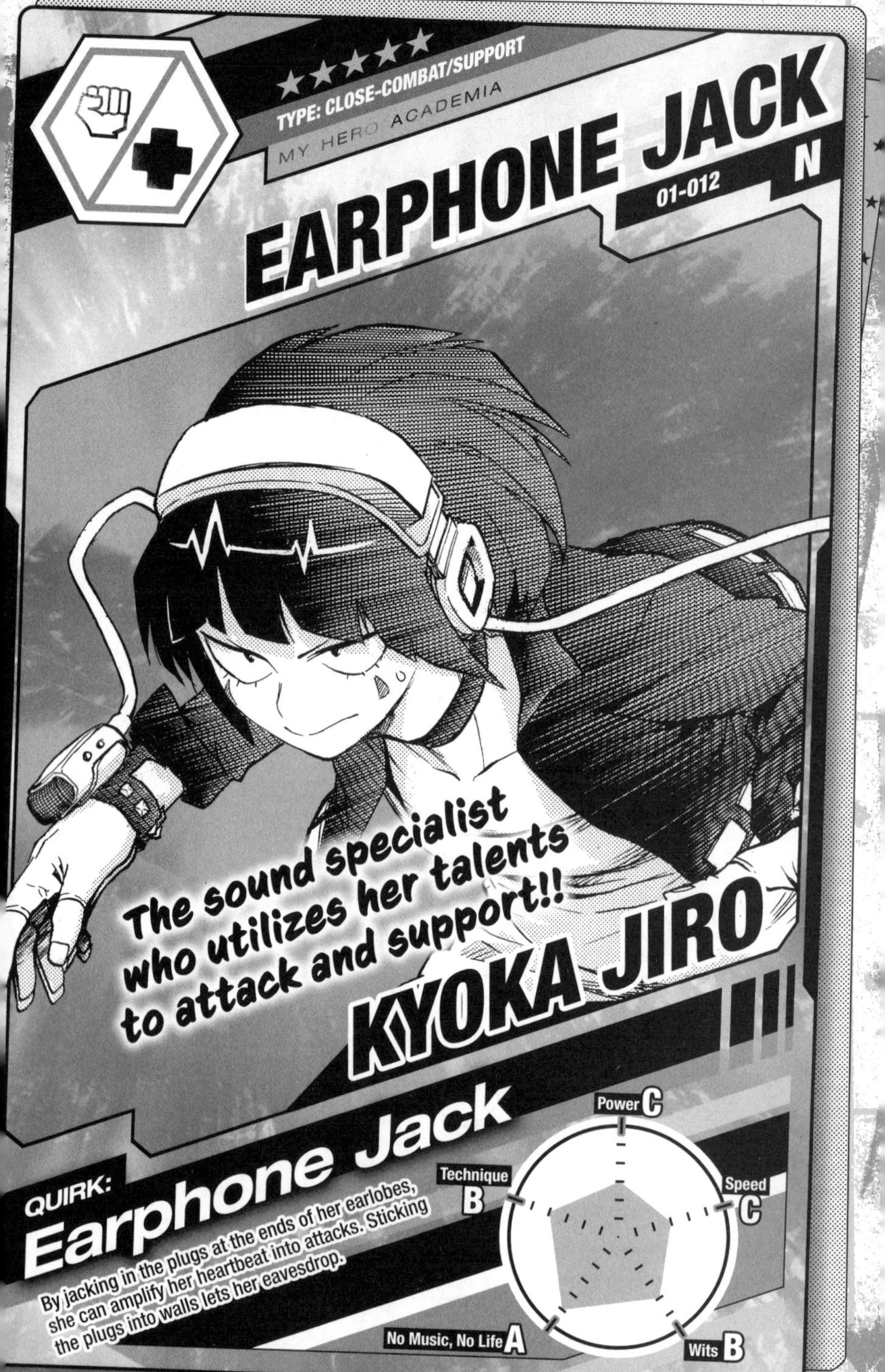

★★★★★
TYPE: CLOSE-COMBAT/SUPPORT
MY HERO ACADEMIA
EARPHONE JACK
01-012
N
The sound specialist who utilizes her talents to attack and support!!
KYOKA JIRO
QUIRK:
Earphone Jack
By jacking in the plugs at the ends of her earlobes, she can amplify her heartbeat into attacks. Sticking the plugs into walls lets her eavesdrop.
Power C
Speed C
Wits B
No Music, No Life A
Technique B

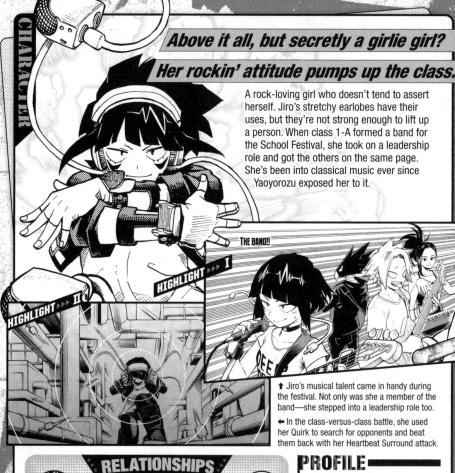

CHARACTER

## Above it all, but secretly a girlie girl?

## Her rockin' attitude pumps up the class.

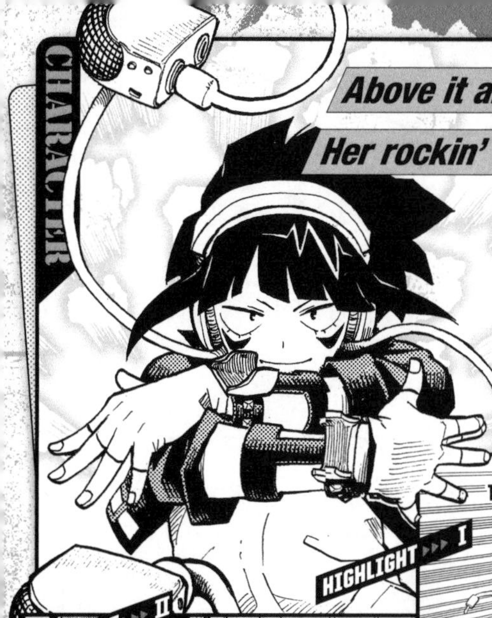

A rock-loving girl who doesn't tend to assert herself. Jiro's stretchy earlobes have their uses, but they're not strong enough to lift up a person. When class 1-A formed a band for the School Festival, she took on a leadership role and got the others on the same page. She's been into classical music ever since Yaoyorozu exposed her to it.

HIGHLIGHT ▸▸▸ I

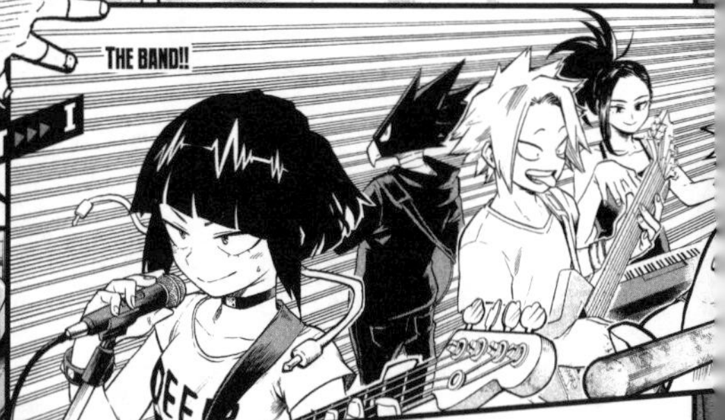

THE BAND!!


HIGHLIGHT ▸▸▸ II

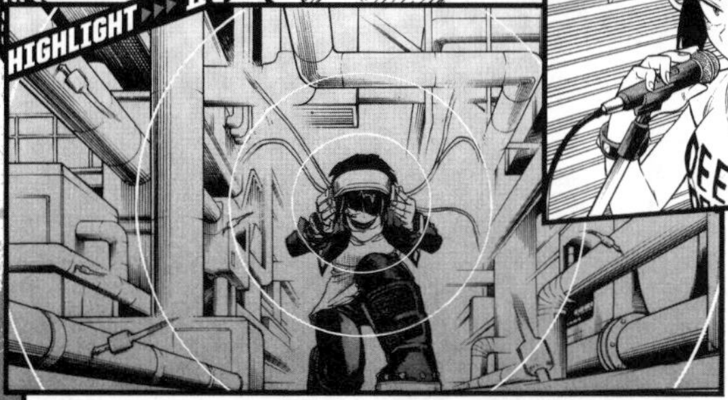

⬆ Jiro's musical talent came in handy during the festival. Not only was she a member of the band—she stepped into a leadership role too.

⬅ In the class-versus-class battle, she used her Quirk to search for opponents and beat them back with her Heartbeat Surround attack.

## RELATIONSHIPS

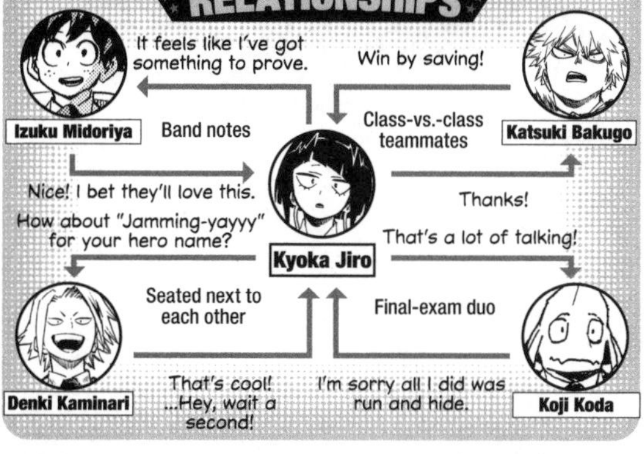

It feels like I've got something to prove.
Win by saving!
Izuku Midoriya
Band notes
Class-vs.-class teammates
Katsuki Bakugo
Nice! I bet they'll love this.
How about "Jamming-yayyy" for your hero name?
Thanks!
That's a lot of talking!
Kyoka Jiro
Seated next to each other
Final-exam duo
Denki Kaminari
That's cool! ...Hey, wait a second!
I'm sorry all I did was run and hide.
Koji Koda


## PROFILE

Name: **Kyoka Jiro**
Hero name: **Earphone Jack**
Quirk: **Earphone Jack**
Birthday: **August 1**
Height: **154 cm**
Blood type: **A**
Birthplace: **Shizuoka Prefecture**
Personality: **Shy rock fan**
Ultimate moves: **Heartbeat Distortion, Heartbeat Surround**

- "I'm the only one he didn't mention." (vol. 7, chap. 59)
- "You wanna be a hero, don't you?! Then let's pass this test." (vol. 8, chap. 66)
- "Turning down all these requests wouldn't make me much of a rock star." (vol. 19, chap. 169)
- "The set list's decided! Now it's nothing but practice time so we can kill it onstage!!" (vol. 19, chap. 173)

Jiro's Notable Quotables

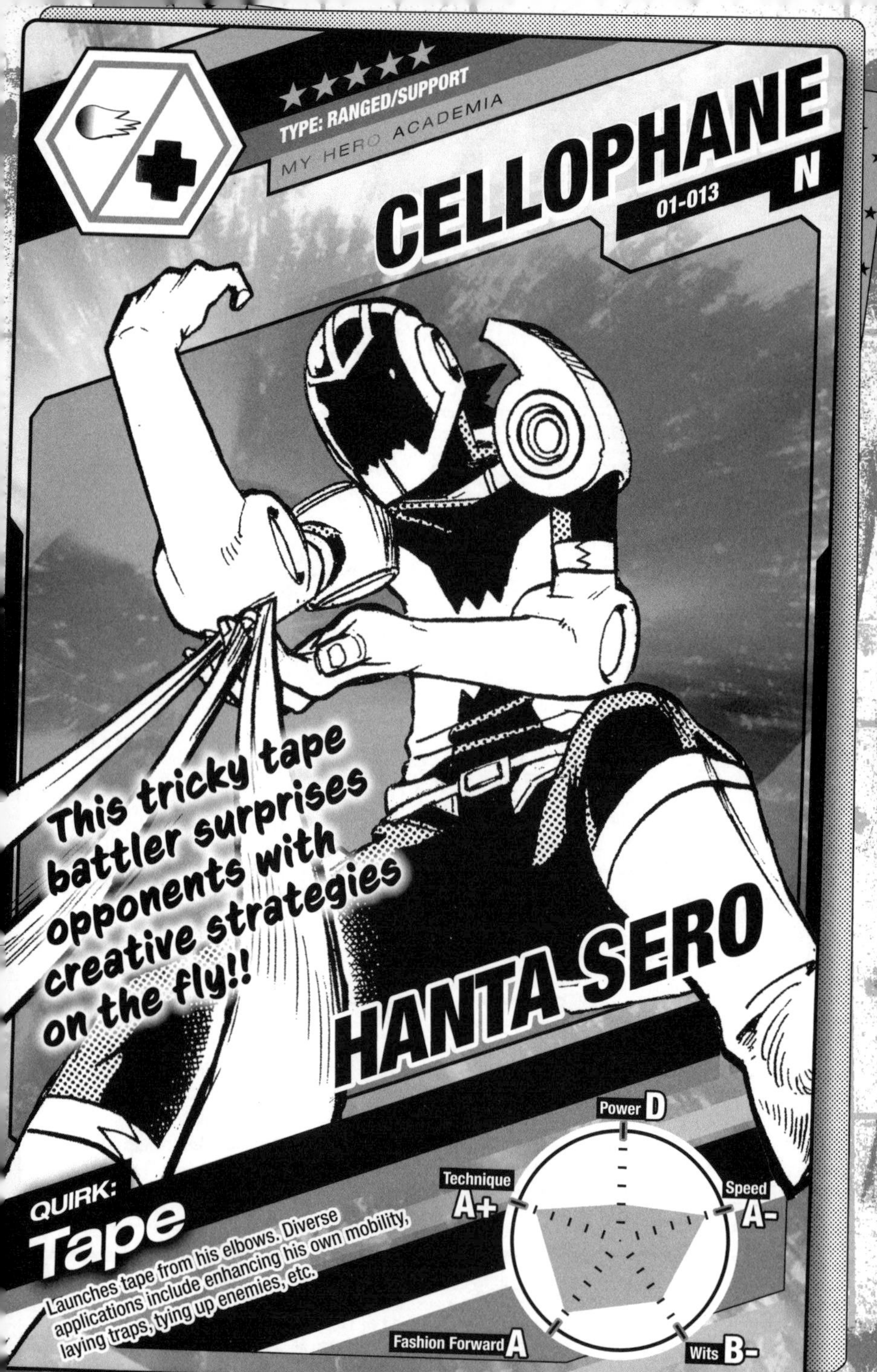
TYPE: RANGED/SUPPORT
MY HERO ACADEMIA
CELLOPHANE
N
01-013
This tricky tape battler surprises opponents with creative strategies on the fly!!
HANTA SERO
Power D
Technique A+
Speed A-
Fashion Forward A
Wits B-
QUIRK:
Tape
Launches tape from his elbows. Diverse applications include enhancing his own mobility, laying traps, tying up enemies, etc.

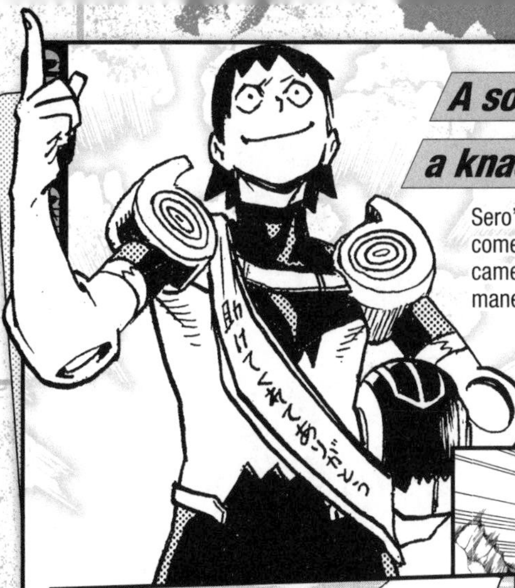

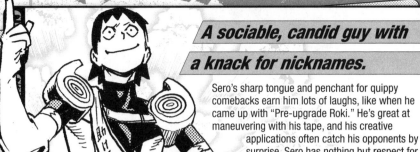

## A sociable, candid guy with a knack for nicknames.

Sero's sharp tongue and penchant for quippy comebacks earn him lots of laughs, like when he came up with "Pre-upgrade Roki." He's great at maneuvering with his tape, and his creative applications often catch his opponents by surprise. Sero has nothing but respect for a certain American web-slinging hero.

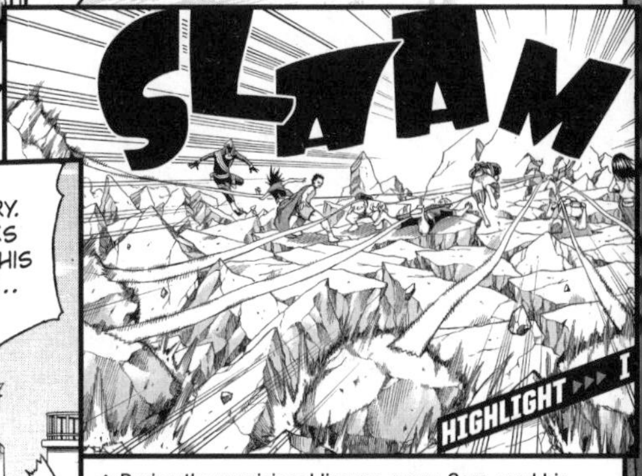
SLAM
HIGHLIGHT ▸▸▸ I

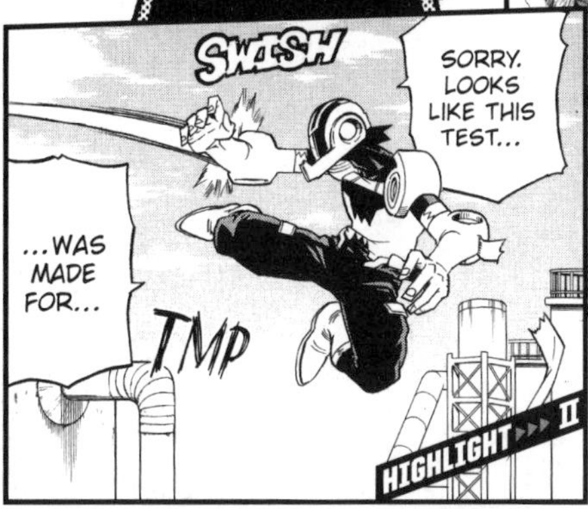
SWISH
SORRY. LOOKS LIKE THIS TEST...
...WAS MADE FOR...
TMP
HIGHLIGHT ▸▸▸ II

⬆ During the provisional license exam, Sero used his tape and some rubble to set a trap that pinned down his rivals.

⬅ Sero's tape allowed him to soar over obstacles with ease. He took first place in the rescue training race.

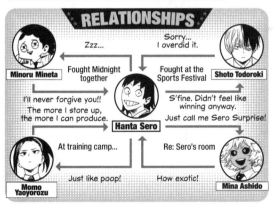

## RELATIONSHIPS

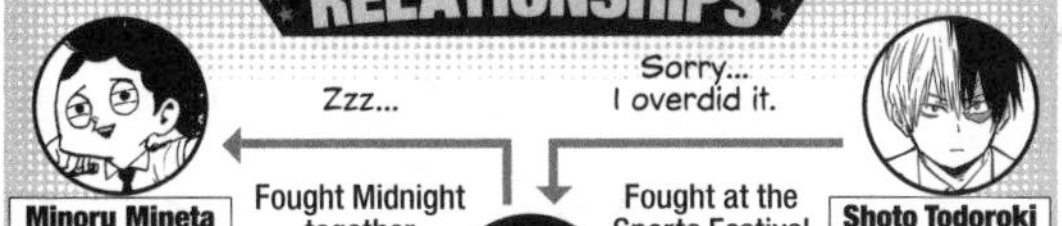
Minoru Mineta
Zzz...
Fought Midnight together
I'll never forgive you!!
Sorry... I overdid it.
Fought at the Sports Festival
Shoto Todoroki
S'fine. Didn't feel like winning anyway.
Hanta Sero
The more I store up, the more I can produce.
Just call me Sero Surprise!
At training camp...
Just like poop!
Momo Yaoyorozu
Re: Sero's room
How exotic!
Mina Ashido

## PROFILE

Name: **Hanta Sero**
Hero name: **Cellophane**
Quirk: **Tape**
Birthday: **July 28**
Height: **177 cm**
Blood type: **B**
Birthplace: **Tokyo**
Personality: **Guy who can read the room**
Ultimate moves: **Barricade Tape, Tape Shot: Trident**

- "Hrm… I don't really feel much like winning… But I don't feel like losing either!!" (vol. 4, chap. 34)
- "It's a perfect 2:8 hair ratio!! Bwa ha ha ha ha!" (vol. 7, chap. 58)
- "I got 84!! Pretty awesome, huh?! See, the simpler you are, the better!" (vol. 13, chap. 114)

### Sero's Notable Quotables

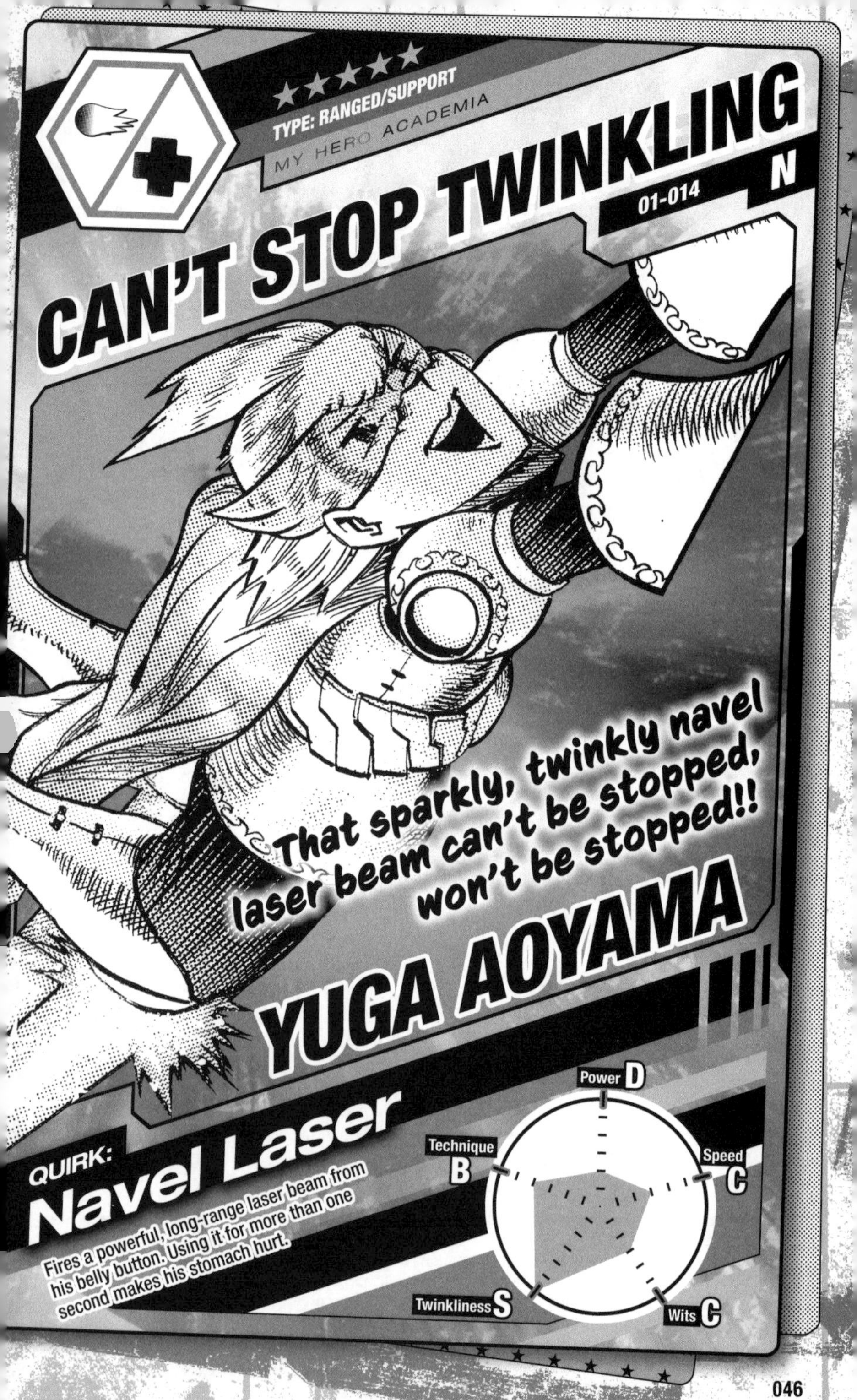
TYPE: RANGED/SUPPORT
MY HERO ACADEMIA
CAN'T STOP TWINKLING
01-014
N
That sparkly, twinkly navel laser beam can't be stopped, won't be stopped!!
YUGA AOYAMA
QUIRK:
Navel Laser
Fires a powerful, long-range laser beam from his belly button. Using it for more than one second makes his stomach hurt.
Power D
Speed C
Wits C
Twinkliness S
Technique B

CHARACTER

# Smug?! Obnoxious?! The mysterious princely dandy!

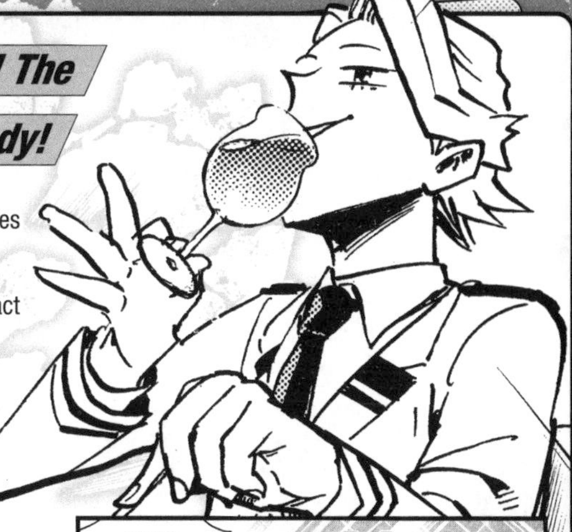

This inscrutable narcissist lives in his own world, and there's nothing he loves like his own sparkly self. It's tough to nail down Aoyama's personality since he rarely goes out of his way to interact with others. Still, he watches people closely and sees right through them. On occasion, Aoyama will blurt out the truth.

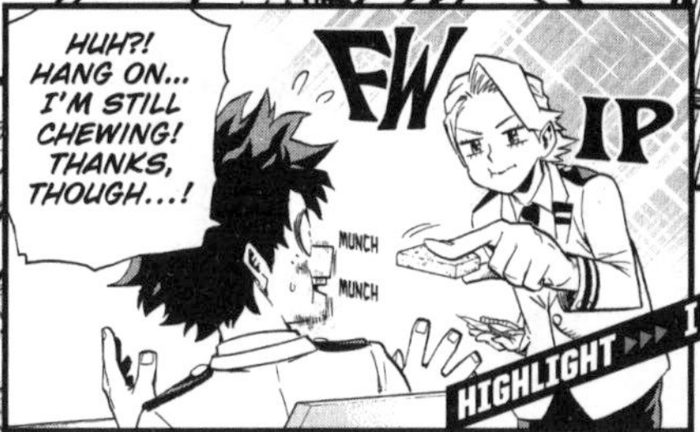

HUH?! HANG ON... I'M STILL CHEWING! THANKS, THOUGH...!
FWIP
MUNCH
MUNCH
HIGHLIGHT ▸▸▸ I


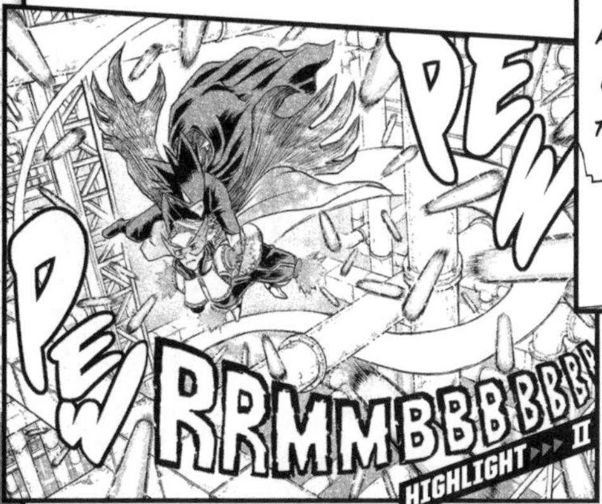

PEW
PEW
RRMMBBBBB
HIGHLIGHT ▸▸▸ II


⬆ Aoyama senses that he and Midoriya share similar struggles, so he begins to open up. Giving someone cheese is his idea of a fun surprise.

⬅ Since strengthening his Quirk, Aoyama can shoot lasers from his shoulders and knees as well, creating a multidirectional barrage.

## RELATIONSHIPS

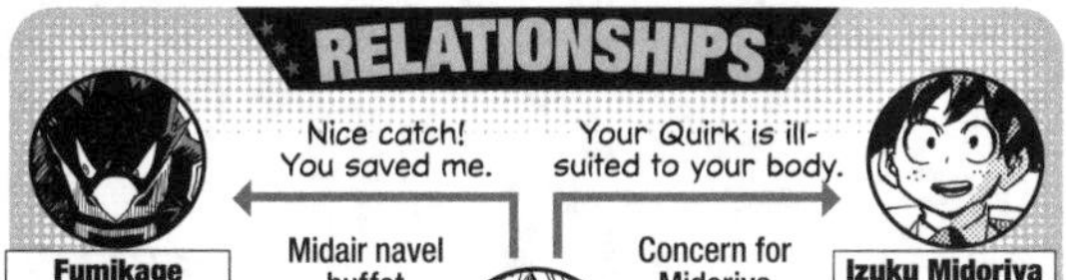

Fumikage Tokoyami
Nice catch! You saved me.
Midair navel buffet
We strike back from the skies! It's my gift to you.☆
Izuku Midoriya
Your Quirk is ill-suited to your body.
Concern for Midoriya
So sharp...Aoyama...
Yuga Aoyama
Tenya Ida
Cooperated during the licensing exam
This is all thanks to you.
Ochaco Uraraka
You like Midoriya, don't you?
Intuitive Aoyama
Huh?!


## PROFILE

Name: **Yuga Aoyama**
Hero name: **Can't Stop Twinkling**
Quirk: **Navel Laser**
Birthday: **May 30**
Height: **168 cm**
Blood type: **O**
Birthplace: **France (or so he claims)**
Personality: **Narcissistic free spirit**
Ultimate move: **Navel Buffet☆ Laser**

- "Non, non… Not shiny. Twinkly!" (vol. 11, chap. 98)
- "I always wanted to feel equal." (vol. 12, chap. 108)
- "Have some cheese." (vol. 18, chap. 167)
- "Did you enjoy my surprise?! ☆" (vol. 19, chap. 168)

## Aoyama's Notable Quotables

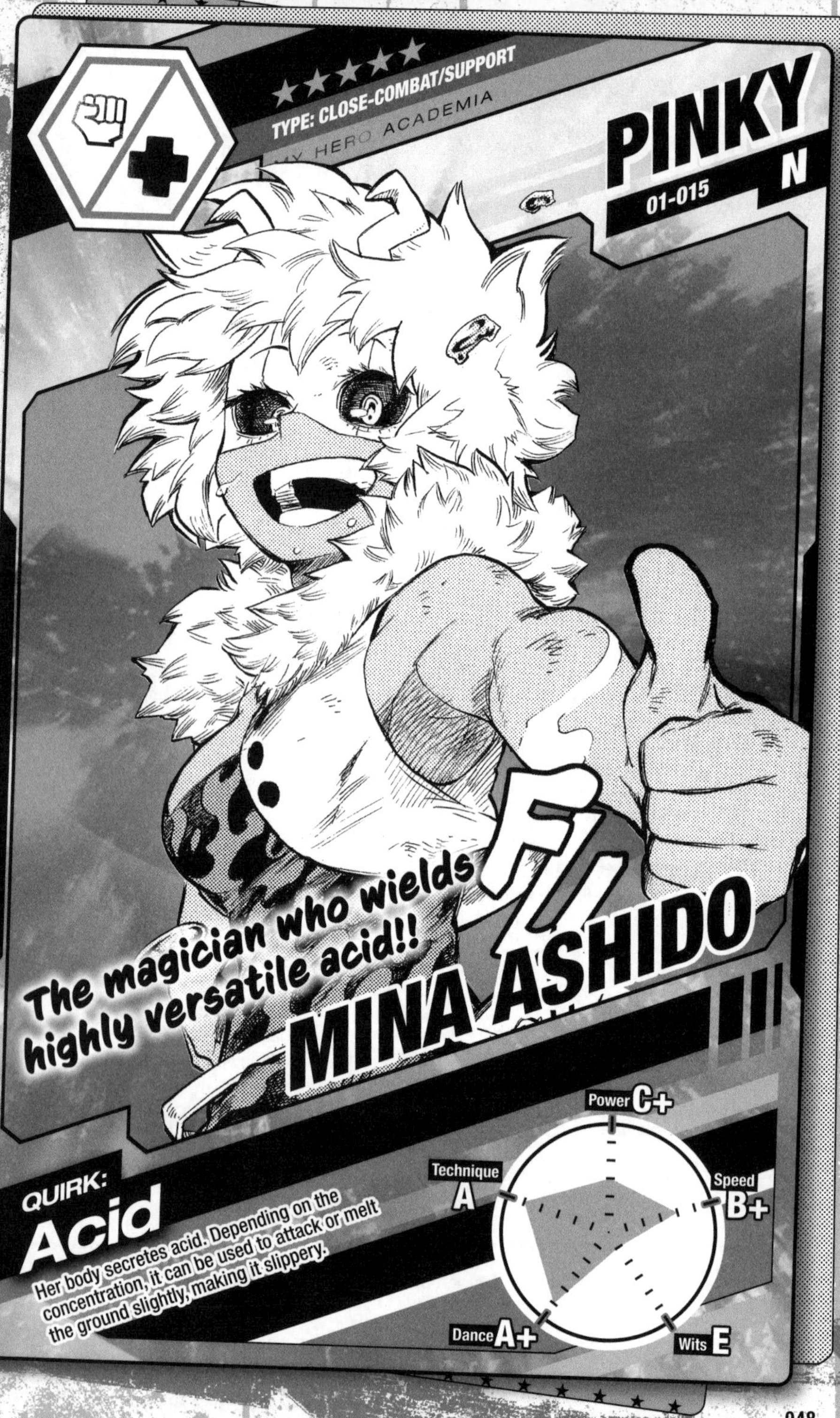
TYPE: CLOSE-COMBAT/SUPPORT
MY HERO ACADEMIA
PINKY
N
01-015
The magician who wields highly versatile acid!!
MINA ASHIDO
QUIRK:
Acid
Her body secretes acid. Depending on the concentration, it can be used to attack or melt the ground slightly, making it slippery.
Power C+
Technique A
Speed B+
Dance A+
Wits E

CHARACTER

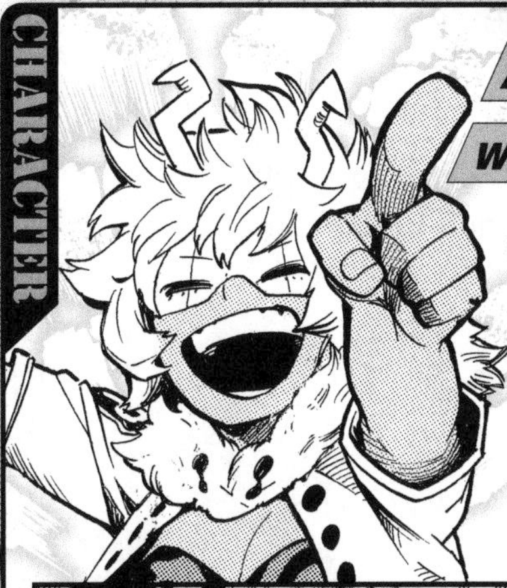

# An amazingly athletic girl who's friendly to all.

Ashido is anything but bashful. She's equally ready to make a new friend or stand up to danger in the name of courage and justice. She pays closer attention than others expect, making her especially good at coming up with team attacks. Fun fact: Ashido has never fallen in love, but she goes gaga over romance.

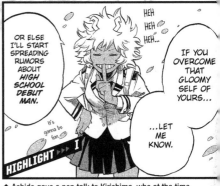

HEH HEH HEH...
IF YOU OVERCOME THAT GLOOMY SELF OF YOURS...
...LET ME KNOW.
OR ELSE I'LL START SPREADING RUMORS ABOUT *HIGH SCHOOL DEBUT MAN.*
It's gonna be fun.
HIGHLIGHT ▸▸▸ I

ACID VEIL!
SH
HIGHLIGHT ▸▸▸ II

⬆ Ashido gave a pep talk to Kirishima, who at the time was held back by regrets and an inferiority complex. Her kindness and consideration really worked.

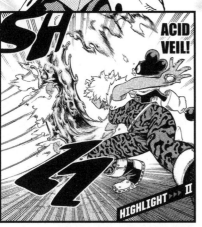

⬅ By upping the acid's viscosity, she can create a defensive wall as one of her ultimate moves. When it's big enough, it can even protect her allies.

## RELATIONSHIPS

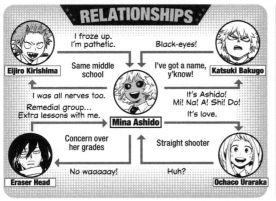

Eijiro Kirishima
I froze up. I'm pathetic.
Same middle school
I was all nerves too.
Katsuki Bakugo
Black-eyes!
I've got a name, y'know!
It's Ashido! Mi! Na! A! Shi! Do!
Mina Ashido
Eraser Head
Remedial group... Extra lessons with me.
Concern over her grades
No waaaaay!
Ochaco Uraraka
It's love.
Straight shooter
Huh?

## PROFILE

Name: **Mina Ashido**
Hero name: **Pinky**
Quirk: **Acid**
Birthday: **July 30**
Height: **159 cm**
Blood type: **AB**
Birthplace: **Chiba Prefecture**
Personality: **Pure energy**
Ultimate moves: **Acid Veil, Acid Shot, Acid Layback, Grape-Pinky Combo: Mineta Bounce**

- "As long as you don't get a tummy ache!" (vol. 2, chap. 13)
- "What the…? You're not looking very uraraka, Uraraka." (vol. 3, chap. 22)
- "Is that for our high school debut?! You got horns! Just like me!" (vol. 16, chap. 145)
- "The old you's not going anywhere with that emo look on your face!" (vol. 16, chap. 145)

## Ashido's Notable Quotables

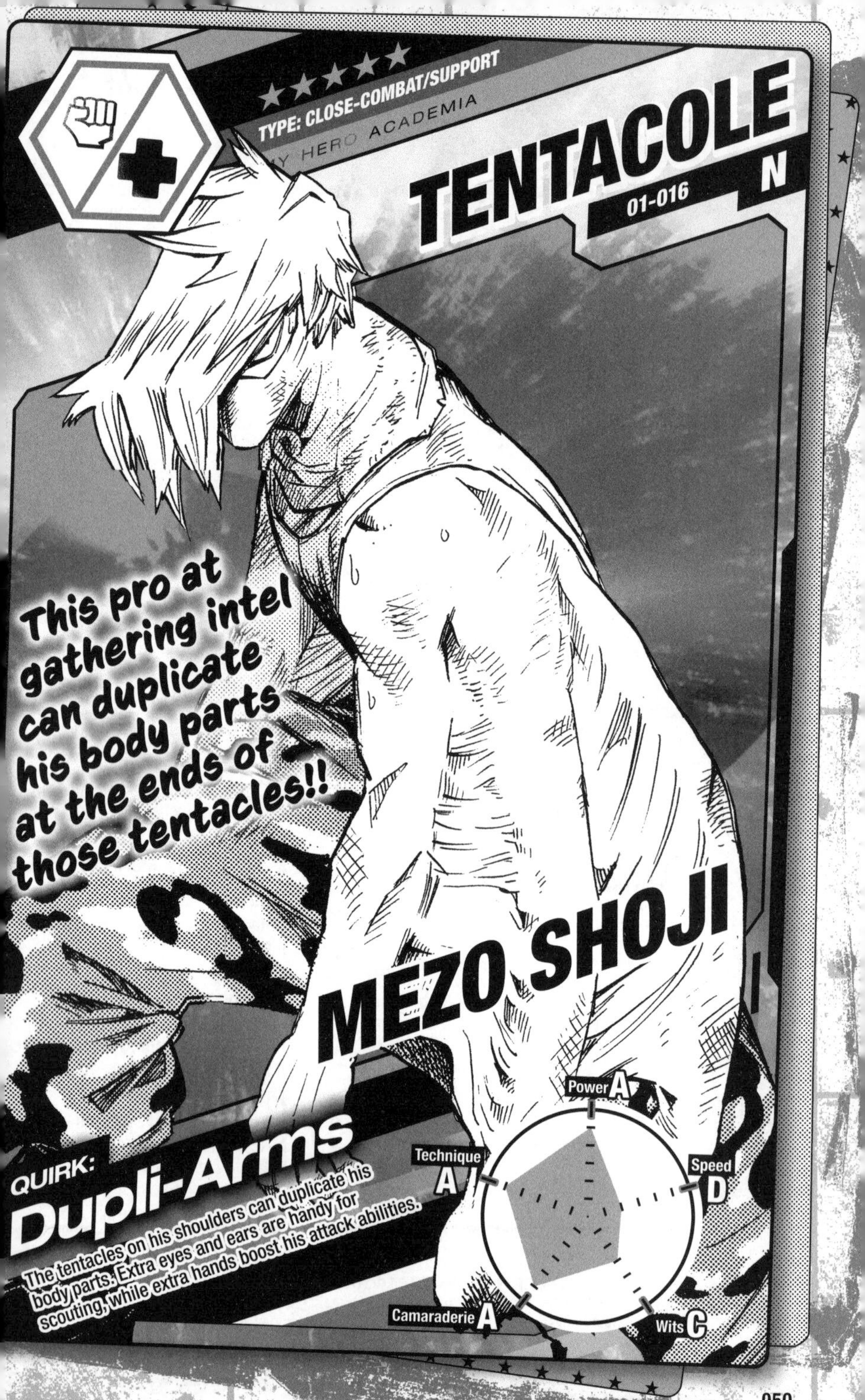
TYPE: CLOSE-COMBAT/SUPPORT
MY HERO ACADEMIA
TENTACOLE
N
01-016
This pro at gathering intel can duplicate his body parts at the ends of those tentacles!!
MEZO SHOJI
Power A
Technique A
Speed D
Camaraderie A
Wits C
QUIRK:
Dupli-Arms
The tentacles on his shoulders can duplicate his body parts. Extra eyes and ears are handy for scouting, while extra hands boost his attack abilities.

## *Always ready to shield his allies, this coolheaded guy cares.*

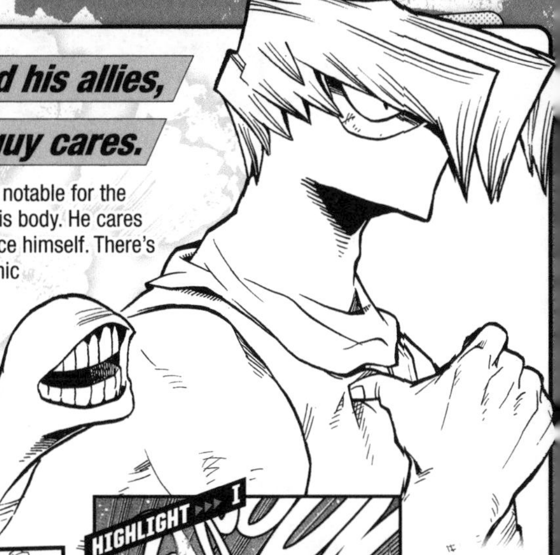

Shoji is the strong and silent type, notable for the winglike tentacles growing from his body. He cares about his friends enough to sacrifice himself. There's still prejudice against heteromorphic types in Shoji's home region, so he often encountered people who were scared of him. He's worn a face mask ever since the time his bare face terrified a little girl to the point of tears.

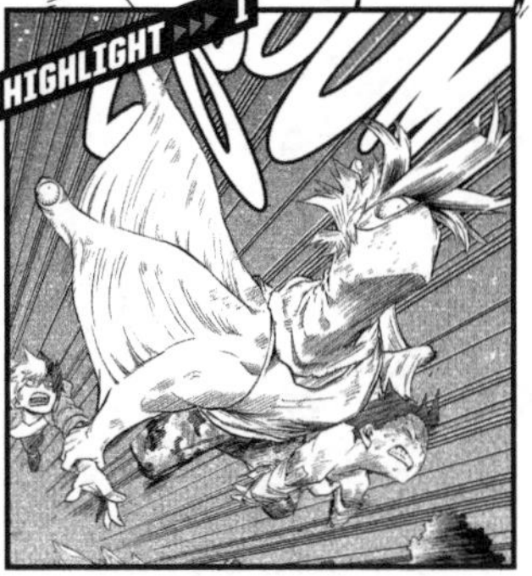
HIGHLIGHT ▸▸▸ I

⬆ With Uraraka's and Asui's help, a desperate Shoji resorted to using his dupli-arms as wings, transforming him into a glider.

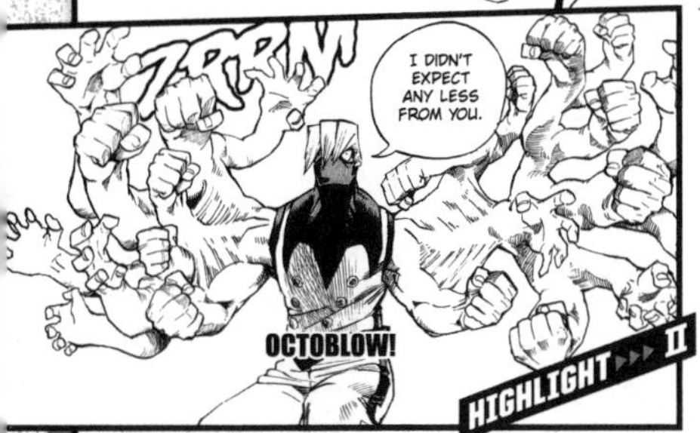
I DIDN'T EXPECT ANY LESS FROM YOU.
OCTOBLOW!
HIGHLIGHT ▸▸▸ II

⬆ He demonstrated superior combat capabilities during his fight against class B's Tsunotori. His new move gives him over 20 arms.

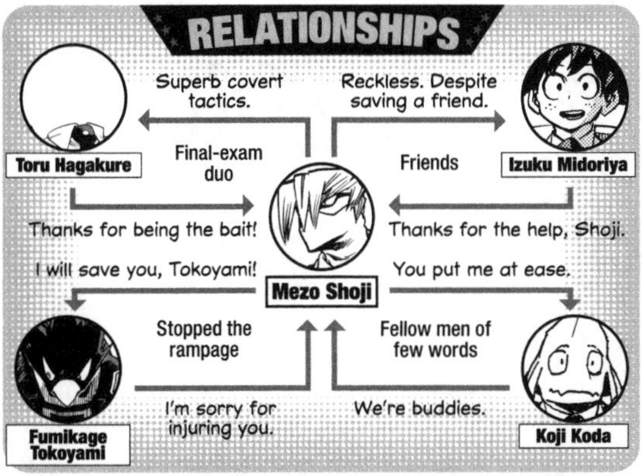
RELATIONSHIPS
Toru Hagakure
Superb covert tactics.
Final-exam duo
Thanks for being the bait!
Izuku Midoriya
Reckless. Despite saving a friend.
Friends
Thanks for the help, Shoji.
Mezo Shoji
I will save you, Tokoyami!
Fumikage Tokoyami
Stopped the rampage
I'm sorry for injuring you.
You put me at ease.
Koji Koda
Fellow men of few words
We're buddies.

## PROFILE

Name: **Mezo Shoji**
Hero name: **Tentacole**
Quirk: **Dupli-Arms**
Birthday: **February 15**
Height: **187 cm**
Blood type: **B**
Birthplace: **Fukuoka Prefecture**
Personality: **Silent gentleman**
Ultimate moves: **Octo-Searcher, Octoblow**

- "No matter what I'm up against, I'll never be the kind of guy who abandons a suffering friend." (vol. 9, chap. 79)
- "Saving someone always comes with risks. Heroes aren't called heroes for nothing." (vol. 9, chap. 79)
- "Save that for later. I know that's what *you* would say." (vol. 9, chap. 80)

**Shoji's Notable Quotables**

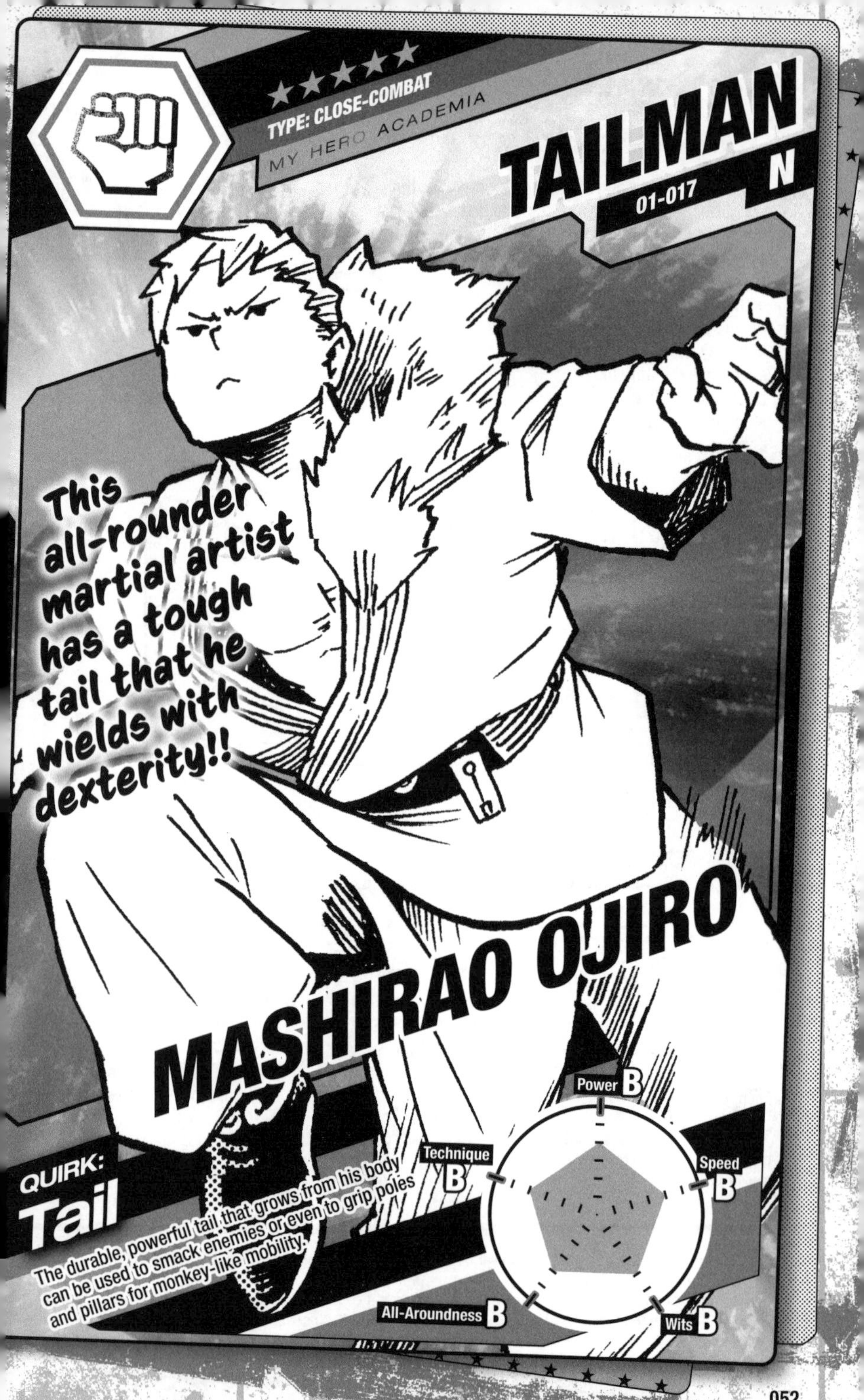
TYPE: CLOSE-COMBAT
MY HERO ACADEMIA
TAILMAN
N
01-017
This all-rounder martial artist has a tough tail that he wields with dexterity!!
MASHIRAO OJIRO
QUIRK:
Tail
The durable, powerful tail that grows from his body can be used to smack enemies or even to grip poles and pillars for monkey-like mobility.
Power B
Speed B
Wits B
All-Aroundness B
Technique B

## An upstanding young man who's always straightforward.

Ojiro is an unaffected sort who takes advantage of his muscular tail to create his own form of martial arts. He doesn't let his emotions get the better of him, and he showed integrity during the Sports Festival when he withdrew from the tournament for the top 16. Ojiro made great use of his instincts during the match against class B, where he faced Kaibara and assisted Shoji.

... OJIRO!
TORNADO...
...TAIL DANCE!!
HIGHLIGHT ▸▸▸ II

UGH!
OUCH! WHAT IS THIS HEAVY FEELING IN MY CHEST?
HIGHLIGHT ▸▸▸ I

⬆ Ojiro couldn't literally hear his classmates' comments during the battle against Kaibara, but somehow he still felt the sting.

⬅ A powerful sneak attack against Tsunotori, who was distracted by Shoji!! This brutal move used the centripetal force provided by Ojiro's long tail.

### RELATIONSHIPS

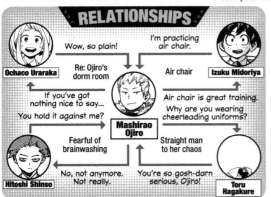

Ochaco Uraraka
Wow, so plain!
Re: Ojiro's dorm room
If you've got nothing nice to say...
Izuku Midoriya
I'm practicing air chair.
Air chair
Air chair is great training.
Mashirao Ojiro
Hitoshi Shinso
You hold it against me?
Fearful of brainwashing
No, not anymore. Not really.
Toru Hagakure
Why are you wearing cheerleading uniforms?
Straight man to her chaos
You're so gosh-darn serious, Ojiro!

### PROFILE

Name: **Mashirao Ojiro**
Hero name: **Tailman**
Quirk: **Tail**
Birthday: **May 28**
Height: **169 cm**
Blood type: **O**
Birthplace: **Tokyo**
Personality: **Plain old hard worker**
Ultimate moves: **Tornado Tail Dance, Fist of the Tail: Swamp Smack Spin**

- "But this final tournament… Everyone else made it here by their own strength. Yet I'm standing here, and I don't even know how or why. I just can't take it." (vol. 4, chap. 32)
- "Why me…?" (vol. 9, chap. 73)
- "Basically, I'm too plain… (*sniffle*)" (vol. 12, chap. 100)

Ojiro's Notable Quotables

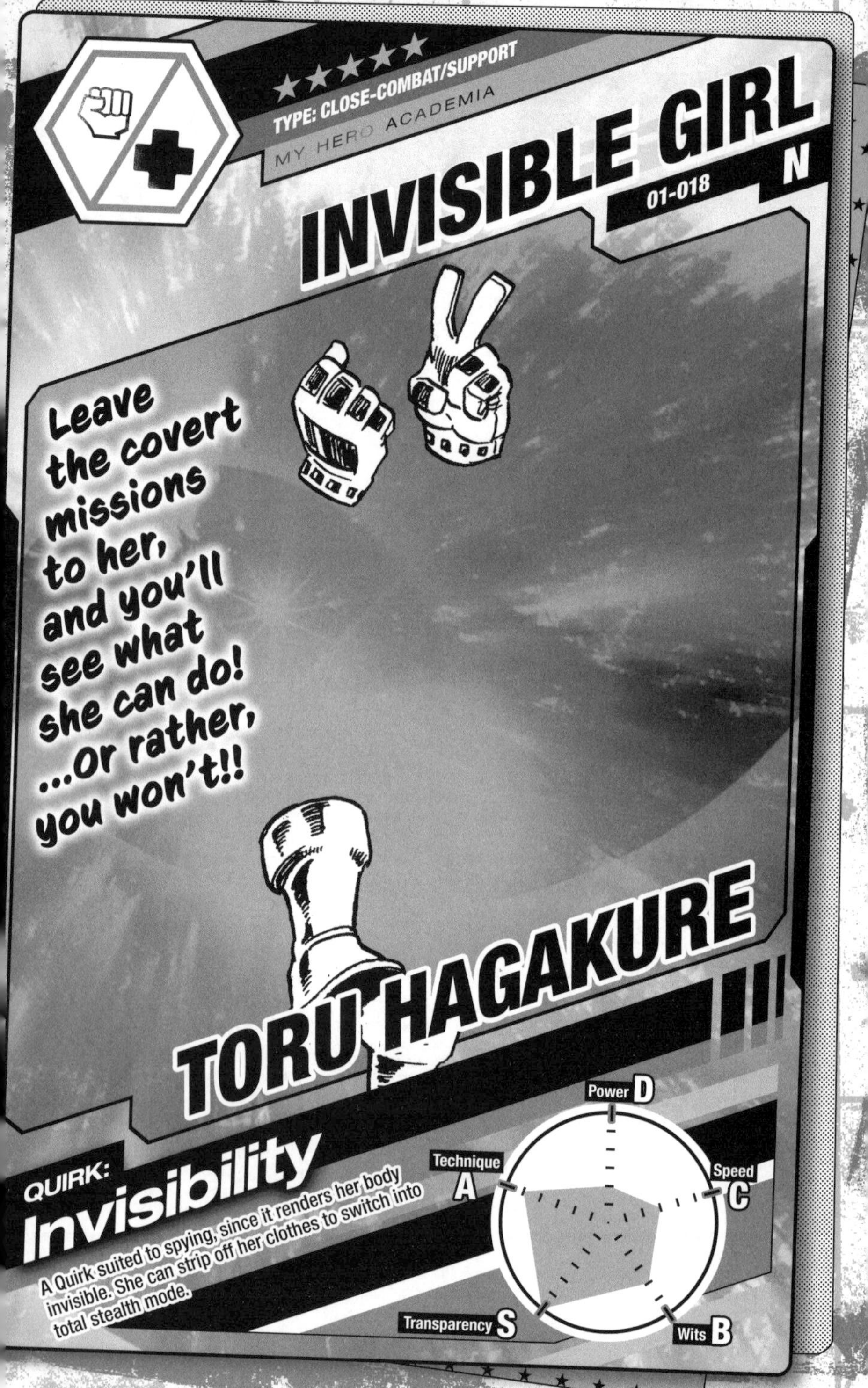
★★★★★
TYPE: CLOSE-COMBAT/SUPPORT
MY HERO ACADEMIA
INVISIBLE GIRL
01-018
N
Leave the covert missions to her, and you'll see what she can do! ...Or rather, you won't!!
TORU HAGAKURE
QUIRK:
Invisibility
A Quirk suited to spying, since it renders her body invisible. She can strip off her clothes to switch into total stealth mode.
Power D
Technique A
Speed C
Transparency S
Wits B

## Invincibility due to invisibility?!

## Always trying to stand out.

Hagakure is almost aggressive in her attempts to draw attention to herself via cheery outbursts and wild movements. In battle, she uses her invisibility to sneak around stealthily, but she can also gather and warp light. She is bold enough to go fully nude if need be! In the competition against class B, she challenged Fukidashi and nearly beat him into submission with a flurry of blows.

HIGHLIGHT ▸▸▸ I
HAGAKURE'S ROOM
WELL ?!

⬆ During the dorm room contest, Hagakure made girliness her selling point. She's the most stereotypical high school girl in the class.

FWASH
WARP REFRACTION: SAY CHEESE!
GAH! TOO BRIGHT...
HIGHLIGHT ▸▸▸ II

⬆ Since strengthening her Quirk, Hagakure is now able to adjust the refractive index of light to blind her opponents.

RELATIONSHIPS
Kyoka Jiro
Your singing was super-duper cool!
Friendly
C'mon... Stop making things harder!
Manga Fukidashi
Hiyahhh!!
Class-vs.-class battle
Wha?! I can't see her!
Toru Hagakure
Todoroki's crazy strong.
The dangers of invisibility
I could've frozen her. Yikes.
Shoto Todoroki
Time to strip down and go full power!
Going full power
But she's a girl. Damn. This feels unethical.
Mashirao Ojiro

## PROFILE

Name: **Toru Hagakure**
Hero name: **Invisible Girl**
Quirk: **Invisibility**
Birthday: **June 16**
Height: **152 cm**
Blood type: **A**
Birthplace: **Tokyo**
Personality: **Bright and cheery**
Ultimate move: **Warp**
**Refraction: Say Cheese**

- "I'm going all out, Ojiro. The gloves and boots are coming off." (vol. 2, chap. 11)
- "How about we all go shopping together, class A?" (vol. 8, chap. 68)
- "You don't beat around the bush, huh, Mineta?!" (vol. 11, chap. 99)
- "Invisible is invincible!!" (vol. 22, chap. 201)

**Hagakure's Notable Quotables**

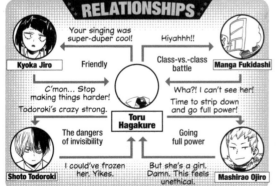

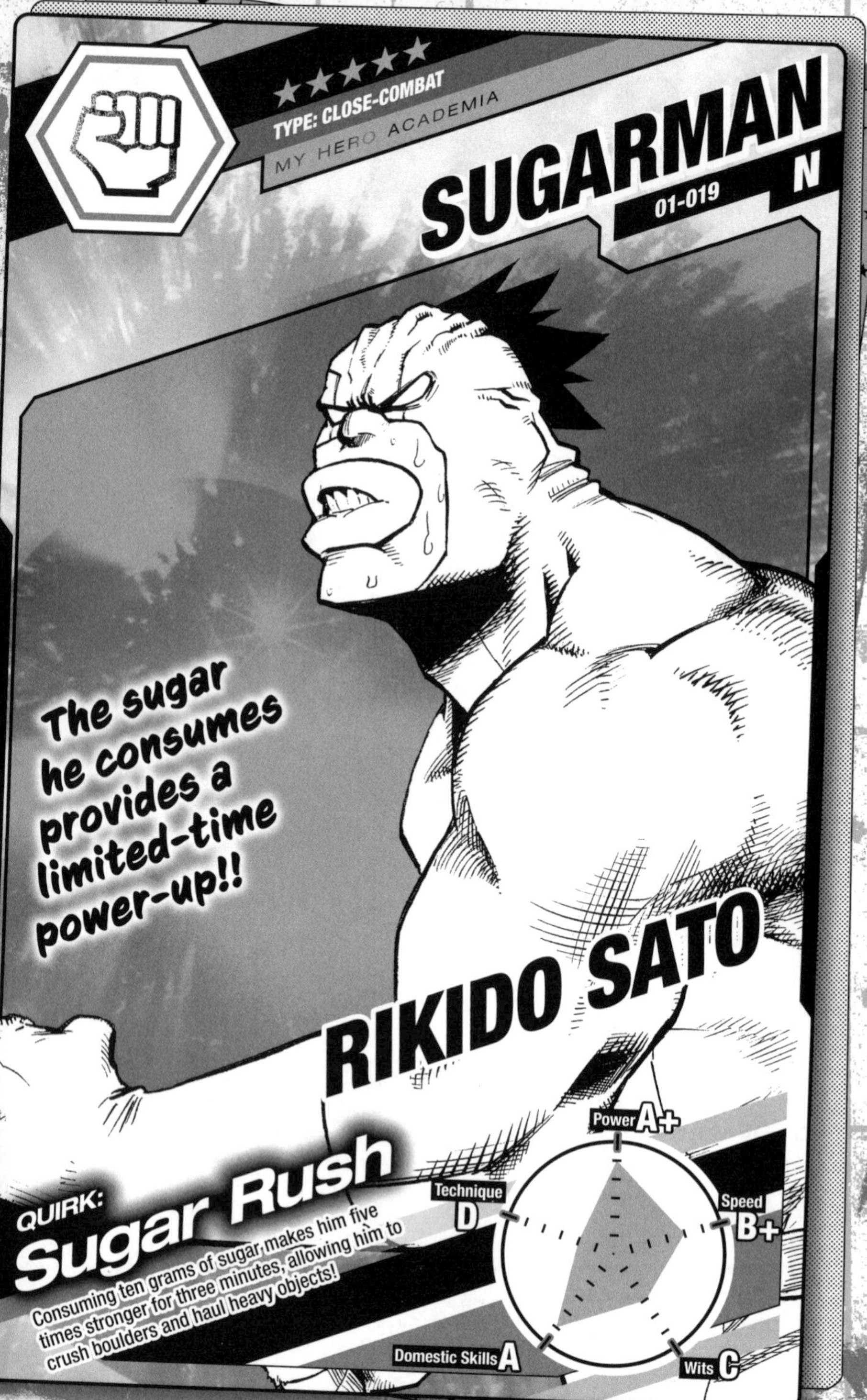

★★★★★
TYPE: CLOSE-COMBAT
MY HERO ACADEMIA
SUGARMAN
01-019
N
The sugar he consumes provides a limited-time power-up!!
RIKIDO SATO
QUIRK:
Sugar Rush
Consuming ten grams of sugar makes him five times stronger for three minutes, allowing him to crush boulders and haul heavy objects!
Power A+
Speed B+
Wits C
Domestic Skills A
Technique D

CHARACTER

# A ripped giant whose confectionary creations power up his Quirk.

This strapping lad may look like a pro wrestler, but his Quirk relies on sugar to boost his strength, so he has to constantly consume sweets. Now that the class lives in a dorm building, the others always look forward to “Sugarman’s Sugar Time”!! Sato’s sweets and Yaoyorozu’s fine tea make for some indulgent evenings.

HIGHLIGHT ▸▸▸ I
H
HH
SMASH PAST YOUR LIMITS!

HIGHLIGHT ▸▸▸ II
SUGAR
RUSH!!
CRASH
GET GOING!

⬆ Sato’s Quirk allows for a barrage of hard-hitting punches. In the blink of an eye, he freed Bakugo from Awase’s welded joints.

⬆ Sato did strength training while scarfing down cake. This regimen simultaneously boosted the duration of his power-up and honed his muscles.

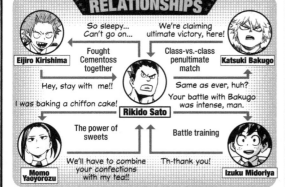

## RELATIONSHIPS

Eijiro Kirishima
So sleepy... Can't go on...
Fought Cementoss together
Hey, stay with me!!
Katsuki Bakugo
We're claiming ultimate victory, here!
Class-vs.-class penultimate match
Same as ever, huh?
Rikido Sato
I was baking a chiffon cake!
Your battle with Bakugo was intense, man.
Momo Yaoyorozu
The power of sweets
We'll have to combine your confections with my tea!!
Izuku Midoriya
Battle training
Th-thank you!

## PROFILE

Name: **Rikido Sato**
Hero name: **Sugarman**
Quirk: **Sugar Rush**
Birthday: **June 19**
Height: **185 cm**
Blood type: **O**
Birthplace: **Tottori Prefecture**
Personality: **Just the sweetest boy**
Ultimate move: **Sugar Rush**

- “Sleepy… Tired…” (vol. 8, chap. 67)
- “I was baking a chiffon cake! I wanted to share it with everyone…” (vol. 11, chap. 99)
- “It’d really be better with frosting, but…want some?” (vol. 11, chap. 99)

Sato’s Notable Quotables

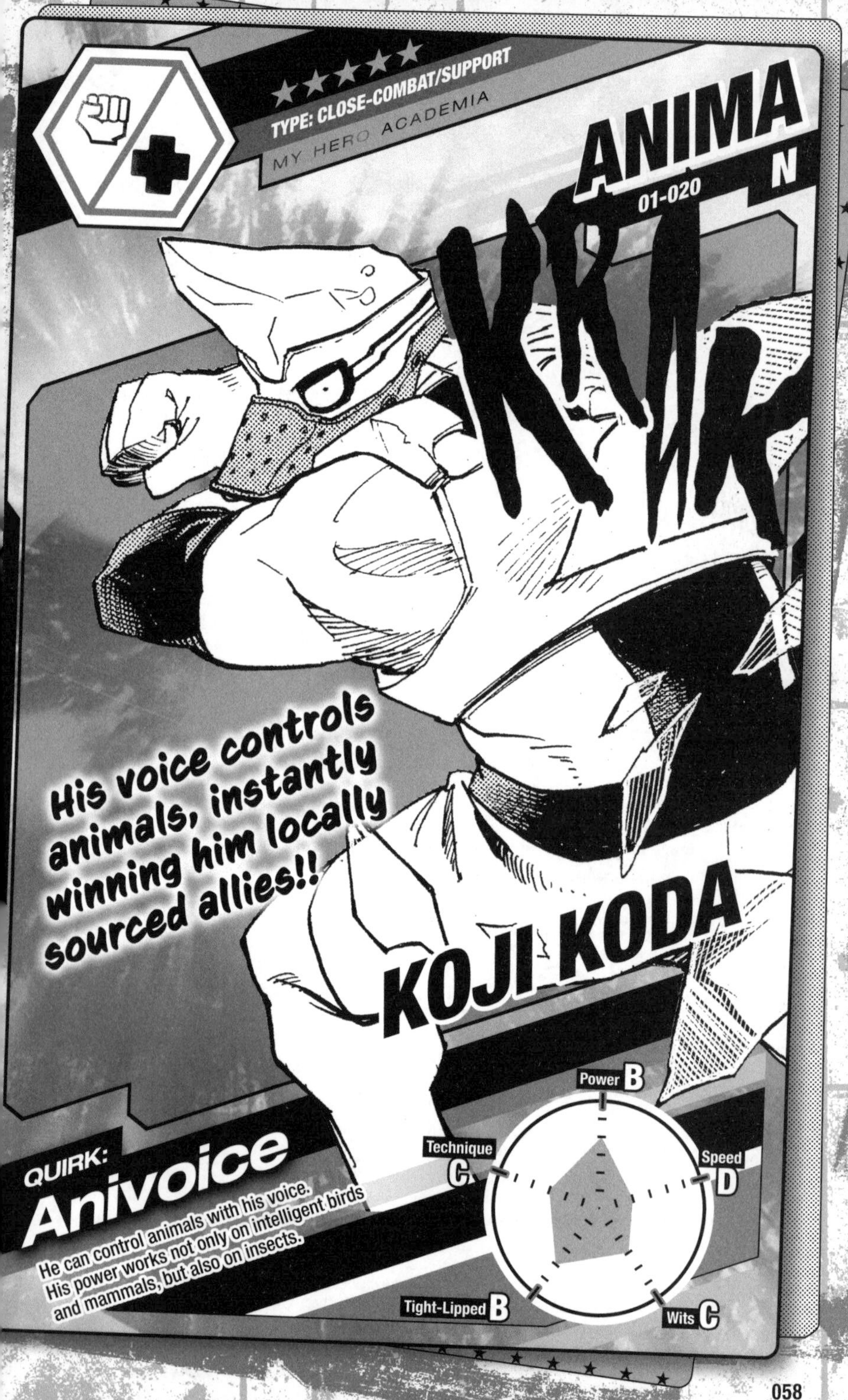

TYPE: CLOSE-COMBAT/SUPPORT
MY HERO ACADEMIA
ANIMA
N
01-020
KRAK
His voice controls animals, instantly winning him locally sourced allies!!
KOJI KODA
QUIRK:
Anivoice
He can control animals with his voice. His power works not only on intelligent birds and mammals, but also on insects.
Power B
Speed D
Wits C
Tight-Lipped B
Technique C

## The kindly Petting Hero is a nature lover with a fondness for animals.

Despite Koda's bulky body, he's extremely introverted and soft-spoken. His pet rabbit Yuwai is wildly popular with the girls, who think he's simply adorable. Other members of Koda's family have horns, but his haven't grown in yet.

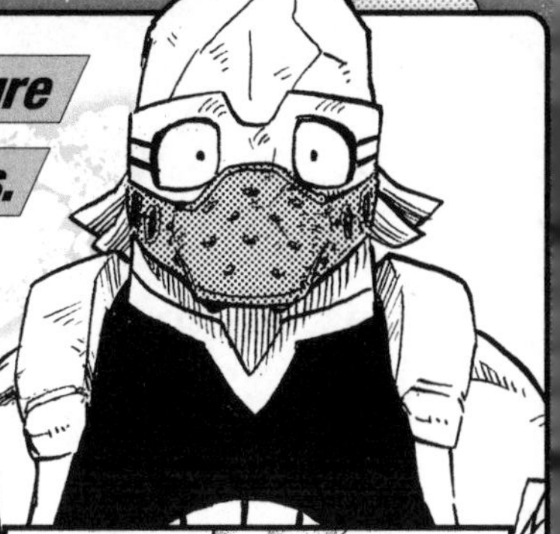

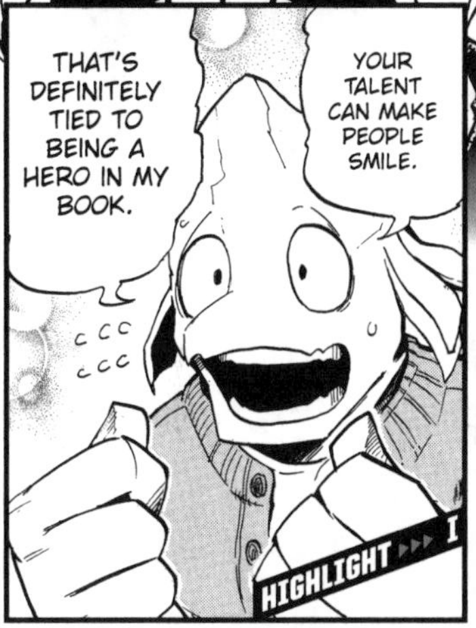
HIGHLIGHT ▸▸▸ I
THAT'S DEFINITELY TIED TO BEING A HERO IN MY BOOK.
YOUR TALENT CAN MAKE PEOPLE SMILE.

⬆ Being a hero is about keeping people smiling. Jiro was hesitant about leading the band, but Koda's thoughts on heroism encouraged her.

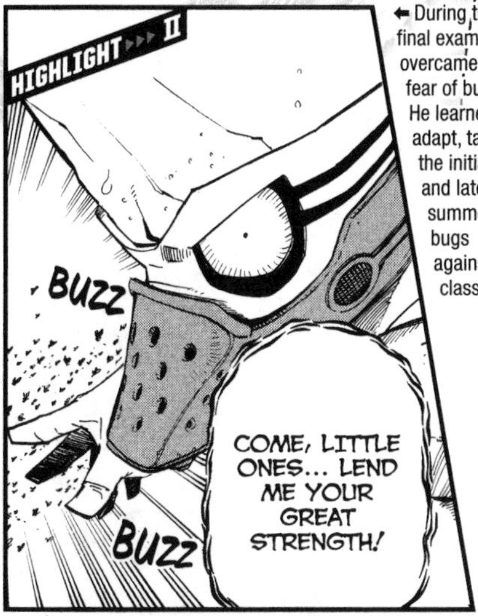
HIGHLIGHT ▸▸▸ II
BUZZ
BUZZ
COME, LITTLE ONES... LEND ME YOUR GREAT STRENGTH!

⬅ During the final exam, Koda overcame his fear of bugs. He learned to adapt, take the initiative, and later, summon bugs against class B.

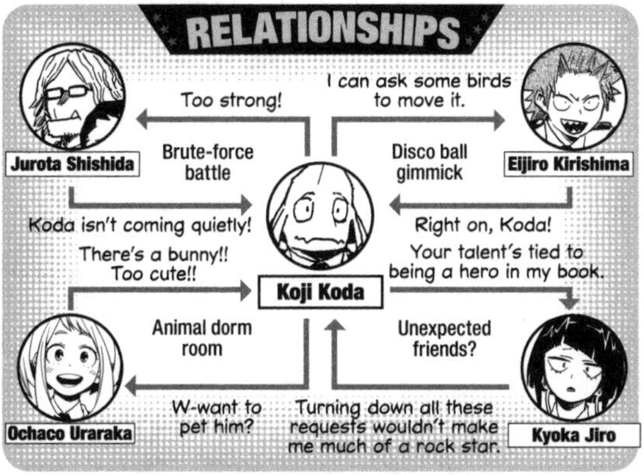
RELATIONSHIPS
Jurota Shishida
Too strong!
Brute-force battle
Koda isn't coming quietly!
Eijiro Kirishima
I can ask some birds to move it.
Disco ball gimmick
Right on, Koda!
Koji Koda
There's a bunny!! Too cute!!
Animal dorm room
W-want to pet him?
Ochaco Uraraka
Your talent's tied to being a hero in my book.
Unexpected friends?
Turning down all these requests wouldn't make me much of a rock star.
Kyoka Jiro

## PROFILE

Name: **Koji Koda**
Hero name: **Anima**
Quirk: **Anivoice**
Birthday: **February 1**
Height: **186 cm**
Blood type: **A**
Birthplace: **Iwate Prefecture**
Personality: **Tenderhearted**
Ultimate moves: **Hitchcock Birds, Bugging Out**

- "Please, go forth, little ones. It's time to take down the source of all that big, bad noise. Won't you help me out...?" (vol. 8, chap. 66)
- "Calm yourself, creature. Please, back down." (vol. 8, chap. 70)
- "Now, my feathered friends. Move those lights up, down, side to side!" (vol. 20, chap. 182)

**Koda's Notable Quotables**

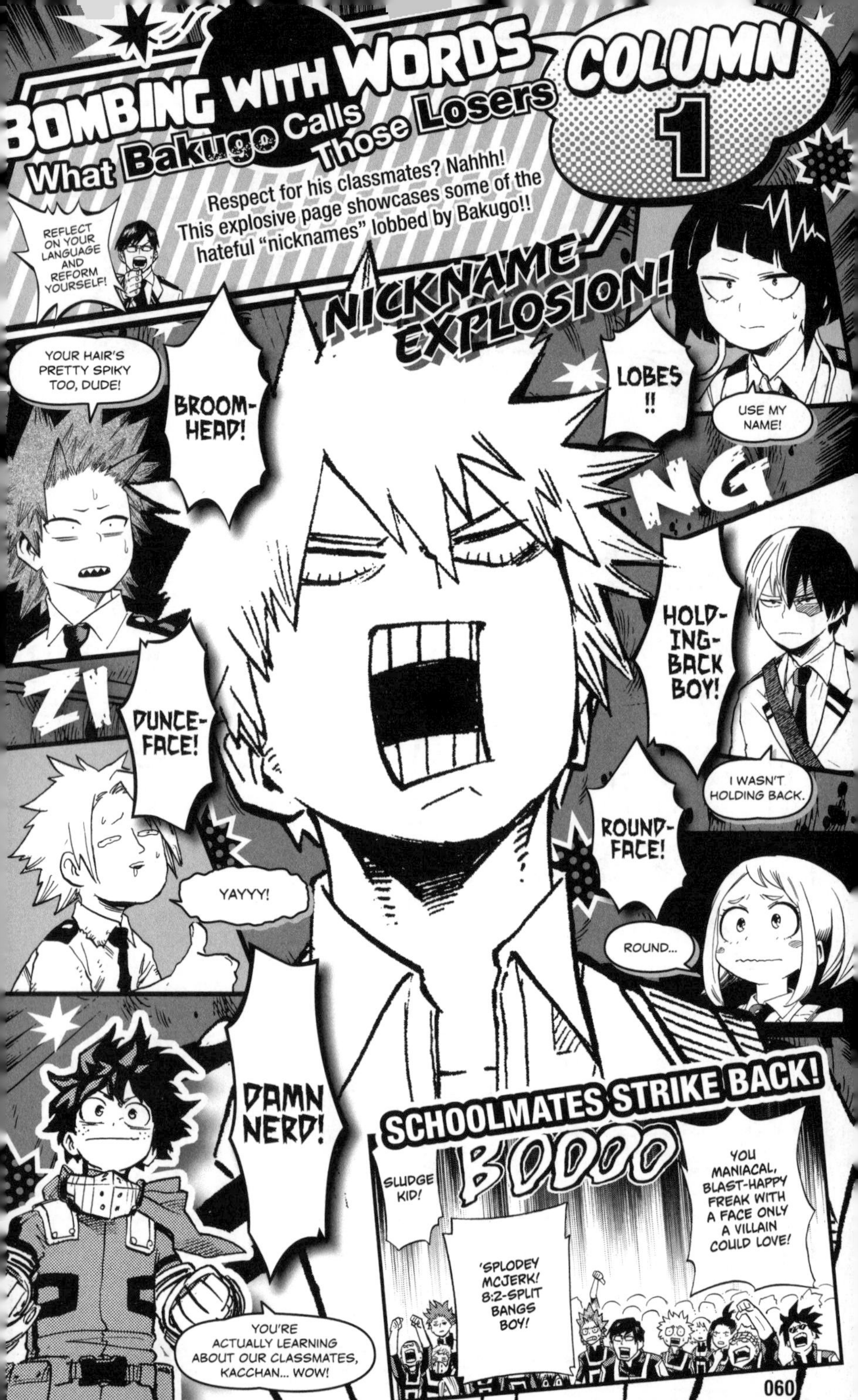
BOMBING WITH WORDS
What Bakugo Calls Those Losers
COLUMN 1
Respect for his classmates? Nahhh! This explosive page showcases some of the hateful "nicknames" lobbed by Bakugo!!
REFLECT ON YOUR LANGUAGE AND REFORM YOURSELF!
NICKNAME EXPLOSION!
LOBES!!
USE MY NAME!
BROOM-HEAD!
YOUR HAIR'S PRETTY SPIKY TOO, DUDE!
NG
HOLD-ING-BACK BOY!
I WASN'T HOLDING BACK.
ZI
DUNCE-FACE!
YAYYY!
ROUND-FACE!
ROUND...
DAMN NERD!
YOU'RE ACTUALLY LEARNING ABOUT OUR CLASSMATES, KACCHAN... WOW!
SCHOOLMATES STRIKE BACK!
BOOOO
YOU MANIACAL, BLAST-HAPPY FREAK WITH A FACE ONLY A VILLAIN COULD LOVE!
'SPLODEY MCJERK! 8:2-SPLIT BANGS BOY!
SLUDGE KID!

# 2nd EDITION

## NEW HEROES II

The kids of class 1-B make great rivals for class 1-A, as they're striving just as hard to be heroes. Here, we break down the personalities and Quirks of all 20 members.

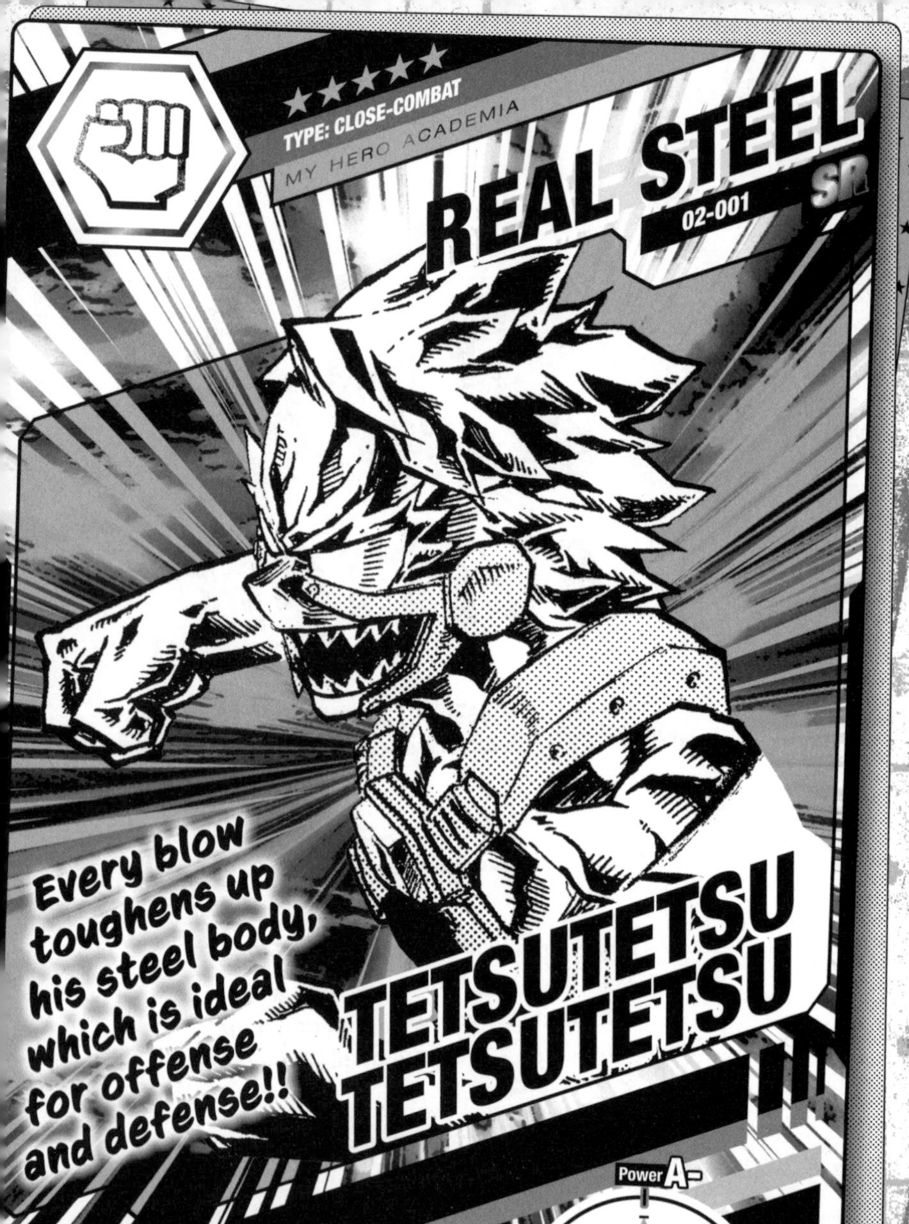
TYPE: CLOSE-COMBAT
MY HERO ACADEMIA
REAL STEEL
02-001
SR
Every blow toughens up his steel body, which is ideal for offense and defense!!
TETSUTETSU TETSUTETSU
QUIRK:
Steel
Turns his body into metal, allowing him to function in extreme temperatures. The more iron in his diet, the tougher he gets and the longer the effect lasts.
Power A-
Speed D
Wits C
Chivalrous Spirit A
Technique D

## This hot-blooded guy loves his friends and sticks to his convictions with a will of steel.

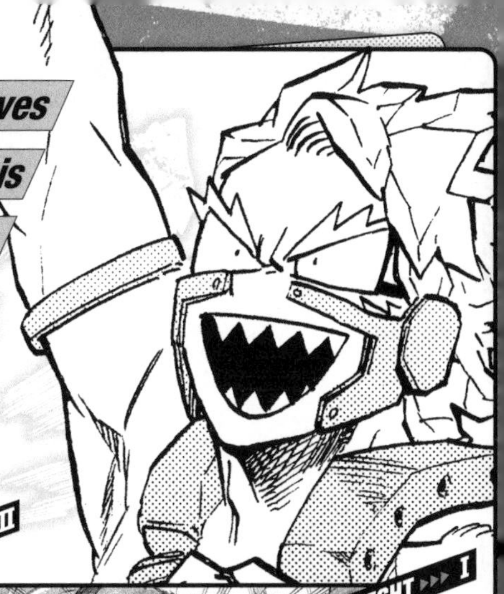

Class B's boss brawler. Tetsutetsu didn't get asked back to Fourth Kind's agency for his work study, so he was bitter upon learning that Kirishima got to work with Fat Gum. The "Tetsutetsu BBQ" that class B put together came to a grinding halt when he declared that his sweat provided the salty seasoning.

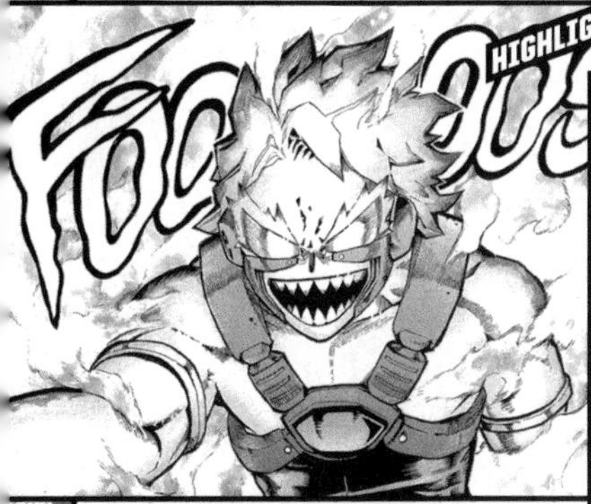
HIGHLIGHT ▸▸▸ II

⬆ During the class-versus-class battle, Tetsutetsu proved that he could endure Todoroki's blazing heat and chilling cold. Intense Quirk training was responsible for this massive endurance boost.

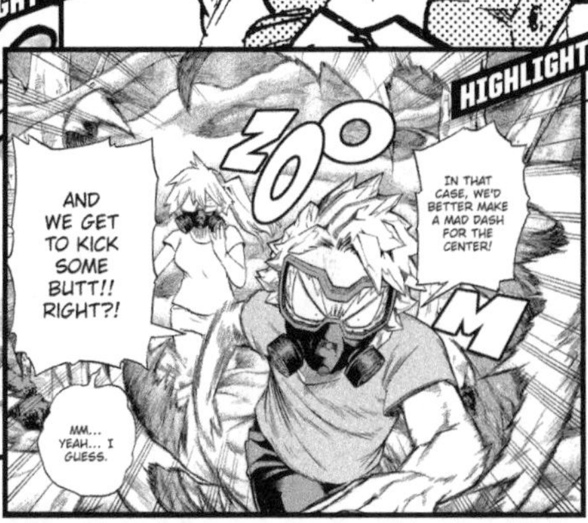
HIGHLIGHT ▸▸▸ I
IN THAT CASE, WE'D BETTER MAKE A MAD DASH FOR THE CENTER!
ZOOOM
AND WE GET TO KICK SOME BUTT!! RIGHT?!
MM... YEAH... I GUESS.

⬆ When Mustard's poison gas threatened Tetsutetsu's friends during their training camp, he bravely stood up to the villain.

## RELATIONSHIPS

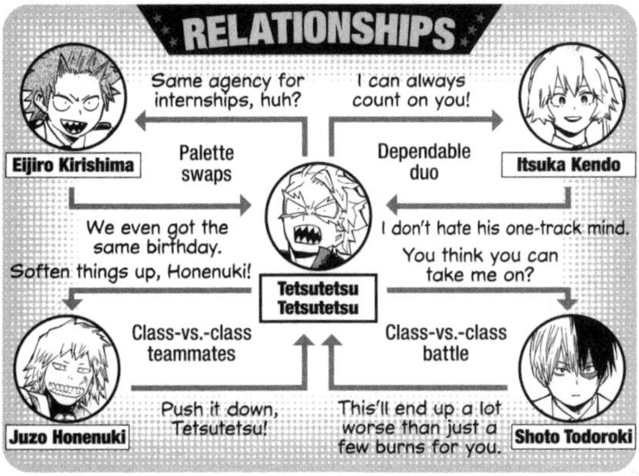
Eijiro Kirishima
Same agency for internships, huh?
Palette swaps
We even got the same birthday.
Itsuka Kendo
I can always count on you!
Dependable duo
I don't hate his one-track mind.
Tetsutetsu Tetsutetsu
Soften things up, Honenuki!
Juzo Honenuki
Class-vs.-class teammates
Push it down, Tetsutetsu!
You think you can take me on?
Shoto Todoroki
Class-vs.-class battle
This'll end up a lot worse than just a few burns for you.

## PROFILE

Name: **Tetsutetsu Tetsutetsu**
Hero name: **Real Steel**
Quirk: **Steel**
Birthday: **October 16**
Height: **174 cm**
Blood type: **B**
Birthplace: **Saitama Prefecture**
Personality: **Scorchingly hot-blooded**
Ultimate moves: **My Fist, Horn Dash Hammer, Heatetsu**

- "Don't try to stop me, Kendo! I'm in class 1-B of the Hero Course! If I don't stand up here, what's the point?!" (vol. 9, chap. 74)
- "Tricks 'n' schemes won't work here! Gonna be a straight-up brawl, so let's bring the pain!!" (vol. 22, chap. 202)
- "Time to strike while the iron is hot!!" (vol. 22, chap. 204)

**Tetsutetsu's Notable Quotables**

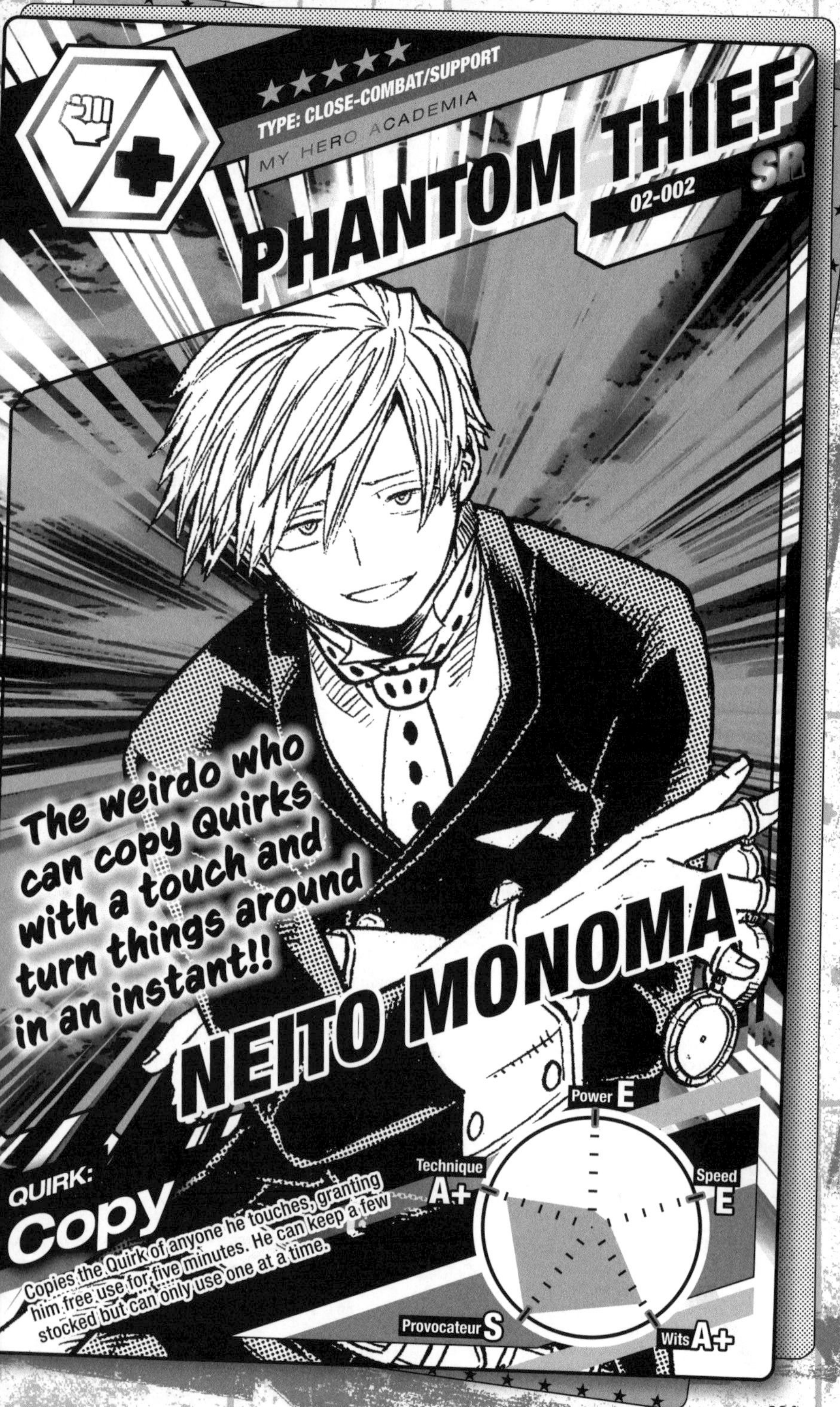
TYPE: CLOSE-COMBAT/SUPPORT
MY HERO ACADEMIA
PHANTOM THIEF
SR
02-002
The weirdo who can copy Quirks with a touch and turn things around in an instant!!
NEITO MONOMA
QUIRK:
Copy
Copies the Quirk of anyone he touches, granting him free use for five minutes. He can keep a few stocked but can only use one at a time.
Power E
Speed E
Wits A+
Provocateur S
Technique A+

CHARACTER

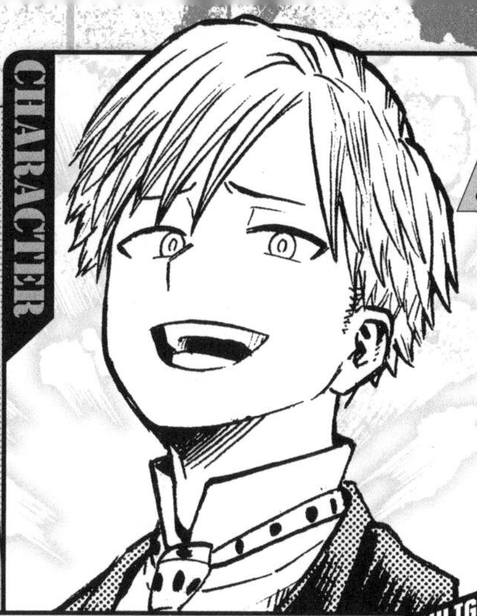

## This snide bigmouth always has something to prove to class A.

Despite his snarky, scheming nature, Monoma is a sharp thinker with a strategic mind and has a way with words, so the rest of class B respects him. He can stock up to four different copied Quirks. Monoma feels so competitive with class A that he sometimes walks into their dorm, unloads a nasty speech on them, and goes home… That's not normal.

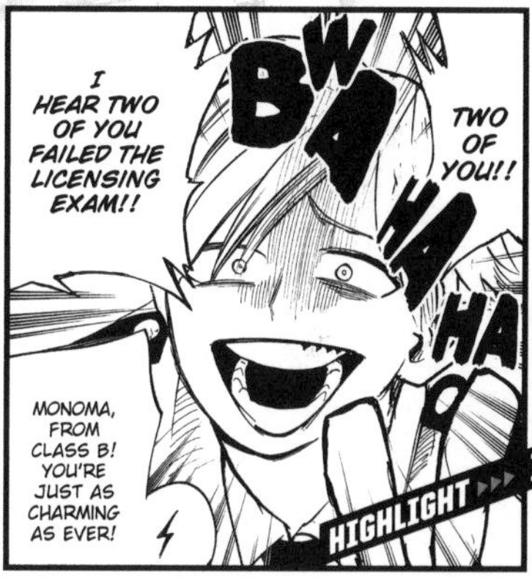
I HEAR TWO OF YOU FAILED THE LICENSING EXAM!!
BWAHAHAHA
TWO OF YOU!!
MONOMA, FROM CLASS B! YOU'RE JUST AS CHARMING AS EVER!
HIGHLIGHT I

⬆ Monoma hates on class A while ignoring his own studies. What is it that gives him such strength (?) of character…?

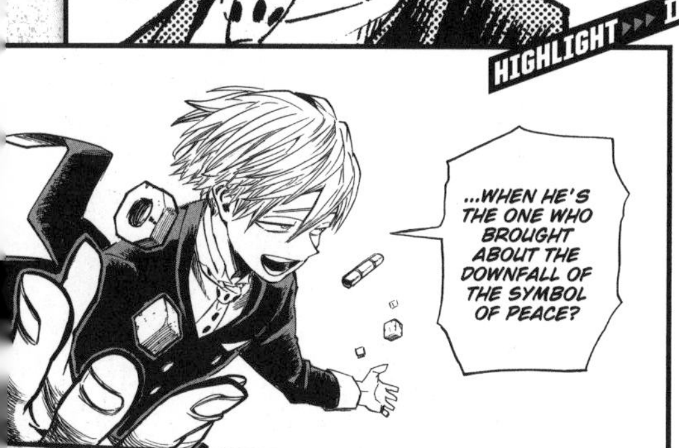
HIGHLIGHT II
...WHEN HE'S THE ONE WHO BROUGHT ABOUT THE DOWNFALL OF THE SYMBOL OF PEACE?

⬆ Monoma can turn the tables through effective use of Quirks he's copied, whether they come from ally or enemy.

## RELATIONSHIPS

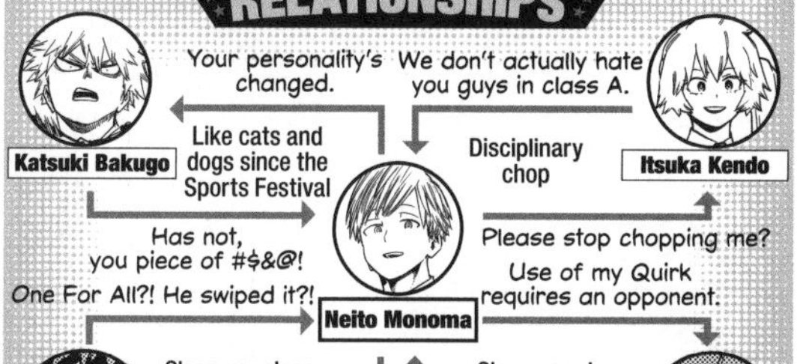
Katsuki Bakugo
Your personality's changed.
Like cats and dogs since the Sports Festival
Has not, you piece of #$&@!
Itsuka Kendo
We don't actually hate you guys in class A.
Disciplinary chop
Please stop chopping me?
Neito Monoma
Izuku Midoriya
One For All?! He swiped it?!
Class-vs.-class battle
Your Quirk gave me a "blank."
Hitoshi Shinso
Use of my Quirk requires an opponent.
Class-vs.-class teammates
I'm in the same boat, basically.

## PROFILE

Name: **Neito Monoma**
Hero name: **Phantom Thief**
Quirk: **Copy**
Birthday: **May 13**
Height: **170 cm**
Blood type: **A**
Birthplace: **Kanagawa Prefecture**
Personality: **Kind to his allies**
Ultimate move: **Scanners**

## Monoma's Notable Quotables

- "Class A thinks it's so great. Well, let's show 'em why we in class B hung back and placed low in the preliminaries." (vol. 4, chap. 27)
- "Hey, have you all heard?! About how half of those taking the licensing test fail it?" (vol. 12, chap. 102)
- "We are all, to the last, merely bit players in the lives of others, and the stars of only our own!" (vol. 22, chap. 209)

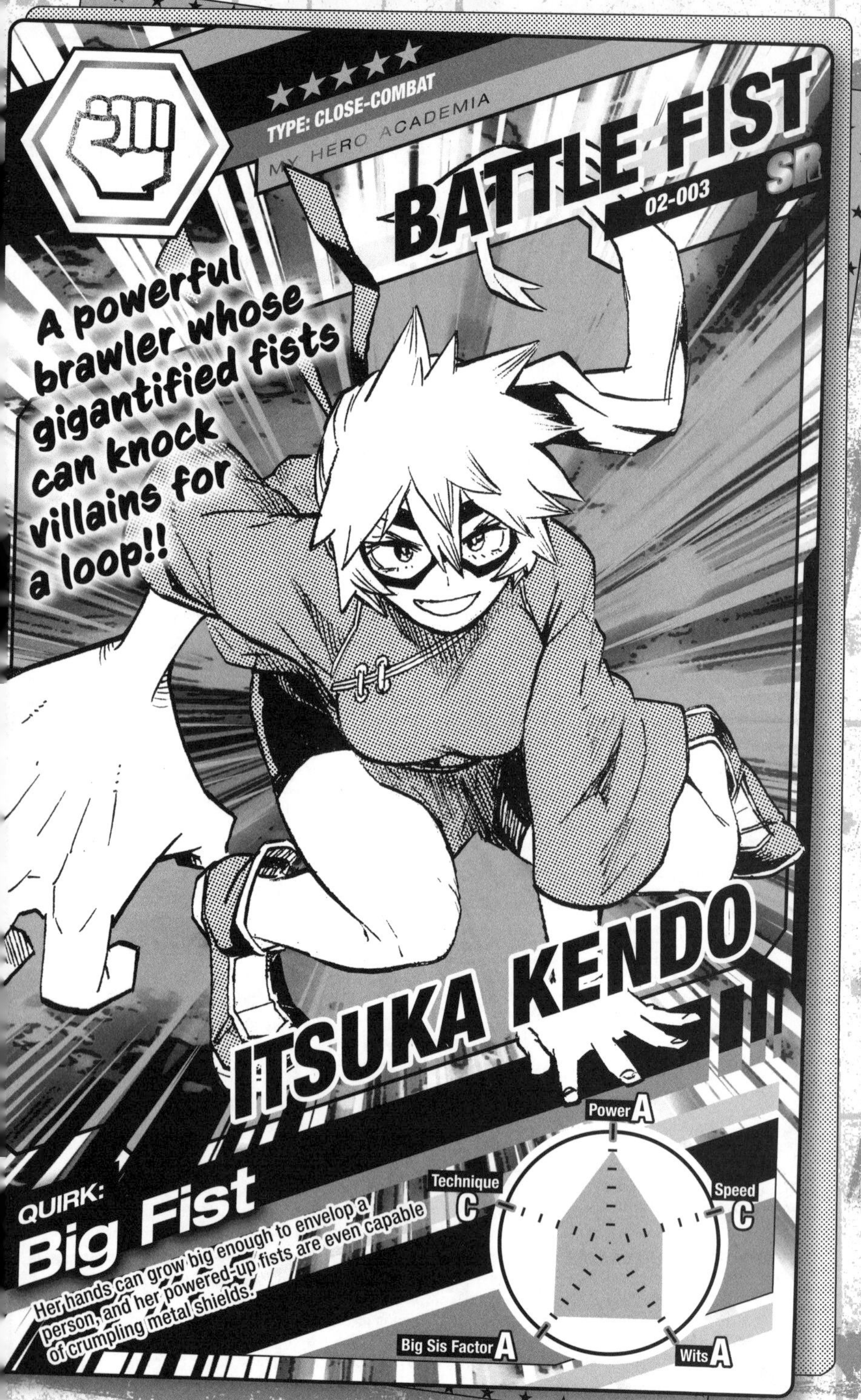
★★★★★★
TYPE: CLOSE-COMBAT
MY HERO ACADEMIA
BATTLE FIST
SR
02-003
A powerful brawler whose gigantified fists can knock villains for a loop!!
ITSUKA KENDO
QUIRK:
Big Fist
Her hands can grow big enough to envelop a person, and her powered-up fists are even capable of crumpling metal shields.
Power A
Technique C
Speed C
Big Sis Factor A
Wits A

CHARACTER

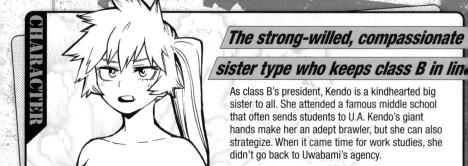

## The strong-willed, compassionate sister type who keeps class B in lin[e]

As class B's president, Kendo is a kindhearted big sister to all. She attended a famous middle school that often sends students to U.A. Kendo's giant hands make her an adept brawler, but she can also strategize. When it came time for work studies, she didn't go back to Uwabami's agency.

WHAM
HIGHLIGHT ▸▸▸ I

⬆ Kendo's massive hand crushes a tungsten shield with ease. If she lures the opponent into a hand-to-hand fight, she's got the advantage.

I'M JUST WORRIED THAT, ONE OF THESE DAYS, WE'RE ALL GONNA GET CAUGHT UP IN SOME OF YOUR ANTICS! SCARY...
PRETTY SCARY!
WHAP
THAT'S NOT FUNNY. DIDN'T YOU HEAR WHAT HAPPENED TO IDA?
GAH!!
HIGHLIGHT ▸▸▸ II

⬆ One of Kendo's key roles is keeping Monoma from riling up class A. He goes down with a single, clean WHAP every time—she's just that good.

## RELATIONSHIPS

Neito Monoma
I can't wait to show up class A...
Presidential punishment
C'mon! (chops) Sorry about him, class A.
Momo Yaoyorozu
I've been itching to go head-to-head!
Put in the same box?
I wholeheartedly accept!
Itsuka Kendo
Tetsutetsu Tetsutetsu
Don't be reckless, now!
Skill repects skill
Sure, sure! I got it handled!
Bibimi Kenranzaki
Nothing beats my splen-diferous gorgeousness!
Beauty pageant rivals
So over-the-top...

## PROFILE

Name: **Itsuka Kendo**
Hero name: **Battle Fist**
Quirk: **Big Fist**
Birthday: **September 9**
Height: **166 cm**
Blood type: **0**
Birthplace: **Chiba Prefecture**
Personality: **Refreshingly easygoing**
Ultimate move: **Double Jumbo Fist**

## Kendo's Notable Quotables

- "I can't say I don't like that about him." (vol. 9, chap. 78)
- "Well… If I'm gonna do it, might as well try to win." (vol. 20, chap. 178)
- "Your Quirk and grades are way better than mine, but they still lump us together. Honestly, I don't like it." (vol. 21, chap. 198)

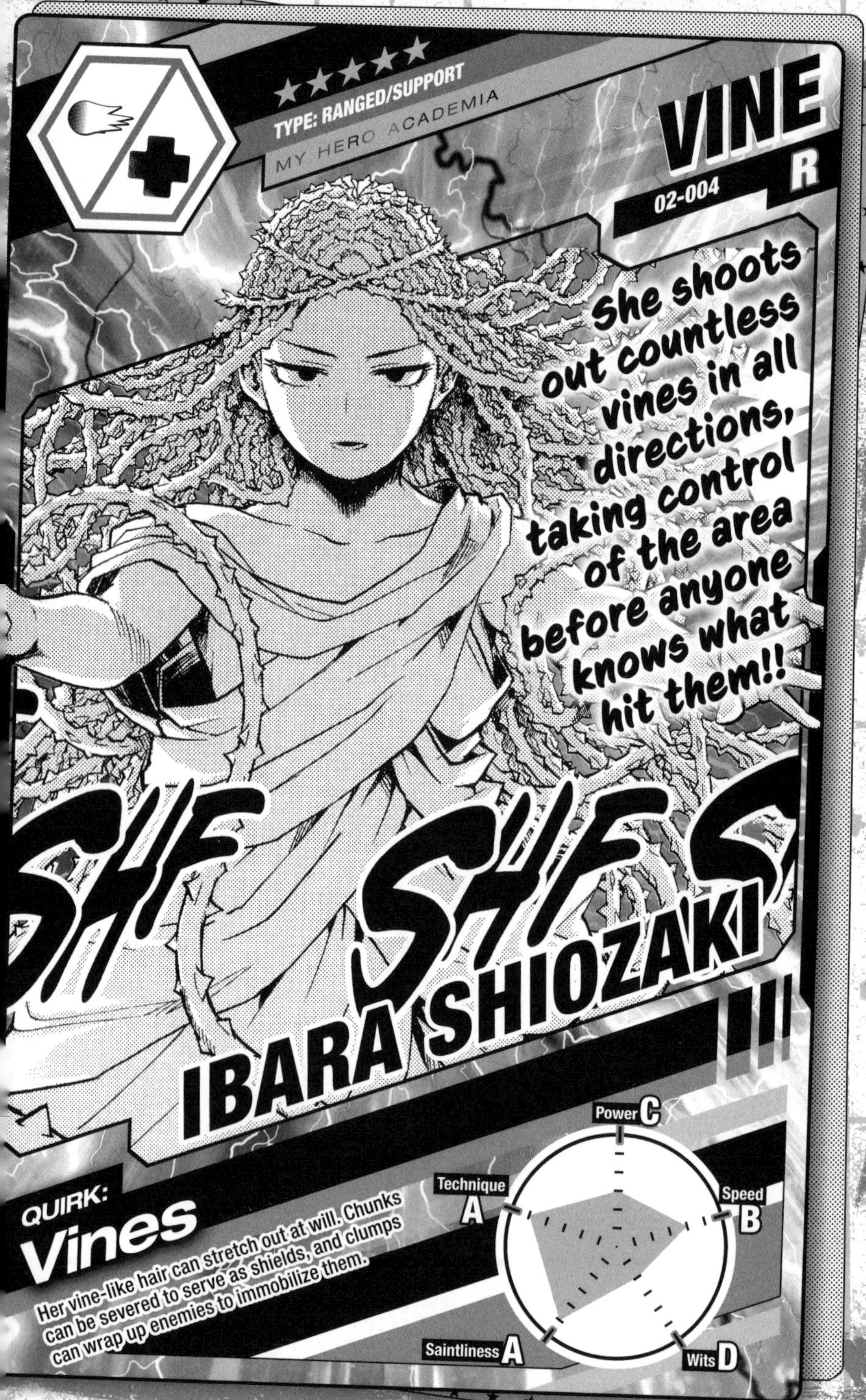
★★★★★★
TYPE: RANGED/SUPPORT
MY HERO ACADEMIA
VINE
R
02-004
She shoots out countless vines in all directions, taking control of the area before anyone knows what hit them!!
SHF SHF
IBARA SHIOZAKI
QUIRK:
Vines
Her vine-like hair can stretch out at will. Chunks can be severed to serve as shields, and clumps can wrap up enemies to immobilize them.
Power C
Speed B
Wits D
Saintliness A
Technique A

## With mercy and compassion in her heart, she can't bring herself to deceive others.

Shiozaki is straitlaced and compassionate, and would rather show mercy than deceive. She crushed Kaminari during the Sports Festival and demonstrated great leadership in the battle against class A. Drawing all those hair vines is a pain, so whenever she leaps into action, the author really needs to psych himself up.

I SWEA
ON MY NAME, VINE..
...THAT THE SCHEMERS WILL BE JUDGED.
VOOOOM
VIA DOLOROSA!
HIGHLIGHT I

⬆ One of Shiozaki's ultimate moves, acquired through Quirk strengthening. By sending her vines in every direction, she can create a barrier.

HIGHLIGHT II
A BEREFT LITTLE LAMB FROM THE HEAVENS.

⬆ Shiozaki tries to be polite and courteous to all. Even during battle, she speaks like some kind of holy woman.

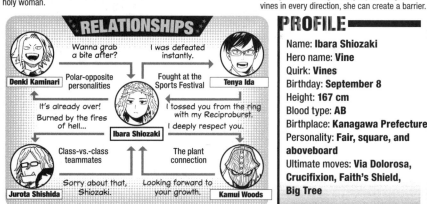

## RELATIONSHIPS

Denki Kaminari
Wanna grab a bite after?
Polar-opposite personalities
It's already over! Burned by the fires of hell...
Tenya Ida
I was defeated instantly.
Fought at the Sports Festival
I tossed you from the ring with my Reciproburst. I deeply respect you.
Ibara Shiozaki
Jurota Shishida
Class-vs.-class teammates
Sorry about that, Shiozaki.
Kamui Woods
The plant connection
Looking forward to your growth.

## PROFILE

Name: **Ibara Shiozaki**
Hero name: **Vine**
Quirk: **Vines**
Birthday: **September 8**
Height: **167 cm**
Blood type: **AB**
Birthplace: **Kanagawa Prefecture**
Personality: **Fair, square, and aboveboard**
Ultimate moves: **Via Dolorosa, Crucifixion, Faith's Shield, Big Tree**

- "Pardon my objection, but what exactly did you mean by 'assassin'? I have merely come this far seeking victory..." (vol. 4, chap. 35)
- "I shall have to teach them that such schemes are steeped in sin." (vol. 21, chap. 196)
- "Their positions now, o Apocalypse Beast!" (vol. 21, chap. 197)

**Shiozaki's Notable Quotables**

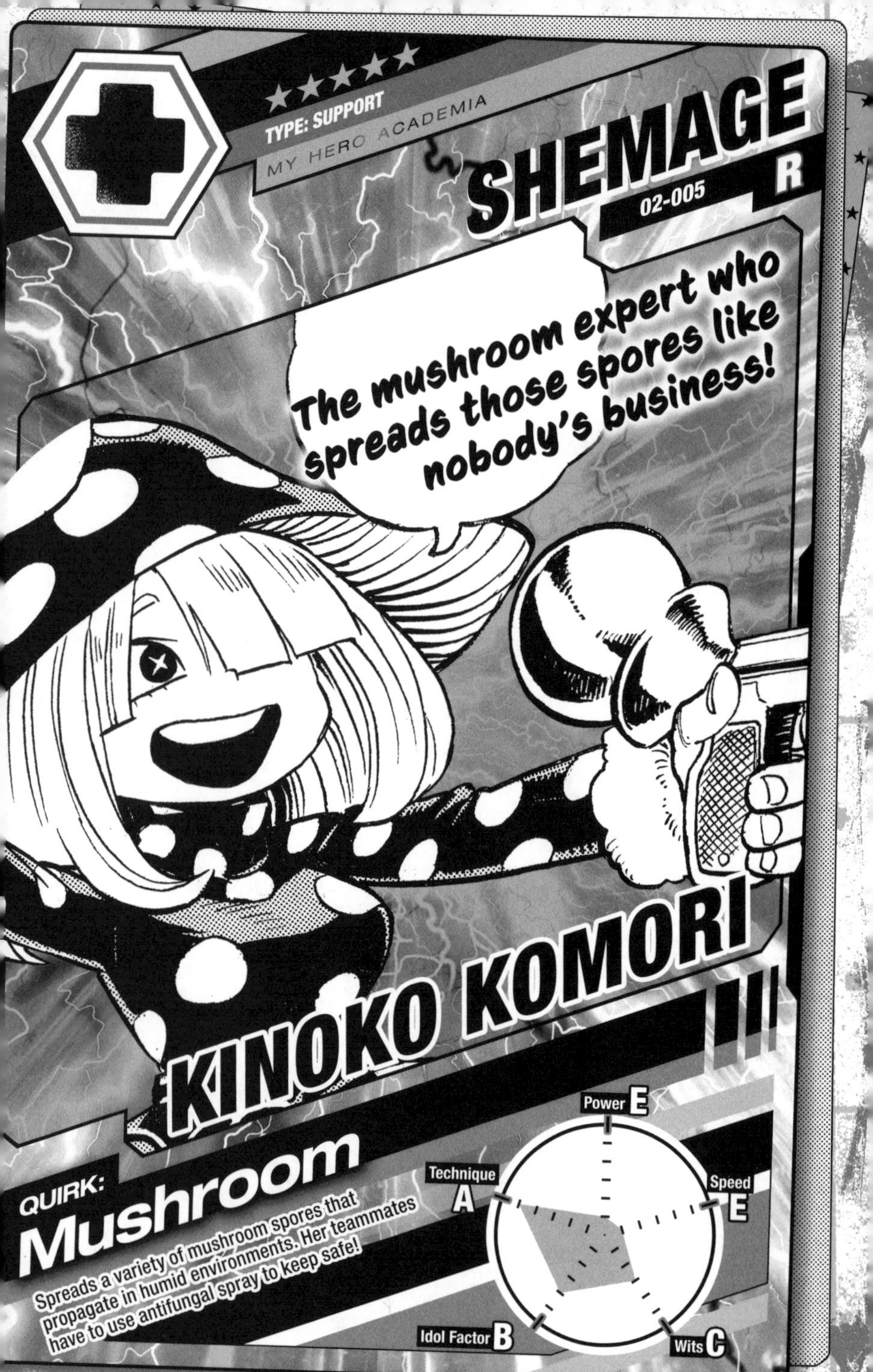
TYPE: SUPPORT
MY HERO ACADEMIA
SHEMAGE
R
02-005
The mushroom expert who spreads those spores like nobody's business!
KINOKO KOMORI
QUIRK:
Mushroom
Spreads a variety of mushroom spores that propagate in humid environments. Her teammates have to use antifungal spray to keep safe!
Power E
Technique A
Speed E
Idol Factor B
Wits C

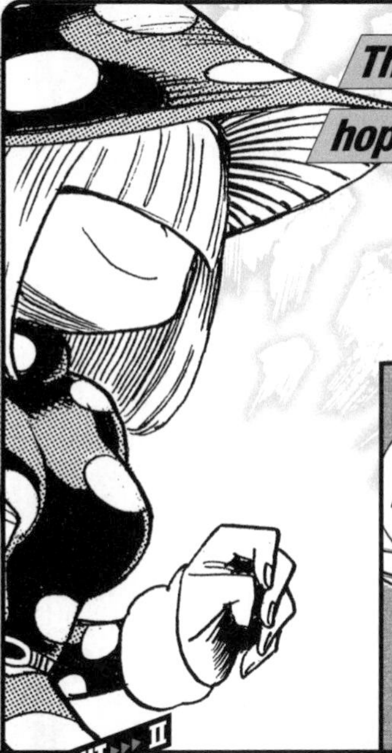

## This mischief-prone Gothic Lolita hopes to become an idol hero, shroom.

Upbeat and irreverent, Komori prefers Lolita fashion, is always up on the latest fad, and wants to be an idol hero. Her first attempt at a hero name was "Much Mush Muse," but that was hard to say, so she started over.

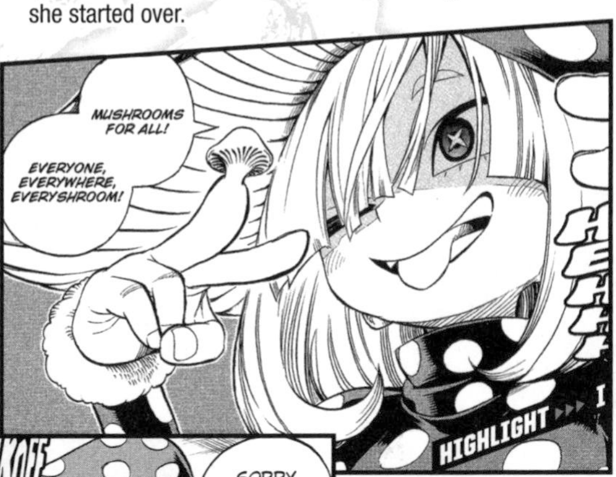
MUSHROOMS FOR ALL!
EVERYONE, EVERYWHERE, EVERYSHROOM!
HIGHLIGHT ▸▸▸ I

⬆ She might look docile, but Komori can be mischievous. Her speech is peppered with shroomy language.

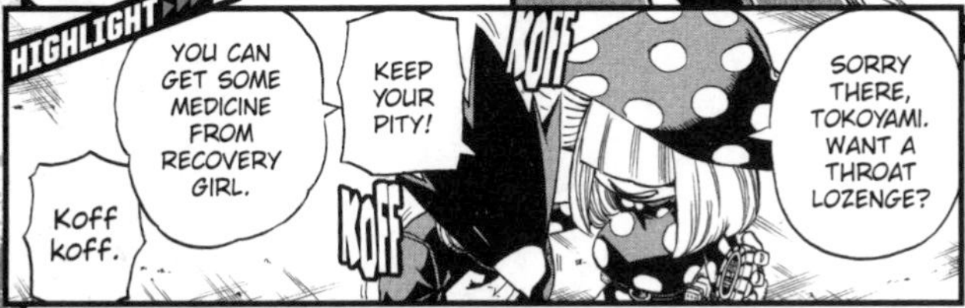
HIGHLIGHT ▸▸▸ II
SORRY THERE, TOKOYAMI. WANT A THROAT LOZENGE?
KOFF
KEEP YOUR PITY!
YOU CAN GET SOME MEDICINE FROM RECOVERY GIRL.
KOFF
Koff koff.

⬆ After the match, Komori showed a softer side to Tokoyami, whose lungs had been attacked by her splitgill mushroom spores.

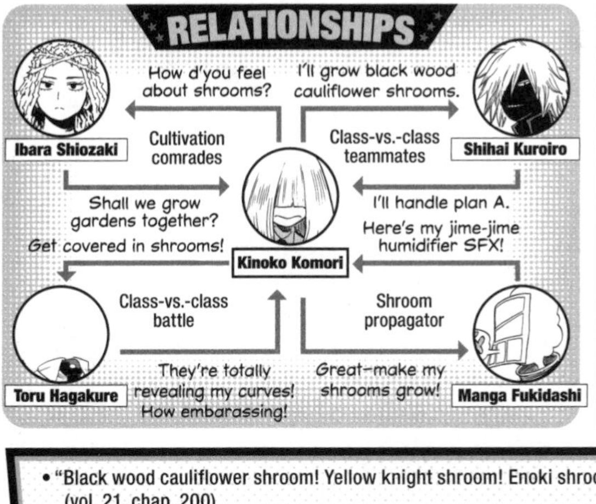
RELATIONSHIPS
How d'you feel about shrooms?
I'll grow black wood cauliflower shrooms.
Ibara Shiozaki
Cultivation comrades
Class-vs.-class teammates
Shihai Kuroiro
Shall we grow gardens together?
Get covered in shrooms!
I'll handle plan A.
Here's my jime-jime humidifier SFX!
Kinoko Komori
Class-vs.-class battle
Shroom propagator
Toru Hagakure
They're totally revealing my curves! How embarassing!
Great—make my shrooms grow!
Manga Fukidashi

## PROFILE

Name: **Kinoko Komori**
Hero name: **Shemage**
Quirk: **Mushroom**
Birthday: **December 2**
Height: **152 cm**
Blood type: **A**
Birthplace: **Gunma Prefecture**
Personality: **Mischievous scamp**
Ultimate move: **Splitgill Lung Strike**

- "Black wood cauliflower shroom! Yellow knight shroom! Enoki shroom, inky cap shroom!" (vol. 21, chap. 200)
- "Grow, grow! Cover the earth with me! Make it shroomtastic!" (vol. 21, chap. 200)
- "Sorrrry! I kept those under wraps because they're not as cute. But if we're about to lose… then I guess I have no other option. Splitgill shrooms attack the lungs!" (vol. 22, chap. 201)

**Komori's Notable Quotables**

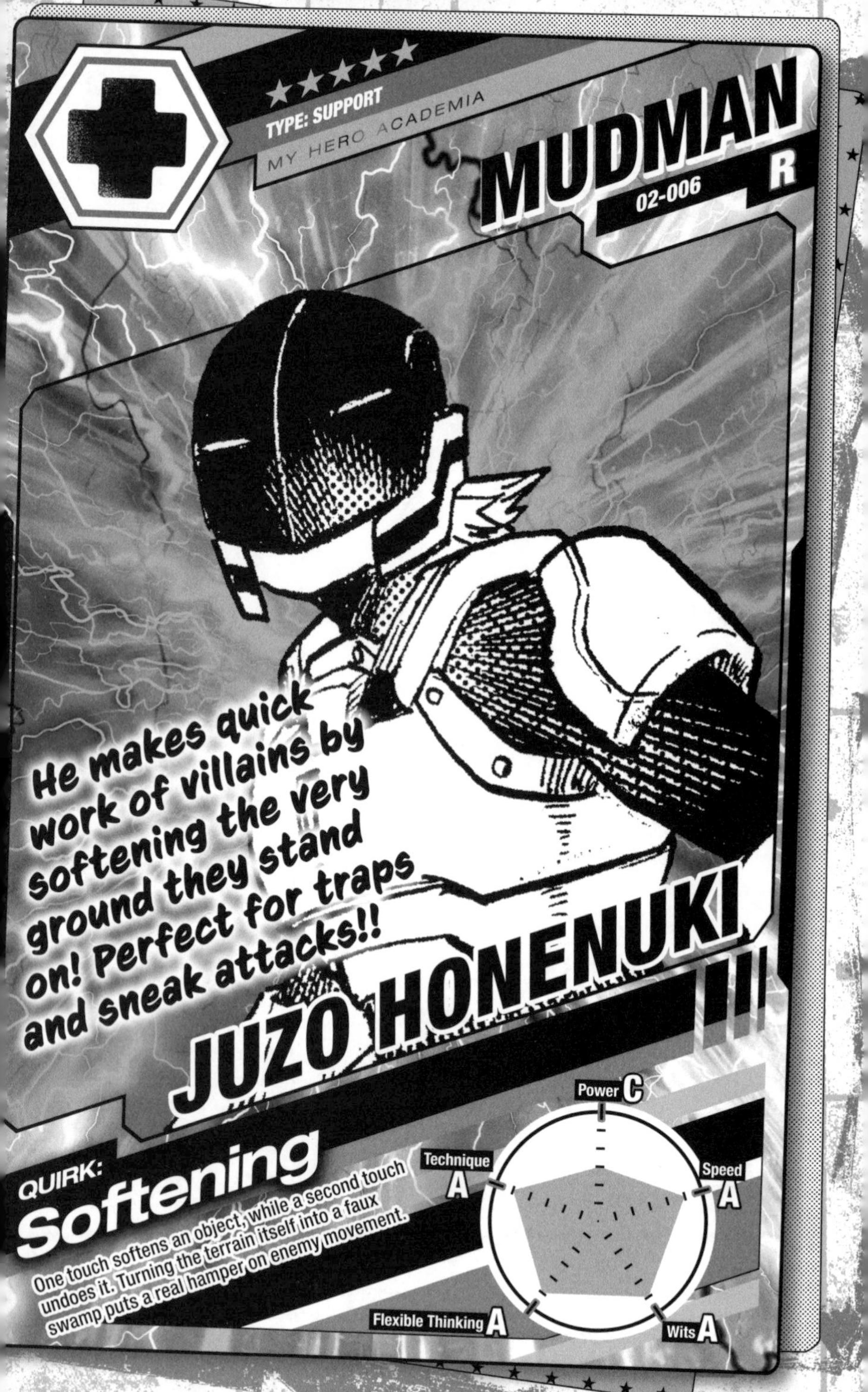
TYPE: SUPPORT
MY HERO ACADEMIA
MUDMAN
R
02-006
He makes quick work of villains by softening the very ground they stand on! Perfect for traps and sneak attacks!!
JUZO HONENUKI
QUIRK:
Softening
One touch softens an object, while a second touch undoes it. Turning the terrain itself into a faux swamp puts a real hamper on enemy movement.
Power C
Speed A
Wits A
Flexible Thinking A
Technique A

CHARACTER

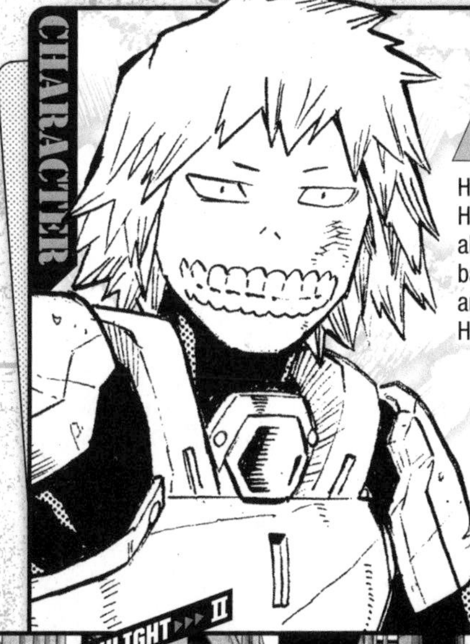

## An intellectual with a scary fac
## who has a trademark soft way.

Honenuki got into the school on special recommendation. He also did a work study. His thinking and conduct are always flexible, so he's great at coming up with ad hoc battle strategies. He can hold a pleasant conversation with anyone, but when Monoma grumbles about class A, Honenuki merely says, "Why not just say it to their faces?"

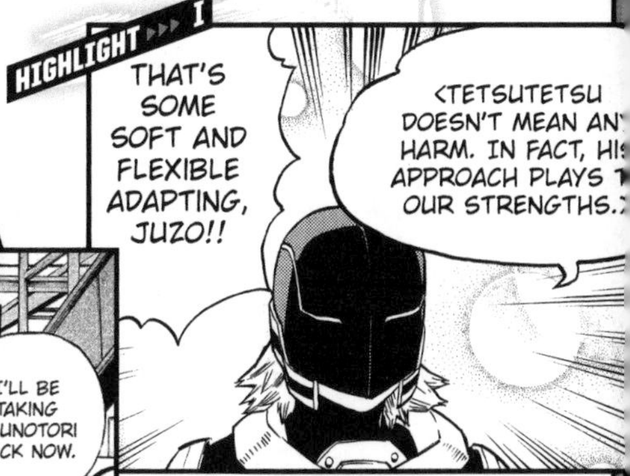
HIGHLIGHT ▸▸▸ I
<TETSUTETSU DOESN'T MEAN AN HARM. IN FACT, HI APPROACH PLAYS T OUR STRENGTHS.>
THAT'S SOME SOFT AND FLEXIBLE ADAPTING, JUZO!!

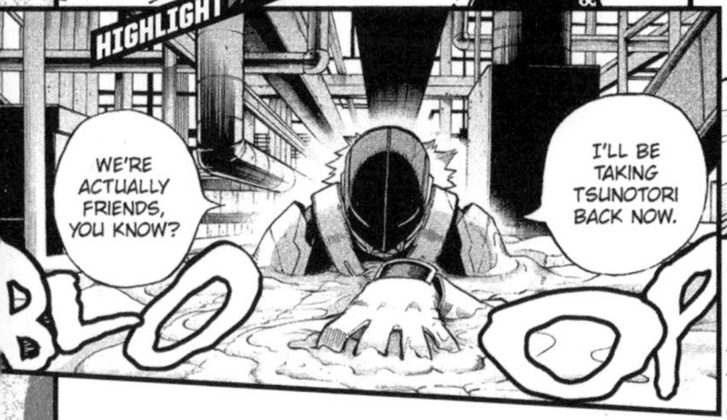
HIGHLIGHT ▸▸▸ II
I'LL BE TAKING TSUNOTORI BACK NOW.
WE'RE ACTUALLY FRIENDS, YOU KNOW?
BLOOP

⬆ When Tsunotori gets mad and speaks English, the ever-flexible Honenuki responds in English without missing a beat.

⬅ Creepy face or not, Honenuki cares about his friends. He's also earnest and ambitious enough for a rematch against Ida and Todoroki.

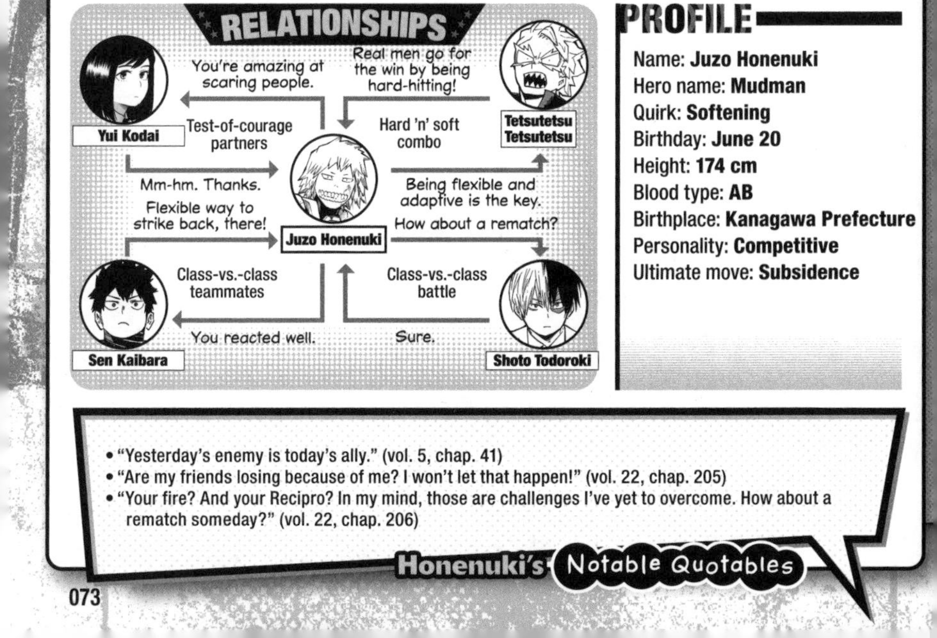
RELATIONSHIPS
Yui Kodai
You're amazing at scaring people.
Test-of-courage partners
Mm-hm. Thanks.
Tetsutetsu Tetsutetsu
Real men go for the win by being hard-hitting!
Hard 'n' soft combo
Being flexible and adaptive is the key.
Juzo Honenuki
Flexible way to strike back, there!
Class-vs.-class teammates
You reacted well.
Sen Kaibara
How about a rematch?
Class-vs.-class battle
Sure.
Shoto Todoroki

## PROFILE

Name: **Juzo Honenuki**
Hero name: **Mudman**
Quirk: **Softening**
Birthday: **June 20**
Height: **174 cm**
Blood type: **AB**
Birthplace: **Kanagawa Prefecture**
Personality: **Competitive**
Ultimate move: **Subsidence**

- "Yesterday's enemy is today's ally." (vol. 5, chap. 41)
- "Are my friends losing because of me? I won't let that happen!" (vol. 22, chap. 205)
- "Your fire? And your Recipro? In my mind, those are challenges I've yet to overcome. How about a rematch someday?" (vol. 22, chap. 206)

**Honenuki's Notable Quotables**

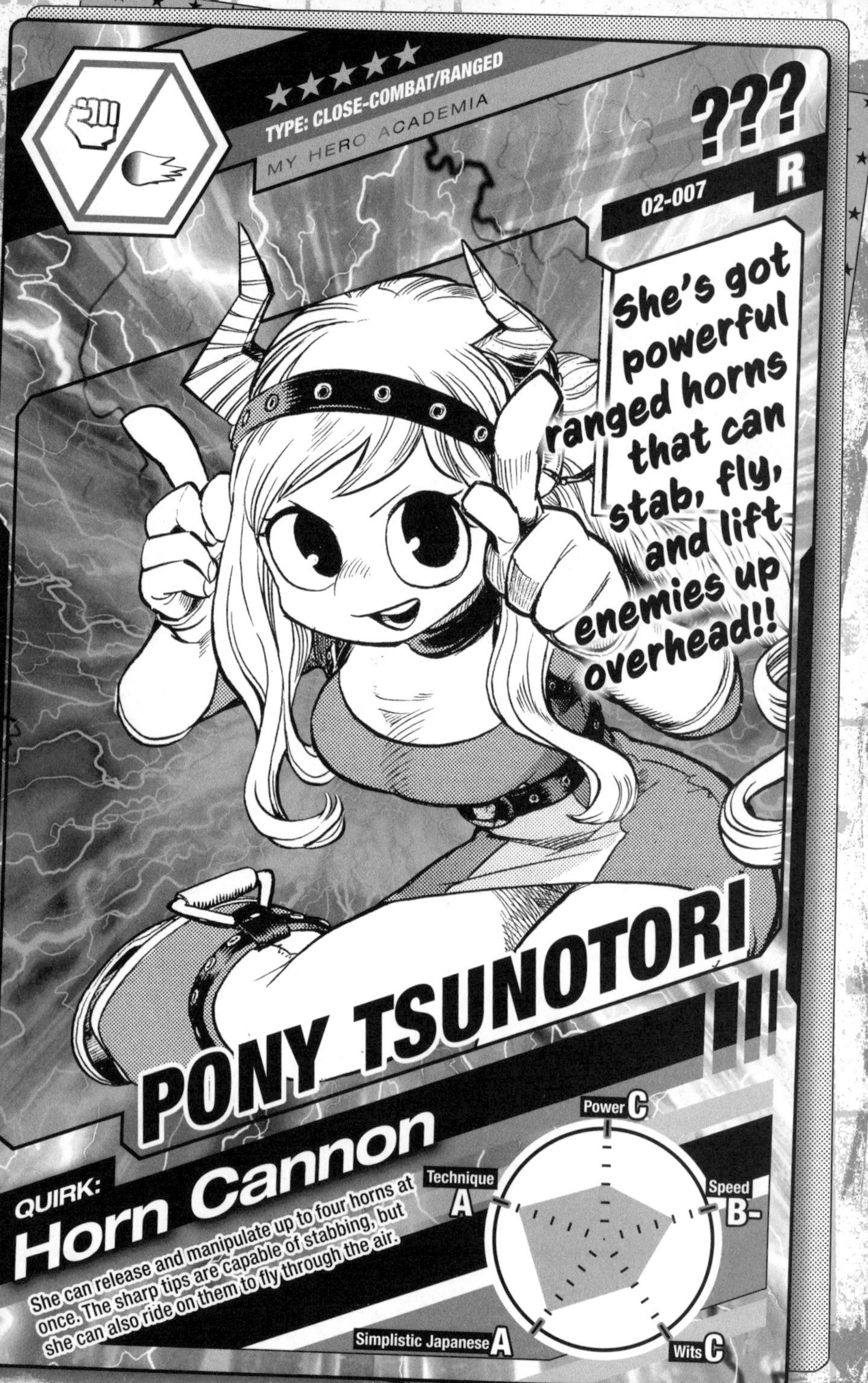
TYPE: CLOSE-COMBAT/RANGED
MY HERO ACADEMIA
???
R
02-007
She's got powerful ranged horns that can stab, fly, and lift enemies up overhead!!
PONY TSUNOTORI
QUIRK:
Horn Cannon
She can release and manipulate up to four horns at once. The sharp tips are capable of stabbing, but she can also ride on them to fly through the air.
Power C
Speed B-
Wits C
Simplistic Japanese A
Technique A

## The blond American who starts speaking English when she's mad.

Tsunotori is a Japanese American hero who hails from the U.S.—the land of heroes. She isn't 100 percent fluent in Japanese yet, so when she's worked up, she inadvertently switches to English. She loves anime, and after Yanagi started holding horror-movie parties, she decided to do anime parties of her own. That's why class B knows so much about anime.

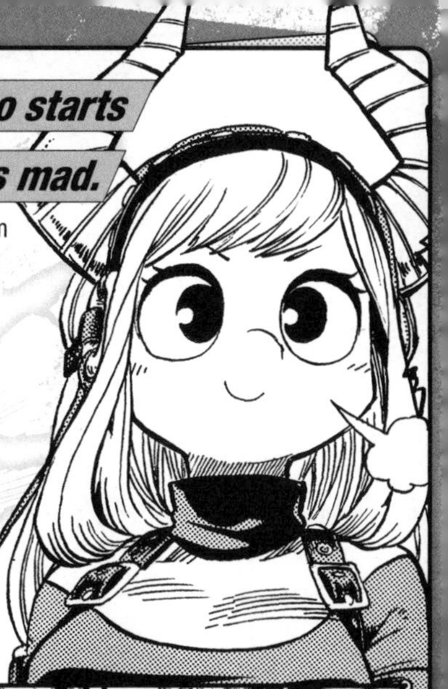

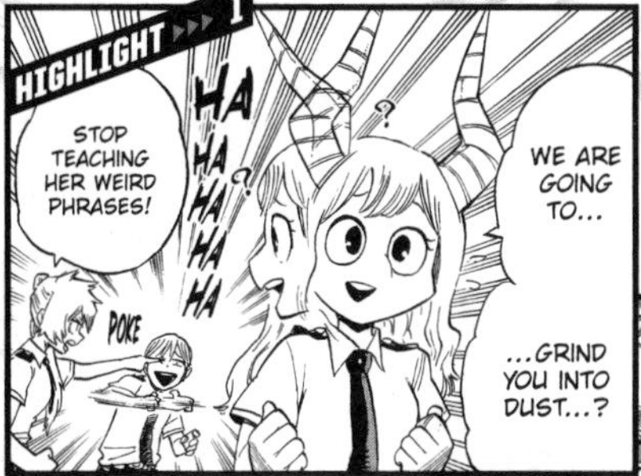
HIGHLIGHT ▸▸▸ I
WE ARE GOING TO...
...GRIND YOU INTO DUST...?
HA HA HA HA HA HA
STOP TEACHING HER WEIRD PHRASES!
POKE

⬆ Tsunotori's classmates teach her Japanese, so when she says something really nasty, you know Monoma is to blame!!

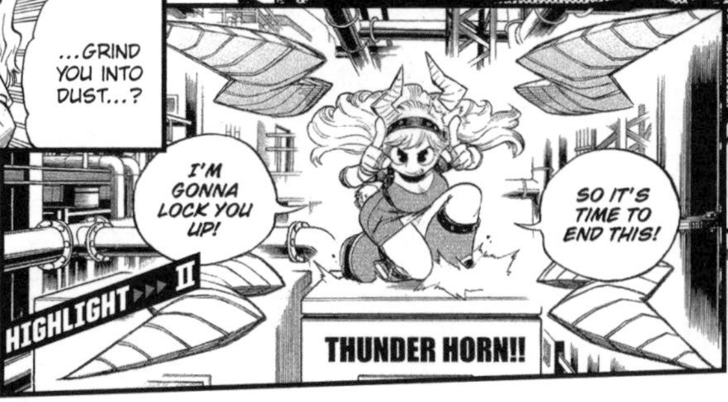
SO IT'S TIME TO END THIS!
I'M GONNA LOCK YOU UP!
HIGHLIGHT ▸▸▸ II
THUNDER HORN!!

➡ An ultimate move that involves launching four horns at once. The horns pack enough power to push back even Shoji.

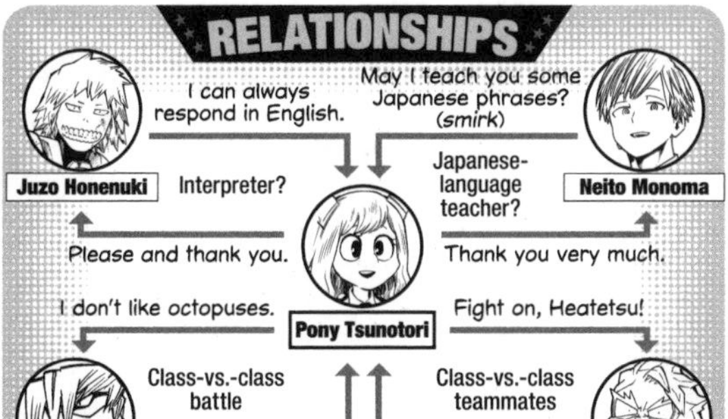
RELATIONSHIPS
Juzo Honenuki
I can always respond in English.
Interpreter?
Please and thank you.
Neito Monoma
May I teach you some Japanese phrases? (smirk)
Japanese-language teacher?
Thank you very much.
Pony Tsunotori
Mezo Shoji
I don't like octopuses.
Class-vs.-class battle
I'm no stranger to being feared.
Tetsutetsu Tetsutetsu
Fight on, Heatetsu!
Class-vs.-class teammates
Gonna be a straight-up brawl!

## PROFILE

Name: **Pony Tsunotori**
Hero name: **Undecided**
Quirk: **Horn Cannon**
Birthday: **April 21**
Height: **155 cm**
Blood type: **O**
Birthplace: **United States**
Personality: **Very sociable**
Ultimate moves: **Thunder Horn, Horn Dash Hammer, Horn Surf**

- "<Geez! Don't keep us in the dark like that!>" (vol. 22, chap. 202)
- "Sorry, Tentacole. But I always trot right past the octopus tank at the aquarium. I can't stand the things." (vol. 22, chap. 205)
- "<We may not win…but I refuse to let us lose.>" (vol. 22, chap. 206)

### Tsunotori's Notable Quotables

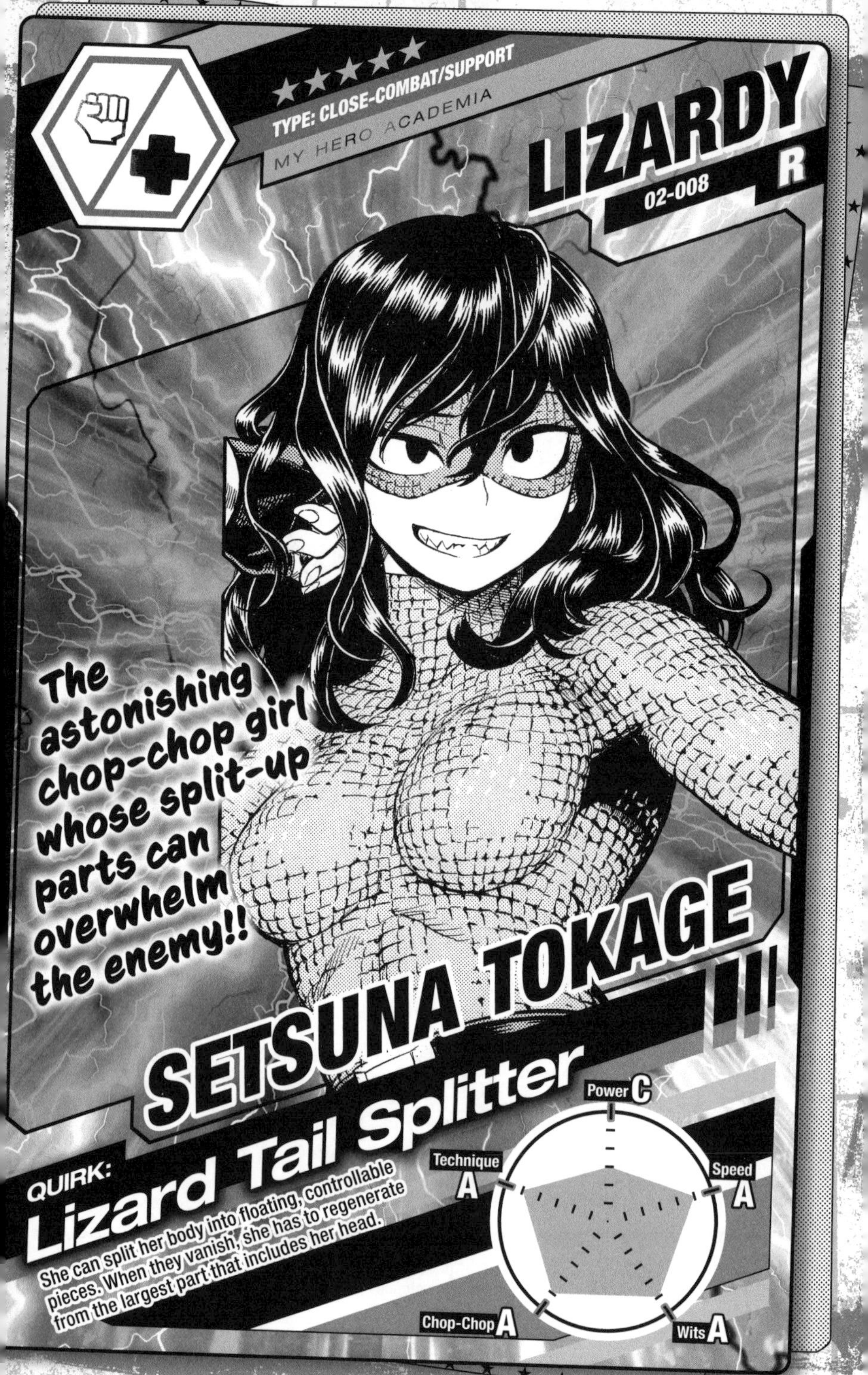
★★★★★
TYPE: CLOSE-COMBAT/SUPPORT
MY HERO ACADEMIA
LIZARDY
R
02-008
The astonishing chop-chop girl whose split-up parts can overwhelm the enemy!!
SETSUNA TOKAGE
QUIRK:
Lizard Tail Splitter
She can split her body into floating, controllable pieces. When they vanish, she has to regenerate from the largest part that includes her head.
Power C
Technique A
Speed A
Chop-Chop A
Wits A

# This special-recommendation student has a sharp mind.

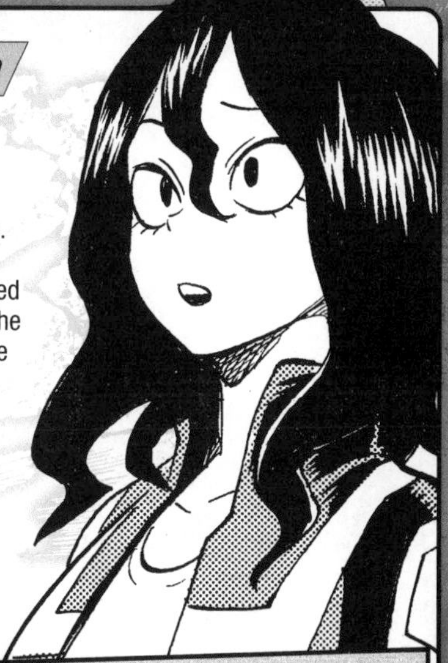

Tokage was a “gyaru” in middle school, and now she’s an upbeat girl who wears her heart on her sleeve. She’s highly calculating in a fight, with a talent for exploiting weaknesses. As such, Tokage is often annoyed by the class B boys who have less strategic minds. In the battle against class A, she made Jiro’s scouting move backfire with her split-apart parts.

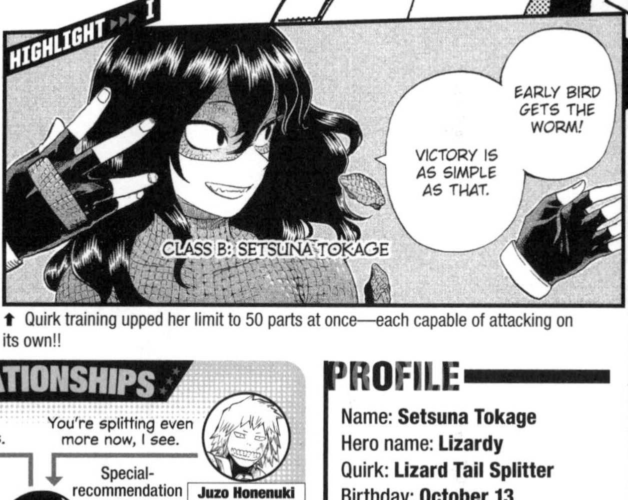
HIGHLIGHT ▸▸▸ I
EARLY BIRD GETS THE WORM!
VICTORY IS AS SIMPLE AS THAT.
CLASS B: SETSUNA TOKAGE

⬆ Quirk training upped her limit to 50 parts at once—each capable of attacking on its own!!

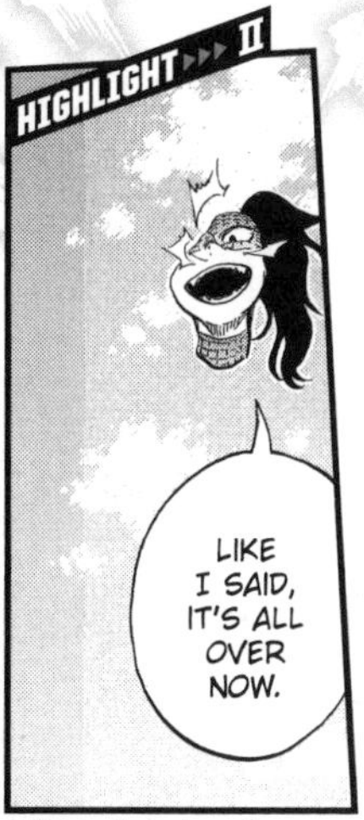
HIGHLIGHT ▸▸▸ II
LIKE I SAID, IT’S ALL OVER NOW.

⬆ Tokage’s costume is a bodysuit with a lizard-scale motif. The costume regenerates too, just like her body parts.

## RELATIONSHIPS

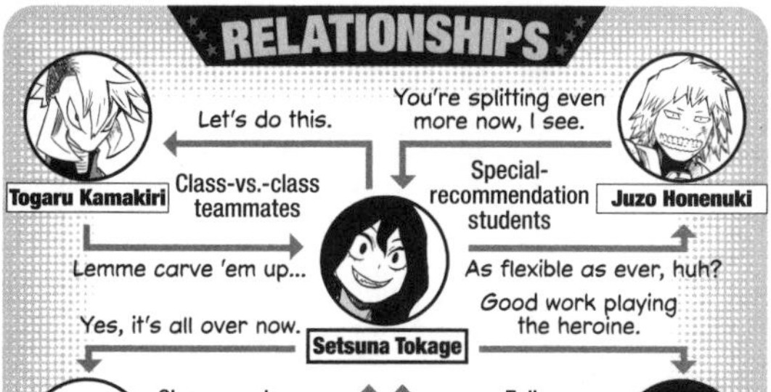
Togaru Kamakiri
Let’s do this.
Class-vs.-class teammates
Lemme carve ’em up...
Juzo Honenuki
You’re splitting even more now, I see.
Special-recommendation students
As flexible as ever, huh?
Setsuna Tokage
Katsuki Bakugo
Yes, it’s all over now.
Class-vs.-class battle
Ugh! Still too small to target!
Yui Kodai
Good work playing the heroine.
Fellow thespians
That sword fight... Cool.

## PROFILE

Name: **Setsuna Tokage**
Hero name: **Lizardy**
Quirk: **Lizard Tail Splitter**
Birthday: **October 13**
Height: **158 cm**
Blood type: **B**
Birthplace: **Saitama Prefecture**
Personality: **Kind of detached**
Ultimate moves: **Part-Powered Punch, Cast-Away**

- “For real?!” (vol. 22, chap. 208)
- “Why’d you go and change so much?!” (vol. 22, chap. 208)
- “Sorry for dragging you all down with me…” (vol. 22, chap. 209)

**Tokage’s Notable Quotables**

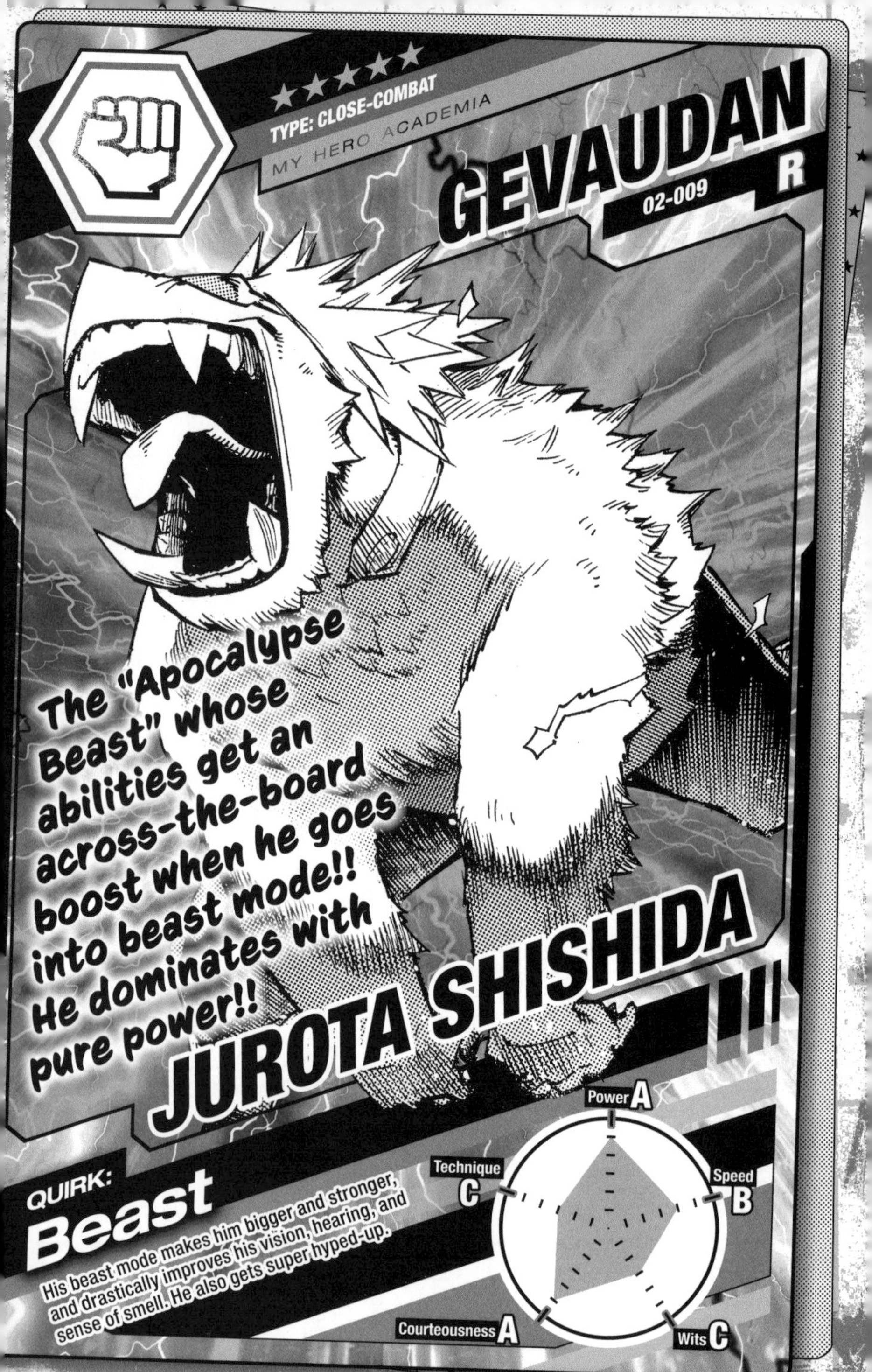

TYPE: CLOSE-COMBAT
MY HERO ACADEMIA
GEVAUDAN
R
02-009
The "Apocalypse Beast" whose abilities get an across-the-board boost when he goes into beast mode!! He dominates with pure power!!
JUROTA SHISHIDA
QUIRK:
Beast
His beast mode makes him bigger and stronger, and drastically improves his vision, hearing, and sense of smell. He also gets super hyped-up.
Power A
Speed B
Wits C
Courteousness A
Technique C

CHARACTER

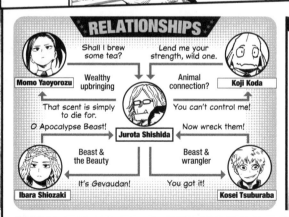

# A refined boy whose exterior belies his courteous personality.

It's Shishida's beast-like appearance that makes him seem rough, gruff, and violent. He looks up to Hound Dog and tries to use animal instincts the way his favorite teacher does, but his proper upbringing gets in the way. He's quite straitlaced otherwise, and he participated in the work-study program.

HIGHLIGHT ▸▸▸ I
ROARING RAGE!!
SHP
TLAK

HIGHLIGHT ▸▸▸ II
JUROTA SHISHIDA
QUIRK: BEAST
GOING INTO BEAST MODE GRANTS HIM A MASSIVE BOOST TO HIS STRENGTH, HEARING, VISION AND SENSE OF SMELL! BUT THE TRANSFORMATION ALSO MAKES HIM WILDLY ENTHUSIASTIC!
I'VE GOT A NOSE FOR THESE THINGS!!
GAH HA HA HA HA

⬆ Shishida captured Kirishima in an instant during the battle against class A. He freed Tsuburaba from Asui's grasp just as quickly.

⬅ Shishida takes his hero name from the "Beast of Gévaudan," a French legend, but his friends call him "Apocalypse Beast" or "Apocabeast."

RELATIONSHIPS
Momo Yaoyorozu
Koji Koda
Jurota Shishida
Ibara Shiozaki
Kosei Tsuburaba
Shall I brew some tea?
Wealthy upbringing
That scent is simply to die for.
Lend me your strength, wild one.
Animal connection?
You can't control me!
O Apocalypse Beast!
Beast & the Beauty
It's Gevaudan!
Now wreck them!
Beast & wrangler
You got it!

## PROFILE

Name: **Jurota Shishida**
Hero name: **Gevaudan**
Quirk: **Beast**
Birthday: **March 26**
Height: **174 cm**
Blood type: **O**
Birthplace: **Akita Prefecture**
Personality: **Reckless rusher**
Ultimate move: **Roaring Rage**

- "And once more, beast mode!" (vol. 21, chap. 196)
- "Could you not call me that? It's Gevaudan!" (vol. 21, chap. 197)
- "However!! Not enough to take down most villains!" (vol. 21, chap. 197)

Shishida's Notable Quotables

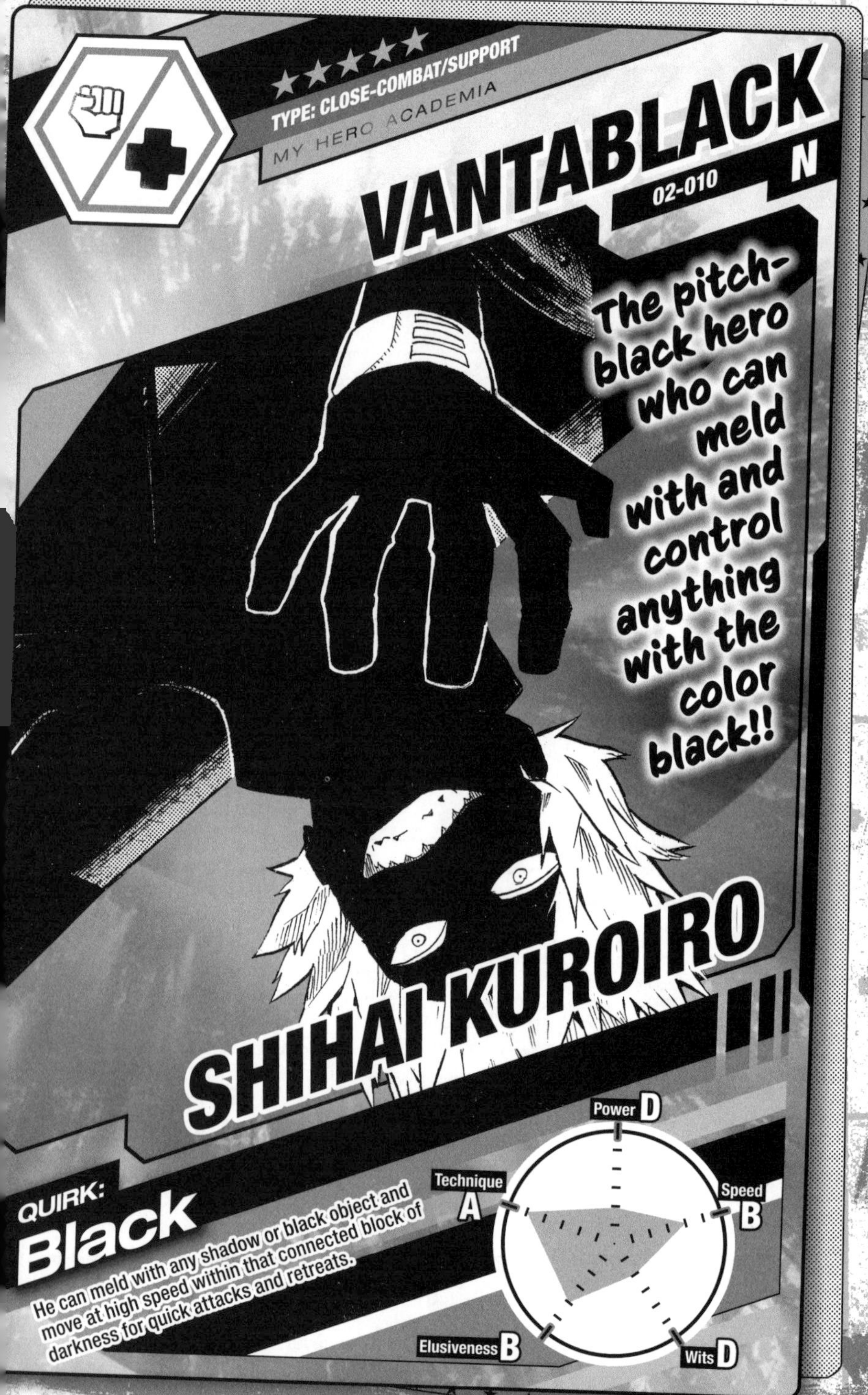
TYPE: CLOSE-COMBAT/SUPPORT
MY HERO ACADEMIA
VANTABLACK
02-010
N
The pitch-black hero who can meld with and control anything with the color black!!
SHIHAI KUROIRO
Power D
Technique A
Speed B
Elusiveness B
Wits D
QUIRK:
Black
He can meld with any shadow or black object and move at high speed within that connected block of darkness for quick attacks and retreats.

CHARACTER

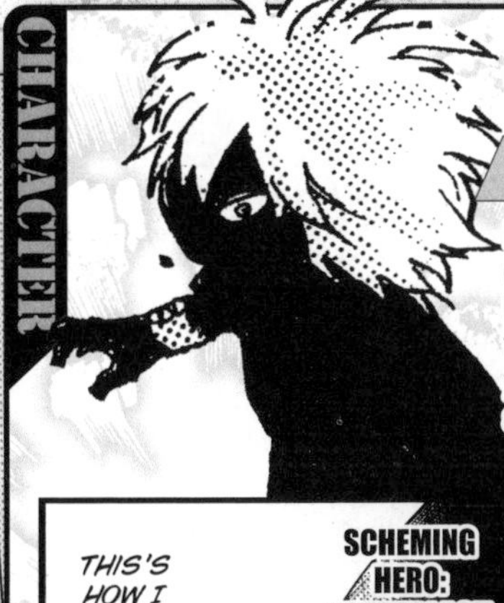

## Tokoyami's rival or ally? Their "darkness" is an edgy connection.

Kuroiro has pitch-black skin and silver hair. He feels a connection with Tokoyami, since both of their Quirks have to do with darkness. Kuroiro isn't great at talking to girls. He just goes straight for the kill and asks, "Are you into me?" At the moment, he is into Komori, but she barely knows he exists.

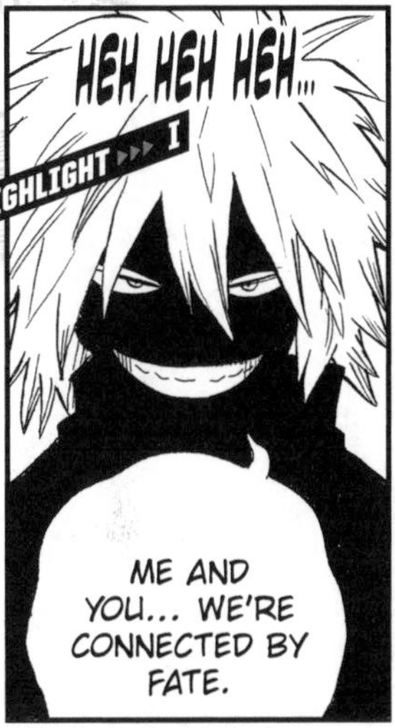
HIGHLIGHT ▸▸▸ I
HEH HEH HEH...
ME AND YOU... WE'RE CONNECTED BY FATE.

⬆ Kuroiro has been harboring a perceived rivalry with Tokoyami for a while. Right before the class-versus-class battle, he basically declared war.

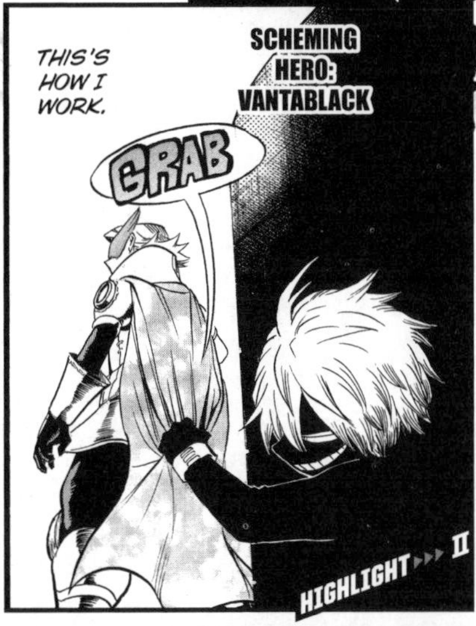
SCHEMING HERO: VANTABLACK
THIS'S HOW I WORK.
GRAB
HIGHLIGHT ▸▸▸ II

⬅ He uses his Quirk to lurk in the shadows before unleashing sneak attacks. He's also strong enough to whisk Aoyama away at lightning speed.

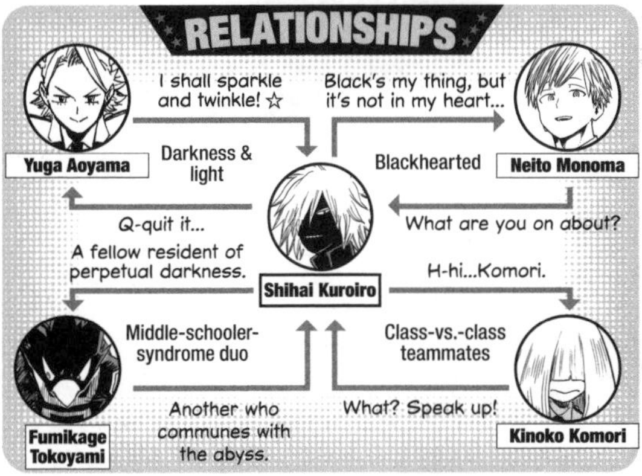
RELATIONSHIPS
Yuga Aoyama
I shall sparkle and twinkle! ☆
Darkness & light
Q-quit it...
Neito Monoma
Black's my thing, but it's not in my heart...
Blackhearted
What are you on about?
Shihai Kuroiro
A fellow resident of perpetual darkness.
H-hi...Komori.
Fumikage Tokoyami
Middle-schooler-syndrome duo
Another who communes with the abyss.
Kinoko Komori
Class-vs.-class teammates
What? Speak up!

## PROFILE

Name: **Shihai Kuroiro**
Hero name: **Vantablack**
Quirk: **Black**
Birthday: **November 1**
Height: **176 cm**
Blood type: **A**
Birthplace: **Fukushima Prefecture**
Personality: **Schemer**
Ultimate move: **Darkseek**

- "Tokoyami... You're...like me." (vol. 21, chap. 198)
- "Fumikage Tokoyami... I'm gonna wear you like a suit." (vol. 21, chap. 198)
- "Keh heh heh! Black Fallen Angel?! Sounds cool. Why don'tcha show me?!" (vol. 21, chap. 199)

**Kuroiro's Notable Quotables**

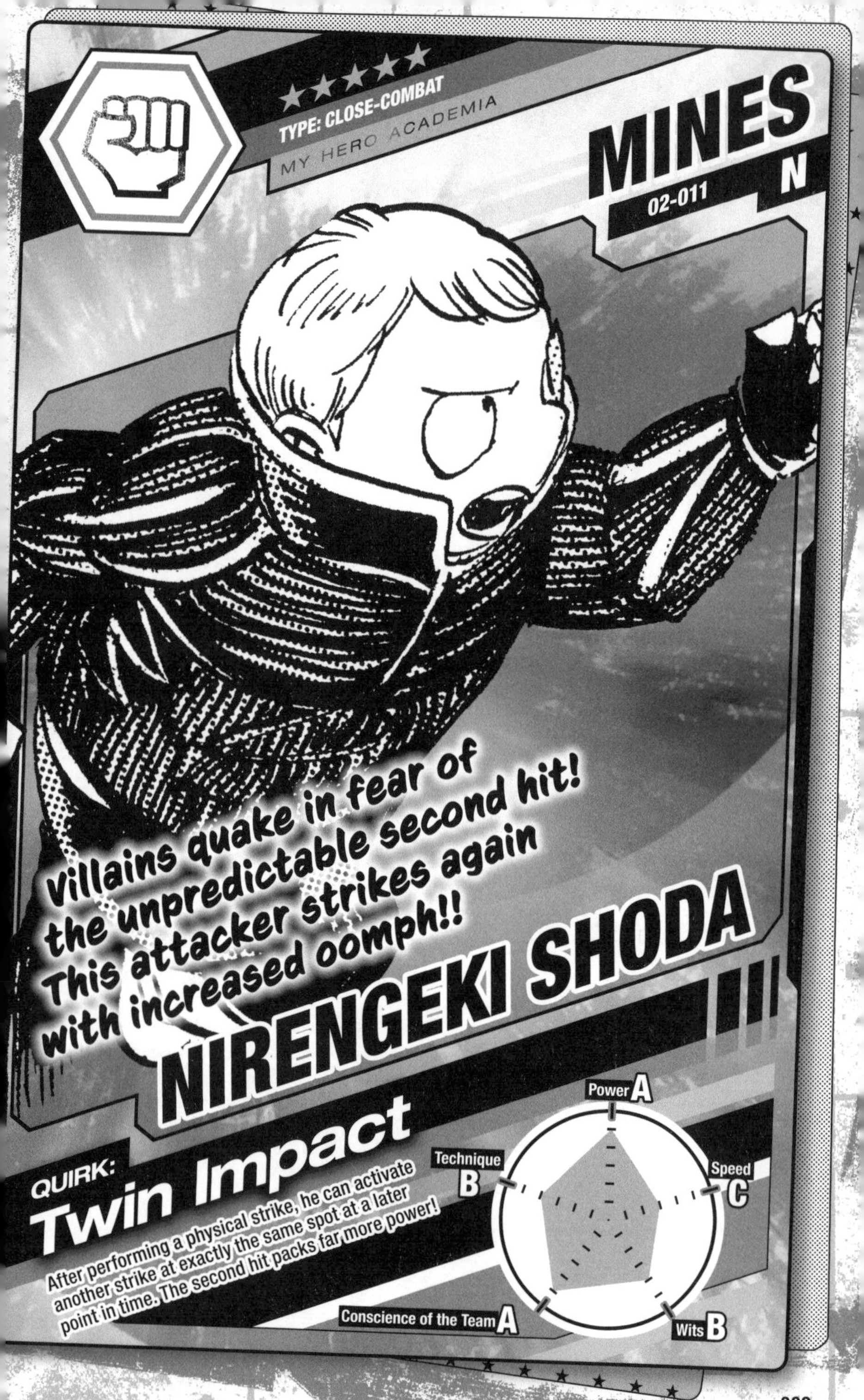
TYPE: CLOSE-COMBAT
MY HERO ACADEMIA
MINES
N
02-011
Villains quake in fear of the unpredictable second hit! This attacker strikes again with increased oomph!!
NIRENGEKI SHODA
QUIRK:
Twin Impact
After performing a physical strike, he can activate another strike at exactly the same spot at a later point in time. The second hit packs far more power!
Power A
Speed C
Wits B
Conscience of the Team A
Technique B

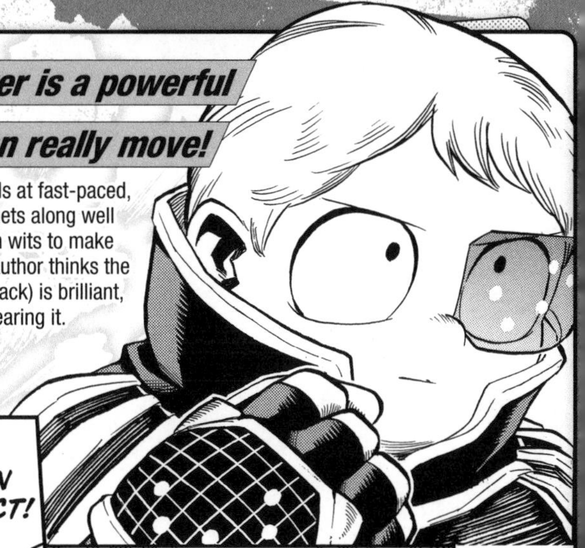

## This little chubster is a powerful fighter who can really move!

Despite his build, Shoda excels at fast-paced, one-on-one combat, and he gets along well with Ida. He's also got enough wits to make him a decent strategist. The author thinks the name "Nirengeki" (two-hit attack) is brilliant, but the editor scoffed upon hearing it.

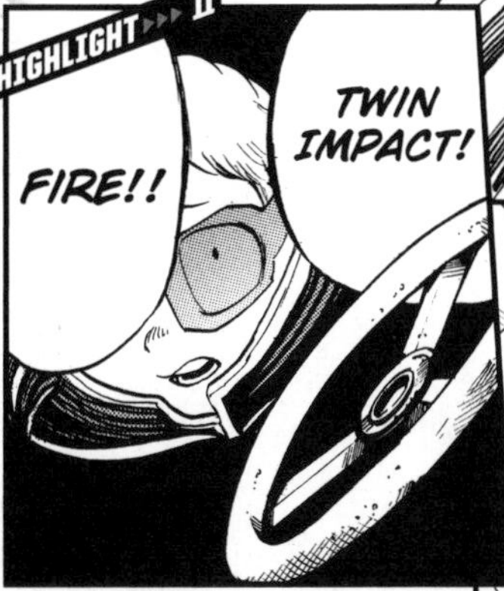
HIGHLIGHT ▸▸▸ II
TWIN IMPACT!
FIRE!!

⬆ The second hit can be activated at will. Part of his strategy is striking fear into the hearts of opponents with an unpredictable follow-up.

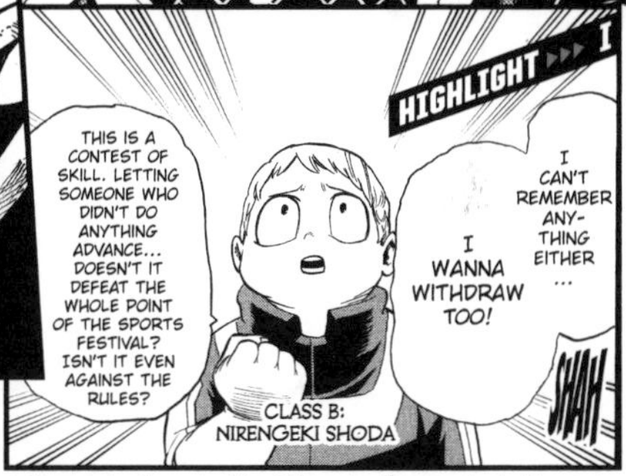
HIGHLIGHT ▸▸▸ I
I CAN'T REMEMBER ANY-THING EITHER...
I WANNA WITHDRAW TOO!
THIS IS A CONTEST OF SKILL. LETTING SOMEONE WHO DIDN'T DO ANYTHING ADVANCE... DOESN'T IT DEFEAT THE WHOLE POINT OF THE SPORTS FESTIVAL? ISN'T IT EVEN AGAINST THE RULES?
SHAH
CLASS B: NIRENGEKI SHODA

⬆ He was brainwashed by Shinso for the cavalry battle, so he withdrew from the final tournament. In doing so, he demonstrated integrity.

## RELATIONSHIPS

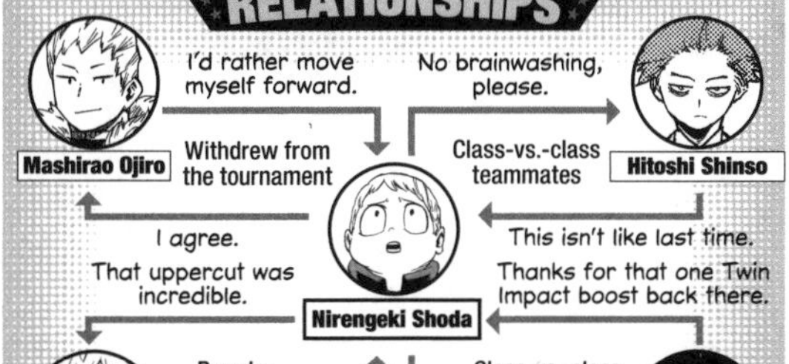
Mashirao Ojiro
I'd rather move myself forward.
Withdrew from the tournament
I agree.
Hitoshi Shinso
No brainwashing, please.
Class-vs.-class teammates
This isn't like last time.
Nirengeki Shoda
Mina Ashido
That uppercut was incredible.
Brawler showdown
Right? I gotcha good there.
Minoru Mineta
Thanks for that one Twin Impact boost back there.
Class-vs.-class teammates
Huh? What are you thanking me for?

## PROFILE

Name: **Nirengeki Shoda**
Hero name: **Mines**
Quirk: **Twin Impact**
Birthday: **February 2**
Height: **165 cm**
Blood type: **O**
Birthplace: **Tokyo**
Personality: **Strong-willed**
Ultimate move: **Twin Impact: Fire**

- "That's her way of calling him scary." (vol. 22, chap. 209)
- "I wish we could regroup, but they're coming at us so quick! There's no time to come up with a plan!!" (vol. 23, chap. 214)
- "They call me the *Mobile Adonis*!" (vol. 23, chap. 215)

**Shoda's Notable Quotables**

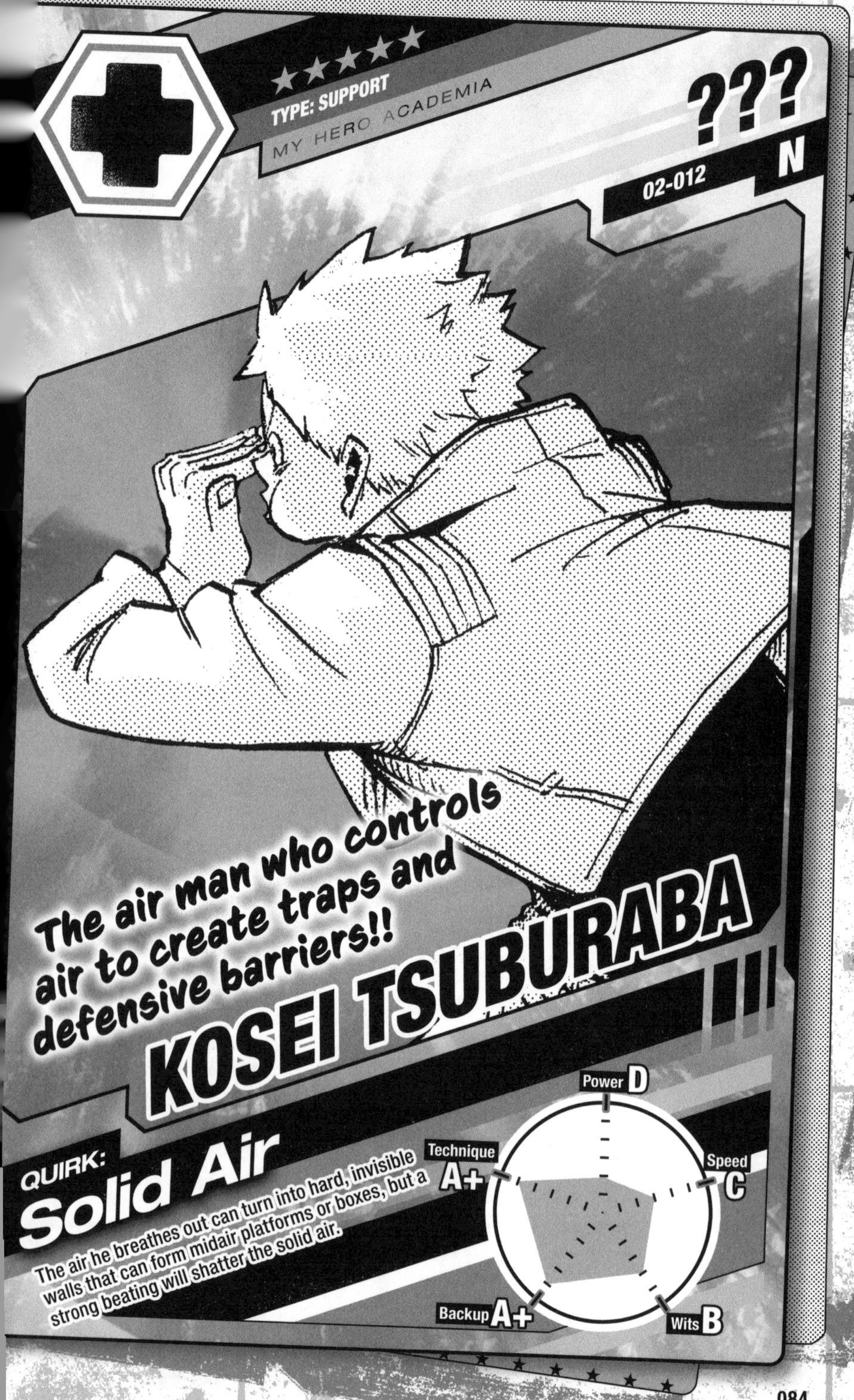
TYPE: SUPPORT
MY HERO ACADEMIA
???
N
02-012
The air man who controls air to create traps and defensive barriers!!
KOSEI TSUBURABA
QUIRK:
Solid Air
The air he breathes out can turn into hard, invisible walls that can form midair platforms or boxes, but a strong beating will shatter the solid air.
Power D
Speed C
Wits B
Backup A+
Technique A+

CHARACTER

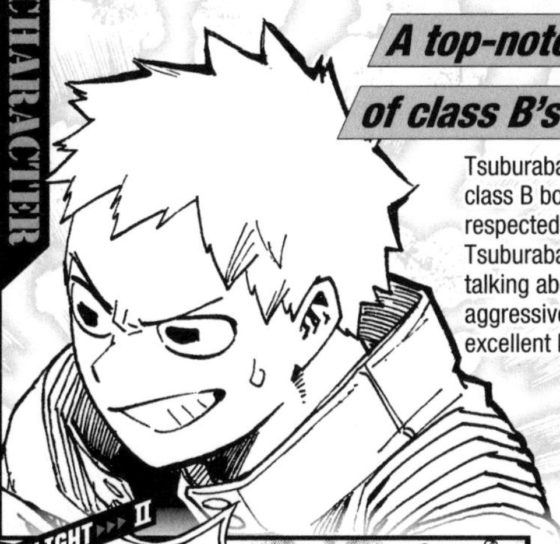

# A top-notch support fighter and one of class B's four Common Sense Lords

Tsuburaba has ellipse-shaped eyes, and he's one of the class B boys with plenty of common sense. He's respected Todoroki ever since the forest training camp. Tsuburaba, Kaibara, and Kuroiro often get worked up talking about girls. Though he's not the type to attack aggressively, Tsuburaba uses his Solid Air to provide excellent backup.

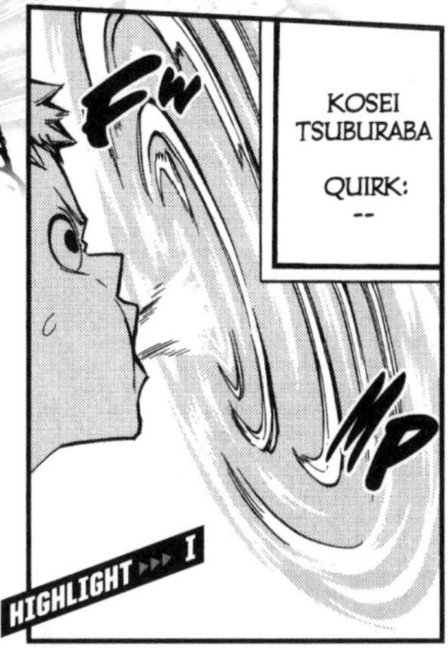
KOSEI TSUBURABA QUIRK: --
FW
MP
HIGHLIGHT ▸▸▸ I

⬆ By upping his lung capacity, Tsuburaba can create more of his Solid Air.

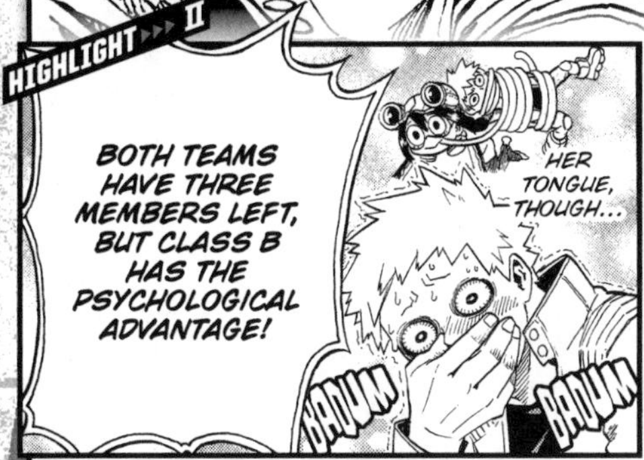
HIGHLIGHT ▸▸▸ II
HER TONGUE, THOUGH...
BOTH TEAMS HAVE THREE MEMBERS LEFT, BUT CLASS B HAS THE PSYCHOLOGICAL ADVANTAGE!
BADUM
BADUM

⬆ He blushed in spite of himself after getting wrapped up by Asui's tongue—surely a heart-pounding experience for any adolescent.

## RELATIONSHIPS

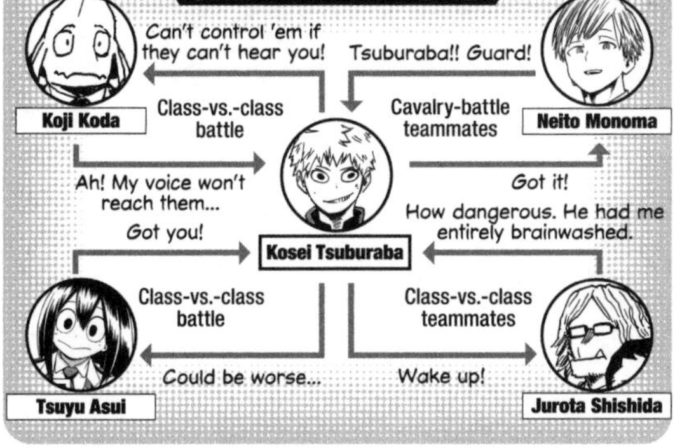
Koji Koda
Can't control 'em if they can't hear you!
Class-vs.-class battle
Ah! My voice won't reach them...
Neito Monoma
Tsuburaba!! Guard!
Cavalry-battle teammates
Got it!
Kosei Tsuburaba
Got you!
Tsuyu Asui
Class-vs.-class battle
Could be worse...
How dangerous. He had me entirely brainwashed.
Class-vs.-class teammates
Wake up!
Jurota Shishida

## PROFILE

Name: **Kosei Tsuburaba**
Hero name: **???**
Quirk: **Solid Air**
Birthday: **May 19**
Height: **170 cm**
Blood type: **O**
Birthplace: **Kanagawa Prefecture**
Personality: **Unsung background hero**
Ultimate move: **Air Prison**

## Tsuburaba's Notable Quotables

- "Ha ha! How d'ya like that? It's an invisible wall!" (vol. 4, chap. 30)
- "It's soundproof solitary confinement!" (vol. 21, chap. 195)
- "She got me good... Her tongue, though..." (vol. 21, chap. 196)

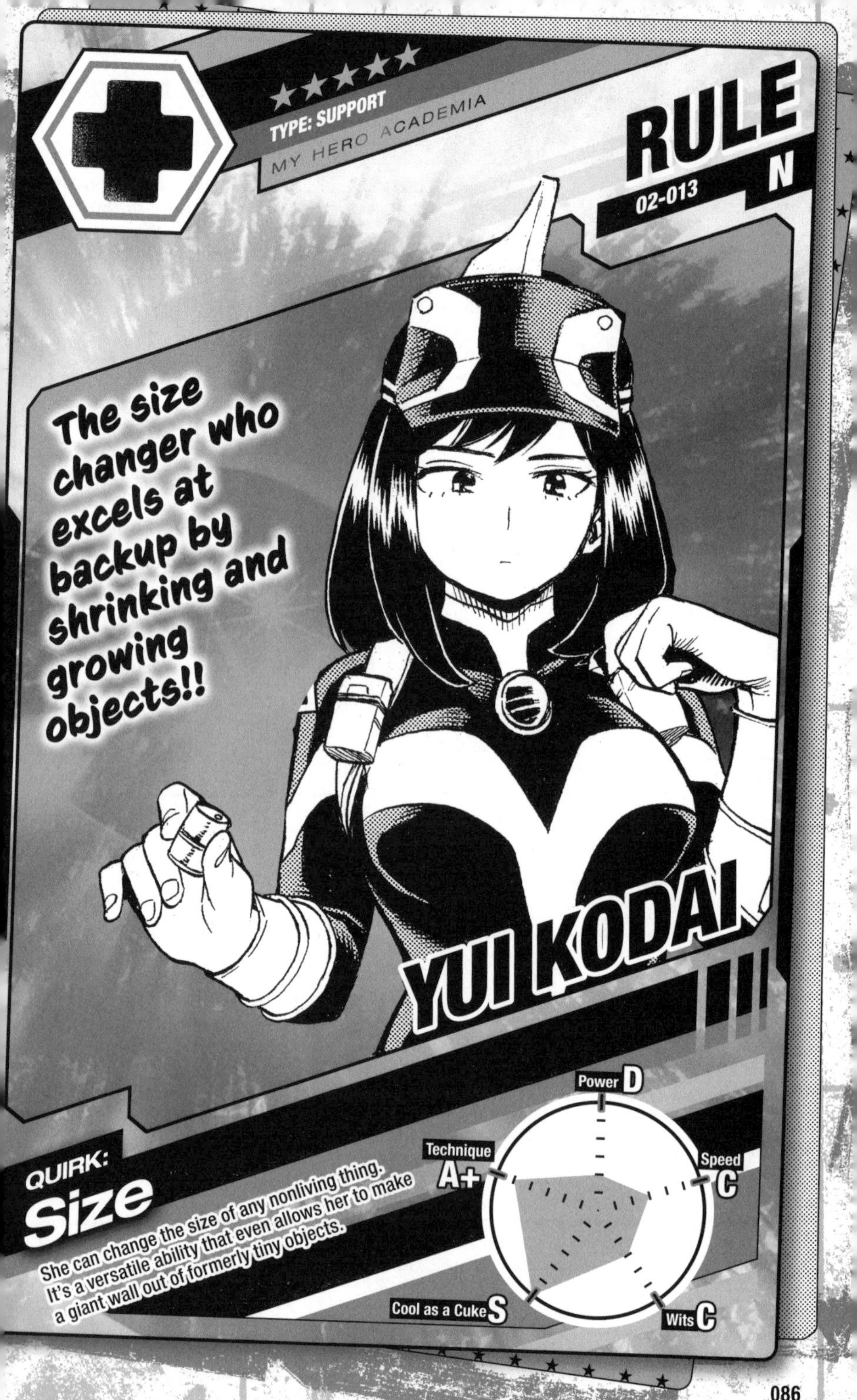

TYPE: SUPPORT
MY HERO ACADEMIA
RULE
N
02-013
The size changer who excels at backup by shrinking and growing objects!!
YUI KODAI
QUIRK:
Size
She can change the size of any nonliving thing. It's a versatile ability that even allows her to make a giant wall out of formerly tiny objects.
Power D
Speed C
Wits C
Cool as a Cuke S
Technique A+

CHARACTER

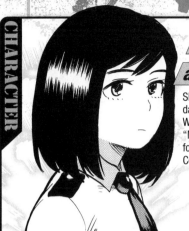

## This poker-faced beauty can say a lot with a series of "Mm"s!

She barely speaks or emotes, but Kodai isn't especially dark or gloomy. When she's happy, she says, "Mm!" When she eats a tomato (her favorite food), she goes, "Mm-mm!" Kodai is especially popular among the boys for being the most attractive first-year in the Hero Course. She can't stand Monoma.

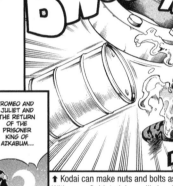

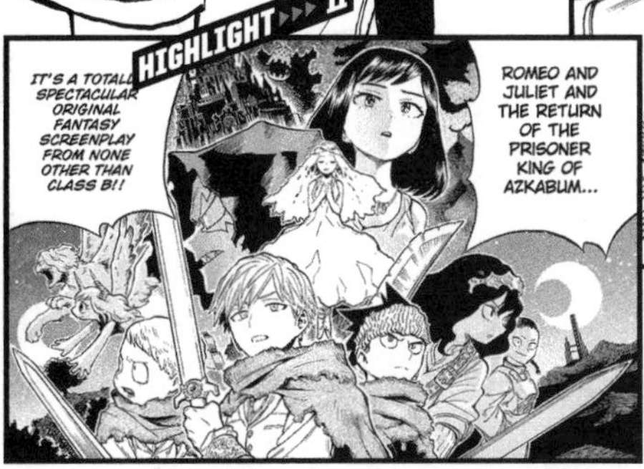

BWOOMP
HIGHLIGHT ▸▸▸ I

HIGHLIGHT ▸▸▸ II
ROMEO AND JULIET AND THE RETURN OF THE PRISONER KING OF AZKABUM...
IT'S A TOTALLY SPECTACULAR ORIGINAL FANTASY SCREENPLAY FROM NONE OTHER THAN CLASS B!!

⬆ Kodai can make nuts and bolts as big as people. With more Quirk training, will she able to make them even bigger?

⬅ Kodai played Juliet in class B's stage play for the School Festival. Her Quirk came in handy when moving the set pieces.

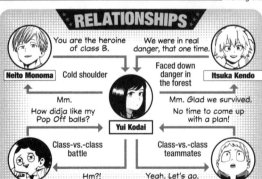

## RELATIONSHIPS

Neito Monoma
You are the heroine of class B.
Cold shoulder
Mm.
Itsuka Kendo
We were in real danger, that one time.
Faced down danger in the forest
Mm. Glad we survived.
Yui Kodai
Minoru Mineta
How didja like my Pop Off balls?
Class-vs.-class battle
Hm?!
Nirengeki Shoda
No time to come up with a plan!
Class-vs.-class teammates
Yeah. Let's go.

## PROFILE

Name: **Yui Kodai**
Hero name: **Rule**
Quirk: **Size**
Birthday: **December 19**
Height: **160 cm**
Blood type: **B**
Birthplace: **Shimane Prefecture**
Personality: **Nerves of steel?**
Ultimate moves: **Unknown**

## Kodai's Notable Quotables

- "Mm." (vol. 8, chap. 70; vol. 9, chap. 73; vol. 23, chap. 213)
- "Hm?!" (vol. 9, chap. 73)
- "Yeah." (vol. 23, chap. 214)

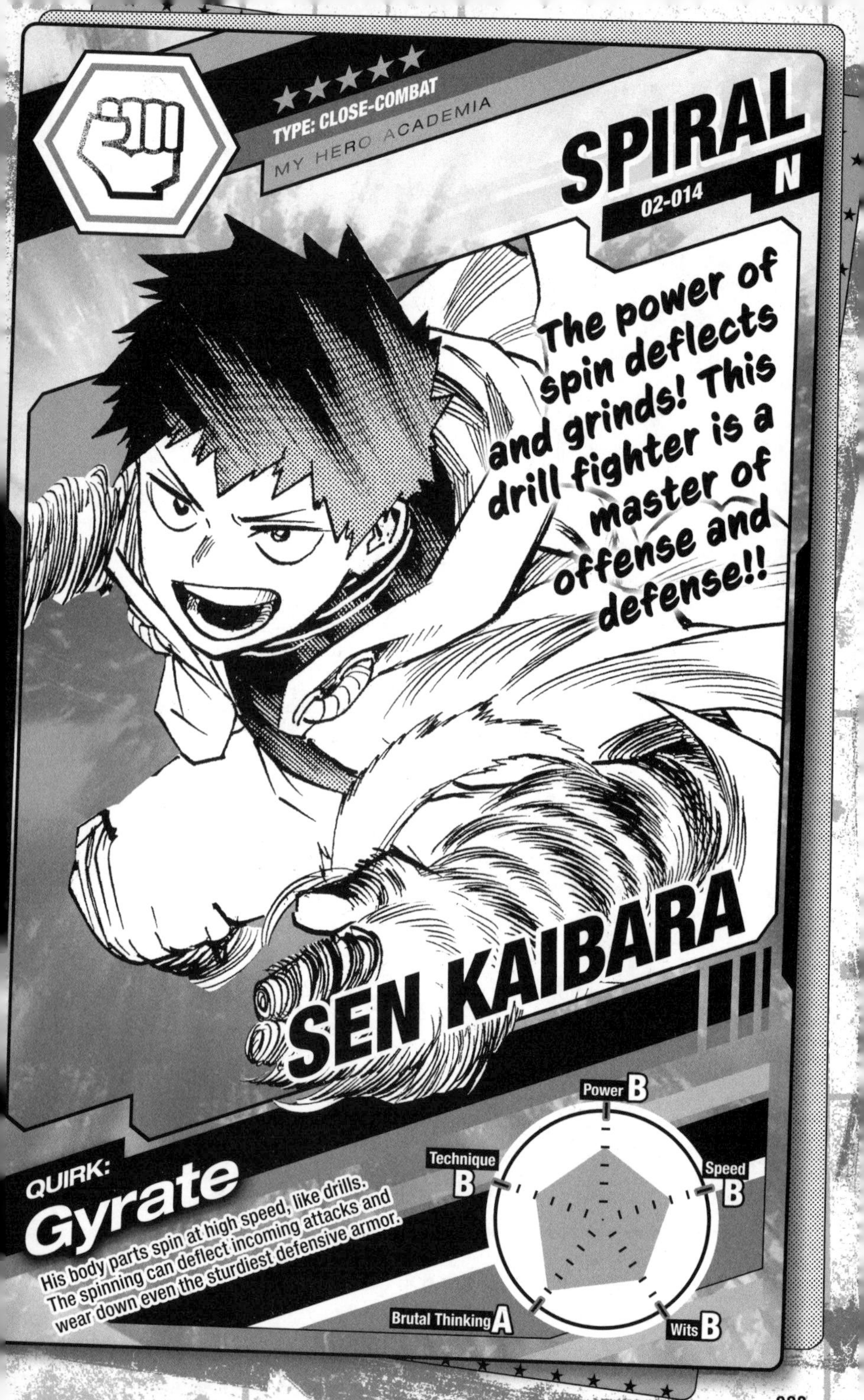
TYPE: CLOSE-COMBAT
MY HERO ACADEMIA
SPIRAL
N
02-014
The power of spin deflects and grinds! This drill fighter is a master of offense and defense!!
SEN KAIBARA
QUIRK:
Gyrate
His body parts spin at high speed, like drills. The spinning can deflect incoming attacks and wear down even the sturdiest defensive armor.
Power B
Speed B
Wits B
Brutal Thinking A
Technique B

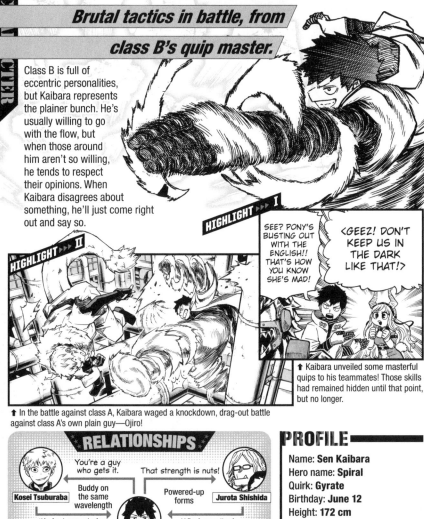

## Brutal tactics in battle, from class B's quip master.

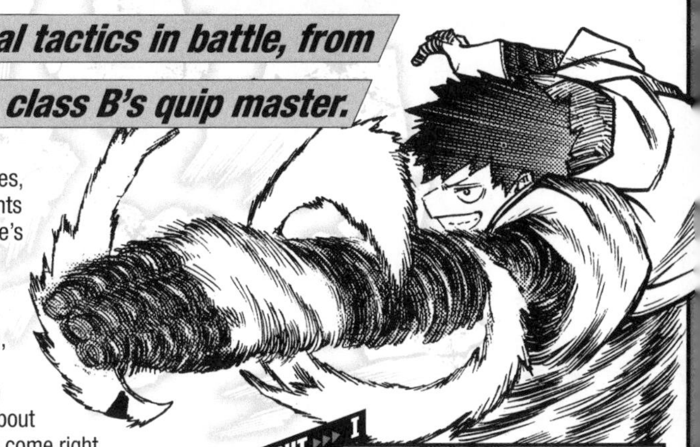

Class B is full of eccentric personalities, but Kaibara represents the plainer bunch. He's usually willing to go with the flow, but when those around him aren't so willing, he tends to respect their opinions. When Kaibara disagrees about something, he'll just come right out and say so.

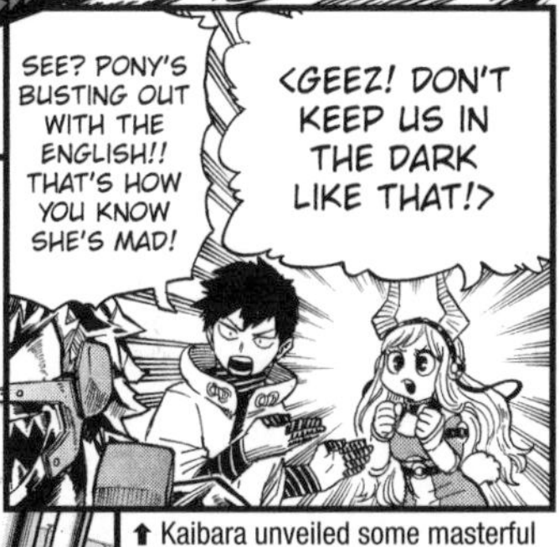
HIGHLIGHT ▸▸▸ I
<GEEZ! DON'T KEEP US IN THE DARK LIKE THAT!>
SEE? PONY'S BUSTING OUT WITH THE ENGLISH!! THAT'S HOW YOU KNOW SHE'S MAD!

⬆ Kaibara unveiled some masterful quips to his teammates! Those skills had remained hidden until that point, but no longer.

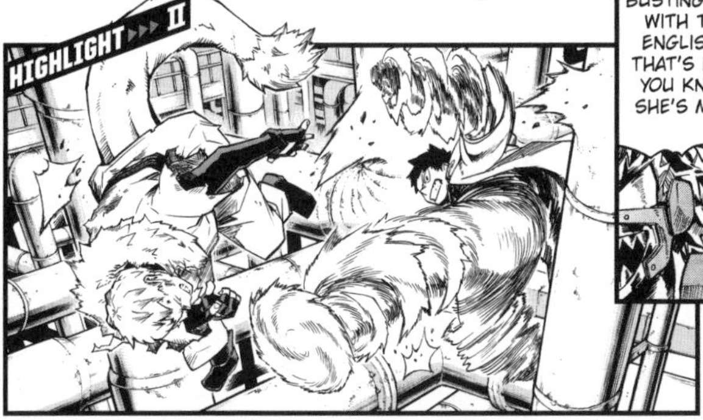
HIGHLIGHT ▸▸▸ II

⬆ In the battle against class A, Kaibara waged a knockdown, drag-out battle against class A's own plain guy—Ojiro!

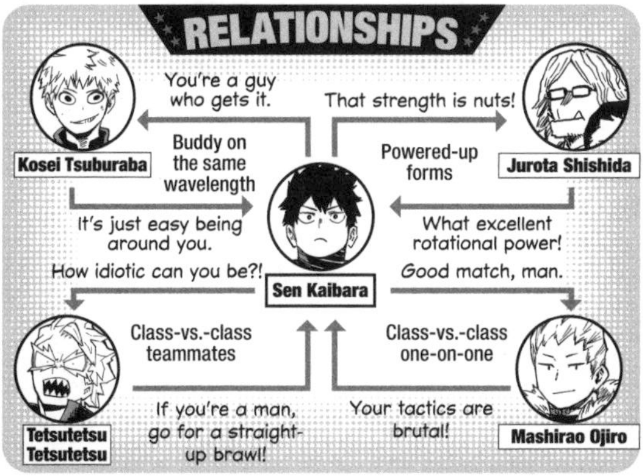
RELATIONSHIPS
Kosei Tsuburaba
You're a guy who gets it.
Buddy on the same wavelength
It's just easy being around you.
Jurota Shishida
That strength is nuts!
Powered-up forms
What excellent rotational power!
Sen Kaibara
How idiotic can you be?!
Good match, man.
Tetsutetsu Tetsutetsu
Class-vs.-class teammates
If you're a man, go for a straight-up brawl!
Mashirao Ojiro
Class-vs.-class one-on-one
Your tactics are brutal!

## PROFILE

Name: **Sen Kaibara**
Hero name: **Spiral**
Quirk: **Gyrate**
Birthday: **June 12**
Height: **172 cm**
Blood type: **B**
Birthplace: **Tokyo**
Personality: **Amenable**
Ultimate moves: **Unknown**

- "Thanks, Juzo! That's one soft and flexible counterattack!" (vol. 22, chap. 203)
- "Dodging alone won't win this fight!" (vol. 22, chap. 204)
- "Get offa me! I didn't get to really show off yet!" (vol. 22, chap. 204)

### Kaibara's Notable Quotables

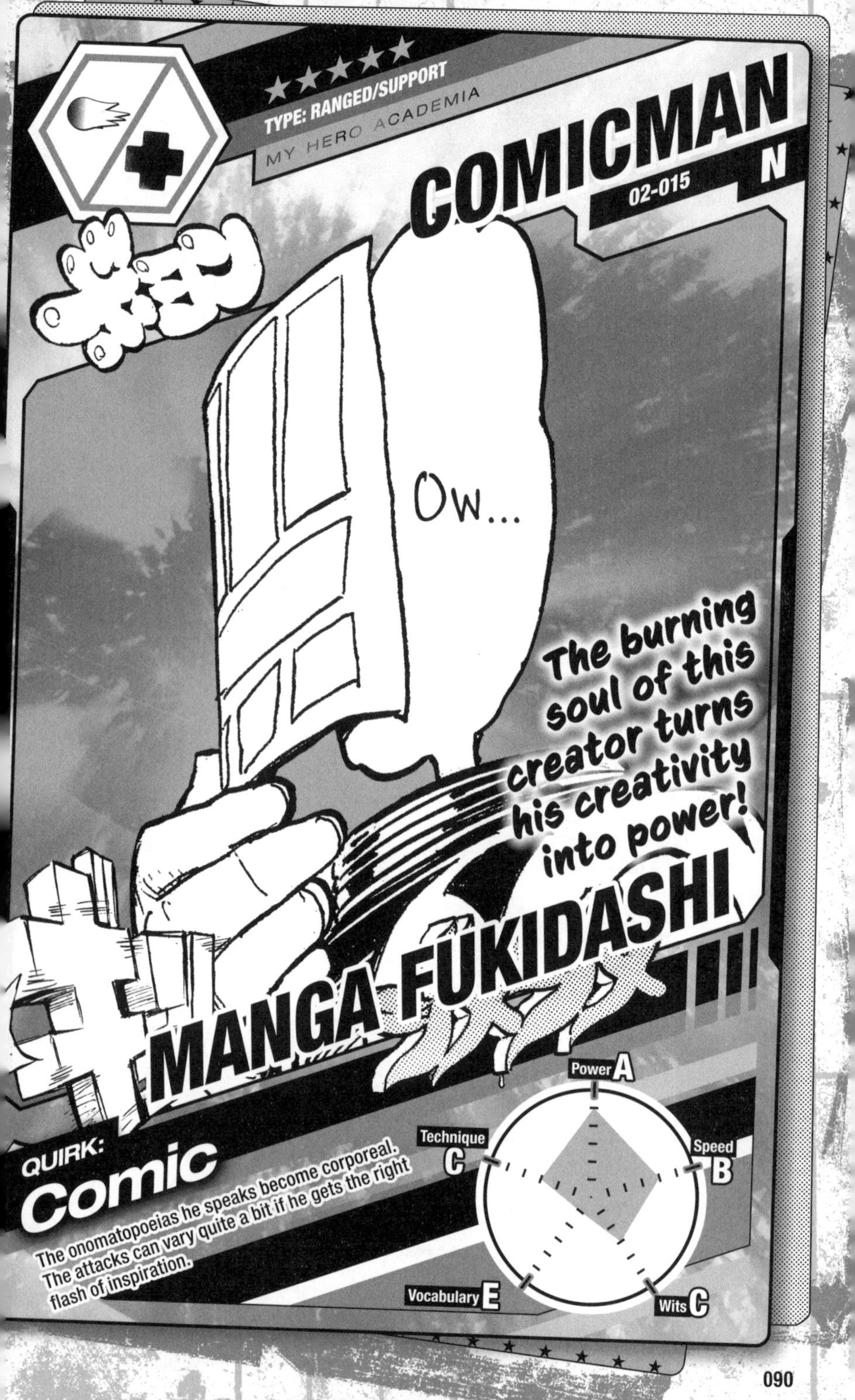
TYPE: RANGED/SUPPORT
MY HERO ACADEMIA
COMICMAN
N
02-015
Ow...
The burning soul of this creator turns his creativity into power!
MANGA FUKIDASHI
QUIRK:
Comic
The onomatopoeias he speaks become corporeal. The attacks can vary quite a bit if he gets the right flash of inspiration.
Power A
Speed B
Wits C
Vocabulary E
Technique C

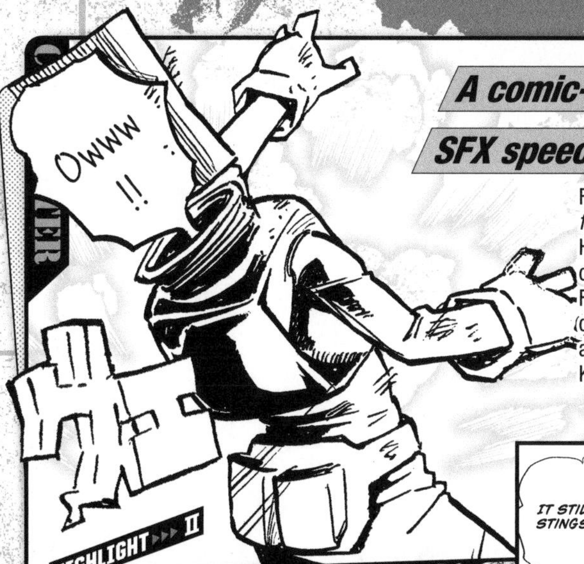

OWWW !!


## A comic-al explosion?! His SFX speech can't be stopped!

Fukidashi is a positive guy with a *fukidashi* (speech bubble) for a head. His dream is to bring joy to the children of the world with his Quirk. Fukidashi often gets into animated conversations with Tsunotori about anime, but he's head over heels for Kenranzaki—an older student.

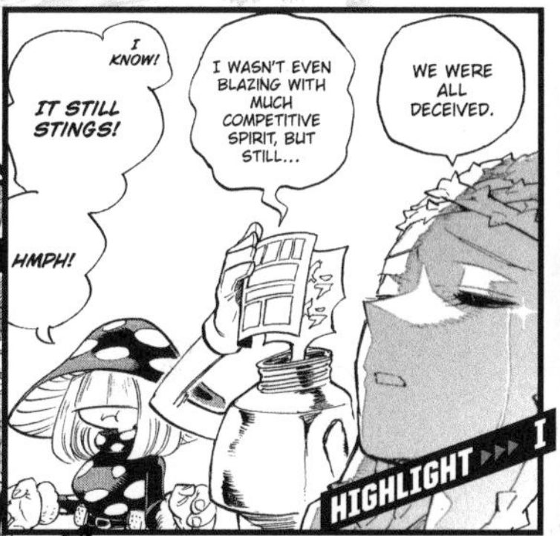

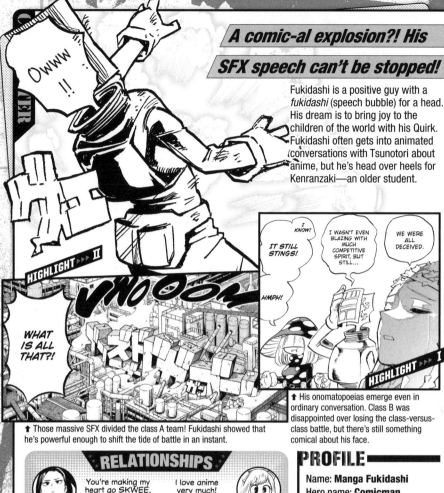

HIGHLIGHT ▸▸▸ I
WE WERE ALL DECEIVED.
I WASN'T EVEN BLAZING WITH MUCH COMPETITIVE SPIRIT, BUT STILL...
I KNOW! IT STILL STINGS!
HMPH!


⬆ His onomatopoeias emerge even in ordinary conversation. Class B was disappointed over losing the class-versus-class battle, but there's still something comical about his face.

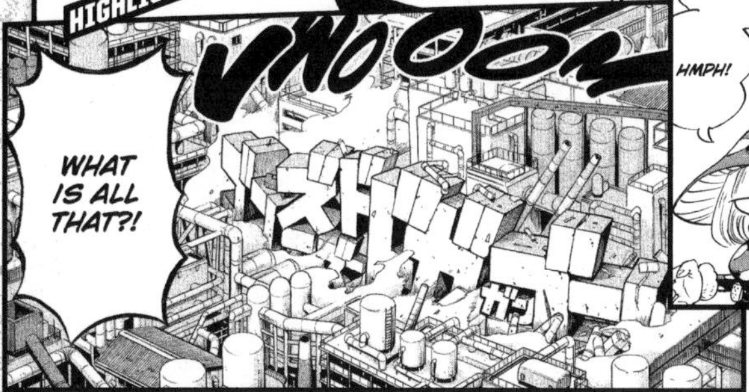

HIGHLIGHT ▸▸▸ II
VNOOOM
WHAT IS ALL THAT?!


⬆ Those massive SFX divided the class A team! Fukidashi showed that he's powerful enough to shift the tide of battle in an instant.

## RELATIONSHIPS

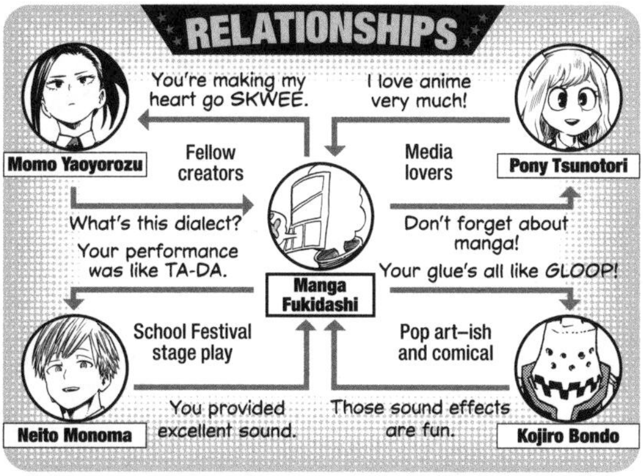

Momo Yaoyorozu
You're making my heart go SKWEE.
Fellow creators
What's this dialect?
Pony Tsunotori
I love anime very much!
Media lovers
Don't forget about manga!
Manga Fukidashi
Your performance was like TA-DA.
Neito Monoma
School Festival stage play
You provided excellent sound.
Your glue's all like GLOOP!
Kojiro Bondo
Pop art–ish and comical
Those sound effects are fun.


## PROFILE

Name: **Manga Fukidashi**
Hero name: **Comicman**
Quirk: **Comic**
Birthday: **February 2**
Height: **140–160 cm**
Blood type: **A**
Birthplace: **Wakayama Prefecture**
Personality: **Ultra positive**
Ultimate moves: **KRASH, WHAMABAM**

- "KRASH! BOOM! Um… WHAMABAM!" (vol. 21, chap. 200)
- "I'm on top of my game! That 'BOOM' was more like 'KERBOOSH'! Made my heart go 'BADUM'!" (vol. 21, chap. 200)

**Fukidashi's Notable Quotables**

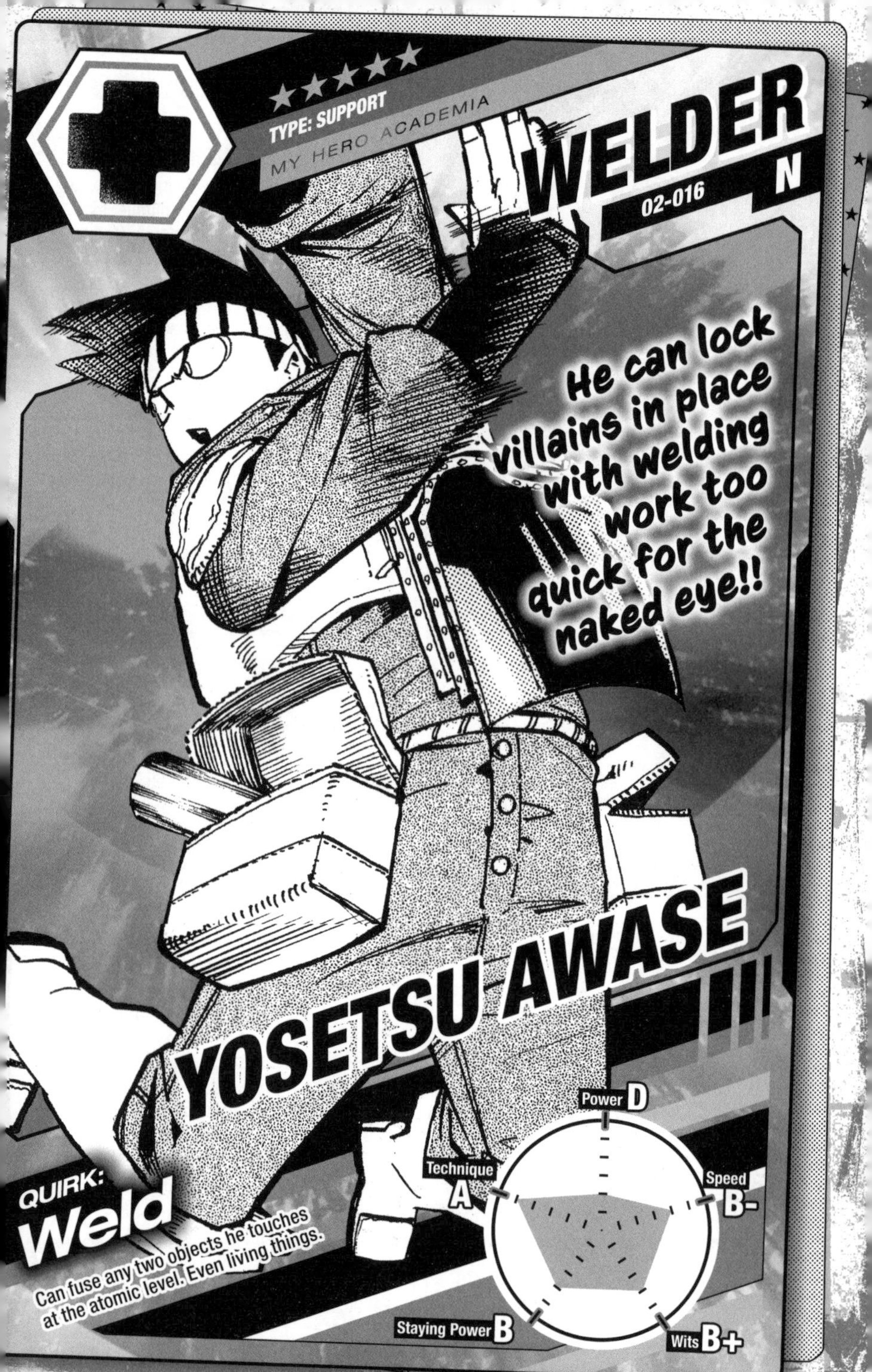
TYPE: SUPPORT
MY HERO ACADEMIA
WELDER
N
02-016
He can lock villains in place with welding work too quick for the naked eye!!
YOSETSU AWASE
Power D
Technique A
Speed B-
Staying Power B
Wits B+
QUIRK:
Weld
Can fuse any two objects he touches at the atomic level. Even living things.

## Class B's super assist man boasts top-notch judgment and efficacy.

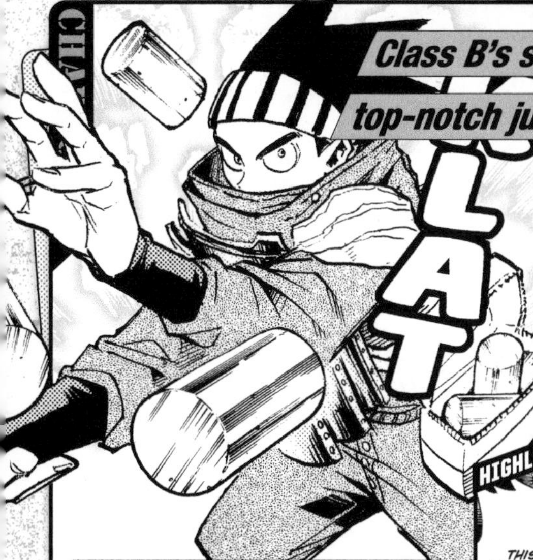

Awase's family owns a small-town factory. He does his best work from the sidelines and often supports Monoma and Kendo. Awase also did a work study. At the School Festival and when the villains attacked during the training camp, he proved just how reliable he can be. He's kind of smitten with Yaoyorozu.

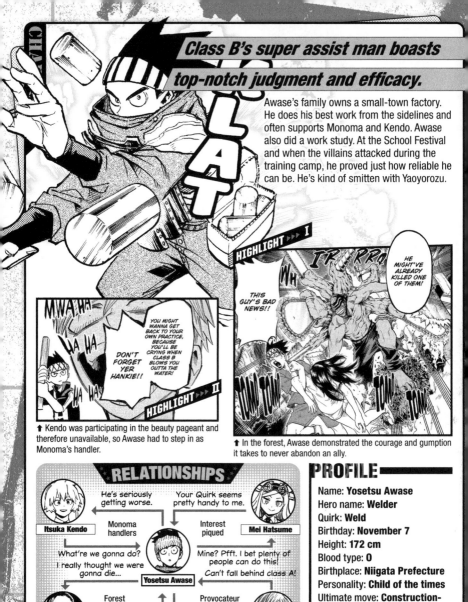

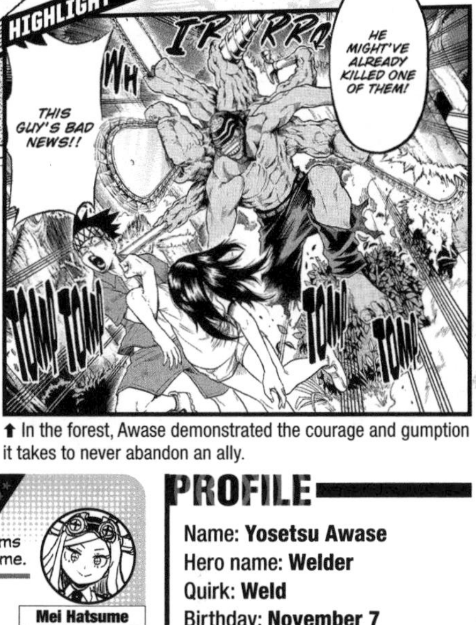
HIGHLIGHT I
HE MIGHT'VE ALREADY KILLED ONE OF THEM!
IRRRQ
WH
THIS GUY'S BAD NEWS!!
TOM TOM
TOM TOM

⬆ In the forest, Awase demonstrated the courage and gumption it takes to never abandon an ally.

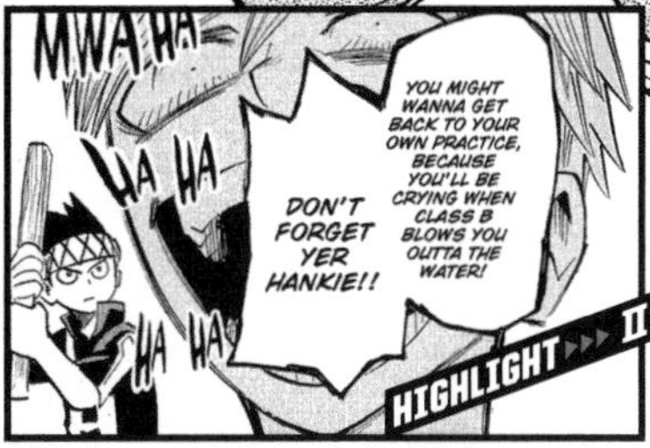
MWA HA
YOU MIGHT WANNA GET BACK TO YOUR OWN PRACTICE, BECAUSE YOU'LL BE CRYING WHEN CLASS B BLOWS YOU OUTTA THE WATER!
DON'T FORGET YER HANKIE!!
HA HA
HA HA
HIGHLIGHT II

⬆ Kendo was participating in the beauty pageant and therefore unavailable, so Awase had to step in as Monoma's handler.

### RELATIONSHIPS

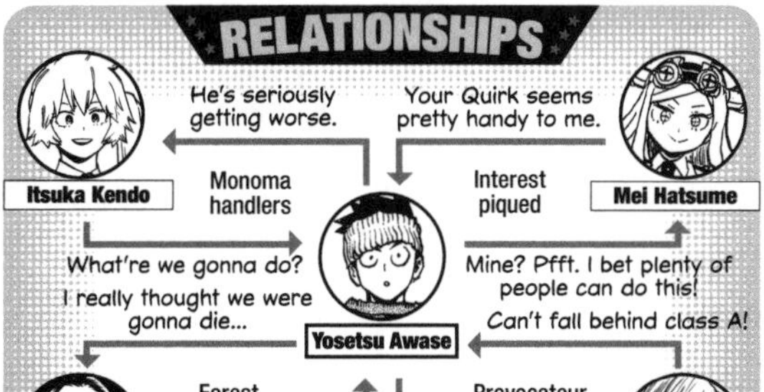
Itsuka Kendo
He's seriously getting worse.
Monoma handlers
What're we gonna do? I really thought we were gonna die...
Mei Hatsume
Your Quirk seems pretty handy to me.
Interest piqued
Mine? Pfft. I bet plenty of people can do this! Can't fall behind class A!
Yosetsu Awase
Momo Yaoyorozu
Forest connection
I appreciate your saving me.
Neito Monoma
Provocateur inhibitor
You're really pushing the envelope, bud.

### PROFILE

Name: **Yosetsu Awase**
Hero name: **Welder**
Quirk: **Weld**
Birthday: **November 7**
Height: **172 cm**
Blood type: **O**
Birthplace: **Niigata Prefecture**
Personality: **Child of the times**
Ultimate move: **Construction-Done-Kwik: Weldcraft**

- "Crap! Craaap!! This guy's bad news!!" (vol. 10, chap. 81)
- "Sorry, class A guy. His usual handler isn't around, so he's got no filter." (vol. 19, chap. 173)

### Awase's Notable Quotables

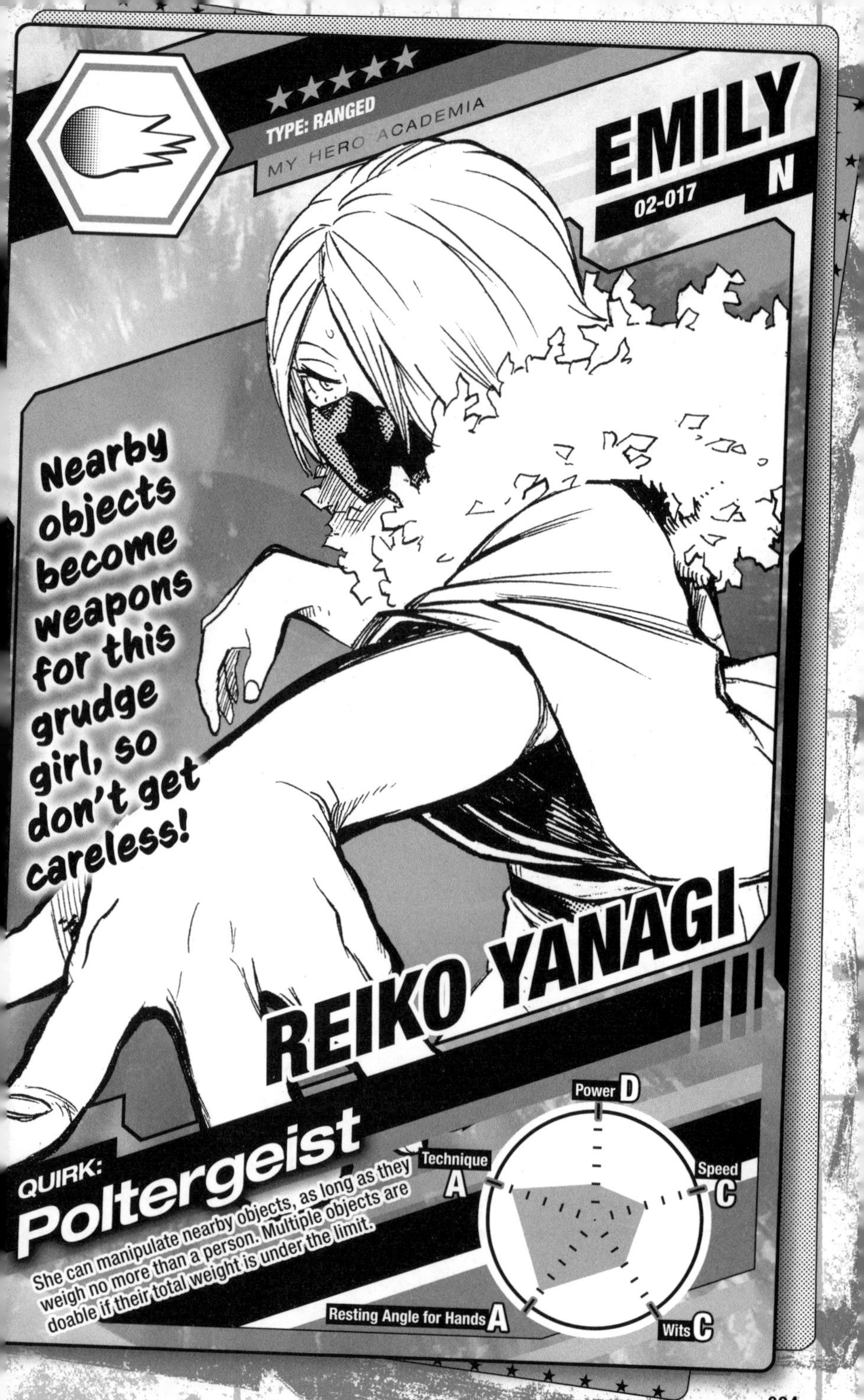
TYPE: RANGED
MY HERO ACADEMIA
EMILY
N
02-017
Nearby objects become weapons for this grudge girl, so don't get careless!
REIKO YANAGI
QUIRK:
Poltergeist
She can manipulate nearby objects, as long as they weigh no more than a person. Multiple objects are doable if their total weight is under the limit.
Power D
Technique A
Speed C
Resting Angle for Hands A
Wits C

CHARACTER

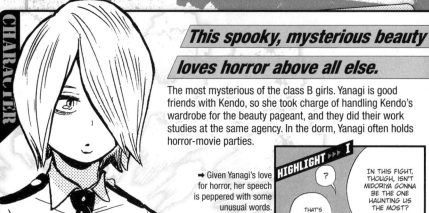

## This spooky, mysterious beauty loves horror above all else.

The most mysterious of the class B girls. Yanagi is good friends with Kendo, so she took charge of handling Kendo's wardrobe for the beauty pageant, and they did their work studies at the same agency. In the dorm, Yanagi often holds horror-movie parties.

➡ Given Yanagi's love for horror, her speech is peppered with some unusual words.

HIGHLIGHT ▸▸▸ I
IN THIS FIGHT, THOUGH, ISN'T MIDORIYA GONNA BE THE ONE HAUNTING US THE MOST?
?
THAT'S HER WAY OF CALLING HIM SCARY.

⬇ In the class-versus-class battle, Yanagi combined her Quirk with those of her teammates Kodai and Shoda to overwhelm Uraraka, Ashido, and Mineta!

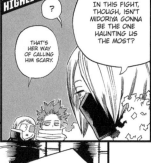

HIGHLIGHT ▸▸▸ II
IT'S YANAGI'S POLTER-GEIST!
FWISH
FWISH

RELATIONSHIPS
Itsuka Kendo
Thanks for picking my outfit.
Beauty pageant
Only the best, of course.
Yui Kodai
You did amazing in the test of courage.
Stylish beauties
Mm. You too, Reiko.
Reiko Yanagi
Minoru Mineta
I got my pick of the litter!
Hunter & prey
Mineta... Scary.
Yuyu Haya
Congrats on your girl's win.
Beauty pageant helpers
Good luck next year, you guys.

## PROFILE

Name: **Reiko Yanagi**
Hero name: **Emily**
Quirk: **Poltergeist**
Birthday: **February 11**
Height: **165 cm**
Blood type: **B**
Birthplace: **Aichi Prefecture**
Personality: **Mysterious**
Ultimate moves: **Unknown**

- "You're scary, Monoma." (vol. 8, chap. 70)
- "You boys had better stop rushing in here." (vol. 20, chap. 178)

Yanagi's Notable Quotables

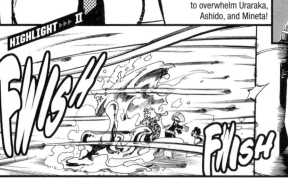

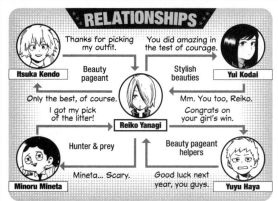

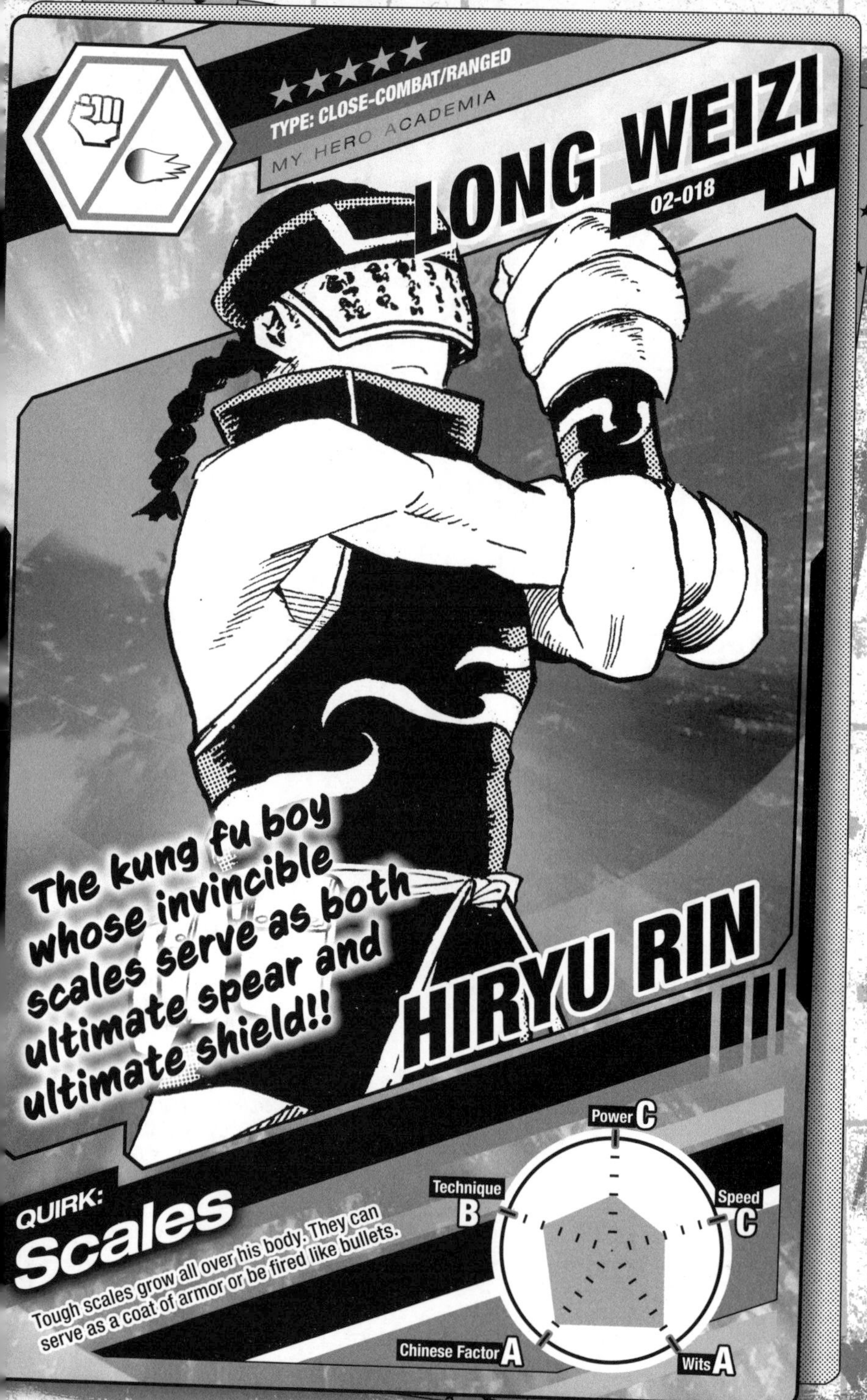

★★★★★★
TYPE: CLOSE-COMBAT/RANGED
MY HERO ACADEMIA
LONG WEIZI
02-018
N
The kung fu boy whose invincible scales serve as both ultimate spear and ultimate shield!!
HIRYU RIN
QUIRK:
Scales
Tough scales grow all over his body. They can serve as a coat of armor or be fired like bullets.
Power C
Technique B
Speed C
Chinese Factor A
Wits A

## A hardworking, straitlaced stude
## and a Common Sense Lord!

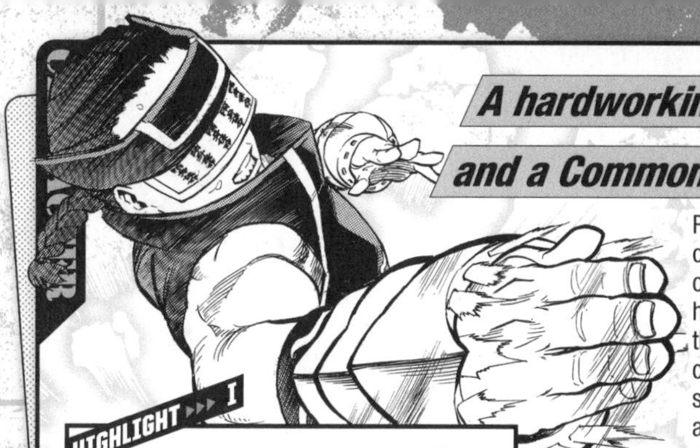

Rin always has it together, so his classmates know they can count on him. The others like to hear him cry "Aiyah!"—so he humors them. Rin needs collagen and calcium to grow his trademark scales, which is why he carries around supplements during battle.

HIGHLIGHT ▸▸▸ I

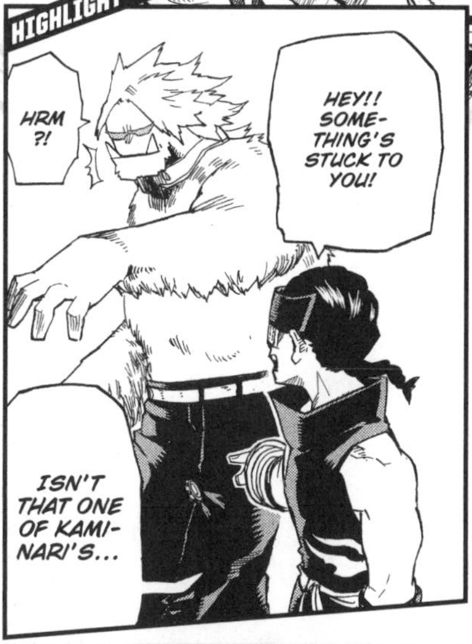
HEY!! SOME-THING'S STUCK TO YOU!
HRM ?!
ISN'T THAT ONE OF KAMI-NARI'S...

⬅ Rin spotted Kaminari's target device that was stuck on Shishida. Even in a crisis, he showed remarkable focus and attention to detail.

HIGHLIGHT ▸▸▸ II

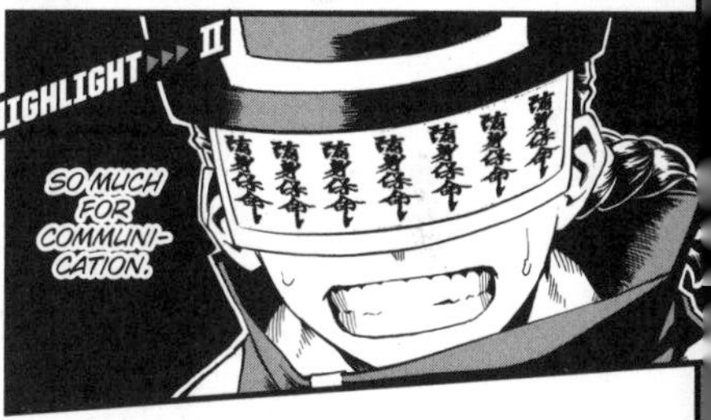
SO MUCH FOR COMMUNI-CATION.

⬇ Even when Shinso's Brainwashing ruined any hope of effective teamwork, Rin kept calm and analyzed the situation until the bitter end.

## RELATIONSHIPS

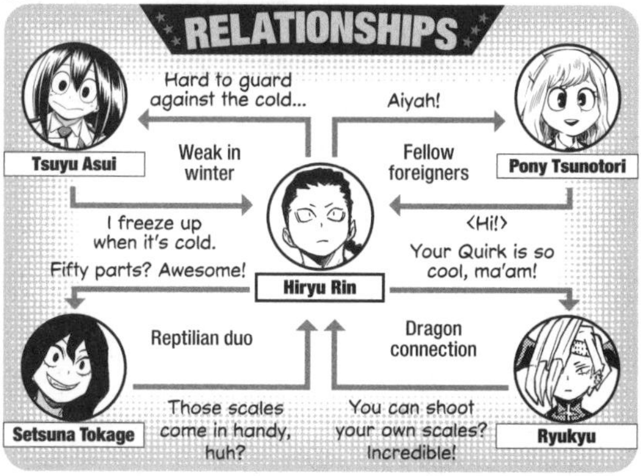
Tsuyu Asui
Hard to guard against the cold...
Weak in winter
I freeze up when it's cold.
Pony Tsunotori
Aiyah!
Fellow foreigners
<Hi!>
Hiryu Rin
Fifty parts? Awesome!
Your Quirk is so cool, ma'am!
Setsuna Tokage
Reptilian duo
Those scales come in handy, huh?
Ryukyu
Dragon connection
You can shoot your own scales? Incredible!

## PROFILE

Name: **Hiryu Rin**
Hero name: **Long Weizi**
Quirk: **Scales**
Birthday: **July 14**
Height: **170 cm**
Blood type: **A**
Birthplace: **China**
Personality: **Calm and composed**
Ultimate moves: **Leafy Scales, Scales of Wrath, Inner Carapace**

- "Let's team up for now so we can carve a path through!" (vol. 3, chap. 25)
- "Aiyah! I know it's safer when we can see each other's lips flapping, but!!" (vol. 21, chap. 197)
- "Down, Apocabeast!!" (vol. 21, chap. 197)

Rin's Notable Quotables

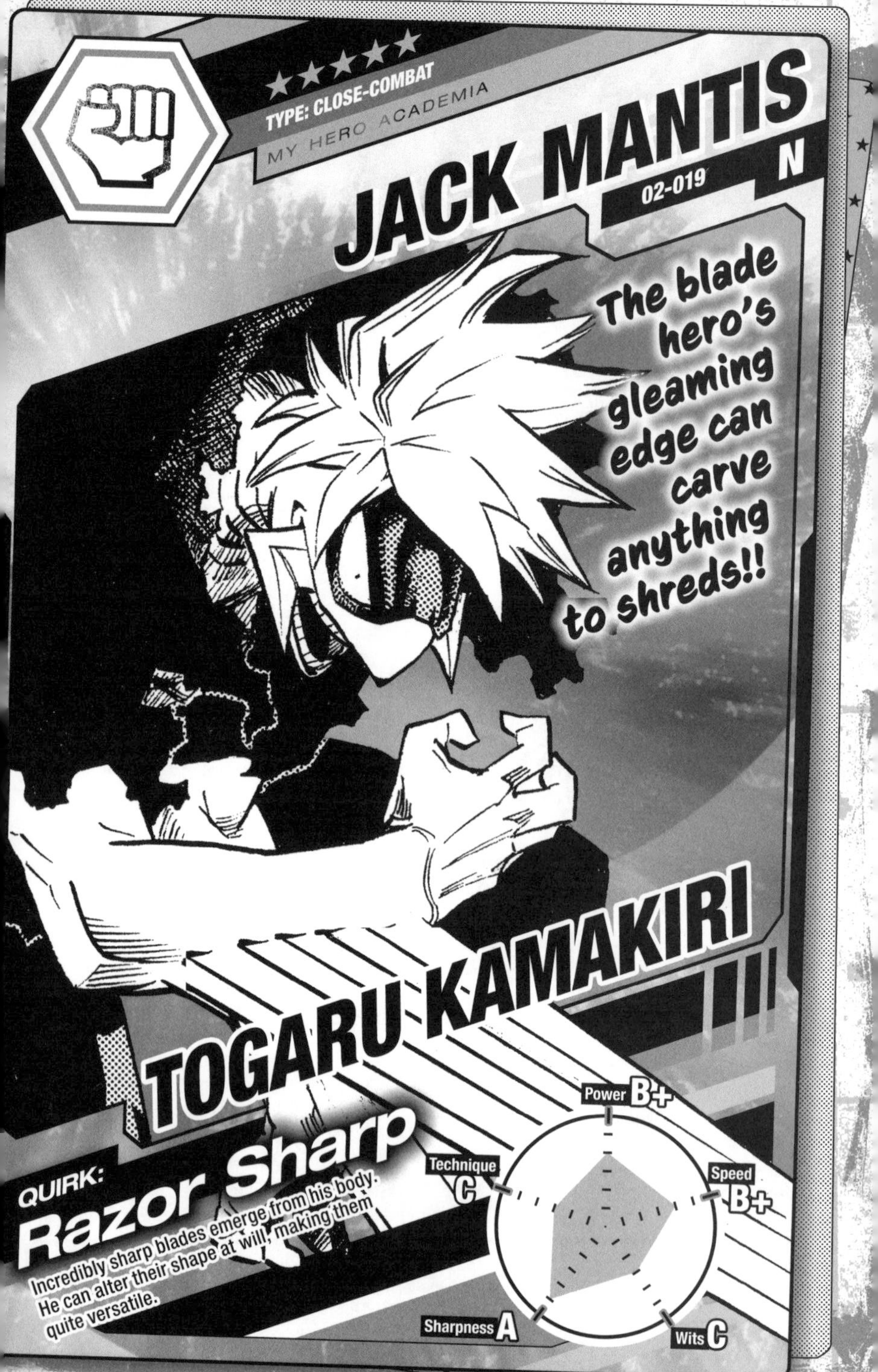
TYPE: CLOSE-COMBAT
MY HERO ACADEMIA
JACK MANTIS
N
02-019
The blade hero's gleaming edge can carve anything to shreds!!
TOGARU KAMAKIRI
QUIRK:
Razor Sharp
Incredibly sharp blades emerge from his body. He can alter their shape at will, making them quite versatile.
Power B+
Speed B+
Wits C
Sharpness A
Technique C

## Cutting words and actions from the carve-happy warrior!

Kamakiri looks like a praying mantis, and he's all about the carving. He makes a great training partner for Tetsutetsu. Given Kamakiri's agility and offensive abilities, he often serves as the vanguard in team battles. He has a lot in common with Bakugo and views him as his rival. It's a one-sided rivalry, though.

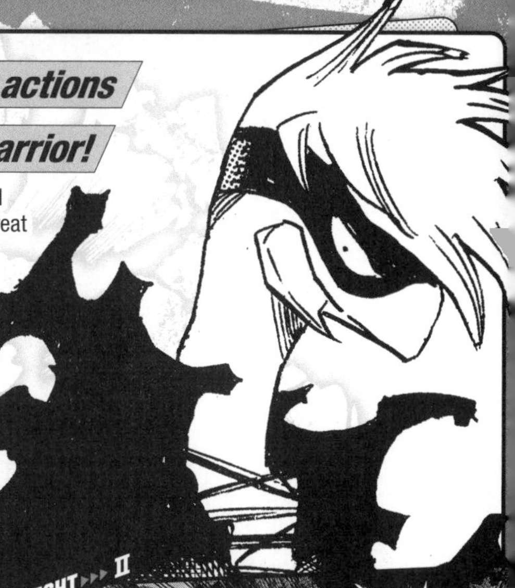

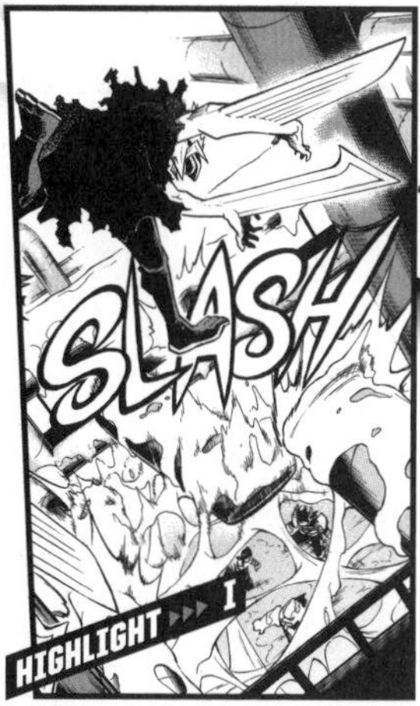
SLASH
HIGHLIGHT ▸▸▸ I

⬆ A sturdy pipe, cleaved in a flash! Kamakiri's combo attack with the glue-spewing Bondo temporarily immobilized the class A team.

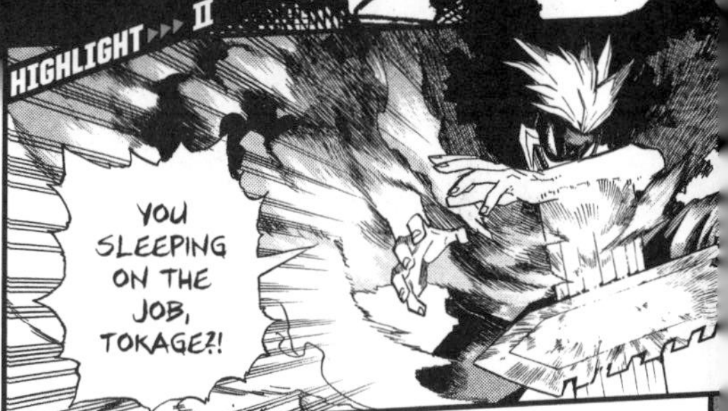
HIGHLIGHT ▸▸▸ II
YOU SLEEPING ON THE JOB, TOKAGE?!

⬆ Kamakiri guarded against Bakugo's explosive attack with his blades. He's got the killer reflexes needed to respond instantly to sneak attacks.

### RELATIONSHIPS

**Togaru Kamakiri**

- **Setsuna Tokage** — Chop-chop duo
  - Kamakiri → Tokage: No point in carving you up...
  - Tokage → Kamakiri: Quit thinking about cutting your classmates...
- **Manga Fukidashi** — Tech crew for the play
  - Kamakiri → Fukidashi: Such explosive taste...
  - Fukidashi → Kamakiri: You worked those stage lights like KAFLASH!
- **Yosetsu Awase** — Carving inhibitor
  - Kamakiri → Awase: Carve... Gotta carve...
  - Awase → Kamakiri: That's enough outta you.
- **Tetsutetsu Tetsutetsu** — Battle-loving boys
  - Kamakiri → Tetsutetsu: I can carve anything!
  - Tetsutetsu → Kamakiri: My Fist'll break your blades!

### PROFILE

Name: **Togaru Kamakiri**
Hero name: **Jack Mantis**
Quirk: **Razor Sharp**
Birthday: **January 7**
Height: **189 cm**
Blood type: **A**
Birthplace: **Nagasaki Prefecture**
Personality: **Battle fiend**
Ultimate moves: **Unknown**

### Kamakiri's Notable Quotables

- "Who cares about all that? Just lemme carve 'em up…" (vol. 22, chap. 207)
- "Hya hya hya! Too slow, too slow!" (vol. 22, chap. 207)
- "We'll carve this brutal loss into our souls…" (vol. 22, chap. 209)

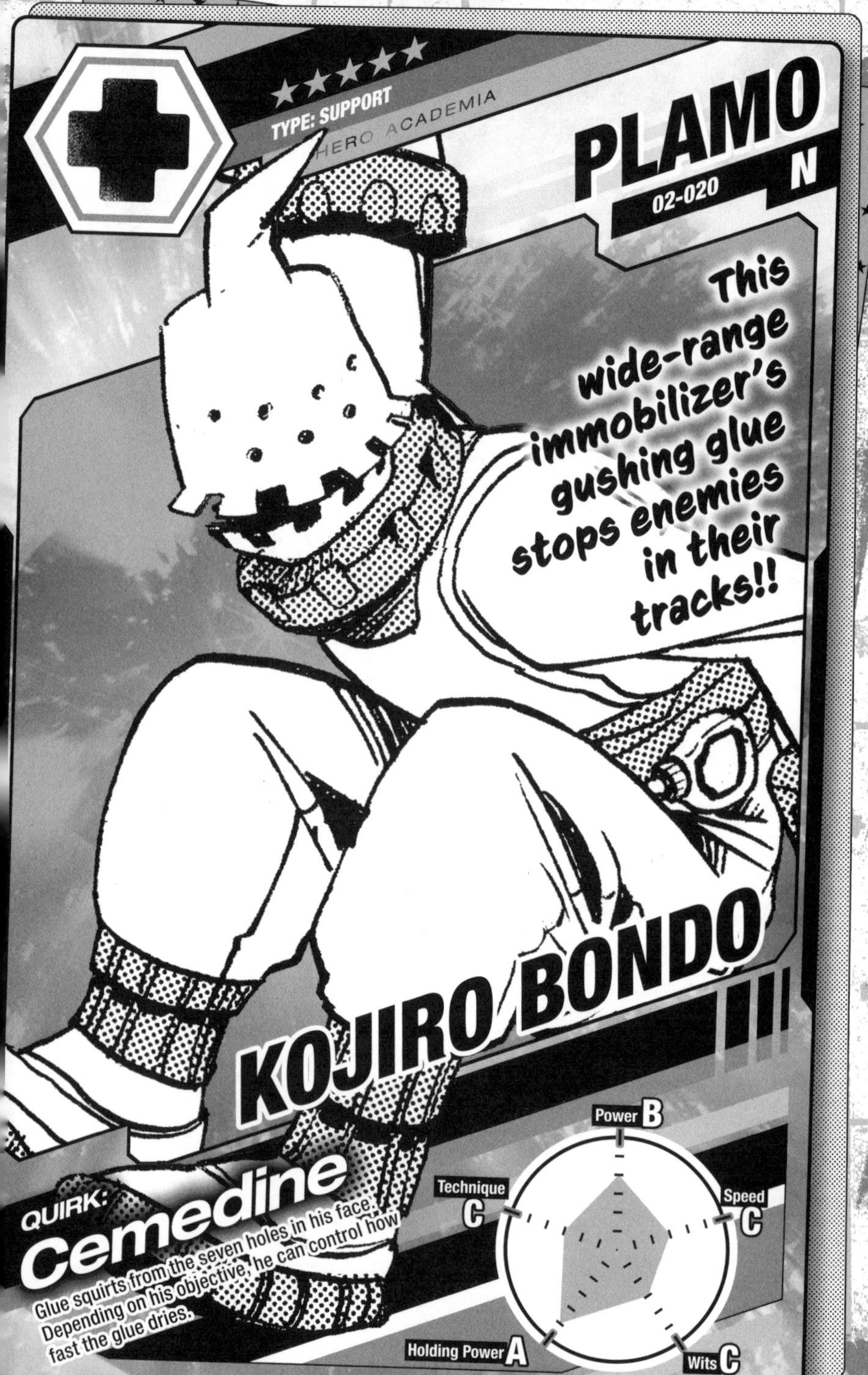
TYPE: SUPPORT
HERO ACADEMIA
PLAMO
N
02-020
This wide-range immobilizer's gushing glue stops enemies in their tracks!!
KOJIRO BONDO
QUIRK: Cemedine
Glue squirts from the seven holes in his face. Depending on his objective, he can control how fast the glue dries.
Power B
Speed C
Wits C
Holding Power A
Technique C

CHARACTER

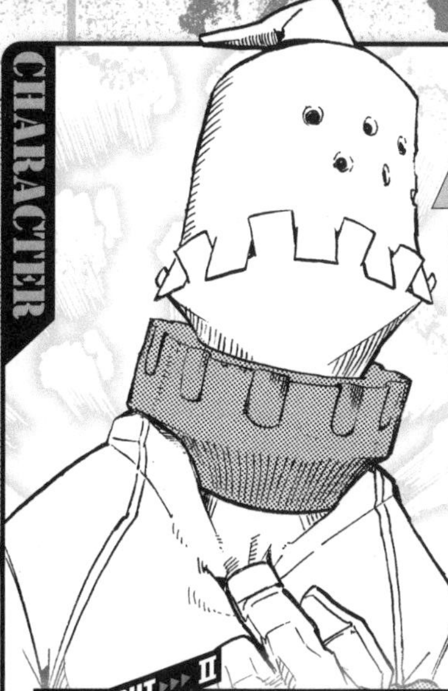

## This easygoing fellow can unleash his talents when the time comes.

Bondo is usually content to take it nice and easy, but once he's called into battle, he analyzes the situation with sharp insight. He and Awase have talked about building a giant model together, but they haven't found the time to make it happen yet…

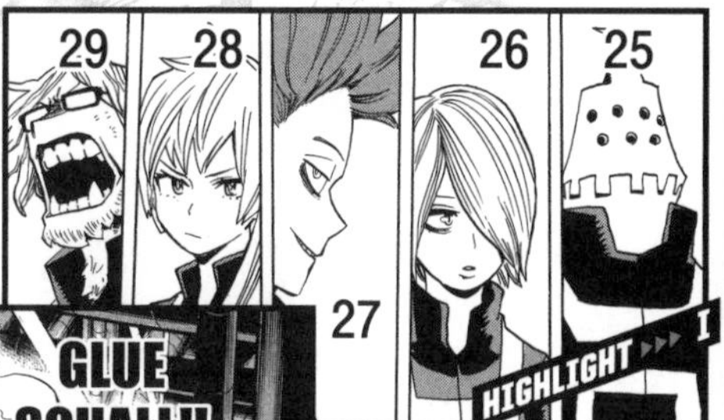
29
28
27
26
25
HIGHLIGHT ▸▸▸ I

⬆ In the Sports Festival's obstacle race, Bondo somehow placed higher than the beastly Shishida and the remarkably athletic Kendo. He's got a lot of potential.

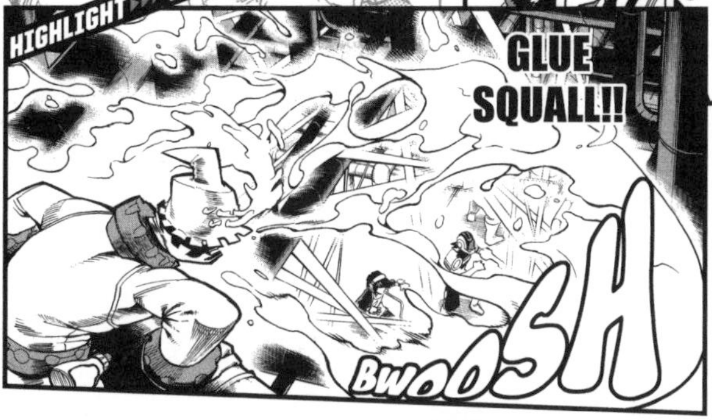
HIGHLIGHT ▸▸▸ II
GLUE SQUALL!!
BWOOOSH

⬅ With this ultimate move, Bondo releases a massive wave of glue! It's sticky enough that one touch means you're not going anywhere!

## RELATIONSHIPS

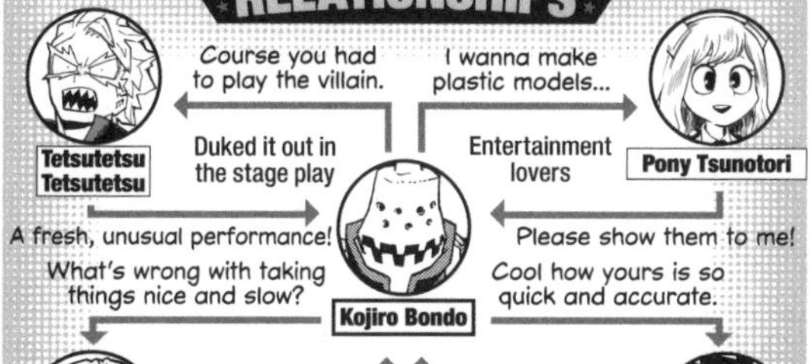
Tetsutetsu Tetsutetsu
Course you had to play the villain.
Duked it out in the stage play
A fresh, unusual performance!
Pony Tsunotori
I wanna make plastic models...
Entertainment lovers
Please show them to me!
Kojiro Bondo
What's wrong with taking things nice and slow?
Easygoing guys
Nothing quite like a good afternoon nap.
Jurota Shishida
Cool how yours is so quick and accurate.
Similar Quirks
Cool how yours has such a wide range.
Yosetsu Awase

## PROFILE

Name: **Kojiro Bondo**
Hero name: **Plamo**
Quirk: **Cemedine**
Birthday: **December 23**
Height: **191 cm**
Blood type: **AB**
Birthplace: **Tokyo**
Personality: **Relaaaxed**
Ultimate move: **Glue Squall**

- "On this terrain, Sero and Jiro are definitely gonna be trouble." (vol. 22, chap. 207)
- "Woo! I did it! Just like Setsuna planned." (vol. 22, chap. 207)

**Bondo's Notable Quotables**

# Best Jeanist Chooses the Best Costumes

COLUMN 2

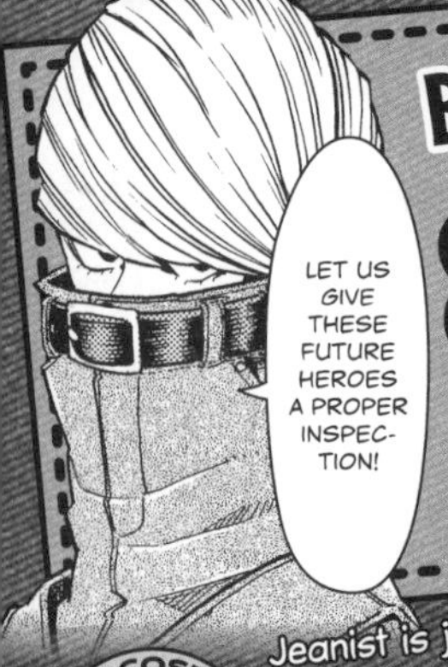

LET US GIVE THESE FUTURE HEROES A PROPER INSPECTION!


Jeanist is judging four different categories! Who shone brightest in each?

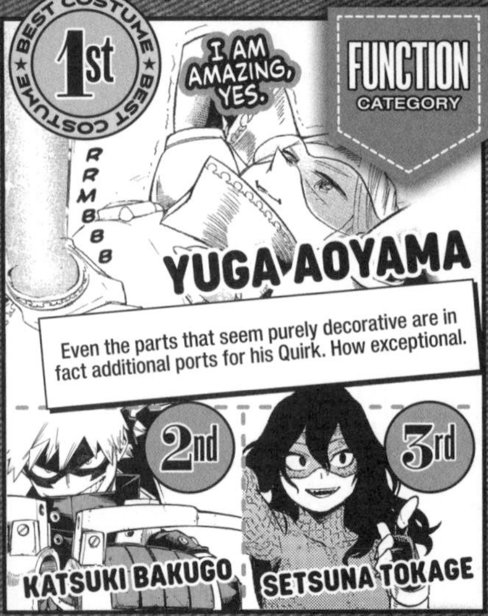

BEST COSTUME
1st
FUNCTION CATEGORY
I AM AMAZING, YES.
RRMBBB
YUGA AOYAMA
Even the parts that seem purely decorative are in fact additional ports for his Quirk. How exceptional.
2nd
KATSUKI BAKUGO
3rd
SETSUNA TOKAGE


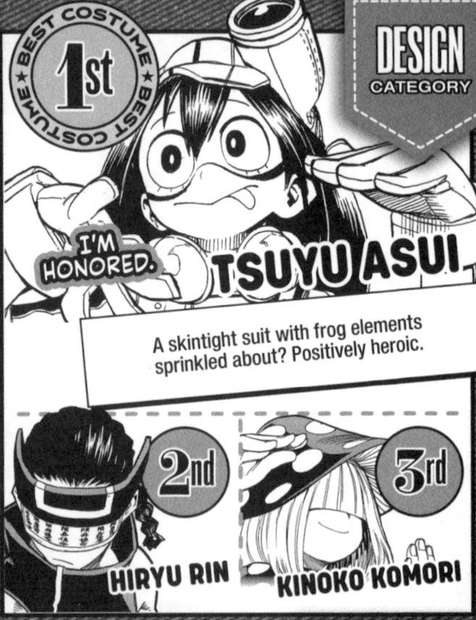

BEST COSTUME
1st
DESIGN CATEGORY
I'M HONORED.
TSUYU ASUI
A skintight suit with frog elements sprinkled about? Positively heroic.
2nd
HIRYU RIN
3rd
KINOKO KOMORI


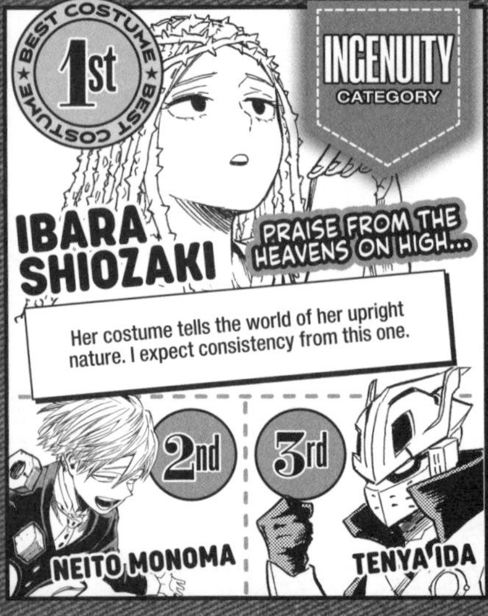

BEST COSTUME
1st
INGENUITY CATEGORY
IBARA SHIOZAKI
PRAISE FROM THE HEAVENS ON HIGH...
Her costume tells the world of her upright nature. I expect consistency from this one.
2nd
NEITO MONOMA
3rd
TENYA IDA


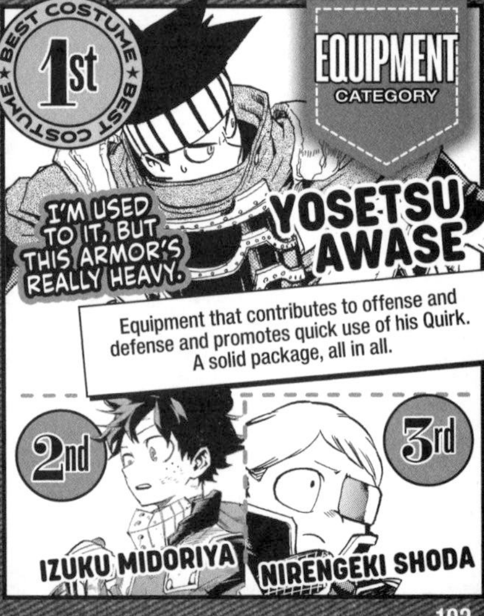

BEST COSTUME
1st
EQUIPMENT CATEGORY
I'M USED TO IT, BUT THIS ARMOR'S REALLY HEAVY.
YOSETSU AWASE
Equipment that contributes to offense and defense and promotes quick use of his Quirk. A solid package, all in all.
2nd
IZUKU MIDORIYA
3rd
NIRENGEKI SHODA

# EX
## EDITION I

**U.A. STUDENTS HIGHLIGHTS**

Ever since starting school at U.A. High,
the students have enjoyed a variety of
school functions and faced off against
deadly villains. Let's take a look back
at their journey so far.

# U.A. Students Highlights

Let us perform a critical review of the events we've experienced!!

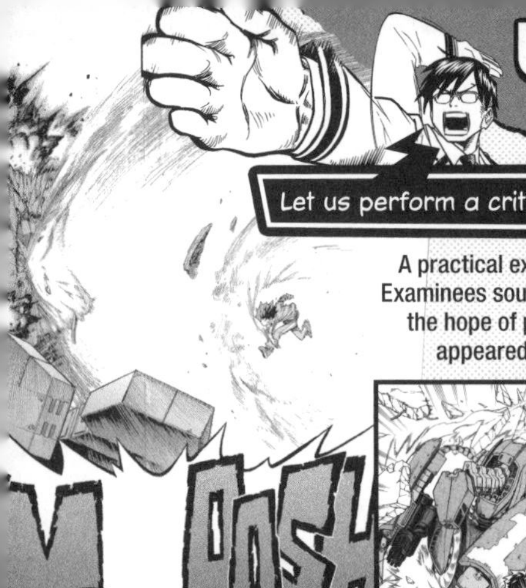
SMASH

## ENTRANCE EXAM

A practical exam that tested basic abilities. Examinees sought to take down faux villains in the hope of passing, but a massive threat appeared to really test their mettle.

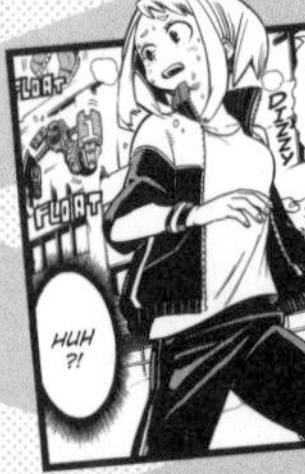
SIGH... 28 POINTS ...
FLOAT
FLOAT
HUH ?!

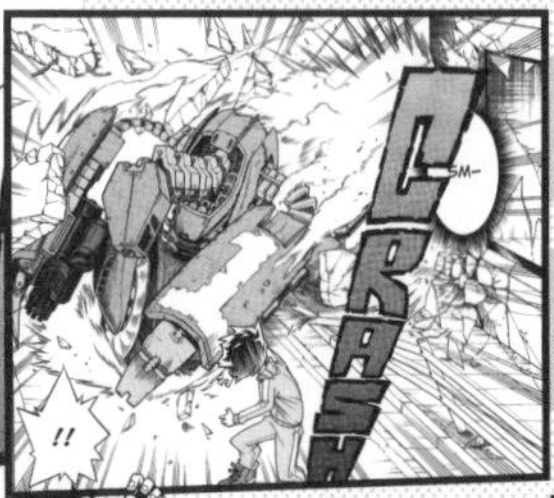
SM-
CRASH
!!

A practical exam, pitting them against faux villains

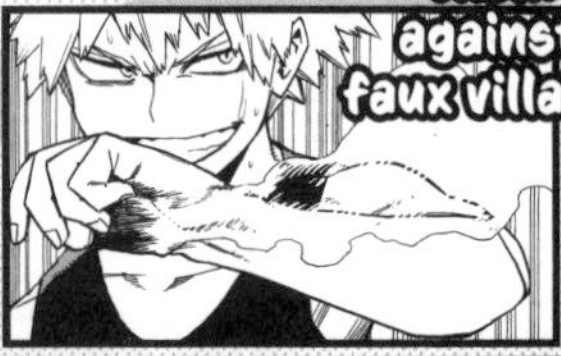

Points are earned through Quirk use

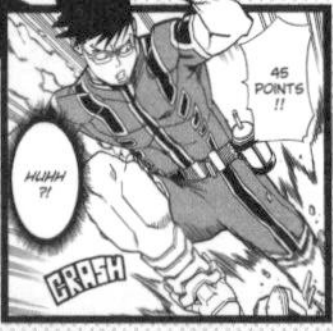
45 POINTS !!
HUHH ?!
CRASH

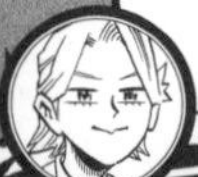

I was taken aback when Midoriya defeated the rampaging gimmick! I could have done so as well, naturally!!

## QUIRK PROFICIENCY TEST

Midoriya and company may have gotten into U.A., but before they could even get excited about school life, they faced a Quirk proficiency test!

One amazing record...

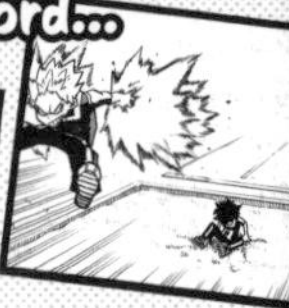

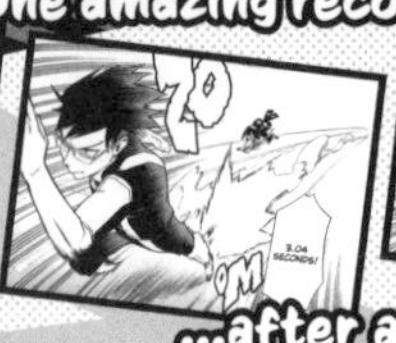
3.04 SECONDS!
OM

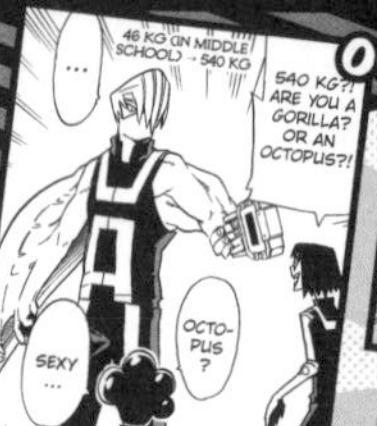
46 KG (IN MIDDLE SCHOOL) → 540 KG
...
540 KG?! ARE YOU A GORILLA? OR AN OCTOPUS?!
OCTO-PUS ?
SEXY ...

...after another

The lowest scorer gets expelled?!

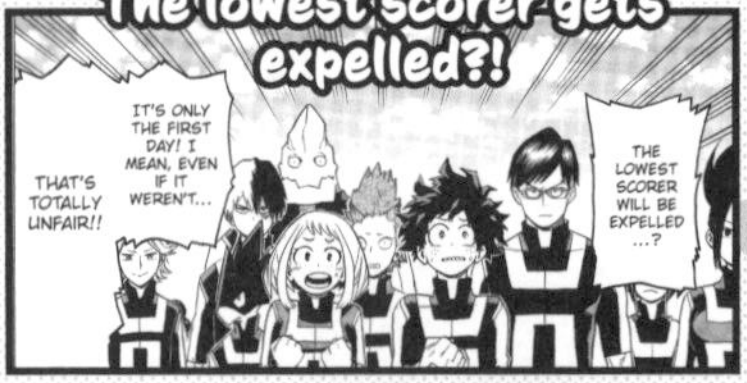
THE LOWEST SCORER WILL BE EXPELLED ...?
IT'S ONLY THE FIRST DAY! I MEAN, EVEN IF IT WEREN'T...
THAT'S TOTALLY UNFAIR!!

Still unable to regulate his new Quirk, Midoriya faced quite a trial.

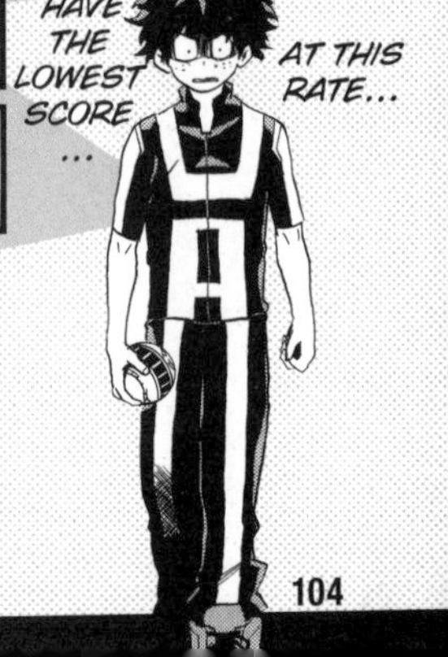
AT THIS RATE...
I'LL HAVE THE LOWEST SCORE ...

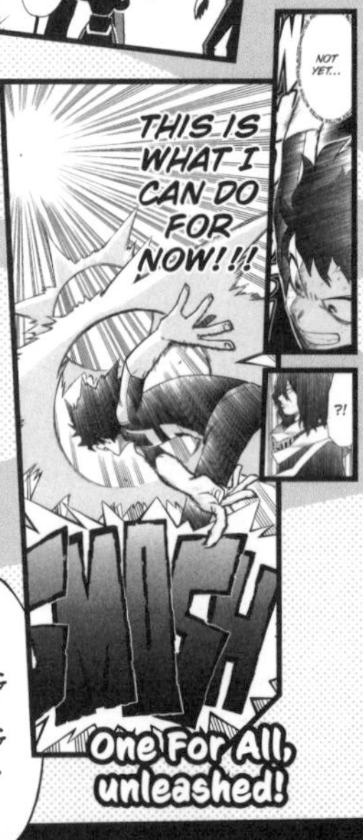
NOT YET...
THIS IS WHAT I CAN DO FOR NOW!!!
?!
SMASH

One For All, unleashed!

?!

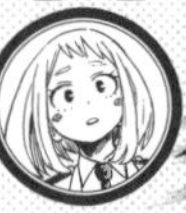

Huh?! The lowest scorer didn't get expelled after all!! That sure made us panic.

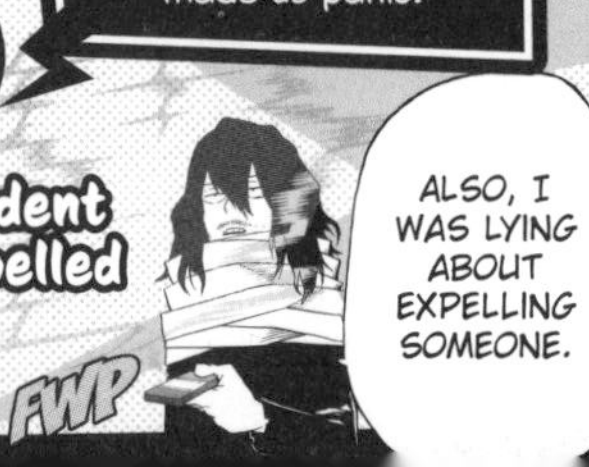
ALSO, I WAS LYING ABOUT EXPELLING SOMEONE.
FWP

No student got expelled

## INDOOR BATTLE TRAINING

The first practical battle training saw the class split into heroes and villains for two-on-two matches! It was time for the costumed students of class A to learn the basics.

**Midoriya and Bakugo clashed**

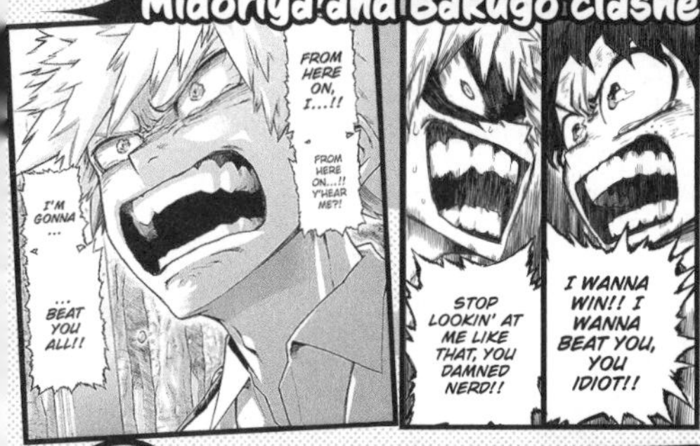
I WANNA WIN!! I WANNA BEAT YOU, YOU IDIOT!!
STOP LOOKIN' AT ME LIKE THAT, YOU DAMNED NERD!!
FROM HERE ON, I...!!
FROM HERE ON...!! Y'HEAR ME?!
I'M GONNA...
...BEAT YOU ALL!!

**Hero costumes—equipped!!**

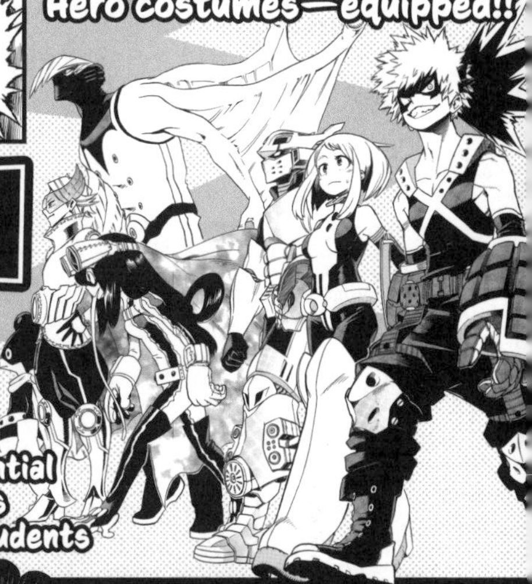

Midoriya and Bakugo's battle got extra heated!! I was practically on fire just watching them.

**The true potential of class A's recommended students**

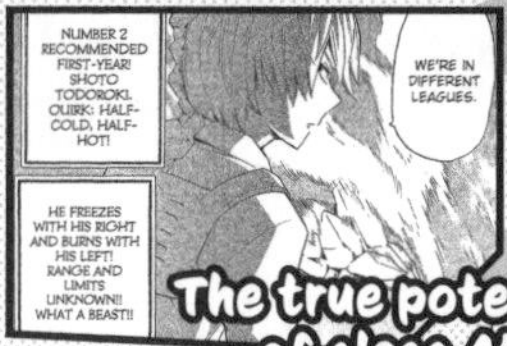
NUMBER 2 RECOMMENDED FIRST-YEAR! SHOTO TODOROKI. QUIRK: HALF-COLD, HALF-HOT!
WE'RE IN DIFFERENT LEAGUES.
HE FREEZES WITH HIS RIGHT AND BURNS WITH HIS LEFT! RANGE AND LIMITS UNKNOWN!! WHAT A BEAST!!

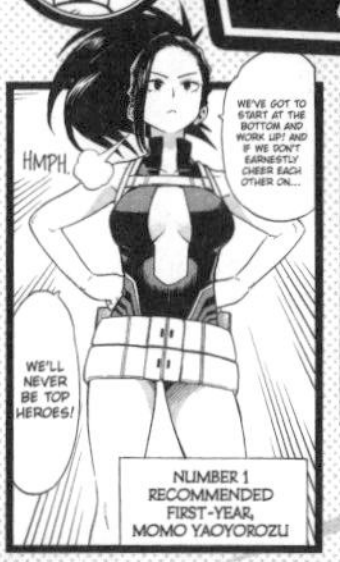
WE'VE GOT TO START AT THE BOTTOM AND WORK UP! AND IF WE DON'T EARNESTLY CHEER EACH OTHER ON...
HMPH.
WE'LL NEVER BE TOP HEROES!
NUMBER 1 RECOMMENDED FIRST-YEAR, MOMO YAOYOROZU

## U.S.J. VILLAIN ATTACK

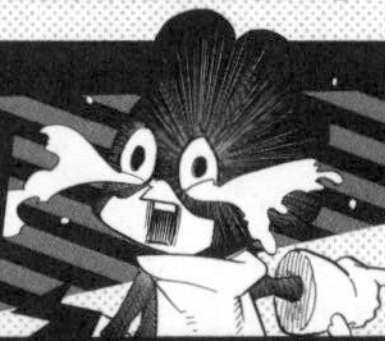

Right before rescue training was set to begin, a bunch of villains attacked U.A., putting the students in a real pinch!!

**Versus villains**

Scary! Nobody told me we'd hafta be prepared to die after getting into this school!!

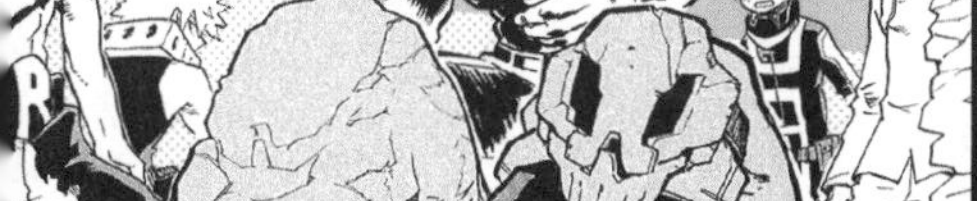

**Dealing with the warper**

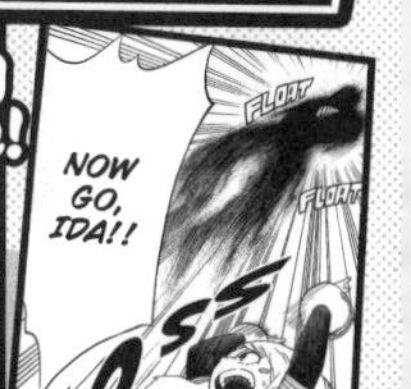
FLOAT
FLOAT
NOW GO, IDA!!
TOSS

**Daring escape!**

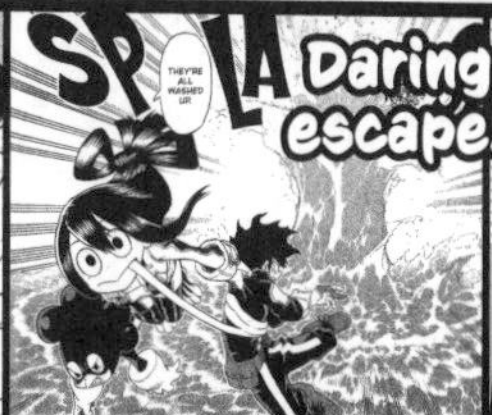
SP LA
THEY'RE ALL WASHED UP.

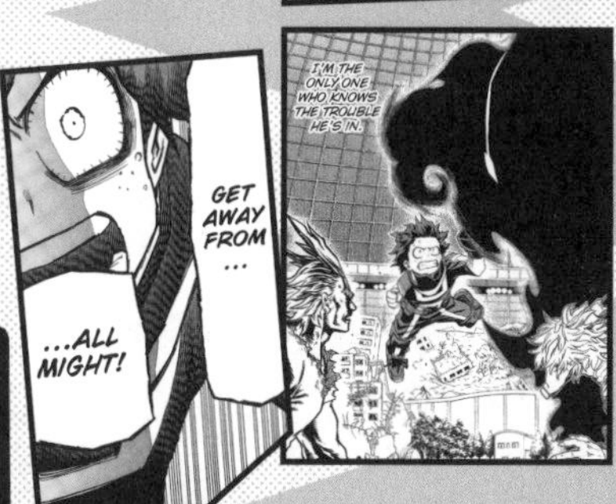
I'M THE ONLY ONE WHO KNOWS THE TROUBLE HE'S IN.
GET AWAY FROM...
...ALL MIGHT!

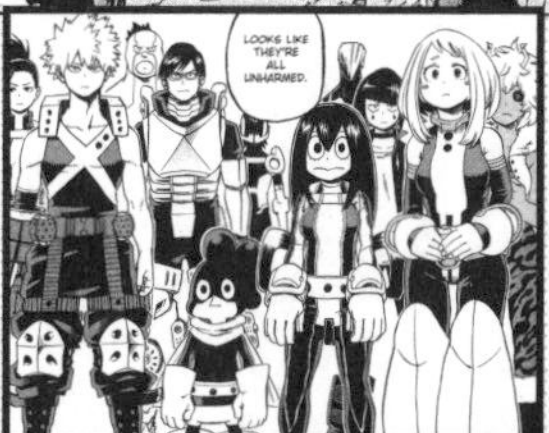
LOOKS LIKE THEY'RE ALL UNHARMED.

**Defending with Electrification**

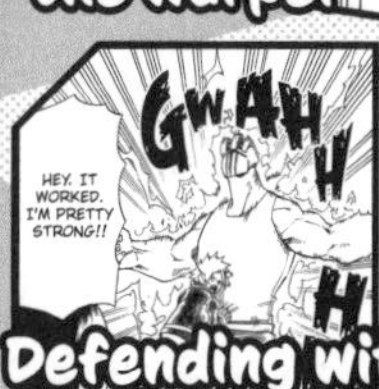
GWAHHH
HEY. IT WORKED. I'M PRETTY STRONG!!

I had to survive all alone. Good thing everyone else managed to too.

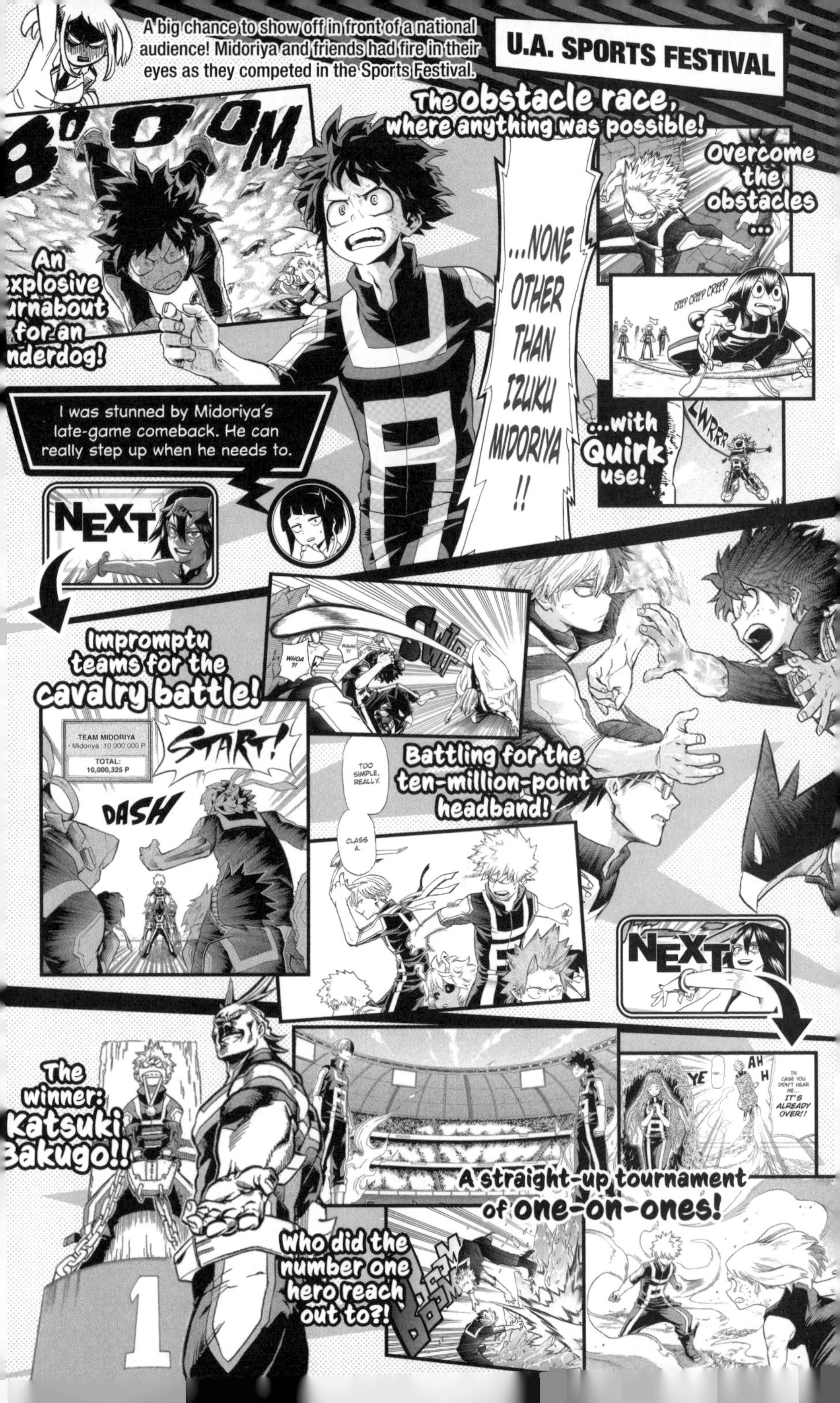
A big chance to show off in front of a national audience! Midoriya and friends had fire in their eyes as they competed in the Sports Festival.
U.A. SPORTS FESTIVAL
The obstacle race, where anything was possible!
BOOOM
An xplosive urnabout for an nderdog!
...NONE OTHER THAN IZUKU MIDORIYA !!
Overcome the obstacles ...
CREEP CREEP CREEP
...with Quirk use!
LWRRR
I was stunned by Midoriya's late-game comeback. He can really step up when he needs to.
NEXT
Impromptu teams for the cavalry battle!
WHOA ?!
WAHH ?!
SWIP
TEAM MIDORIYA
Midoriya: 10,000,000 P
TOTAL: 10,000,325 P
START!
DASH
TOO SIMPLE, REALLY.
Battling for the ten-million-point headband!
CLASS A.
NEXT
The winner: atsuki akugo!!
1
A straight-up tournament of one-on-ones!
YE
AH H
IN CASE YOU DIDN'T HEAR ME... IT'S ALREADY OVER!!
Who did the number one hero reach out to?!
BOOM

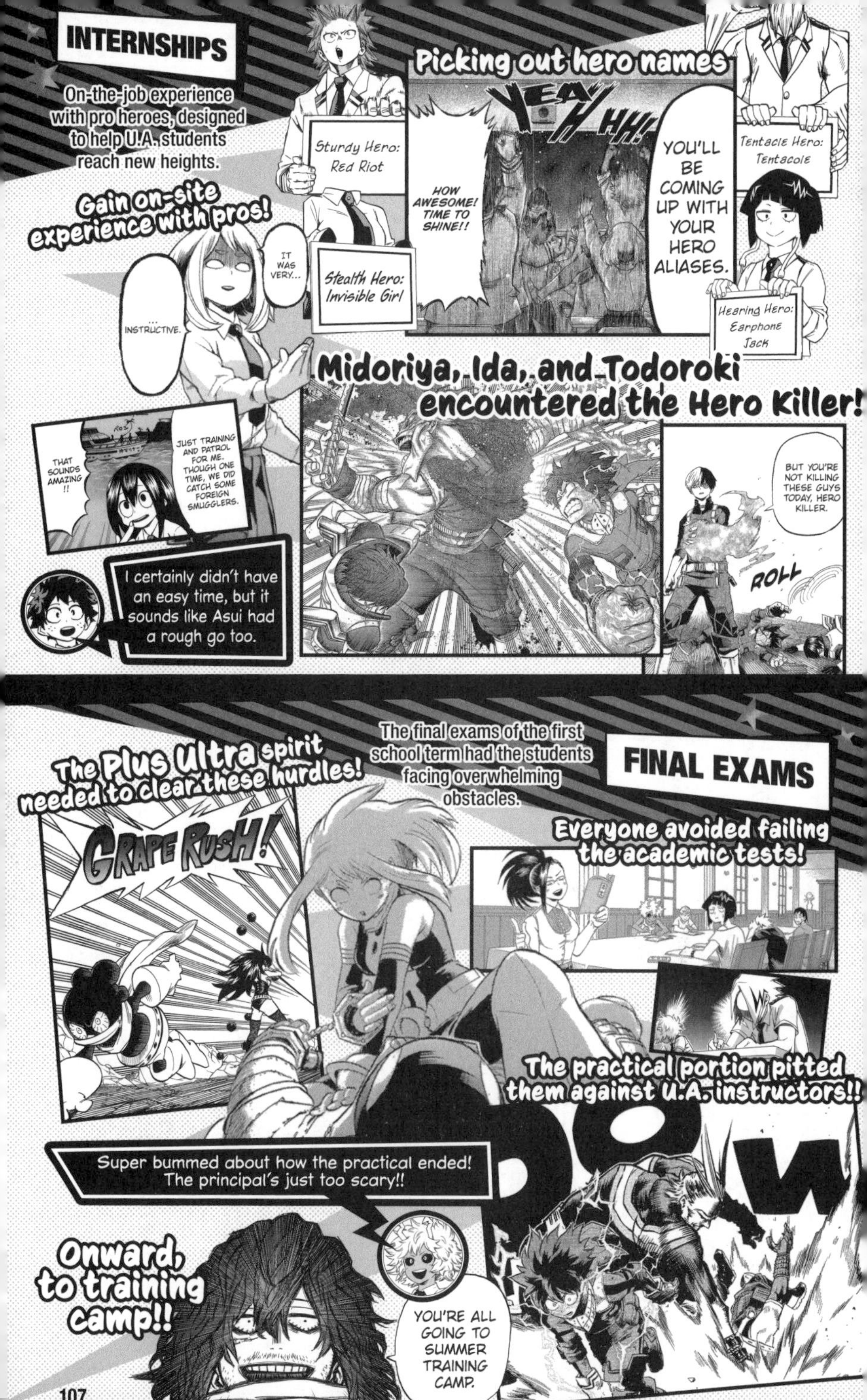
INTERNSHIPS
On-the-job experience with pro heroes, designed to help U.A. students reach new heights.
Picking out hero names
YEAAHHH!
YOU'LL BE COMING UP WITH YOUR HERO ALIASES.
Tentacle Hero: Tentacole
HOW AWESOME! TIME TO SHINE!!
Sturdy Hero: Red Riot
Hearing Hero: Earphone Jack
Stealth Hero: Invisible Girl
Gain on-site experience with pros!
IT WAS VERY...
... INSTRUCTIVE.
JUST TRAINING AND PATROL FOR ME. THOUGH ONE TIME, WE DID CATCH SOME FOREIGN SMUGGLERS.
THAT SOUNDS AMAZING!!
I certainly didn't have an easy time, but it sounds like Asui had a rough go too.
Midoriya, Ida, and Todoroki encountered the Hero Killer!
BUT YOU'RE NOT KILLING THESE GUYS TODAY, HERO KILLER.
ROLL
FINAL EXAMS
The final exams of the first school term had the students facing overwhelming obstacles.
The Plus Ultra spirit needed to clear these hurdles!
GRAPE RUSH!
Everyone avoided failing the academic tests!
The practical portion pitted them against U.A. instructors!!
Super bummed about how the practical ended! The principal's just too scary!!
Onward, to training camp!!
YOU'RE ALL GOING TO SUMMER TRAINING CAMP.

# THE KAMINO NIGHTMARE

During the forest training camp, villains attacked the U.A. students and kidnapped Bakugo!!

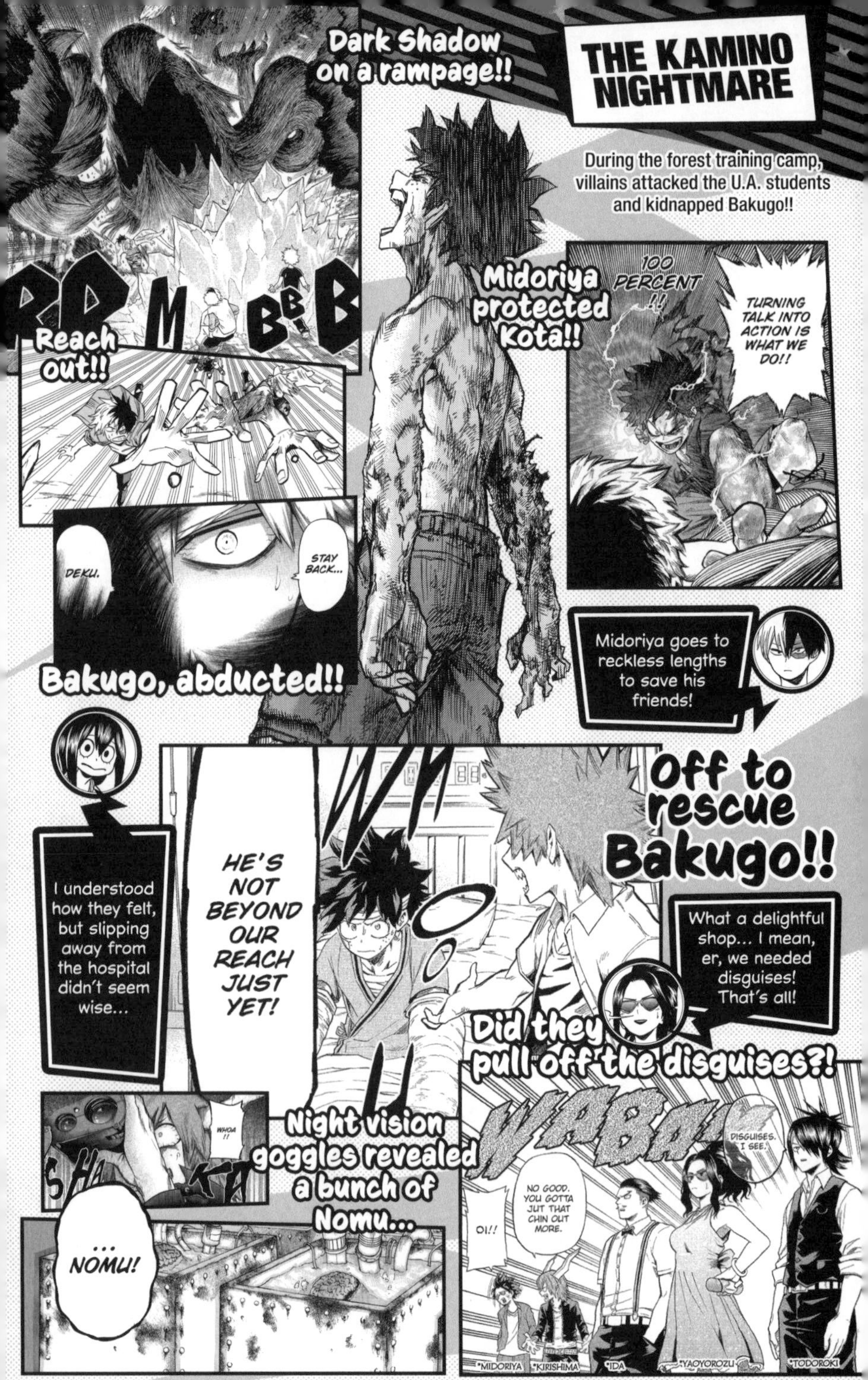
Dark Shadow on a rampage!!
RRMBBB
Reach out!!
DEKU.
STAY BACK...
Bakugo, abducted!!
Midoriya protected Kota!!
100 PERCENT!!
TURNING TALK INTO ACTION IS WHAT WE DO!!
Midoriya goes to reckless lengths to save his friends!
Off to rescue Bakugo!!
HE'S NOT BEYOND OUR REACH JUST YET!
I understood how they felt, but slipping away from the hospital didn't seem wise...
What a delightful shop... I mean, er, we needed disguises! That's all!
Did they pull off the disguises?!
WABAM
DISGUISES. I SEE.
NO GOOD. YOU GOTTA JUT THAT CHIN OUT MORE.
OI!!
*MIDORIYA
*KIRISHIMA
*IDA
*YAOYOROZU
*TODOROKI
Night vision goggles revealed a bunch of Nomu...
WHOA!!
SHA
KA
... NOMU!

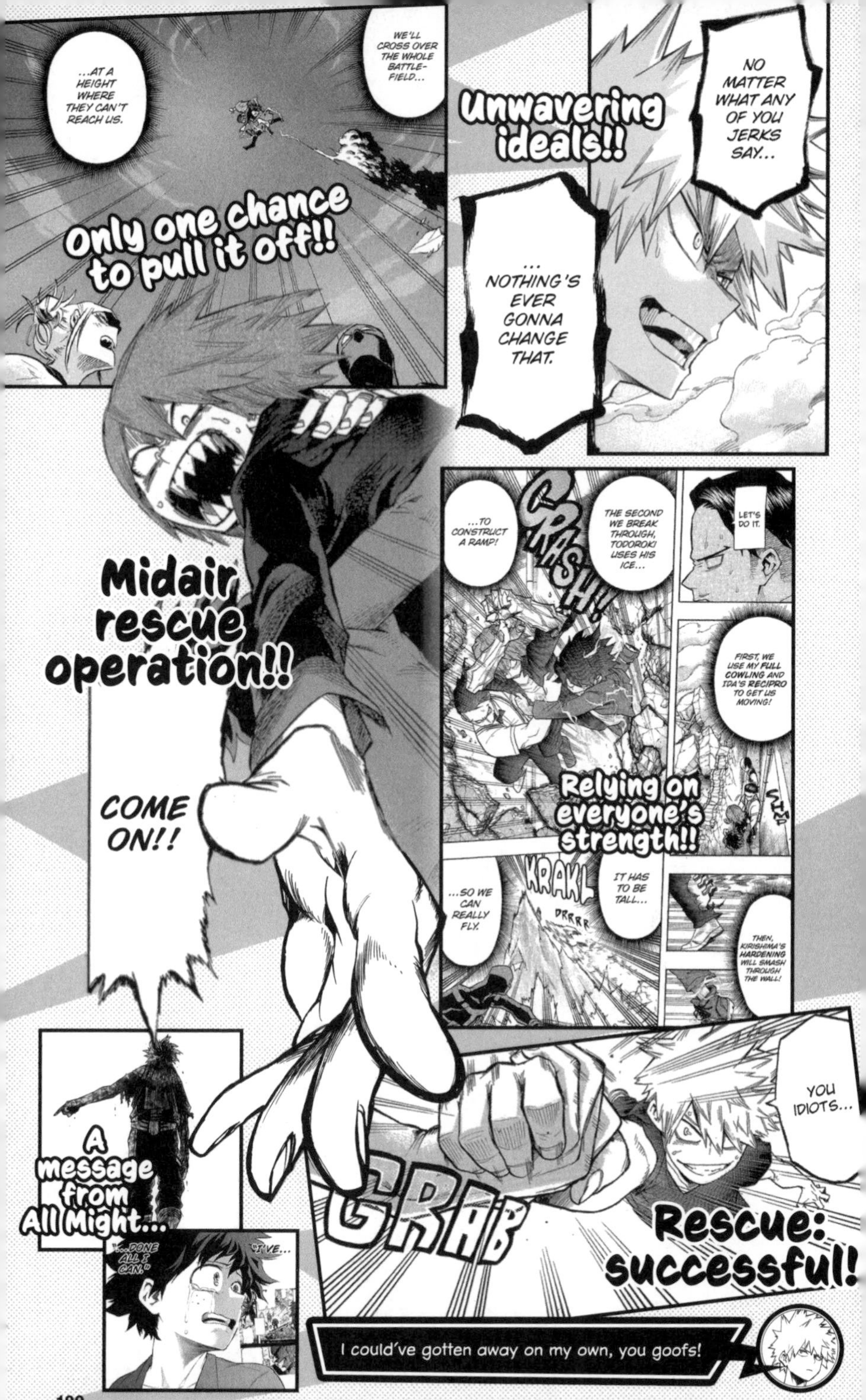
NO MATTER WHAT ANY OF YOU JERKS SAY...
...NOTHING'S EVER GONNA CHANGE THAT.
Unwavering ideals!!
WE'LL CROSS OVER THE WHOLE BATTLE-FIELD...
...AT A HEIGHT WHERE THEY CAN'T REACH US.
Only one chance to pull it off!!
LET'S DO IT.
FIRST, WE USE MY FULL COWLING AND IDA'S RECIPRO TO GET US MOVING!
THE SECOND WE BREAK THROUGH, TODOROKI USES HIS ICE...
...TO CONSTRUCT A RAMP!
CRASH!!
THEN, KIRISHIMA'S HARDENING WILL SMASH THROUGH THE WALL!
IT HAS TO BE TALL...
...SO WE CAN REALLY FLY.
KRAKL
DRRRR
Relying on everyone's strength!!
Midair rescue operation!!
COME ON!!
YOU IDIOTS...
GRAB
Rescue: successful!
A message from All Might...
"I'VE...
...DONE ALL I CAN."
I could've gotten away on my own, you goofs!

# PROVISIONAL LICENSE EXAM

## PUT TOGETHER THOSE ULTIMATE MOVES!!

With the exam coming up, class A worked on creating ultimate moves!!

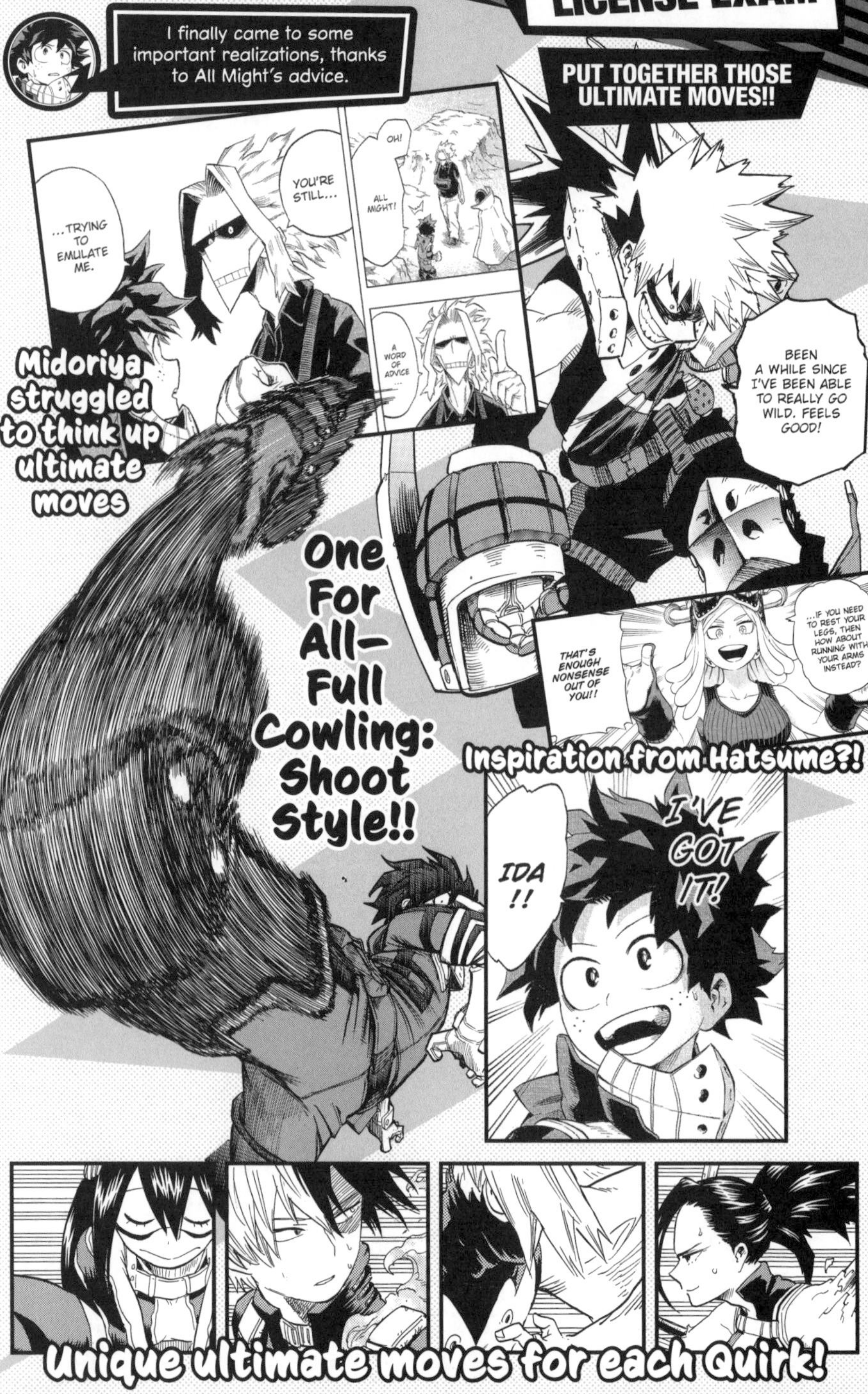
I finally came to some important realizations, thanks to All Might's advice.
OH!
ALL MIGHT!
YOU'RE STILL...
...TRYING TO EMULATE ME.
A WORD OF ADVICE...
Midoriya struggled to think up ultimate moves
BEEN A WHILE SINCE I'VE BEEN ABLE TO REALLY GO WILD. FEELS GOOD!
One For All—Full Cowling: Shoot Style!!
...IF YOU NEED TO REST YOUR LEGS, THEN HOW ABOUT RUNNING WITH YOUR ARMS INSTEAD?
THAT'S ENOUGH NONSENSE OUT OF YOU!!
Inspiration from Hatsume?!
I'VE GOT IT!
IDA!!
Unique ultimate moves for each Quirk!

# PROVISIONAL LICENSE EXAM: ROUND ONE

It was school versus school in round one, where examinees had to hit their rivals with balls to win and move on!

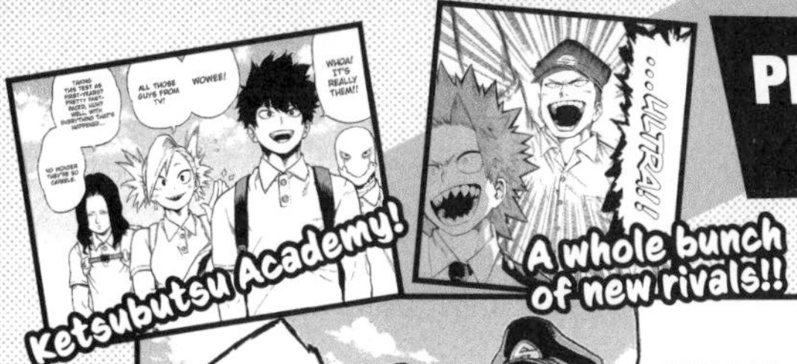

...ULTRA!!
A whole bunch of new rivals!!
WHOA! IT'S REALLY THEM!!
WOWEE!
ALL THOSE GUYS FROM TV!
TAKING THIS TEST AS FIRST-YEARS? PRETTY FAST-PACED, HUH? WELL, WITH EVERYTHING THAT'S HAPPENED...
NO WONDER THEY'RE SO CAPABLE.
Ketsubutsu Academy!


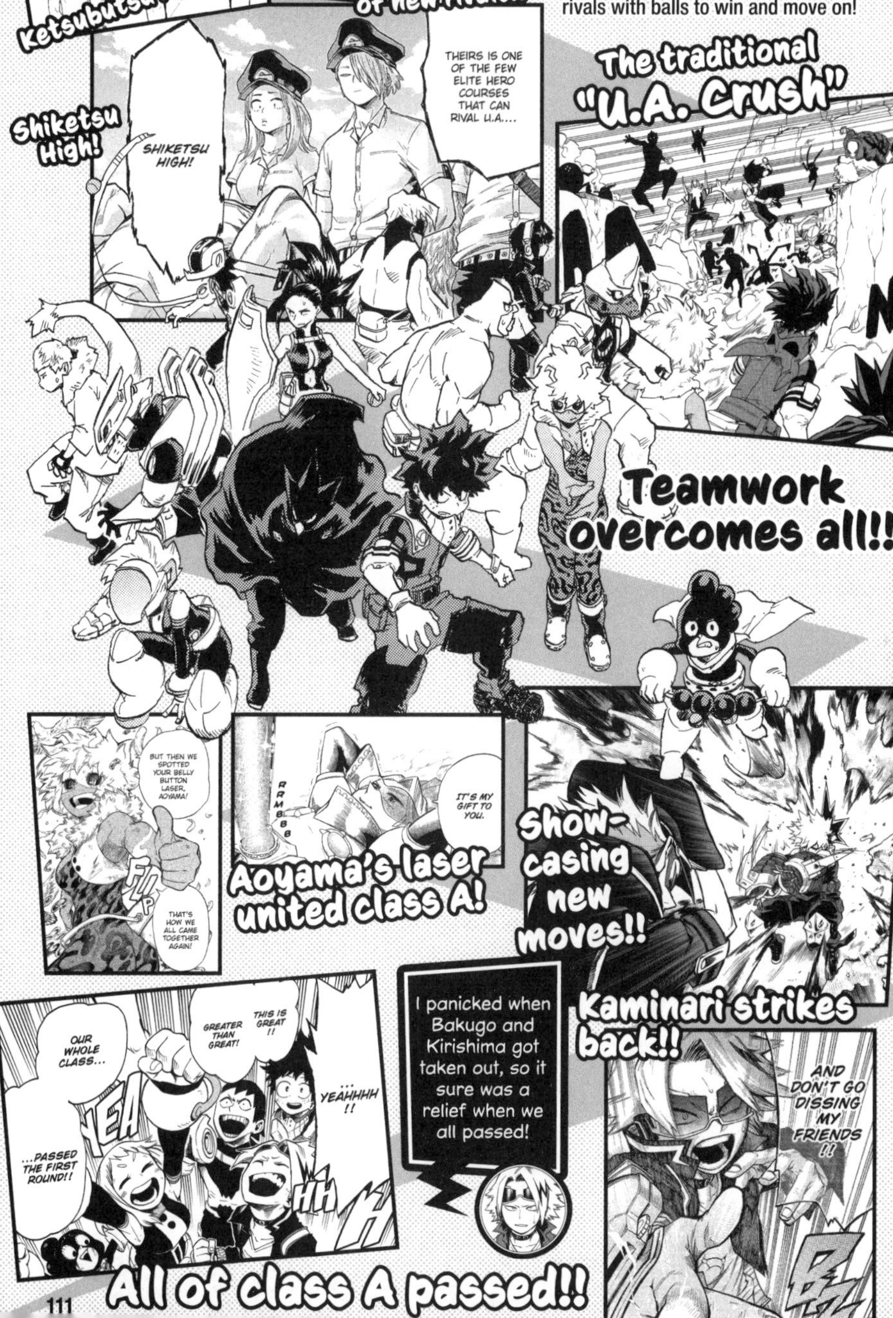

The traditional "U.A. Crush"
THEIRS IS ONE OF THE FEW ELITE HERO COURSES THAT CAN RIVAL U.A....
SHIKETSU HIGH!
Shiketsu High!
Teamwork overcomes all!!
IT'S MY GIFT TO YOU.
RRMBBB
BUT THEN WE SPOTTED YOUR BELLY BUTTON LASER, AOYAMA!
FLIP
THAT'S HOW WE ALL CAME TOGETHER AGAIN!
Aoyama's laser united class A!
Show-casing new moves!!
Kaminari strikes back!!
AND DON'T GO DISSING MY FRIENDS!!
I panicked when Bakugo and Kirishima got taken out, so it sure was a relief when we all passed!
THIS IS GREAT!!
GREATER THAN GREAT!
OUR WHOLE CLASS...
...YEAHHHH!!
YEAHH
...PASSED THE FIRST ROUND!!
All of class A passed!!

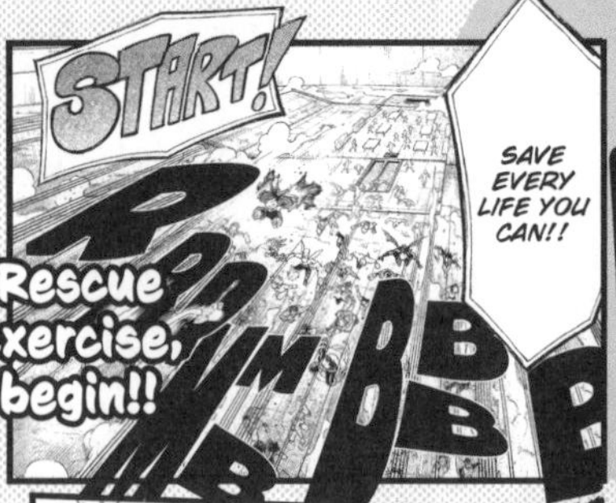
START!
SAVE EVERY LIFE YOU CAN!!
RRRUMBBB
Rescue exercise, begin!!
Just like in a real disaster, quick responses were vital.

## PROVISIONAL LICENSE EXAM: ROUND TWO

Round two was a rescue exercise in a disaster zone with a subtractive scoring system. Examinees were tested on basic knowledge and split-second judgment.

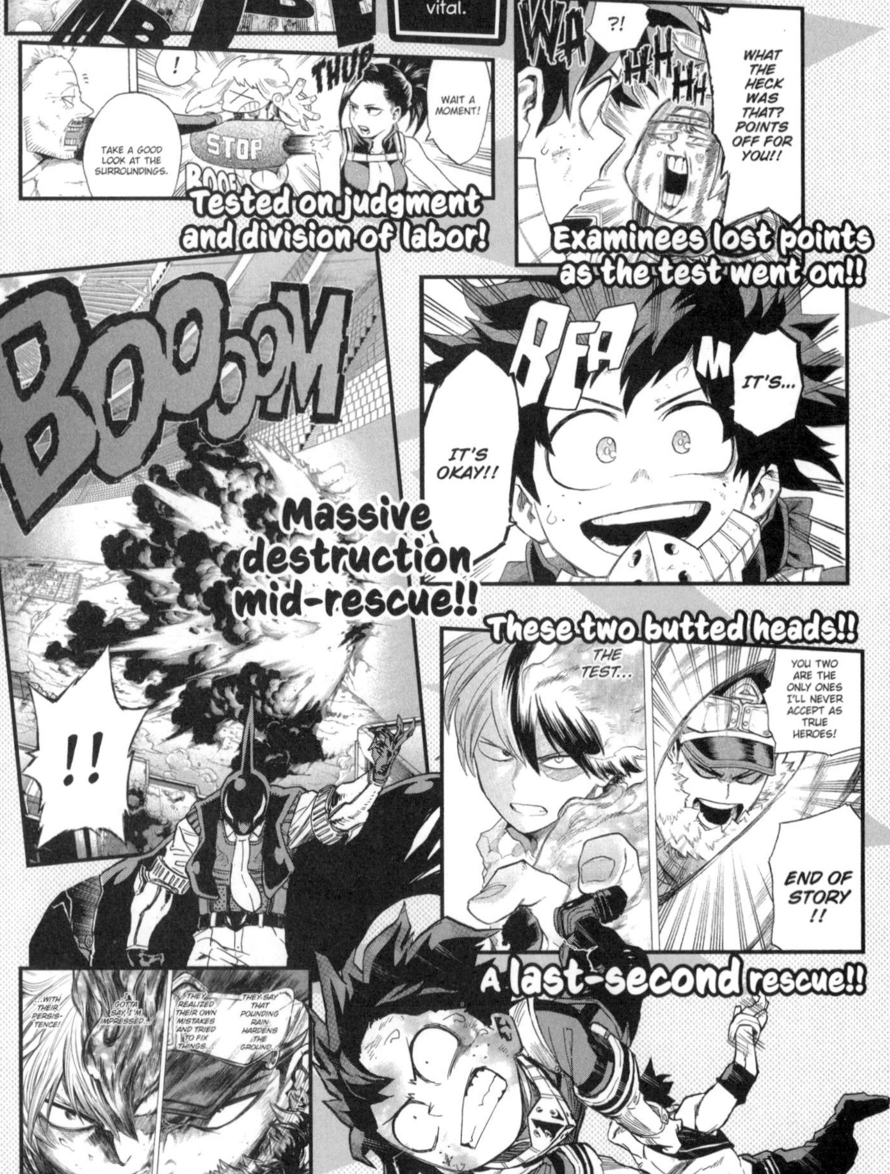
WAHHH
?!
WHAT THE HECK WAS THAT? POINTS OFF FOR YOU!!
Examinees lost points as the test went on!!
THUP
WAIT A MOMENT!
!
TAKE A GOOD LOOK AT THE SURROUNDINGS.
STOP
Tested on judgment and division of labor!
BEAM
IT'S...
IT'S OKAY!!
BOOOOM
Massive destruction mid-rescue!!
!!
These two butted heads!!
YOU TWO ARE THE ONLY ONES I'LL NEVER ACCEPT AS TRUE HEROES!
THE TEST...
END OF STORY !!
A last-second rescue!!
THEY SAY THAT POUNDING RAIN HARDENS THE GROUND.
THEY REALIZED THEIR OWN MISTAKES AND TRIED TO FIX THINGS...
GOTTA SAY, I'M IMPRESSED...
...WITH THEIR PERSISTENCE!
Then, awaiting the results...

## PROVISIONAL LICENSE EXAM RESULTS

All of class A passed…except Todoroki and Bakugo! With those licenses in hand, the students felt like they'd taken the first big step toward their dreams.

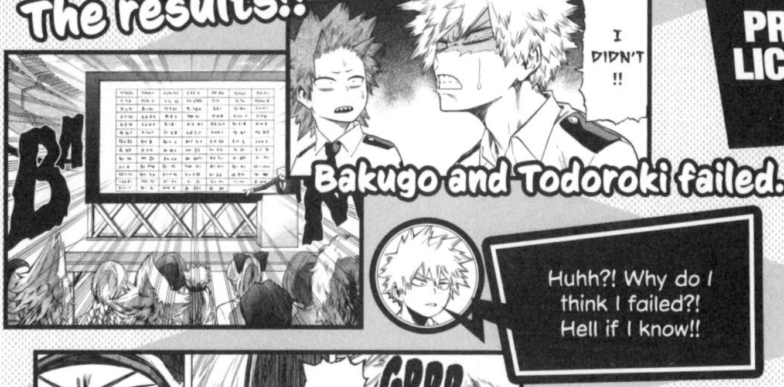
The results!!
B
I DIDN'T !!
Bakugo and Todoroki failed...
Huhh?! Why do I think I failed?! Hell if I know!!

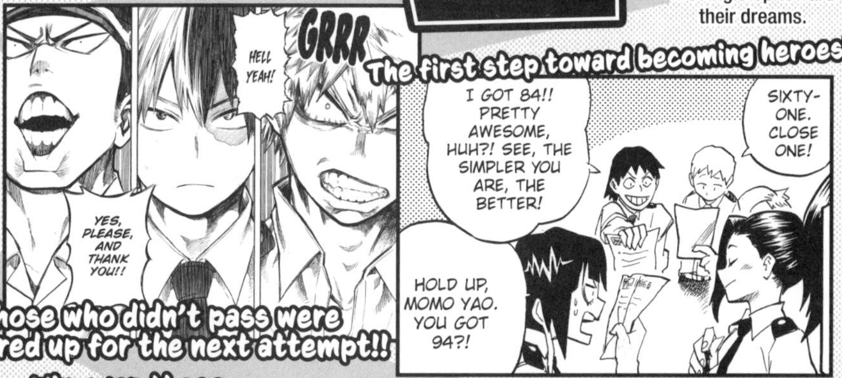
The first step toward becoming heroes!!
SIXTY-ONE. CLOSE ONE!
I GOT 84!! PRETTY AWESOME, HUH?! SEE, THE SIMPLER YOU ARE, THE BETTER!
HOLD UP, MOMO YAO. YOU GOT 94?!
GRRR
HELL YEAH!
YES, PLEASE, AND THANK YOU!!
Those who didn't pass were fired up for the next attempt!!

## SUPPLEMENTARY COURSE

Those who failed the licensing exam had to take a three-month supplementary course… It was their chance to redeem themselves.

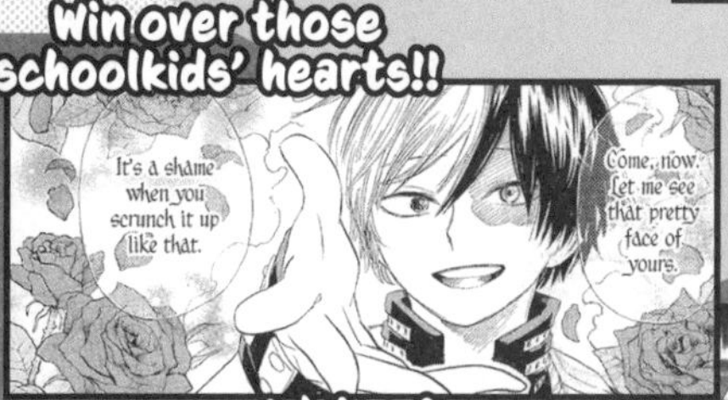
Win over those schoolkids' hearts!!
Come, now. Let me see that pretty face of yours.
It's a shame when you scrunch it up like that.

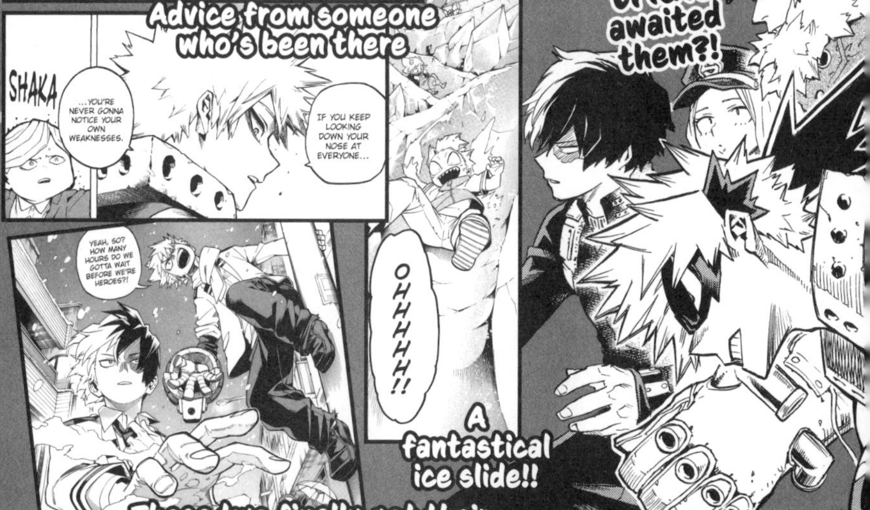
What brutal trials awaited them?!
Advice from someone who's been there
IF YOU KEEP LOOKING DOWN YOUR NOSE AT EVERYONE…
…YOU'RE NEVER GONNA NOTICE YOUR OWN WEAKNESSES.
SHAKA
OHHHHHH!!
YEAH, SO? HOW MANY HOURS DO WE GOTTA WAIT BEFORE WE'RE HEROES?!
A fantastical ice slide!!
Those two finally got their provisional licenses!!

# WORK STUDIES

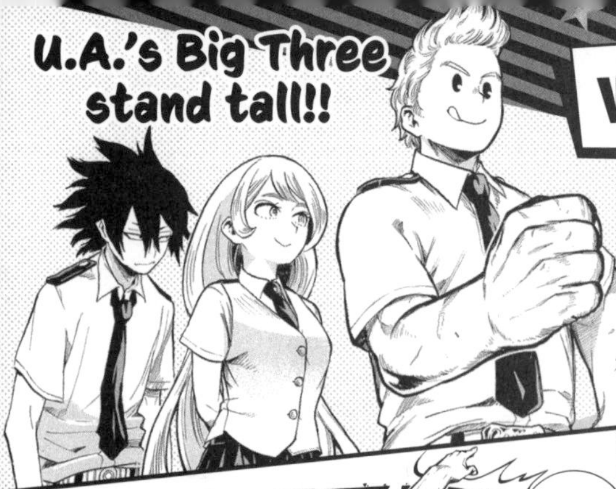

U.A.'s Big Three stand tall!!

## INFO SESSION

U.A.'s Big Three gave a short lecture about work studies, and class A sparred with Togata.

He was all the more convincing once we saw what he was capable of!

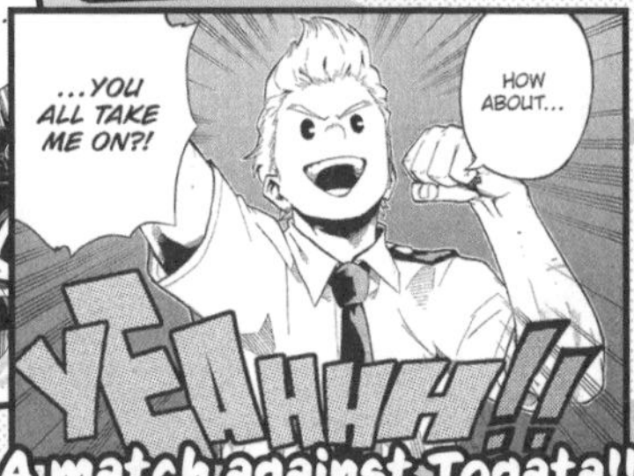

HOW ABOUT...
...YOU ALL TAKE ME ON?!
YEAHHH!!


A match against Togata!!

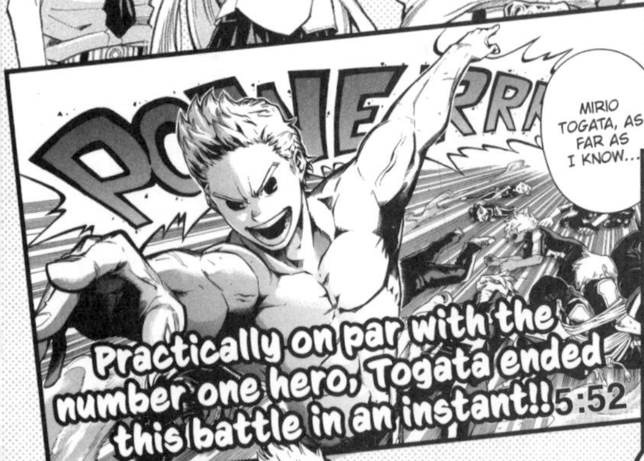

MIRIO TOGATA, AS FAR AS I KNOW...
POWERRR


Practically on par with the number one hero, Togata ended this battle in an instant!! 5:52

## OFF TO SIR NIGHTEYE'S AGENCY

In part thanks to an introduction by Togata, Midoriya got to do his work study with Sir Nighteye's agency.

Sir Nighteye's interview included a practical portion!!

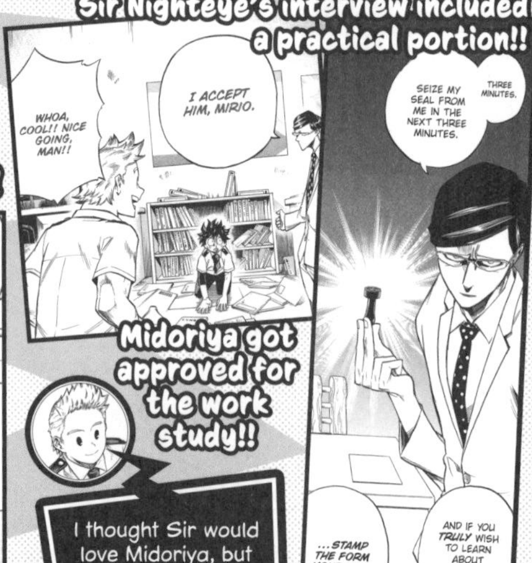

THREE MINUTES.
SEIZE MY SEAL FROM ME IN THE NEXT THREE MINUTES.
AND IF YOU TRULY WISH TO LEARN ABOUT HEROISM AT MY SIDE...
...STAMP THE FORM YOURSELF.
I ACCEPT HIM, MIRIO.
WHOA, COOL!! NICE GOING, MAN!!


Midoriya got approved for the work study!!

I thought Sir would love Midoriya, but the kid kinda flubbed it.

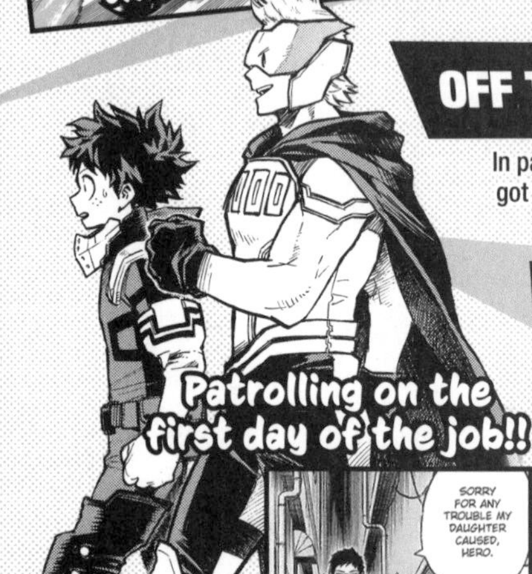

Patrolling on the first day of the job!!

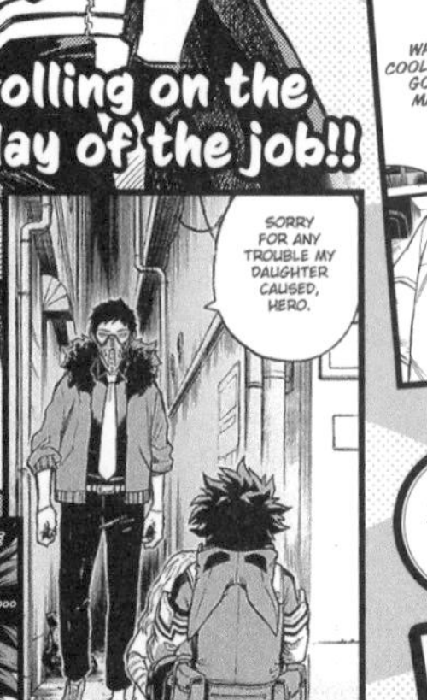

SORRY FOR ANY TROUBLE MY DAUGHTER CAUSED, HERO.


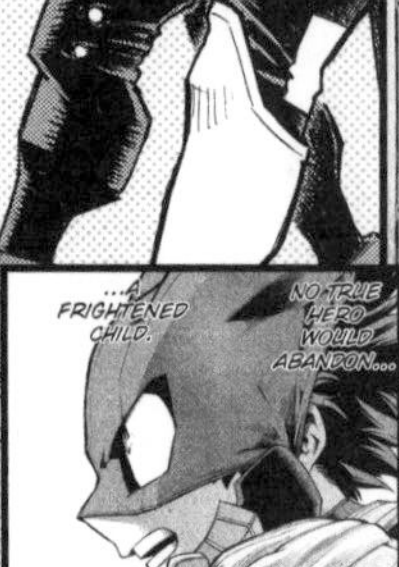

NO TRUE HERO WOULD ABANDON...
...A FRIGHTENED CHILD.
WHAT ARE YOU DOING TO THIS GIRL?


A chance encounter with the target of the investigation!!

# TEAM-UP WITH OTHER AGENCIES

Other work-study trainees spent time at agencies of their own and joined the big investigation.

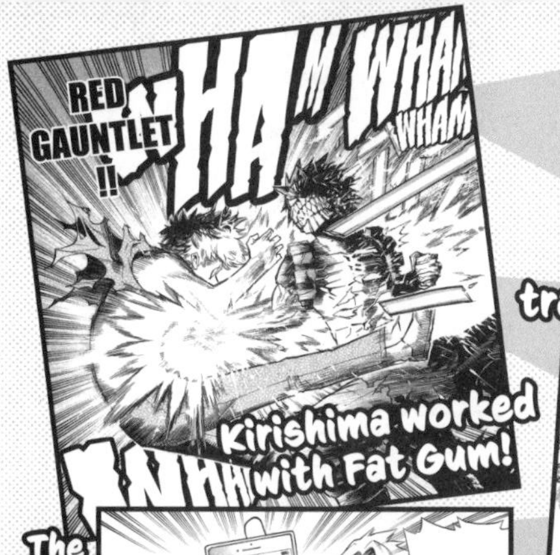
RED GAUNTLET!!
WHAM WHAM WHAM
Kirishima worked with Fat Gum!

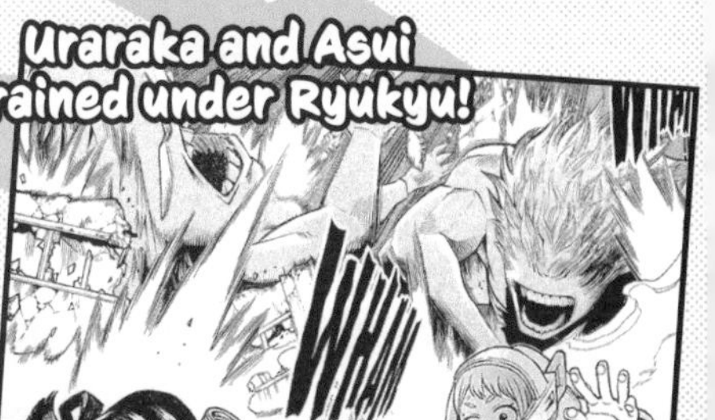
Uraraka and Asui trained under Ryukyu!

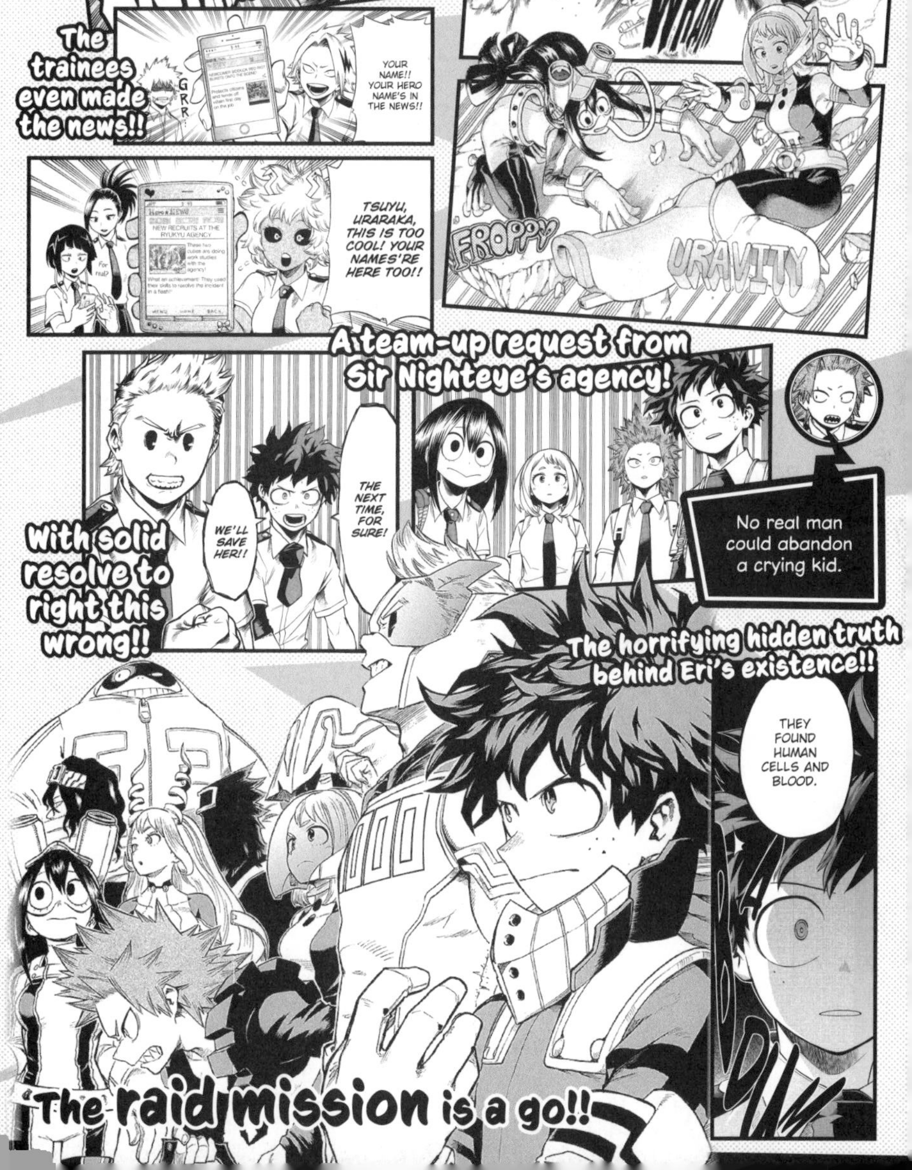
FROPPY
URAVITY
The trainees even made the news!!
YOUR NAME!! YOUR HERO NAME'S IN THE NEWS!!
GRR
TSUYU, URARAKA, THIS IS TOO COOL! YOUR NAMES'RE HERE TOO!!
NEW RECRUITS AT THE RYUKYU AGENCY
These two cuties are doing work studies with the agency!
What an achievement! They used their skills to resolve the incident in a flash!
For real?
A team-up request from Sir Nighteye's agency!
No real man could abandon a crying kid.
THE NEXT TIME, FOR SURE!
WE'LL SAVE HER!!
With solid resolve to right this wrong!!
The horrifying hidden truth behind Eri's existence!!
THEY FOUND HUMAN CELLS AND BLOOD.
The raid mission is a go!!

There is no sense in clinging to regret. Rather, one must find the conviction to act.

# RAIDING THE SHIE HASSAIKAI COMPOUND

With hero assistance, the police raided the Hassaikai hideout to round up the conspirators!

SHIE HASSAIKAI COMPOUND

Aboveground, an ordinary building

**SHIE HASSAIKAI OFFICES/RESIDENCE**

Aboveground

Belowground

Basement

tangled labyrinth!!

## AT THE GATES

| HEROES | | VILLAIN |
|---|---|---|
| Ryukyu | Nejire | |
| Uravity | Froppy | Rikiya Katsukame |

VS

Crushing the villain with four-way teamwork!!

### UNDERGROUND MAZE

| HERO | VILLAIN |
|---|---|
| Suneater | Toya Setsuno |
| | Soramitsu Tabe |
| | Yu Hojo |

VS

...BUT TRASH CAN FORM SOLID BONDS.

WE MIGHT BE TRASH...

Capturing this trio!!

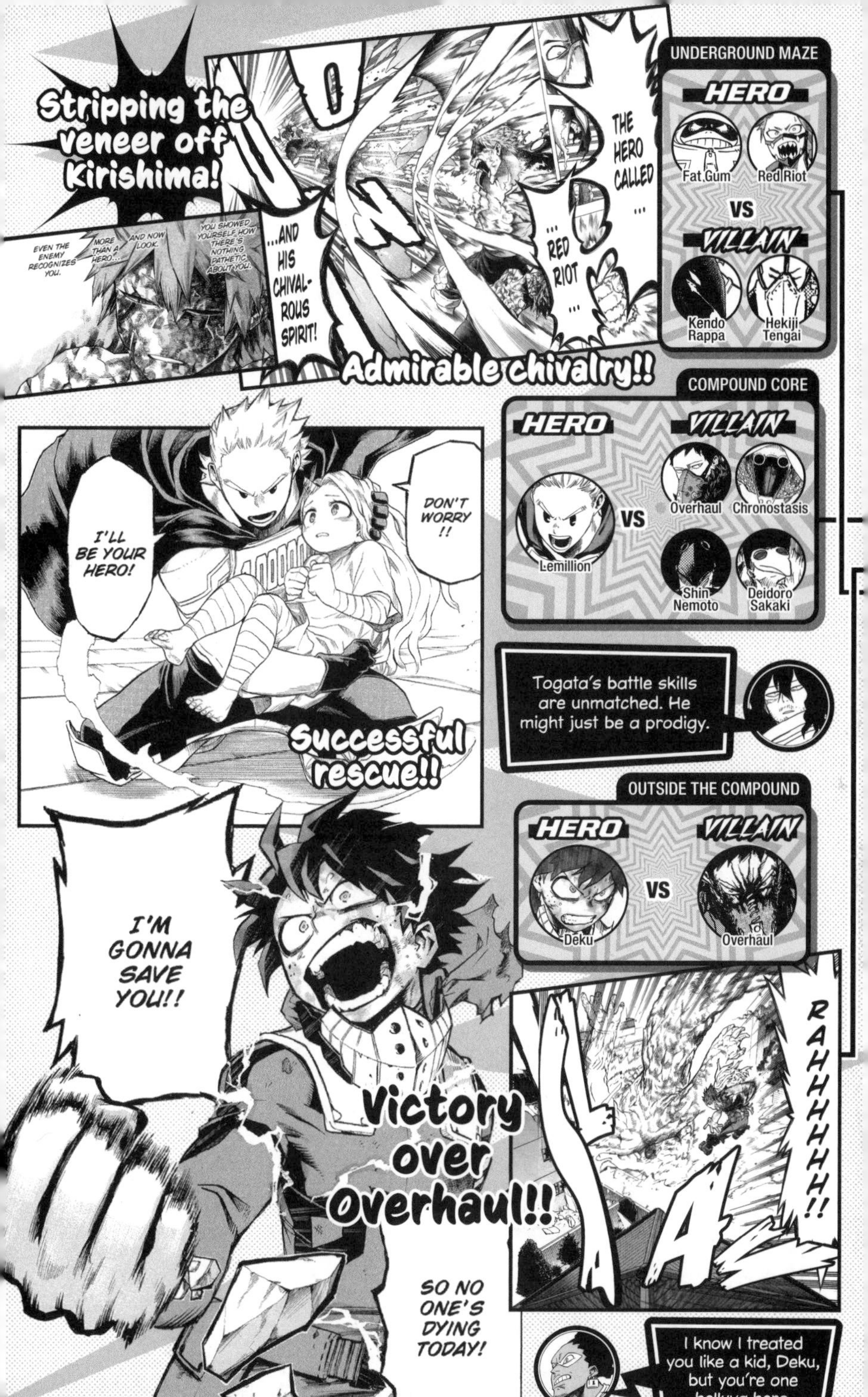
UNDERGROUND MAZE
HERO
Fat Gum
Red Riot
VS
VILLAIN
Kendo Rappa
Hekiji Tengai
Stripping the veneer off Kirishima!
THE HERO CALLED ...
... RED RIOT ...
...AND HIS CHIVALROUS SPIRIT!
YOU SHOWED YOURSELF HOW THERE'S NOTHING PATHETIC ABOUT YOU.
AND NOW LOOK.
MORE THAN A HERO...
EVEN THE ENEMY RECOGNIZES YOU.
Admirable chivalry!!
COMPOUND CORE
HERO
Lemillion
VS
VILLAIN
Overhaul
Chronostasis
Shin Nemoto
Deidoro Sakaki
Togata's battle skills are unmatched. He might just be a prodigy.
DON'T WORRY!!
I'LL BE YOUR HERO!
Successful rescue!!
OUTSIDE THE COMPOUND
HERO
Deku
VS
VILLAIN
Overhaul
RAHHHHHHH!!
I'M GONNA SAVE YOU!!
Victory over Overhaul!!
SO NO ONE'S DYING TODAY!
I know I treated you like a kid, Deku, but you're one helluva hero.

# SCHOOL FESTIVAL

## EVENT-PLANNING MEETING

It is my duty as class president to consolidate our ideas in a smooth and orderly fashion!!

Class A got Plus Ultra excited about planning their event!!

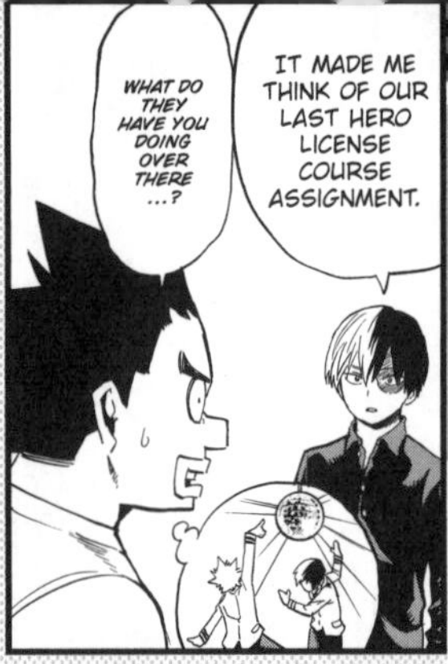

IT MADE ME THINK OF OUR LAST HERO LICENSE COURSE ASSIGNMENT.
WHAT DO THEY HAVE YOU DOING OVER THERE ...?


**A fiery, passionate class meeting!!**

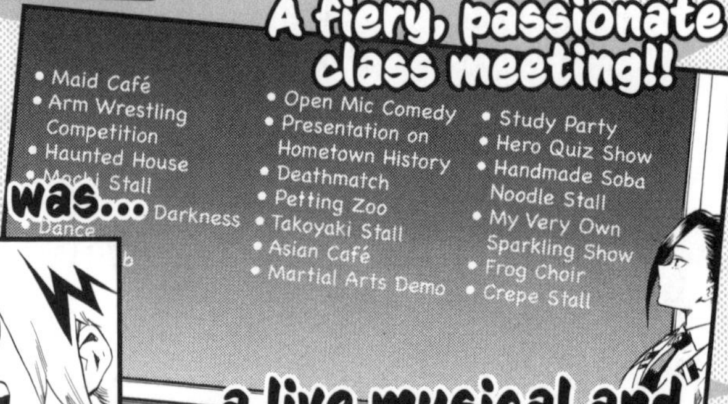

• Maid Café
• Arm Wrestling Competition
• Haunted House
Darkness
Dance
• Open Mic Comedy
• Presentation on Hometown History
• Deathmatch
• Petting Zoo
• Takoyaki Stall
• Asian Café
• Martial Arts Demo
• Study Party
• Hero Quiz Show
• Handmade Soba Noodle Stall
• My Very Own Sparkling Show
• Frog Choir
• Crepe Stall


**Class A's event was...**

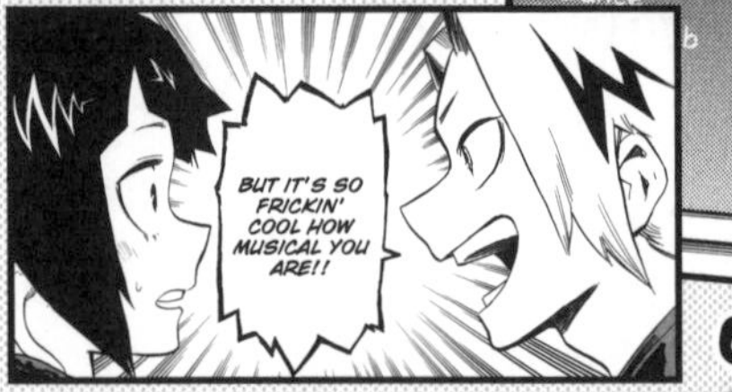

BUT IT'S SO FRICKIN' COOL HOW MUSICAL YOU ARE!!


**...a live musical and dance performance!!**

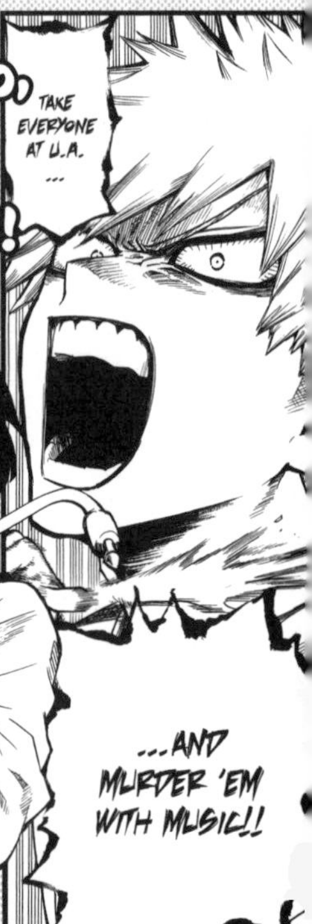

TAKE EVERYONE AT U.A. ...
...AND MURDER 'EM WITH MUSIC!!


**Bakugo, out for blood!!**

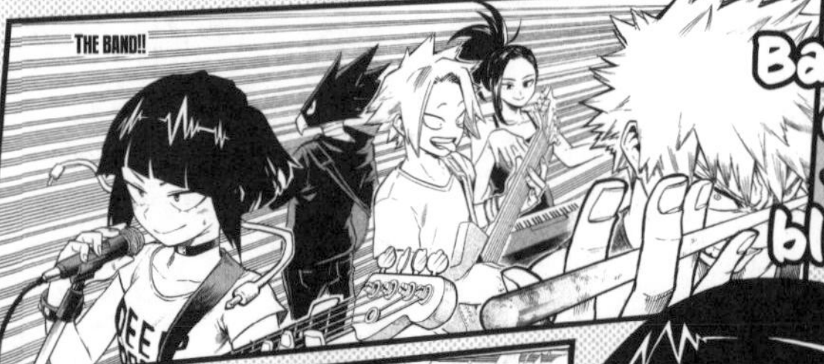

THE BAND!!


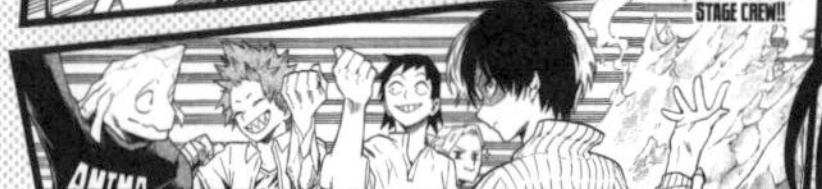

STAGE CREW!!


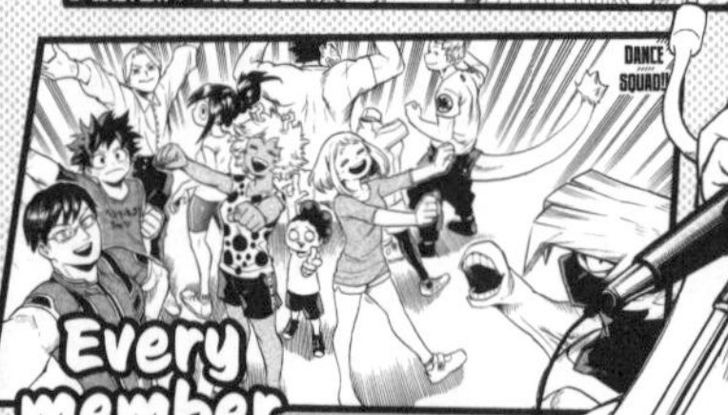

DANCE SQUAD!!


**Every member of the class had a role to play!!**

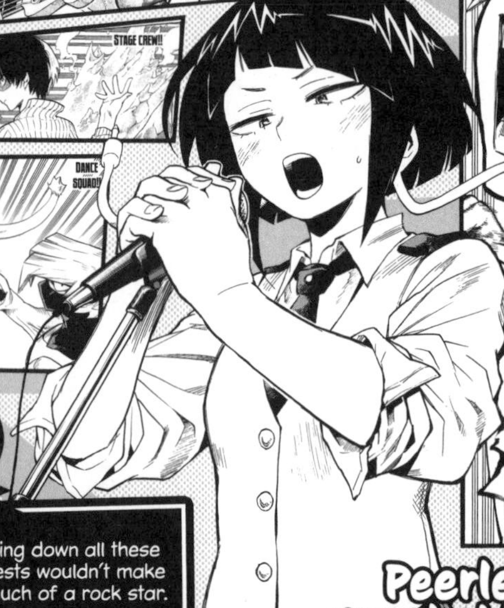

Turning down all these requests wouldn't make me much of a rock star.

**Peerless vocal ability!!**

## PREP TIME

Planning started a month in advance! In the meantime, Eri paid a visit to the school.

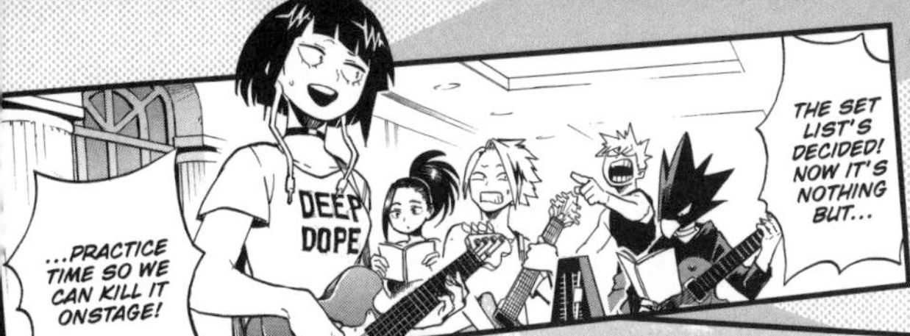
THE SET LIST'S DECIDED! NOW IT'S NOTHING BUT...
...PRACTICE TIME SO WE CAN KILL IT ONSTAGE!
DEEP DOPE

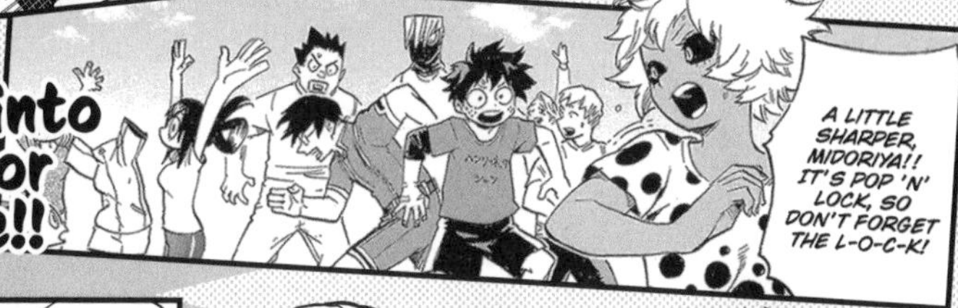
A LITTLE SHARPER, MIDORIYA!! IT'S POP 'N' LOCK, SO DON'T FORGET THE L-O-C-K!

**Splitting into teams for practice!!**

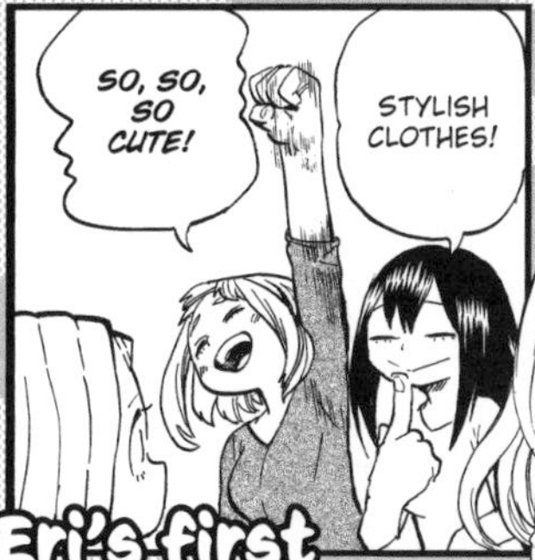
STYLISH CLOTHES!
SO, SO, SO CUTE!

**Eri's first school visit!!**

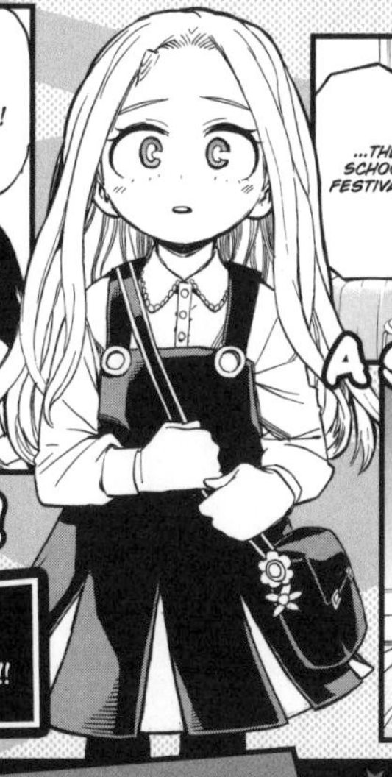

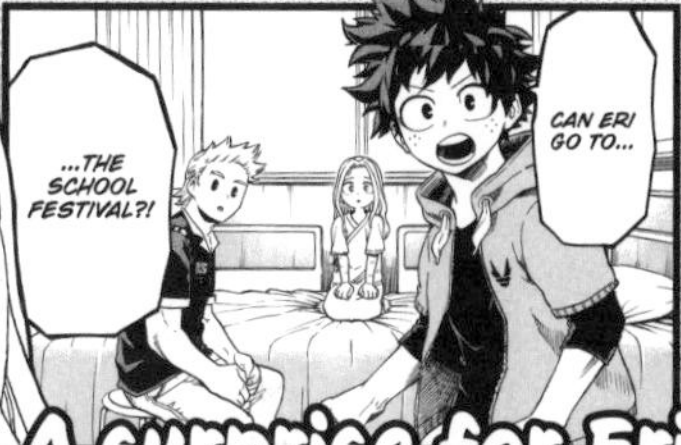
CAN ERI GO TO...
...THE SCHOOL FESTIVAL?!

**A surprise for Eri!!**

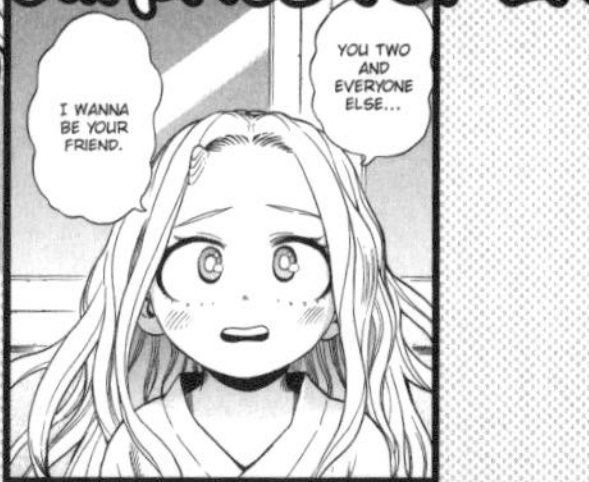
YOU TWO AND EVERYONE ELSE...
I WANNA BE YOUR FRIEND.

I sure hope Eri starts smiling again!!

## What Exactly is U.A.'s SCHOOL FESTIVAL?

Unlike in past years, this festival is limited to students and staff.

An event that showcases the Support Course, General Studies, and the Business Course. Each class gets to create an exhibit or event of some kind.

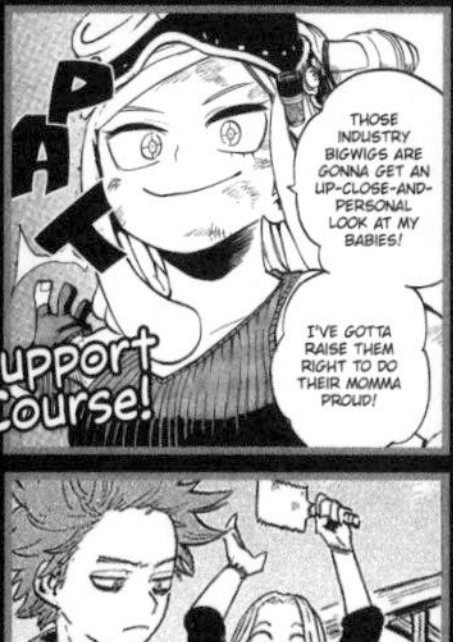
PAT
THOSE INDUSTRY BIGWIGS ARE GONNA GET AN UP-CLOSE-AND-PERSONAL LOOK AT MY BABIES!
I'VE GOTTA RAISE THEM RIGHT TO DO THEIR MOMMA PROUD!

**Support Course!**

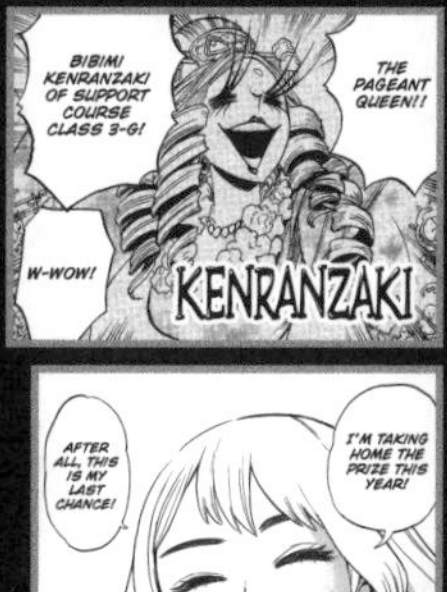
THE PAGEANT QUEEN!!
BIBIMI KENRANZAKI OF SUPPORT COURSE CLASS 3-G!
W-WOW!
KENRANZAKI

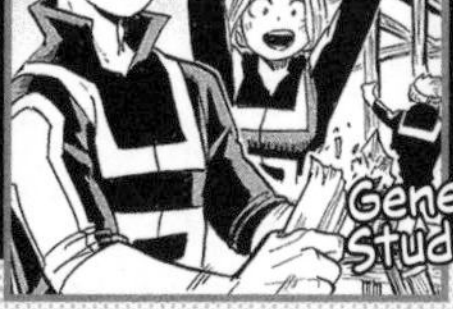

**General Studies!**

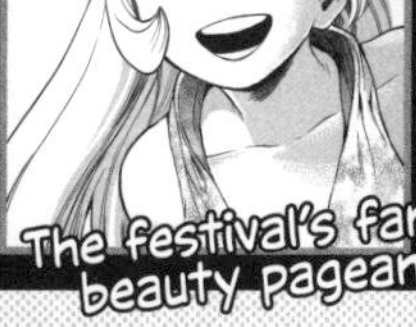
I'M TAKING HOME THE PRIZE THIS YEAR!
AFTER ALL, THIS IS MY LAST CHANCE!

**The festival's famous beauty pageant!!**

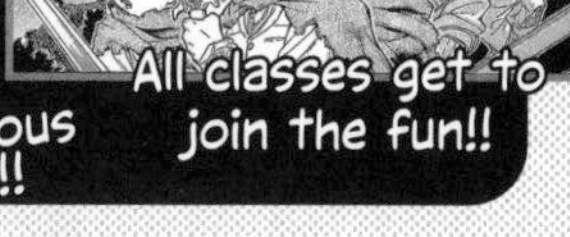
ROMEO AND JULIET AND THE RETURN OF THE PRISONER KING OF AZKABUM...
IT'S A TOTALLY SPECTACULAR ORIGINAL FANTASY SCREENPLAY FROM NONE OTHER THAN CLASS B!!

**All classes get to join the fun!!**

## THE DAY OF

U.A.'s School Festival kicked off without issue!! That Plus Ultra spirit gave rise to an event even more exciting than in years past.

### Mineta and Kaminari's U.A. School Festival Schedule

| | |
|---|---|
| 9:00 | School Festival starts |
| 10:00 | Class 1-A's "A Band" performance |
| 12:00 | Class 1-A tidies up, breaks for lunch |
| 1:00 | Watch the beauty pageant |
| 2:00 | Challenge the Labyrinth of Doom |
| | Check out the cosplay cafe |
| | Join the Super Ball scooping contest |
| | Watch the short films |
| | Line up at the boba stall |
| | Join the singing contest |
| | Recharge with a hamburger |
| 5:00 | Attend beauty pageant results |
| 6:00 | School Festival ends |

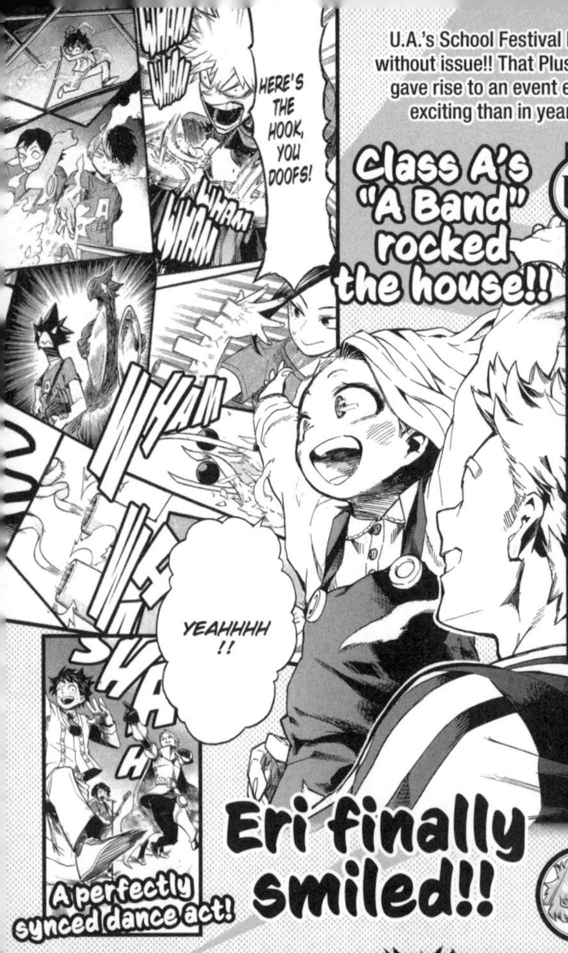
HERE'S THE HOOK, YOU DOOFS!
WHAM
Class A's "A Band" rocked the house!!
YEAHHHH !!
Eri finally smiled!!
A perfectly synced dance act!

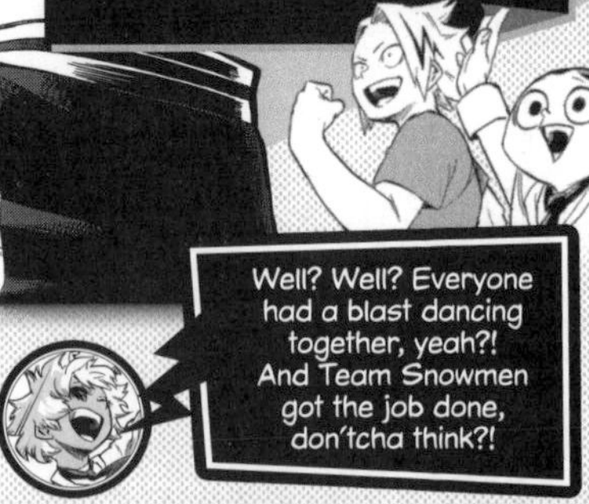
Well? Well? Everyone had a blast dancing together, yeah?! And Team Snowmen got the job done, don'tcha think?!

## VERSUS GENTLE

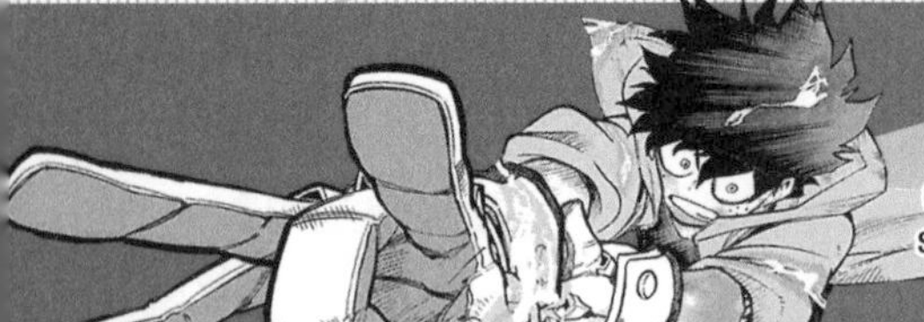

Only Midoriya realized that someone was out to spoil the festival!! Unbeknownst to all, he waged a fierce battle to stop the intruder.

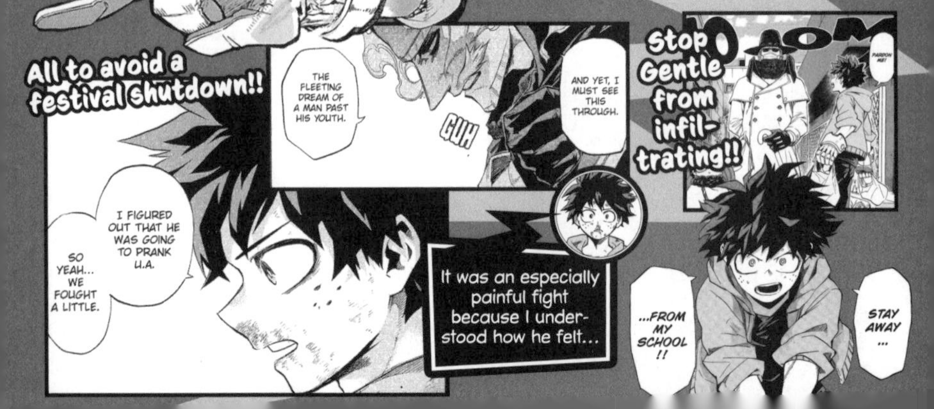
Stop Gentle from infil-trating!!
PARDON ME!
AND YET, I MUST SEE THIS THROUGH.
GUH
THE FLEETING DREAM OF A MAN PAST HIS YOUTH.
All to avoid a festival shutdown!!
STAY AWAY ...
...FROM MY SCHOOL !!
It was an especially painful fight because I under-stood how he felt...
I FIGURED OUT THAT HE WAS GOING TO PRANK U.A.
SO YEAH... WE FOUGHT A LITTLE.

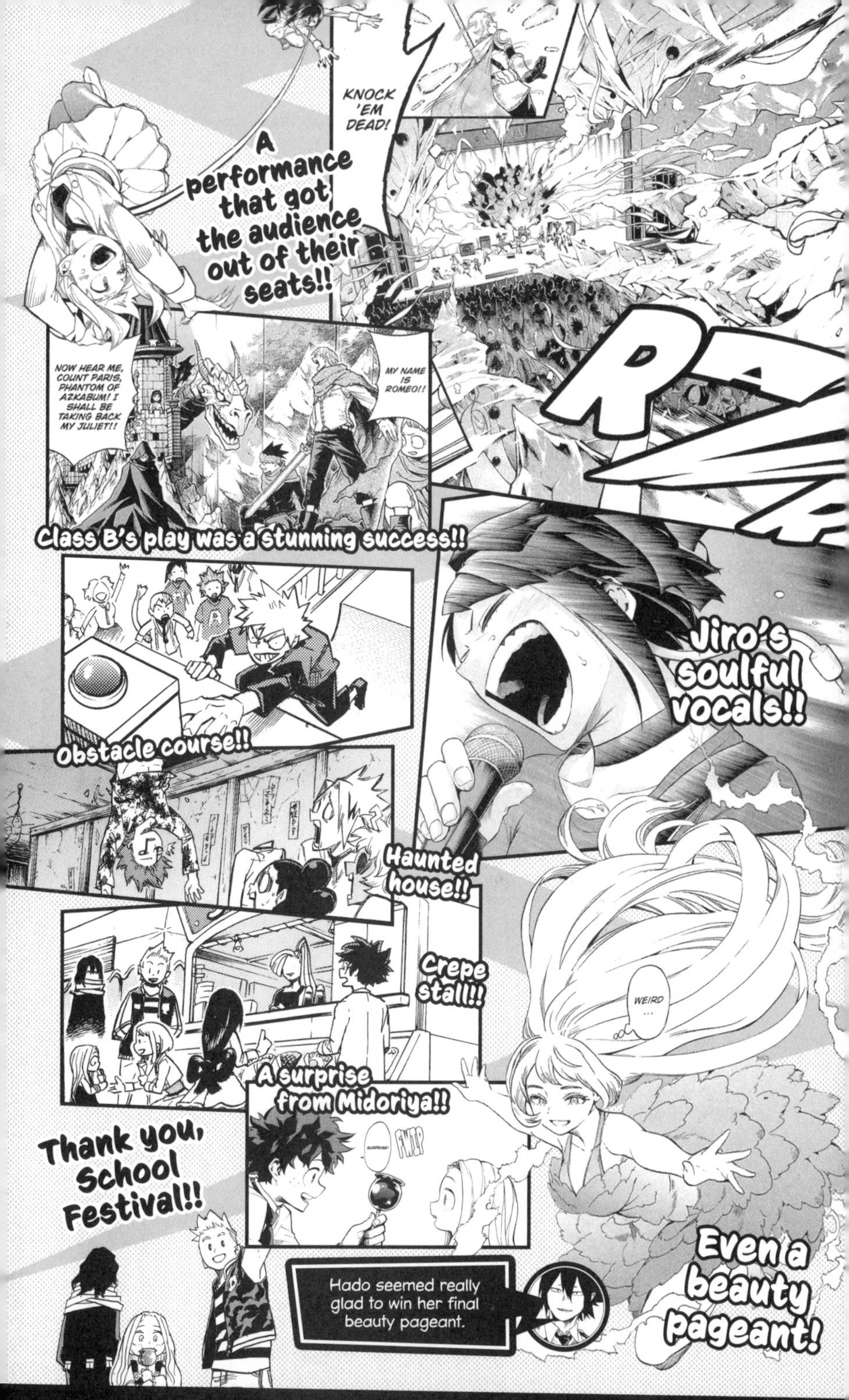
KNOCK 'EM DEAD!
A performance that got the audience out of their seats!!
MY NAME IS ROMEO!!
NOW HEAR ME, COUNT PARIS, PHANTOM OF AZKABUM! I SHALL BE TAKING BACK MY JULIET!!
Class B's play was a stunning success!!
Jiro's soulful vocals!!
Obstacle course!!
Haunted house!!
Crepe stall!!
WEIRD...
A surprise from Midoriya!!
Even a beauty pageant!
Thank you, School Festival!!
Hado seemed really glad to win her final beauty pageant.

# Newcomer!

## Class A vs. Class B

PERSONA CORDS!

CLIK

Ah... Persona Cords. A sound to stir the very soul.

### MATCH 1

| A | | B |
|---|---|---|
| ASUI | | SHIOZAKI |
| KODA | | SHISHIDA |
| KIRISHIMA | VS | RIN |
| KAMINARI | | TSUBURABA |
| SHINSO | | |

## Class B's fierce assault shaped the battle!!

### Standing up to Shishida's sheer power!

KRIK

Even those two couldn't stop him? Shishida's terrifying...

### Kaminari's decoy strategy!

DING DING DING! LEMME TELL YOU WHAT YOU'VE WON!

YANK

Kaminari's electric attacks have really wide range. I wouldn't wanna go up against that.

GRRR. MATCH 1 ...GOES TO CLASS A AND SHINSO!!

I NEED TO GO PRO ON MY STRENGTHS ALONE.

R 99,999 YEARS

### BATTLE REPORT
**Class 1-A's Denki Kaminari**

We woulda lost real bad without Tsuyu and Shinso! I gotta learn to keep my wits about me during battle!!

### BATTLE REPORT
**Class 1-B's Ibara Shiozaki**

Our lack of leadership was exploited in a monumental way. I must devote myself to improvement...

## Winner Class A

THIS'S HOW I WORK.

SCHEMING HERO: VANTABLACK

GRAB

...IS SCOPE US OUT!

**Tokoyami was the early bird!**

JIII

## MATCH 2

| A | | B |
|---|---|---|
| YAOYOROZU | | KENDO |
| TOKOYAMI | VS | KUROIRO |
| HAGAKURE | | KOMORI |
| AOYAMA | | FUKIDASHI |

**Kuroiro, lurking in darkness!**

Kuroiro's Quirk-powered tactics...were quite troublesome.

IT'S A HUMIDIFIER! THE SHROOMS ARE GROWING OUTTA CONTROL!

POP POP POP

The mushrooms revealed Hagakure's location!

**A humid mushroom festival!**

**Strat versus Strat!**

Komori's terrifying ultimate move involves making mushrooms sprout from people's orifices.

BLEH

SORRRRY! I KEPT THOSE UNDER WRAPS BECAUSE THEY'RE NOT AS CUTE.

BUT IF WE'RE ABOUT TO LOSE... THEN I GUESS I HAVE NO OTHER OPTION.

**Scary splitgill spores attack the lungs!**

**A battle about out-maneuvering the enemy!!**

KAPOW WHAP POW KRAK POW MIYAHHH!!

**Hagakure strikes back with a vengeance!**

Check out those punches! Without Kendo, Fukidashi woulda been in real trouble.

IT'S KINDA HARD TO GET AROUND WITH THIS.

AND TIED ME TO HER CANNON.

KRR KRR

**BATTLE REPORT**
Class 1-A's
Momo Yaoyorozu

We lost this battle. I am still an inexperienced fool who must hone her Quirk!!

**BATTLE REPORT**
Class 1-B's
Itsuka Kendo

Sure, we won this match, but she read my strategy so well that it kinda feels like I lost...

**Winner** Class **B**

Did Ida get even faster?! My eyes can barely keep up!

Same old ice blast? Weak stuff.

**MATCH 3**

| A | | B |
|---|---|---|
| TODOROKI | VS | TETSUTETSU |
| IDA | | HONENUKI |
| SHOJI | | TSUNOTORI |
| OJIRO | | KAIBARA |

Covering the battlefield with ice in a flash!

Invading enemy territory at top speed!

Spiral's regrets...

If only Ida hadn't interfered... Walk it off, Kaibara.

RAISE YOUR BODY HEAT RIGHT UP TO THE LIMIT!

Dupli-Arms versus Horn Cannon!

Surpassing limits and never budging in close combat!!

All those attacks, zip-zooping around! I couldn't tell what was going on!!

BUT THEY'RE NOT TECHNICALLY OUT OF THE GAME UNTIL THEY'RE THROWN IN PRISON!

ALL FIGHTERS ARE DOWN FOR THE COUNT!

**BATTLE REPORT**
**Class 1-A's Shoto Todoroki**

I tend to start off with a big ice blast—it's a habit that's hard to shake. I really have to use my fire too.

**BATTLE REPORT**
**Class 1-B's Juzo Honenuki**

We could have won this match if I hadn't left Ida to his devices when I ran off to aid Tetsutetsu and the others.

Draw!!

124

Tokage's strategy to break her body into many pieces is very reliable!

Seek them out via sound!

Jiro is so good at searching for foes...

YES. IT'S ALL OVER NOW.

Tokage's sneak attack!

MATCH 4

| A | | VS | | B |
|---|---|---|---|---|
| BAKUGO | | | TOKAGE | |
| JIRO | | | AWASE | |
| SERO | | | KAMAKIRI | |
| SATO | | | BONDO | |

The tenacious members of class B!

WELDCRAFT!!

JOB. COMPLETE!!

un-expected team-work...

That ultimate move is quick and has real holding power. I wouldn't mind having him on our side.

Unstoppable advance!

Bakugo... Strong. Bondo is haunted by that instant defeat.

BUT NOW I'M FINALLY STARTING TO HEAT UP!

...over-whelmed the quirky class B team!!

TO SURPASS ALL MIGHT AND BE THE NUMBER ONE HERO!

TWITCH

DURRR

**BATTLE REPORT**
Class 1-A's
**Kyoka Jiro**

I was anxious about this fight at first, but when Bakugo's your ally, you can actually count on the guy!

**BATTLE REPORT**
Class 1-B's
**Setsuna Tokage**

Our strategy was too rigid. Not adaptable enough. I'm sorry for making my teammates look bad like that.

Winner Class A

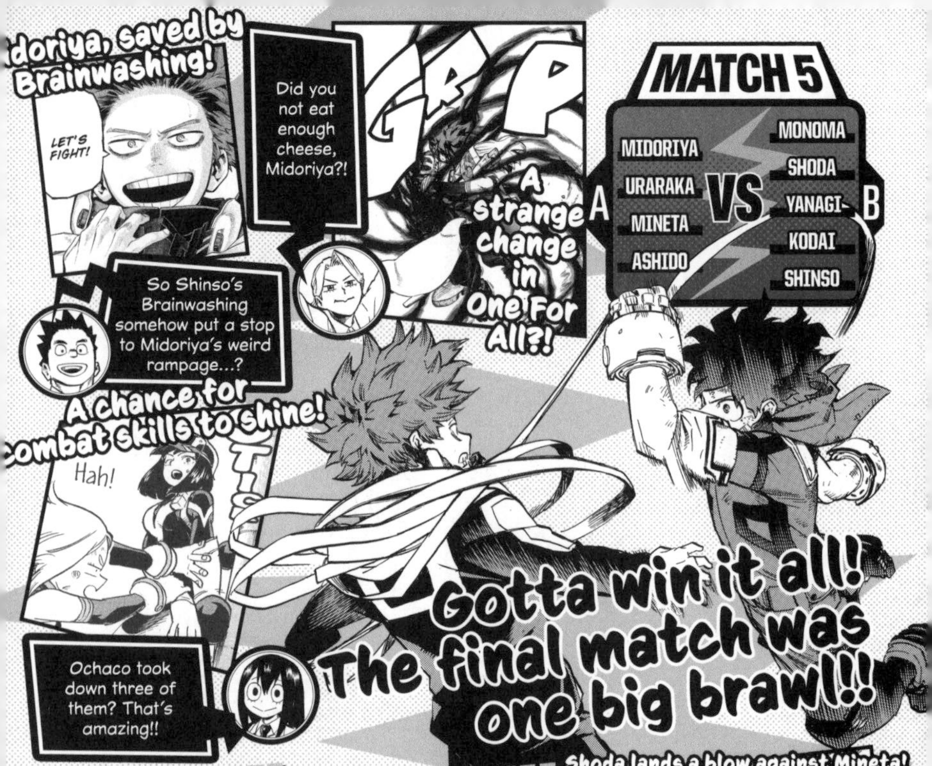
Midoriya, saved by Brainwashing!
LET'S FIGHT!
Did you not eat enough cheese, Midoriya?!
A strange change in One For All?!
MATCH 5
A
MIDORIYA
URARAKA
MINETA
ASHIDO
VS
B
MONOMA
SHODA
YANAGI
KODAI
SHINSO
So Shinso's Brainwashing somehow put a stop to Midoriya's weird rampage...?
A chance for combat skills to shine!
Hah!
Ochaco took down three of them? That's amazing!!
Gotta win it all! The final match was one big brawl!!

**BATTLE REPORT**
**Class 1-C's Hitoshi Shinso**

I faced this challenge with all at my disposal, but I still came up short, by my own standards.

**BATTLE REPORT**
**Class 1-A's Izuku Midoriya**

I never expected my Quirk to go wild like that... I'll have to work hard to get it under my control.

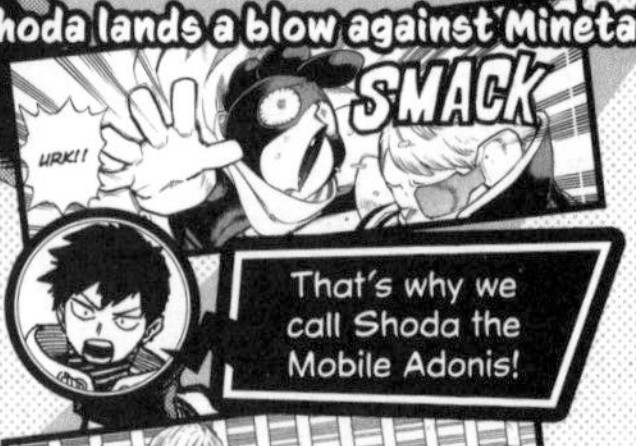
Shoda lands a blow against Mineta!
SMACK
URK!!
That's why we call Shoda the Mobile Adonis!

## MATCH RESULTS

| | | | |
|---|---|---|---|
| Match 1 | A | W–L | B |
| Match 2 | A | L–W | B |
| Match 3 | A | DRAW! | B |
| Match 4 | A | W–L | B |
| Match 5 | A | W–L | B |

**Class A wins it all!**

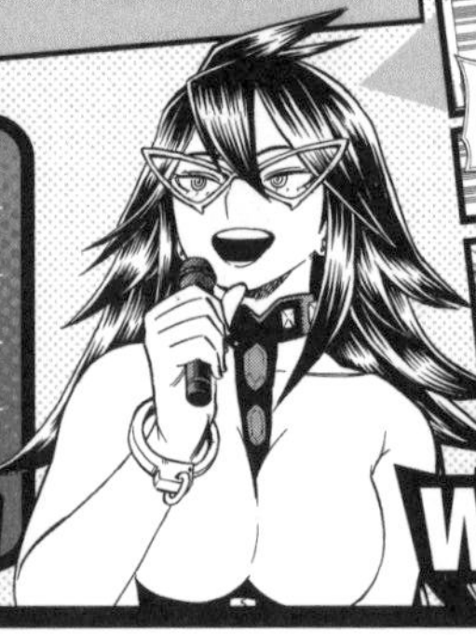

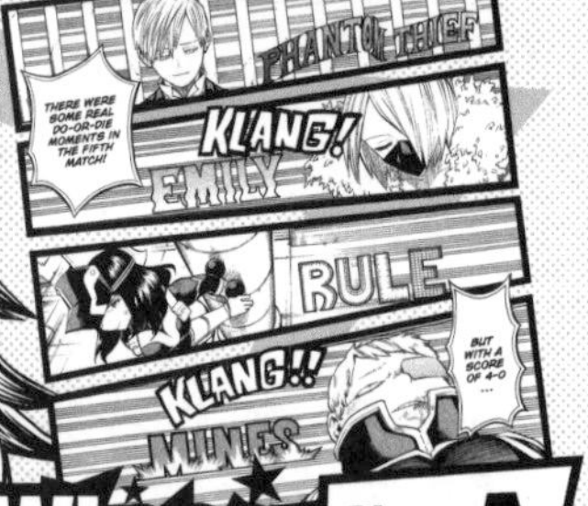
THERE WERE SOME REAL DO-OR-DIE MOMENTS IN THE FIFTH MATCH!
PHANTOM THIEF
KLANG!
EMILY
RULE
BUT WITH A SCORE OF 4-0 ...
KLANG!!
MINES

**Winner Class A**

## Comments

Class A may have won, but you guys have plenty of room for improvement in many regards. There are no take-backs or redos for pros when it really counts, so you need to take the criticisms to heart and put in the effort. That's all from me.

Class B has come a long way in terms of strength and skill, but class A has you beat when it comes to quick decisions and adaptability. I believe that's what led to your downfall. That said, I'm excited to watch your progress!!

# 3rd EDITION

## NEW HEROES III

Introducing other capable members of the next generation, including U.A.'s Big Three third-years, members of General Studies and the Support Course, and students from other schools altogether.

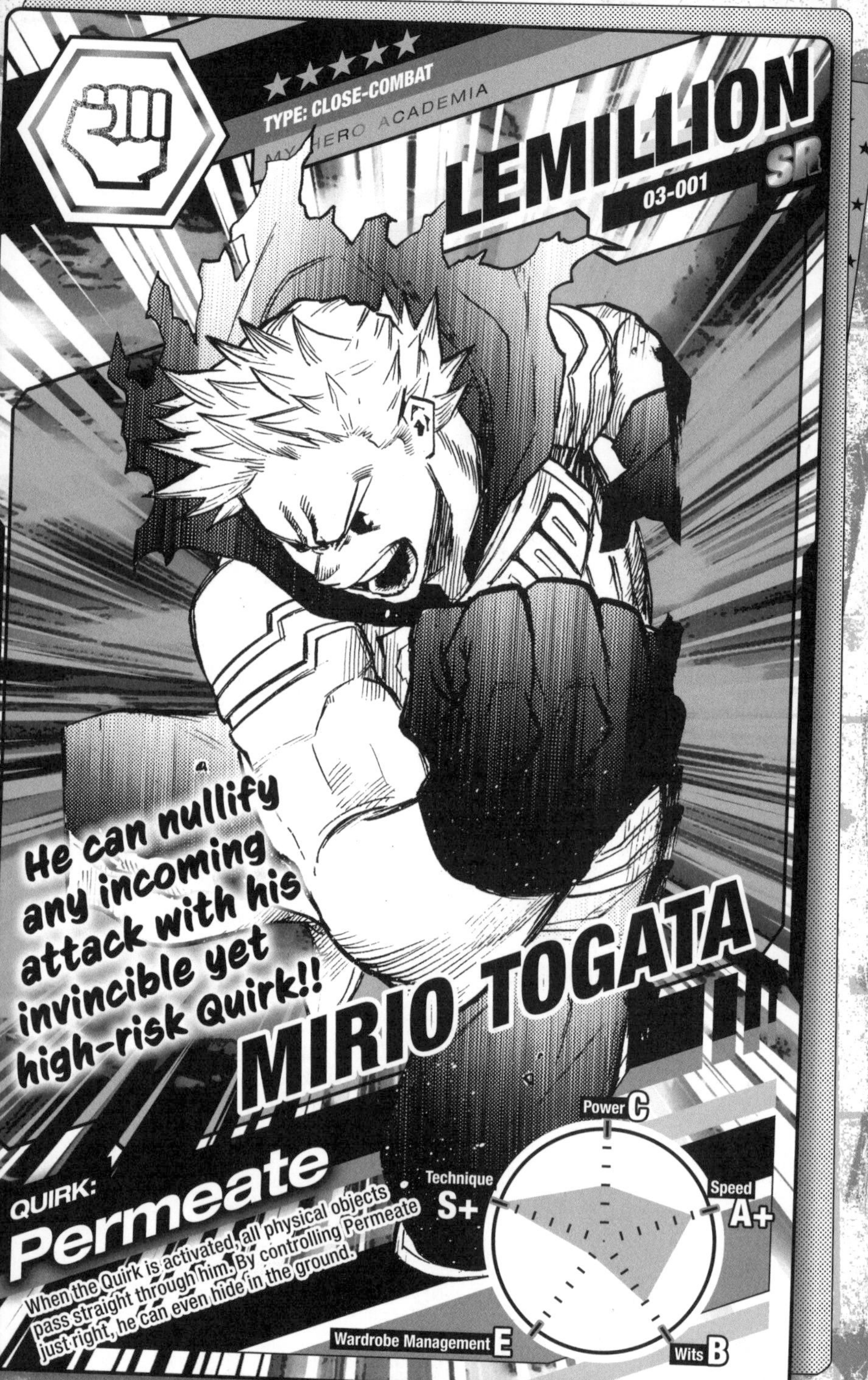
TYPE: CLOSE-COMBAT
MY HERO ACADEMIA
LEMILLION
SR
03-001
He can nullify any incoming attack with his invincible yet high-risk Quirk!!
MIRIO TOGATA
QUIRK:
Permeate
When the Quirk is activated, all physical objects pass straight through him. By controlling Permeate just right, he can even hide in the ground.
Power C
Technique S+
Speed A+
Wits B
Wardrobe Management E

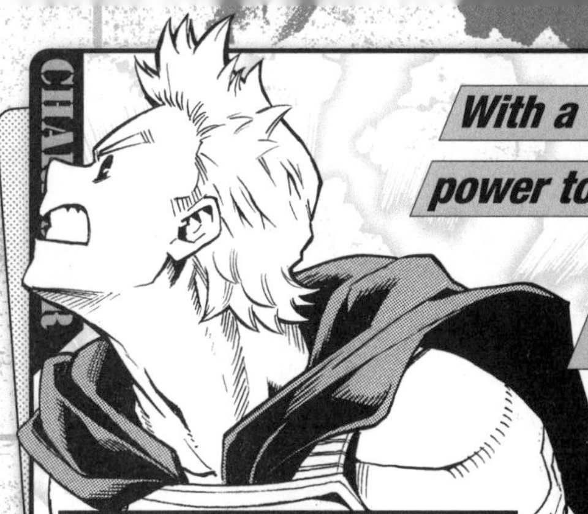

## *With a drive for justice and the power to back it up…he's the closes to being on par with the number one pro hero.*

Learning to control his Quirk was an uphill battle, and Togata was the unlikeliest hero candidate. Thanks to working under Sir Nighteye and putting in some good old-fashioned effort, he's become one of U.A.'s Big Three!! Unfortunately, Togata's Quirk was deleted during the battle with Overhaul. His signature "full moon" gag lost a good 70 percent of the fun factor after that.

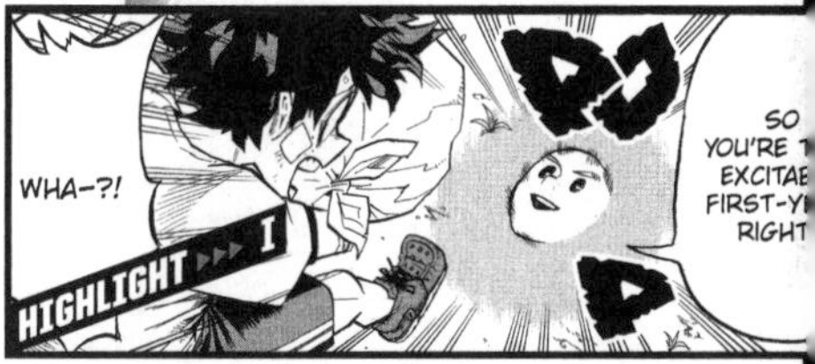
SO YOU'RE
WHA-?!
HIGHLIGHT ▸▸▸ I

⬆ Togata disables his Quirk only for the part of his body he wants exposed!! Supporting his whole body with his face is extremely painful, but hey—anything for a laugh!!

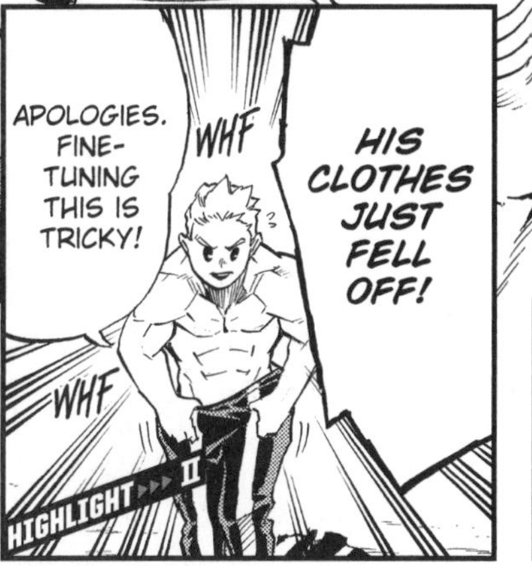
HIS CLOTHES JUST FELL OFF!
WHF
APOLOGIES. FINE-TUNING THIS IS TRICKY!
WHF
HIGHLIGHT ▸▸▸ II

⬆ When Togata's Quirk activates, everything passes straight through him. Even the clothes he's wearing…

## RELATIONSHIP

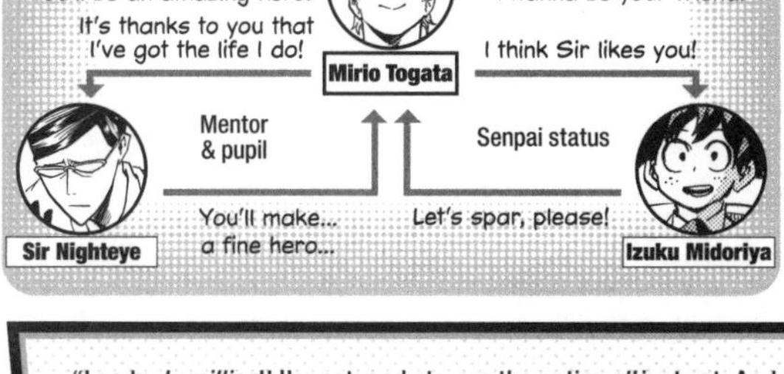
Tamaki Amajiki
I don't wanna lose to you!
Best buds & rivals
You'll be an amazing hero.
Eri
Let's see that smile.
Always hanging out
I wanna be your friend.
Mirio Togata
It's thanks to you that I've got the life I do!
Mentor & pupil
You'll make... a fine hero...
Sir Nighteye
I think Sir likes you!
Senpai status
Let's spar, please!
Izuku Midoriya

## PROFILE

Name: **Mirio Togata**
Hero name: **Lemillion**
Quirk: **Permeate**
Birthday: **July 15**
Height: **181 cm**
Blood type: **O**
Birthplace: **Chiba Prefecture**
Personality: **Sunny disposition**
Ultimate moves: **Blinder Touch Eyeball Crush, Phantom Menace**

- "I go by *Lemillion*!! I'm not ready to use the entire *all* just yet. And the *million* is because that's how many people I wanna save, someday!" (vol. 15, chap. 129)
- "Don't worry!! I'll be your hero!!" (vol. 17, chap. 150)
- "The reason heroes wear capes is to wrap up and protect little girls in pain!" (vol. 17, chap. 151)

**Togata's Notable Quotables**

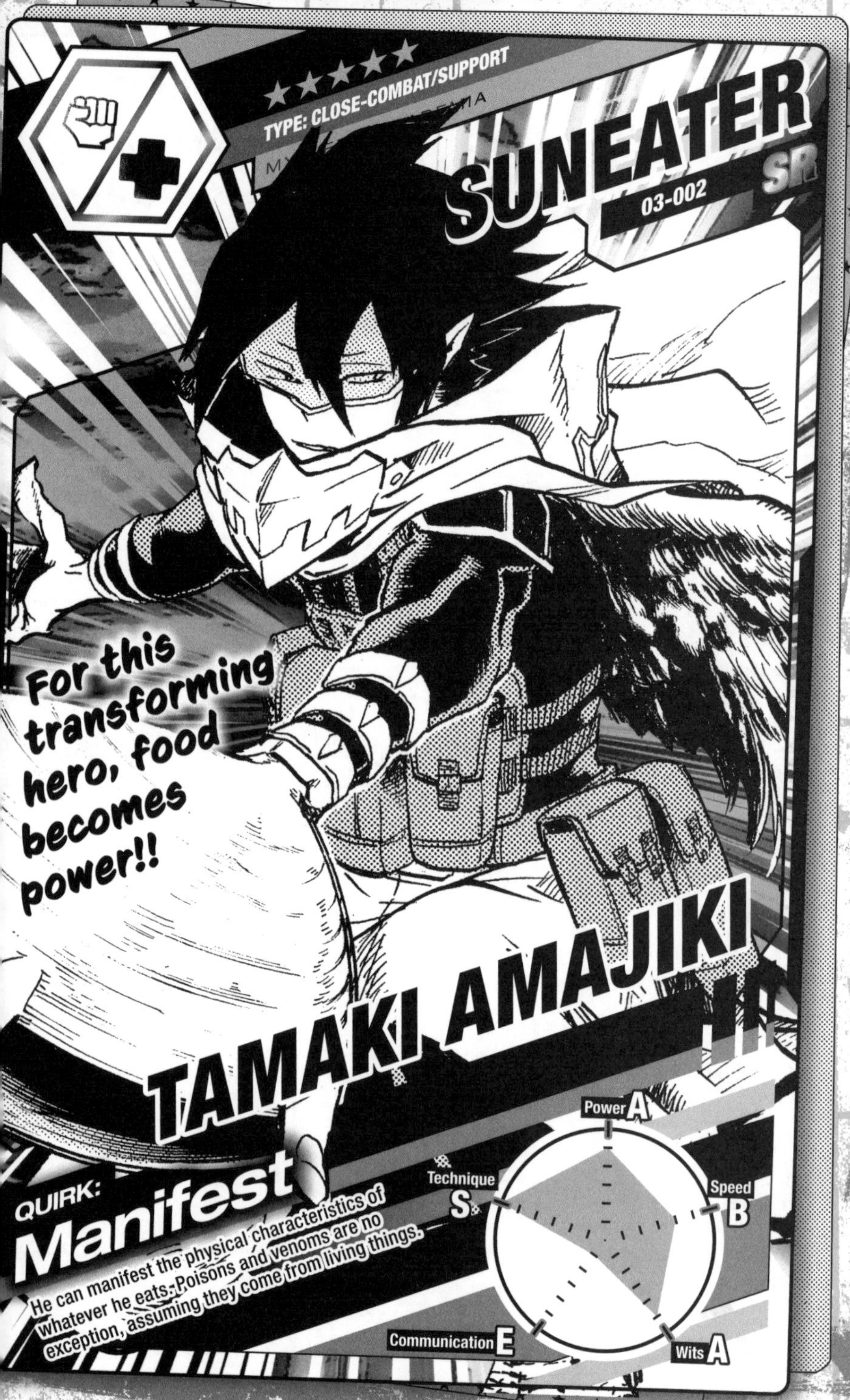
★★★★★★
TYPE: CLOSE-COMBAT/SUPPORT
SUNEATER
SR
03-002
For this transforming hero, food becomes power!!
TAMAKI AMAJIKI
QUIRK:
Manifest
He can manifest the physical characteristics of whatever he eats. Poisons and venoms are no exception, assuming they come from living things.
Power A
Technique S
Speed B
Communication E
Wits A

CHARACTER

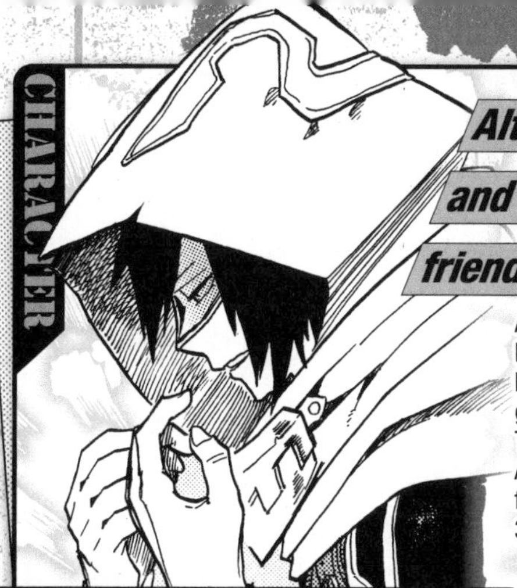

## Although marked by awkwardness and a weak psyche, he is Togata's friend and rival.

Amajiki's insecurity and nerves are matched only by his tendency to crumble under pressure. But he's been training his Quirk hard ever since getting into U.A., and he's become one of the Big Three. His own pro hero mentor, Fat Gum, thinks Amajiki's skills are better than most pros. He and fellow Big Three member Hado are both in class 3-A, while Togata is in class 3-B.

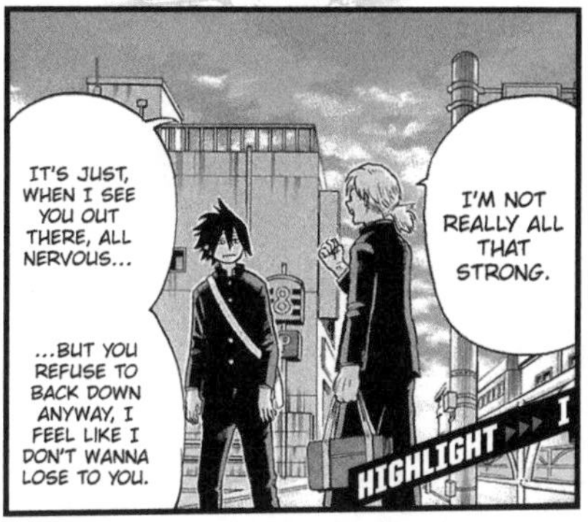
I'M NOT REALLY ALL THAT STRONG.
IT'S JUST, WHEN I SEE YOU OUT THERE, ALL NERVOUS...
...BUT YOU REFUSE TO BACK DOWN ANYWAY, I FEEL LIKE I DON'T WANNA LOSE TO YOU.
HIGHLIGHT ▸▸▸ I

⬆ Tamaki likens Togata—his polar opposite—to a bright and shining sun. In response, Togata dubs Amajiki "Suneater."

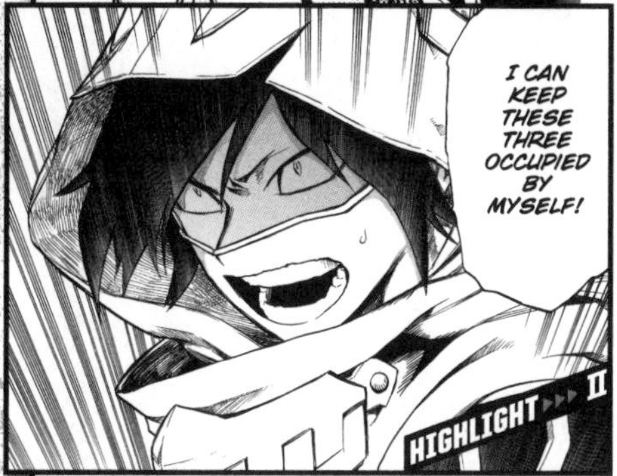
I CAN KEEP THESE THREE OCCUPIED BY MYSELF!
HIGHLIGHT ▸▸▸ II

⬆ Amajiki immediately decides to take on three Hassaikai goons! When his life is in real danger, he manages to conquer his own weakness.

## RELATIONSHIP

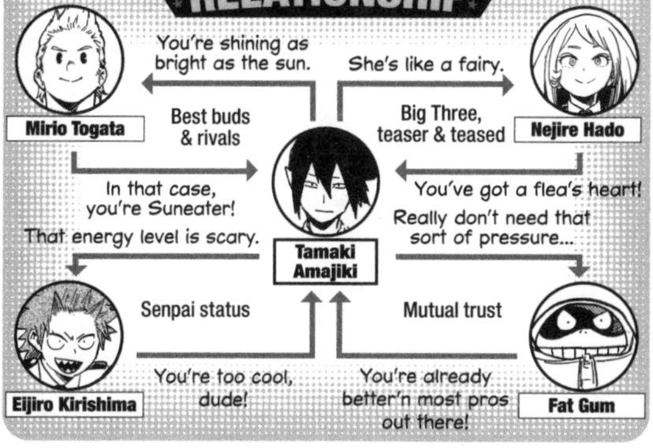
Mirio Togata
You're shining as bright as the sun.
Best buds & rivals
In that case, you're Suneater!
That energy level is scary.
Nejire Hado
She's like a fairy.
Big Three, teaser & teased
You've got a flea's heart!
Really don't need that sort of pressure...
Tamaki Amajiki
Eijiro Kirishima
Senpai status
You're too cool, dude!
Fat Gum
Mutual trust
You're already better'n most pros out there!

## PROFILE

Name: **Tamaki Amajiki**
Hero name: **Suneater**
Quirk: **Manifest**
Birthday: **March 4**
Height: **177 cm**
Blood type: **AB**
Birthplace: **Chiba Prefecture**
Personality: **Ultra Negative Man**
Ultimate move: **Vast Hybrid Chimera: Kraken**

- "That sort of pressure sends me spiraling even deeper." (vol. 15, chap. 132)
- "Give it up... Because I'm Suneater!" (vol. 16, chap. 140)
- "Help out Mirio! I just know...he's gonna take things too far and need saving." (vol. 16, chap. 140)

**Amajiki's Notable Quotables**

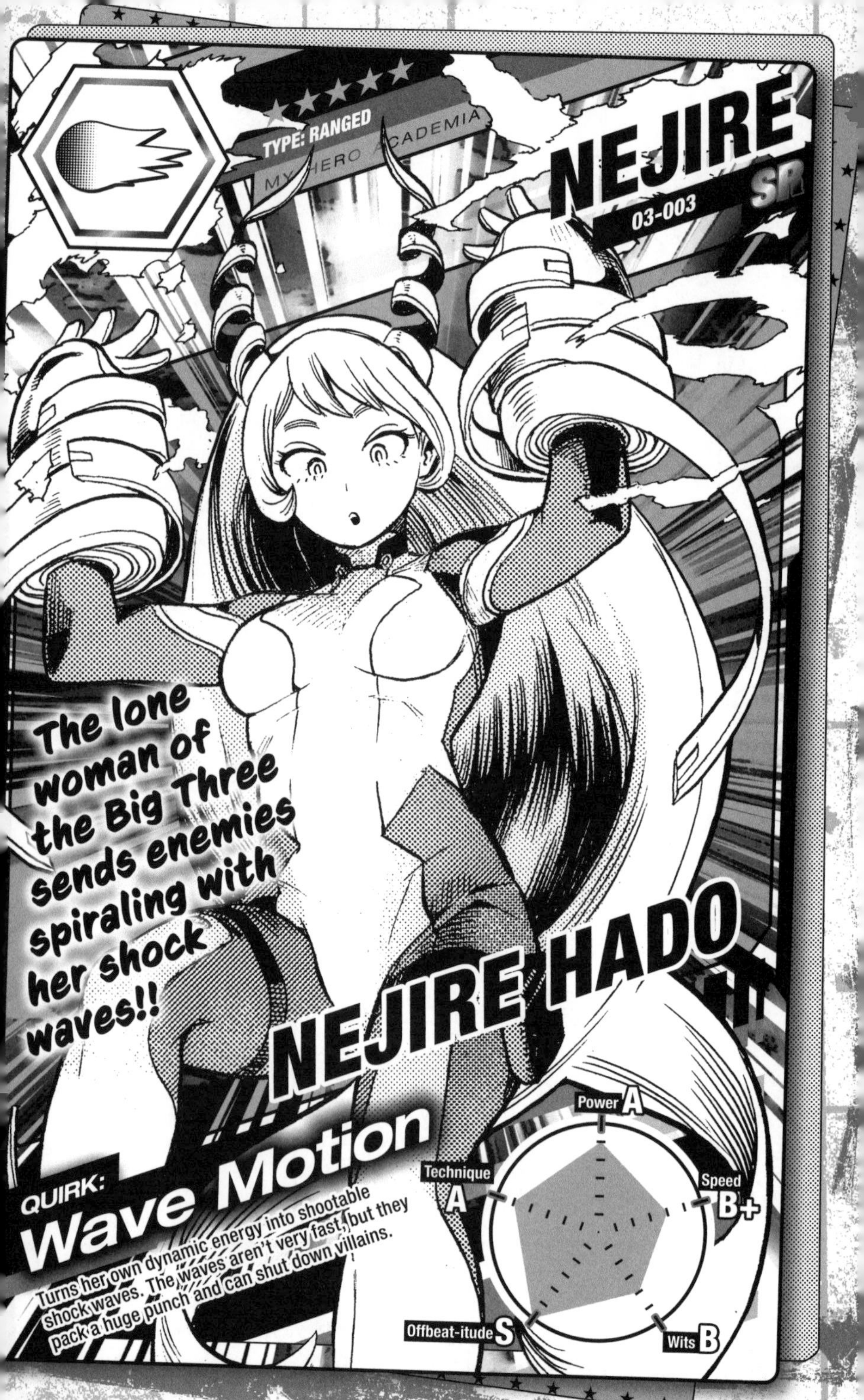
TYPE: RANGED
MY HERO ACADEMIA
NEJIRE
SR
03-003
The lone woman of the Big Three sends enemies spiraling with her shock waves!!
NEJIRE HADO
QUIRK:
Wave Motion
Turns her own dynamic energy into shootable shock waves. The waves aren't very fast, but they pack a huge punch and can shut down villains.
Power A
Technique A
Speed B+
Offbeat-itude S
Wits B

## Quirky and very curious, she'll ask every question that pops into her hea

Hado is in class 3-A with Amajiki and stands tall as the only female member of U.A.'s Big Three. She's innocent, a little naive, and full of curiosity, which leads her to ask some pretty blunt questions regarding whatever she happens to be wondering about. By fine-tuning her Quirk, Hado can launch unpredictable attacks.

➡ Hado had been defeated by Kenranzaki's ostentatious beauty, but during her third and final beauty pageant, she claimed victory in a very Hado-esque way.

SHE'S LIKE A PURE AND INNOCENT FAIRY...
WEIRD ...
HIGHLIGHT ▸▸▸ II

HEY, ASHIDO. IF YOU BROKE THOSE HORNS, WOULD THEY GROW BACK? CAN THEY MOVE?! TELL ME!
AND, MINETA, THOSE BALLS OF YOURS... IS IT HAIR?! HOW D'YOU GET A HAIRCUT?!
ARE YOU LIKE A TREE FROG, ASUI? OR MORE OF A TOAD?
SO MANY CURIOUS THINGS ABOUT ALL OF YOU! DOWNRIGHT CURIOUS.
HIGHLIGHT ▸▸▸ I

⬆ Her free-spirited, rapid-fire speech can leave others flustered. Hado will ask every question that occurs to her, and she isn't actually all too interested in answers.

## RELATIONSHIP

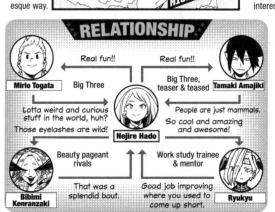

Mirio Togata
Real fun!!
Big Three
Lotta weird and curious stuff in the world, huh?
Tamaki Amajiki
Real fun!!
Big Three, teaser & teased
People are just mammals.
Those eyelashes are wild!
Nejire Hado
So cool and amazing and awesome!
Bibimi Kenranzaki
Beauty pageant rivals
That was a splendid bout.
Ryukyu
Work study trainee & mentor
Good job improving where you used to come up short.

## PROFILE

Name: **Nejire Hado**
Hero name: **Nejire**
Quirk: **Wave Motion**
Birthday: **October 6**
Height: **164 cm**
Blood type: **B**
Birthplace: **Akita Prefecture**
Personality: **Curiouser and curiouser**
Ultimate move: **Nejire Wave**

- "Listen, Amajiki! Isn't it funny that people call that having the heart of a flea? So weird!" (vol. 14, chap. 123)
- "Hey, hey, why're you fighting? Is it cuz you both have the same Quirk?" (vol. 15, chap. 131)
- "Dealing with big ones is tricky." (vol. 18, chap. 161)

**Hado's Notable Quotables**

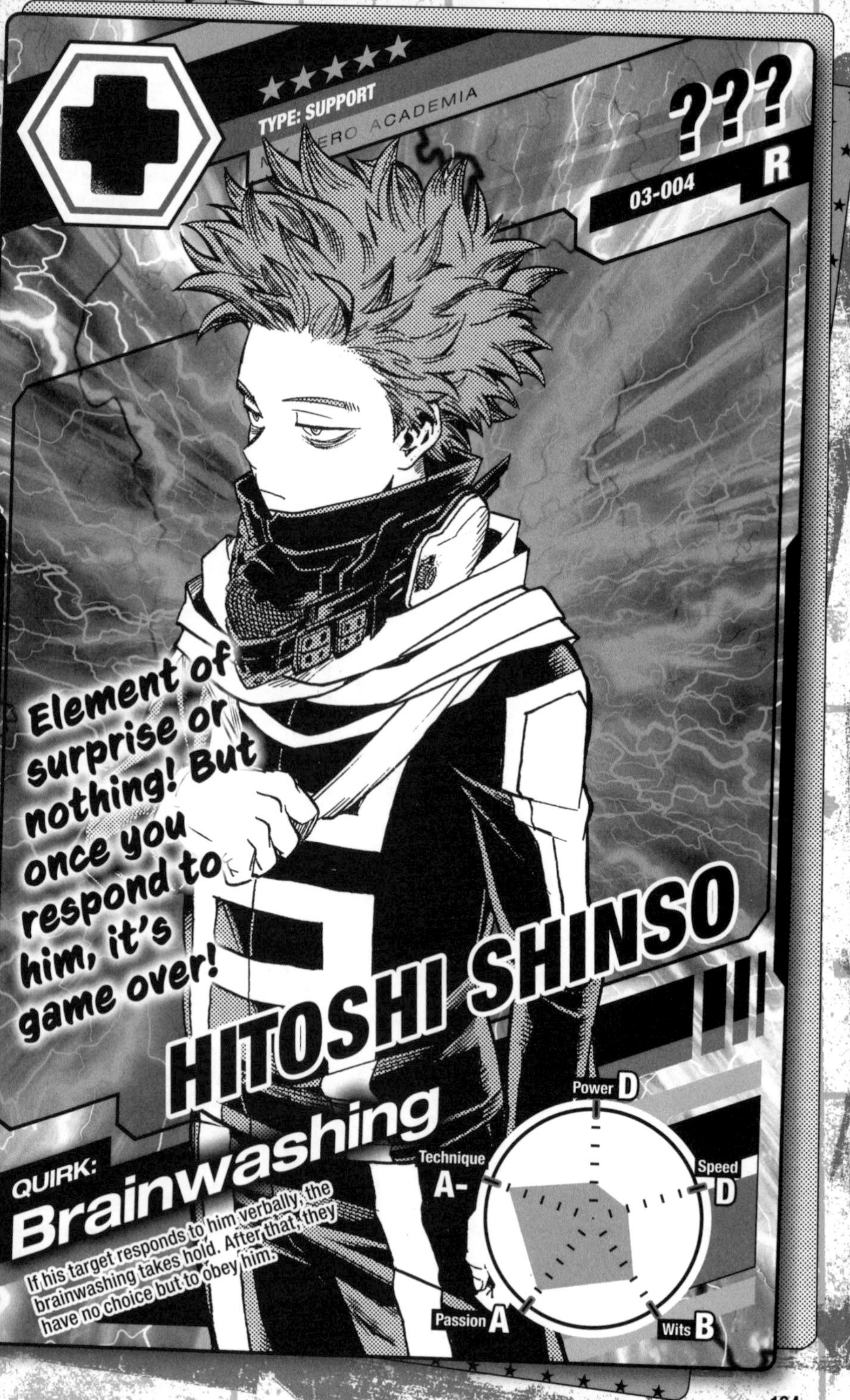

TYPE: SUPPORT
???
R
03-004
Element of surprise or nothing! But once you respond to him, it's game over!
HITOSHI SHINSO
QUIRK:
Brainwashing
If his target responds to him verbally, the brainwashing takes hold. After that, they have no choice but to obey him.
Power D
Technique A-
Speed D
Passion A
Wits B

CHARACTER

## Working on a Hero Course transfer!

## A candidate with a ton of passion!

Shinso is a General Studies student who dreams of joining the Hero Course. He didn't impress during the entrance exam, but after the Sports Festival, he was called the rising star of General Studies. He's been training under Eraser Head ever since, and at this point, his transfer is basically a sure bet. He doesn't know that his current classmates are planning a send-off party.

SLAM
BINDING CLOTH!!
HIGHLIGHT ▸▸▸ I

➡ During the class-versus-class battles, Shinso showed off Eraser Head's binding cloth, passed from mentor to mentee.

HIGHLIGHT ▸▸▸ II
I'M NOT THE TYPE...
...FOR DISPLAYS OF GOOD SPORTSMANSHIP LIKE THAT. I'M ALREADY SO FAR BEHIND YOU ALL...
I'M DOING EVERYTHING I CAN TO CATCH UP.

⬆ Shinso is getting a much later start than the others, and he understands that the path he seeks to tread won't be an easy one.

## RELATIONSHIP

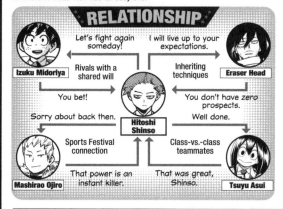

Let's fight again someday!
I will live up to your expectations.
Izuku Midoriya
Rivals with a shared will
Inheriting techniques
Eraser Head
You bet!
You don't have zero prospects.
Sorry about back then.
Hitoshi Shinso
Well done.
Sports Festival connection
Class-vs.-class teammates
That power is an instant killer.
That was great, Shinso.
Mashirao Ojiro
Tsuyu Asui

## PROFILE

Name: **Hitoshi Shinso**
Hero name: **Undecided**
Quirk: **Brainwashing**
Birthday: **July 1**
Height: **177 cm**
Blood type: **AB**
Birthplace: **Saitama Prefecture**
Personality: **Stoic**
Ultimate moves: **Persona Cords, Eraser Head's Binding Cloth**

- "If you've got any kind of vision for your future, there's no sense in worrying about how you get there." (vol. 4, chap. 32)
- "Even with this Quirk of mine, I've still got dreams." (vol. 4, chap. 33)
- "You wouldn't get that. You're naturally blessed. You people…born with your awesome Quirks… Getting to follow all your dreams!" (vol. 4, chap. 33)
- "I'll be a great hero someday and strive to use my Quirk to help people." (vol. 21, chap. 195)

**Shinso's Notable Quotables**

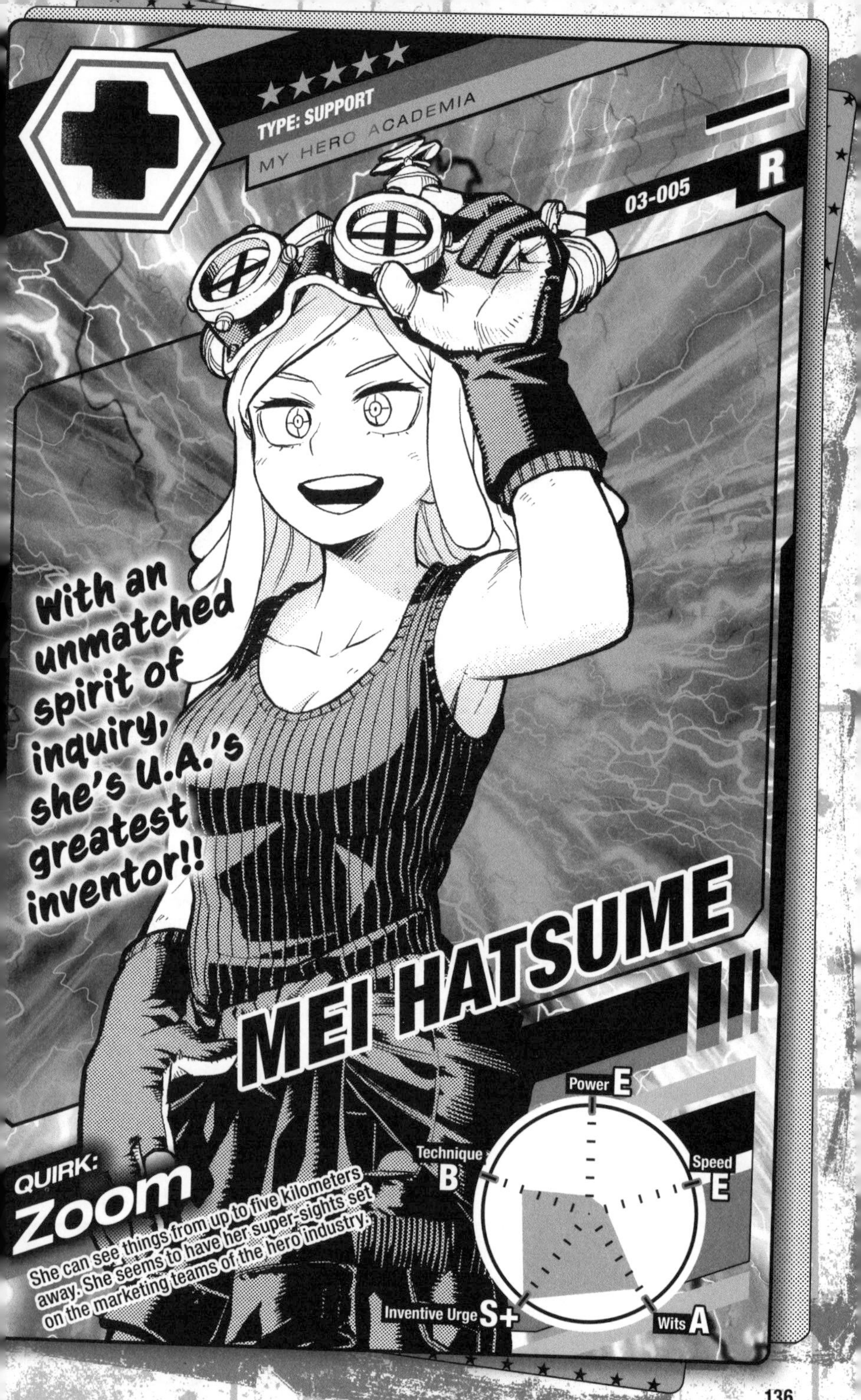
TYPE: SUPPORT
MY HERO ACADEMIA
R
03-005
With an unmatched spirit of inquiry, she's U.A.'s greatest inventor!!
MEI HATSUME
Power E
Technique B
Speed E
Wits A
Inventive Urge S+
QUIRK:
Zoom
She can see things from up to five kilometers away. She seems to have her super-sights set on the marketing teams of the hero industry.

## Now with over 200 "babies"!

## She's holed up in the studio every day.

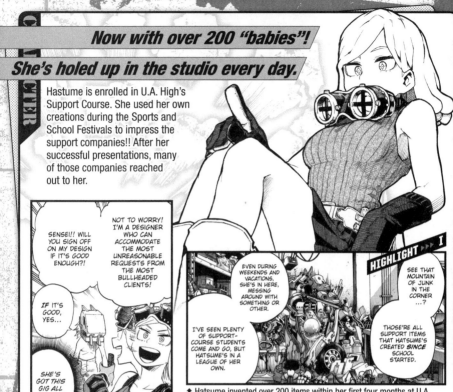

Hastume is enrolled in U.A. High's Support Course. She used her own creations during the Sports and School Festivals to impress the support companies!! After her successful presentations, many of those companies reached out to her.

HIGHLIGHT ▸▸▸ I
SEE THAT MOUNTAIN OF JUNK IN THE CORNER ...?
THOSE'RE ALL SUPPORT ITEMS THAT HATSUME'S CREATED *SINCE* SCHOOL STARTED.
EVEN DURING WEEKENDS AND VACATIONS, SHE'S IN HERE, MESSING AROUND WITH SOMETHING OR OTHER.
I'VE SEEN PLENTY OF SUPPORT-COURSE STUDENTS COME AND GO, BUT HATSUME'S IN A LEAGUE OF HER OWN.

⬆ Hatsume invented over 200 items within her first four months at U.A. While that's certainly impressive, a massive number of unfinished items have been abandoned in a heap.

NOT TO WORRY! I'M A DESIGNER WHO CAN ACCOMMODATE THE MOST UNREASONABLE REQUESTS FROM THE MOST BULLHEADED CLIENTS!
SENSEI!! WILL YOU SIGN OFF ON MY DESIGN IF IT'S GOOD ENOUGH?!
*IF* IT'S GOOD, YES...
SHE'S GOT THIS GIG ALL FIGURED OUT!
HIGHLIGHT ▸▸▸ II

⬅ Hatsume takes pride in her role as a creator. When it comes to the wellspring of ideas inside her, she doesn't have a pause button!

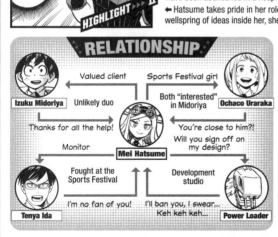

RELATIONSHIP
Izuku Midoriya
Valued client
Unlikely duo
Thanks for all the help!
Ochaco Uraraka
Sports Festival girl
Both "interested" in Midoriya
You're close to him?!
Mei Hatsume
Monitor
Will you sign off on my design?
Tenya Ida
Fought at the Sports Festival
I'm no fan of you!
Power Loader
Development studio
I'll ban you, I swear... Keh keh keh...

## PROFILE

Name: **Mei Hatsume**
Hero name: **None**
Quirk: **Zoom**
Birthday: **April 18**
Height: **157 cm**
Blood type: **O**
Birthplace: **Kyoto Prefecture**
Personality: **Undaunted challenger**
Ultimate move: **Trial and error**

- "Take a look, all you national support companies!!" (vol. 3, chap. 25)
- "I don't know you, but I could be useful to someone in your position." (vol. 4, chap. 27)
- "I'm a designer who can accommodate the most unreasonable requests from the most bullheaded clients!" (vol. 12, chap. 102)
- "Those industry bigwigs are gonna get an up-close-and-personal look at my babies! I've gotta raise them right to do their momma proud!" (vol. 19, chap. 173)

**Hatsume's Notable Quotables**

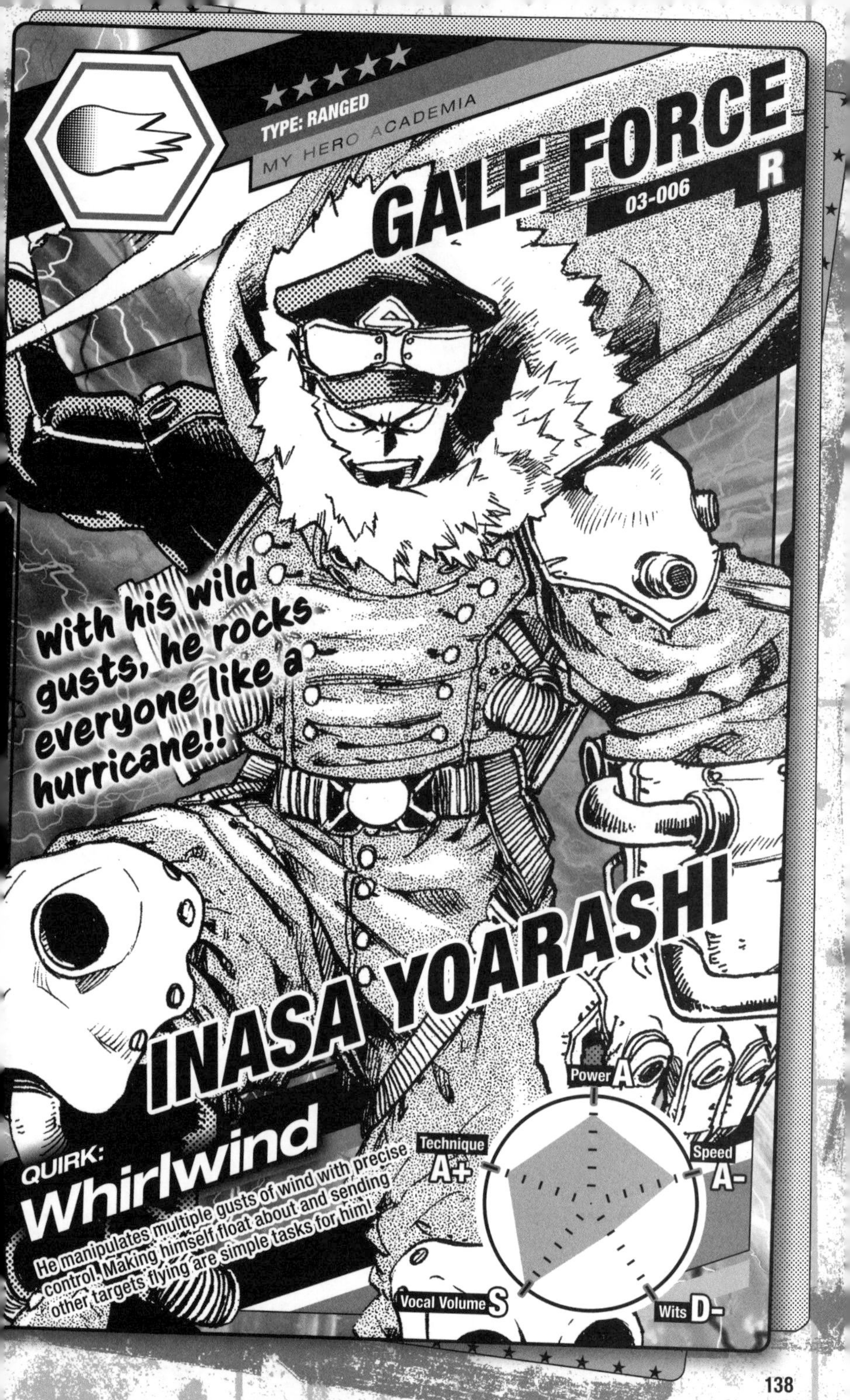

TYPE: RANGED
MY HERO ACADEMIA
GALE FORCE
03-006
R
With his wild gusts, he rocks everyone like a hurricane!!
INASA YOARASHI
QUIRK:
Whirlwind
He manipulates multiple gusts of wind with precise control. Making himself float about and sending other targets flying are simple tasks for him!
Power A
Technique A+
Speed A-
Vocal Volume S
Wits D-

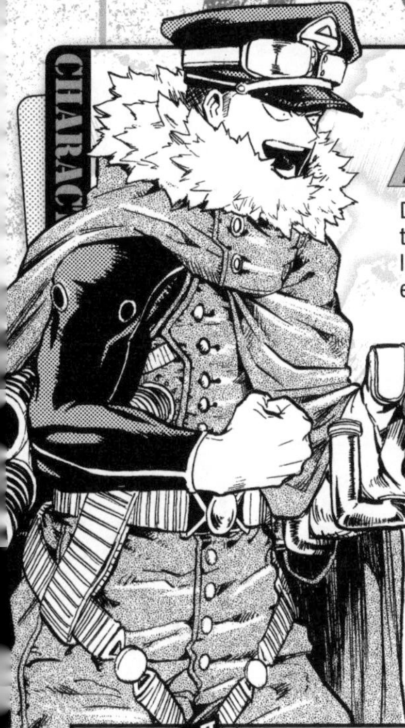

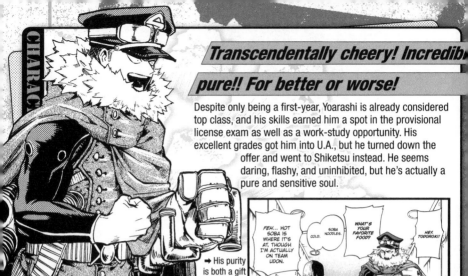

## Transcendentally cheery! Incredib
## pure!! For better or worse!

Despite only being a first-year, Yoarashi is already considered top class, and his skills earned him a spot in the provisional license exam as well as a work-study opportunity. His excellent grades got him into U.A., but he turned down the offer and went to Shiketsu instead. He seems daring, flashy, and uninhibited, but he's actually a pure and sensitive soul.

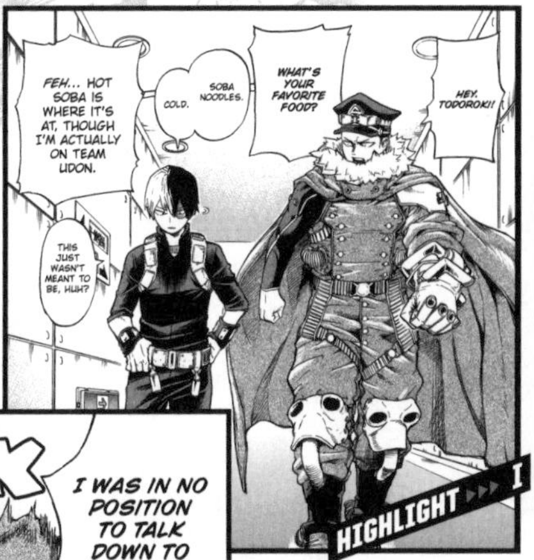
HEY. TODOROKI!!
WHAT'S YOUR FAVORITE FOOD?
SOBA NOODLES.
COLD.
FEH... HOT SOBA IS WHERE IT'S AT, THOUGH I'M ACTUALLY ON TEAM UDON.
THIS JUST WASN'T MEANT TO BE, HUH?
HIGHLIGHT ▸▸▸ I

➡ His purity is both a gift and a curse, to the extent that even elementary school kids can see through him.

⬅ After ending his grudge against Todoroki, he has tried to force an unlikely friendship.

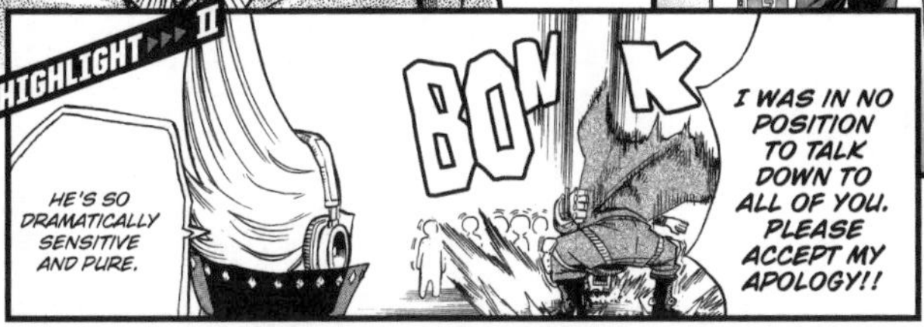
HIGHLIGHT ▸▸▸ II
I WAS IN NO POSITION TO TALK DOWN TO ALL OF YOU. PLEASE ACCEPT MY APOLOGY!!
HE'S SO DRAMATICALLY SENSITIVE AND PURE.

## RELATIONSHIP

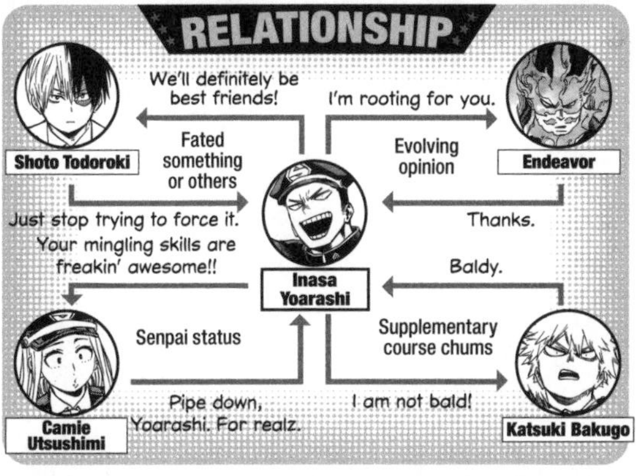
Shoto Todoroki
We'll definitely be best friends!
Fated something or others
Just stop trying to force it. Your mingling skills are freakin' awesome!!
Endeavor
I'm rooting for you.
Evolving opinion
Thanks.
Inasa Yoarashi
Camie Utsushimi
Senpai status
Pipe down, Yoarashi. For realz.
Katsuki Bakugo
Baldy.
Supplementary course chums
I am not bald!

## PROFILE

Name: **Inasa Yoarashi**
Hero name: **Gale Force**
Quirk: **Whirlwind**
Birthday: **September 26**
Height: **190 cm**
Blood type: **B**
Birthplace: **Yamanashi Prefecture**
Personality: **Stupidly straightforward**
Ultimate moves: **Slicing Gust: Fury, Mountain Haze: Majesty**

- "I just always wanted to try saying it!! Plus Ultra!! I freakin' love U.A. High!!" (vol. 12, chap. 102)
- "I believe heroes should be hot-blooded!! So good job with this hot-blooded battle, guys! I freakin' love it!!" (vol. 12, chap. 104)
- "A villain incursion, is it?! What a heated turn of events they've decided to go with!!" (vol. 13, chap. 111)

**Yoarashi's Notable Quotables**

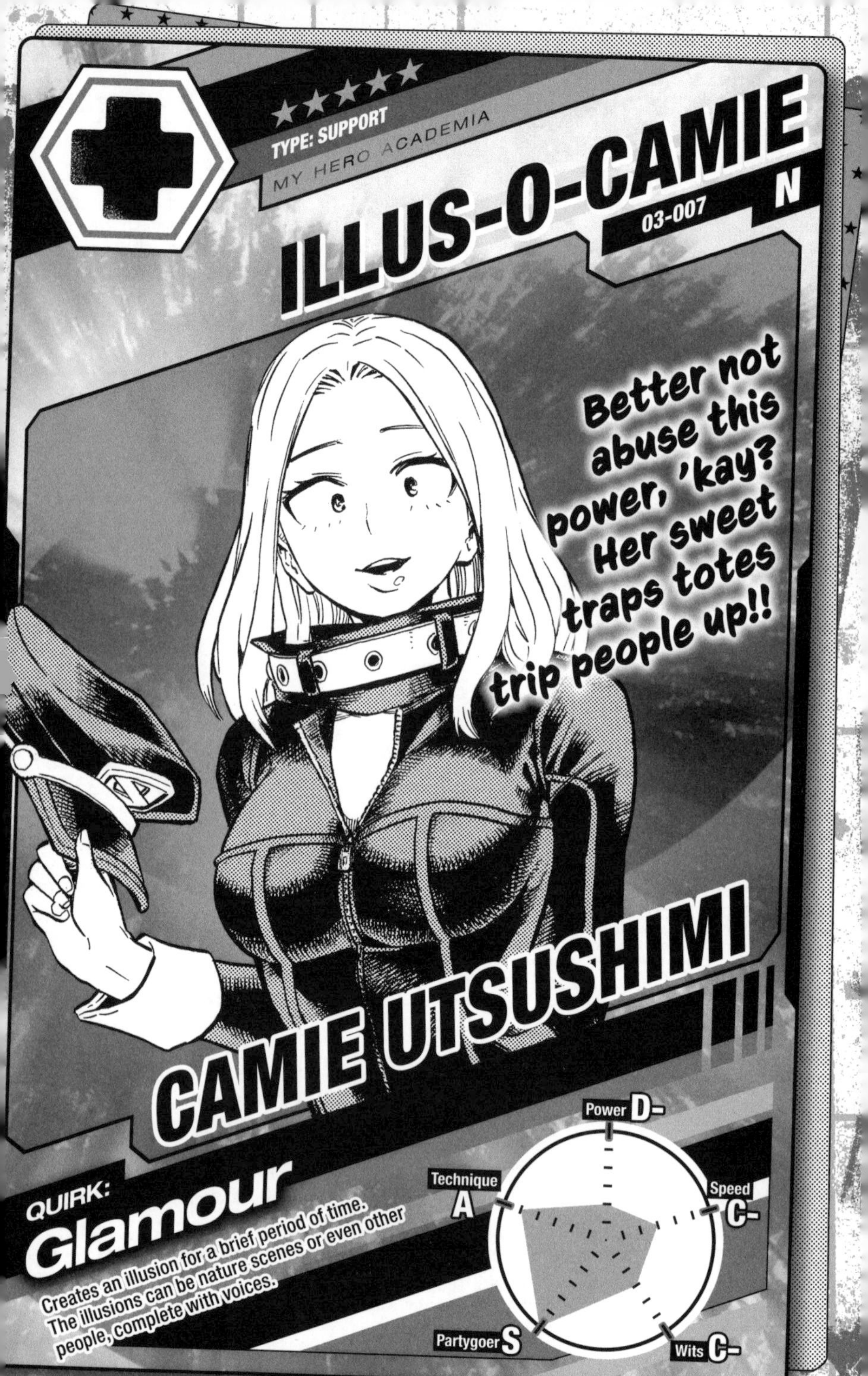
TYPE: SUPPORT
MY HERO ACADEMIA
ILLUS-O-CAMIE
03-007
N
Better not abuse this power, 'kay? Her sweet traps totes trip people up!!
CAMIE UTSUSHIMI
QUIRK:
Glamour
Creates an illusion for a brief period of time. The illusions can be nature scenes or even other people, complete with voices.
Power D-
Speed C-
Wits C-
Partygoer S
Technique A

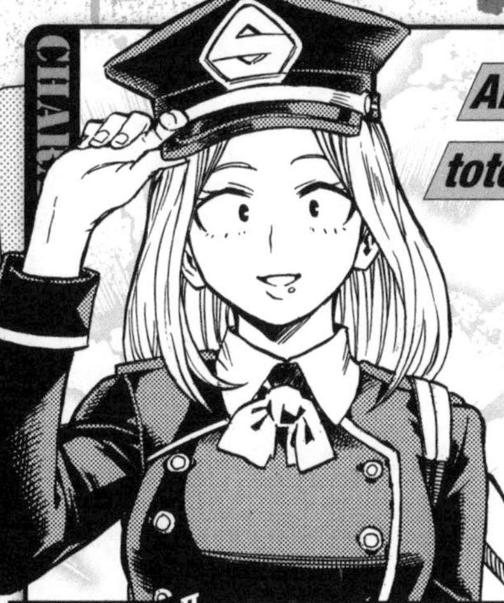

## Armed with modern slang, she's totes hoping to become a hero.

She lives in her own world and doesn't know the meaning of code-switching, which can result in misunderstandings! When the League of Villains—fearing further investigation by the authorities—kidnapped Utsushimi, Himiko Toga purposely made use of her, knowing that she would be slow to realize what had happened, thereby delaying the investigation. Utsushimi was targeted due to her airheaded nature, as it suited Toga's goals.

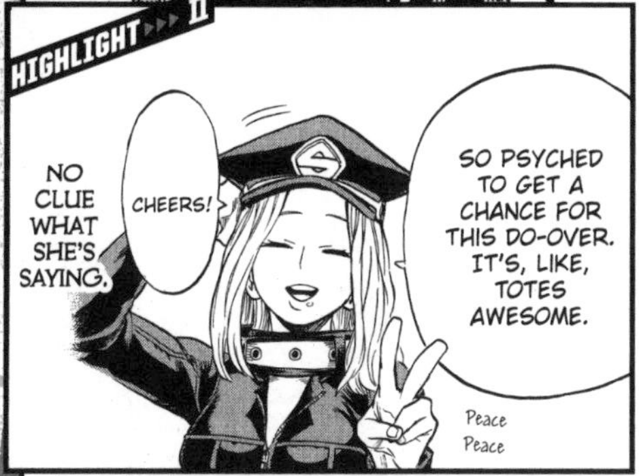
HIGHLIGHT ▸▸▸ II
SO PSYCHED TO GET A CHANCE FOR THIS DO-OVER. IT'S, LIKE, TOTES AWESOME.
CHEERS!
NO CLUE WHAT SHE'S SAYING.
Peace
Peace

⬆ Utsushimi constantly slips modern slang into her conversations with anyone and everyone. When she overdoes it, people lose track of what she's saying.

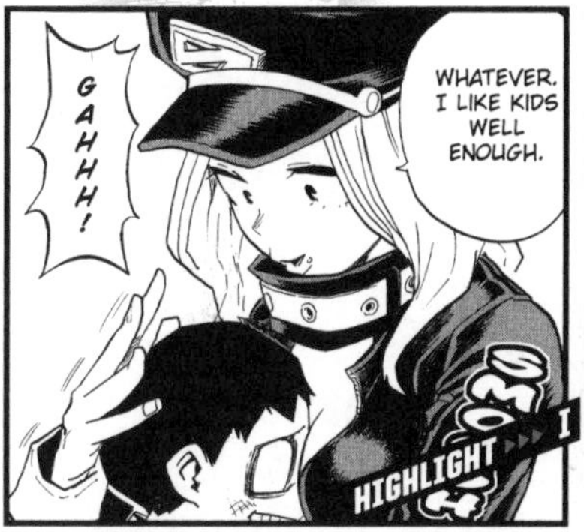
WHATEVER. I LIKE KIDS WELL ENOUGH.
GAHHH!
HIGHLIGHT ▸▸▸ I

⬆ Utsushimi isn't big on boundaries, which helped her win over some of the children quite easily. She uses her communication skills as a weapon.

## RELATIONSHIP

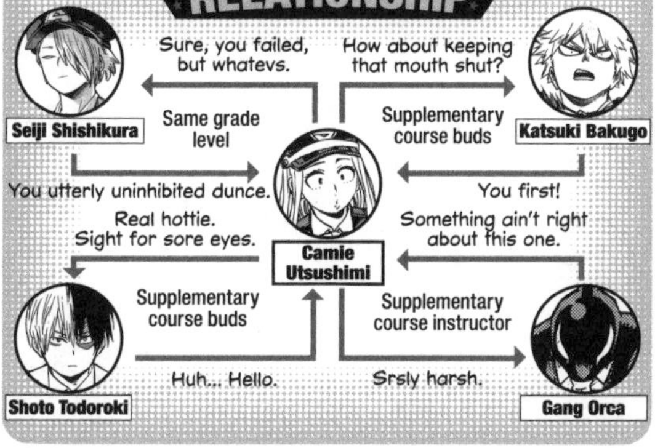
Camie Utsushimi
Seiji Shishikura
Sure, you failed, but whatevs.
Same grade level
You utterly uninhibited dunce.
Katsuki Bakugo
How about keeping that mouth shut?
Supplementary course buds
You first!
Shoto Todoroki
Real hottie. Sight for sore eyes.
Supplementary course buds
Huh... Hello.
Gang Orca
Something ain't right about this one.
Supplementary course instructor
Srsly harsh.

## PROFILE

Name: **Camie Utsushimi**
Hero name: **Illus-o-Camie**
Quirk: **Glamour**
Birthday: **August 15**
Height: **161 cm**
Blood type: **O**
Birthplace: **Saitama Prefecture**
Personality: **Uninhibited dummy**
Ultimate moves: **Doppelviber, High-Key Mirage**

## Utsushimi's Notable Quotables

- "You've got some nerve." (vol. 18, chap. 164)
- "Nothing like a handsome dude to brighten my day." (vol. 18, chap. 165)
- "What's this? Shishikura's chatting with the symbol himself, All Might?" (vol. 18, chap. 167)

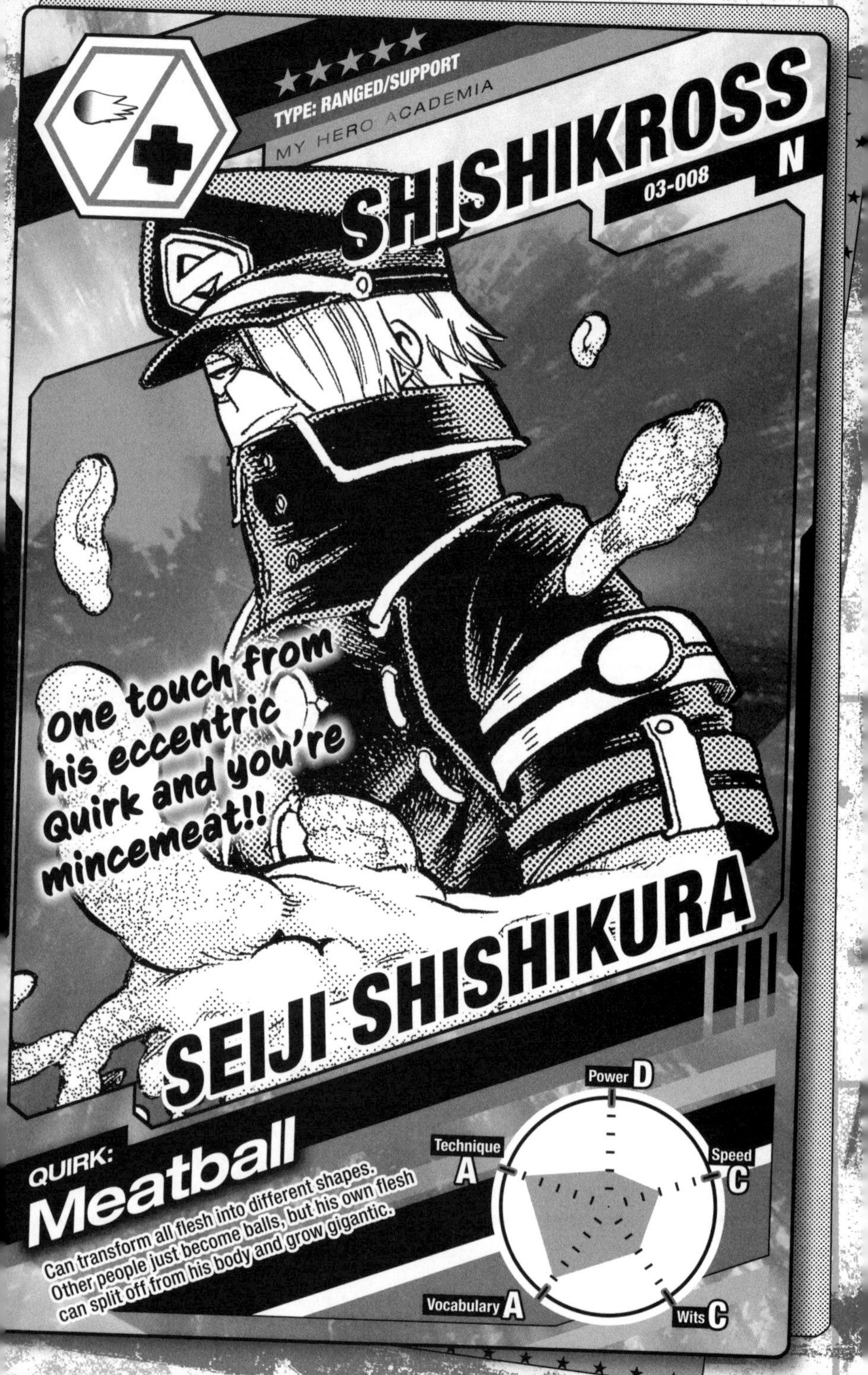
★★★★★
TYPE: RANGED/SUPPORT
MY HERO ACADEMIA
SHISHIKROSS
03-008
N
One touch from his eccentric Quirk and you're mincemeat!!
SEIJI SHISHIKURA
QUIRK:
Meatball
Can transform all flesh into different shapes. Other people just become balls, but his own flesh can split off from his body and grow gigantic.
Power D
Speed C
Wits C
Vocabulary A
Technique A

CHARACTER

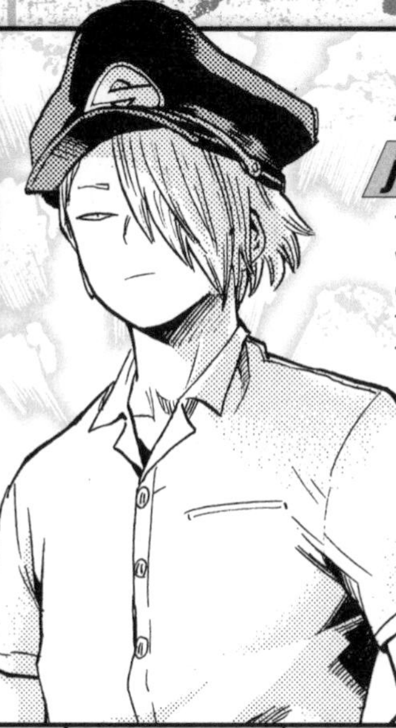

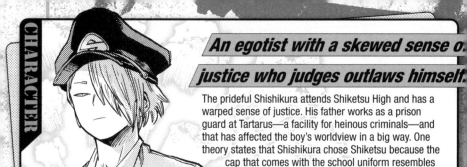

## An egotist with a skewed sense of justice who judges outlaws himself.

The prideful Shishikura attends Shiketsu High and has a warped sense of justice. His father works as a prison guard at Tartarus—a facility for heinous criminals—and that has affected the boy's worldview in a big way. One theory states that Shishikura chose Shiketsu because the cap that comes with the school uniform resembles those worn by Tartarus guards.

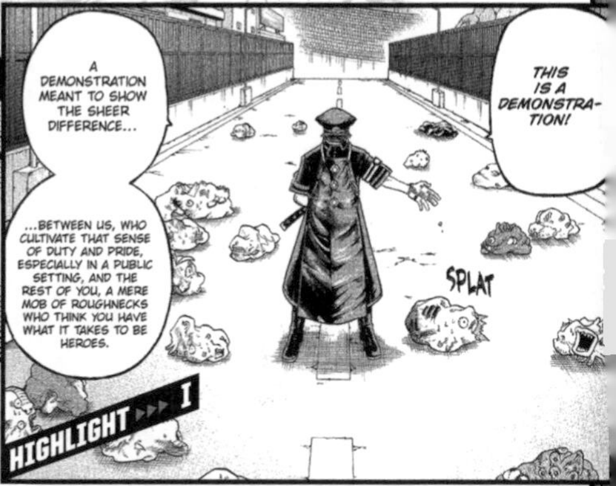
THIS IS A DEMONSTRATION!
A DEMONSTRATION MEANT TO SHOW THE SHEER DIFFERENCE...
...BETWEEN US, WHO CULTIVATE THAT SENSE OF DUTY AND PRIDE, ESPECIALLY IN A PUBLIC SETTING, AND THE REST OF YOU, A MERE MOB OF ROUGHNECKS WHO THINK YOU HAVE WHAT IT TAKES TO BE HEROES.
SPLAT
HIGHLIGHT ▸▸▸ I

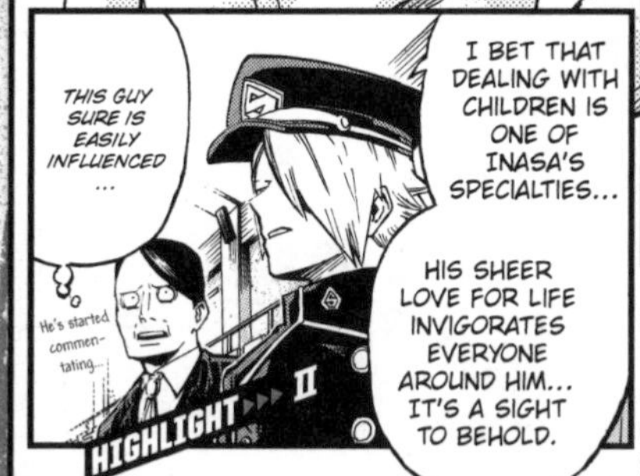
I BET THAT DEALING WITH CHILDREN IS ONE OF INASA'S SPECIALTIES...
HIS SHEER LOVE FOR LIFE INVIGORATES EVERYONE AROUND HIM... IT'S A SIGHT TO BEHOLD.
THIS GUY SURE IS EASILY INFLUENCED...
He's started commentating...
HIGHLIGHT ▸▸▸ II

⬆ In order to show off his warped worldview, Shishikura transformed a number of examinees into meatballs. He may be a nasty tyrant, but his skills aren't lacking!

⬅ Shishikura observed the supplementary course just to keep an eye on his schoolmates from Shiketsu. Though he seems to possess unshakable convictions, he's actually easily influenced.

## RELATIONSHIP

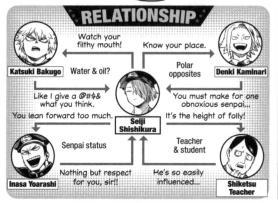

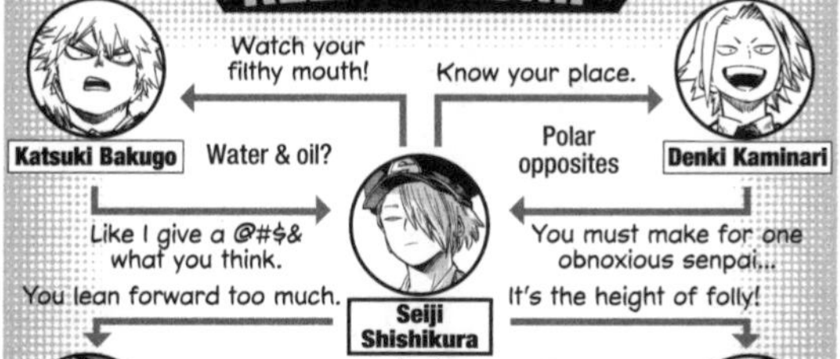
Seiji Shishikura
Katsuki Bakugo
Watch your filthy mouth!
Water & oil?
Like I give a @#$& what you think.
Denki Kaminari
Know your place.
Polar opposites
You must make for one obnoxious senpai...
Inasa Yoarashi
You lean forward too much.
Senpai status
Nothing but respect for you, sir!!
Shiketsu Teacher
It's the height of folly!
Teacher & student
He's so easily influenced...

## PROFILE

Name: **Seiji Shishikura**
Hero name: **Shishikross**
Quirk: **Meatball**
Birthday: **February 9**
Height: **172 cm**
Blood type: **A**
Birthplace: **Okayama Prefecture**
Personality: **Persuadable**
Ultimate moves: **Meatball, Chorizo**

- "My eyes are big and handsome!" (vol. 12, chap. 106)
- "The League of Villains… To think I never realized my own comrade was being impersonated… It's shameful!" (vol. 18, chap. 164)
- "Sinking to their level is the height of folly!!" (vol. 18, chap. 166)

**Shishikura's Notable Quotables**

## The elite student who unifies Shiketsu's collection of weirdos.

President and unifier of class 2-1 at the famous Shiketsu High, in the west. The controllable hair is one thing, but his appearance was inspired by a fuzzy alien featured in a certain saga about wars among the stars.

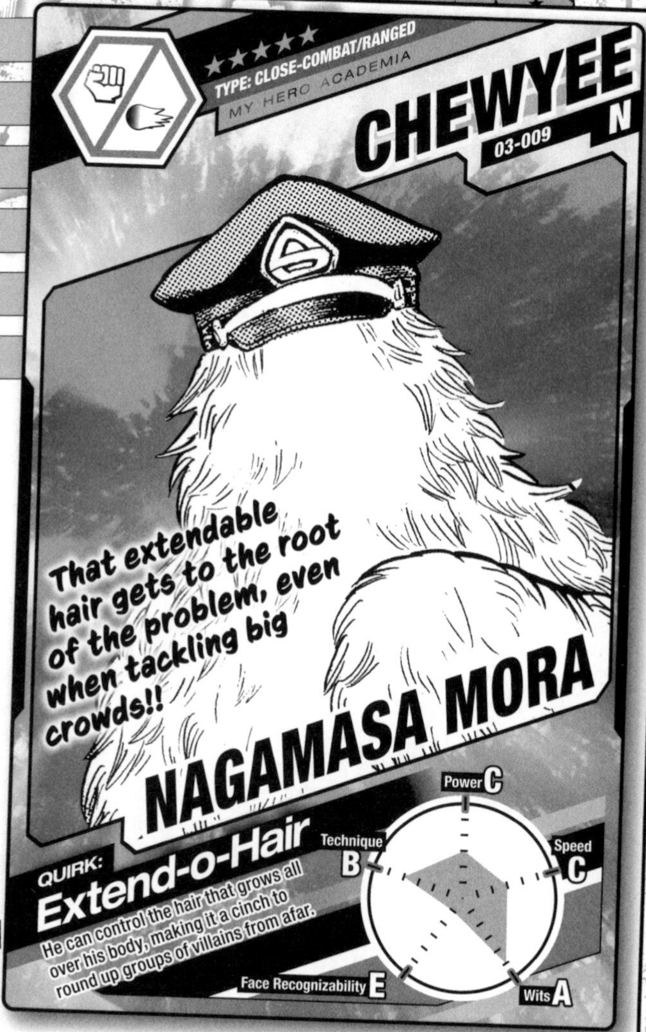

★★★★★ TYPE: CLOSE-COMBAT/RANGED
MY HERO ACADEMIA
CHEWYEE
N
03-009
That extendable hair gets to the root of the problem, even when tackling big crowds!!
NAGAMASA MORA
QUIRK:
Extend-o-Hair
He can control the hair that grows all over his body, making it a cinch to round up groups of villains from afar.
Power C
Speed C
Wits A
Face Recognizability E
Technique B


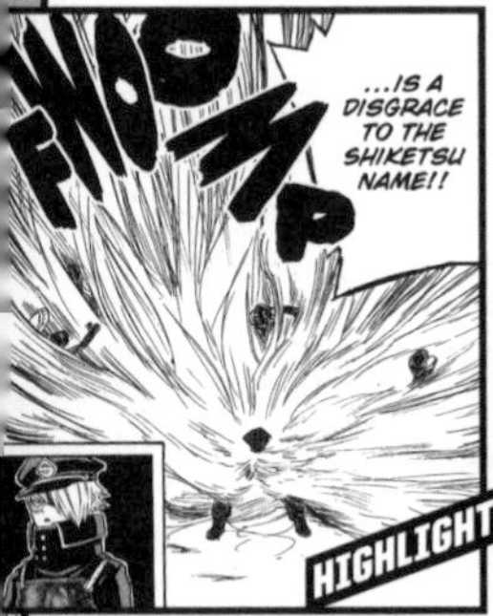

FWOOMP
...IS A DISGRACE TO THE SHIKETSU NAME!!
HIGHLIGHT


⬆ Mora gets enraged when his school's honor is besmirched, and that rage triggers his Quirk.

## RELATIONSHIP

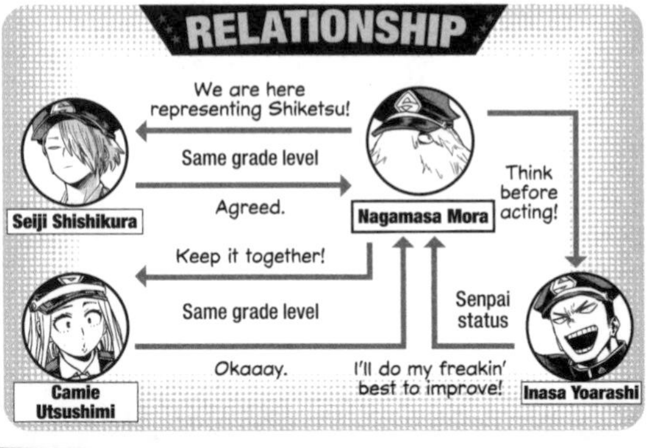

We are here representing Shiketsu!
Same grade level
Agreed.
Seiji Shishikura
Nagamasa Mora
Think before acting!
Keep it together!
Same grade level
Okaaay.
Camie Utsushimi
Senpai status
I'll do my freakin' best to improve!
Inasa Yoarashi


## PROFILE

Name: **Nagamasa Mora**
Hero name: **Chewyee**
Quirk: **Extend-o-Hair**
Birthday: **November 13**
Height: **180 cm**
Blood type: **O**
Birthplace: **Okayama Prefecture**
Personality: **Exemplary leader**
Ultimate move: **Hell-Hair**

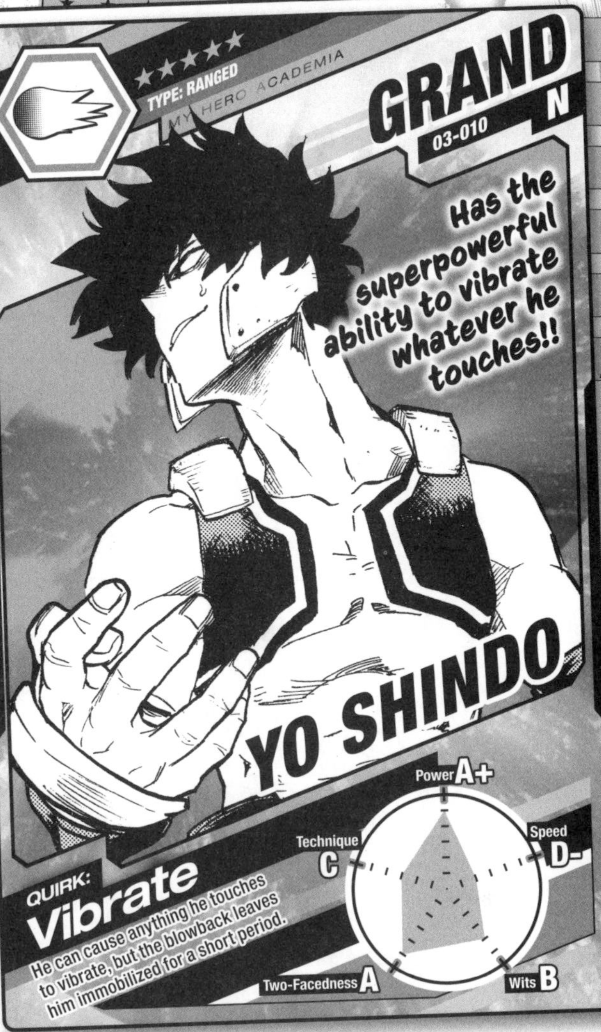
★★★★★
TYPE: RANGED
MY HERO ACADEMIA
GRAND
N
03-010
Has the superpowerful ability to vibrate whatever he touches!!
YO SHINDO
Power A+
Speed D-
Technique C
Two-Facedness A
Wits B
QUIRK:
Vibrate
He can cause anything he touches to vibrate, but the blowback leaves him immobilized for a short period.

## Being two-faced is a strategy?! This schemer isn't picky about how to get the job done.

A smooth, good-looking dude. In round one of the test, Shindo used his Quirk to split the earth and throw the other examinees into chaos. His headgear is there to reduce the vibrations that reach his own brain.

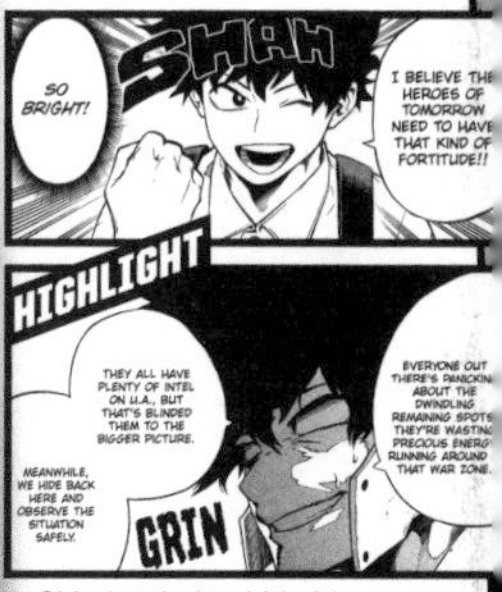
I BELIEVE THE HEROES OF TOMORROW NEED TO HAVE THAT KIND OF FORTITUDE!!
SHAH
SO BRIGHT!
HIGHLIGHT
EVERYONE OUT THERE'S PANICKIN ABOUT THE DWINDLING REMAINING SPOTS THEY'RE WASTIN PRECIOUS ENERG RUNNING AROUND THAT WAR ZONE.
THEY ALL HAVE PLENTY OF INTEL ON U.A., BUT THAT'S BLINDED THEM TO THE BIGGER PICTURE.
MEANWHILE, WE HIDE BACK HERE AND OBSERVE THE SITUATION SAFELY.
GRIN

⬆ Shindo tried to hide his ambitions upon first contact with the U.A. students, but Bakugo saw right through the act.

## RELATIONSHIP

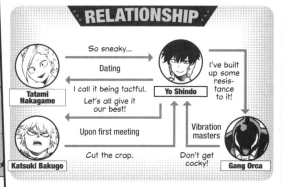

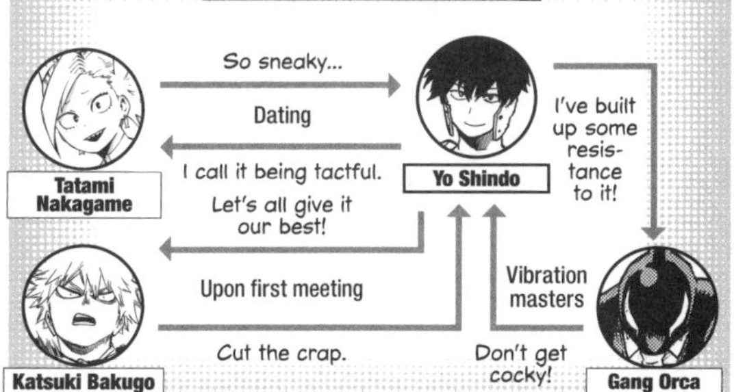
Tatami Nakagame
Yo Shindo
Katsuki Bakugo
Gang Orca
So sneaky...
Dating
I call it being tactful.
Let's all give it our best!
Upon first meeting
Cut the crap.
I've built up some resis-tance to it!
Vibration masters
Don't get cocky!

## PROFILE

Name: **Yo Shindo**
Hero name: **Grand**
Quirk: **Vibrate**
Birthday: **May 13**
Height: **176 cm**
Blood type: **AB**
Birthplace: **Shizuoka Prefecture**
Personality: **Pretty-boy troll**
Ultimate move: **Tremoring Earth**

## Her collapsible body is perfect for rescue missions!!

A girl in class 2-2 at Ketsubutsu Academy. Nakagame tends to jump on the bandwagon, like when she asked Todoroki for his autograph because he became a minor celebrity after the Sports Festival. But don't get the wrong idea—she's already dating Shindo.

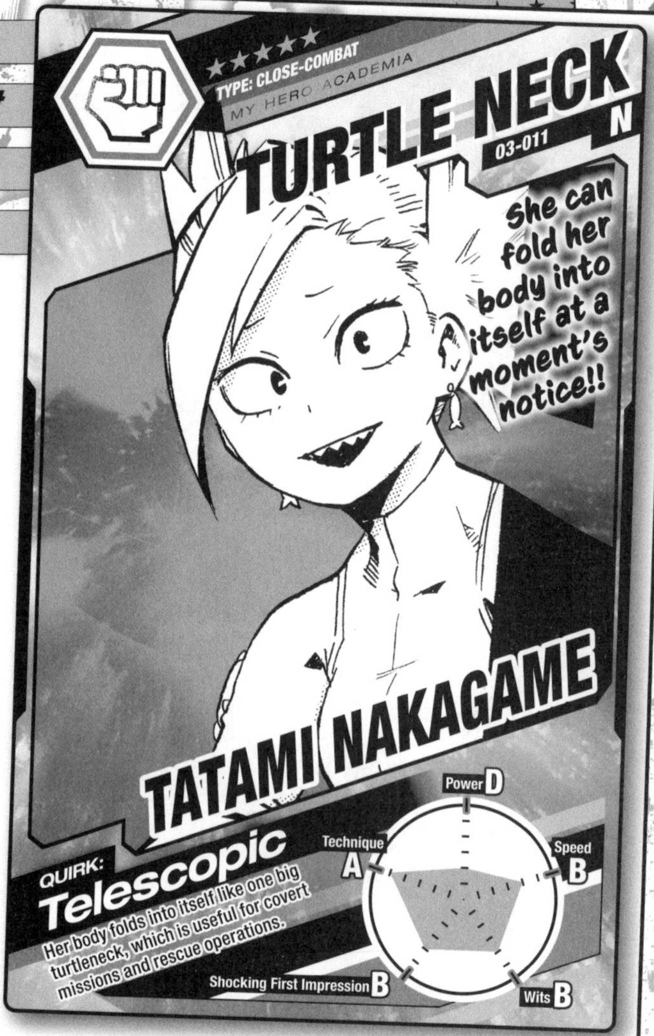

★★★★★
TYPE: CLOSE-COMBAT
MY HERO ACADEMIA
TURTLE NECK
03-011
N
She can fold her body into itself at a moment's notice!!
TATAMI NAKAGAME
QUIRK:
Telescopic
Her body folds into itself like one big turtleneck, which is useful for covert missions and rescue operations.
Power D
Speed B
Wits B
Shocking First Impression B
Technique A


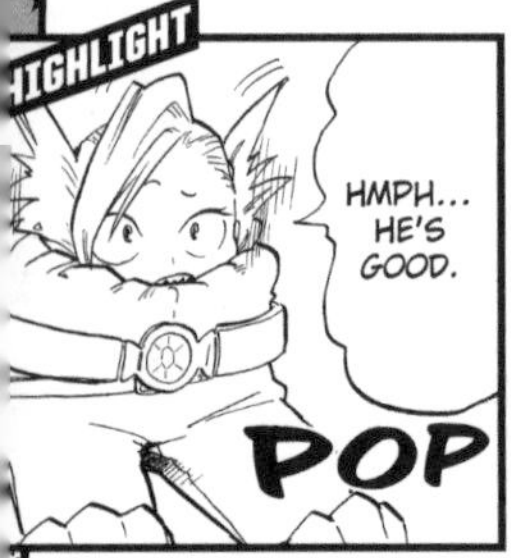

HIGHLIGHT
HMPH... HE'S GOOD.
POP


⬆ Nakagame activates her Quirk in the blink of an eye to evade incoming attacks. Now that she's got her provisional license, she's doing hero stuff with Shindo.

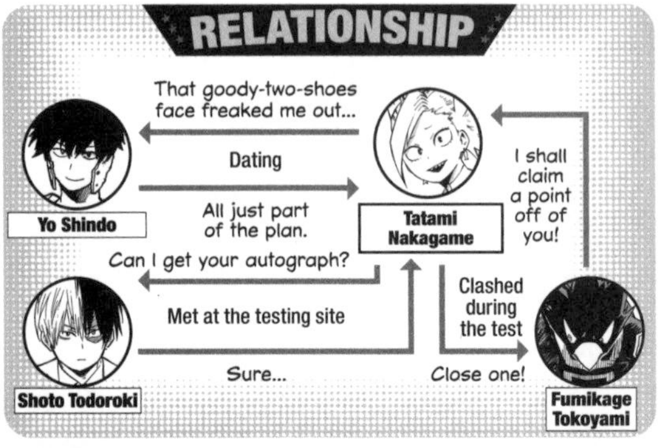

RELATIONSHIP
That goody-two-shoes face freaked me out...
Dating
All just part of the plan.
Yo Shindo
Tatami Nakagame
I shall claim a point off of you!
Can I get your autograph?
Met at the testing site
Sure...
Shoto Todoroki
Clashed during the test
Close one!
Fumikage Tokoyami


### PROFILE

Name: **Tatami Nakagame**
Hero name: **Turtle Neck**
Quirk: **Telescopic**
Birthday: **January 23**
Height: **155 cm**
Blood type: **A**
Birthplace: **Aichi Prefecture**
Personality: **Follow-the-crowd type**
Ultimate moves: **Rocket Punch, Rocket Dash**

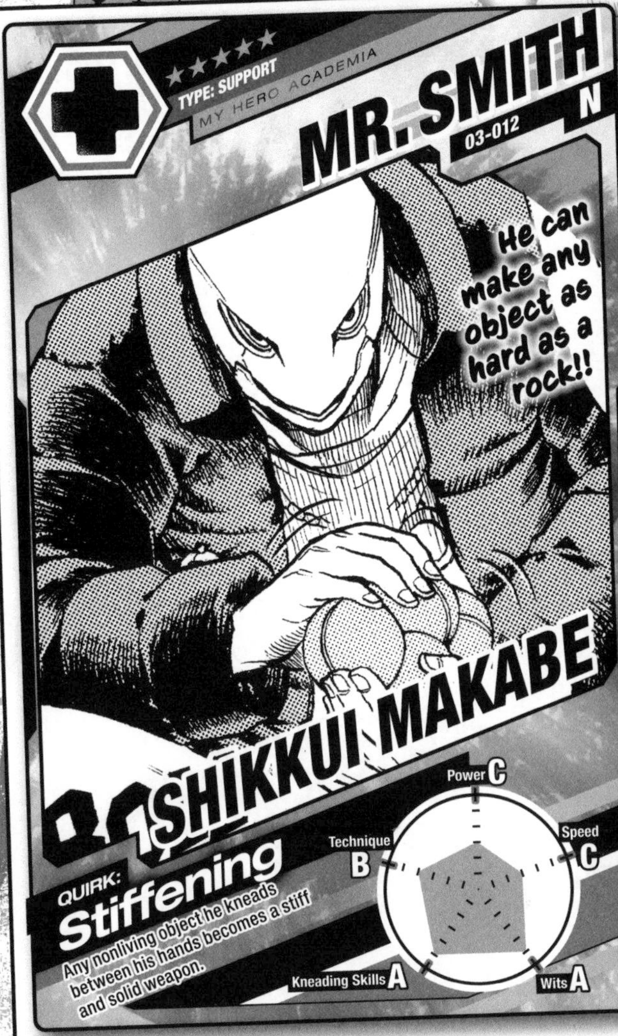
★★★★★
TYPE: SUPPORT
MY HERO ACADEMIA
MR. SMITH
N
03-012
He can make any object as hard as a rock!!
SHIKKUI MAKABE
QUIRK:
Stiffening
Any nonliving object he kneads between his hands becomes a stiff and solid weapon.
Power C
Speed C
Wits A
Kneading Skills A
Technique B

## The weapon crafter whose talents shine when he's paired up with others.

Makabe can turn any object on hand into a weapon, and his ability to keep calm and analyze the state of battle makes him a capable leader. When he was little, he accidentally worked his magic on some rice balls and shattered his father's teeth…

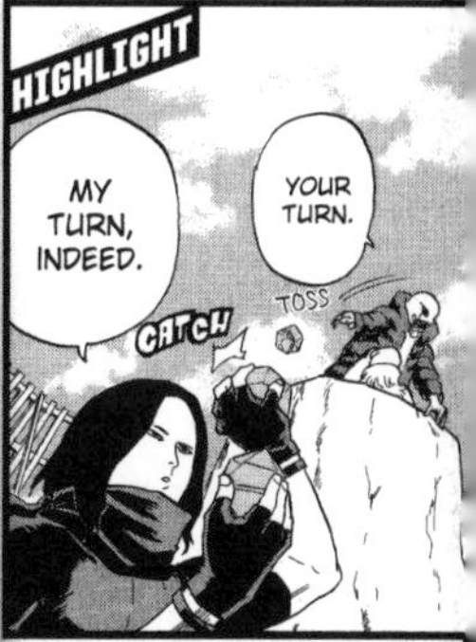
HIGHLIGHT
YOUR TURN.
MY TURN, INDEED.
TOSS
CATCH

⬆ This smooth combo move with Toteki gave the U.A. kids a run for their money.

## RELATIONSHIP

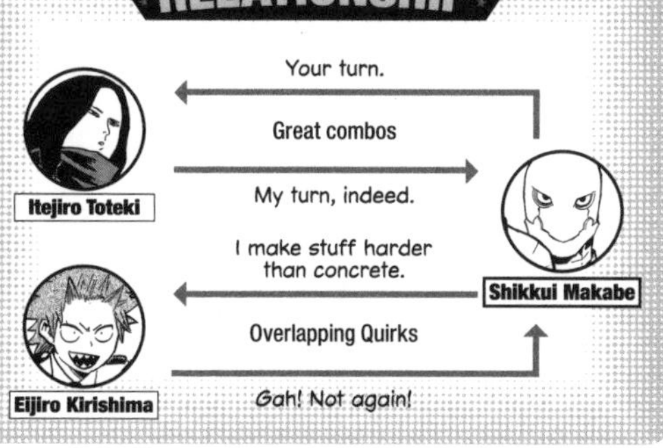
Your turn.
Great combos
My turn, indeed.
Itejiro Toteki
Shikkui Makabe
I make stuff harder than concrete.
Overlapping Quirks
Gah! Not again!
Eijiro Kirishima

## PROFILE

Name: **Shikkui Makabe**
Hero name: **Mr. Smith**
Quirk: **Stiffening**
Birthday: **March 30**
Height: **180 cm**
Blood type: **B**
Birthplace: **Iwate Prefecture**
Personality: **Stiff**
Ultimate move: **Forge Shield**

## Powerful analytical abilities hidden behind a poker face.

In round one of the test, Toteki launched a bevy of brutal ranged attacks at the U.A. students. Despite being an introvert, he actually talks a lot. Toteki bears a strong resemblance to manga author Kohei Horikoshi, but shhh—that's a state secret.

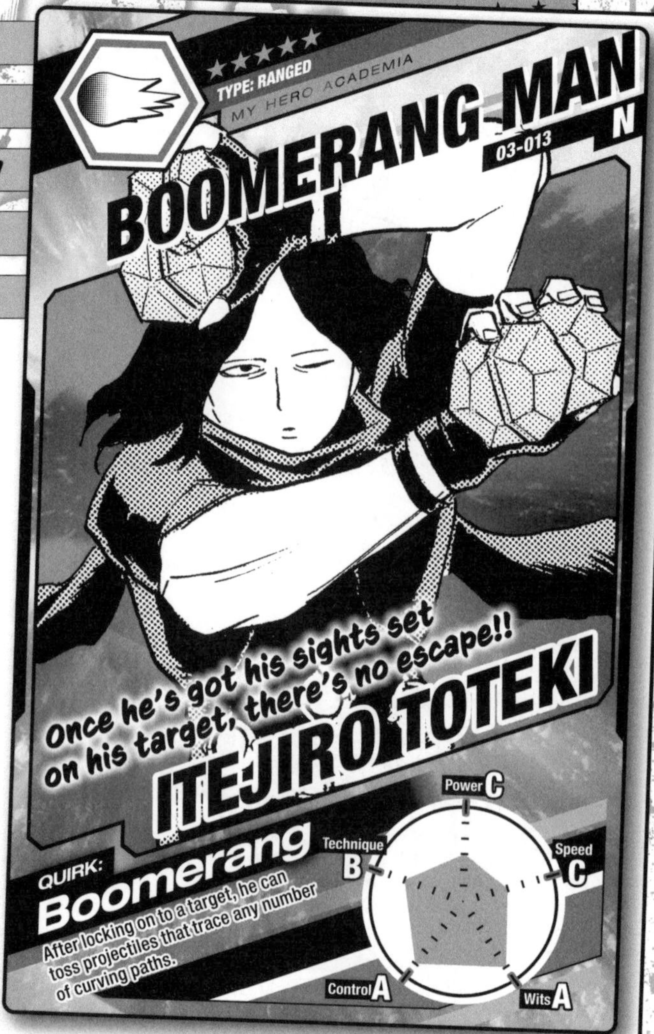
TYPE: RANGED
MY HERO ACADEMIA
BOOMERANG MAN
03-013
N
Once he's got his sights set on his target, there's no escape!!
ITEJIRO TOTEKI
QUIRK:
Boomerang
After locking on to a target, he can toss projectiles that trace any number of curving paths.
Power C
Speed C
Wits A
Control A
Technique B

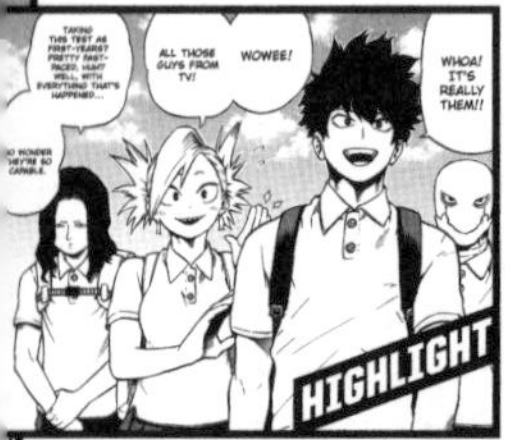
WHOA! IT'S REALLY THEM!!
WOWEE!
ALL THOSE GUYS FROM TV!
TAKING THIS TEST AS FIRST-YEARS? PRETTY FAST-PACED, HUH? WELL, WITH EVERYTHING THAT'S HAPPENED...
HIGHLIGHT

⬆ Toteki's first time meeting the U.A. kids. Was that when he locked on to them as targets?

## RELATIONSHIP

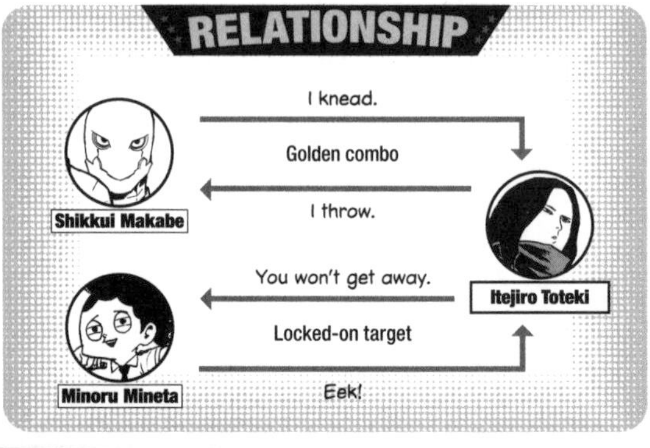
I knead.
Golden combo
I throw.
Shikkui Makabe
Itejiro Toteki
You won't get away.
Locked-on target
Eek!
Minoru Mineta

## PROFILE

Name: **Itejiro Toteki**
Hero name: **Boomerang Man**
Quirk: **Boomerang**
Birthday: **December 20**
Height: **171 cm**
Blood type: **B**
Birthplace: **Aichi Prefecture**
Personality: **High-strung**
Ultimate moves: **Crescent Moon, Full Moon**

## Bibimi Kenranzaki

A Support Course student marked by her absurdly long eyelashes. Everything about Kenranzaki is gaudy. That aesthetic, combined with her tech skills, made her the beauty pageant queen two years running. In her final beauty pageant, Kenranzaki showed off a splendiferous transforming mecha.

## Yuyu Haya

Nejire Hado's good friend. Haya thinks that Hado is the cutest thing in the galaxy, and she's been urging her friend to join the beauty pageant for years. For the third and final beauty pageant, Haya coordinated everything—from outfit to performance—leading Hado to victory.

## Chikuchi Togeike

A General Studies girl with a spiky hair tie. She and Agoyamato attended class 1-A's show in order to express their resentment, but they were so moved that they apologized.

## Tsutsutaka Agoyamato

A General Studies boy marked by his rigid pompadour and elongated chin. Upon hearing that class 1-A was doing a live music performance, Agoyamato showed up to boo but ended up blown away!!

## General Course Students

Shinso's admirable performance at the Sports Festival unified his class. During the School Festival, they created the Labyrinth of Doom, which won high praise from attendees.

## Business Course Students

These students watched the highest-ranked performers during the Sports Festival and came up with strategies. They also put their skills to work by setting up stalls, allowing them to rake in serious money.

# Others

## Eri

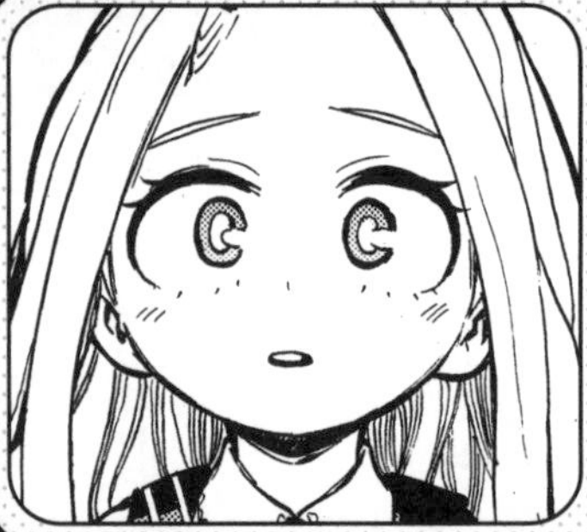

The granddaughter of the Shie Hassaikai gang boss. Eri's Quirk appeared as a sudden mutation and turned out to be capable of destroying the Quirk factor in people, giving rise to Kai Chisaki's grand plan. Eri was once resigned to her horrible fate, but ever since Togata and Midoriya saved her, she's been living at the U.A. dorms.

## Shiketsu High Teacher

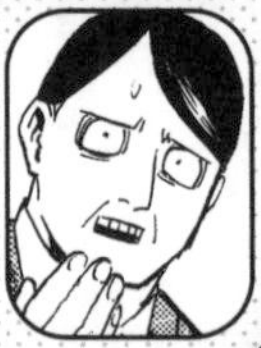

A man with a discerning eye for evaluating his students. Always brings his hand to his mouth.

## Teruo Hazukashi

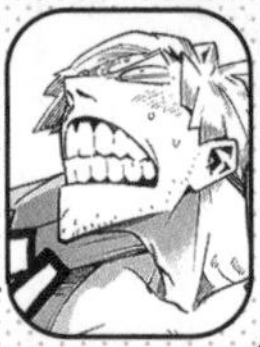

A man who was arrested after an attempt to destroy the company that employed him.

## Hiroshi Tameda

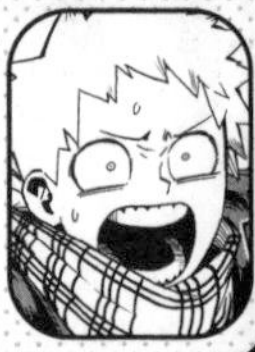

A megafan of Endeavor's. Experienced 15 minutes of fame as the Can'tcha See Kid.

## Kota Izumi

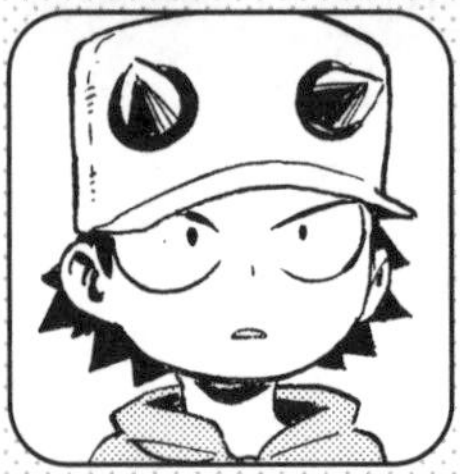

The only son of the hero duo Water Hose, who were killed in the line of duty. Kota began to hate heroes after their deaths but had a change of heart after Midoriya saved him during the training camp. Now he's a big-time Midoriya fan.

## Miyashita

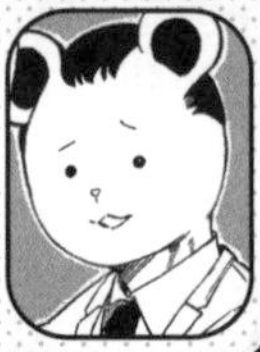

An employee at Detnerat. Killed for bad-mouthing the Meta Liberation Army ideals.

## Habuko Mongoose

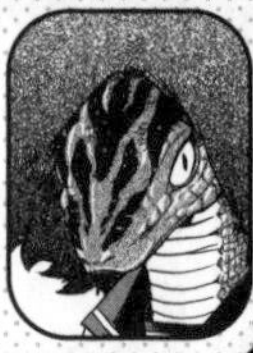

Tsuyu Asui's friend. Her Quirk paralyzes people for three seconds with a glare.

## Shimura Family: Kotaro, Mother, In-Laws, Hana

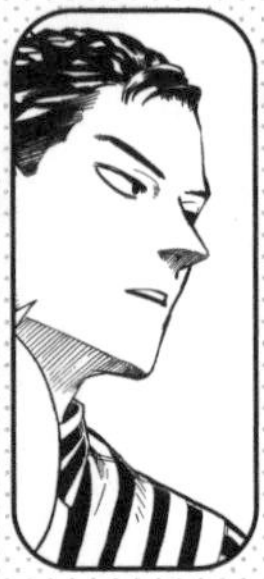
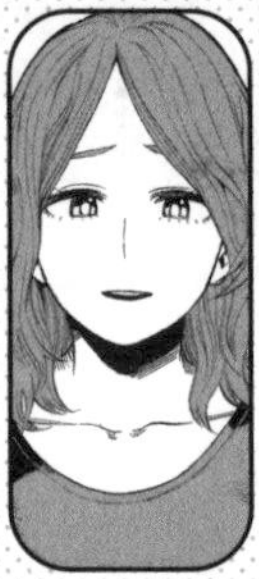
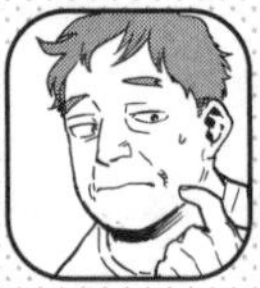
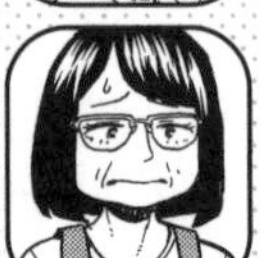
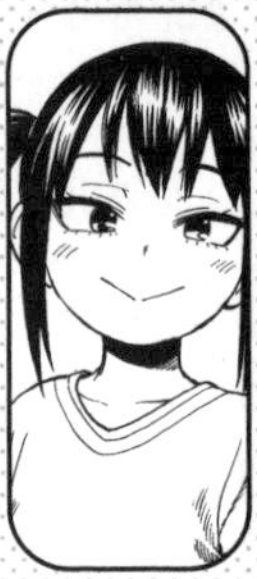

Tomura Shigaraki's family. Despite being Nana Shimura's son, Kotaro never allowed any talk about heroes in his household, and he firmly objected to Shigaraki's dream of becoming a hero.

## Tsubasa

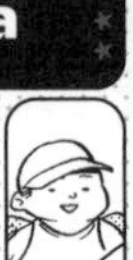

Midoriya and Bakugo's friend from elementary school. They lost touch with him during middle school...

### Inko Midoriya

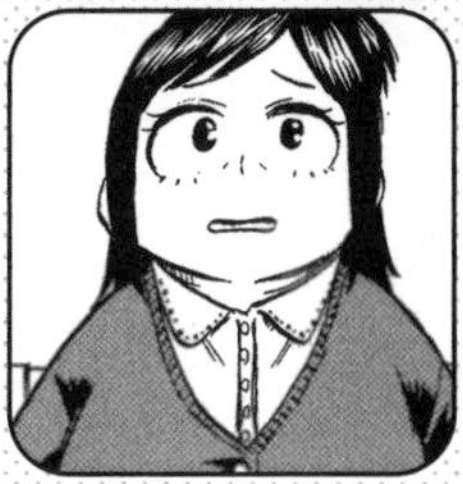

Izuku's mother. His constant injuries drove her to recommend that he change schools, but after All Might gained her trust, she gave Izuku her blessing.

### Masaru and Mitsuki Bakugo

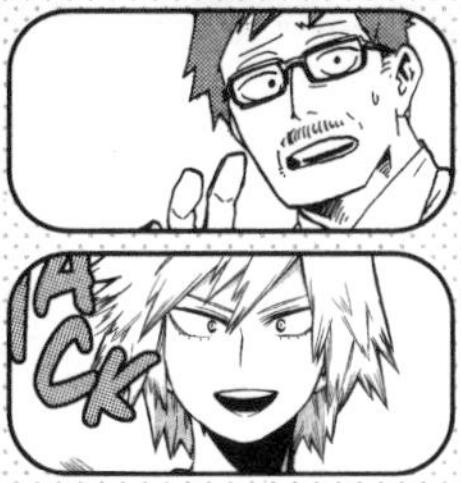

Katsuki's parents. Back in the day, Masaru worked at a design company and the strong-willed Mitsuki chased him. They get along just fine as husband and wife.

### Mr. and Mrs. Uraraka

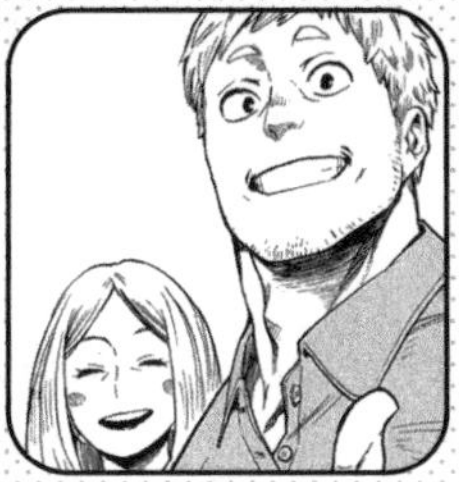

They run a construction business but don't have much to show for it. After the Sports Festival, they showed up at Ochaco's apartment to celebrate.

### Kyotoku and Mika Jiro

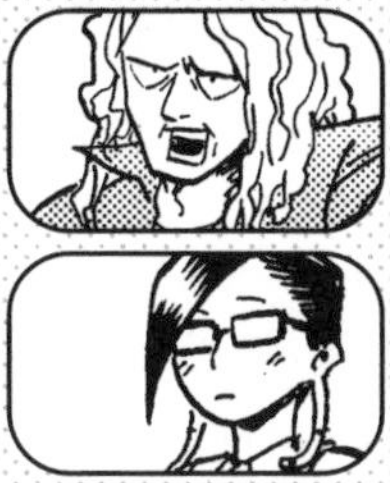

Kyoka's parents, who both work in the music industry. They're no strangers to doing what they love, so they support their daughter's dream of being a hero.

### Todoroki Family: Rei, Fuyumi, Natsuo

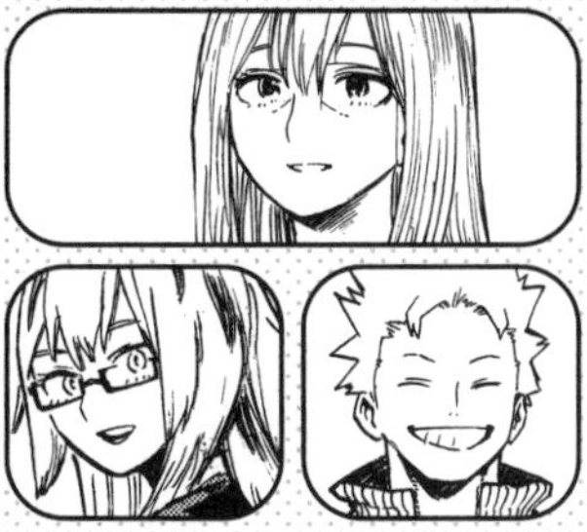

Shoto's family. The Todoroki family also had an eldest son named Toya, making Shoto the third son and the youngest child of the four.

### Mrs. Ida

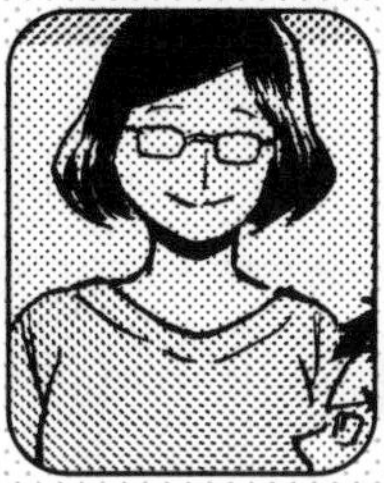

Currently helping with her older son Tensei's rehab in the wake of him being attacked by Stain. She was once a hero too.

### Asui Family: Ganma, Bell, Samidare, Satsuki

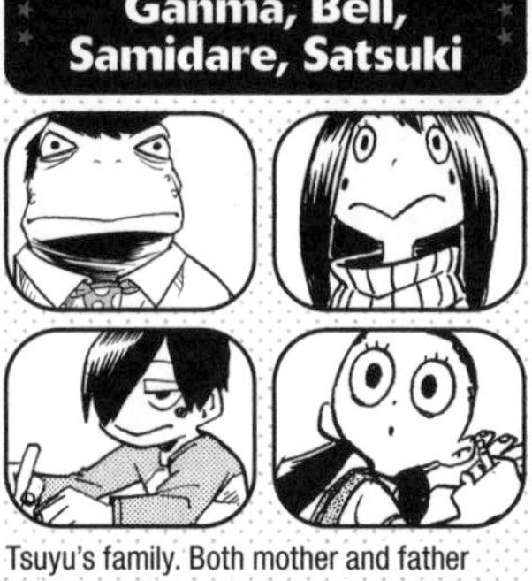

Tsuyu's family. Both mother and father used to work busy jobs, but things have calmed down now, and the family gets to spend a lot more time together.

### Mrs. Aoyama

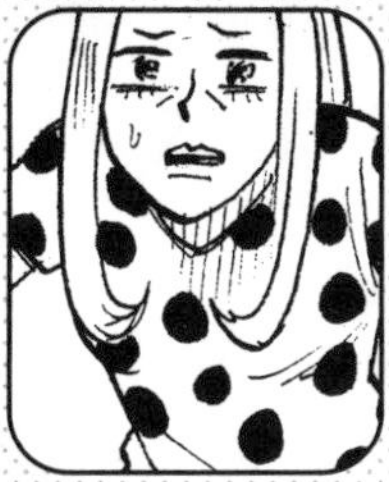

Her face is identical to Yuga's. She and her son watched on live TV the battle unfolding in Kamino.

### Mrs. Koda

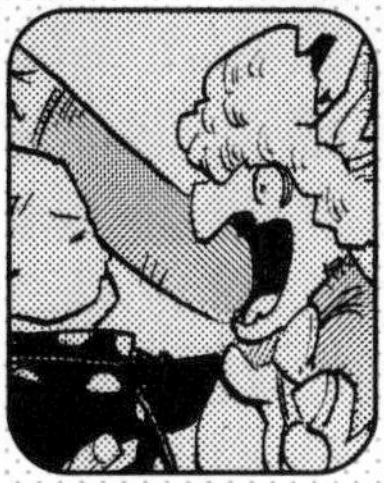

She raised Koji with love and care and was thrilled when she learned that he had gotten into U.A.

## Leader-esque Boy

A cynical, sneering Masegaki student. He has nothing but contempt for adults and is basically the boss of his class.

## Komari Ikoma

A timid newbie teacher at Masegaki Elementary who's prone to crying. Her personality doesn't serve her well when dealing with her up-front and direct students, whom she often finds impossible to teach… Her preferred cure for a stressful day is a can of beer. Cute.

## Girl Who Decided that Utsushimi Is the Enemy

A Masegaki student with a crush on Sho. She ignored Utsushimi but warmed up to the older girl by the time the exercise was over.

## Sho

A Masegaki student who's quite popular with the girls. Easily charmed by Camie Utsushimi's more mature appeal.

## Takuto

Cheery and curious, but with a glass heart that's easily shattered. One second after approaching Bakugo, he began wailing.

## Tongue Tank Boy

Has a tongue that turns into a projectile-firing cannon. He and his classmates attack the older examinees all at once.

## Assault Dust Boy

His Quirk lets him control dust. His classmates rely on him when it comes time to clean the classroom.

## Binging Ball Boy

Controls high-speed balls that attack by biting. He's got a lot of energy, so he tends to set the mood for the class.

## Magnet Missile, King's Ram, and Hula-Hoop Boys

As generations pass, Quirks become more blended, complex, and powerful. Children who ignore the rules and use their Quirks in daily life naturally develop their abilities to the point that they can even overpower adults.

## Viral Cosmos Girl

A Masegaki student with cosmos flowers sprouting from her head. Her Quirk spreads a virus through flower petals.

# 4th
## EDITION

**ULTRA HEROES**

Day and night, heroes battle evil to preserve
peace across the globe. Pro heroes come in
all shapes and sizes, so let's take a look
at the people behind the masks.

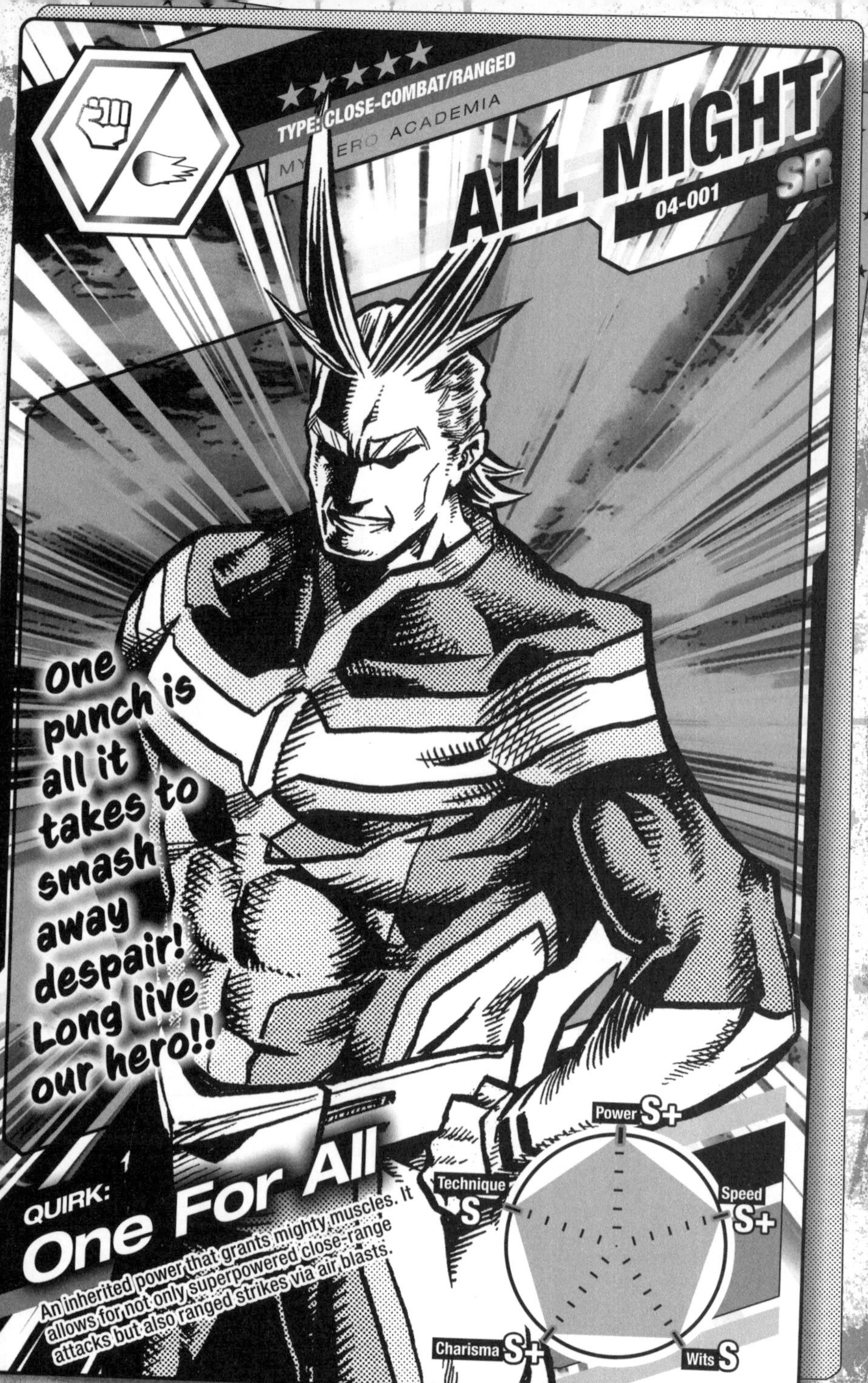
TYPE: CLOSE-COMBAT/RANGED
ALL MIGHT
SR
04-001
One punch is all it takes to smash away despair! Long live our hero!!
Power S+
Technique S
Speed S+
Charisma S+
Wits S
QUIRK:
One For All
An inherited power that grants mighty muscles. It allows for not only superpowered close-range attacks but also ranged strikes via air blasts.

CHARACTER

## His valiant image remains, even as the newcomers inherit his spirit.

The ultimate hero who always saved people with a smile. All Might saw the makings of a pure hero inside Midoriya and passed his Quirk down to the boy. Then, he began teaching at U.A. to help train Midoriya and friends to be heroes. All Might's distinct visual style (when in muscle form) is a result of his time studying abroad in the U.S.

HIGHLIGHT ▸▸▸ I
DETROIT
SMASH!!!!!!!!

⬆ During the operation to rescue Bakugo, All Might fought All For One. He had to smash past his limits to claim victory with one final attack.

FROM NOW ON, I CAN FOCUS ON RAISING YOU RIGHT.
SHP
EVEN THOUGH I'VE BEEN REDUCED TO THIS STATE... LET'S DO OUR BEST, OKAY?
HIGHLIGHT ▸▸▸ II

⬆ Now that All Might's power is gone, he's focusing on educating his successor, Midoriya. The Symbol of Peace's retirement has had major effects on society.

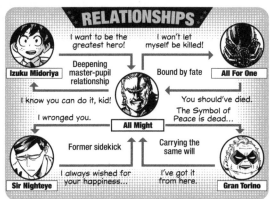

## RELATIONSHIPS

Izuku Midoriya
I want to be the greatest hero!
Deepening master-pupil relationship
I know you can do it, kid!
All For One
I won't let myself be killed!
Bound by fate
You should've died.
All Might
I wronged you.
Former sidekick
I always wished for your happiness...
Sir Nighteye
The Symbol of Peace is dead...
Carrying the same will
I've got it from here.
Gran Torino

## PROFILE

Name: **Toshinori Yagi**
Hero name: **All Might**
Quirk: **One For All**
Birthday: **June 10**
Height: **220 cm**
Blood type: **A**
Birthplace: **Tokyo**
Personality: **Unexpectedly playful**
Ultimate moves: **Texas Smash, Detroit Smash, Missouri Smash, Carolina Smash, etc.**

## All Might's Notable Quotables

- "Fear not, kid!! I am here!!" (vol. 1, chap. 1)
- "Indeed! There are plenty of things…that heroes need to protect, All For One!!" (vol. 11, chap. 92)
- "What purpose does our strength serve? Endeavor, the answer is a simple one." (vol. 18, chap. 166)

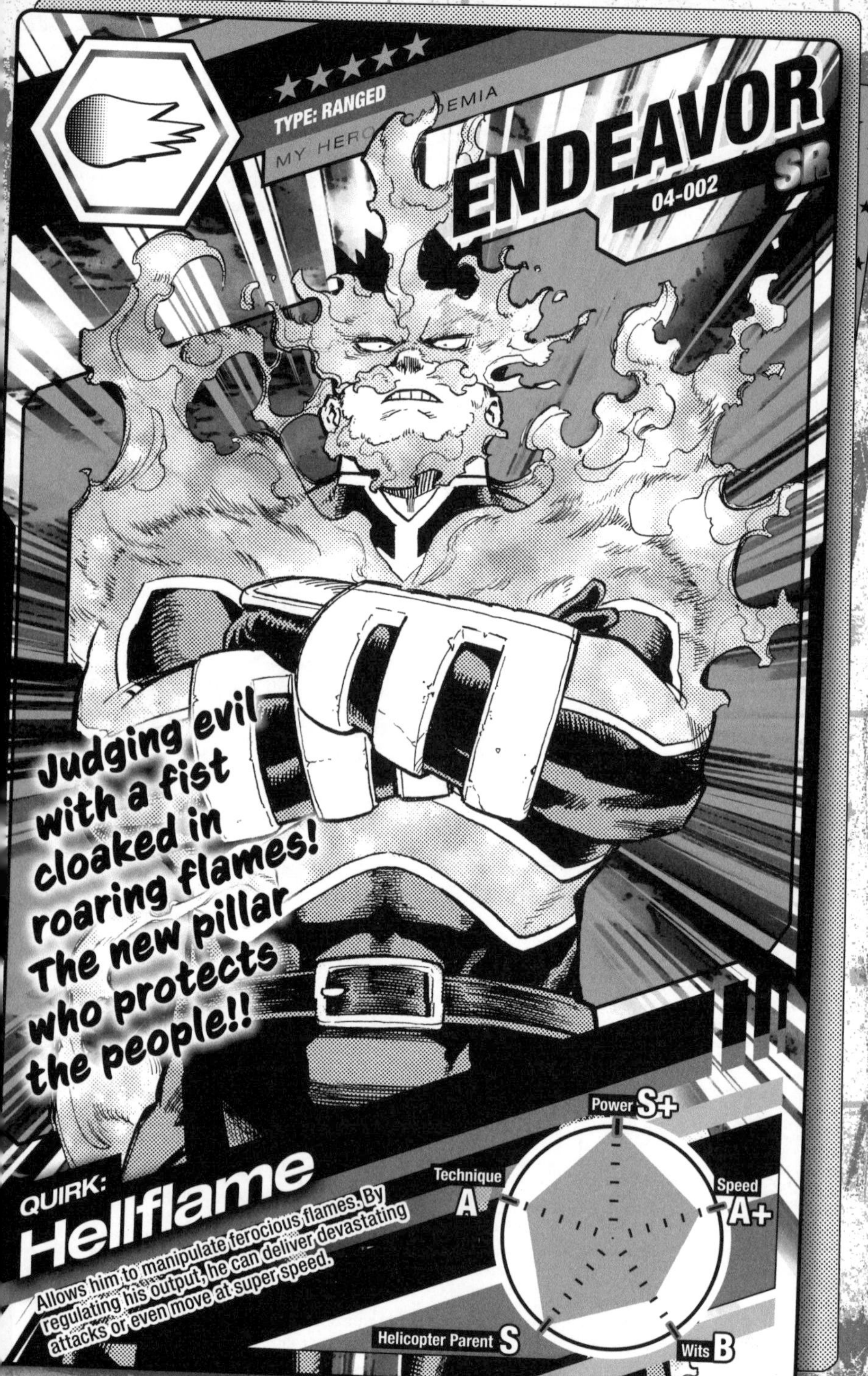

TYPE: RANGED
MY HERO ACADEMIA
ENDEAVOR
SR
04-002
Judging evil with a fist cloaked in roaring flames! The new pillar who protects the people!!
QUIRK:
Hellflame
Allows him to manipulate ferocious flames. By regulating his output, he can deliver devastating attacks or even move at super speed.
Power S+
Speed A+
Wits B
Helicopter Parent S
Technique A

CHARACTER

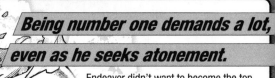

## *Being number one demands a lot, even as he seeks atonement.*

Endeavor didn't want to become the top hero just because All Might retired. He's always been obsessed with power, but now that he's number one, he's questioning the purpose of that strength and seeks to fill the role in his own way. He still can't bring himself to see Rei, his wife, face-to-face.

HIGHLIGHT ▸▸▸ I
I'M HOPING TO BECOME A HERO YOU CAN BE PROUD OF.
ON THAT NOTE...


⬆ Endeavor passed down everything to Shoto, and now he's approaching his son in a different way. He's fully aware of the pain he inflicted on his family and is determined to atone.

HIGHLIGHT ▸▸▸ II
PROMINENCE BURN!!


⬆ Endeavor battled the High-End Nomu that showed up in the city. People were given hope by seeing the new number one fighting valiantly.

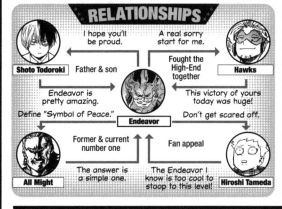

RELATIONSHIPS
Shoto Todoroki
I hope you'll be proud.
Father & son
Endeavor is pretty amazing.
Hawks
A real sorry start for me.
Fought the High-End together
This victory of yours today was huge!
Endeavor
Define "Symbol of Peace."
Former & current number one
The answer is a simple one.
All Might
Don't get scared off.
Fan appeal
The Endeavor I know is too cool to stoop to this level!
Hiroshi Tameda


## PROFILE

Name: **Enji Todoroki**
Hero name: **Endeavor**
Quirk: **Hellflame**
Birthday: **August 8**
Height: **195 cm**
Blood type: **AB**
Birthplace: **Around Shizuoka Prefecture**
Personality: **Pigheaded father**
Ultimate moves: **Flashfire Fist: Jetburn, Flashfire Fist: Hell Spider, Prominence Burn, PLUS ULTRA Prominence Burn**

- "So, number one hero… What's it mean to be the Symbol of Peace?" (vol. 18, chap. 164)
- "After my junior colleague fanned the flames like that, I don't have much to say. Except…just watch me!" (vol. 20, chap. 185)
- "C'mon! You want number one? You got him!" (vol. 20, chap. 186)
- "You think I'm beat? This eye's giving out, but I still see victory up ahead! More firepower!! More!! Beyond!!" (vol. 21, chap. 189)

**Endeavor's Notable Quotables**

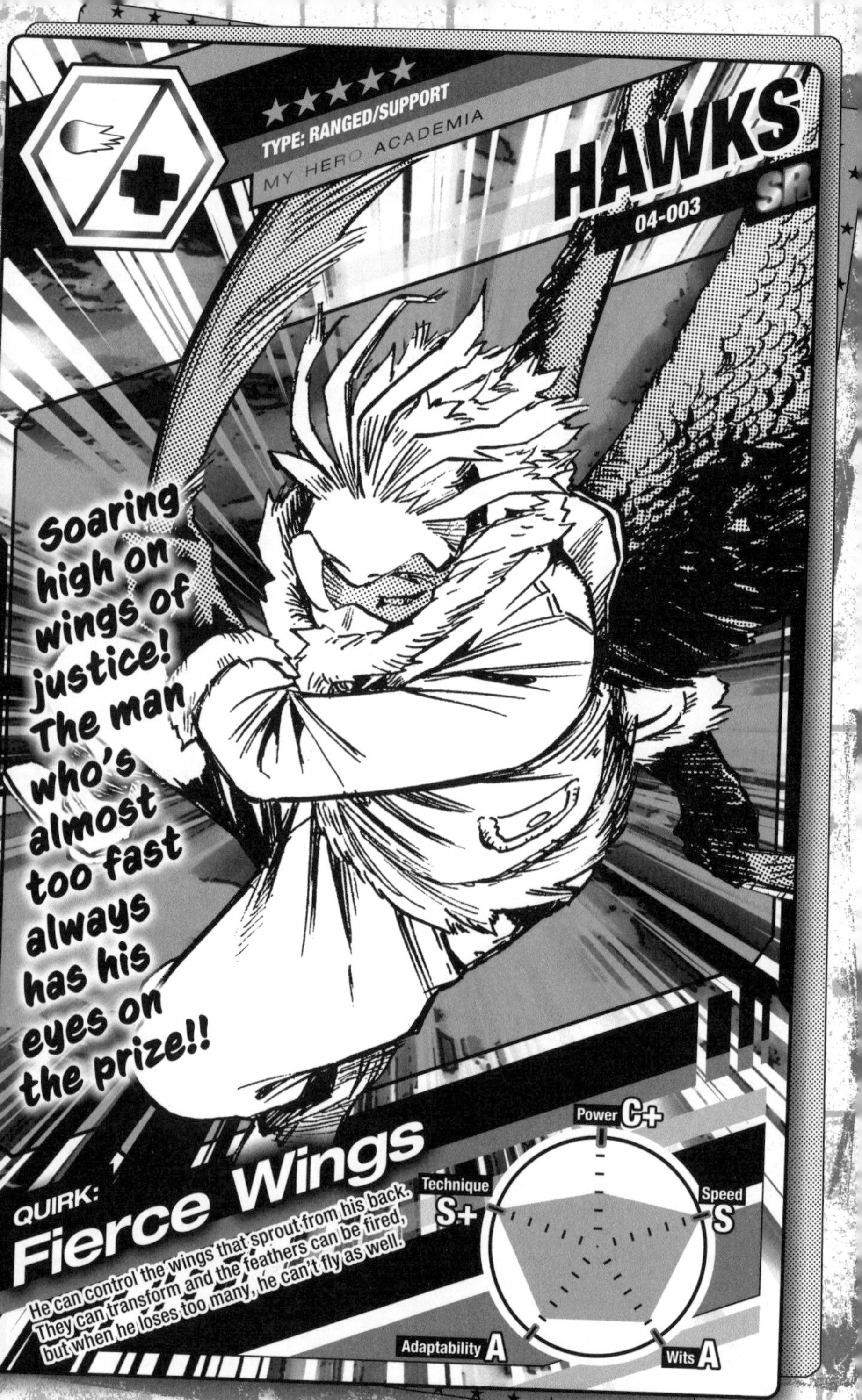
HAWKS
SR
04-003
★★★★★
TYPE: RANGED/SUPPORT
MY HERO ACADEMIA
Soaring high on wings of justice! The man who's almost too fast always has his eyes on the prize!!
QUIRK:
Fierce Wings
He can control the wings that sprout from his back. They can transform and the feathers can be fired, but when he loses too many, he can't fly as well.
Power C+
Technique S+
Speed S
Adaptability A
Wits A

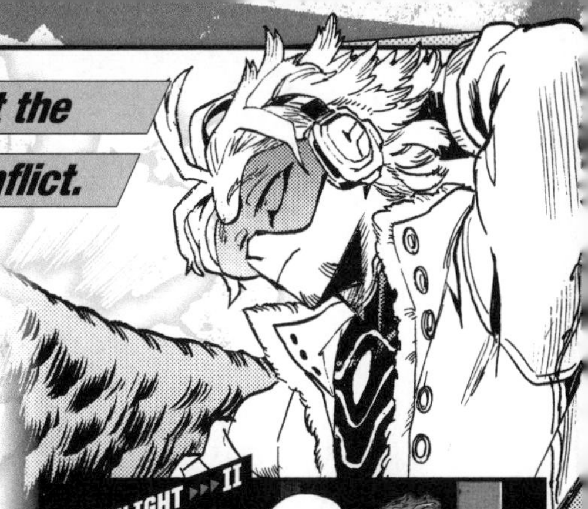

## He fights for peace, but the mask hides his inner conflict.

This supersonic hero was the youngest to ever make it into the top ten. Hawks's real name isn't public knowledge. He accepted a mission from the Heroes Public Safety Commission to gather intel on the League of Villains, which led him to contact Dabi. Then, Hawks suggested a team-up with Endeavor and led the new number one into a fight with a High-End Nomu. He isn't quite like the other heroes, so what has he really set his sights on?

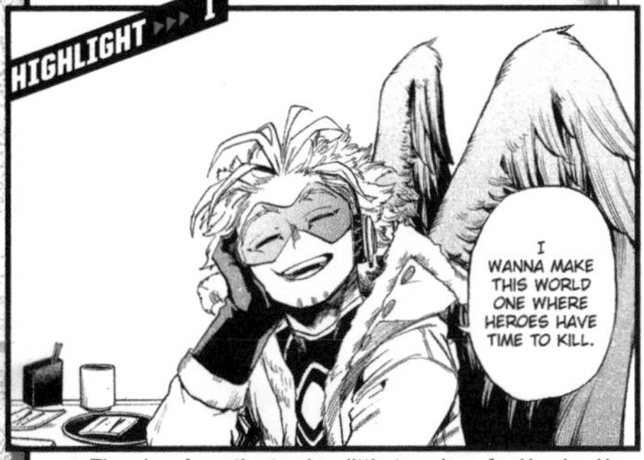
HIGHLIGHT ▸▸▸ I
I WANNA MAKE THIS WORLD ONE WHERE HEROES HAVE TIME TO KILL.

⬆ The view from the top is a little too clear, for Hawks. He smiles from ear to ear when telling the number one about his dream, but is he being entirely truthful…?

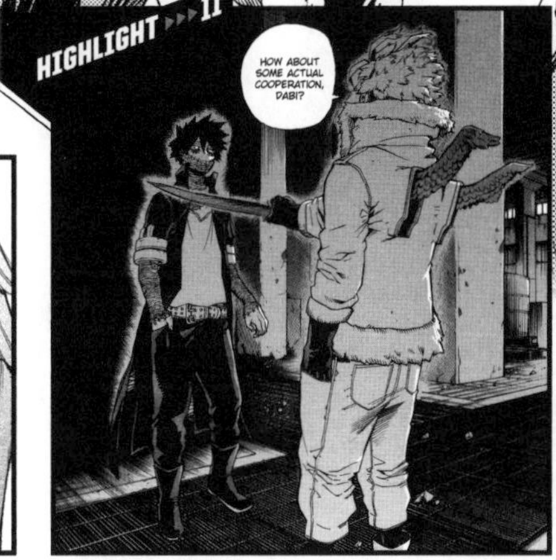
HIGHLIGHT ▸▸▸ II
HOW ABOUT SOME ACTUAL COOPERATION, DABI?

⬆ Dabi doubted the number two hero's intentions, so he went off script as a test. His silver tongue seemed to convince Hawks that he wasn't acting in bad faith.

### RELATIONSHIPS

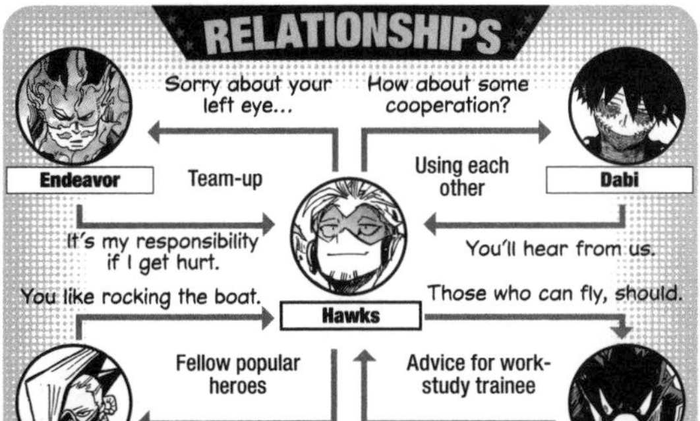
Endeavor
Sorry about your left eye...
Team-up
It's my responsibility if I get hurt.
Dabi
How about some cooperation?
Using each other
You'll hear from us.
Hawks
You like rocking the boat.
Those who can fly, should.
Edgeshot
Fellow popular heroes
I just hate holding back how I feel.
Fumikage Tokoyami
Advice for work-study trainee
I'm grateful to you, Hawks.

### PROFILE

Name: **Keigo Takami**
Hero name: **Hawks**
Quirk: **Fierce Wings**
Birthday: **December 28**
Height: **172 cm**
Blood type: **B**
Birthplace: **Fukuoka Prefecture**
Personality: **Sharp-eyed, sharp-eared**
Ultimate moves: **Weather Vane Wing, Wind-Cutter**

- "You're next. Dude with a lower approval rating than me… Mr. Number One." (vol. 20, chap. 185)
- "My speed…added to your firepower! I'll push you forward, number one!!" (vol. 21, chap. 189)
- "A society where heroes can enjoy a little boredom… I promise I'll make it happen, at my trademark top speed." (vol. 21, chap. 192)

Hawks's Notable Quotables

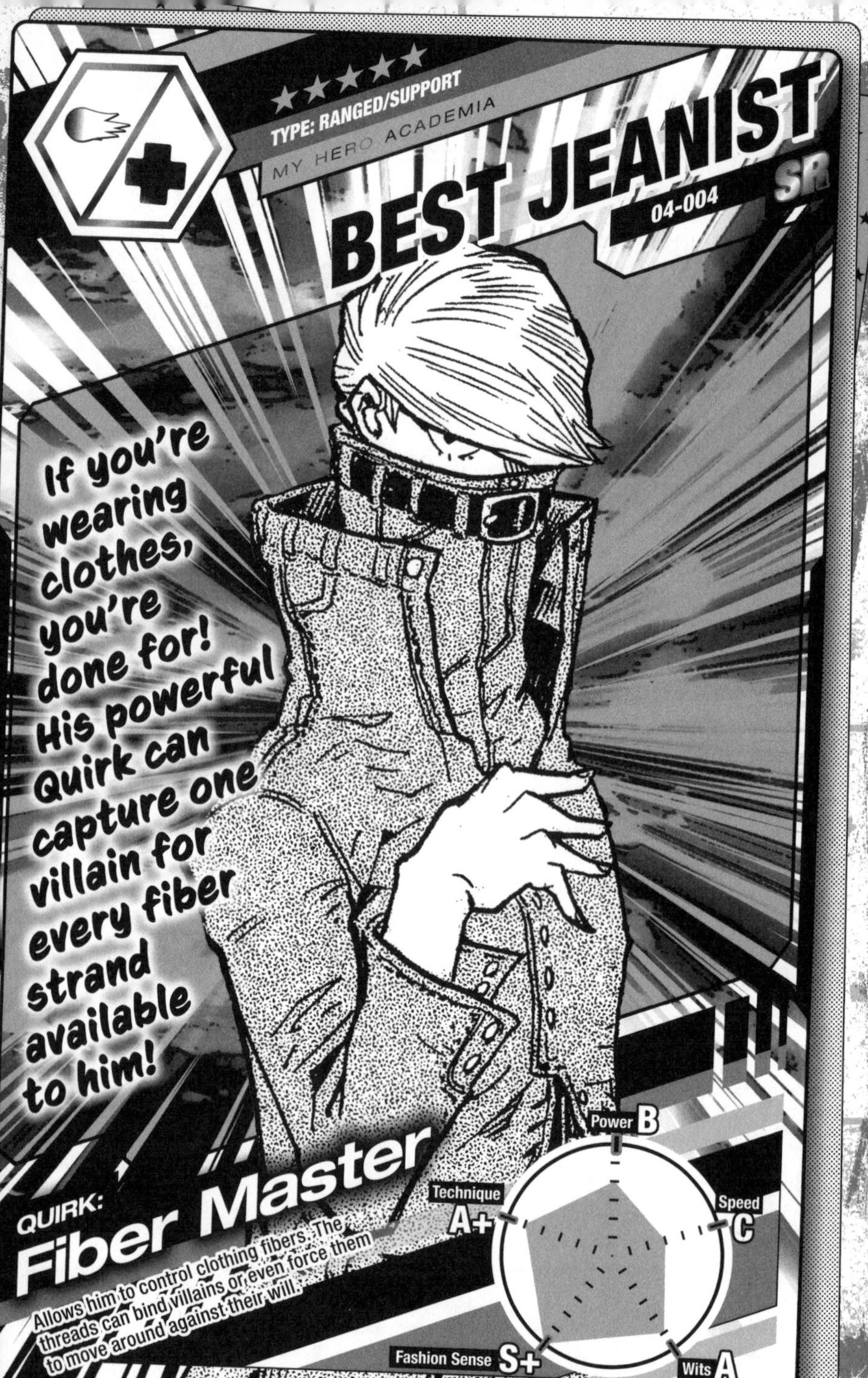
★★★★★
TYPE: RANGED/SUPPORT
MY HERO ACADEMIA
BEST JEANIST
SR
04-004
If you're wearing clothes, you're done for! His powerful Quirk can capture one villain for every fiber strand available to him!
QUIRK:
Fiber Master
Allows him to control clothing fibers. The threads can bind villains or even force them to move around against their will.
Power B
Technique A+
Speed C
Fashion Sense S+
Wits A

CHARACTER

# With unparalleled support, peopl are rooting for his comeback.

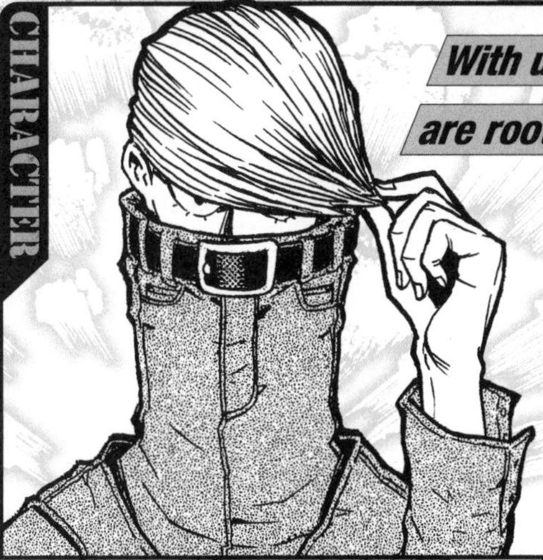

Best Jeanist is a fashion leader clad in pure denim, and he became a hero in order to "reform" ferocious people. He favors the quality offerings of the long-standing brand Onigashima Jeans. Beyond just being a hero, Best Jeanist is also a fashion model with overseas contracts, so his achievements are known both at home and abroad.

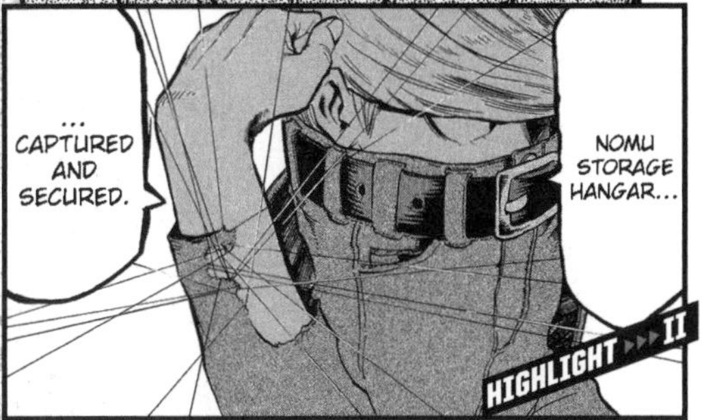
NOMU STORAGE HANGAR...
... CAPTURED AND SECURED.
HIGHLIGHT ▸▸▸ II

⬆ During the Kamino Nightmare, Best Jeanist was assigned to the squad that raided the Nomu hangar. Even during simple missions that require little combat, he gets the job done properly.

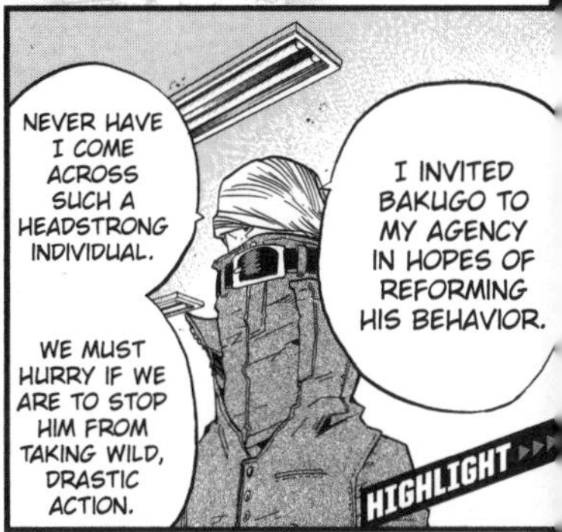
I INVITED BAKUGO TO MY AGENCY IN HOPES OF REFORMING HIS BEHAVIOR.
NEVER HAVE I COME ACROSS SUCH A HEADSTRONG INDIVIDUAL.
WE MUST HURRY IF WE ARE TO STOP HIM FROM TAKING WILD, DRASTIC ACTION.
HIGHLIGHT ▸▸▸

⬆ Best Jeanist recruited Bakugo to reform him. He couldn't best Bakugo's unshakable pride, which even affects the roots of his hair.

## RELATIONSHIPS

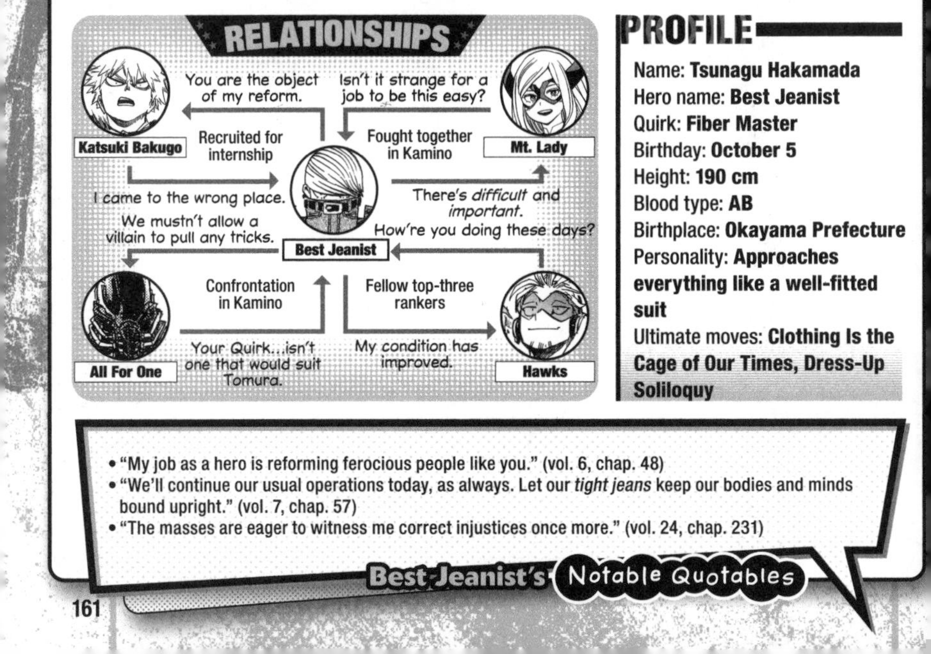
Katsuki Bakugo
You are the object of my reform.
Recruited for internship
I came to the wrong place.
Mt. Lady
Isn't it strange for a job to be this easy?
Fought together in Kamino
There's *difficult* and *important*.
Best Jeanist
We mustn't allow a villain to pull any tricks.
How're you doing these days?
All For One
Confrontation in Kamino
Your Quirk...isn't one that would suit Tomura.
Hawks
Fellow top-three rankers
My condition has improved.

## PROFILE

Name: **Tsunagu Hakamada**
Hero name: **Best Jeanist**
Quirk: **Fiber Master**
Birthday: **October 5**
Height: **190 cm**
Blood type: **AB**
Birthplace: **Okayama Prefecture**
Personality: **Approaches everything like a well-fitted suit**
Ultimate moves: **Clothing Is the Cage of Our Times, Dress-Up Soliloquy**

- "My job as a hero is reforming ferocious people like you." (vol. 6, chap. 48)
- "We'll continue our usual operations today, as always. Let our *tight jeans* keep our bodies and minds bound upright." (vol. 7, chap. 57)
- "The masses are eager to witness me correct injustices once more." (vol. 24, chap. 231)

**Best Jeanist's Notable Quotables**

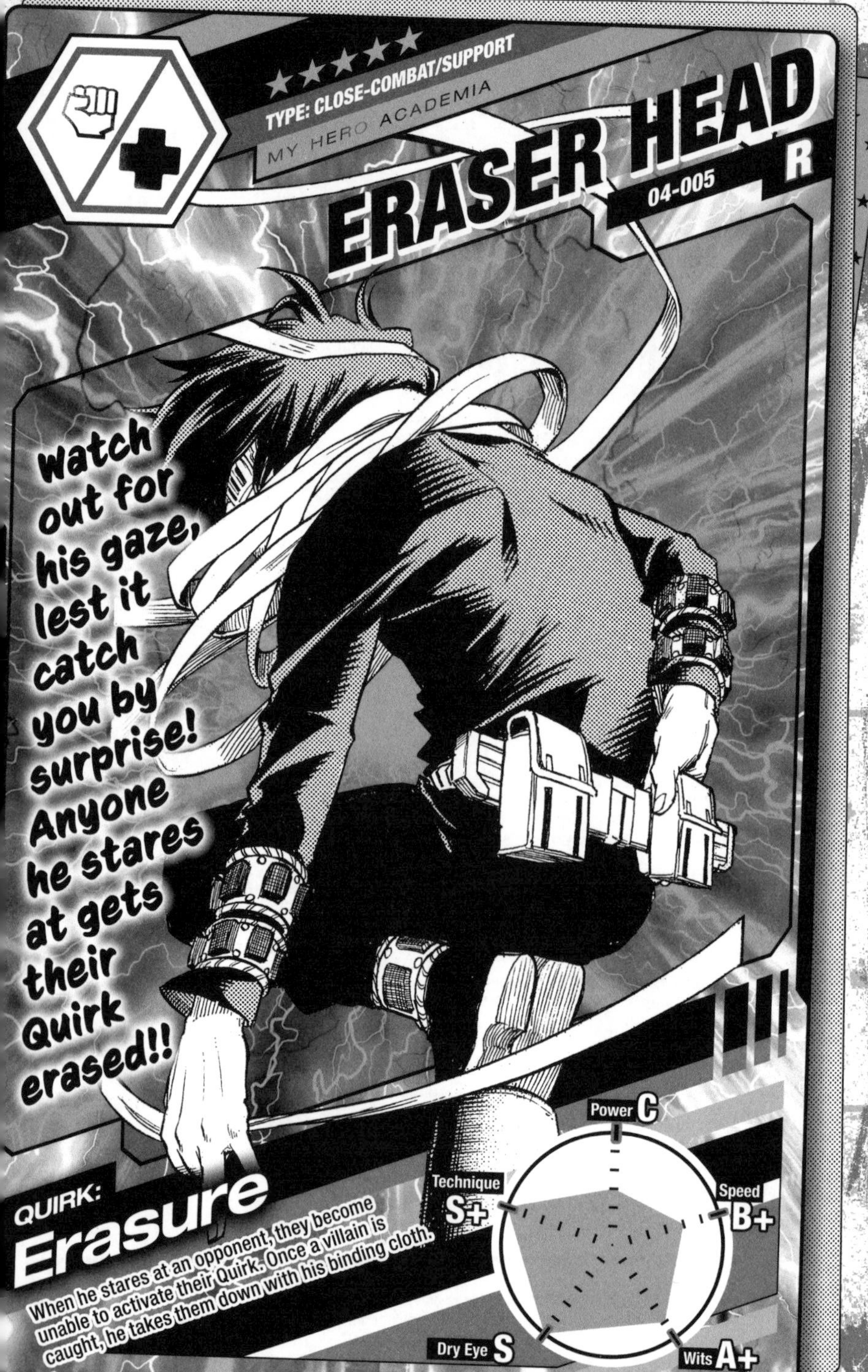
TYPE: CLOSE-COMBAT/SUPPORT
MY HERO ACADEMIA
ERASER HEAD
R
04-005
Watch out for his gaze, lest it catch you by surprise! Anyone he stares at gets their Quirk erased!!
QUIRK:
Erasure
When he stares at an opponent, they become unable to activate their Quirk. Once a villain is caught, he takes them down with his binding cloth.
Power C
Speed B+
Wits A+
Dry Eye S
Technique S+

CHARACTER

## *Seeing the truth with sharp eyes, this teacher cares for his students.*

The pro hero who serves as homeroom teacher to Midoriya and the others of U.A.'s class 1-A. Eraser Head experienced the death of a friend back during his school days, which makes him all the more strict with his would-be hero students. Meanwhile, he's personally mentoring Shinso from General Studies and teaching the boy how to use the binding cloth weapon, which took Eraser Head six years to master. Once he decides to look after someone, he'll give them as much support as humanly possible.

HIGHLIGHT ▸▸▸ I

CRASH

⬆ While rushing off to protect his students, Eraser Head got attacked by Dabi and took the villain down in an instant with his binding cloth. No motion is wasted!

MORE THAN ANYONE, HE PURSUES THE TITLE OF TOP HERO WITH EVERYTHING HE'S GOT.
IF THE VILLAINS HAVE MISTAKEN THAT FOR A WEAKNESS...
...THEN THEIR THOUGHT PROCESS IS INDEED SUPERFICIAL.

HIGHLIGHT ▸▸▸ II

⬆ Eraser Head is always calm, whether he's dealing with school duties or provocative members of the media. For the sake of protecting his students, he'll always act rationally.

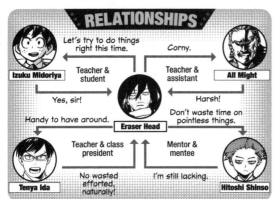

## RELATIONSHIPS

Izuku Midoriya
Let's try to do things right this time.
Teacher & student
Yes, sir!
All Might
Corny.
Teacher & assistant
Harsh!
Eraser Head
Handy to have around.
Tenya Ida
Teacher & class president
No wasted efforted, naturally!
Don't waste time on pointless things.
Hitoshi Shinso
Mentor & mentee
I'm still lacking.

## PROFILE

Name: **Shota Aizawa**
Hero name: **Eraser Head**
Quirk: **Erasure**
Birthday: **November 8**
Height: **183 cm**
Blood type: **B**
Birthplace: **Tokyo**
Personality: **Actually kind of doting**
Ultimate move: **Binding Cloth**

- "Don't let them get you while we're still in the dark, future heroes!" (vol. 9, chap. 77)
- "No offense, but compared to the rest of you, we're looking towards the future." (vol. 12, chap. 103)
- "I'll watch over you. Let's try to do things right this time, Midoriya." (vol. 15, chap. 136)
- "Otherwise, we're doing a regular class open house." (vol. 19, chap. 169)

### Eraser Head's Notable Quotables

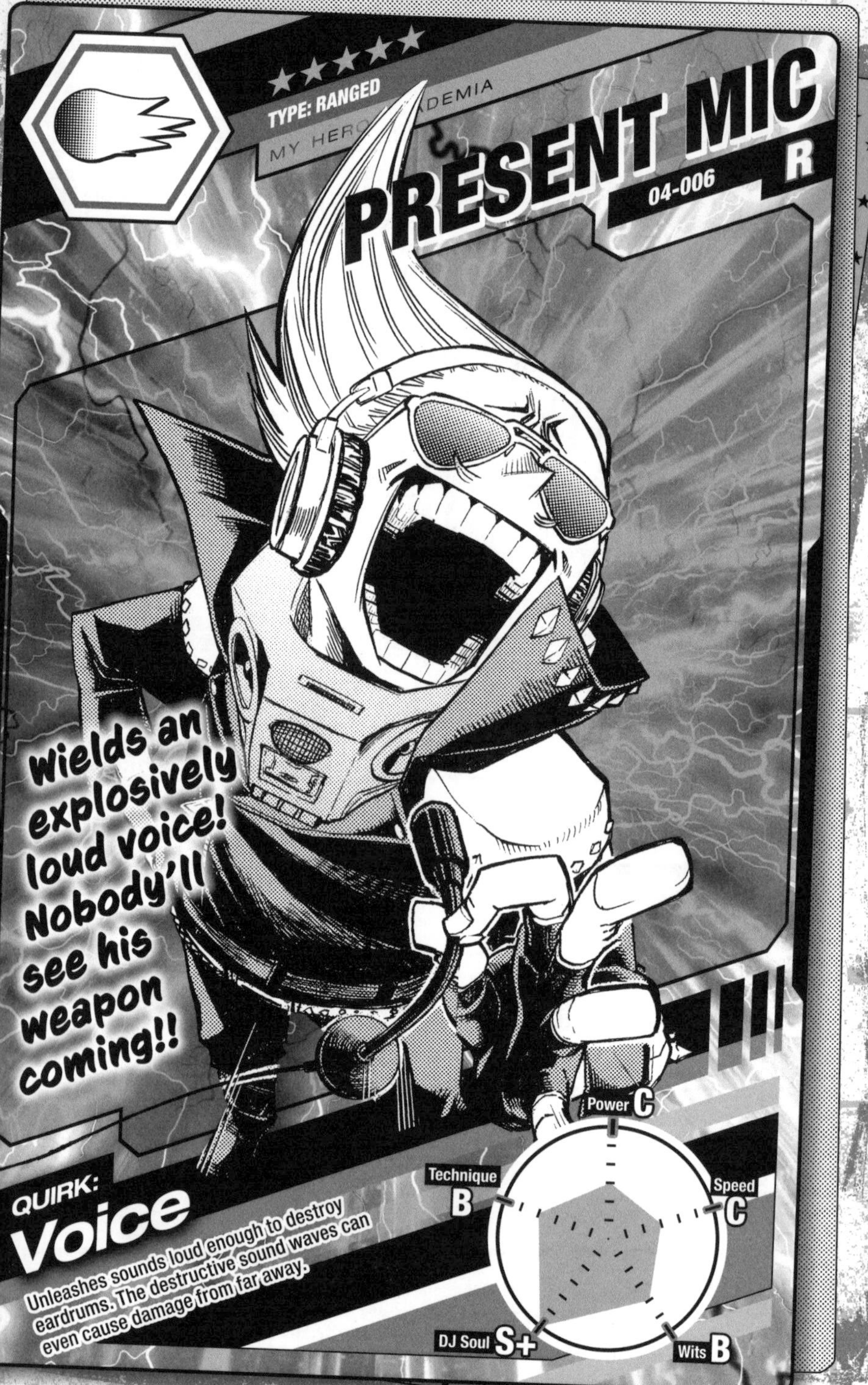
TYPE: RANGED
MY HERO ACADEMIA
PRESENT MIC
R
04-006
Wields an explosively loud voice! Nobody'll see his weapon coming!!
Power C
Technique B
Speed C
DJ Soul S+
Wits B
QUIRK:
Voice
Unleashes sounds loud enough to destroy eardrums. The destructive sound waves can even cause damage from far away.

# As a radio DJ and commentator, he always provides a good time.

A pro hero who works as a teacher at U.A. and is a radio DJ. Present Mic is in charge of live commentary for school events and always livens up the venue with his lighthearted play-by-play. He's been friends with Eraser Head since they attended school together and even came up with his hero name. They seem to be close.

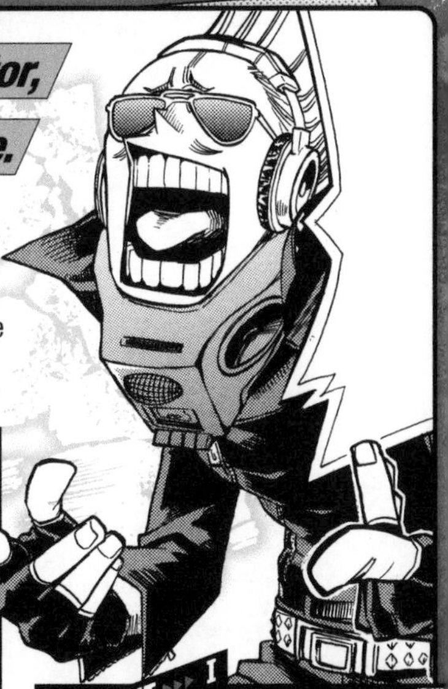

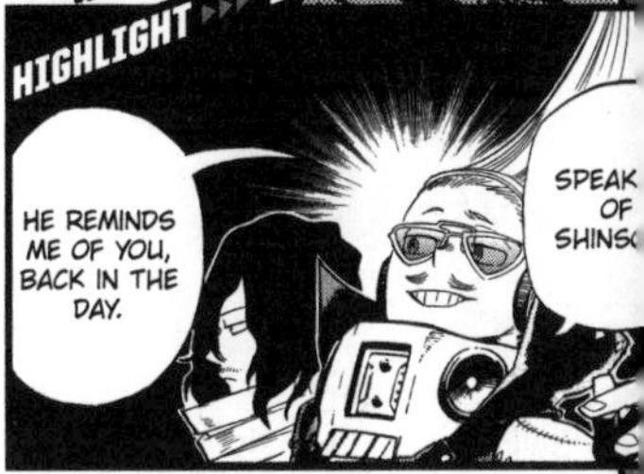
HIGHLIGHT I
HE REMINDS ME OF YOU, BACK IN THE DAY.
SPEAK OF

⬆ After seeing Shinso perform, Present Mic noticed a resemblance between Shinso and young Eraser Head.

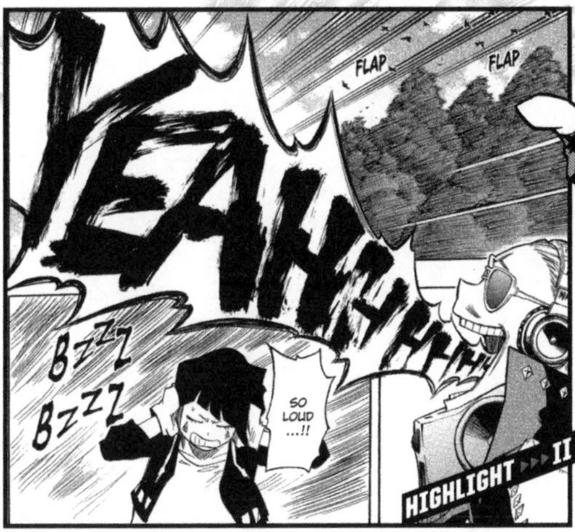
FLAP
FLAP
SO LOUD ...!!
BZZZ
BZZZ
HIGHLIGHT II

⬆ Jiro wasn't able to cancel out Present Mic's powerful sound waves with her own sound attacks. She couldn't even approach him, which just goes to show the gap between pro heroes and everyone else.

## RELATIONSHIPS

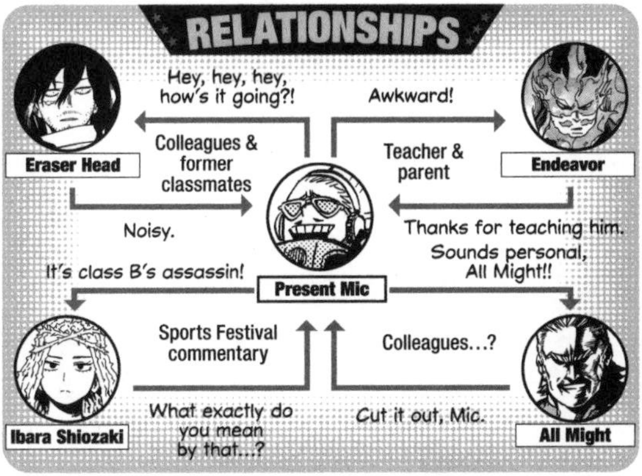
Eraser Head
Hey, hey, hey, how's it going?!
Colleagues & former classmates
Noisy.
Endeavor
Awkward!
Teacher & parent
Thanks for teaching him.
Present Mic
It's class B's assassin!
Sports Festival commentary
What exactly do you mean by that...?
Ibara Shiozaki
Sounds personal, All Might!!
Colleagues...?
Cut it out, Mic.
All Might

## PROFILE

Name: **Hizashi Yamada**
Hero name: **Present Mic**
Quirk: **Voice**
Birthday: **July 7**
Height: **185 cm**
Blood type: **B**
Birthplace: **Tokyo**
Personality: **Extremely excitable**
Ultimate moves: **Echo Voice, High Shout**

- "Welcome to today's live performance!! Everybody say 'Hey'!!" (vol. 1, chap. 3)
- "Where's the music? The live commentary? Without those, an event's got no soul!" (vol. 18, chap. 164)
- "Get those good vibes flowing and let's say...Yeaahhh!!" (vol. 18, chap. 164)

**Present Mic's Notable Quotables**

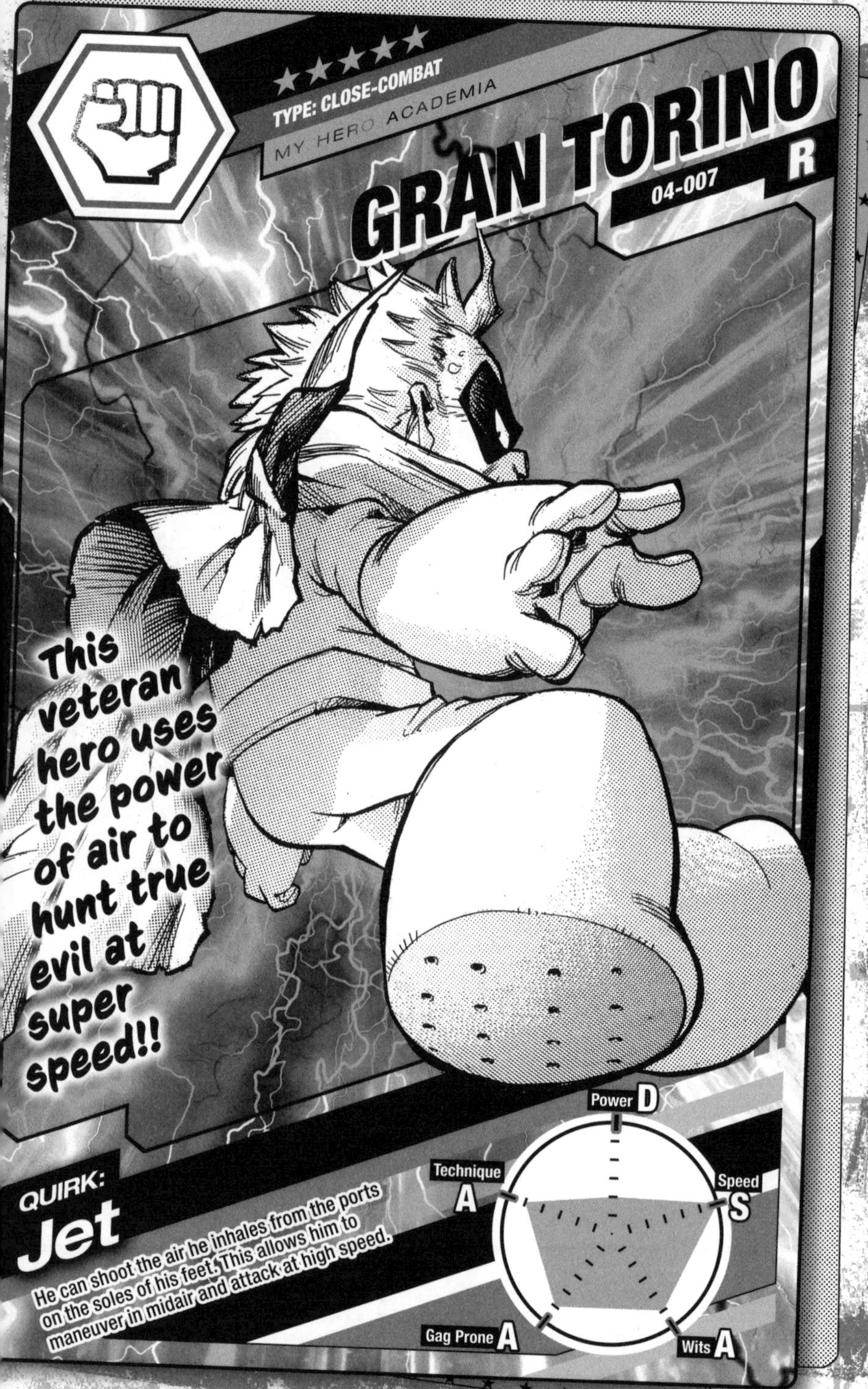
★★★★★
TYPE: CLOSE-COMBAT
MY HERO ACADEMIA
GRAN TORINO
R
04-007
This veteran hero uses the power of air to hunt true evil at super speed!!
Power D
Technique A
Speed S
Gag Prone A
Wits A
QUIRK:
Jet
He can shoot the air he inhales from the ports on the soles of his feet. This allows him to maneuver in midair and attack at high speed.

CHARACTER

## An unsung, mysterious hero, with ties to One For All.

Gran Torino used to team up with Nana Shimura, and at her request, he taught at U.A. for one year in order to train the young All Might. His propensity for goofy gags rubbed off on All Might. Nowadays, people who witness the aged Gran Torino's gags aren't sure whether to laugh or be concerned for his health and well-being…

TMP
TMP
...TRY TO LAND A SINGLE HIT ON ME!!
TMP
HIGHLIGHT ▸▸▸ I

⬆ Gran Torino flustered Midoriya by moving too fast for the naked eye to track! Elderly or not, no one doubts his abilities. Why did he never seek fame and fortune…?

IT'S BECAUSE THIS COUNTRY'S GOT NO "PILLAR" TO SUPPORT IT...
...SO HE SAYS HE'S GONNA BE THAT PILLAR.
HIGHLIGHT ▸▸▸ II

⬆ In his younger days, he worked alongside Shimura. His connection with her led him in later years to keep watch over All Might.

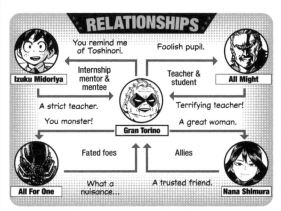

## RELATIONSHIPS

Izuku Midoriya
You remind me of Toshinori.
Internship mentor & mentee
A strict teacher.
All Might
Foolish pupil.
Teacher & student
Terrifying teacher!
Gran Torino
You monster!
Fated foes
What a nuisance...
All For One
A great woman.
Allies
A trusted friend.
Nana Shimura

## PROFILE

Name: **Sorahiko Torino**
Hero name: **Gran Torino**
Quirk: **Jet**
Birthday: **January 28**
Height: **120 cm**
Blood type: **B**
Birthplace: **Yamanashi Prefecture**
Personality: **Carrot-and-stick mentality**
Ultimate move: **Jet V8 Wild Speed**

### Gran Torino's Notable Quotables

- "Who are you?!" (vol. 6, chap. 46)
- "Then I'll tell you once more. Come at me, you *neophyte*." (vol. 6, chap. 46)
- "I couldn't half-ass his training. He was entrusted to me by a dear departed friend." (vol. 6, chap. 48)

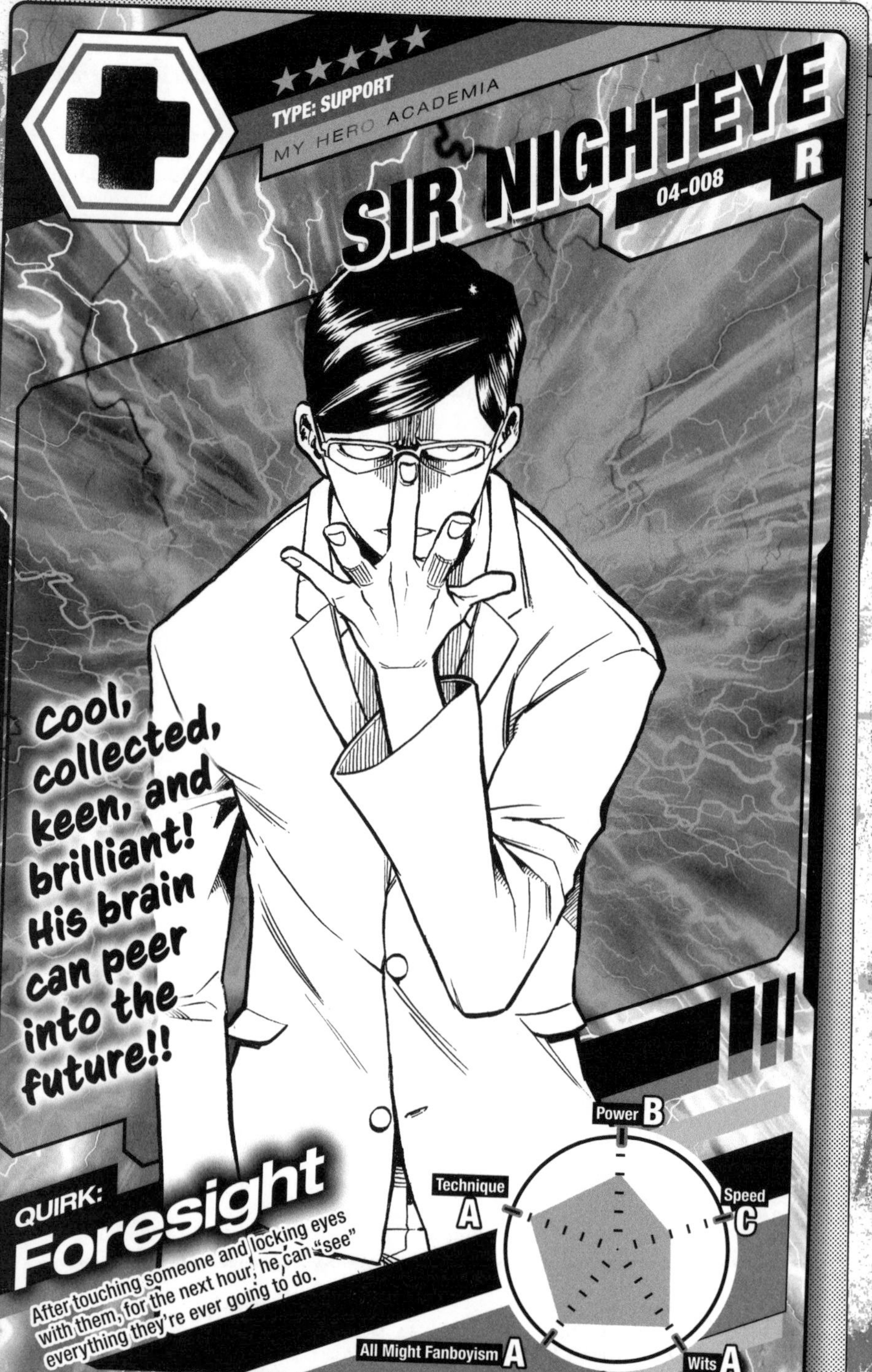
★★★★★★
TYPE: SUPPORT
MY HERO ACADEMIA
SIR NIGHTEYE
R
04-008
Cool, collected, keen, and brilliant! His brain can peer into the future!!
Power B
Technique A
Speed C
All Might Fanboyism A
Wits A
QUIRK:
Foresight
After touching someone and locking eyes with them, for the next hour, he can "see" everything they're ever going to do.

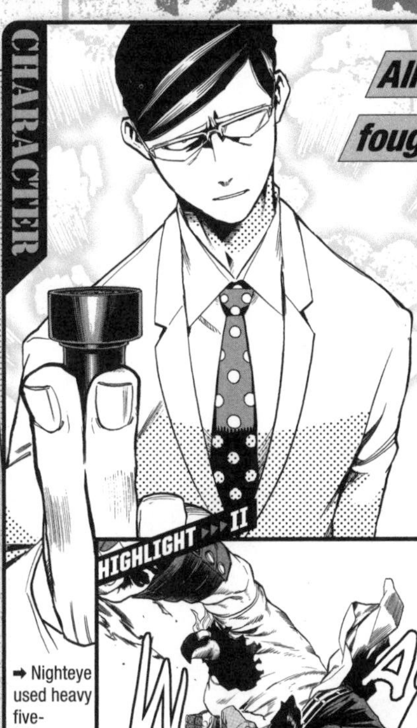
CHARACTER

## All Might's former sidekick!! He fought against his own prediction.

As All Might's sidekick, Nighteye supported the great hero by performing routine tasks behind the scenes. Those yellow streaks in his hair were an homage to All Might. After going independent, Nighteye opened his own agency and started taking on work-study trainees like Midoriya and Togata. He died from wounds received in the battle against Chisaki.

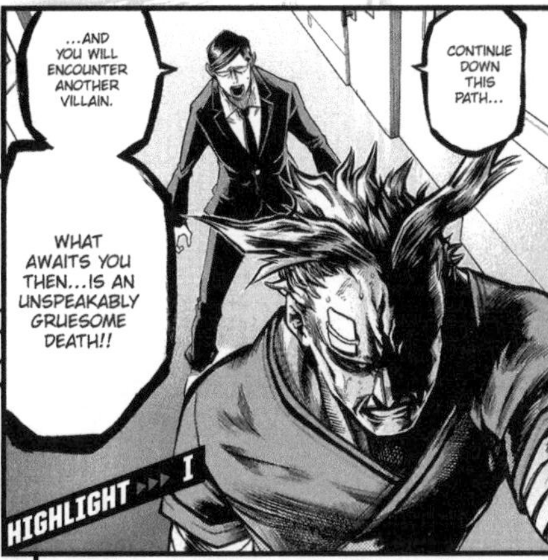
CONTINUE DOWN THIS PATH...
...AND YOU WILL ENCOUNTER ANOTHER VILLAIN.
WHAT AWAITS YOU THEN...IS AN UNSPEAKABLY GRUESOME DEATH!!
HIGHLIGHT ▸▸▸ I

⬆ Nighteye struggled against what he saw in All Might's future. His respect for the man caused the two to go their separate ways...

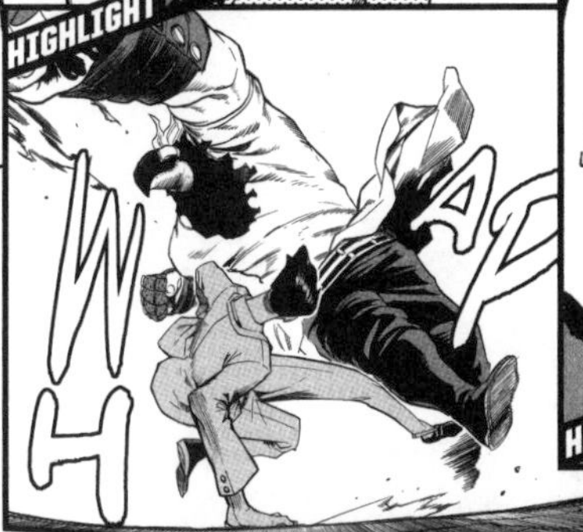
HIGHLIGHT ▸▸▸ II

➡ Nighteye used heavy five-kilogram personal seals and was an elegant brawler in his own right!

## RELATIONSHIPS

- **Mirio Togata** — Mentor & mentee
  - Sir Nighteye → Mirio Togata: "He should have been the successor."
  - Mirio Togata → Sir Nighteye: "Yes, sir!"
- **All Might** — Former duo
  - Sir Nighteye → All Might: "You should have quit as a legend."
  - All Might → Sir Nighteye: "I can't face him."
- **Izuku Midoriya** — Accepted for work study
  - Sir Nighteye → Izuku Midoriya: "I still hadn't accepted you."
  - Izuku Midoriya → Sir Nighteye: "I can change the future!"
- **Bubble Girl** — Boss & underling
  - Sir Nighteye → Bubble Girl: "Once more, with feeling."
  - Bubble Girl → Sir Nighteye: "Yes, sir!"

## PROFILE

Name: **Mirai Sasaki**
Hero name: **Sir Nighteye**
Quirk: **Foresight**
Birthday: **January 2**
Height: **200 cm**
Blood type: **AB**
Birthplace: **Tokyo**
Personality: **Humor lover**
Ultimate move: **Seal Stamp**

- "I believe that a society without humor and spirit has no future." (vol. 14, chap. 126)
- "The cleverest villains out there lurk in the shadows." (vol. 15, chap. 130)
- "You'll make...a fine hero... That...is one part of the future...that mustn't...be changed. So...keep smiling." (vol. 18, chap. 161)

**Sir Nighteye's Notable Quotables**

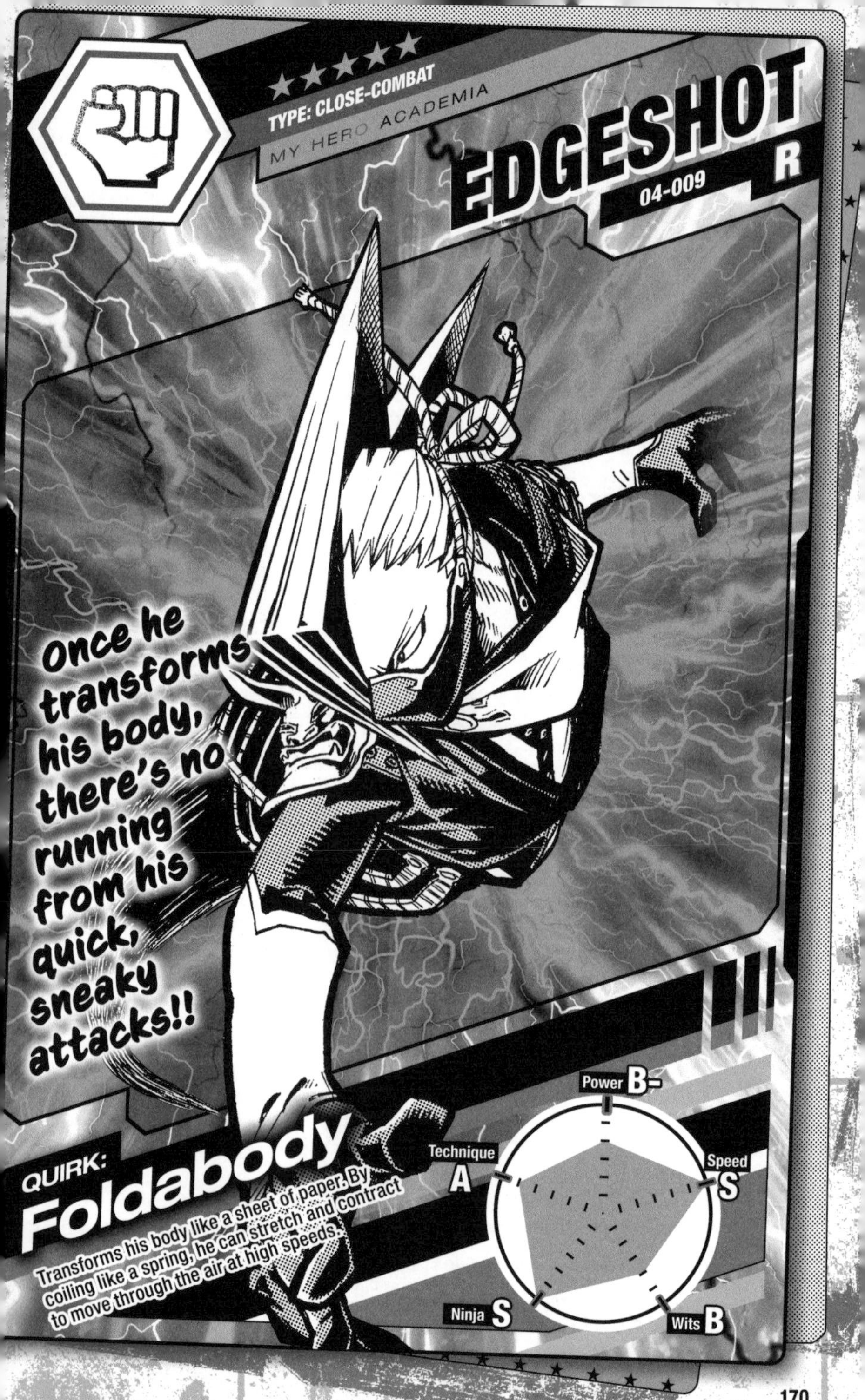
TYPE: CLOSE-COMBAT
MY HERO ACADEMIA
EDGESHOT
R
04-009
Once he transforms his body, there's no running from his quick, sneaky attacks!!
QUIRK:
Foldabody
Transforms his body like a sheet of paper. By coiling like a spring, he can stretch and contract to move through the air at high speeds.
Power B-
Technique A
Speed S
Ninja S
Wits B

# Nothing is known about this mysterious ninja hero's life!

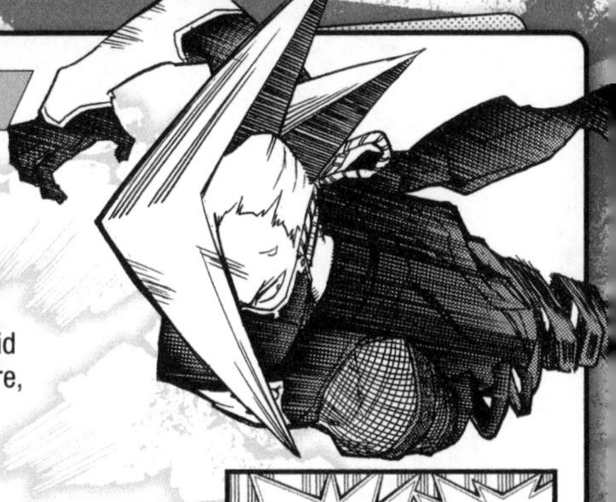

The no. 4 pro hero is known for being a bit old-fashioned. During the operation to rescue Bakugo, Edgeshot slipped through a locked door and secured a route for the rest of the raid team. Though not the type to team up by nature, he formed the Lurkers with Kamui Woods and Mt. Lady. Edgeshot is adaptable and can read the room when it counts.

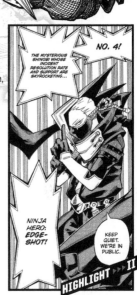

NO. 4!
THE MYSTERIOUS SHINOBI WHOSE INCIDENT RESOLUTION RATE AND SUPPORT ARE SKYROCKETING...
NINJA HERO: EDGE-SHOT!
KEEP QUIET. WE'RE IN PUBLIC.
HIGHLIGHT ▸▸▸ II

➡ Edgeshot shows off those hand seals. He's popular due to his ninja theme and overall aesthetic. He's the genuine article, with plenty of successes to his name.

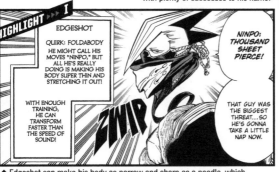

HIGHLIGHT ▸▸▸ I
NINPO: THOUSAND SHEET PIERCE!
THAT GUY WAS THE BIGGEST THREAT...SO HE'S GONNA TAKE A LITTLE NAP NOW.
EDGESHOT
QUIRK: FOLDABODY
HE MIGHT CALL HIS MOVES "NINPO," BUT ALL HE'S REALLY DOING IS MAKING HIS BODY SUPER THIN AND STRETCHING IT OUT!
WITH ENOUGH TRAINING, HE CAN TRANSFORM FASTER THAN THE SPEED OF SOUND!
ZWIP

⬆ Edgeshot can make his body as narrow and sharp as a needle, which allowed him to incapacitate even the mist-like Kurogiri with a swift strike. That kind of skill comes from experience!

## RELATIONSHIPS

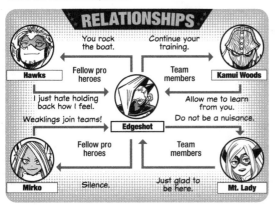

Hawks
You rock the boat.
Fellow pro heroes
I just hate holding back how I feel.
Kamui Woods
Continue your training.
Team members
Allow me to learn from you.
Edgeshot
Mirko
Weaklings join teams!
Fellow pro heroes
Silence.
Mt. Lady
Do not be a nuisance.
Team members
Just glad to be here.

## PROFILE

Name: **Shinya Kamihara**
Hero name: **Edgeshot**
Quirk: **Foldabody**
Birthday: **February 22**
Height: **170 cm**
Blood type: **A**
Birthplace: **Unknown**
Personality: **Private and secretive**
Ultimate move: **Ninpo: Thousand Sheet Pierce**

- "One must never neglect defense. Especially when attacking…" (vol. 10, chap. 87)
- "Not so fast, you destroyer. We're here to do some saving!" (vol. 11, chap. 93)
- "I don't do this job for fame or reputation. The ability to preserve law and order is the true measure of a hero." (vol. 20, chap. 185)

**Edgeshot's Notable Quotables**

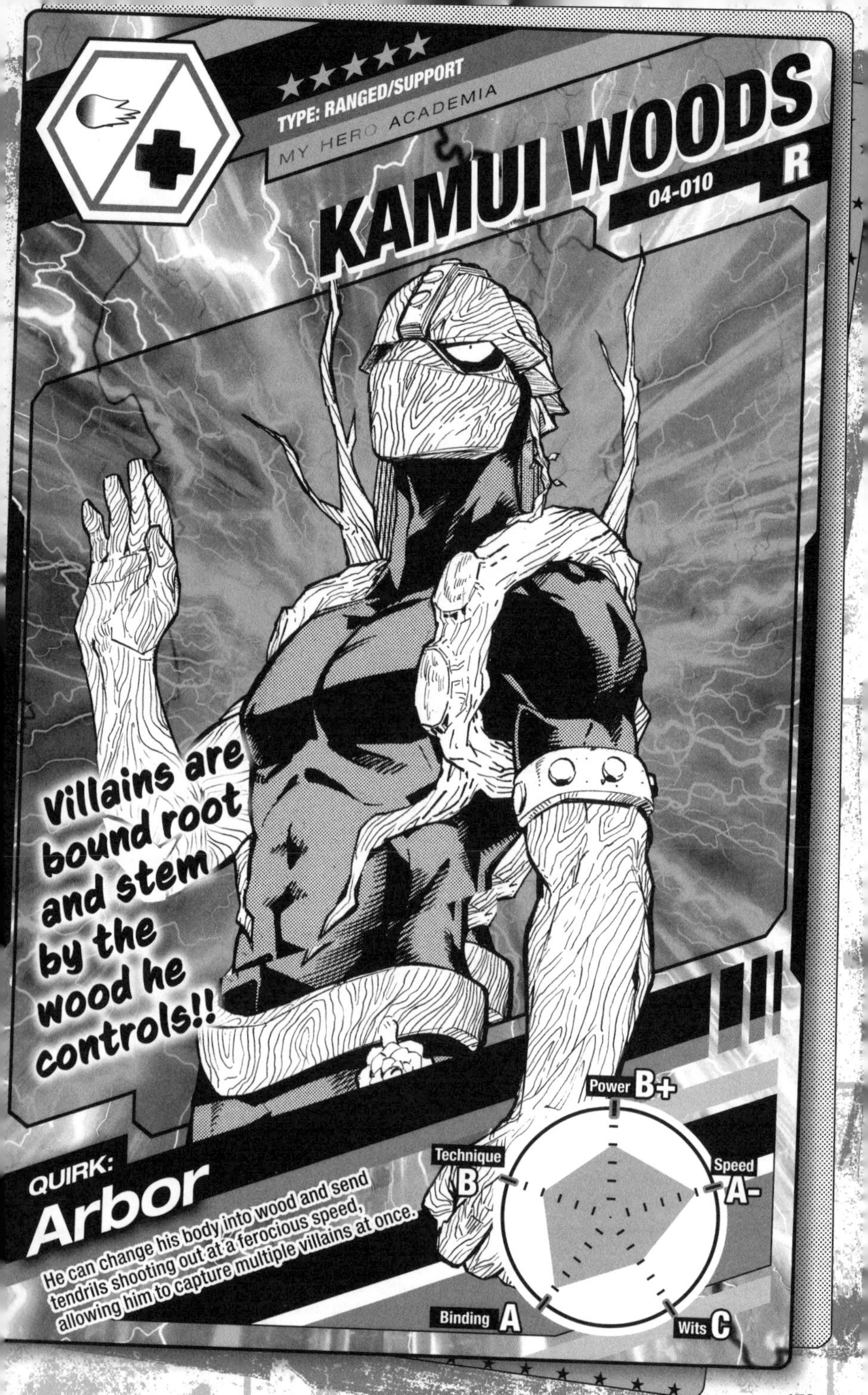

TYPE: RANGED/SUPPORT
MY HERO ACADEMIA
KAMUI WOODS
R
04-010
Villains are bound root and stem by the wood he controls!!
Power B+
Technique B
Speed A-
Binding A
Wits C
QUIRK:
Arbor
He can change his body into wood and send tendrils shooting out at a ferocious speed, allowing him to capture multiple villains at once.

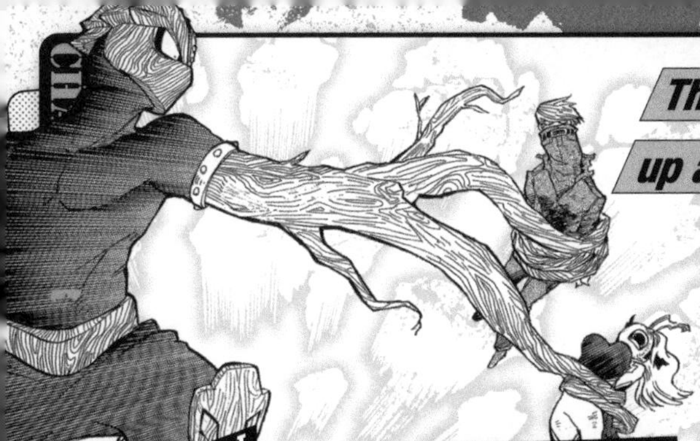

## This sprout is racking up achievements.

A relatively new pro hero whose strength and by-the-book approach to justice earned him a tip of the hat even from All Might. During the raid on the League of Villains' hideout, Kamui Woods proved his mettle by joining the vanguard alongside All Might! His involvement with the events in Kamino sent his notoriety skyrocketing and won him a team-up request from Edgeshot. He was so happy he wept for two hours straight.

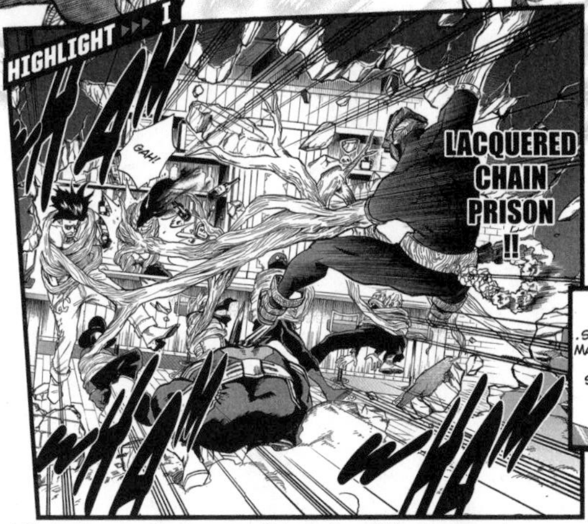
HIGHLIGHT ▸▸▸ I
WHAM
GAAH!!
LACQUERED CHAIN PRISON!!
WHAM
WHAM

↑ During the operation to rescue Bakugo, Kamui Woods captured seven members of the League of Villains! His wide-range attack was too quick for the villains to react to and strong enough to hold them in place.

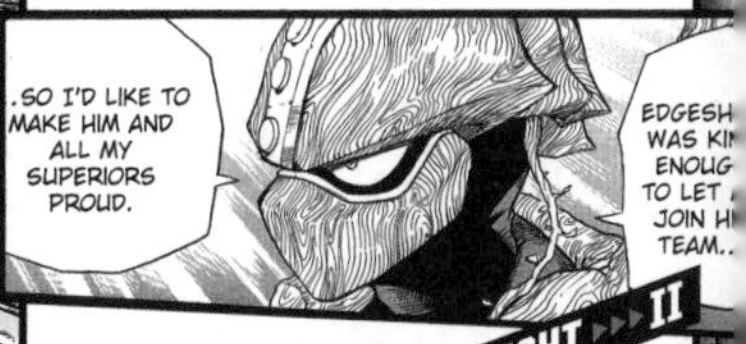
.SO I'D LIKE TO MAKE HIM AND ALL MY SUPERIORS PROUD.
HIGHLIGHT ▸▸▸ II

↑ He doesn't let his new popularity go to his head and always remembers to respect his elders. The public appreciates that modesty.

## RELATIONSHIPS

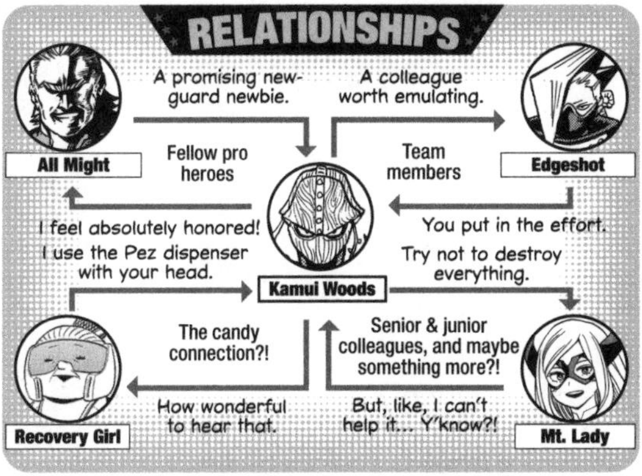
All Might
A promising new-guard newbie.
Fellow pro heroes
I feel absolutely honored! I use the Pez dispenser with your head.
Edgeshot
A colleague worth emulating.
Team members
You put in the effort. Try not to destroy everything.
Kamui Woods
Recovery Girl
The candy connection?!
How wonderful to hear that.
Mt. Lady
Senior & junior colleagues, and maybe something more?!
But, like, I can't help it... Y'know?!

## PROFILE

Name: **Shinji Nishiya**
Hero name: **Kamui Woods**
Quirk: **Arbor**
Birthday: **May 20**
Height: **168 cm**
Blood type: **A**
Birthplace: **Kagoshima Prefecture**
Personality: **Tight-lipped and straitlaced**
Ultimate move: **Preemptive Binding Lacquered Chain Prison**

- "You're pure evil." (vol. 1, chap. 1)
- "You did good, Mt. Lady!!" (vol. 11, chap. 93)
- "I'd like to make him and all my superiors proud." (vol. 20, chap. 185)

**Kamui Woods's Notable Quotables**

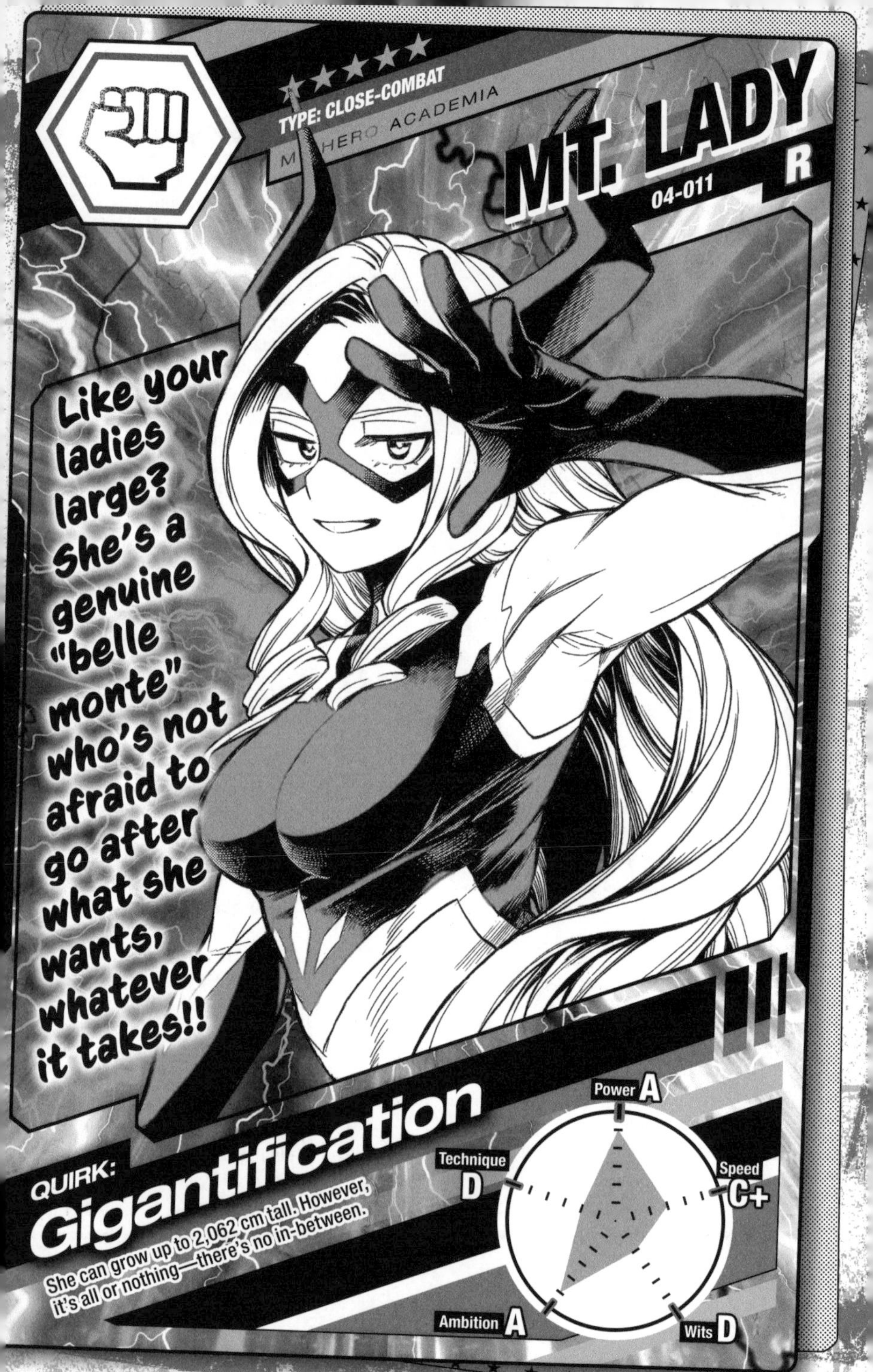
★★★★★★
TYPE: CLOSE-COMBAT
MY HERO ACADEMIA
MT. LADY
R
04-011
Like your ladies large? She's a genuine "belle monte" who's not afraid to go after what she wants, whatever it takes!!
QUIRK:
Gigantification
She can grow up to 2,062 cm tall. However, it's all or nothing—there's no in-between.
Power A
Technique D
Speed C+
Ambition A
Wits D

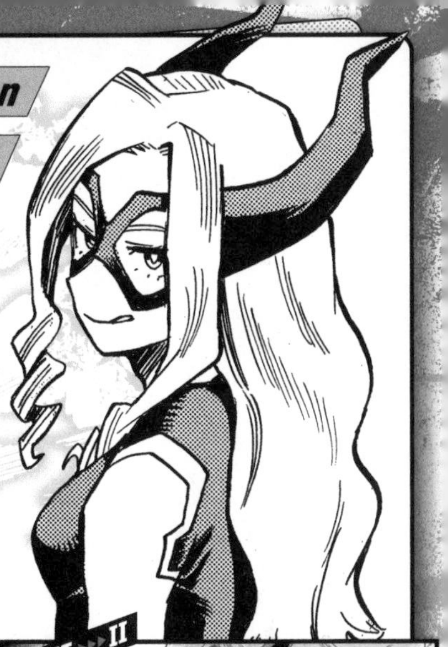

# Her tendencies are attention getting!! And expensive!!

A pro hero who's undeniably gorgeous but can be a little eccentric. When Mt. Lady made her debut, she only cared about fame, but ever since the events in Kamino and her team-up with Edgeshot, her views have been evolving!!

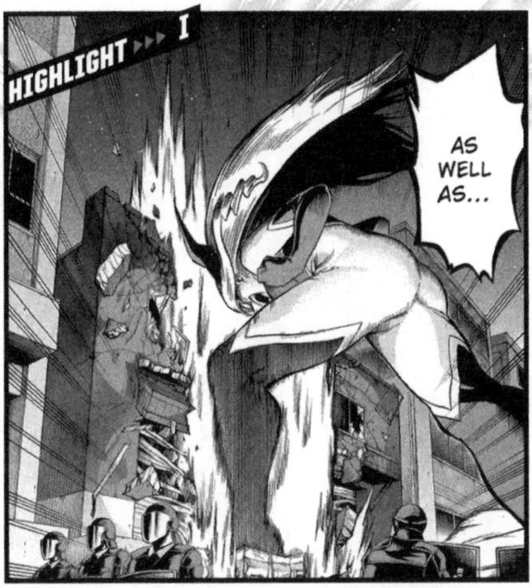
HIGHLIGHT ▸▸▸ I
AS WELL AS...

⬆ After turning giant, Mt. Lady packs enough power to pulverize a building with one attack!! A simple punch becomes strong enough to count as an ultimate move!

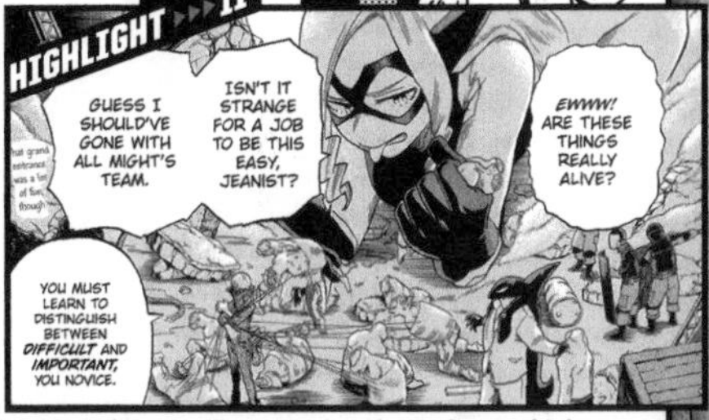
HIGHLIGHT ▸▸▸ II
EWWW! ARE THESE THINGS REALLY ALIVE?
ISN'T IT STRANGE FOR A JOB TO BE THIS EASY, JEANIST?
GUESS I SHOULD'VE GONE WITH ALL MIGHT'S TEAM.
YOU MUST LEARN TO DISTINGUISH BETWEEN *DIFFICULT* AND *IMPORTANT*, YOU NOVICE.

⬆ Mt. Lady sometimes worries about glory and takes a disrespectful attitude toward her senior colleagues… but she always maintains her dignity as a pro hero.

## RELATIONSHIPS

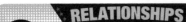

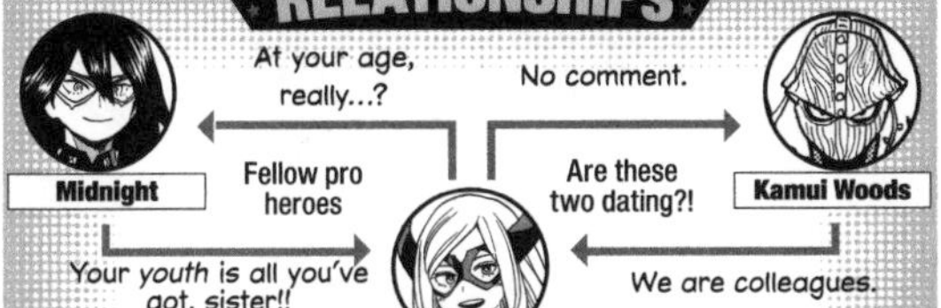
Midnight
At your age, really...?
Fellow pro heroes
Your youth is all you've got, sister!!
Kamui Woods
No comment.
Are these two dating?!
We are colleagues.
Mt. Lady
Best Jeanist
Shush, novice.
Fellow pro heroes
Sorrrry.
Minoru Mineta
You snitch, you die.
Internship mentor & mentee
Women are actually scary, deep down!

## PROFILE

Name: **Yu Takeyama**
Hero name: **Mt. Lady**
Quirk: **Gigantification**
Birthday: **August 11**
Height: **162 cm → 2,062 cm**
Blood type: **B**
Birthplace: **Hokkaido**
Personality: **Self-interested**
Ultimate moves: **Canyon Cannon, Titan Cliff**

- "I wanna make it big!!" (vol. 3, side story)
- "It's just kind of sad to see our *elders* make fools of themselves." (vol. 8, side story)
- "Prioritize…the rescue. Go on…you dumb kids…" (vol. 11, chap. 91)

**Mt. Lady's Notable Quotables**

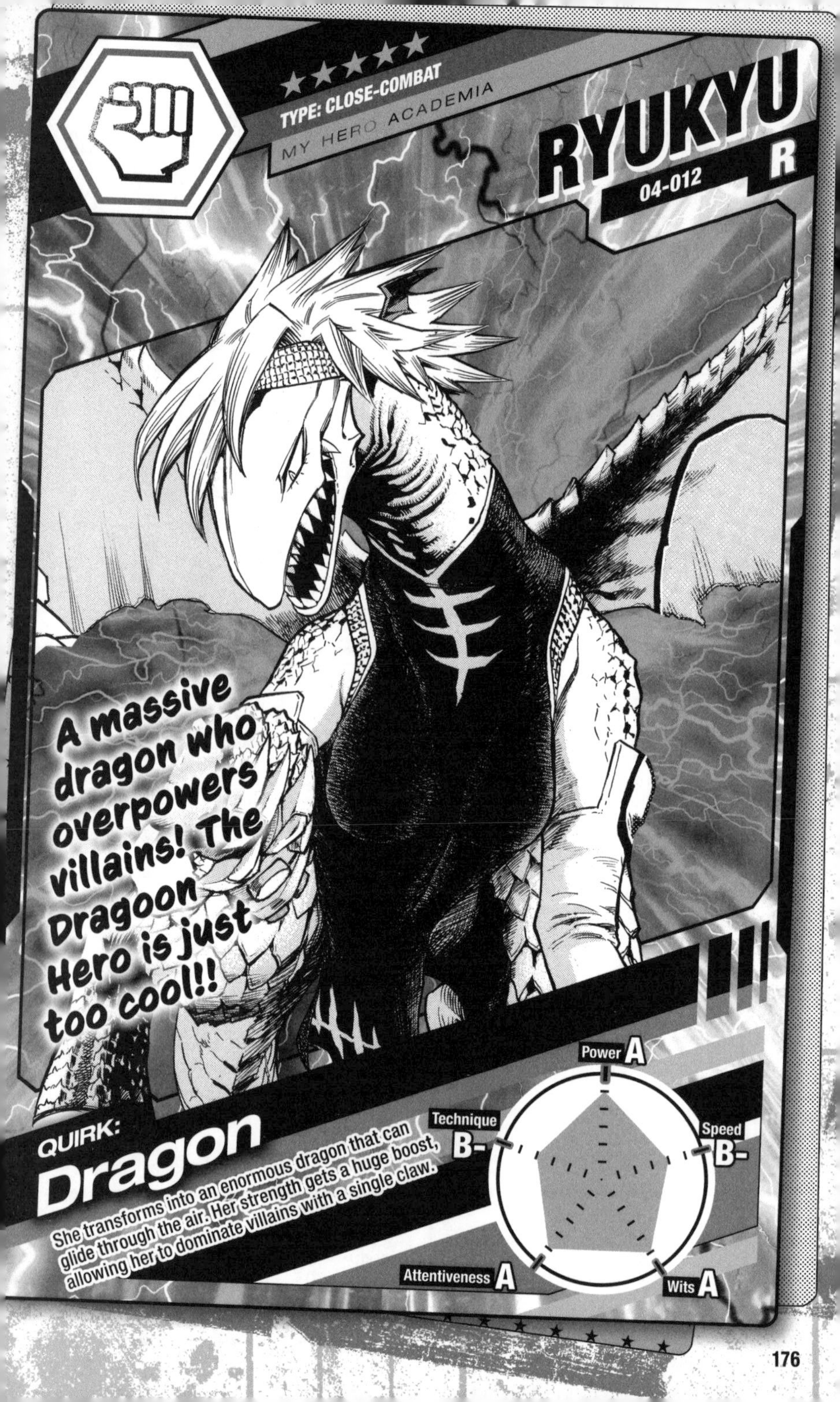
★★★★★★
TYPE: CLOSE-COMBAT
MY HERO ACADEMIA
RYUKYU
R
04-012
A massive dragon who overpowers villains! The Dragoon Hero is just too cool!!
QUIRK:
Dragon
She transforms into an enormous dragon that can glide through the air. Her strength gets a huge boost, allowing her to dominate villains with a single claw.
Power A
Technique B-
Speed B-
Attentiveness A
Wits A

CHARACTER

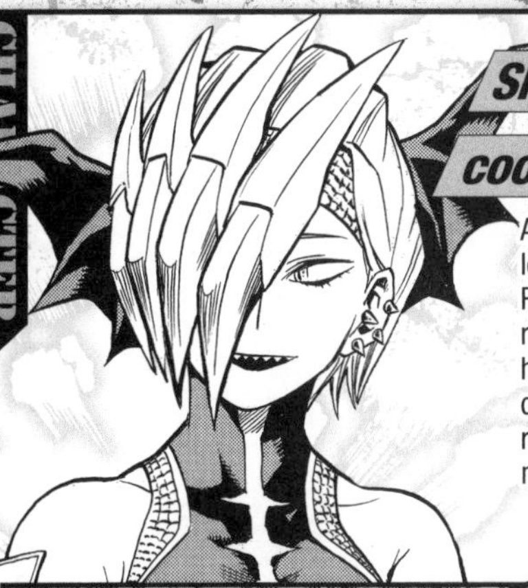

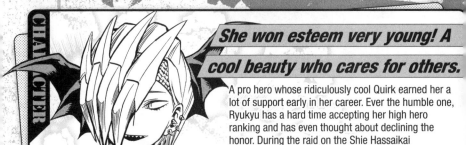

## She won esteem very young! A cool beauty who cares for others.

A pro hero whose ridiculously cool Quirk earned her a lot of support early in her career. Ever the humble one, Ryukyu has a hard time accepting her high hero ranking and has even thought about declining the honor. During the raid on the Shie Hassaikai compound, she protected everyone from the rampaging Katsukame and incapacitated him in one mighty blow.

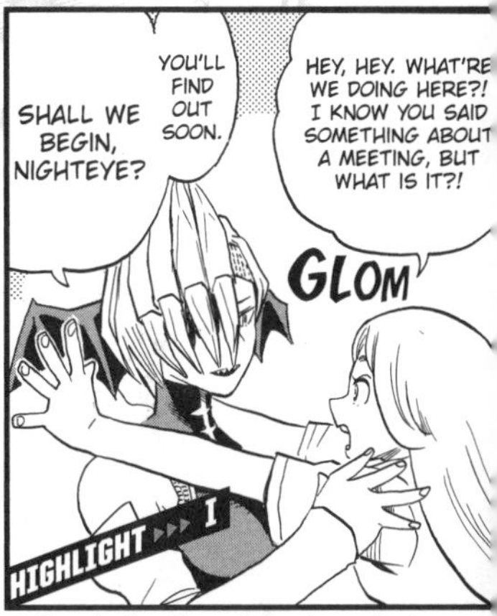
HEY, HEY. WHAT'RE WE DOING HERE?! I KNOW YOU SAID SOMETHING ABOUT A MEETING, BUT WHAT IS IT?!
YOU'LL FIND OUT SOON.
SHALL WE BEGIN, NIGHTEYE?
GLOM
HIGHLIGHT ▸▸▸ I

⬆ Though absurdly cool at a glance, Ryukyu is friendly and has a big heart, which has earned her adoration from many.

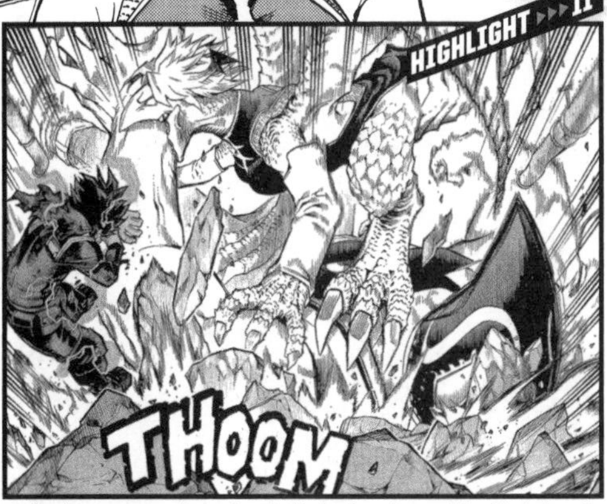
HIGHLIGHT ▸▸▸ II
THOOM

⬆ Ryukyu gave precise orders to Hado, Uraraka, and Asui to help get them through this crisis. The trust she had built with her work-study trainee team really paid off.

## RELATIONSHIPS

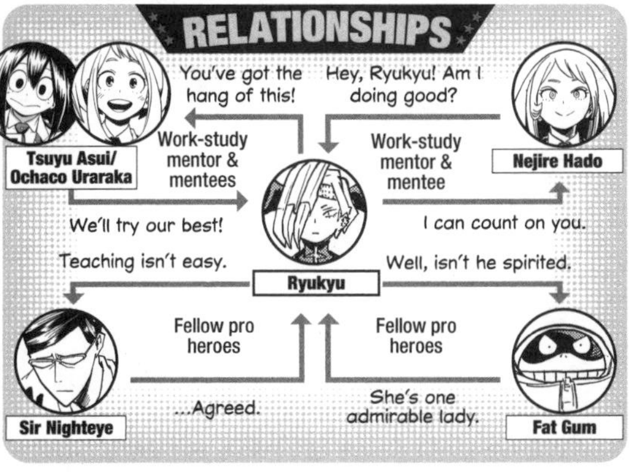
Tsuyu Asui/ Ochaco Uraraka
You've got the hang of this!
Work-study mentor & mentees
We'll try our best!
Hey, Ryukyu! Am I doing good?
Work-study mentor & mentee
Nejire Hado
I can count on you.
Ryukyu
Teaching isn't easy.
Well, isn't he spirited.
Fellow pro heroes
...Agreed.
Sir Nighteye
Fellow pro heroes
She's one admirable lady.
Fat Gum

## PROFILE

Name: **Ryuko Tatsuma**
Hero name: **Ryukyu**
Quirk: **Dragon**
Birthday: **September 22**
Height: **166 cm**
Blood type: **A**
Birthplace: **Okinawa**
Personality: **Dependable big sister**
Ultimate moves: **Dragoon Punish, Wing Slash**

## Ryukyu's Notable Quotables

- "There's a child in need out there. That's what matters most." (vol. 15, chap. 136)
- "There have been lives I couldn't save... So going forward, I'll strive to really earn my ranking." (vol. 20, chap. 185)

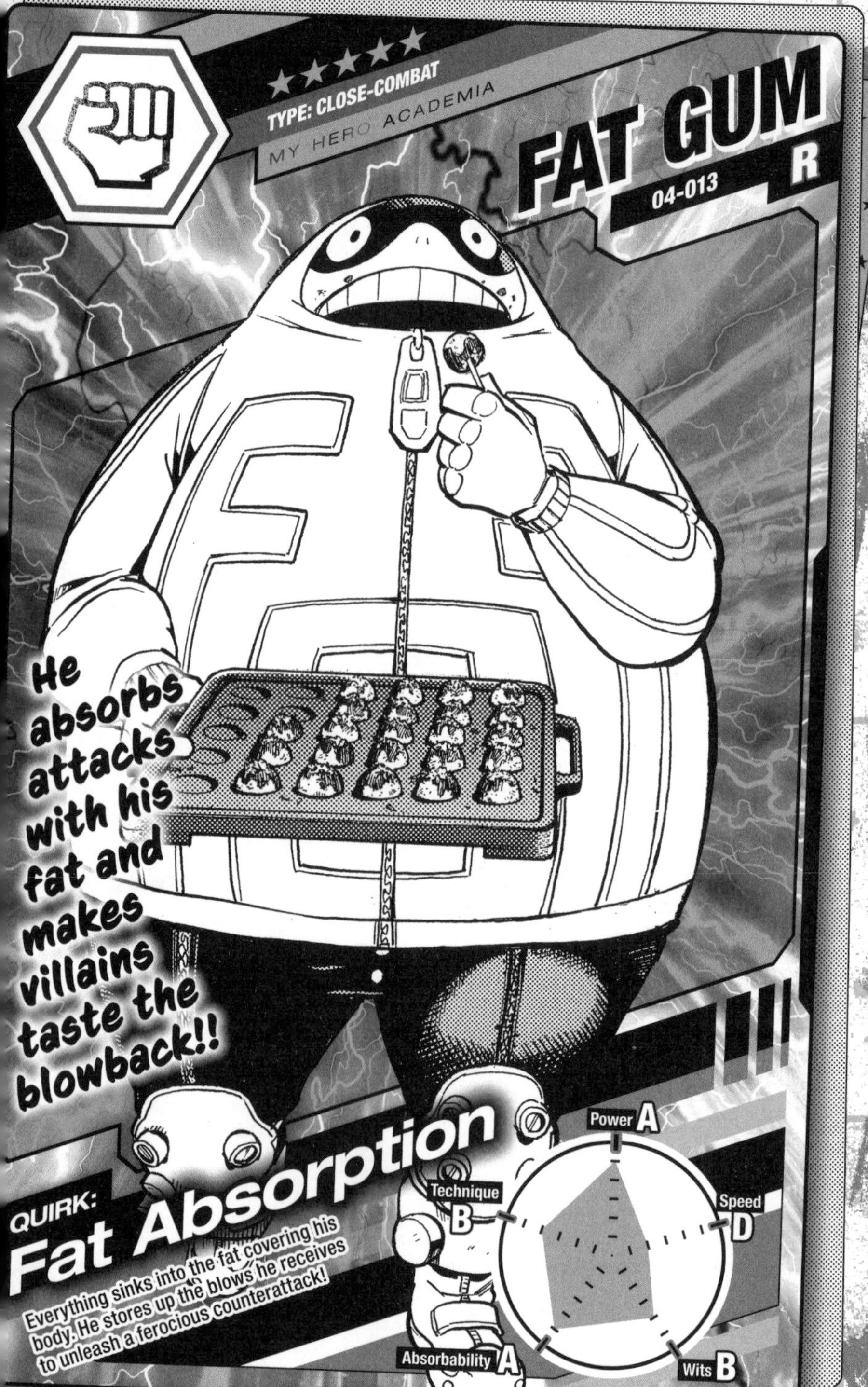
TYPE: CLOSE-COMBAT
MY HERO ACADEMIA
FAT GUM
R
04-013
He absorbs attacks with his fat and makes villains taste the blowback!!
QUIRK:
Fat Absorption
Everything sinks into the fat covering his body. He stores up the blows he receives to unleash a ferocious counterattack!
Power A
Speed D
Wits B
Absorbability A
Technique B

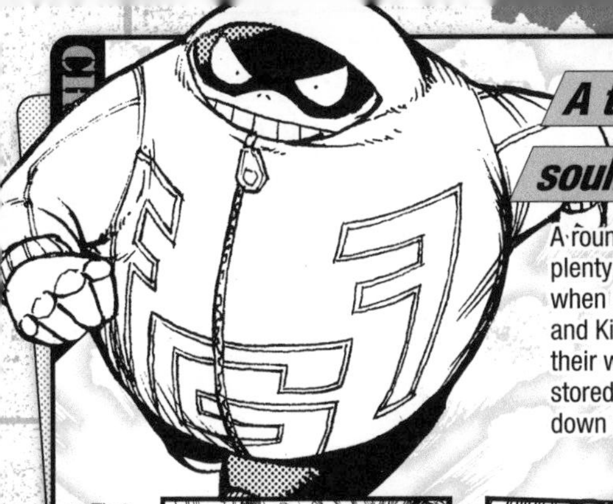

## A thick body plus a passionate soul!! The hero from Kansai!

A round and somewhat adorable pro hero. Fat Gum is plenty approachable, but he gets mighty fired up when it's time for heroics!! He helped teach Amajiki and Kirishima the true meaning of being a hero during their work study. After Fat Gum converts the energy stored in his fat into an attack of his own, he shrinks down and becomes unrecognizable.

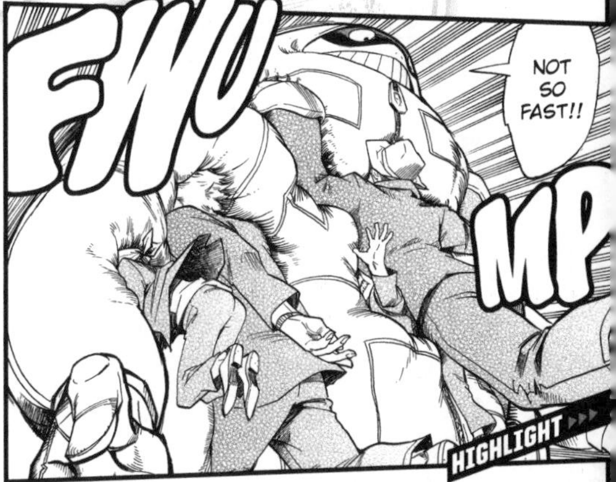

FWU
NOT SO FAST!!
MP
HIGHLIGHT


⬆ A whole gang of villains found themselves sucked into the fat. Fat Gum believes in making evildoers lose the will to fight before they even get a chance to hurt anyone.

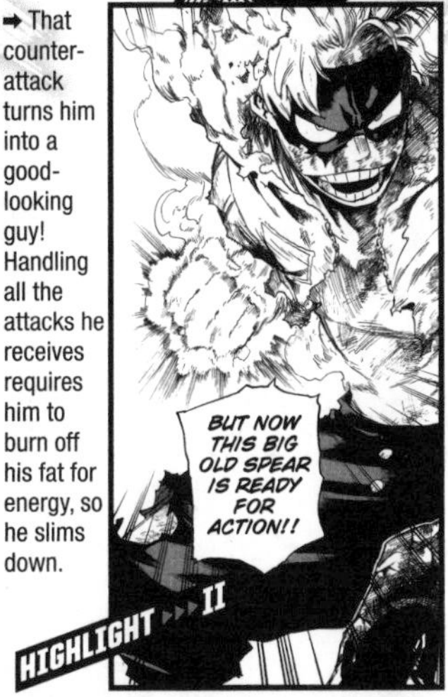

BUT NOW THIS BIG OLD SPEAR IS READY FOR ACTION!!
HIGHLIGHT II


➡ That counter-attack turns him into a good-looking guy! Handling all the attacks he receives requires him to burn off his fat for energy, so he slims down.

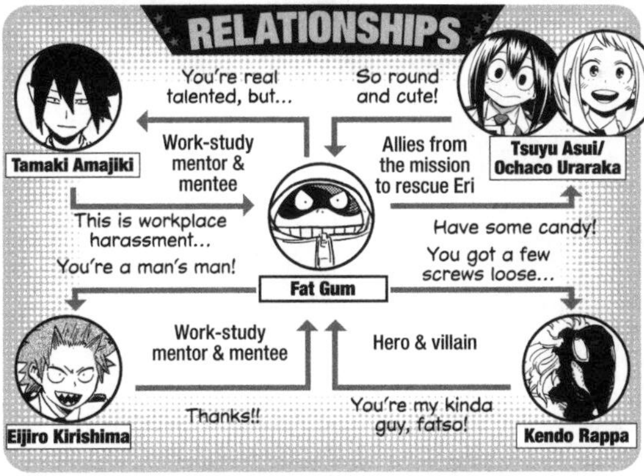

RELATIONSHIPS
You're real talented, but...
So round and cute!
Tamaki Amajiki
Work-study mentor & mentee
Allies from the mission to rescue Eri
Tsuyu Asui/ Ochaco Uraraka
This is workplace harassment...
Have some candy!
You're a man's man!
You got a few screws loose...
Fat Gum
Work-study mentor & mentee
Hero & villain
Eijiro Kirishima
Thanks!!
You're my kinda guy, fatso!
Kendo Rappa


## PROFILE

Name: **Taishiro Toyomitsu**
Hero name: **Fat Gum**
Quirk: **Fat Absorption**
Birthday: **August 8**
Height: **250 cm (?)**
Blood type: **O**
Birthplace: **Osaka**
Personality: **Reliable big brother**
Ultimate moves: **Stuff 'Em In, Calorie Fuel Burn**

- "When fighting villains, quickly making them lose the will to fight is everything!!" (vol. 15, chap. 134)
- "When a guy says he's got your back, a real man has just gotta believe!!" (vol. 16, chap. 142)
- "You wanna know why you're gonna lose?! Because all of us—including me—underestimated him!! The hero called Red Riot and his chivalrous spirit!" (vol. 16, chap. 145)

### Fat Gum's Notable Quotables

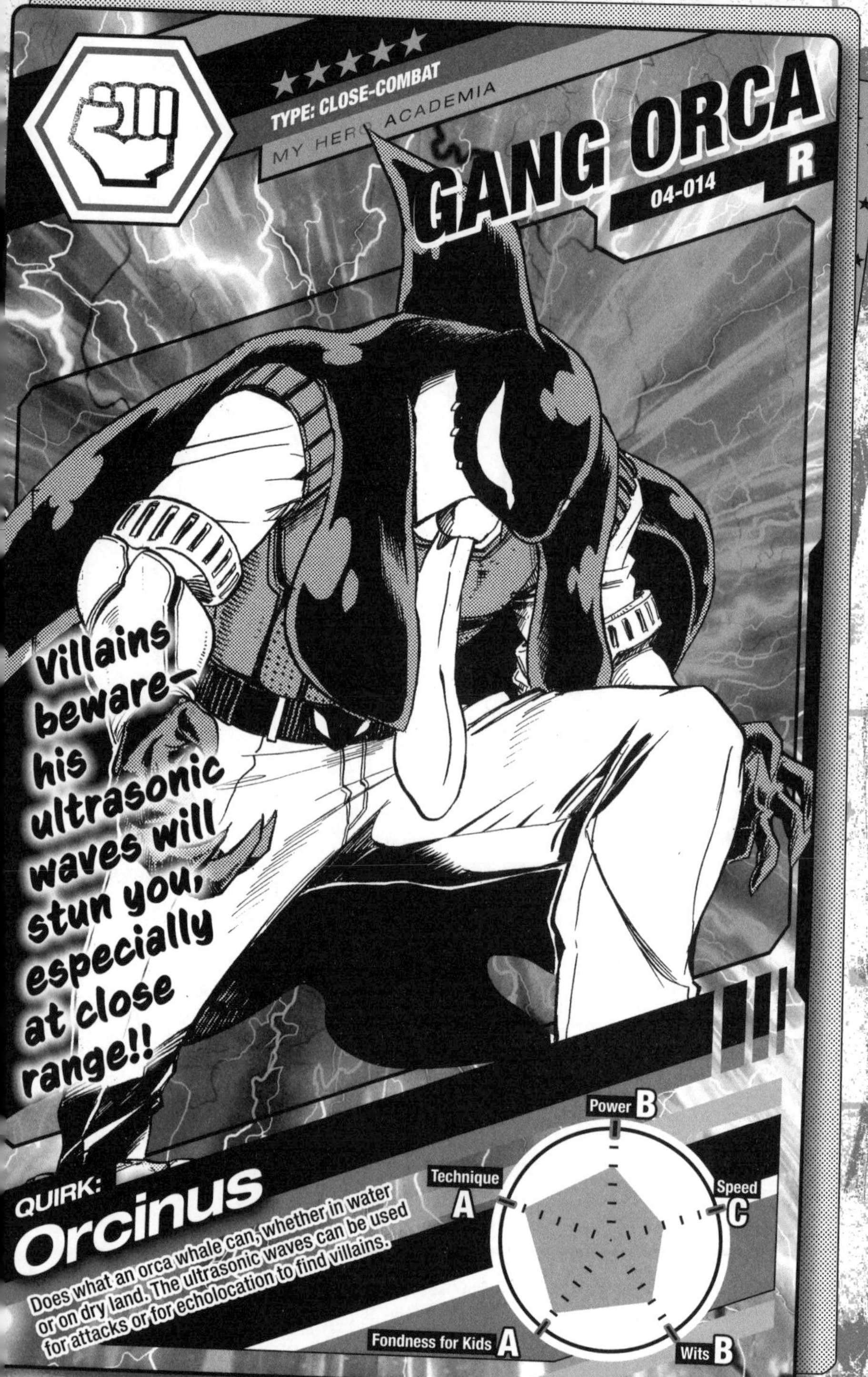
TYPE: CLOSE-COMBAT
MY HERO ACADEMIA
GANG ORCA
R
04-014
Villains beware—his ultrasonic waves will stun you, especially at close range!!
QUIRK:
Orcinus
Does what an orca whale can, whether in water or on dry land. The ultrasonic waves can be used for attacks or for echolocation to find villains.
Power B
Technique A
Speed C
Fondness for Kids A
Wits B

## That intimidating exterior hides a kind heart.

A hero powerful and skilled enough to be invited to the Bakugo rescue mission to work alongside Endeavor. Gang Orca employs a large number of sidekicks at his agency. They love him and call him “Big Fish,” but because he’s never revealed much about his background, some have their doubts that he’s human.

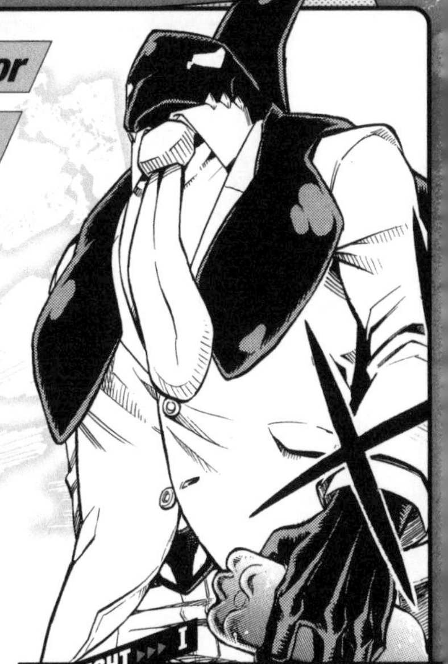

➡ Gang Orca ranks third on the list of heroes who look like villains. He feels bad when his terrifying appearance makes small children cry.

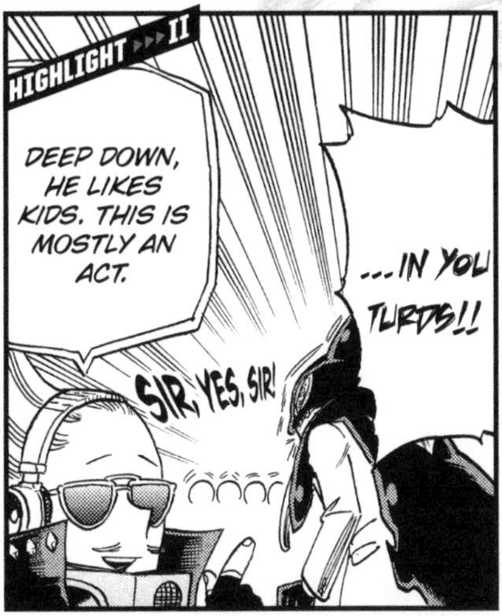
HIGHLIGHT ▸▸▸ II
...IN YOU TURDS!!
DEEP DOWN, HE LIKES KIDS. THIS IS MOSTLY AN ACT.
SIR, YES, SIR!

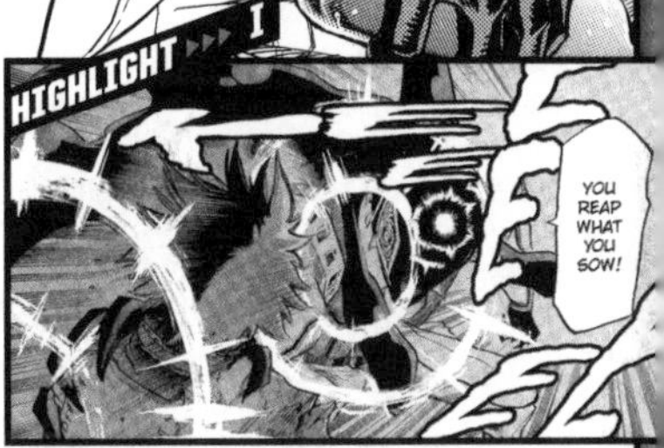
HIGHLIGHT ▸▸▸ I
YOU REAP WHAT YOU SOW!

⬆ During round two of the provisional license exam, Todoroki and pals learned the hard way what sort of power the no. 10 hero was packing.

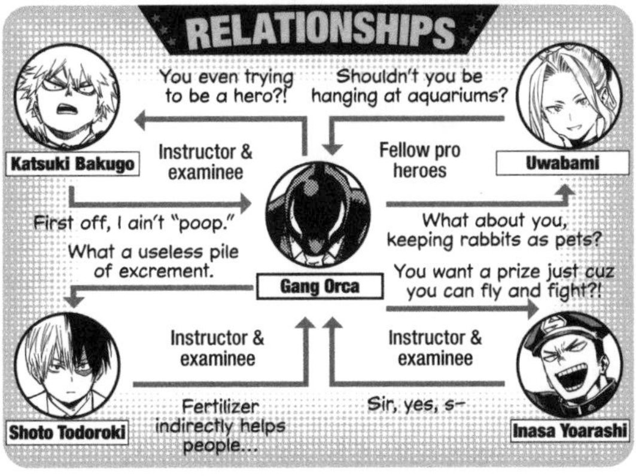
RELATIONSHIPS
You even trying to be a hero?!
Shouldn’t you be hanging at aquariums?
Katsuki Bakugo
Instructor & examinee
Fellow pro heroes
Uwabami
First off, I ain’t “poop.”
What about you, keeping rabbits as pets?
What a useless pile of excrement.
Gang Orca
You want a prize just cuz you can fly and fight?!
Instructor & examinee
Instructor & examinee
Fertilizer indirectly helps people...
Sir, yes, s—
Shoto Todoroki
Inasa Yoarashi

## PROFILE

Name: **Kugo Sakamata**
Hero name: **Gang Orca**
Quirk: **Orcinus**
Birthday: **October 29**
Height: **202 cm**
Blood type: **O**
Birthplace: **Kanagawa Prefecture**
Personality: **Drill sergeant**
Ultimate move: **Ultrasonic Waves**

- “They realized their own mistakes and tried to fix things… I gotta say, I’m impressed with their persistence!” (vol. 13, chap. 113)
- “Y’know, I’ve learned something from helping out with this course. You wastes of oxygen aren’t cut out to be plankton, let alone heroes!! You’re lower than fish poop!!” (vol. 18, chap. 164)
- “You lack discipline!!” (vol. 18, chap. 164)

**Gang Orca’s Notable Quotables**

## With her superior judgment, she can provide instant aid to far-off allies.

One of the four members of the Wild, Wild Pussycats—a hero team that specializes in mountain rescues. Mandalay had trouble opening up during her college years, but Pixie-Bob and the others were there for her.

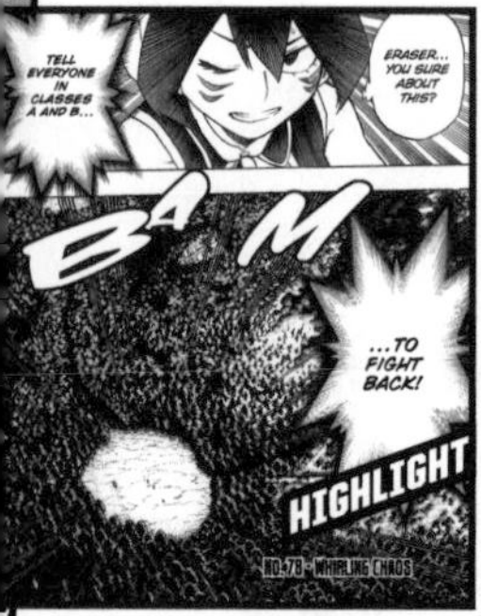
ERASER... YOU SURE ABOUT THIS?
TELL EVERYONE IN CLASSES A AND B...
BAM
...TO FIGHT BACK!
HIGHLIGHT
NO.78 - WHIRLING CHAOS

⬆ Mandalay gave a "commence combat" message to the scattered students, turning the battle around.

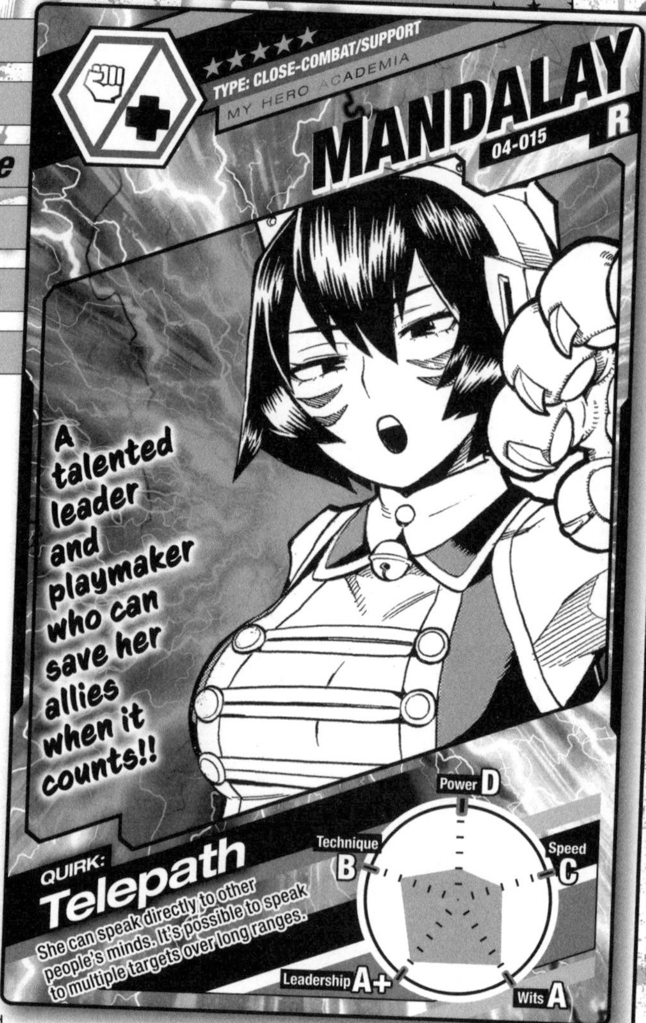
★★★★★★
TYPE: CLOSE-COMBAT/SUPPORT
MY HERO ACADEMIA
MANDALAY
R
04-015
A talented leader and playmaker who can save her allies when it counts!!
QUIRK:
Telepath
She can speak directly to other people's minds. It's possible to speak to multiple targets over long ranges.
Power D
Speed C
Wits A
Leadership A+
Technique B

## RELATIONSHIPS

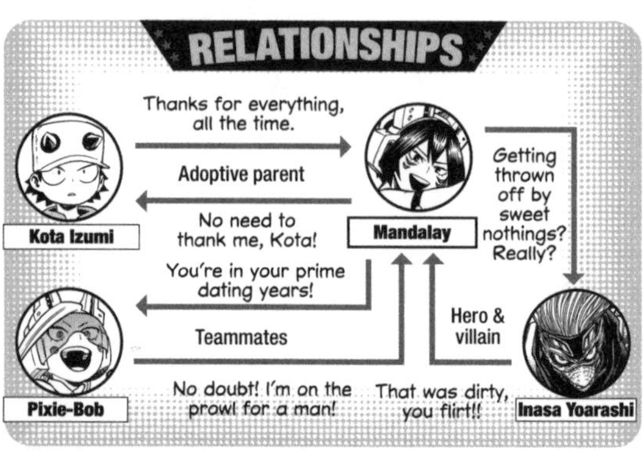
Thanks for everything, all the time.
Adoptive parent
No need to thank me, Kota!
Kota Izumi
Mandalay
Getting thrown off by sweet nothings? Really?
You're in your prime dating years!
Teammates
Hero & villain
No doubt! I'm on the prowl for a man!
That was dirty, you flirt!!
Pixie-Bob
Inasa Yoarashi

## PROFILE

Name: **Shino Sozaki**
Hero name: **Mandalay**
Quirk: **Telepath**
Birthday: **May 1**
Height: **168 cm**
Blood type: **A**
Birthplace: **Miyagi Prefecture**
Personality: **Loves her cousin's kid**
Ultimate move: **Cat Claw**

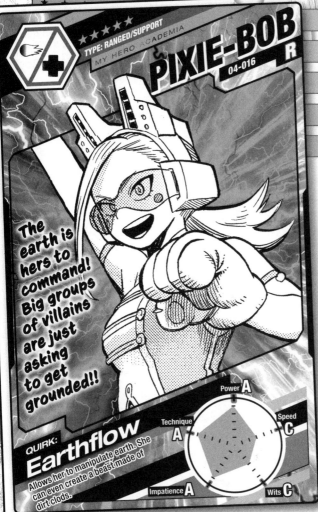

TYPE: RANGED/SUPPORT
MY HERO ACADEMIA
PIXIE-BOB
R
04-016
The earth is hers to command! Big groups of villains are just asking to get grounded!!
Power A
Speed C
Technique A
Impatience A
Wits C
QUIRK:
Earthflow
Allows her to manipulate earth. She can even create a beast made of dirt clods.

## "We're 18 at heart!!" She'd rather be a damsel than a hero?!

The Pussycats member who came up with the team concept and name. Mandalay was a big introvert during college, but Pixie-Bob was always there to drag her out to have fun.

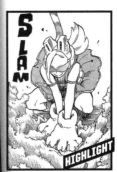

SLAM
HIGHLIGHT

⬆ By transforming the very topography around her, Pixie-Bob can get the upper paw in battle!

## RELATIONSHIPS

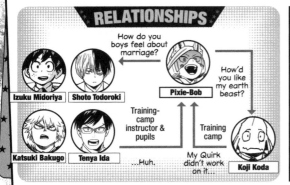

How do you boys feel about marriage?
Izuku Midoriya
Shoto Todoroki
Pixie-Bob
How'd you like my earth beast?
Training-camp instructor & pupils
Training camp
Katsuki Bakugo
Tenya Ida
...Huh.
My Quirk didn't work on it...
Koji Koda

## PROFILE

Name: **Ryuko Tsuchikawa**
Hero name: **Pixie-Bob**
Quirk: **Earthflow**
Birthday: **June 26**
Height: **167 cm**
Blood type: **AB**
Birthplace: **Ehime Prefecture**
Personality: **Animated**
Ultimate moves: **Earth Beast, Landslide**

# The combat specialist! A trans man whose spirit shines bright.

Tiger is a transgender man whose rippling muscles make him the team's only combat specialist. His original video series, "My Boot Camp," has gained a lot of popularity on the internet.

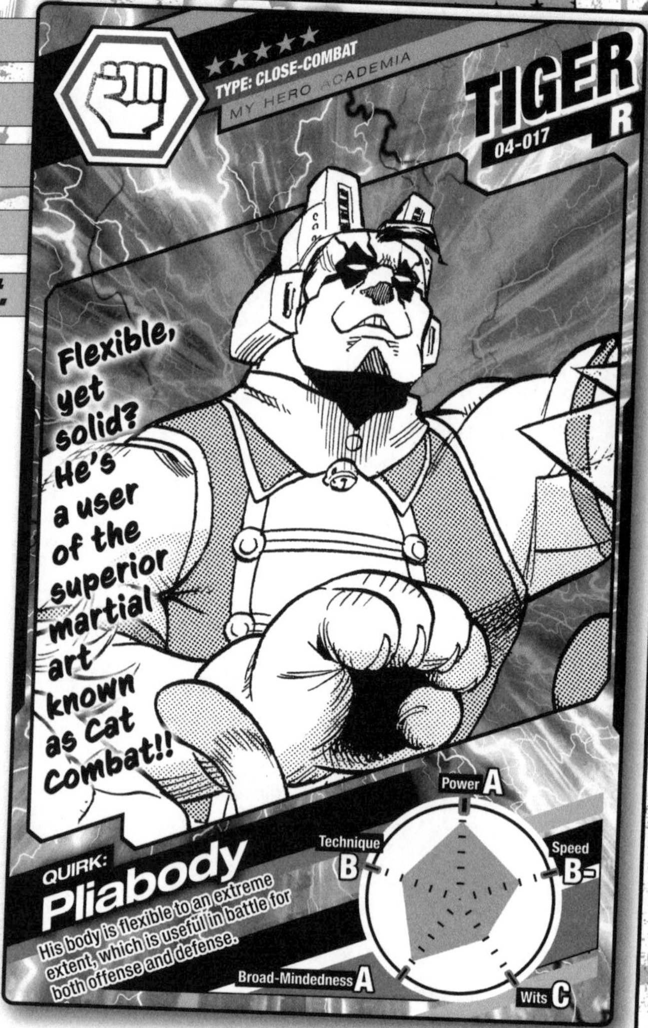

★★★★★★
TYPE: CLOSE-COMBAT
MY HERO ACADEMIA
TIGER
R
04-017
Flexible, yet solid? He's a user of the superior martial art known as Cat Combat!!
QUIRK:
Pliabody
His body is flexible to an extreme extent, which is useful in battle for both offense and defense.
Power A
Speed B
Wits C
Broad-Mindedness A
Technique B


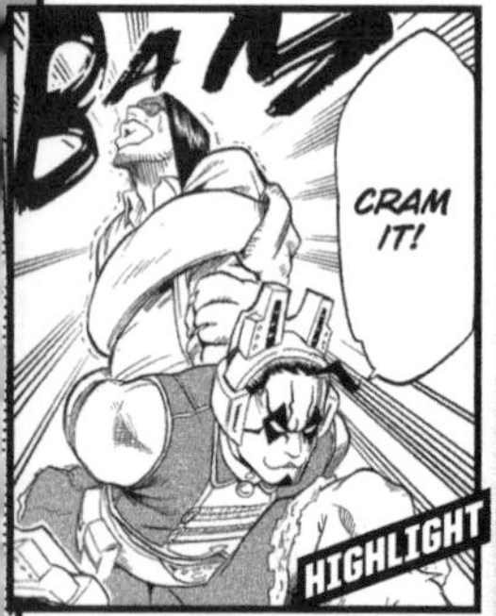

BAM
CRAM IT!
HIGHLIGHT


⬆ Tiger's Quirk is suited to both combat and capture.

## RELATIONSHIPS

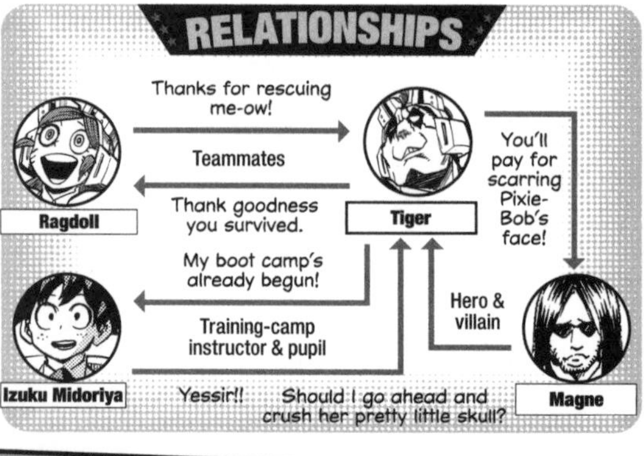

Thanks for rescuing me-ow!
Teammates
Thank goodness you survived.
Ragdoll
Tiger
You'll pay for scarring Pixie-Bob's face!
My boot camp's already begun!
Training-camp instructor & pupil
Hero & villain
Izuku Midoriya
Yessir!!
Should I go ahead and crush her pretty little skull?
Magne


## PROFILE

Name: **Yawara Chatora**
Hero name: **Tiger**
Quirk: **Pliabody**
Birthday: **February 29**
Height: **190 cm**
Blood type: **A**
Birthplace: **Kagoshima Prefecture**
Personality: **A true friend**
Ultimate move: **Cat Combat**

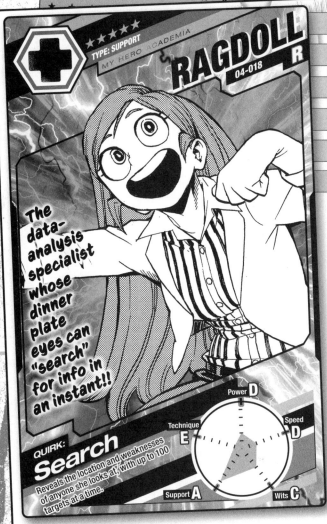

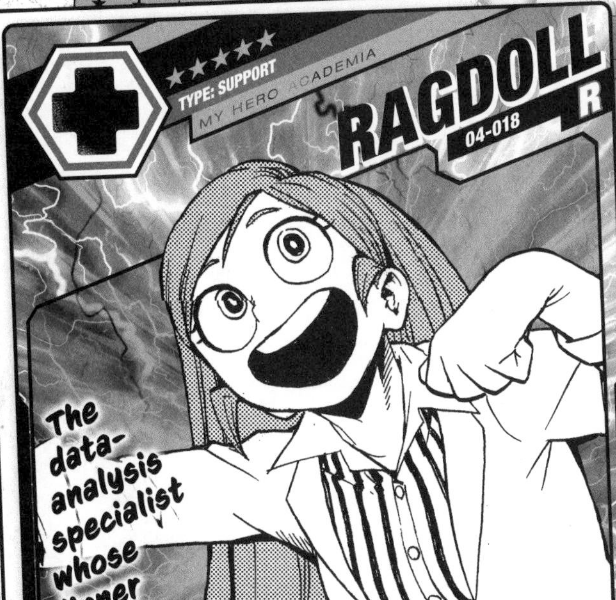
★★★★★
TYPE: SUPPORT
MY HERO ACADEMIA
RAGDOLL
R
04-018
The data-analysis specialist whose dinner plate eyes can "search" for info in an instant!!
Power D
Speed D
Technique E
Support A
Wits C
QUIRK:
Search
Reveals the location and weaknesses of anyone she looks at, with up to 100 targets at a time.

## With a mind made for data, she provides support for the Pussycats.

Everyone loves Ragdoll, especially since the four-member team was her idea to start with. Her Quirk may have been stolen, but All For One couldn't steal her positive attitude. Even now, Ragdoll provides data analysis for the team.

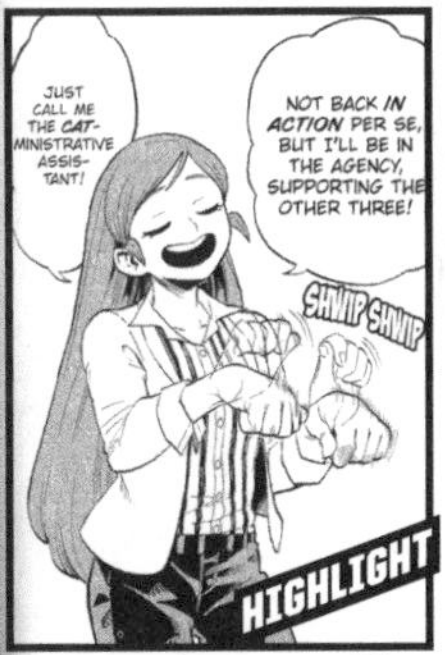
NOT BACK *IN ACTION* PER SE, BUT I'LL BE IN THE AGENCY, SUPPORTING THE OTHER THREE!
JUST CALL ME THE *CAT*-MINISTRATIVE ASSISTANT!
SHWIP SHWIP
HIGHLIGHT

⬆ Still as upbeat as ever! Now, Ragdoll helps out from behind a desk!!

## RELATIONSHIPS

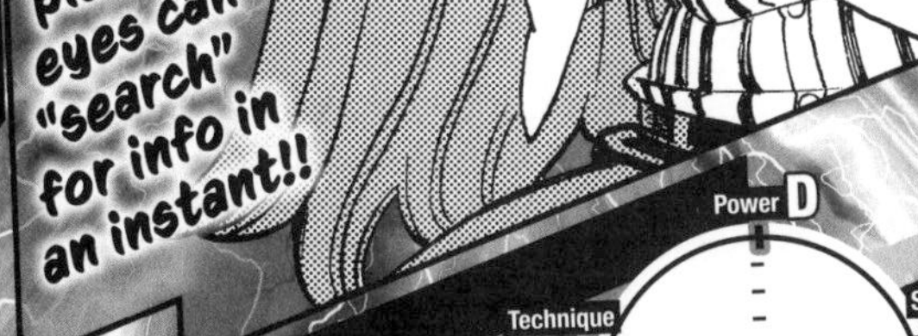
The Wild, Wild Pussycats are dudes among dudes!
Training-camp instructor & pupil
We can't stop moving forward!!
Eijiro Kirishima
Ragdoll
Just call me the cat-mini-strative assistant!
Woulda loved to team up with you, meow!
Training-camp instructor & pupil
Your Search and my own Quirk would be an ideal pairing.
Momo Yaoyorozu
Team-mates
We appreciate all the support!
Mandalay

## PROFILE

Name: **Tomoko Shiretoko**
Hero name: **Ragdoll**
Quirk: **Search**
Birthday: **April 8**
Height: **166 cm**
Blood type: **O**
Birthplace: **Tokyo**
Personality: **Perceptive**
Ultimate move: **Cat Outta Hell**

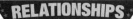

## Her unabashed manner is backed by confidence in her strength.

A pro hero with an eye-catchingly muscular body. Mirko takes great pride in her strength and represents a new type of hero—a pioneer who doesn't have an agency of her own.

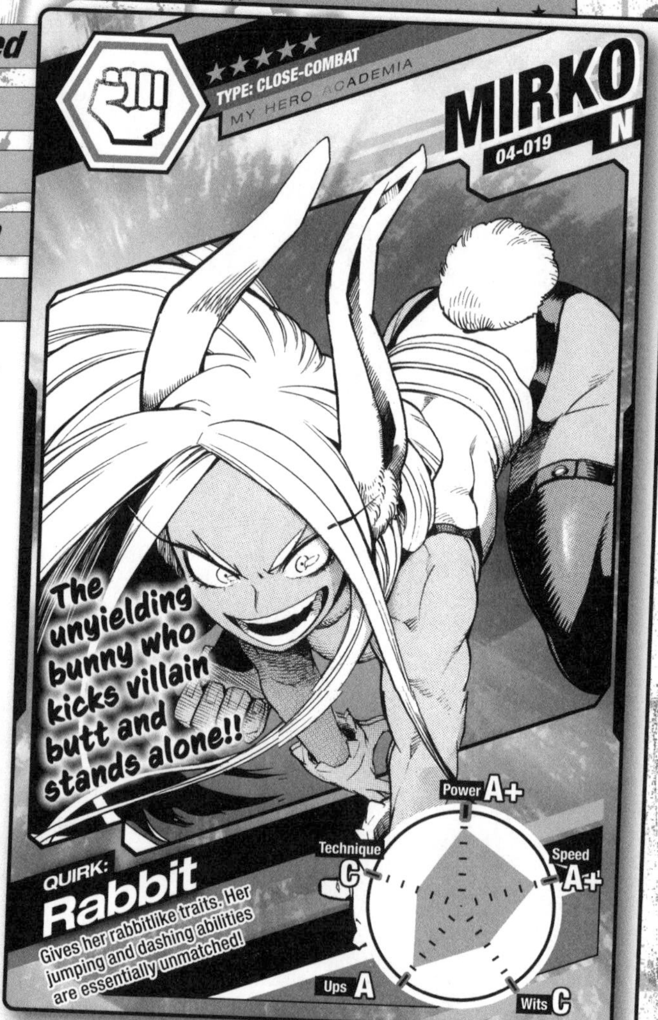
TYPE: CLOSE-COMBAT
MY HERO ACADEMIA
MIRKO
N
04-019
The unyielding bunny who kicks villain butt and stands alone!!
Power A+
Speed A+
Wits C
Ups A
Technique C
QUIRK:
Rabbit
Gives her rabbitlike traits. Her jumping and dashing abilities are essentially unmatched!

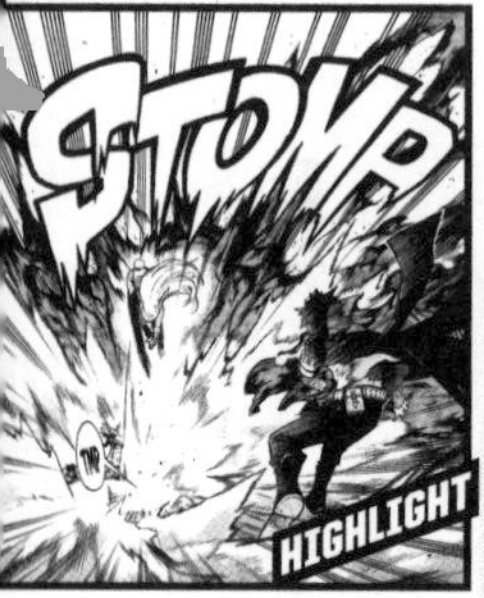
STOMP
HIGHLIGHT

⬆ Backed by Mirko's powerful legs, this stomp is strong enough to be considered an ultimate move!

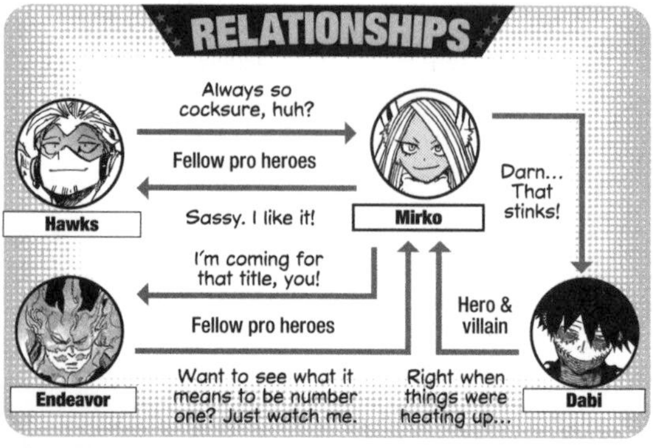
RELATIONSHIPS
Always so cocksure, huh?
Fellow pro heroes
Sassy. I like it!
Hawks
Mirko
Darn... That stinks!
I'm coming for that title, you!
Fellow pro heroes
Want to see what it means to be number one? Just watch me.
Hero & villain
Right when things were heating up...
Endeavor
Dabi

## PROFILE

Name: **Rumi Usagiyama**
Hero name: **Mirko**
Quirk: **Rabbit**
Birthday: **March 1**
Height: **159 cm**
Blood type: **O**
Birthplace: **Hiroshima Prefecture**
Personality: **Strong-minded**
Ultimate move: **Luna Crescent**

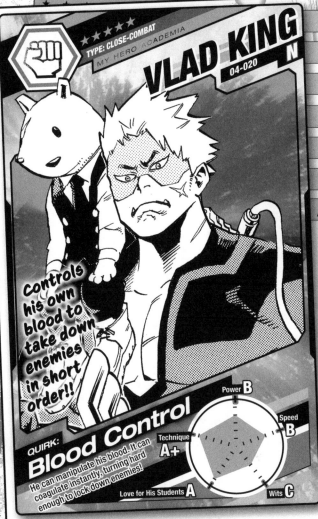

TYPE: CLOSE-COMBAT
MY HERO ACADEMIA
VLAD KING
N
04-020
Controls his own blood to take down enemies in short order!!
QUIRK:
Blood Control
He can manipulate his blood. It can coagulate instantly, turning hard enough to lock down enemies!
Power B
Speed B
Technique A+
Love for His Students A
Wits C


***His love borders on madness! This teacher is strict, kind, and always hot-blooded.***

A pro hero who prides himself on his rippling muscles and is homeroom teacher to U.A.'s class 1-B. Vlad King tends to let his blood boil at every little thing when instructing his students, but most enthusiastic teachers don't actually wear their blood on the outside!

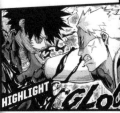

HIGHLIGHT


⬆ After making sure the kids were safe, Vlad King wasted no time in pinning down Dabi.

## RELATIONSHIPS

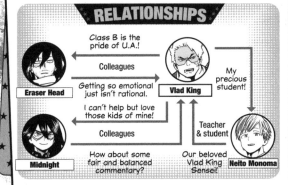

Class B is the pride of U.A.!
Colleagues
Getting so emotional just isn't rational.
Eraser Head
Vlad King
My precious student!
I can't help but love those kids of mine!
Colleagues
Teacher & student
Midnight
How about some fair and balanced commentary?
Our beloved Vlad King Sensei!
Neito Monoma


## PROFILE

Name: **Sekijiro Kan**
Hero name: **Vlad King**
Quirk: **Blood Control**
Birthday: **November 10**
Height: **194 cm**
Blood type: **B**
Birthplace: **Aomori Prefecture**
Personality: **Hot-blooded man's man**
Ultimate move: **Blood Blade**

## A super sadist who loves to psychologically torment the weak.

Midnight is a captivating pro hero with a bad habit of torturing partially awake targets… When that rumor started to spread, some villains emerged from the woodwork, all too eager to be her next "victims."

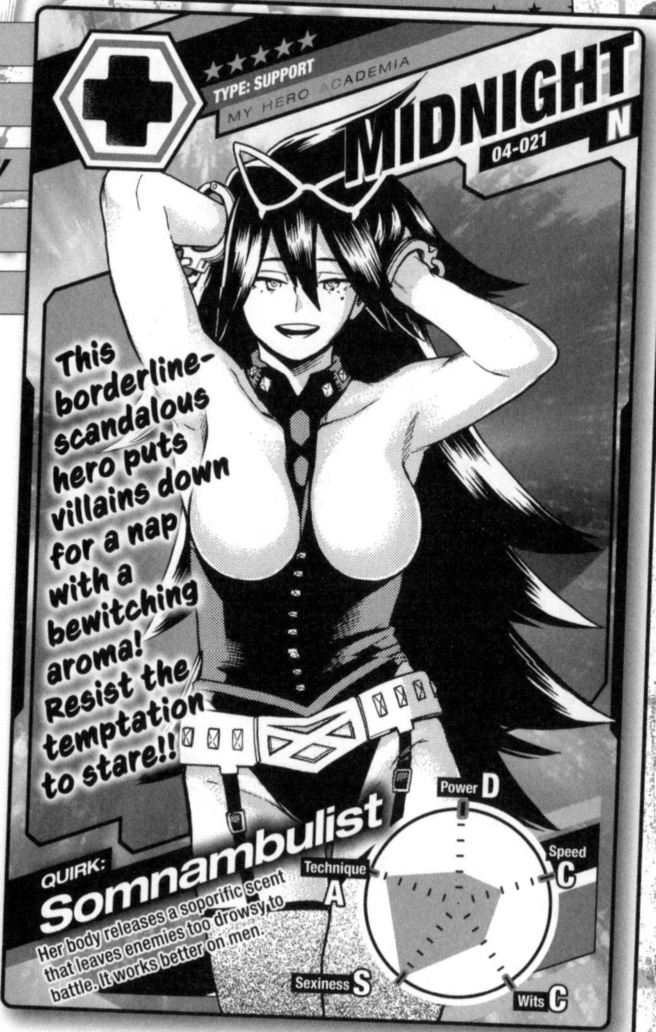
TYPE: SUPPORT
MY HERO ACADEMIA
MIDNIGHT
N
04-021
This borderline-scandalous hero puts villains down for a nap with a bewitching aroma! Resist the temptation to stare!!
QUIRK:
Somnambulist
Her body releases a soporific scent that leaves enemies too drowsy to battle. It works better on men.
Power D
Speed C
Wits C
Sexiness S
Technique A

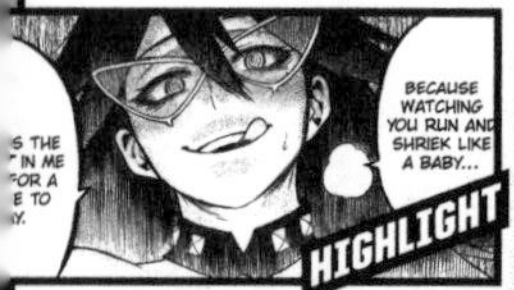
BECAUSE WATCHING YOU RUN AND SHRIEK LIKE A BABY…
HIGHLIGHT

⬆ Typically, Midnight takes her job seriously and does it well. Only occasionally does her inner sadist emerge…

## RELATIONSHIPS

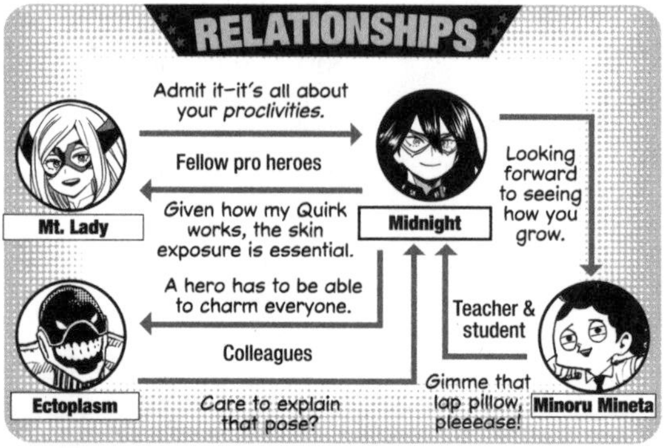
Admit it—it's all about your *proclivities.*
Fellow pro heroes
Given how my Quirk works, the skin exposure is essential.
Mt. Lady
Midnight
Looking forward to seeing how you grow.
A hero has to be able to charm everyone.
Teacher & student
Colleagues
Ectoplasm
Care to explain that pose?
Gimme that lap pillow, pleeease!
Minoru Mineta

## PROFILE

Name: **Nemuri Kayama**
Hero name: **Midnight**
Quirk: **Somnambulist**
Birthday: **March 9**
Height: **175 cm**
Blood type: **A**
Birthplace: **Saitama Prefecture**
Personality: **Super sadist**
Ultimate move: **Sleepy Hollow**

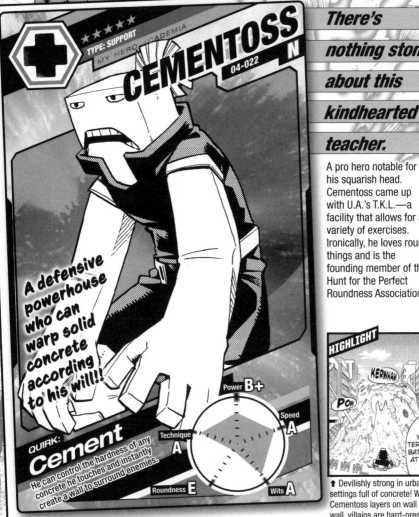

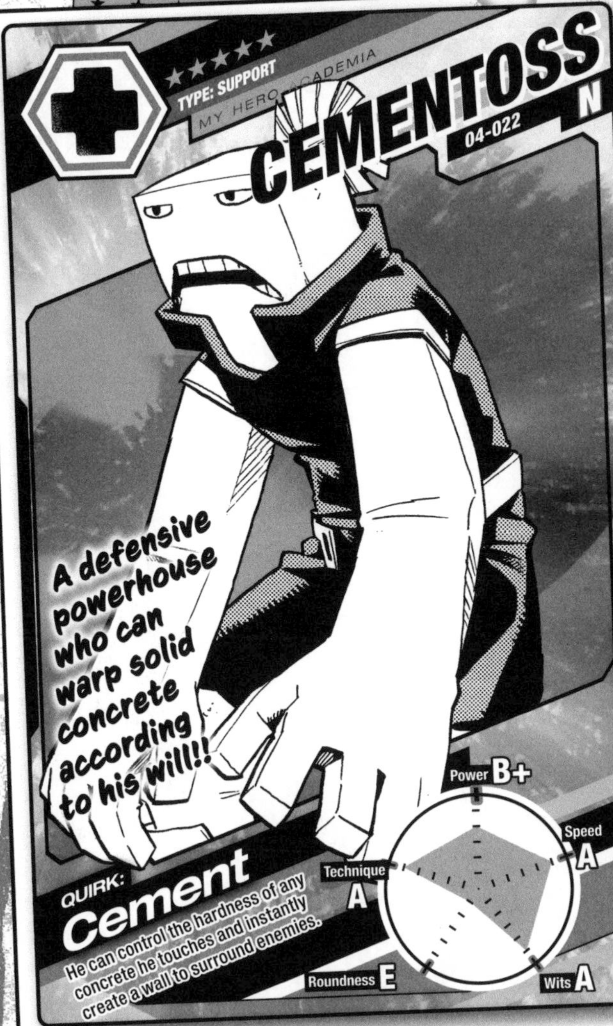
TYPE: SUPPORT
MY HERO ACADEMIA
CEMENTOSS
N
04-022
A defensive powerhouse who can warp solid concrete according to his will!!
QUIRK:
Cement
He can control the hardness of any concrete he touches and instantly create a wall to surround enemies.
Power B+
Speed A
Technique A
Roundness E
Wits A

## *There's nothing stony about this kindhearted teacher.*

A pro hero notable for his squarish head. Cementoss came up with U.A.'s T.K.L.—a facility that allows for a variety of exercises. Ironically, he loves round things and is the founding member of the Hunt for the Perfect Roundness Association.

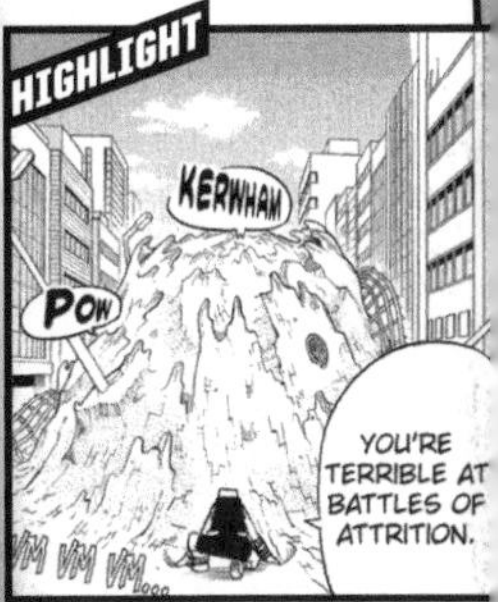
HIGHLIGHT
KERWHAM
POW
YOU'RE TERRIBLE AT BATTLES OF ATTRITION.
VM VM VM...

⬆ Devilishly strong in urban settings full of concrete! When Cementoss layers on wall after wall, villains are hard-pressed to escape!!

## RELATIONSHIPS

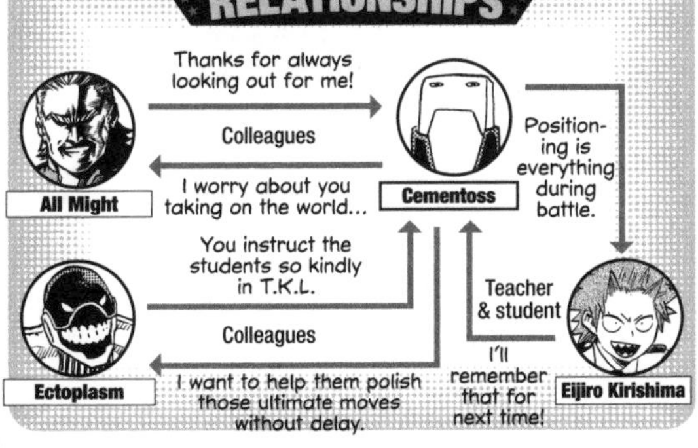
Thanks for always looking out for me!
Colleagues
I worry about you taking on the world...
All Might
Cementoss
Position-ing is everything during battle.
You instruct the students so kindly in T.K.L.
Colleagues
I want to help them polish those ultimate moves without delay.
Ectoplasm
Teacher & student
I'll remember that for next time!
Eijiro Kirishima

## PROFILE

Name: **Ken Ishiyama**
Hero name: **Cementoss**
Quirk: **Cement**
Birthday: **March 22**
Height: **185 cm**
Blood type: **B**
Birthplace: **Yamagata Prefecture**
Personality: **Unflappable**
Ultimate move: **Battering Ram**

**A peculiar voice, villainous appearance, and desire to help students grow!**

A U.A. teacher who makes frequent appearances on the "heroes who look like villains" list. Ectoplasm's clones are all capable of independent thought and action, so he can easily give one-on-one training to all 20 students in class 1-A simultaneously.

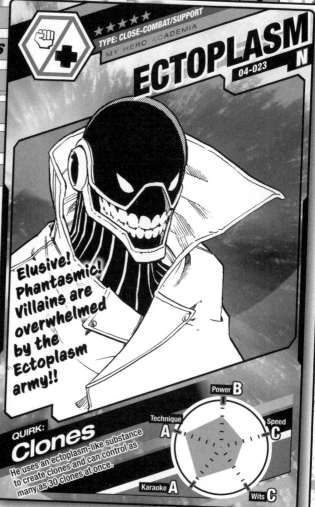

TYPE: CLOSE-COMBAT/SUPPORT

MY HERO ACADEMIA

# ECTOPLASM

04-023 N

Elusive! Phantasmic! Villains are overwhelmed by the Ectoplasm army!!

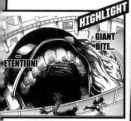

HIGHLIGHT
GIANT BITE...
...ETENTION!

⬆ This ultimate move uses a colossal clone to swallow up opponents!

QUIRK: **Clones**

He uses an ectoplasm-like substance to create clones and can control as many as 30 clones at once.

Power B
Speed C
Wits C
Karaoke A
Technique A

## RELATIONSHIPS

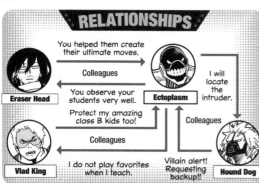

You helped them create their ultimate moves.
Colleagues
You observe your students very well.
Eraser Head
Ectoplasm
I will locate the intruder.
Protect my amazing class B kids too!
Colleagues
Colleagues
Vlad King
I do not play favorites when I teach.
Villain alert! Requesting backup!!
Hound Dog

## PROFILE

Name: **Unknown**
Hero name: **Ectoplasm**
Quirk: **Clones**
Birthday: **March 23**
Height: **180 cm**
Blood type: **AB**
Birthplace: **Okinawa Prefecture**
Personality: **Hard knocks adherent**
Ultimate move: **Giant Bite Detention**

★★★★★
TYPE: SUPPORT
MY HERO ACADEMIA
???
N
04-024
Intelligent enough to trap villains like rats! Everyone loves this smarty-pants mouse!!
QUIRK:
High Specs
His unprecedented Quirk gives this animal intelligence exceeding that of most humans.
Power E
Speed D
Technique A
Loveliness A
Wits S


## A true mouse of character, the only animal to manifest a Quirk.

As the principal of an elite educational institution for heroes, Nezu shows unparalleled humanity (?) in the way he cares for the students. The sharp thinker has even earned All Might's trust and respect. Nezu loves squirming into tight, confined spaces (following his instincts, perhaps?), and the folds of Eraser Head's binding cloth make for an especially comfy hiding spot.

CURRENTLY, I AM PERSONALLY COOPERATING WITH THE POLICE IN THEIR ONGOING INVESTIGATION.
WE'RE HARDLY APPROACHIN THIS PASSIVELY
HIGHLIGHT


⬆ Nezu often bears the brunt of public criticism. He defends U.A. with smooth responses to harsh questioning.

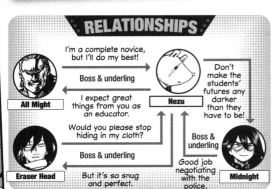

## RELATIONSHIPS

All Might
Nezu
Eraser Head
Midnight
I'm a complete novice, but I'll do my best!
Boss & underling
I expect great things from you as an educator.
Would you please stop hiding in my cloth?
Boss & underling
But it's so snug and perfect.
Don't make the students' futures any darker than they have to be!
Boss & underling
Good job negotiating with the police.


## PROFILE

Name: **Nezu**
Hero name: **Unknown**
Quirk: **High Specs**
Birthday: **January 1**
Height: **85 cm**
Blood type: **A**
Birthplace: **Tokyo**
Personality: **Refined yet friendly**
Ultimate move: **Brain Break**

*Leave expansion and development to him! Also, he's Hatsume's watchdog.*

A pro hero notable for his steam shovel mask. Power Loader has an official license for costume development. Given his mad-genius personality, he has few friends, and even his fellow educators think he's rather eccentric.

WELL DONE, GIVEN THE BAD FOOTING HERE...

**HIGHLIGHT**

↑ Power Loader does construction projects without using equipment. When watching over the damage-prone Hatsume, he's always helpful and caring.

TYPE: SUPPORT

MY HERO ACADEMIA

# POWER LOADER
04-025

He's proud of his Iron Claws, which can reshape the ground itself and steal away villains' footing!!

QUIRK:
## Iron Claws
The claws growing from his fingers are as hard as steel, allowing him to tunnel through the earth.

Power A

Technique D

Speed B−

Height D

Wits D

## RELATIONSHIPS

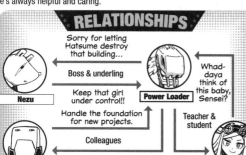

Sorry for letting Hatsume destroy that building...

Boss & underling

Keep that girl under control!!

**Nezu**

Whadda-daya think of this baby, Sensei?

**Power Loader**

Handle the foundation for new projects.

Teacher & student

Colleagues

**Cementoss**

I'm your guy for excavation jobs.

You're too egocentric...

**Mei Hatsume**

## PROFILE

Name: **Higari Maijima**
Hero name: **Power Loader**
Quirk: **Iron Claws**
Birthday: **September 17**
Height: **155 cm**
Blood type: **A**
Birthplace: **Osaka**
Personality: **Eccentric genius**
Ultimate move: **Mole Sink**

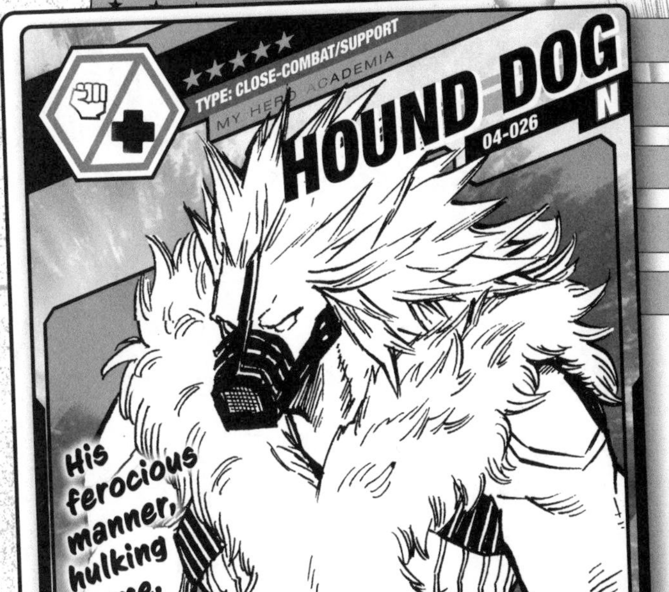
TYPE: CLOSE-COMBAT/SUPPORT
MY HERO ACADEMIA
HOUND DOG
N
04-026
His ferocious manner, hulking frame, and keen sense of smell allow for a rapid response!!
Power A+
Speed A
Technique D-
Wits B
Loyalty A
QUIRK:
Dog
Enhances his sense of smell, which lets him identify far-off targets right down to an exact head count.

## The school life supervisor forgets how to speak when enraged.

U.A. High's school life supervisor loses the ability to speak when he gets angry and can only communicate with a series of vicious barks. This has earned Hound Dog a terrifying reputation among the students. When things get out of hand, his friend Vlad King is always there to interpret and mediate.

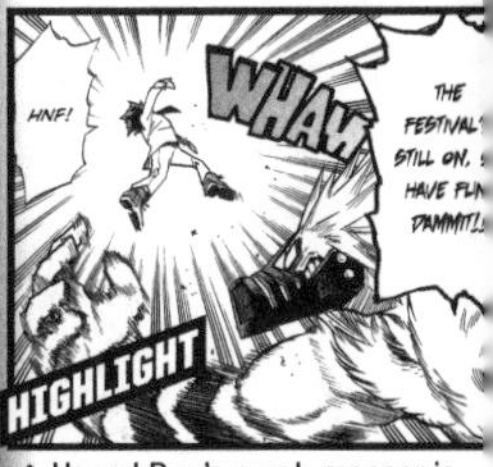
HIGHLIGHT
HNF!
WHAM

⬆ Hound Dog's rough manner is just his way of showing his love.

## RELATIONSHIPS

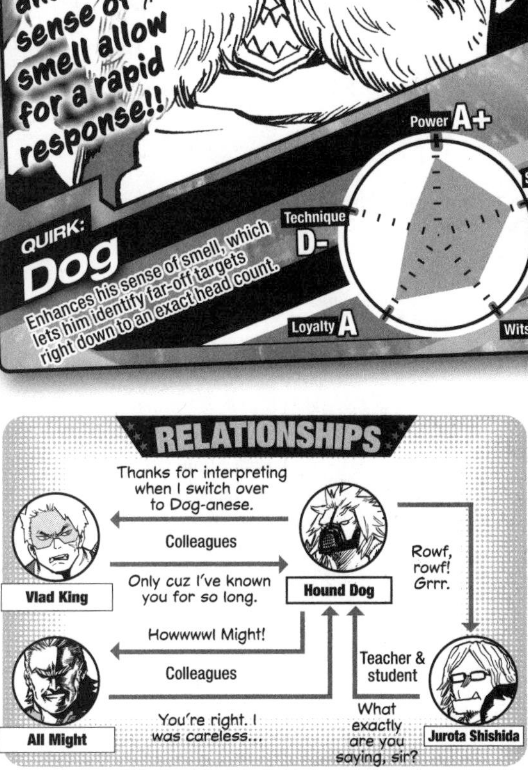
Thanks for interpreting when I switch over to Dog-anese.
Colleagues
Only cuz I've known you for so long.
Vlad King
Hound Dog
Rowf, rowf! Grrr.
Howwwwl Might!
Colleagues
You're right. I was careless...
All Might
Teacher & student
What exactly are you saying, sir?
Jurota Shishida

## PROFILE

Name: **Ryo Inui**
Hero name: **Hound Dog**
Quirk: **Dog**
Birthday: **November 15**
Height: **196 cm**
Blood type: **A**
Birthplace: **Tokyo**
Personality: **Workaholic**
Ultimate move: **Wild Hunt**

## U.A.'s number two pillar. Her voice is just as influential as the principal's!

U.A. High's nurse is the school's longest-tenured employee. Recovery Girl also knows about All Might's personal history. In addition to nursing students back to health, she travels the country and works her healing magic at hospitals.

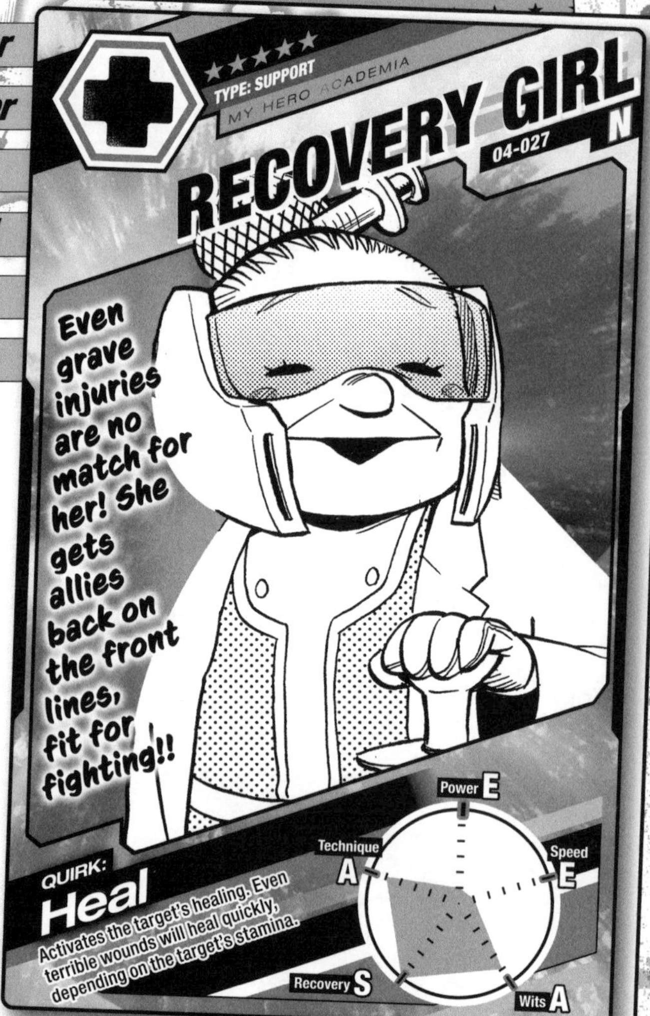

TYPE: SUPPORT
MY HERO ACADEMIA
RECOVERY GIRL
04-027
N
Even grave injuries are no match for her! She gets allies back on the front lines, fit for fighting!!
QUIRK:
Heal
Activates the target's healing. Even terrible wounds will heal quickly, depending on the target's stamina.
Power E
Speed E
Wits A
Recovery S
Technique A


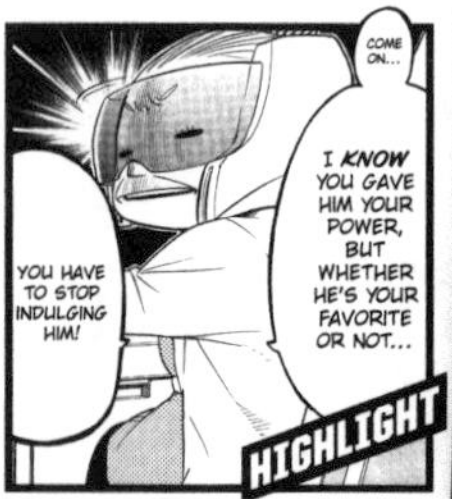

COME ON...
I KNOW YOU GAVE HIM YOUR POWER, BUT WHETHER HE'S YOUR FAVORITE OR NOT...
YOU HAVE TO STOP INDULGING HIM!
HIGHLIGHT


⬆ Recovery Girl is one of the few people who can give All Might a good scolding.

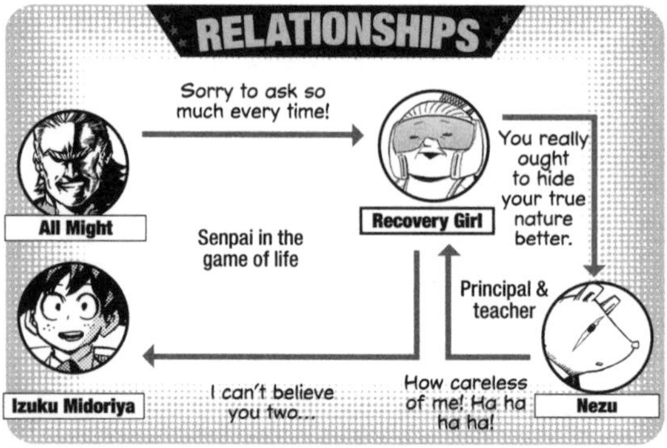

RELATIONSHIPS
Sorry to ask so much every time!
All Might
Recovery Girl
You really ought to hide your true nature better.
Senpai in the game of life
Principal & teacher
Izuku Midoriya
I can't believe you two...
How careless of me! Ha ha ha ha!
Nezu


## PROFILE

Name: **Chiyo Shuzenji**
Hero name: **Recovery Girl**
Quirk: **Heal**
Birthday: **April 4**
Height: **115 cm**
Blood type: **B**
Birthplace: **Tokyo**
Personality: **Brisk and lucid**
Ultimate move: **Healing**

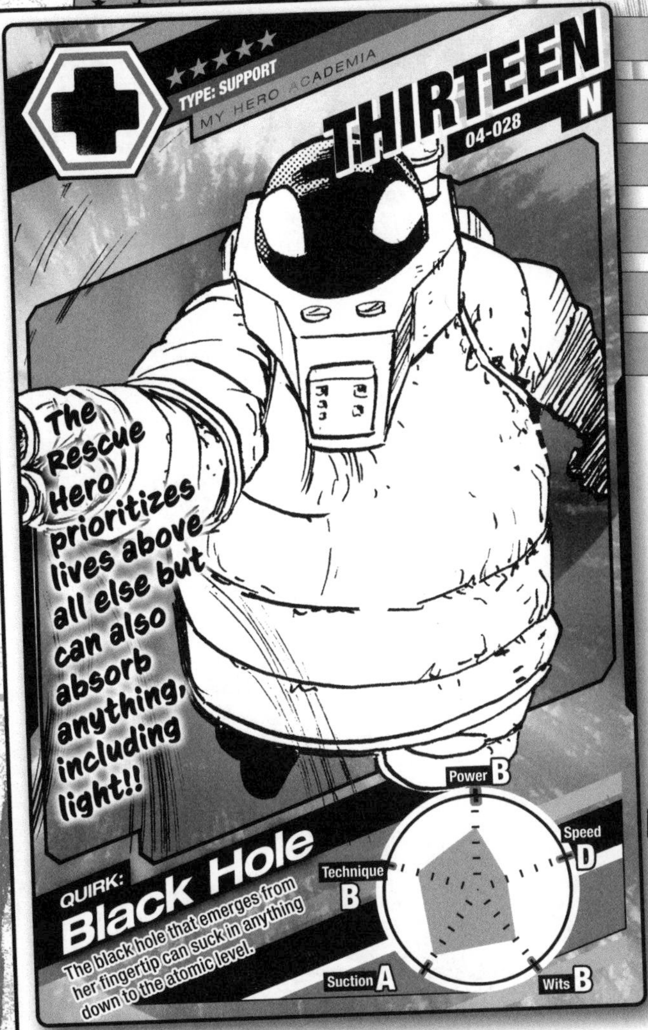

TYPE: SUPPORT
MY HERO ACADEMIA
THIRTEEN
N
04-028
The Rescue Hero prioritizes lives above all else but can also absorb anything, including light!!
QUIRK:
Black Hole
The black hole that emerges from her fingertip can suck in anything down to the atomic level.
Power B
Speed D
Technique B
Suction A
Wits B


# The founder of U.S.J. discusses the danger of powerful Quirks.

A U.A. educator and pro hero who specializes in disaster-scenario rescues. Thirteen is beloved among students for her kind personality and manner of speech. It's hard to tell much about her physical appearance with that costume hiding everything, but yes—Thirteen is indeed a woman.

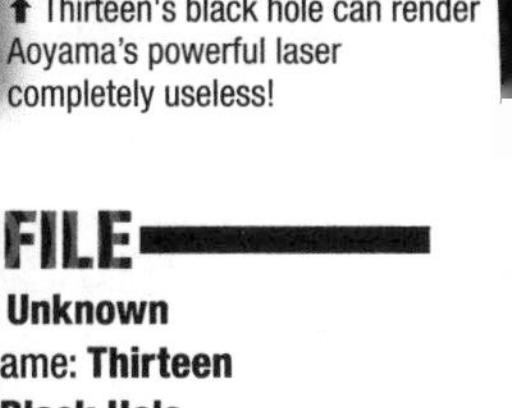

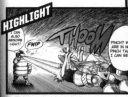

HIGHLIGHT
I CAN ALSO ABSORB LIGHT!
FWIP
THOOM


⬆ Thirteen's black hole can render Aoyama's powerful laser completely useless!

## RELATIONSHIPS

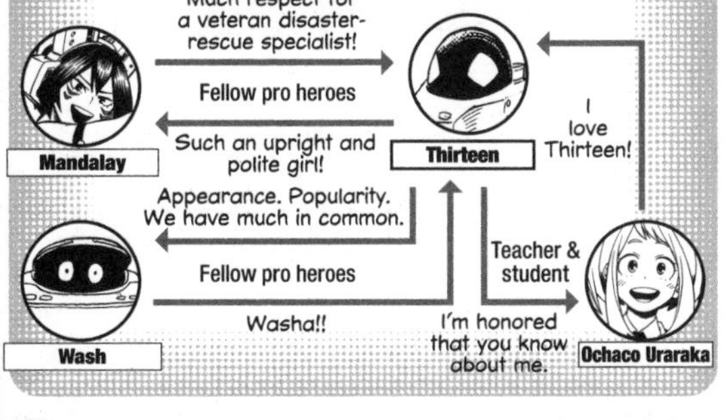

Much respect for a veteran disaster-rescue specialist!
Fellow pro heroes
Such an upright and polite girl!
Mandalay
Thirteen
I love Thirteen!
Appearance. Popularity. We have much in common.
Teacher & student
Fellow pro heroes
Washa!!
I'm honored that you know about me.
Wash
Ochaco Uraraka


## PROFILE

Name: **Unknown**
Hero name: **Thirteen**
Quirk: **Black Hole**
Birthday: **February 3**
Height: **180 cm**
Blood type: **A**
Birthplace: **Kagoshima Prefecture (Tanegashima)**
Personality: **Gentle**
Ultimate move: **Black Hole**

## This sidekick at Nighteye's agency is still training in the ways of humor.

As a sidekick employed at Nighteye's hero agency, Bubble Girl is all by the book around her boss but is cheery and relaxed otherwise. Thanks to training from her senior heroes and sidekicks, she's growing by leaps and bounds!

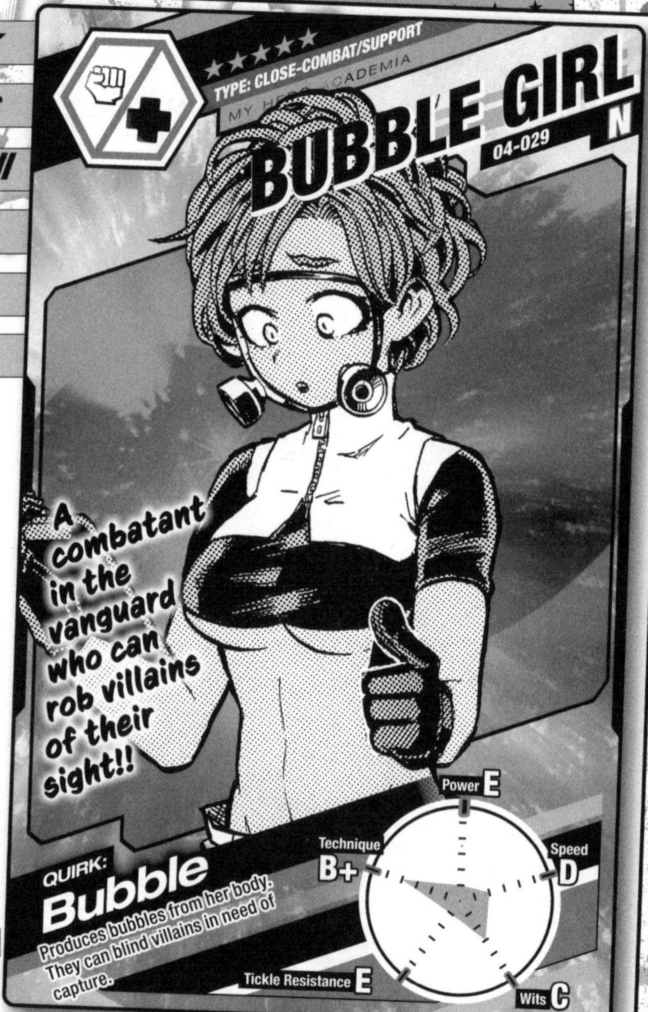
TYPE: CLOSE-COMBAT/SUPPORT
MY HERO ACADEMIA
BUBBLE GIRL
N
04-029
A combatant in the vanguard who can rob villains of their sight!!
QUIRK:
Bubble
Produces bubbles from her body. They can blind villains in need of capture.
Power E
Speed D
Wits C
Tickle Resistance E
Technique B+

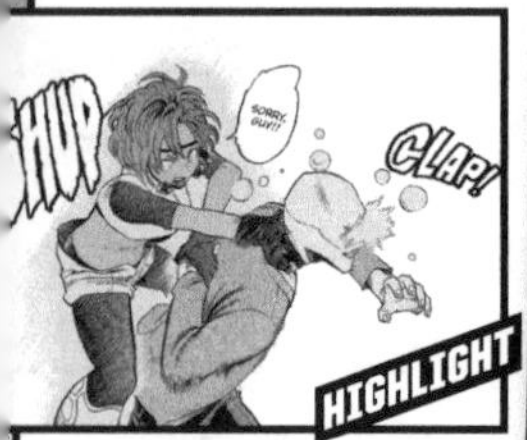
SHUP
CLAP!
HIGHLIGHT

⬆ Bubble Girl might have been nervous before the raid, but she's smooth on the battlefield!

## RELATIONSHIPS

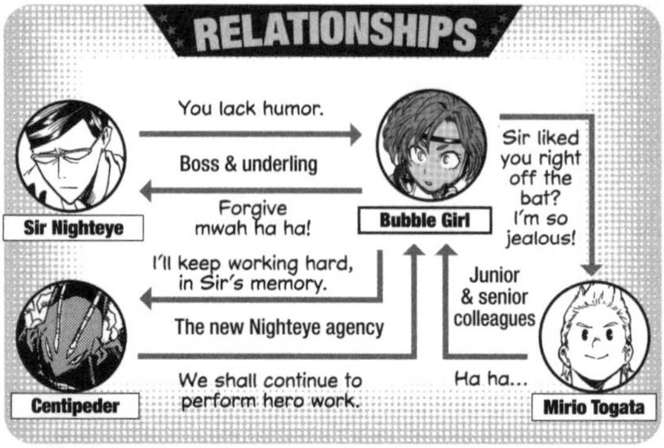
Sir Nighteye
Bubble Girl
Centipeder
Mirio Togata
You lack humor.
Boss & underling
Forgive mwah ha ha!
Sir liked you right off the bat? I'm so jealous!
I'll keep working hard, in Sir's memory.
The new Nighteye agency
We shall continue to perform hero work.
Junior & senior colleagues
Ha ha...

## PROFILE

Name: **Kaoruko Awata**
Hero name: **Bubble Girl**
Quirk: **Bubble**
Birthday: **April 23**
Height: **167 cm**
Blood type: **B**
Birthplace: **Ehime Prefecture**
Personality: **Get-it-done attitude**
Ultimate move: **Perfume Bubble**

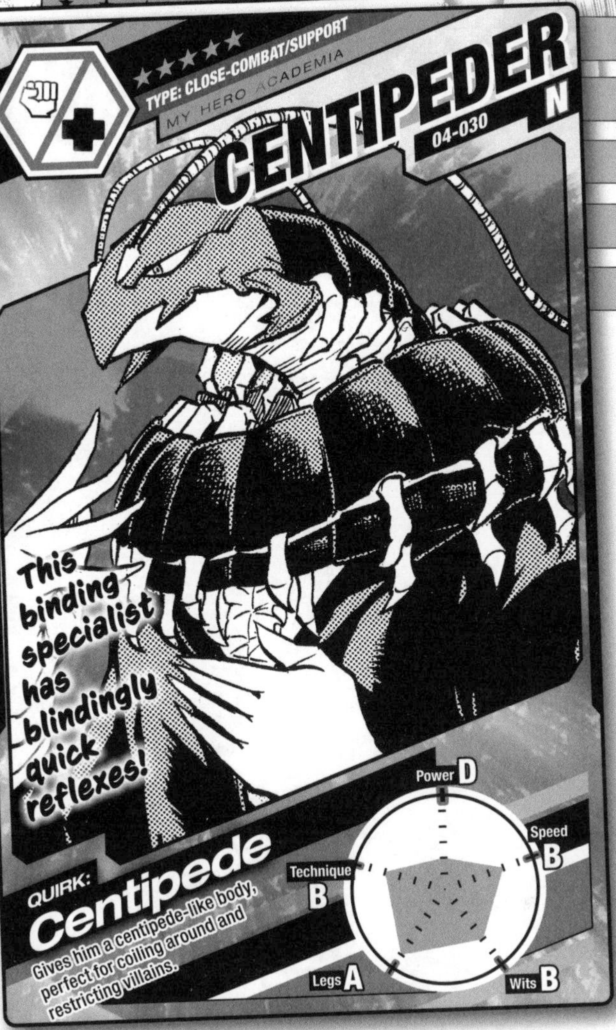
★★★★★★
TYPE: CLOSE-COMBAT/SUPPORT
MY HERO ACADEMIA
CENTIPEDER
N
04-030
This binding specialist has blindingly quick reflexes!
Power D
Speed B
Technique B
Legs A
Wits B
QUIRK:
Centipede
Gives him a centipede-like body, perfect for coiling around and restricting villains.

**A gentleman who makes sound judgments no matter what.**

This sidekick at Nighteye's agency is a gentleman who's always cool and composed. Centipeder is also in charge of training Bubble Girl. He's taken over the agency since Nighteye's death.

⬇ Centipeder had no trouble apprehending two of the Shie Hassaikai goons who attacked from the shadows.

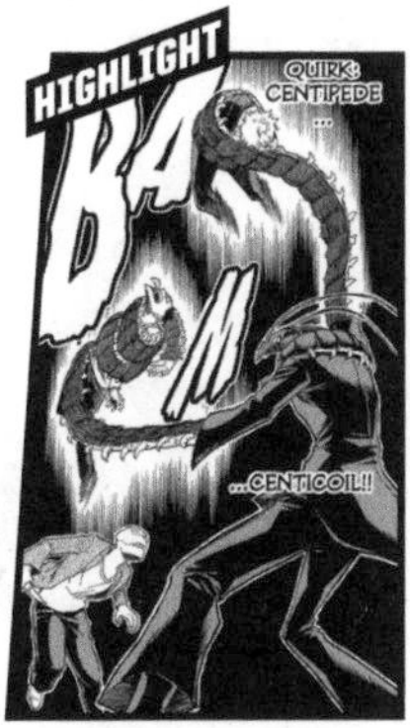
HIGHLIGHT
QUIRK: CENTIPEDE
...
BAM
...CENTICOIL!!

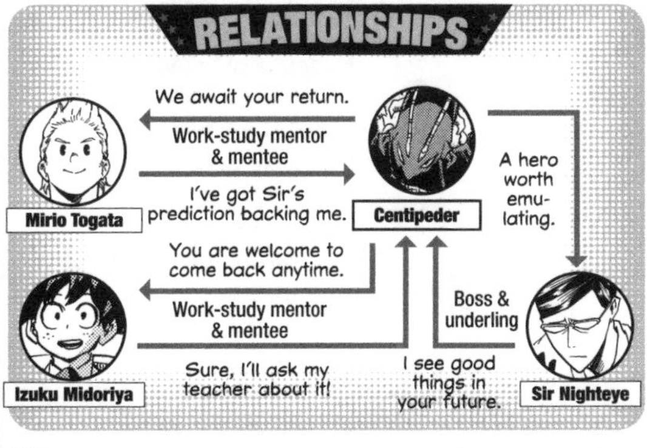
RELATIONSHIPS
We await your return.
Work-study mentor & mentee
I've got Sir's prediction backing me.
Mirio Togata
Centipeder
A hero worth emulating.
You are welcome to come back anytime.
Work-study mentor & mentee
Sure, I'll ask my teacher about it!
Izuku Midoriya
Boss & underling
I see good things in your future.
Sir Nighteye

## PROFILE

Name: **Juzo Moashi**
Hero name: **Centipeder**
Quirk: **Centipede**
Birthday: **June 4**
Height: **205 cm**
Blood type: **A**
Birthplace: **Niigata Prefecture**
Personality: **Composed gentleman**
Ultimate move: **Centicoil**

## Foulmouthed, but a kindhearted and devoted husband.

A pro hero with dreadlocks. Rock Lock often has a bad attitude (as shown at the pre-raid meeting), but deep down, he's a devoted husband with a big heart. He only wields that sharp tongue because he's worried about his friends and allies getting hurt in battle.

TYPE: CLOSE-COMBAT/SUPPORT

MY HERO ACADEMIA

# ROCK LOCK
04-031

*The Locking Hero can lock down whatever he touches!!*

**QUIRK:**
## Lock Down
Any nonliving thing he touches is locked in place, even if that means it's suspended in midair.

| | |
|---|---|
| Power | C |
| Technique | B |
| Speed | C |
| Cynical Edge | B |
| Wits | A- |

I DON'T GET IT, NIGHTEYE!

...ON. WHY ...N'TCHA ...E A LOOK ...ME? I'LL ...VOID ...ATEVER ...S GOT IN ...RE FOR ...ME!

**HIGHLIGHT**

↑ Rock Lock was so eager to rescue Eri that he berated Nighteye over his reluctance to use his Foresight Quirk.

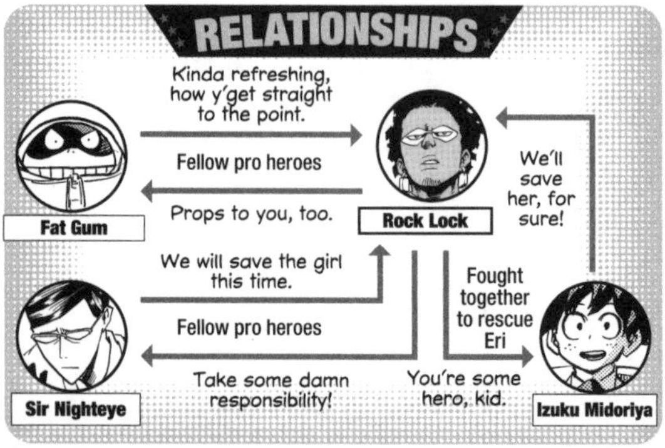

## RELATIONSHIPS

Kinda refreshing, how y'get straight to the point.

Fellow pro heroes → **Rock Lock**

Props to you, too. ← **Fat Gum**

We'll save her, for sure!

We will save the girl this time.

Fellow pro heroes → **Sir Nighteye**

Take some damn responsibility!

Fought together to rescue Eri

You're some hero, kid. → **Izuku Midoriya**

## PROFILE

Name: **Ken Takagi**
Hero name: **Rock Lock**
Quirk: **Lock Down**
Birthday: **June 9**
Height: **173 cm**
Blood type: **B**
Birthplace: **Tokushima Prefecture**
Personality: **Great guy, deep down**
Ultimate move: **Deadbolt**

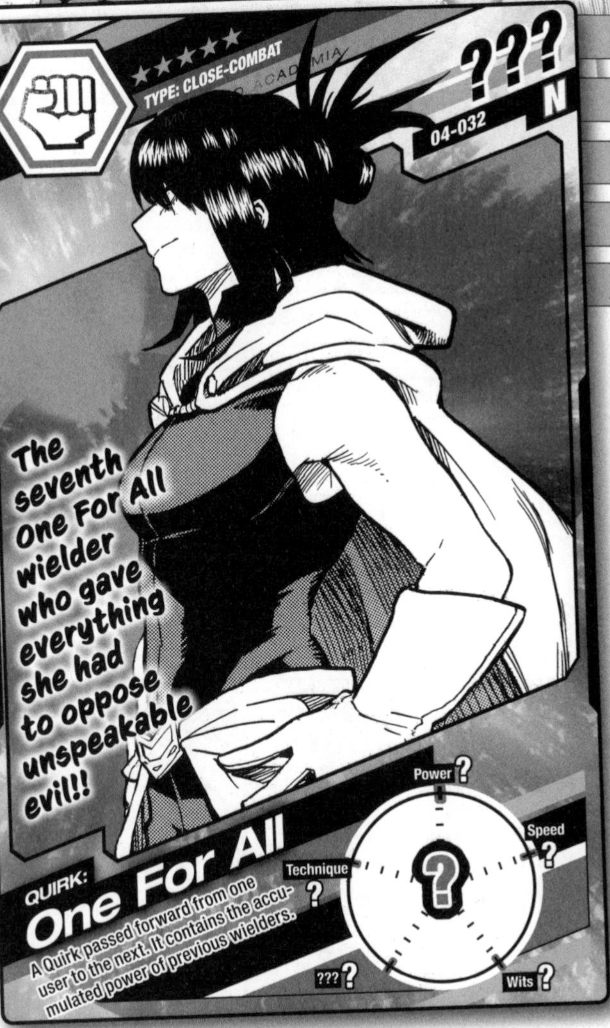
★★★★★★
TYPE: CLOSE-COMBAT
???
N
04-032
The seventh One For All wielder who gave everything she had to oppose unspeakable evil!!
QUIRK:
One For All
A Quirk passed forward from one user to the next. It contains the accumulated power of previous wielders.
Power ?
Speed ?
Technique ?
?
??? ?
Wits ?

## All Might's master, whose indomitable smile never faltered.

All Might's master and Gran Torino's sworn friend. For the sake of peace, Shimura stood up to All For One, but that tenacious evil made light of her convictions and defeated her…

HIGHLIGHT

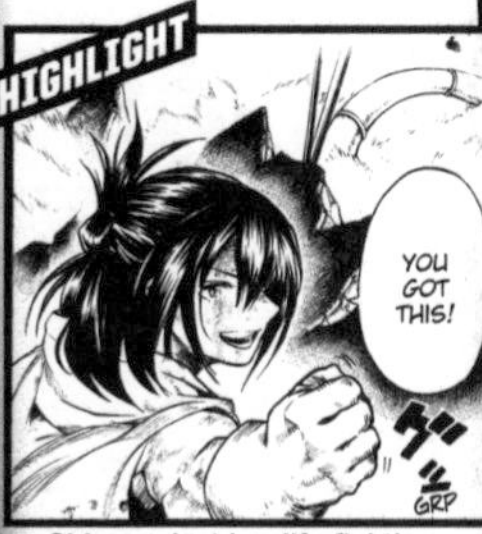
YOU GOT THIS!
GRP

⬆ Shimura lost her life fighting All For One, and All Might inherited her will and mission.

## RELATIONSHIPS

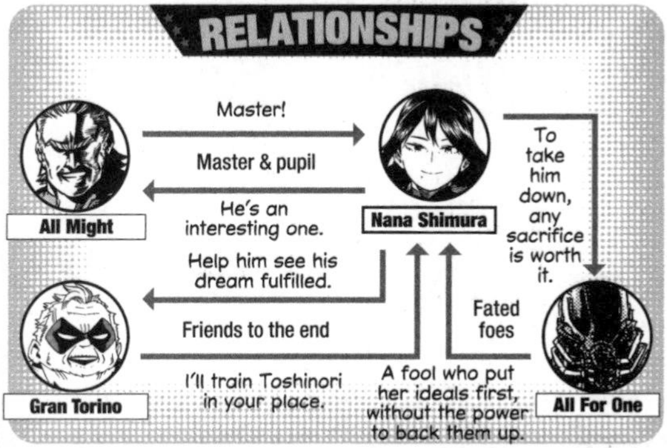
All Might
Nana Shimura
Gran Torino
All For One
Master!
Master & pupil
He's an interesting one.
Help him see his dream fulfilled.
Friends to the end
I'll train Toshinori in your place.
To take him down, any sacrifice is worth it.
Fated foes
A fool who put her ideals first, without the power to back them up.

## PROFILE

Name: **Nana Shimura**
Hero name: **Unknown**
Quirk: **One For All**
Birthday: **Unknown**
Height: **Unknown**
Blood type: **Unknown**
Birthplace: **Unknown**
Personality: **Unyielding smile**
Ultimate move: **Unknown**

## Backdraft

He thrives around conflagrations. Nobody can snuff fires faster than Backdraft.

## Ms. Joke

Homeroom teacher to class 2-2 at Ketsubutsu Academy. Her Quirk, Outburst, forces people to laugh. As the Smile Hero, Ms. Joke creates seas of laughter and chaos. She and Eraser Head are longtime acquaintances, but she's never made him laugh.

## Snipe

He focuses on every student, and his accuracy means villains never get away.

## Lunch Rush

One bite of Lunch Rush's nutritionally balanced food will leave you wanting more.

## Desutegoro

His muscles put him in high demand—whether as a bodyguard or as a fighter.

## Toy-Toy

She booed Bakugo during a festival. Looks like a circus troupe toy poodle.

## Ingenium

The Turbo Hero was a by-the-book leader. He retired after Stain maimed him.

## Airjet

As the Buster Hero, Airjet uses backpack equipment for midair combat.

## Fourth Kind

His Quirk is Quad Arms, and he scares children. Currently seeking a better look.

## Manual

Manual is beloved for his steady, earnest approach and can handle anything.

## Crimson Riot

The Chivalrous Hero admired by Kirishima lived without regret.

## Native

Stain attacked Native in Hosu City but was stopped by Midoriya and friends.

## Uwabami

Her good looks make her the ideal spokesperson. Men love her.

## Gunhead

The soft-spoken Battle Hero and the creator of Gunhead Martial Arts (G.M.A.).

## Mr. Brave

He used his own hair against the Shie Hassaikai, but he fears a receding hairline.

## Kesagiri Man

This mysterious hero teamed up with Mr. Brave against the Shie Hassaikai.

## Water Hose

A hero team, and Kota's parents. They died in a battle against Muscular.

## Crust

A reliable hero who can be overbearing, though many fans appreciate that.

## Takeshita

Gentle's high school classmate. The costume is heavy on the bamboo theme.

## Snatch

Snatch's upper half turns to sand. He died when Chisaki's transport was attacked.

## Slidin' Go

Believed to have a Quirk for sliding around. He led Shigaraki to the M.L.A.'s HQ.

## Yoroi Musha

The Equipped Hero has a stern and severe approach. Military geeks love him.

## Wash

The beloved Laundry Hero! An ad he appeared in turned into an ongoing series.

## Yokumiru Mera

A perpetually overworked member of the Heroes Public Safety Commission, and the man in charge of announcements during the provisional license exam. A lack of staff means Mera is always busy—those dark rings under his eyes come from a lack of sleep. His favorite type of sleep is non-REM, since it allows the brain to take a breather.

## Naomasa Tsukauchi

A capable detective with a knack for profiling, he was put in charge of cases concerning the League of Villains. Tsukauchi is an old friend of All Might's, and he even gets in touch with All Might's mentor Gran Torino for special missions. The two successfully captured Kurogiri when the villain attempted to make contact with Gigantomachia.

## Gori

The detective in charge of interrogating Gentle. When Gentle tried to take all the blame to keep La Brava from being charged, Gori suggested that he might still be capable of rehabilitation.

## Kenji Tsuragamae

Chief Tsuragamae is a gentleman. In order to preserve law and order, he had to cover up the achievements of Midoriya and friends in the Hero Killer case, though he deeply regretted it.

## Heroes Public Safety Commission President

The commission is charged with protecting peace and order, and this woman sits at the top. With a will of steel, she even takes it upon herself to personally deliver the orders for classified missions.

## Sansa Tamagawa

Tsukauchi's reliable underling. Always serious and justice minded, Tamagawa tackles every case earnestly, no matter the scope and scale. On his days off, he grooms himself to relax and relieve stress.

# EX
## EDITION II

Heroes are always ready to stand against villains who threaten peace, and no matter the odds, they never give up. The following is a collection of news stories chronicling their exploits.

# HERO NEWS

## SPOTLIGHT

# MASSIVE DAMAGE WHILE WARDING OFF THE ENEMY!

**Event: Attack on U.S.J.**

## Villains at U.A. High? But Why?!

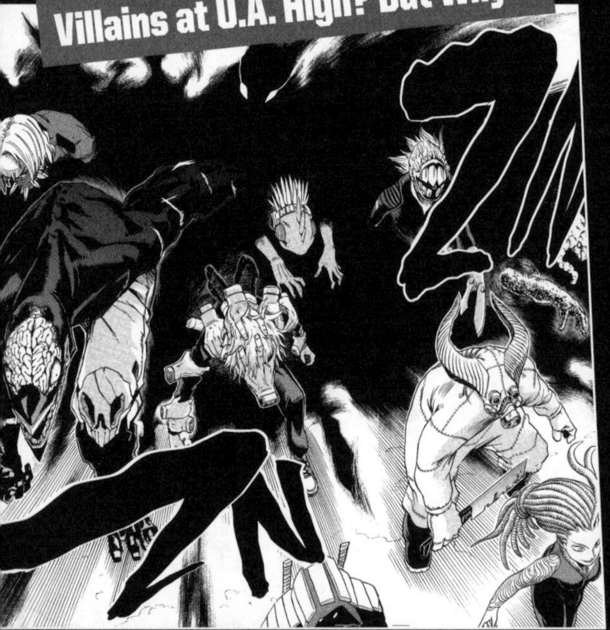

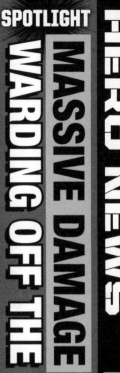

⬆ A small army of villains appeared at U.S.J., hoping to attack All Might!!

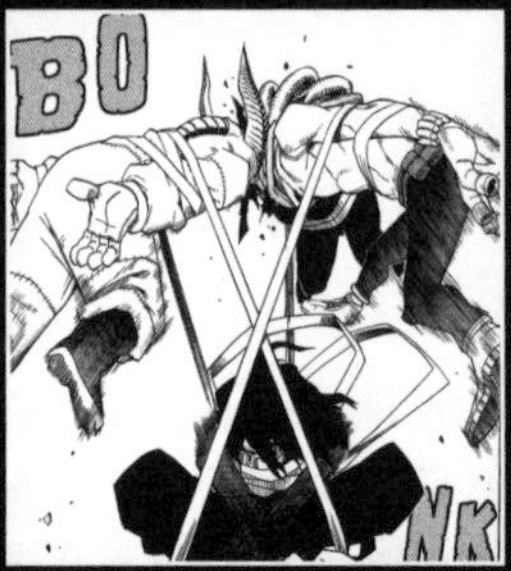
BO
NK

⬆ Lead chaperone Eraser Head engaged the villains in fierce combat to protect his students.

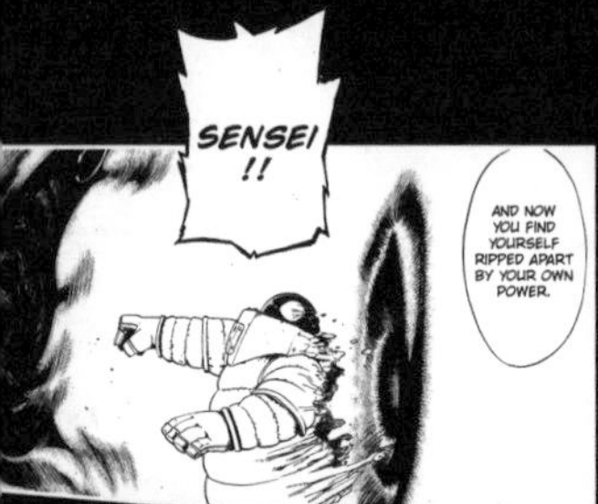
SENSEI !!
AND NOW YOU FIND YOURSELF RIPPED APART BY YOUR OWN POWER.

⬆ Another teacher, Thirteen, faced Kurogiri and was tripped up by a Warp Gate trap.

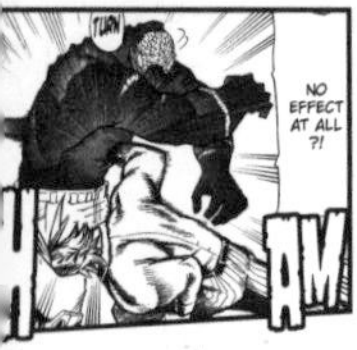
NO EFFECT AT ALL ?!
AM

⬆ The Nomu's Shock Absorption Quirk handily absorbed All Might's blows…

### The grotesque Nomu!!

The League of Villains employed a Nomu—a bioengineered creature possessing multiple Quirks. It was a fearsomely powerful foe, capable of regenerating itself and trading blows with All Might himself.

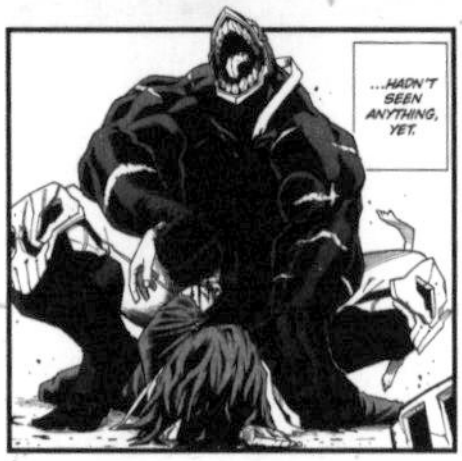
…HADN'T SEEN ANYTHING, YET.

⬆ Even Eraser Head's Erasure Quirk couldn't cancel out the Nomu's unbelievable strength, made possible by bioengineering.

### These two U.A. teachers faced an uphill battle at U.S.J.

The League of Villains sought to bring hero society crumbling down by killing the number one hero and symbol of peace, All Might. Was a traitorous mole instrumental to this meticulously planned sneak attack?

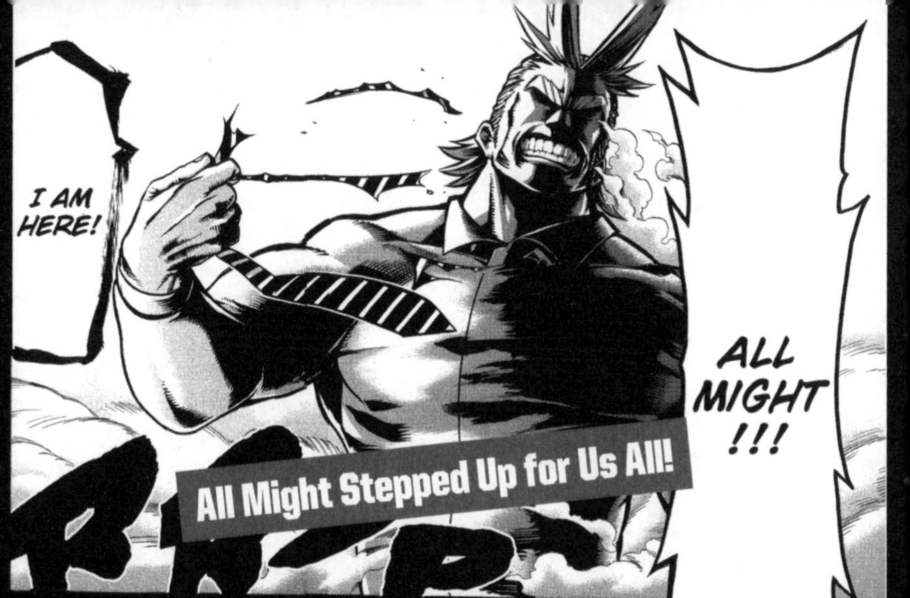
ALL MIGHT !!!
I AM HERE!

## All Might Stepped Up for Us All!

⬆ When both students and teachers were facing certain doom…All Might appeared!! The hero came running when he realized lines of communication with U.S.J. were down, and the students raised a cry of joy upon his arrival.

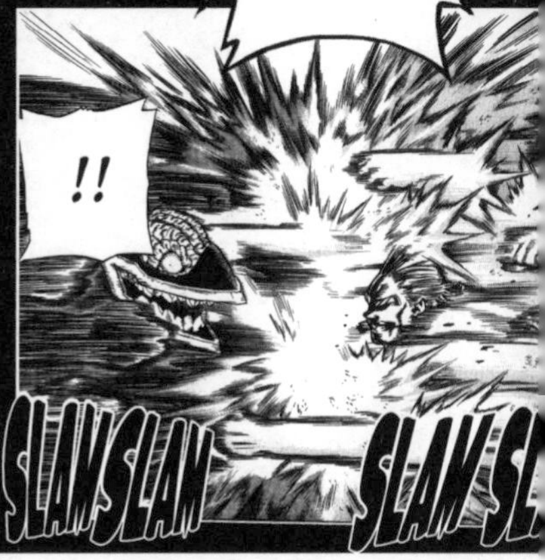
!!
SLAM SLAM
SLAM SL

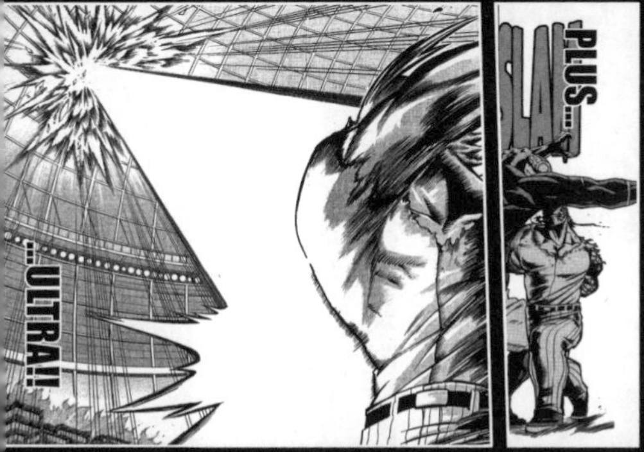
SLAM
PLUS…
…ULTRA!!

⬆ A brutal battle against the ferociously strong Nomu ensued. All Might turned his rage into power and sent the enemy flying off into the sky.

**Student Testimony**

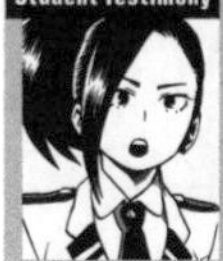

**Momo Yaoyorozu, Class 1-A**
I don't make much of a hero, but I fought with all I had.

**Student Testimony**

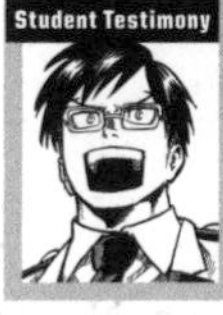

**Tenya Ida, Class 1-A**
I was reluctant to leave the scene, but I'm glad that my actions helped protect everyone.

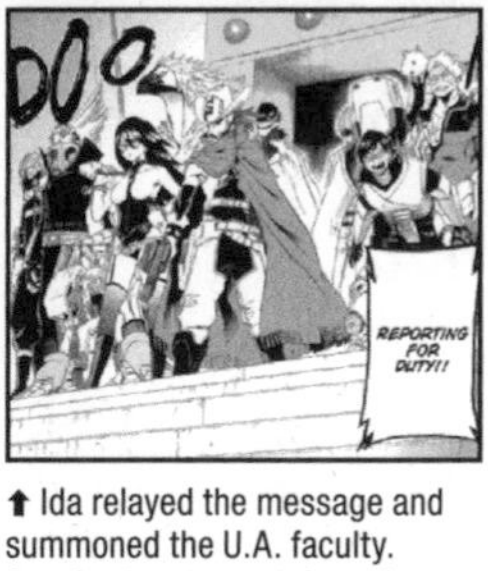
DOO
REPORTING FOR DUTY!!

⬆ Ida relayed the message and summoned the U.A. faculty. Sensing imminent defeat, the League of Villains was forced to retreat.

### Heroes arrived in the nick of time to save the day

In the end, it was the leadership of U.A. faculty member Thirteen that warded off the villains. When Thirteen realized that those present were at a distinct disadvantage against the villains, she ordered the fleet-footed Ida to run back to the school and inform the other faculty members. Their arrival at the scene brought this crisis to a quick conclusion.

# HERO NEWS

SPOTLIGHT

# HERO KILLER: ARRESTED!

Event: Rampage in Hosu City

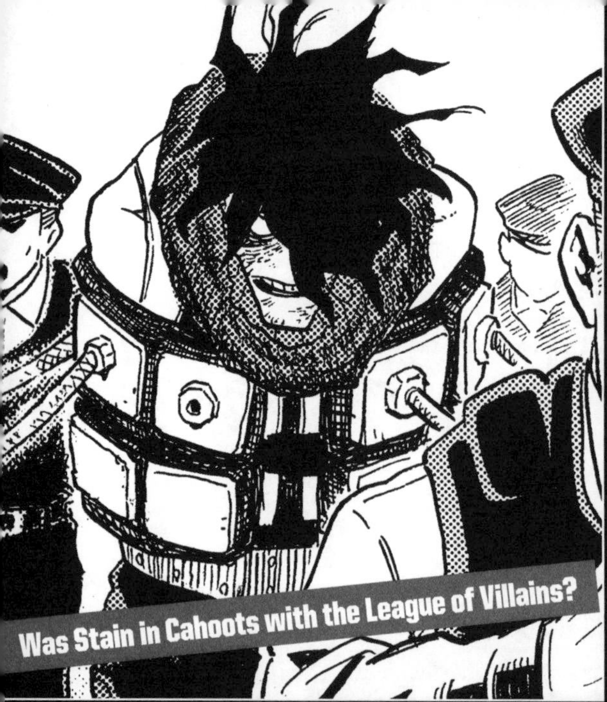

## Was Stain in Cahoots with the League of Villains?

⬆ The vile murderer who terrorized Hosu City—in custody at last!!

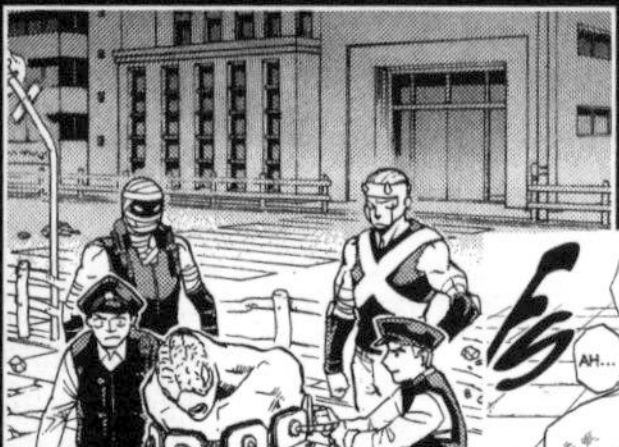

⬆ The presence of Nomu clearly pointed to the League of Villains' involvement.

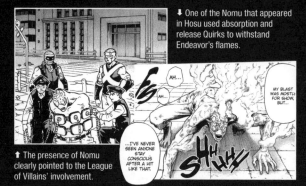

⬇ One of the Nomu that appeared in Hosu used absorption and release Quirks to withstand Endeavor's flames.

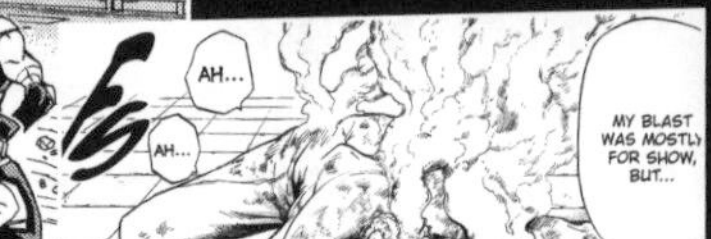
MY BLAST WAS MOSTLY FOR SHOW, BUT...
AH...
AH...
...I'VE NEVER SEEN ANYONE STAY CONSCIOUS AFTER A HIT LIKE THAT.
SHHHHH

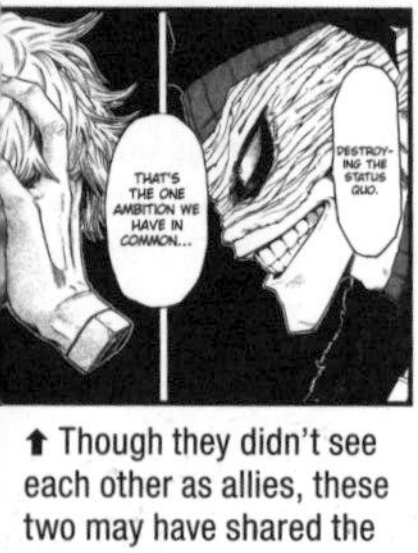
DESTROYING THE STATUS QUO.
THAT'S THE ONE AMBITION WE HAVE IN COMMON...

⬆ Though they didn't see each other as allies, these two may have shared the common goal of destroying the status quo.

### More Nomu? Was this the League of Villains?

Several Nomu appeared in the city without warning. It seems likely that Stain was collaborating with the League of Villains during this attack.

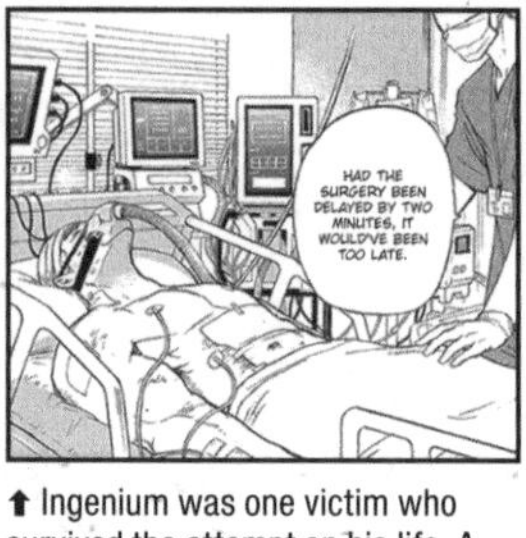
HAD THE SURGERY BEEN DELAYED BY TWO MINUTES, IT WOULD'VE BEEN TOO LATE.

⬆ Ingenium was one victim who survived the attempt on his life. A spinal cord injury left him paralyzed from the waist down.

### A series of killings in Hosu City

Serial killings of heroes rocked Tokyo's Hosu City, and the man behind the murders came to be known as the Hero Killer.

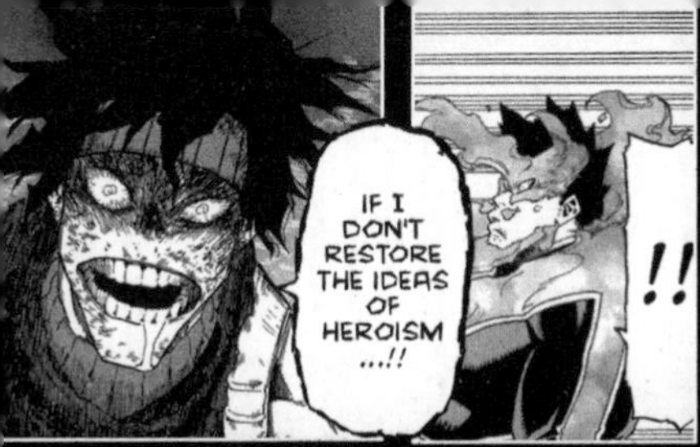
IF I DON'T RESTORE THE IDEAS OF HEROISM ...!!
!!

⬆ Stain's tenet is "reviving the true meaning of hero." In his madness, he advocated for purging all except All Might—the one true hero.

⬇ Gran Torino and Endeavor teamed up to fight back against the Nomu ravaging the city.

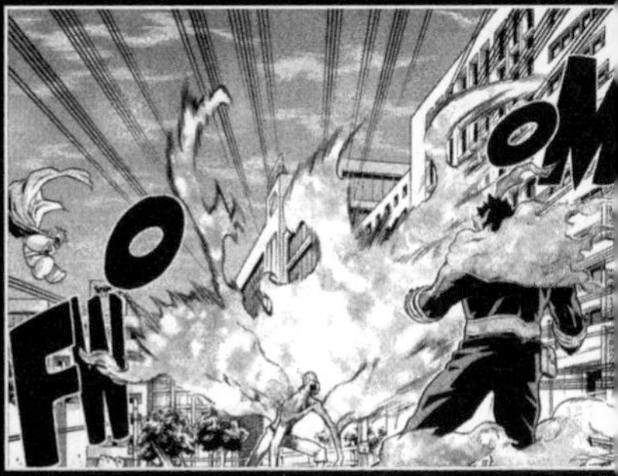
FWOOM

## Endeavor Was the Main Man Who Saved the Day!!

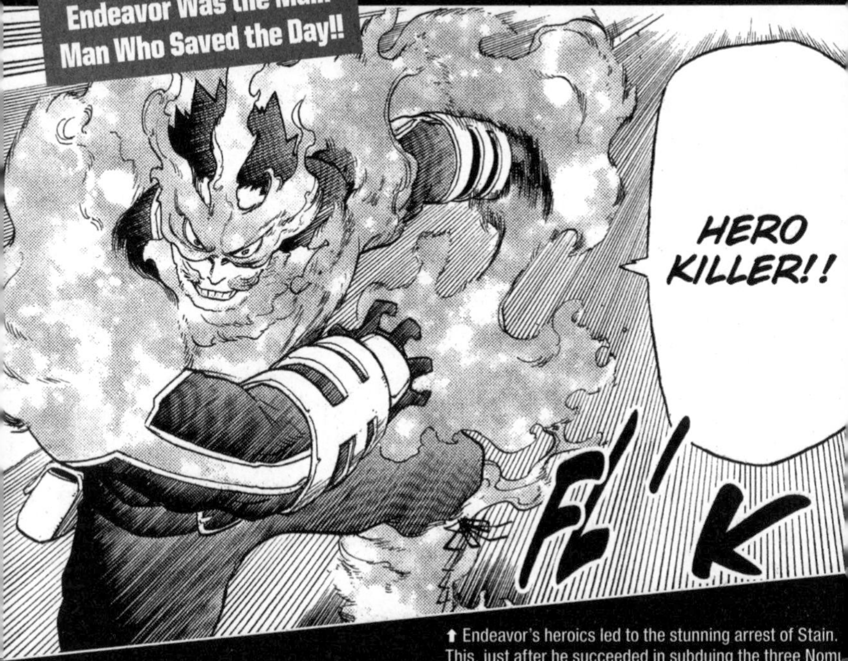
HERO KILLER!!

⬆ Endeavor's heroics led to the stunning arrest of Stain. This, just after he succeeded in subduing the three Nomu that rampaged in Hosu City.

**Hero Testimony**

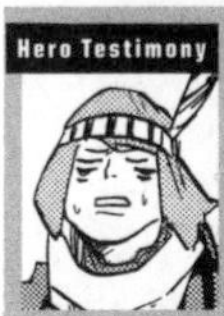

**Native**
Those kids saved me when Stain attacked. I'm really grateful to them.

**Hero Testimony**

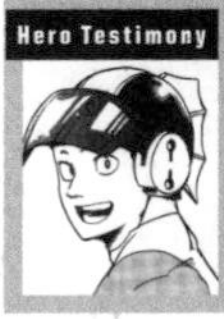

**Manual**
As the ones watching over the children, it was our negligence that got them caught up in this affair. We take responsibility...

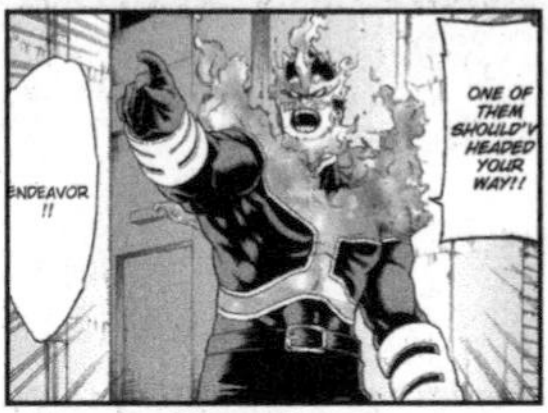
ONE OF THEM SHOULD'VE HEADED YOUR WAY!!
ENDEAVOR !!

⬆ Endeavor's efforts to evacuate the area ended up saving many lives. His sidekicks also contributed and demonstrated incredible teamwork.

## Leadership from Endeavor, the number two hero

Endeavor not only prevented Stain from doing any more harm but also minimized the damage and casualties caused by the Nomu. His battle prowess and leadership in a crisis merited high praise.

## Event: The Kamino Nightmare

# TO RESCUE U.A. STUDENT!!

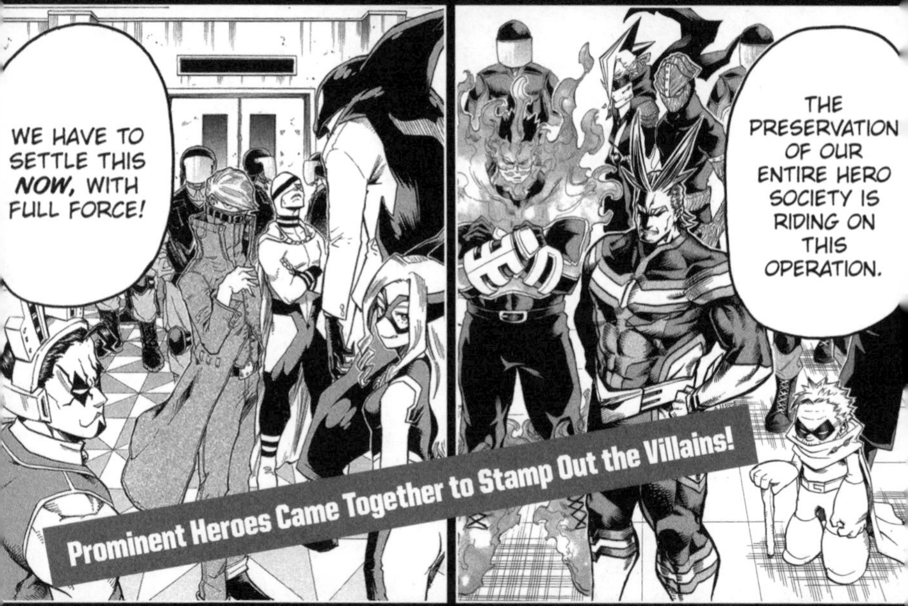
THE PRESERVATION OF OUR ENTIRE HERO SOCIETY IS RIDING ON THIS OPERATION.
WE HAVE TO SETTLE THIS *NOW,* WITH FULL FORCE!

## Prominent Heroes Came Together to Stamp Out the Villains!

↑ The rise of the League of Villains is linked to the downfall of hero society, which prompted this takedown operation.

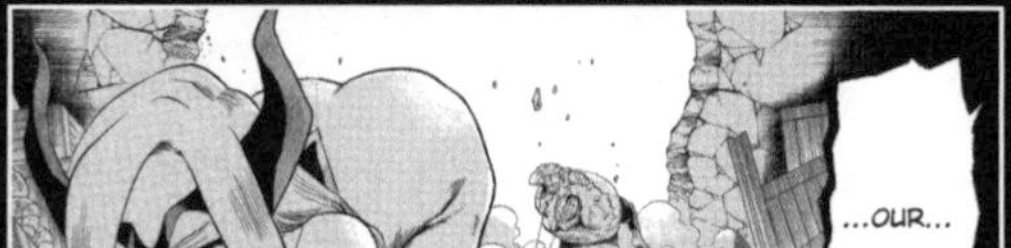
...OUR...
...RAGE!!
ZWF
SWIRL SWIRL

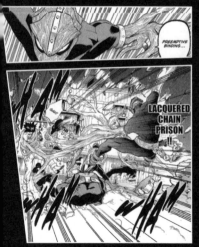

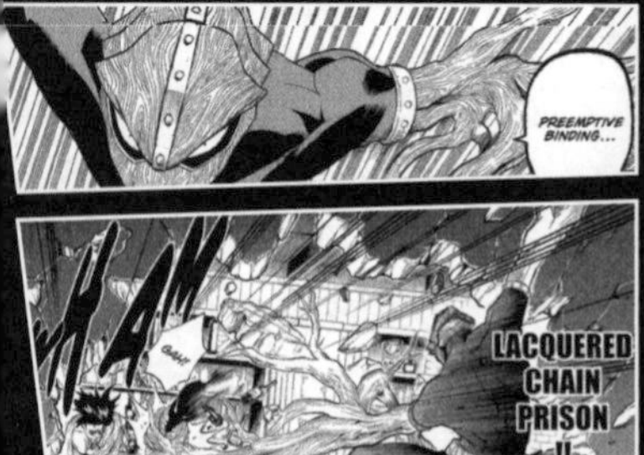
PREEMPTIVE BINDING...
LACQUERED CHAIN PRISON!!
WHAM
WHAM
WHAM

←↑ School staff at the U.A. press conference implied that the investigation hadn't made much headway, but that was a bluff to fool the villains. Quick raids by hero teams took control of multiple hideouts at once, including the Nomu storage hangar.

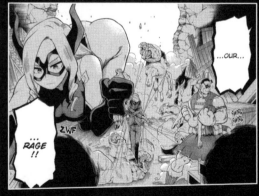

SPOTLIGHT HERO NEWS

# HEROES ASSEMBLE

## U.A. High Press Conference

In light of the attack and the recent abduction of a student during a training camp, the principal and a few teachers held a press conference.

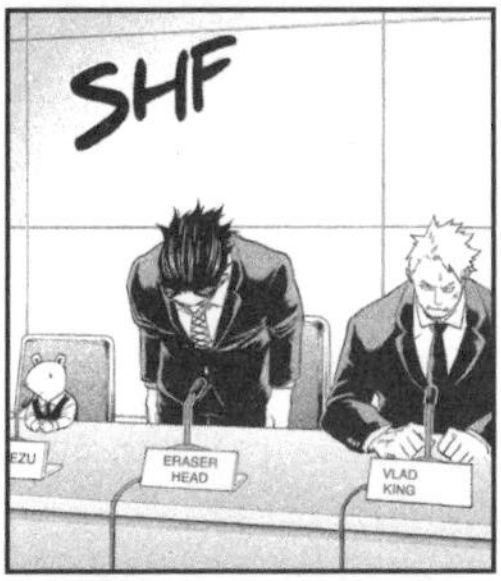
SHF
ERASER HEAD
VLAD KING

## Capable of Stealing Quirks

Legendary villain All For One protected the League of Villains from the authorities. The ruthless, cold-blooded man has the power to steal away the Quirks of others.

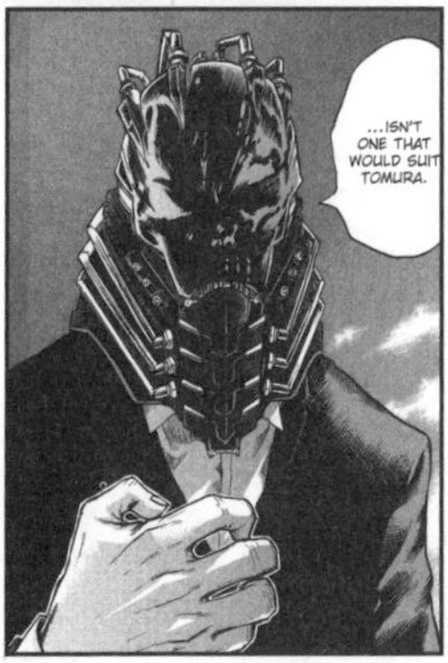
...ISN'T ONE THAT WOULD SUIT TOMURA.

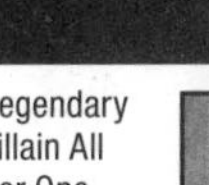

**Hero Testimony** **Kamui Woods**
I failed when I allowed Shigaraki and the others to escape from my clutches. What was that black liquid, anyhow?

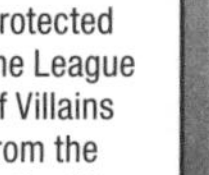

**Hero Testimony** **Best Jeanist**
So that man was the brains behind the league... Still, that's no excuse for my failure...

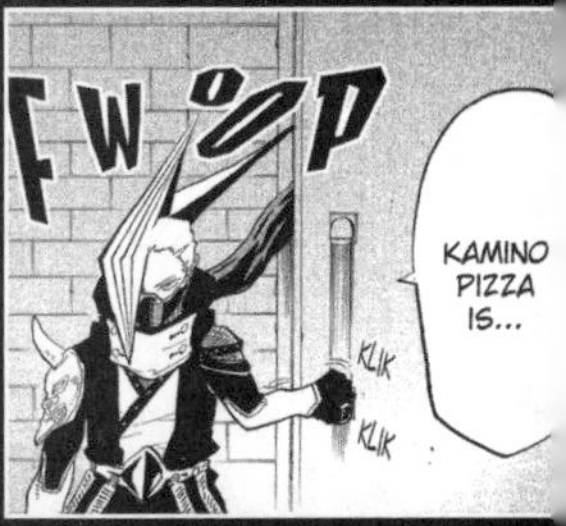
FWOOP
KAMINO PIZZA IS...
KLIK
KLIK

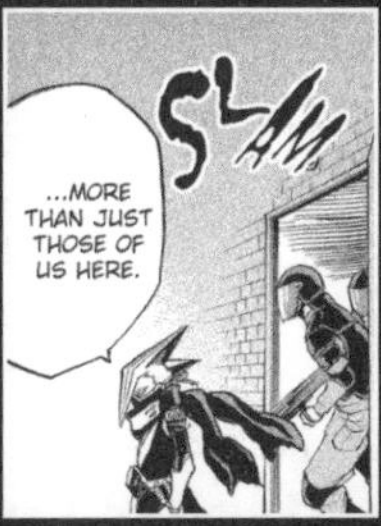
S'LAM
...MORE THAN JUST THOSE OF US HERE.

⬆ All Might and the main forces raided the hideout with the villain commanders, while Endeavor and skilled members of law enforcement formed a perimeter outside.

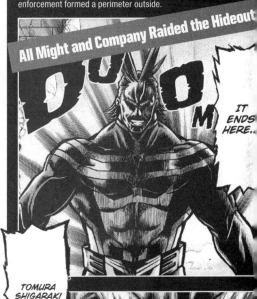

## All Might and Company Raided the Hideout

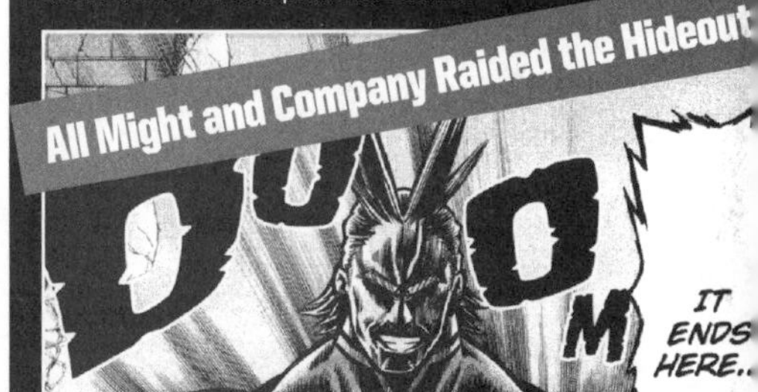
DOOM
IT ENDS HERE..
TOMURA SHIGARAKI !!

⬆ The elite team of heroes instantly cornered the League of Villains commanders—including their leader, Shigaraki—and intended to question the villains concerning the whereabouts of their shadowy string puller.

Event: The Kamino Nightmare

# ALL MIGHT FACED OFF AGAINST EVIL INCARNATE

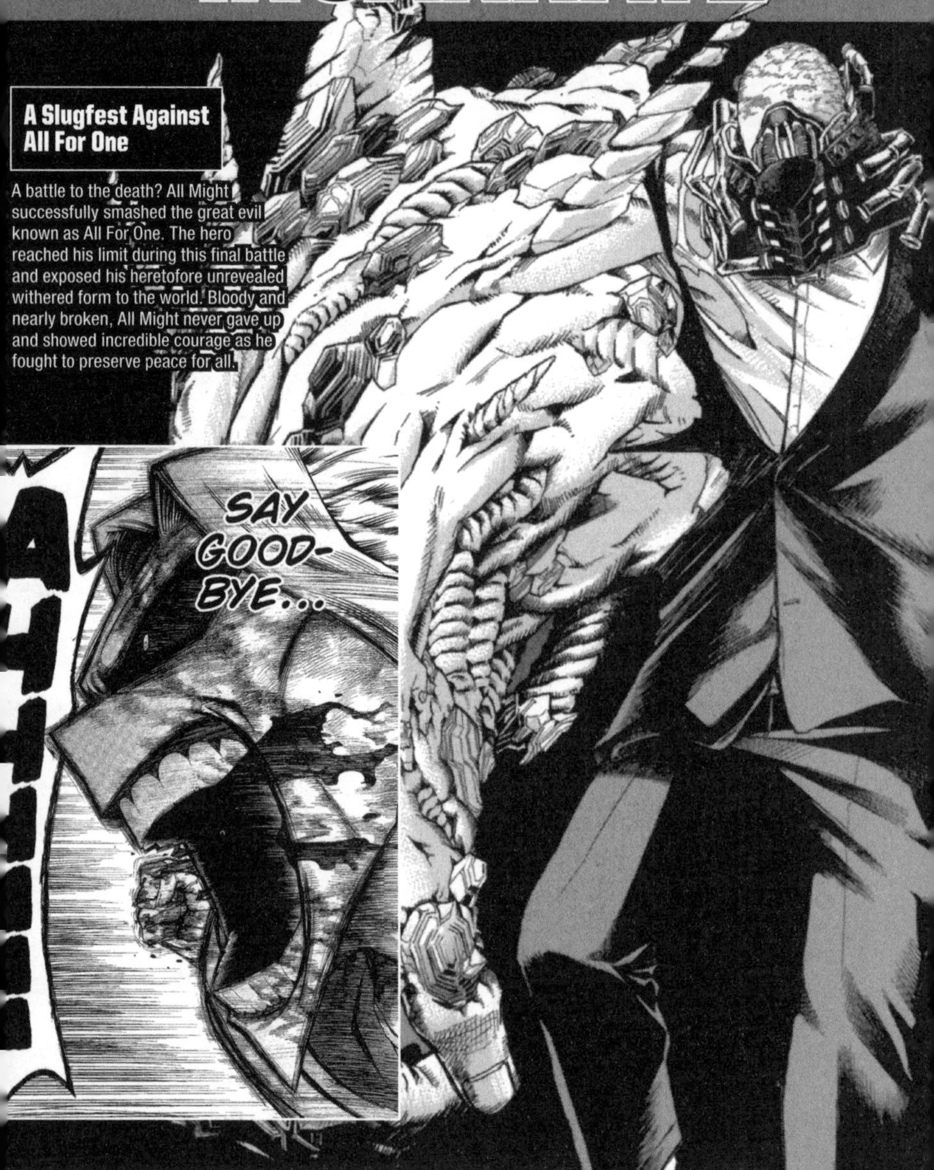
SAY GOOD-BYE...

### A Slugfest Against All For One

A battle to the death? All Might successfully smashed the great evil known as All For One. The hero reached his limit during this final battle and exposed his heretofore unrevealed withered form to the world. Bloody and nearly broken, All Might never gave up and showed incredible courage as he fought to preserve peace for all.

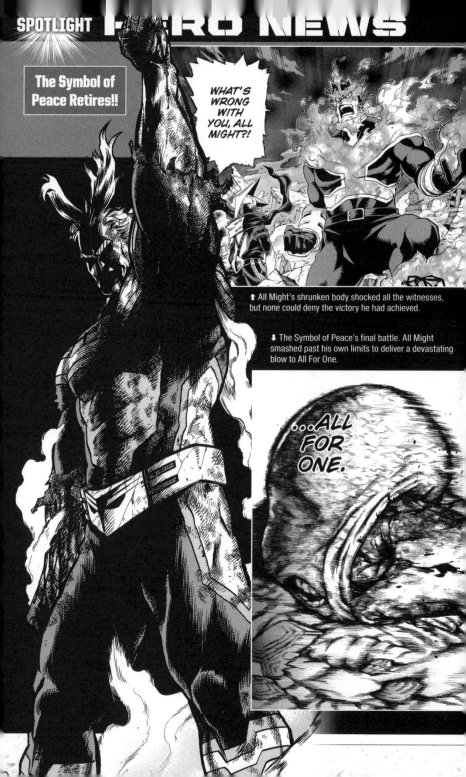

# SPOTLIGHT HERO NEWS

## The Symbol of Peace Retires!!

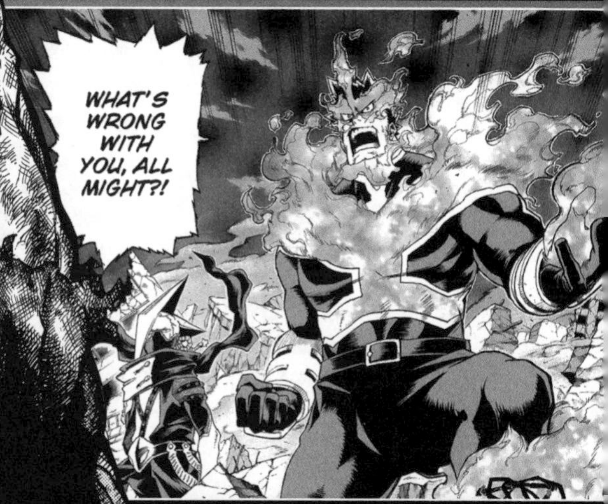
WHAT'S WRONG WITH YOU, ALL MIGHT?!

⬆ All Might's shrunken body shocked all the witnesses, but none could deny the victory he had achieved.

⬇ The Symbol of Peace's final battle. All Might smashed past his own limits to deliver a devastating blow to All For One.

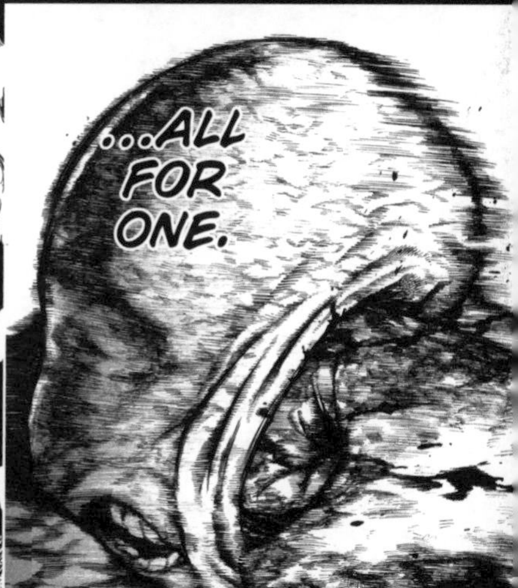
...ALL FOR ONE.

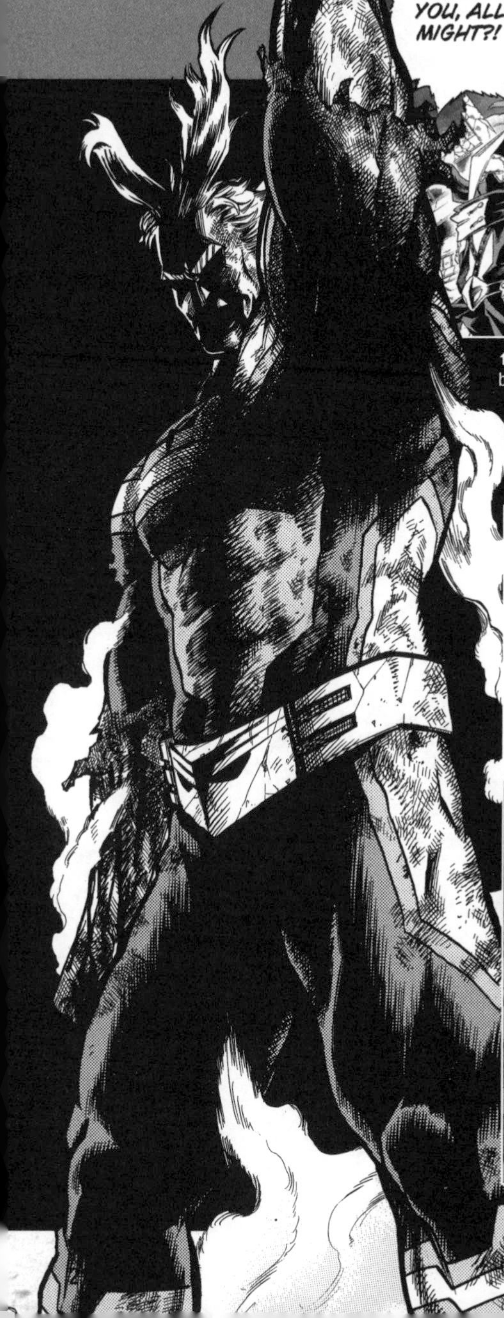

## Event: Shie Hassaikai Compound Raid

# SHIE HASSAIKAI!!

### A Team of Heroes Led by Sir Nighteye

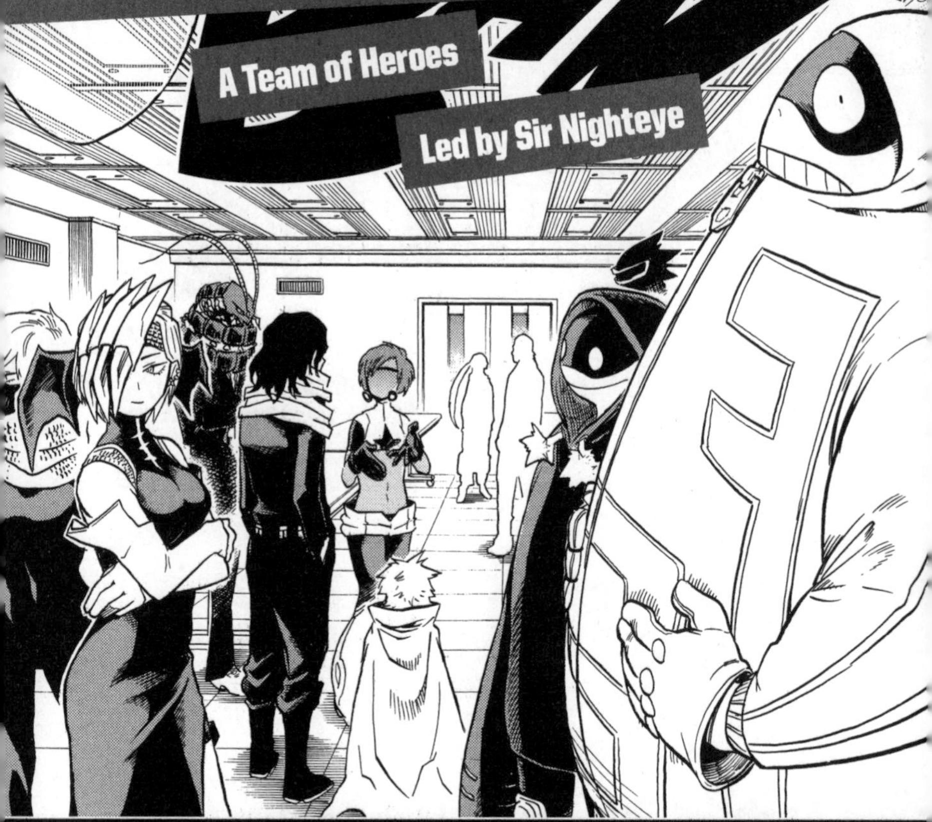

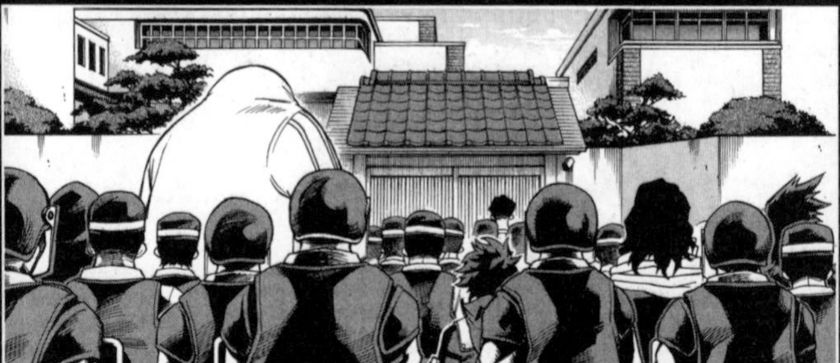

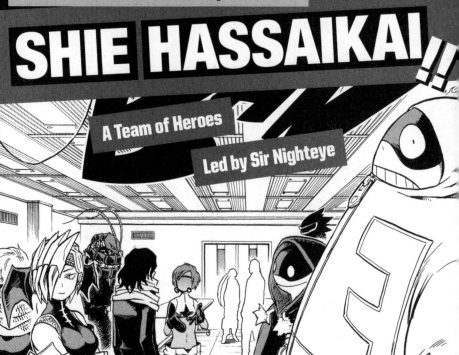

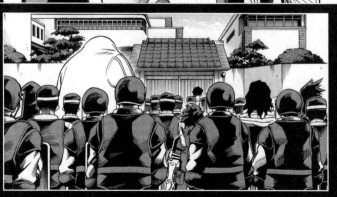

↑ After Sir Nighteye got to the bottom of the illegal drugs being produced and distributed by the Shie Hassaikai gang, a team of heroes was assembled to take action.

← The raid on the gang's main compound brought together heroes and law enforcement.

SPOTLIGHT HERO NEWS

# Raid on the VILLAIN ORGANIZATION:

## The drug produced by Shie Hassaikai

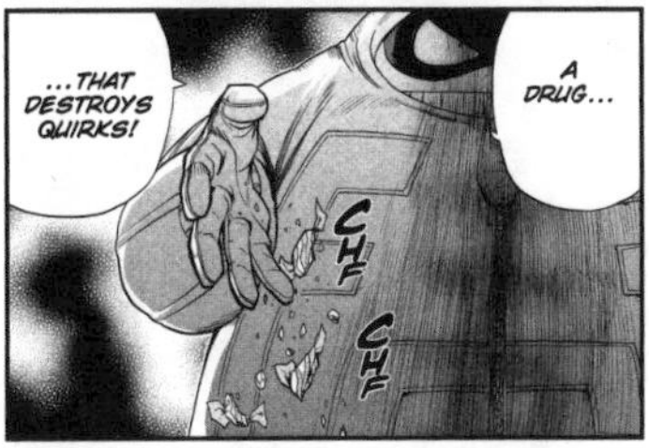
A DRUG...
...THAT DESTROYS QUIRKS!
CHF
CHF

The drugs were made into bullets, and any individual shot by one would lose use of their Quirk for a limited time.

## The grand plan behind the drugs?

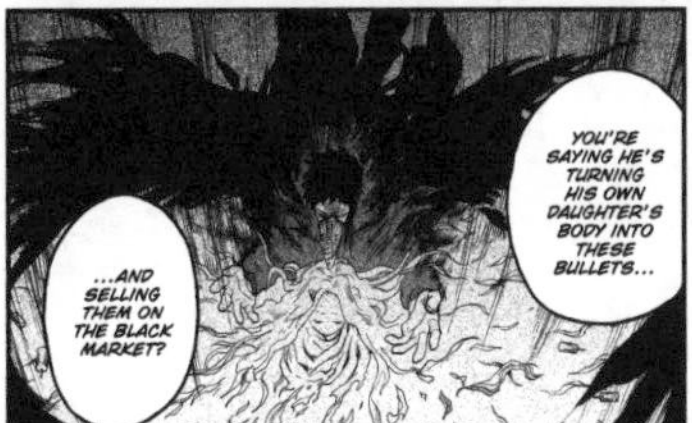
YOU'RE SAYING HE'S TURNING HIS OWN DAUGHTER'S BODY INTO THESE BULLETS...
...AND SELLING THEM ON THE BLACK MARKET?

Chisaki's goal was to distribute a perfected version of the drug capable of destroying a Quirk. It's a safe assumption that the young gang leader sought the utter destruction of hero society.

Hero Testimony

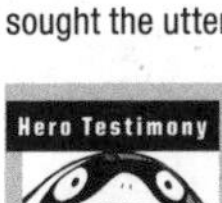

**Fat Gum**
Those Hassaikai punks were creating one nasty drug. They put up a real fight, but nothing I couldn't handle.

Hero Testimony

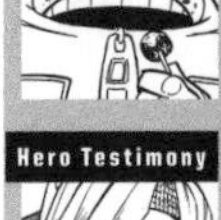

**Ryukyu**
I never imagined they'd be so prepared for us. It seemed as if they were willing to defend their operation to the death.

⬇ Anticipating a siege by heroes and police officers, Shie Hassaikai prepared to do battle and conceal evidence of wrongdoing.

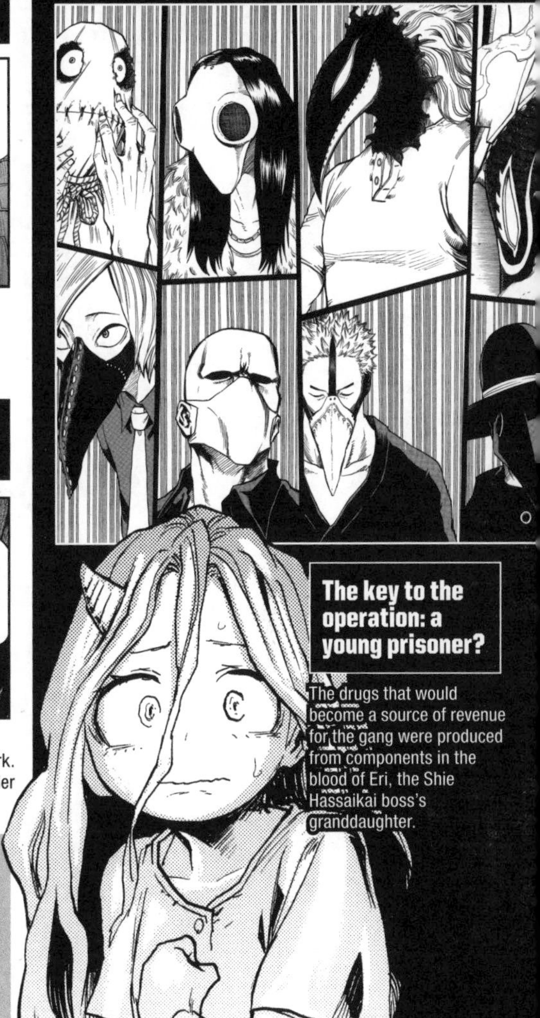

## The key to the operation: a young prisoner?

The drugs that would become a source of revenue for the gang were produced from components in the blood of Eri, the Shie Hassaikai boss's granddaughter.

# HERO NEWS

SPOTLIGHT

## PART TWO OF THE STORY!!

# THE SHIE HASSAIKAI GANG FOUGHT BACK!

**Event: Shie Hassaikai Compound Raid**

During the raid on the compound, the members of the organized crime gang fought back viciously. HQ director Joi Irinaka used his Mimicry Quirk to transform part of the compound into a labyrinth that confounded the raid team. However, the commendable efforts of heroes like Fat Gum succeeded in routing these villains.

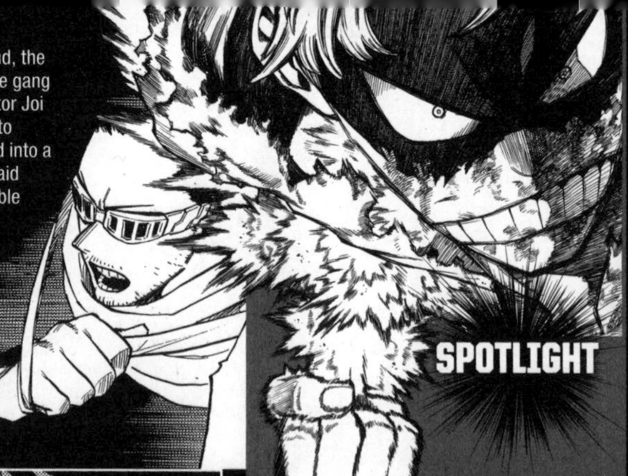

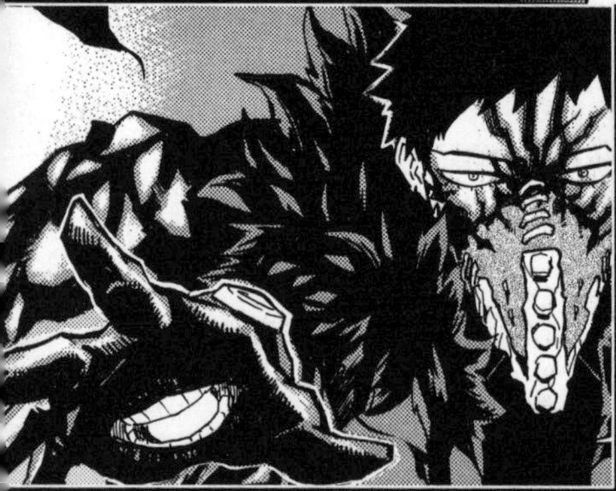

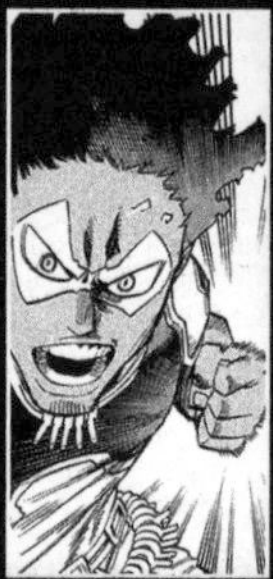

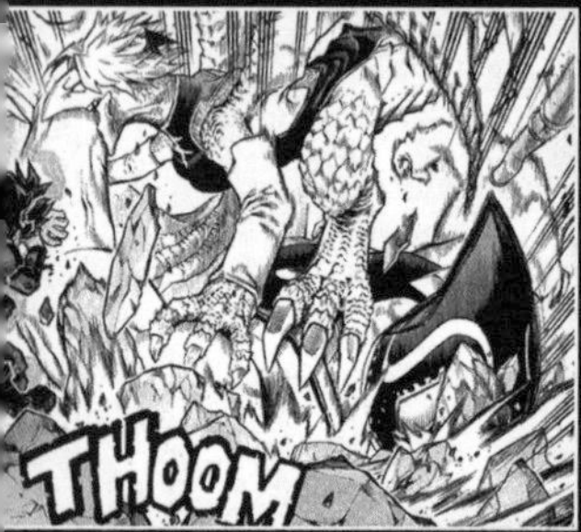
THOOM

### Sir Nighteye, killed in the line of duty

Sir Nighteye was in large part responsible for the operation's success, but shortly after, he succumbed to injuries incurred during the battle.

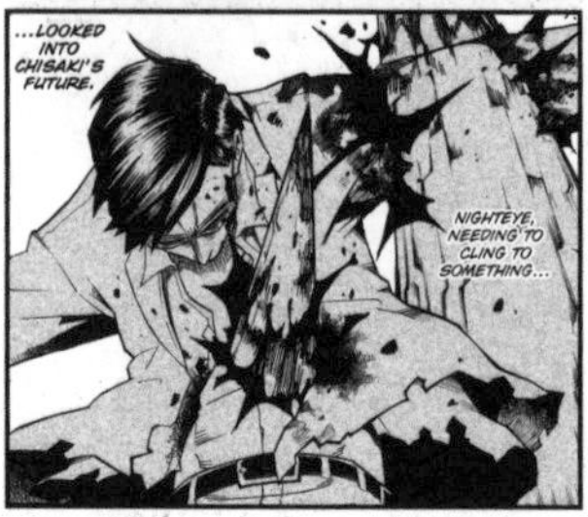
NIGHTEYE, NEEDING TO CLING TO SOMETHING...
...LOOKED INTO CHISAKI'S FUTURE.

⬆ Did Sir Nighteye allow himself to be hit in a valiant attempt to alter the future he had foreseen?

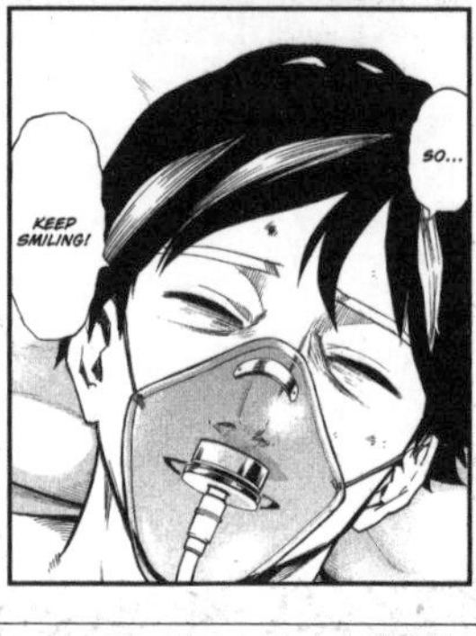
SO...
KEEP SMILING!

➡ This hero passed on while wishing the next generation a bright future full of humor and good cheer.

## Rescue Target:

## Secured!

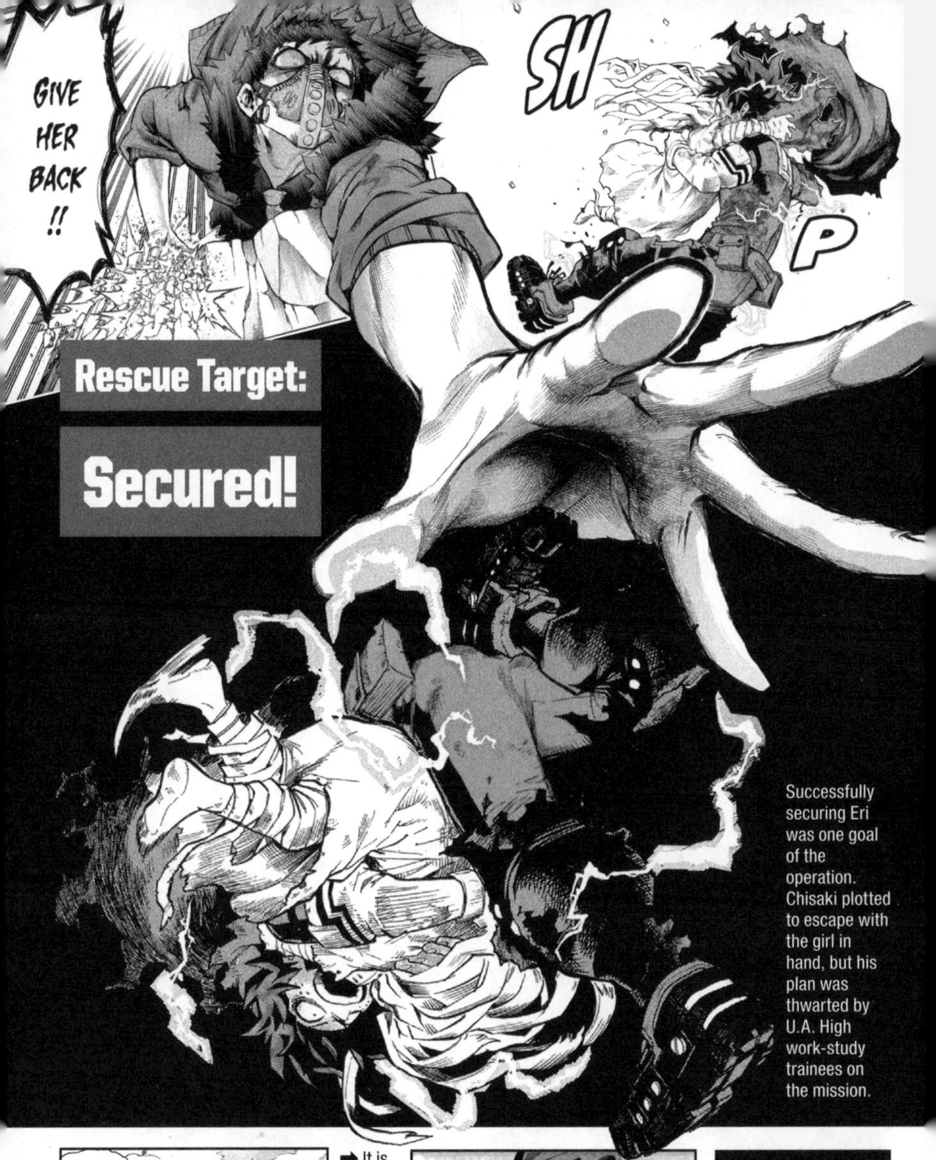
SH
P
GIVE HER BACK !!

Successfully securing Eri was one goal of the operation. Chisaki plotted to escape with the girl in hand, but his plan was thwarted by U.A. High work-study trainees on the mission.

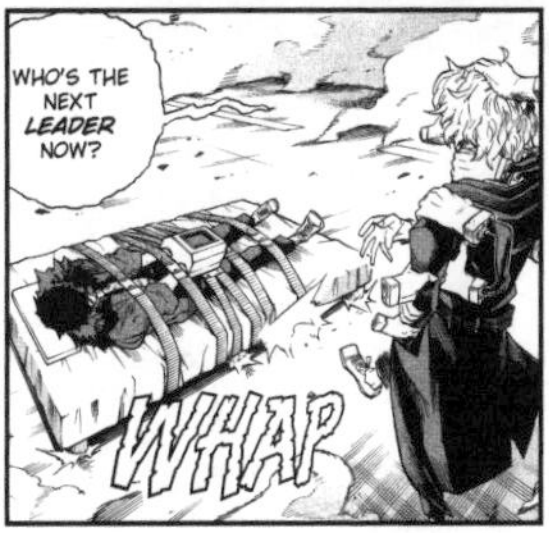
WHO'S THE NEXT LEADER NOW?
WHAP

⬆ By removing both of Chisaki's arms, the league succeeded in physically robbing him of his Quirk.

➡ It is unclear why the league attacked the transport. Did they have a falling out?

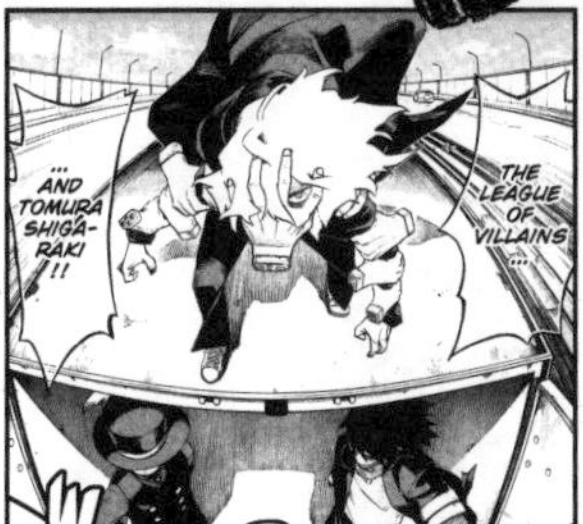
THE LEAGUE OF VILLAINS...
...AND TOMURA SHIGARAKI!!
FWOOSH

### The League of Villains leaps into action

From the start, the League of Villains was suspected of conspiring with the Shie Hassaikai gang. After the raid operation, the league attacked Chisaki's transport vehicle.

**Event: High-End Nomu Battle**

# THE NEW NUMBER ONE FIGHTS BACK!!

**Endeavor!!**

## When a Single Villain Threatened Fukuoka, the Number One Hero Stepped Up!

A new breed of Nomu appeared in the Kyushu region, and it was up to the number one hero, Endeavor, to stop the vicious creature from destroying an entire city. The so-called High-End Nomu possessed multiple Quirks and independent thought, making the encounter a trial that tested Endeavor's strength.

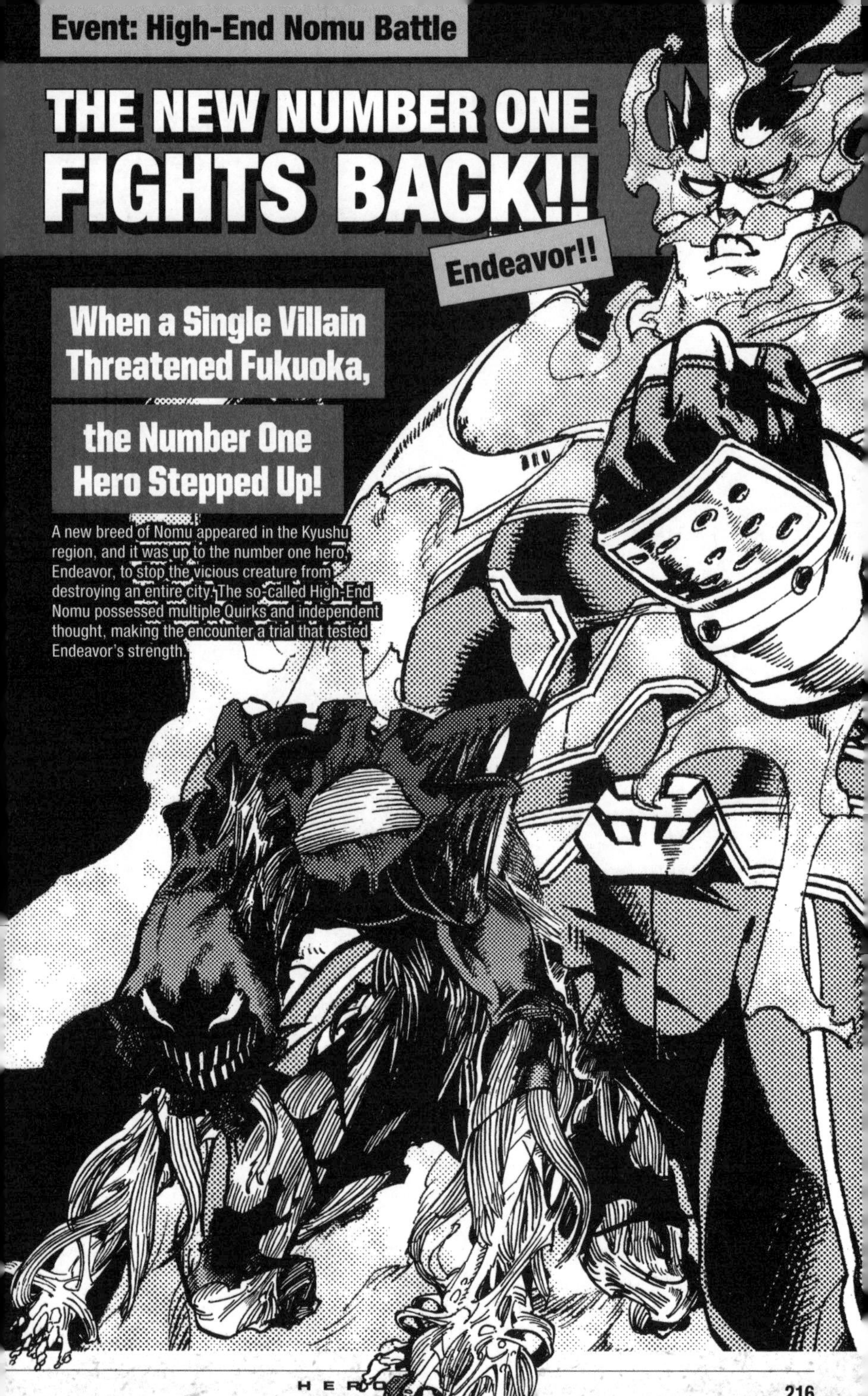

# HIGH-END ATTACKS!

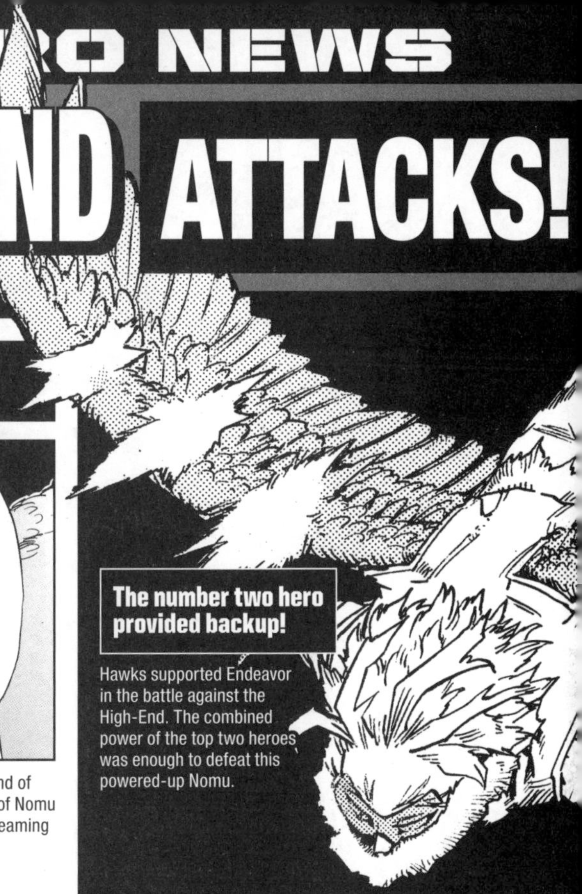

## Rumors of Nomu, and a team-up with Hawks

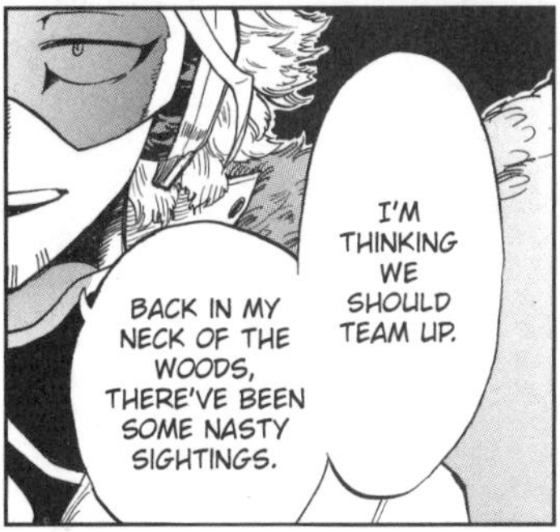
BACK IN MY NECK OF THE WOODS, THERE'VE BEEN SOME NASTY SIGHTINGS.
I'M THINKING WE SHOULD TEAM UP.

Endeavor paid a visit to Hawks's homeland of Kyushu. Given recent rumored sightings of Nomu around Japan, the Wing Hero proposed teaming up to get to the bottom of the matter.

## Endeavor grievously wounded

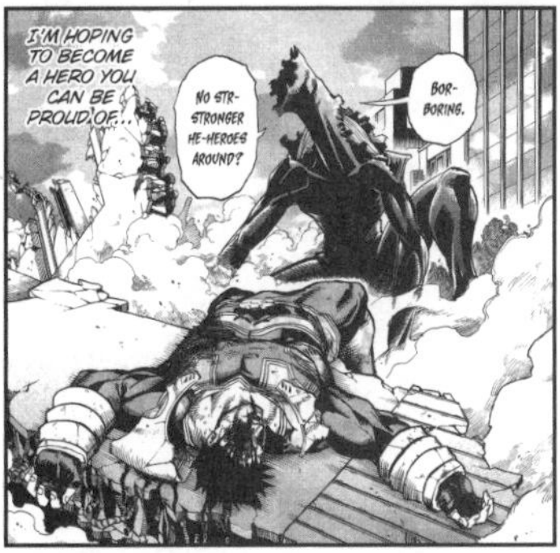
I'M HOPING TO BECOME A HERO YOU CAN BE PROUD OF...
NO STR-STRONGER HE-HEROES AROUND?
BOR-BORING.

Even Endeavor faced an uphill battle against this Nomu and its blend of Quirks. The beast refused to succumb to a powerful Prominence Burn blast and retaliated with regeneration, stretchy limbs, and fission abilities, allowing it to do serious harm to Endeavor.

## The number two hero provided backup!

Hawks supported Endeavor in the battle against the High-End. The combined power of the top two heroes was enough to defeat this powered-up Nomu.

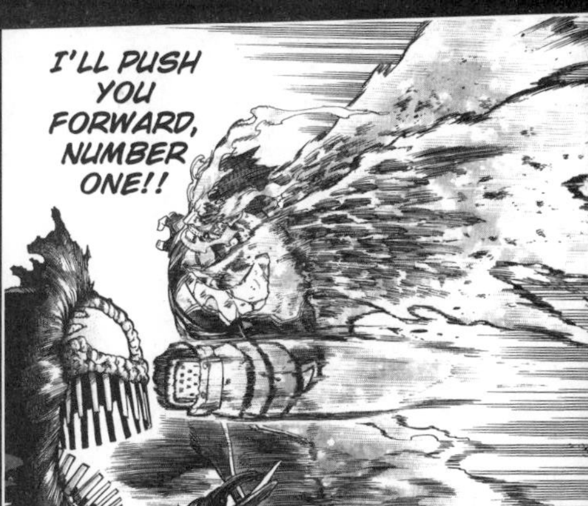
I'LL PUSH YOU FORWARD, NUMBER ONE!!

⬆ Hawks's speedy feathers gave a boost to Endeavor's firepower, allowing the latter to roast the High-End despite the creature's regenerative abilities.

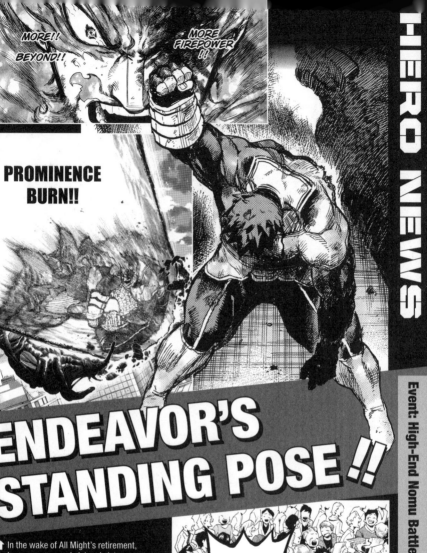

# HERO NEWS

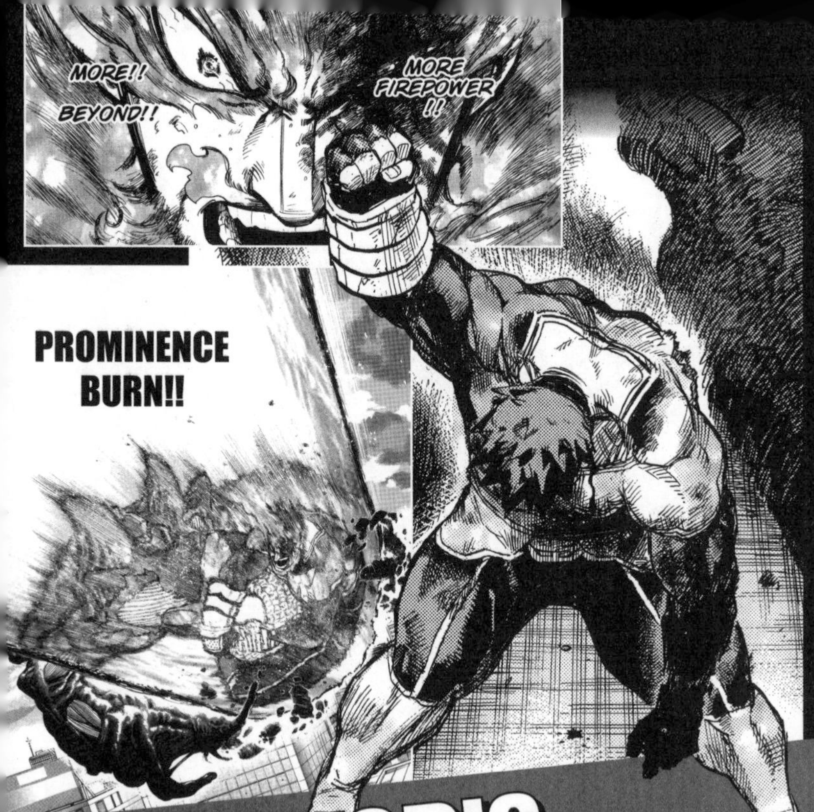
MORE FIREPOWER!!
MORE!!
BEYOND!!
PROMINENCE BURN!!

Event: High-End Nomu Battle

# ENDEAVOR'S STANDING POSE!!

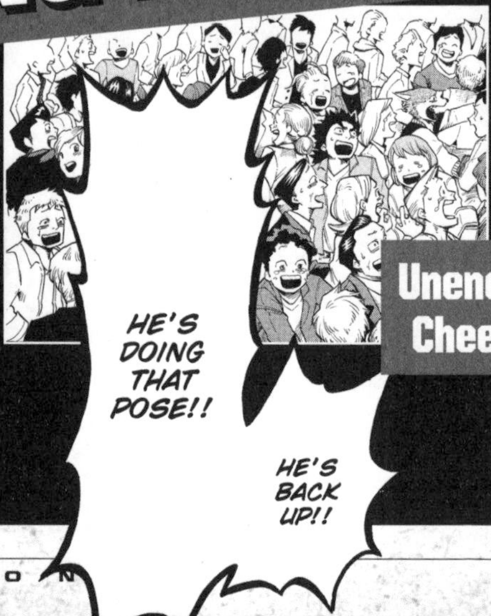
HE'S DOING THAT POSE!!
HE'S BACK UP!!

## Unending Cheers!

⬆ In the wake of All Might's retirement, Endeavor rose up and claimed victory, proving he could meet the people's expectations. Their cheers rang out across the entire nation.

**Family Testimony**

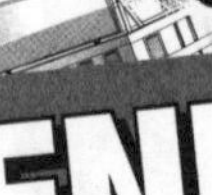

**Natsuo Todoroki**
Sure, my father won. So what? What's that got to do with me? I couldn't care less.

**Family Testimony**

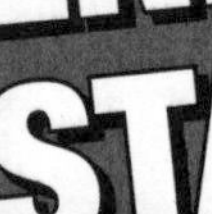

**Fuyumi Todoroki**
I think Dad really stepped up and showed people what he's made of. I'm grateful to everyone who cheered him on.

# WANTED 5th EDITION

## WANTED VILLAINS

Villains gather their forces in the shadows to plot the downfall of hero society and menace the lives of the people. Here are profiles on the villains most in need of a taste of justice.

# TOMURA SHIGARAKI

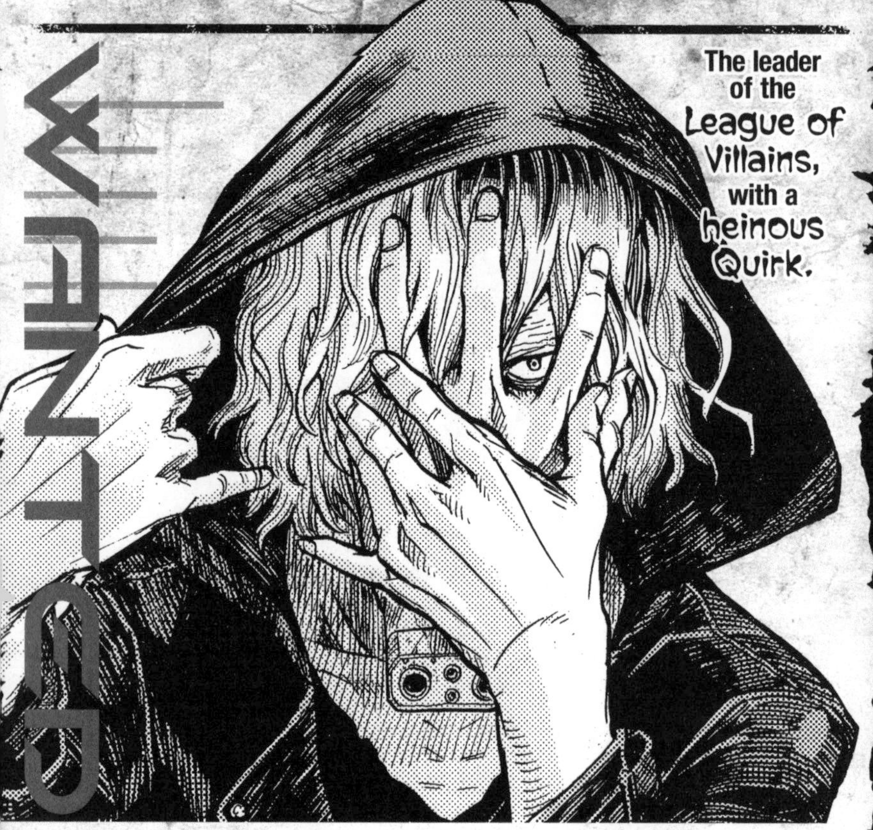
WANTED
The leader of the League of Villains, with a heinous Quirk.

**QUIRK** » **Decay**

**THREAT LEVEL** S

Anything he touches with all five fingers of either hand turns to dust. The target slowly crumbles until nothing is left.

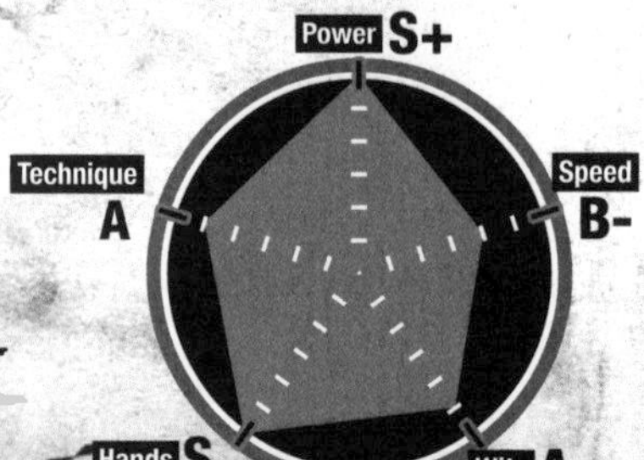
Power S+
Speed B-
Wits A
Hands S
Technique A

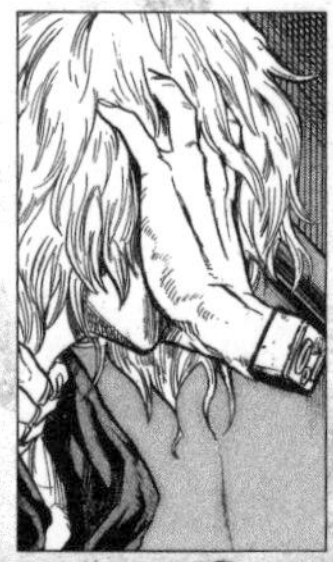

**Profile**

Villain name: **Tomura Shigaraki**
Real name: **Tenko Shimura**
Quirk: **Decay**
Affiliation: **League of Villains**
Birthday: **April 4**
Height: **175 cm**
Blood type: **Unknown**
Personality: **Man-child**

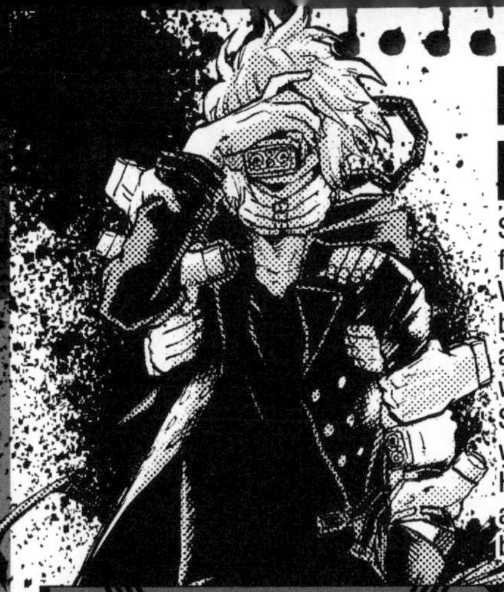

## The young leader of the league despises hero society.

Shigaraki brings together capable villains to form the organization known as the League of Villains. As a child, he lost his entire family because of his own Quirk. In the immediate aftermath, nobody offered the boy any help, which led him to resent heroes as a whole. Shigaraki's current goal is to destroy the entire world through a series of atrocious attacks. He wears his family's hands all over his body, and his bare face has yet to be confirmed by authorities.

### OFFENSE I

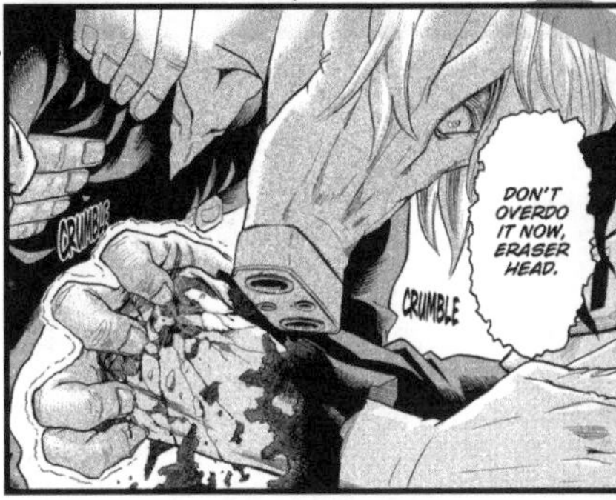
CRUMBLE
DON'T OVERDO IT NOW, ERASER HEAD.
CRUMBLE

**Masterminded the attack on U.A. High**

Shigaraki invaded U.A. with a small army. They wounded Eraser Head, Thirteen, and All Might, and turned the league into a household name.

### OFFENSE II

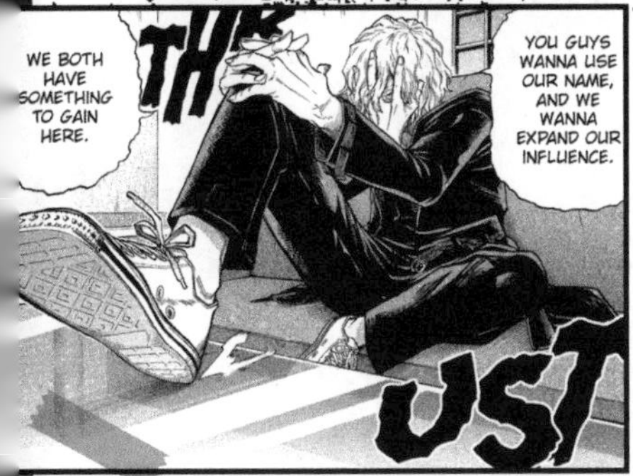
YOU GUYS WANNA USE OUR NAME, AND WE WANNA EXPAND OUR INFLUENCE.
WE BOTH HAVE SOMETHING TO GAIN HERE.

**Conspired with Shie Hassaikai**

He tried and failed to ally with Shie Hassaikai. In the end, he attacked Chisaki while he was being transported by the authorities.

## CONSPIRATORS

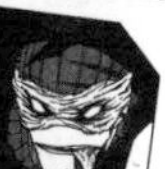

**STAIN**

Possible Shigaraki's ally. Says he isn't a league member.

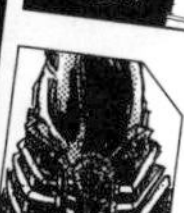

**ALL FOR ONE**

Revealed as the mastermind after Kamino. Imprisoned.

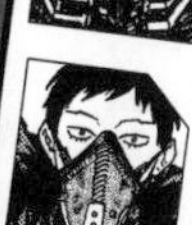

**OVERHAUL**

Attacking Chisaki's transport ended their alliance.

## Tomura Shigaraki's Past

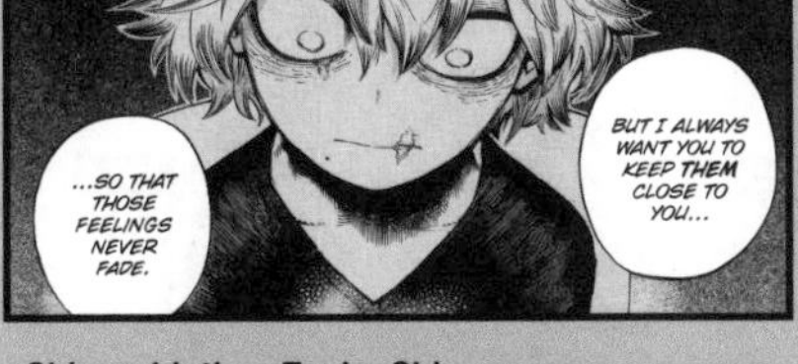
BUT I ALWAYS WANT YOU TO KEEP THEM CLOSE TO YOU...
...SO THAT THOSE FEELINGS NEVER FADE.

Shigaraki, then Tenko Shimura, was unaware how to control his Quirk when it manifested, which led to the deaths of his entire family.

# ALL FOR ONE

WANTED

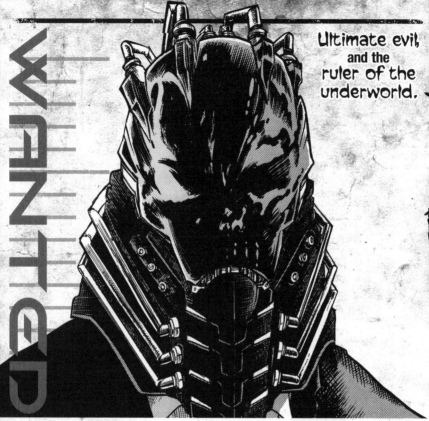

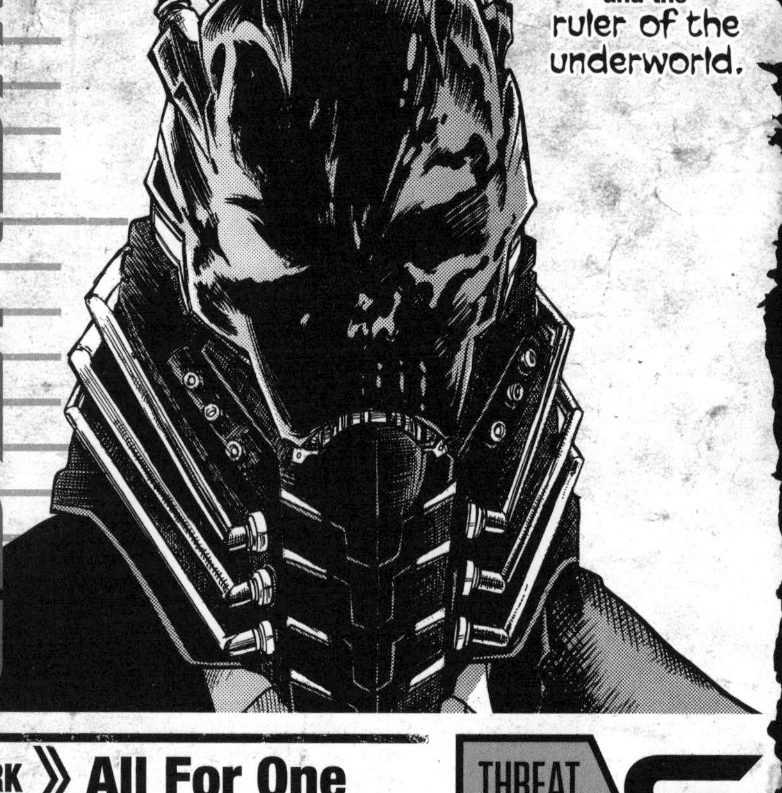
Ultimate evil, and the ruler of the underworld.

## QUIRK 》 All For One

THREAT LEVEL S

The power to steal the Quirks of others and give them away. Stolen Quirks can be stocked up and used several times.

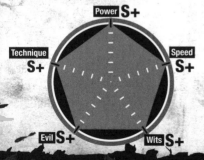

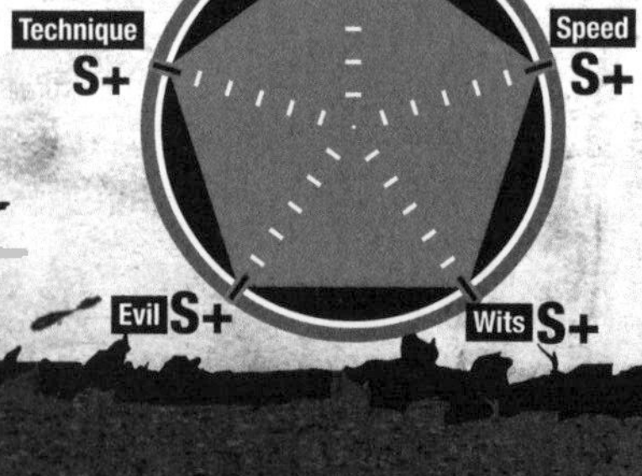
Power S+
Technique S+
Speed S+
Evil S+
Wits S+

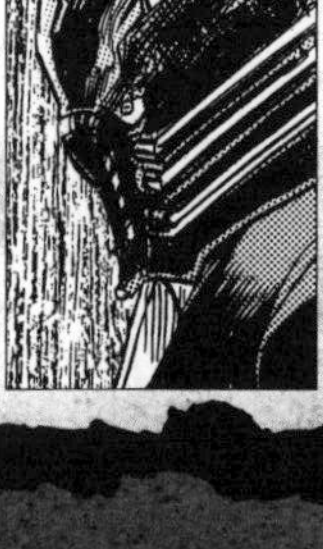

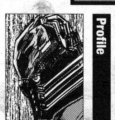

**Profile**

- Villain name: **All For One**
- Real name: **Unknown**
- Quirk: **All For One**
- Affiliation: **League of Villains**
- Birthday: **Unknown**
- Height: **Unknown**
- Blood type: **Unknown**
- Personality: **Unsettling**

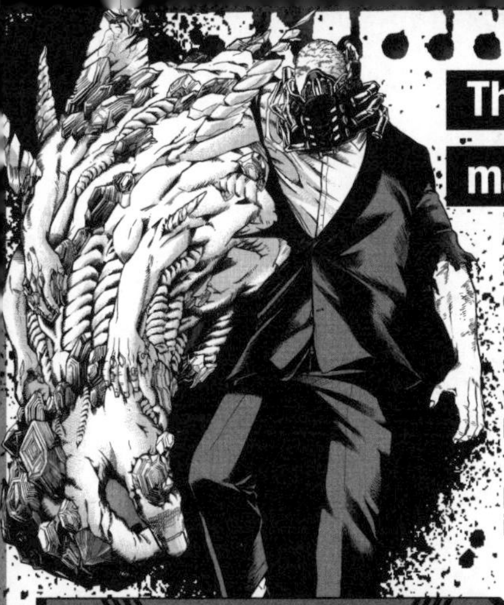

## This root of evil secretly manipulates the league.

A wicked overlord who's been around since the advent of the exceptional, and the true leader of the League of Villains. AFO's identity is shrouded in mystery, and he's used the Quirks stolen from others and his charisma to unify villains around him and get them to do his vile bidding. He was captured and imprisoned following the events in Kamino. According to prison staff, they sometimes spot AFO grinning in his cell, as if recalling something…

### OFFENSE I

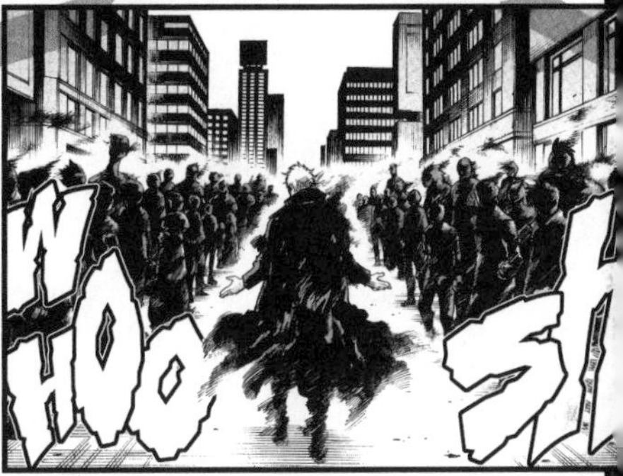

**The Accumulation of Villainous Power**

AFO shows mercy to some and strikes fear in others. By wielding his fiendish power, he put together a massive network, effectively making him the emperor of the underworld.

### OFFENSE II

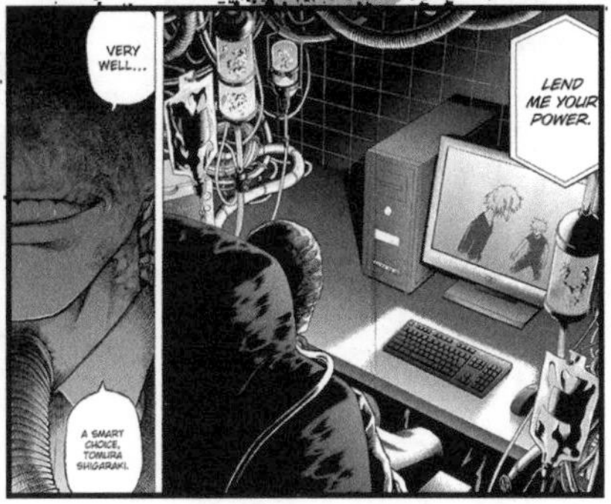
LEND ME YOUR POWER.
VERY WELL...
A SMART CHOICE, TOMURA SHIGARAKI.

**Helping and Guiding the League**

While in hiding, AFO guided Shigaraki toward evil and manipulated the League of Villains. His goals are still unclear.

## CONSPIRATORS

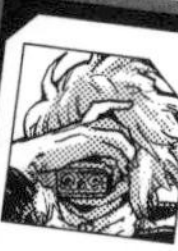

**TOMURA SHIGARAKI**

Highly dangerous and thought to be All For One's successor.

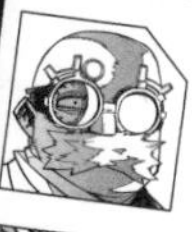

**THE DOCTOR**

All For One's doctor. Co-created the Nomu with him.

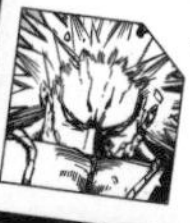

**GIGANTOMACHIA**

This loyal servant has begun to make moves of his

## All For One's Past

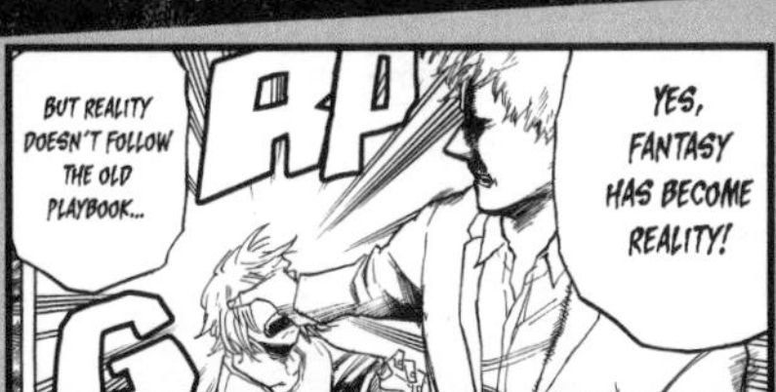
YES, FANTASY HAS BECOME REALITY!
BUT REALITY DOESN'T FOLLOW THE OLD PLAYBOOK...

All For One gave his younger brother a stolen Quirk in the hope of making an ally. That gave rise to One For All.

# DABI

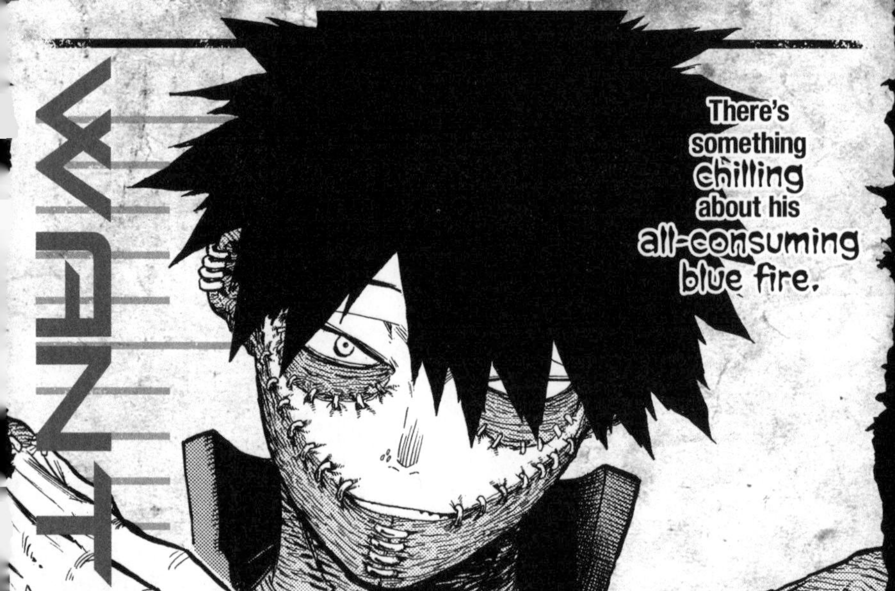
WANTED
There's something chilling about his all-consuming blue fire.

## QUIRK » Unknown

He shoots blue fire from his palms. Despite multiple incidents, the full details of his Quirk still aren't clear.

THREAT LEVEL A

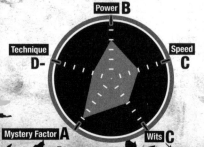

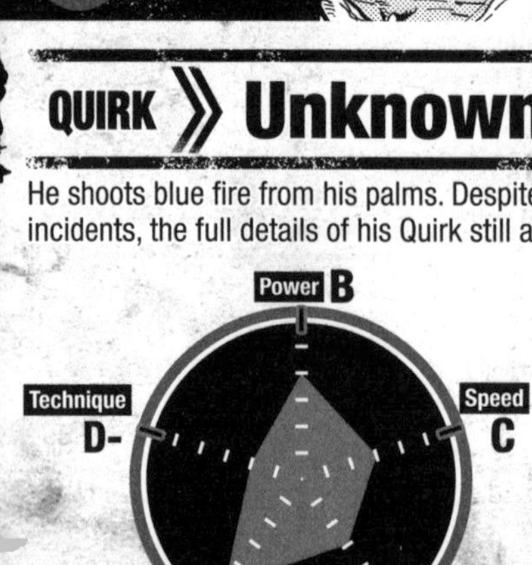
Power B
Speed C
Wits C
Mystery Factor A
Technique D-

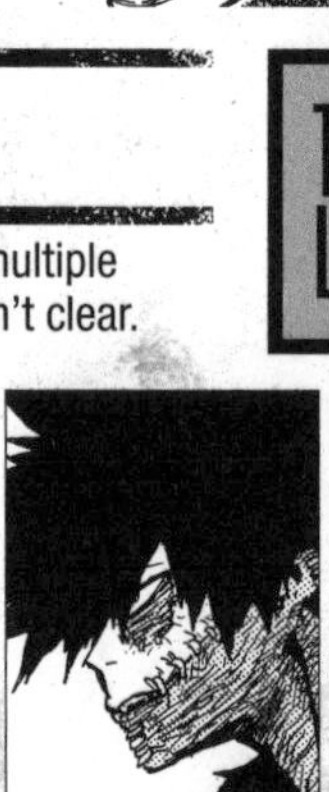

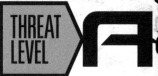

**Profile**

Villain name: **Dabi**
Real name: **Unknown**
Quirk: **Unknown**
Affiliation: **League of Villains**
Birthday: **Unknown**
Height: **Unknown**
Blood type: **Unknown**
Personality: **Inscrutable**

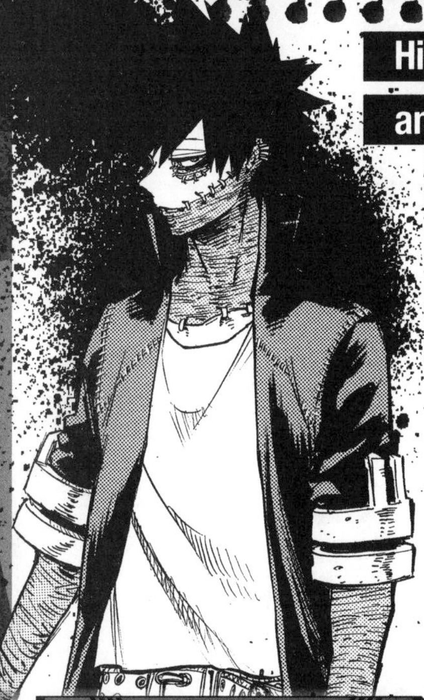

# His motives are a mystery, and his gaze is arrogant.

A man of mystery who sympathizes with Stain's ideals and joined the League of Villains thanks to an introduction by Giran. Dabi doesn't hesitate to burn to a crisp anyone he disagrees with, whether hero or villainous ally. He has experience leading squad-based missions. "Dabi" is a pseudonym, and he never talks about his origin or past, not even with allies.

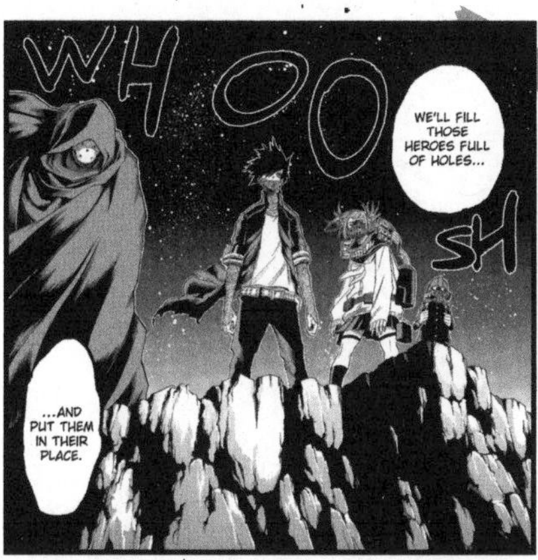
WHOO
SH
WE'LL FILL THOSE HEROES FULL OF HOLES...
...AND PUT THEM IN THEIR PLACE.

## OFFENSE I

**Leading the Training-Camp Attack**

Dabi led the attack on U.A. High's training camp. Some doubles joined the battle to slow down Vlad King and Eraser Head and cause chaos.

## OFFENSE II

**Back Channel with Hawks?!**

Dabi was trusted with utilizing a High-End, and he unleashed the monster in Fukuoka. Hawks connected with Dabi as part of a secret mission.

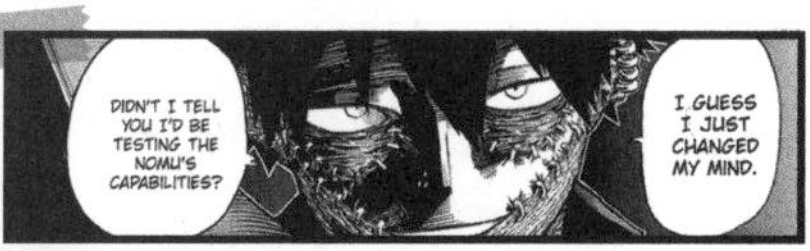
I GUESS I JUST CHANGED MY MIND.
DIDN'T I TELL YOU I'D BE TESTING THE NOMU'S CAPABILITIES?

## CONSPIRATORS

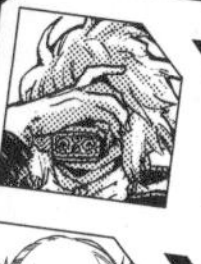

**TOMURA SHIGARAKI**

Their fractious relationship began following Stain's arrest.

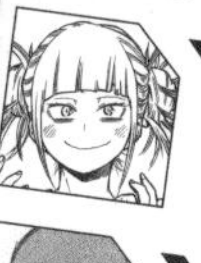

**HIMIKO TOGA**

Joined at the same time as her frequent partner Dabi.

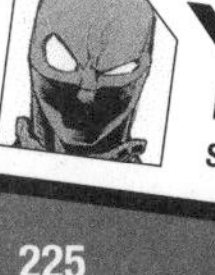

**TWICE**

Has served under Dabi ever since the training camp attack.

## Dabi's Connections

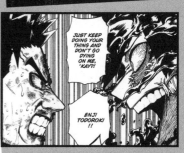

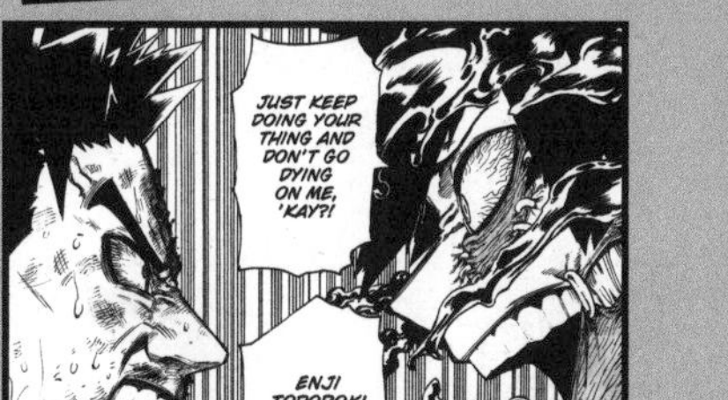
JUST KEEP DOING YOUR THING AND DON'T GO DYING ON ME, 'KAY?!
ENJI TODOROKI !!

Dabi sicced a High-End Nomu on the newly crowned number one hero, Endeavor...

# HIMIKO TOGA

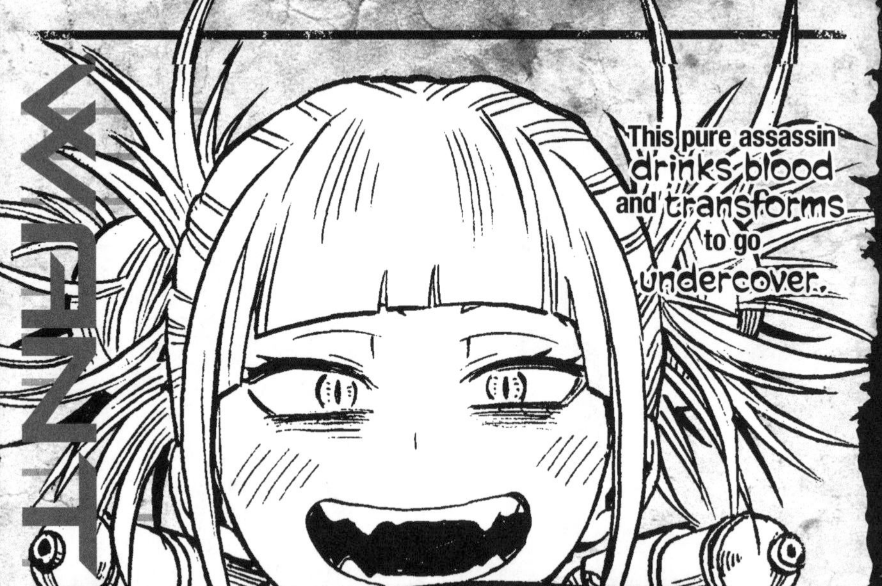
WANTED
This pure assassin drinks blood and transforms to go undercover.

QUIRK 》 **Transform**

She can transform into another person by drinking their blood. Now, she can also use their quirk.

THREAT LEVEL **A**

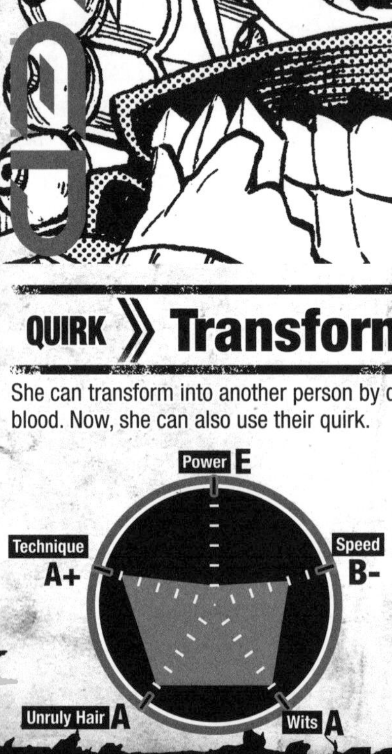
Power E
Technique A+
Speed B-
Unruly Hair A
Wits A

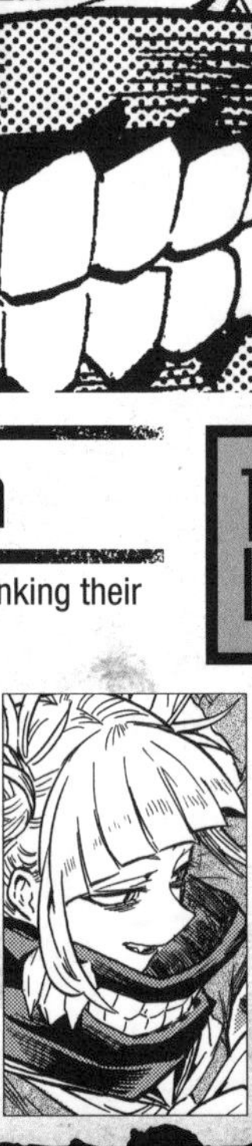

**Profile**

Villain name: **Himiko Toga**
Real name: **Himiko Toga**
Quirk: **Transform**
Affiliation: **League of Villains**
Birthday: **August 7**
Height: **157 cm**
Blood type: **Unknown**
Personality: **Lovestruck**

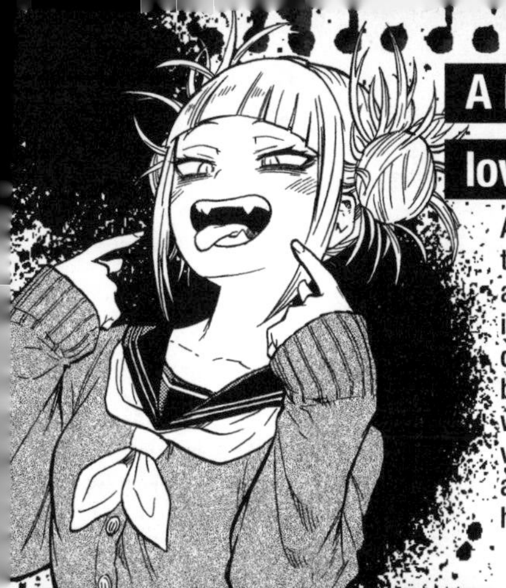

## A blood-starved cutie who loves everything adorable.

An elite member of the League of Villains with the power to transform. Toga is purehearted and quick to fall in love, but she expresses love in an unconventional way. That is to say, she develops an eerie obsession with sucking the blood of those she loves and turning into them, which usually doesn't end well... While society views Toga's actions as criminal, she sees them as normal, which explains why she never hesitates before committing her atrocities.

### OFFENSE I

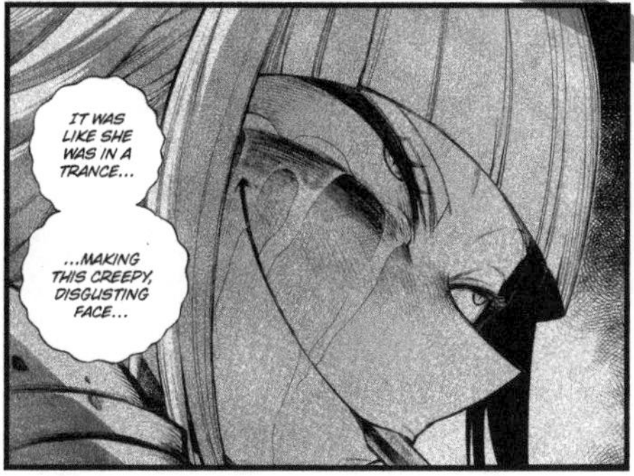
IT WAS LIKE SHE WAS IN A TRANCE...
...MAKING THIS CREEPY, DISGUSTING FACE...

**Serial Bloodsucking Suspect**

On the day of her middle school graduation, she sucked the blood of a classmate. That was the first in a string of deaths which earned Toga "wanted" status.

### OFFENSE II

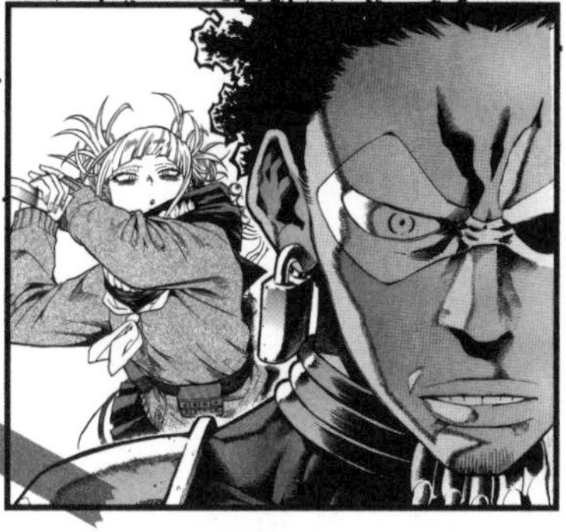

**Work with Shie Hassaikai**

Under Shigaraki's orders, Toga joined the Shie Hassaikai and was tasked with interfering with the raid.

### Himiko Toga's Past

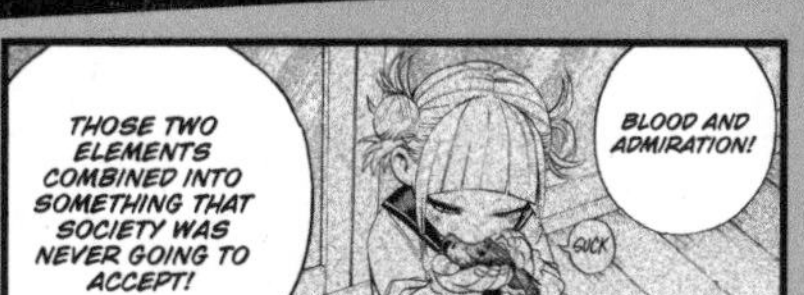
BLOOD AND ADMIRATION!
THOSE TWO ELEMENTS COMBINED INTO SOMETHING THAT SOCIETY WAS NEVER GOING TO ACCEPT!
GLICK

When Toga began sucking the blood of things she loved (such as small birds), her parents were concerned for her future... However, her addiction couldn't be cured, and she wound up isolated and friendless.

### CONSPIRATORS

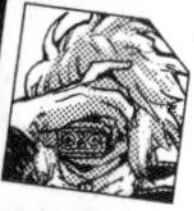

**TOMURA SHIGARAKI**

After clashing, they now recognize each other as allies.

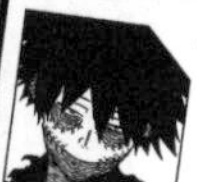

**DABI**

Joined the league at the same time as Toga.

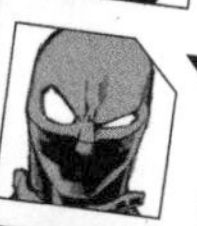

**TWICE**

They get along well since teaming up with the Shie Hassaikai.

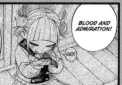

# TWICE

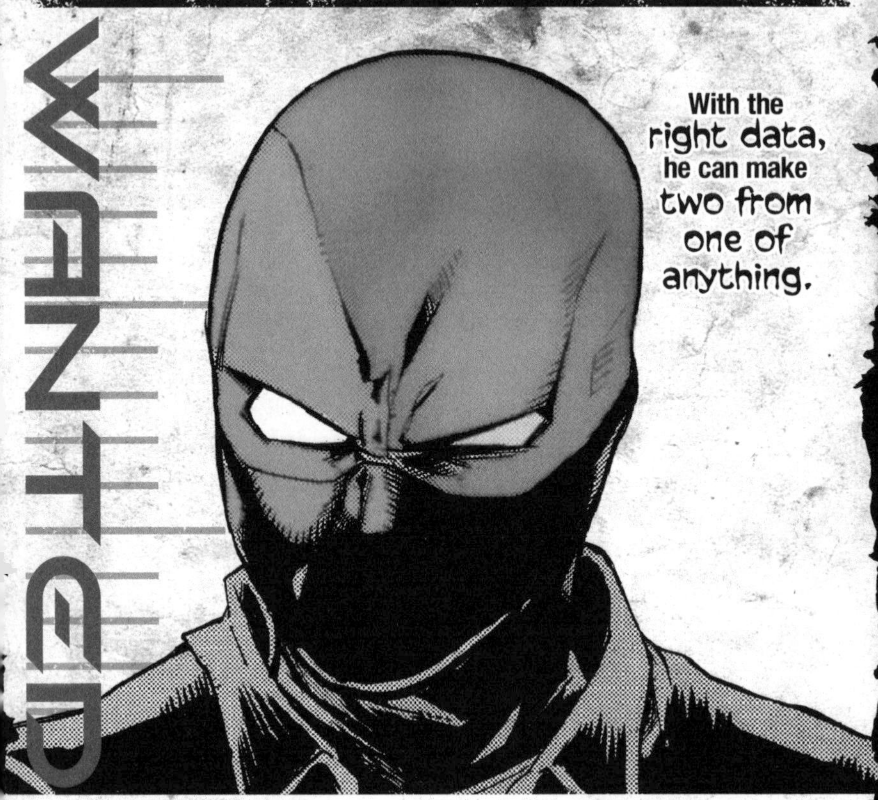
WANTED
With the right data, he can make two from one of anything.

**QUIRK » Double**

With the proper info, he can make a perfect copy of anyone or anything. His doubles can create additional doubles.

**THREAT LEVEL S**

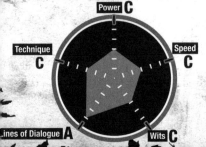

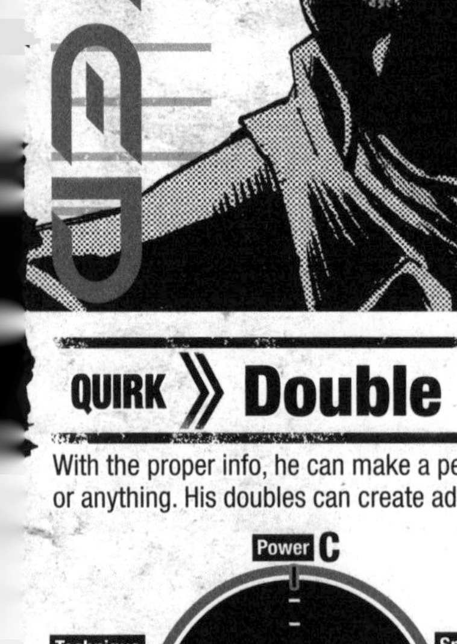
Power C
Speed C
Wits C
Lines of Dialogue A
Technique C

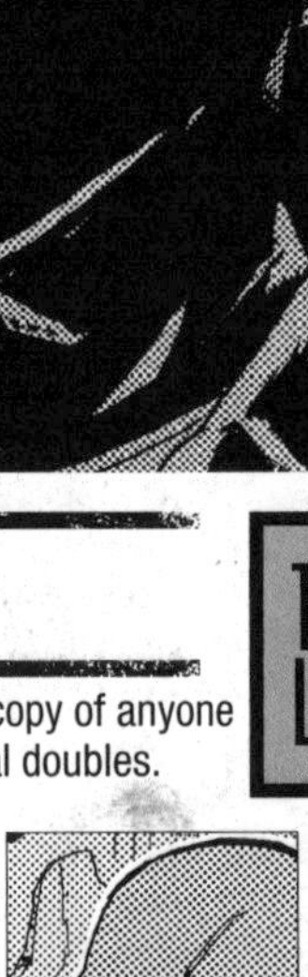

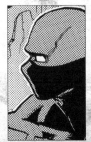

**Profile**

Villain name: **Twice**
Real name: **Jin Bubaigawara**
Quirk: **Double**
Affiliation: **League of Villains**
Birthday: **May 10**
Height: **178 cm**
Blood type: **Unknown**
Personality: **Utterly chaotic**

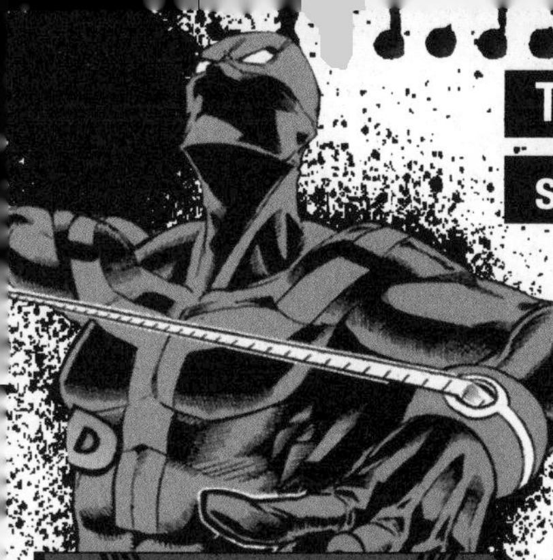

# The mask keeps him whole, soothing his inner turmoil.

Twice lost his parents to a villain attack relatively early in life and wound up creating a gang of doubles to commit crimes with. However, when the doubles rebelled, Twice's sense of self crumbled. Usually, wearing a mask is enough to keep the split personalities under control. Twice feels an incredibly strong sense of camaraderie with the other members of the League of Villains, who accepted him and gave him a place to belong.

## OFFENSE I

### The League and Shie Hassaikai

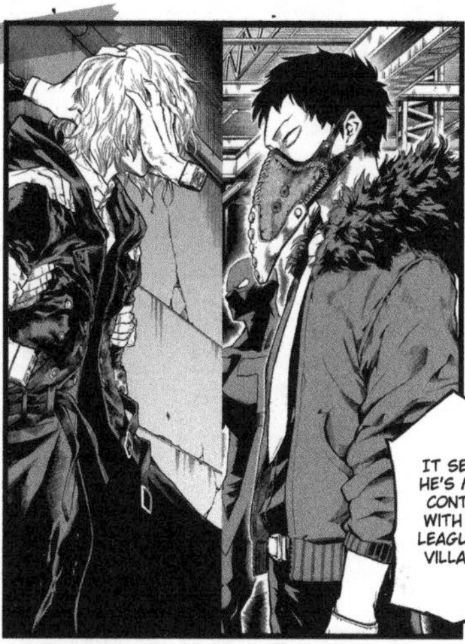
IT SEEMS HE'S MADE CONTACT WITH THE LEAGUE OF VILLAINS!

He introduced Overhaul to Shigaraki, enabling collaboration between the two.

## OFFENSE II

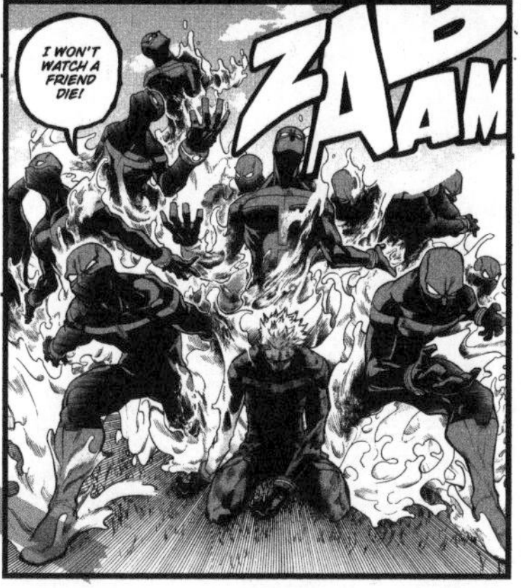
I WON'T WATCH A FRIEND DIE!
ZAAAM

### Fighting the Meta Liberation Army

After anthropomorphs resembling Twice attacked, he overcame his underlying trauma and became able to create an army of doubles.

## CONSPIRATORS

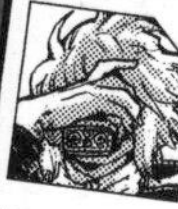

**TOMURA SHIGARAKI**

Accepted Twice into the league and gave him a high rank.

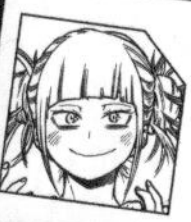

**HIMIKO TOGA**

He feels such an affinity for her that he's willing to risk his life.

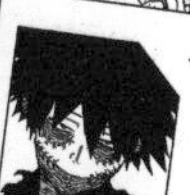

**DABI**

Twice, Toga, and Dabi often operate together.

## Twice's Past

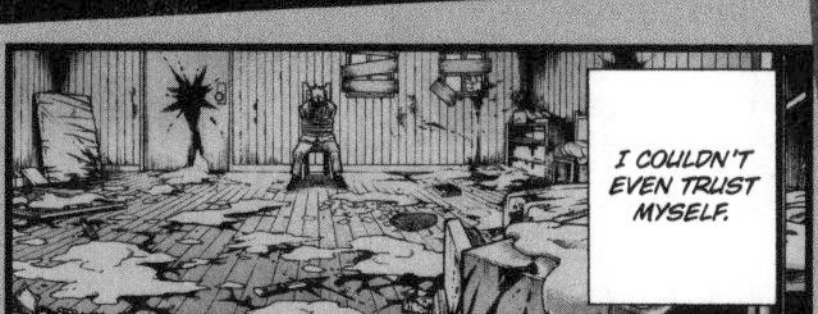
I COULDN'T EVEN TRUST MYSELF.

The doubles Twice created to distract him from his solitude turned on him. He watched them kill each other in a gruesome spectacle. Afterward, he couldn't be sure whether or not he was a double himself.

## The League of Villains' level-headed defense.

# KUROGIRI

WANTED
He bends the fabric of space to summon and banish.

Adviser for the League of Villains and support mechanism for Shigaraki. Kurogiri was plotting to make contact with Gigantomachia but got arrested in the process. He's currently locked up in Tartarus and seems wholly unwilling to talk.

**QUIRK » Warp Gate**

His body transforms into a mist that creates a gate capable of transporting people and objects.

**THREAT LEVEL**

# B

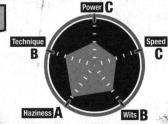

Power C
Speed C
Wits B
Haziness A
Technique B

**Profile**

Villain name: **Kurogiri**
Real name: **Unknown**
Quirk: **Warp Gate**
Affiliation: **League of Villains**
Birthday: **Unknown**
Height: **Unknown**
Blood type: **Unknown**
Personality: **Composed**

## OFFENSE

Kurogiri used his Warp Gate Quirk to allow a gang of villains to invade U.A.'s U.S.J. facility.

ZW

**Major Threat in the Attack on U.A. High**

## CONSPIRATOR

**TOMURA SHIGARAKI**

He is always at Shigaraki's side, ready to aid and abet crimes.

# MR. COMPRESS

## The mad illusionist can shrink anything!

He wears a second face covering under the mask to hide any sign of emotion and flusters opponents with his attitude. Mr. Compress is an entertainer, even during battle, and delights in catching others by surprise. As a phantom thief with quite a rap sheet, he's on the nation's most wanted list.

### Profile

Villain name: **Mr. Compress**
Real name: **Atsuhiro Sako**
Quirk: **Compress**
Affiliation: **League of Villains**
Birthday: **Unknown**
Height: **Unknown**
Blood type: **Unknown**
Personality: **Entertainer**

"Too quick for the naked eye, his hands will steal you away before you can say 'presto.'"

QUIRK » **Compress**

He can compress a chunk of space into a marble. Works on both people and objects.

THREAT LEVEL **B**

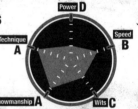

Power D
Technique A
Speed B
Showmanship A
Wits C

---

# SPINNER

## Warped fundamentals and ideals.

He originally joined the League of Villains to carry out Stain's will but wound up sympathizing with Shigaraki's motivations. Still, as the organization continues to push to new extremes, Spinner is actually bewildered that he got caught up in a movement from which there is no going back.

### Profile

Villain name: **Spinner**
Real name: **Shuichi Iguchi**
Quirk: **Gecko**
Affiliation: **League of Villains**
Birthday: **August 8**
Height: **174 cm**
Blood type: **Unknown**
Personality: **Stain zealot**

Every flash of his colossal sword is merciless.

QUIRK » **Gecko**

Allows him to cling to walls. Not a powerful Quirk by any stretch of the imagination.

THREAT LEVEL **C**

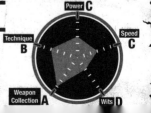

Power C
Technique B
Speed C
Weapon Collection A
Wits D

# MAGNE

## A lady who controls magnetism at will.

Magne is a member of the League of Villains who is a capable martial artist. Despite her bulky body, her speaking style is fairly feminine. During negotiations with Shie Hassaikai, Magne became enraged with Overhaul's attitude and attacked, only to be killed when her plan backfired.

**Profile**

Villain name: **Magne**
Real name: **Kenji Hikiishi**
Quirk: **Magnetism**
Affiliation: **League of Villains**
Birthday: **Unknown**
Height: **Unknown**
Blood type: **Unknown**
Personality: **Feminine**

She makes people into **magnets, turning men into south poles and women into north poles.**

## QUIRK 》 Magnetism

She can magnetize nearby people.

**THREAT LEVEL** B

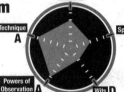

Power **B**
Technique **A**
Speed **C**
Powers of Observation **A**
Wits **D**

---

# MUSCULAR

## Pump up and destroy!!

## A cold-blooded maniac.

A member of the League of Villains who joined the attack on U.A. High's training camp. Muscular was examined by Dr. Ujiko in the past, but it's unknown if their interactions have any connection with the man's Quirk. He was arrested after the training-camp attack and is now imprisoned in Tartarus.

**Profile**

Villain name: **Muscular**
Real name: **Unknown**
Quirk: **Pump Up**
Affiliation: **League of Villains**
Birthday: **Unknown**
Height: **Unknown**
Blood type: **Unknown**
Personality: **Cruel**

Pumps up his own muscles to transform into a **mass of hardened flesh.**

## QUIRK 》 Pump Up

Augments his muscles so they cover his body inside and out and give him major strength.

**THREAT LEVEL** A

Power **S**
Technique **E**
Speed **A**
Bloodlust **S**
Wits **E**

# MOONFISH

## This killer loves the sensation of biting.

A death row inmate who escaped and joined the league just in time to attack U.A.'s training camp. Moonfish wears an unsettling restraining outfit, and by his own admission, this highly dangerous individual loves carving up flesh to view the insides. He is currently imprisoned in Tartarus.

**Profile**

Villain name: **Moonfish**
Real name: **Unknown**
Quirk: **Bladetooth**
Affiliation: **League of Villains**
Birthday: **Unknown**
Height: **Unknown**
Blood type: **Unknown**
Personality: **Sadistic**

WANTED

His razor-sharp teeth carve **everything** to shreds.

**QUIRK ›› Bladetooth**

His teeth can stretch out and transform into blades capable of carving up enemies.

**THREAT LEVEL ›› B**

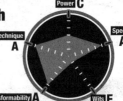

| | Power C | |
|---|---|---|
| Technique A | | Speed A |
| Transformability A | | Wits E |

---

# MUSTARD

## This poison gas user dominates in battles.

A boy wearing a gas mask and school uniform who attacked the training camp. He spread his poison gas in the area to slow down the heroes and aid his fellow villains. After being arrested, he refused to tell the authorities a word about the League of Villains...

**Profile**

Villain name: **Mustard**
Real name: **Unknown**
Quirk: **Gas**
Affiliation: **League of Villains**
Birthday: **Unknown**
Height: **Unknown**
Blood type: **Unknown**
Personality: **Childish smooth talker**

WANTED

Creates a poison gas that pollutes a wide area around him.

**QUIRK ›› Gas**

Releases a poisonous gas into the air. He can fine-tune the toxicity and range.

**THREAT LEVEL ›› C**

| | Power E | |
|---|---|---|
| Technique B | | Speed E |
| Attack Range A | | Wits C |

# NOMU

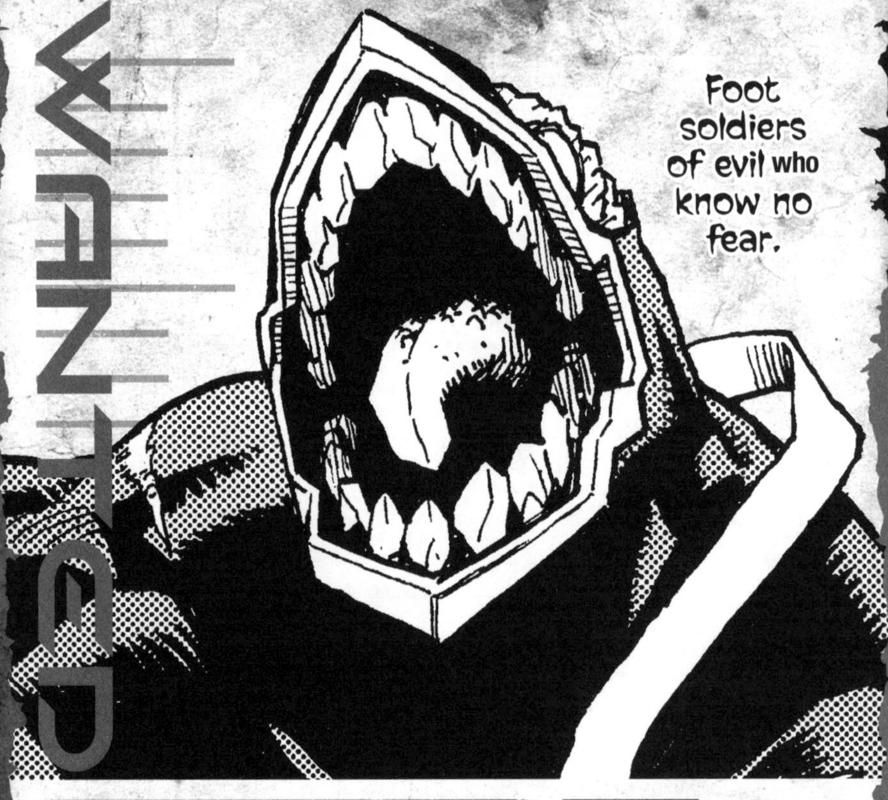
WANTED
Foot soldiers of evil who know no fear.

## QUIRKS » Various Quirks

THREAT LEVEL A

Each individual Nomu is granted different Quirks by All For One. Most are equipped with more than one.

Power ?
Speed ?
Wits ?
??? ?
Technique ?

Profile differs from Nomu to Nomu

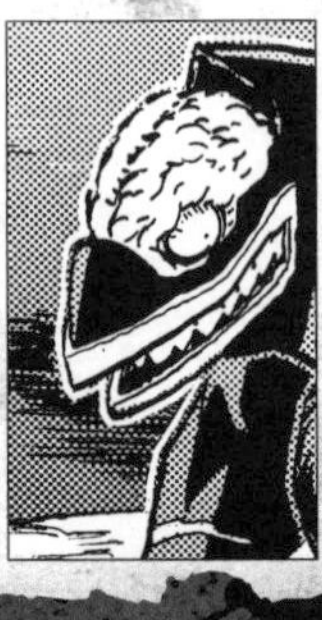

**Profile**

Villain Name: **Nomu**
Real name: **Unknown**
Quirk: **Differs from Nomu to Nomu**
**Profile differs from Nomu to Nomu**
Birthday: **Unknown**
Height: **Unknown**
Blood type: **Unknown**
Personality: **Unknown**

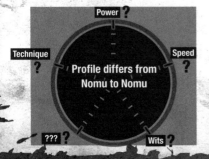

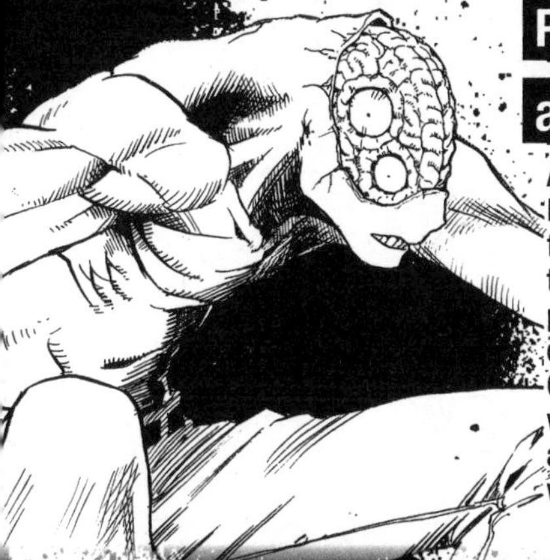

## Pumped full of Quirks, they are remodeled goons.

As battle personnel for the League of Villains, Nomu are programmed to obey orders only from specific people. They lack independent thought and cannot act on their own, but with powerful muscular bodies courtesy of the doctor and multiple Quirks granted by All For One, they're strong enough to go toe-to-toe with All Might. Despite their eerie, off-putting appearance, it's become clear that every Nomu was once human.

### OFFENSE I

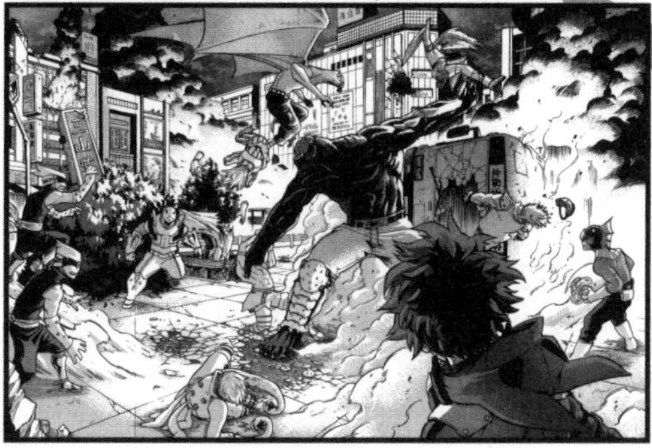

**Joined the Attack on Hosu City**

Three Nomu appeared to attack Hosu City at the same time as Stain and wound up doing battle. They caused huge amounts of damage before Endeavor and Gran Torino took them down.

### OFFENSE II

**Assaulted the Students' Training Camp**

Following Dabi's orders, a Nomu attacked U.A.'s training camp. A tracker placed on this particular Nomu allowed the authorities to locate the hideout.

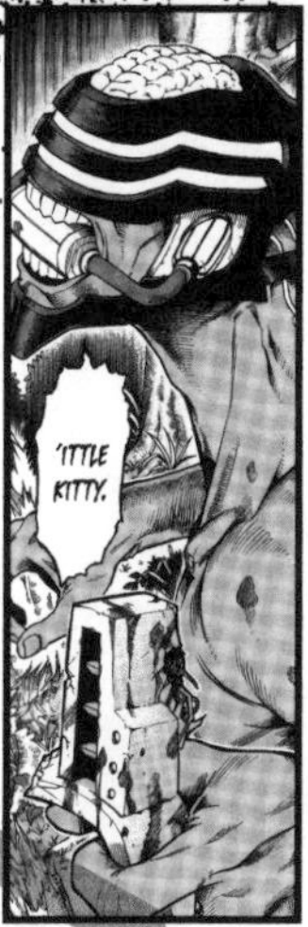
'ITTLE KITTY.

## CONSPIRATORS

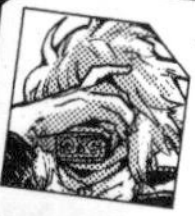

**TOMURA SHIGARAKI**

He most likely ordered them to wreak havoc.

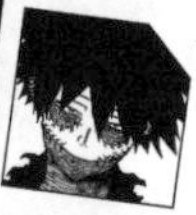

**DABI**

Dabi used a distinct Nomu during the camp attack.

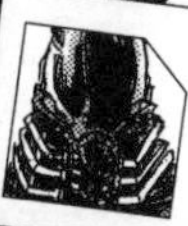

**ALL FOR ONE**

This mastermind and the doctor possibly made the Nomu...

### Nomu Variety

A given Nomu's traits vary widely based on the Quirks it possesses. Remodeling by the doctor has created at least a handful of Nomu that are beyond the standard level.

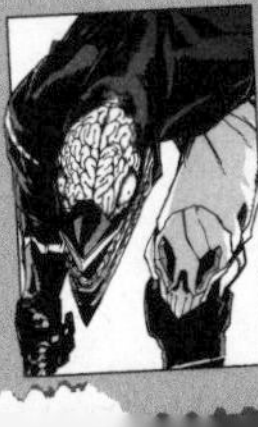
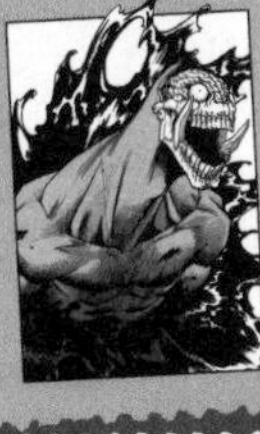
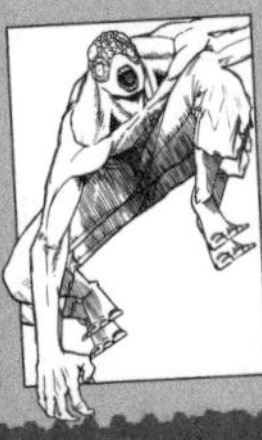

# The Hero Killer stained by a warped sense of justice.

# STAIN

**The terrifying blood licker who paralyzes his victims.**

He considers all heroes except All Might frauds and attacks them in what he views as a righteous purge. His tenets and very existence have since inspired many villains.

**QUIRK >> Bloodcurdle**

He can lick an opponent's blood to paralyze them for a varying amount of time, based on blood type.

## THREAT LEVEL

A

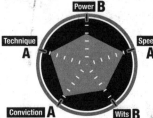

Power **B**
Technique **A**
Speed **A**
Conviction **A**
Wits **B**

---

## OFFENSE

### Serial Attacks on Heroes

Stain attacked a number of heroes in Hosu City, including Ingenium. Endeavor succeeded in apprehending him while out on patrol.

YOU PEOPLE HAVEN'T REALIZED...

**Profile**

Villain name: **Stain**
Real name: **Chizome Akaguro**
Quirk: **Bloodcurdle**
Affiliation: **League of Villains**
Birthday: **Unknown**

Height: **Unknown**
Blood type: **Unknown**
Personality: **All Might zealot**

## CONSPIRATOR

### TOMURA SHIGARAKI

Stain had nothing but contempt for him, but found common ground.

e underworld
oker who provides
erything.

# GIRAN

WANTED

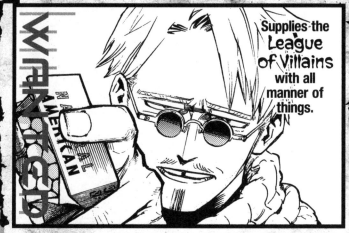

Supplies the League of Villains with all manner of things.

infamous
derworld
oker who
n get his
ands on
ything.
eyond just
roviding
quipment to
e League
f Villains,
iran was
e one who
ntroduced
wice and
Dabi to the
peration.

**QUIRK » Muddied**

By touching a person's head, he can make their memories of the previous and next five minutes hazy.

THREAT LEVEL

C

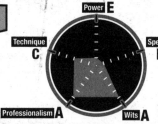

Power E
Speed E
Wits A
Professionalism A
Technique C

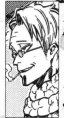

## OFFENSE

**Black Market Conduit**

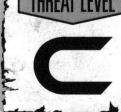

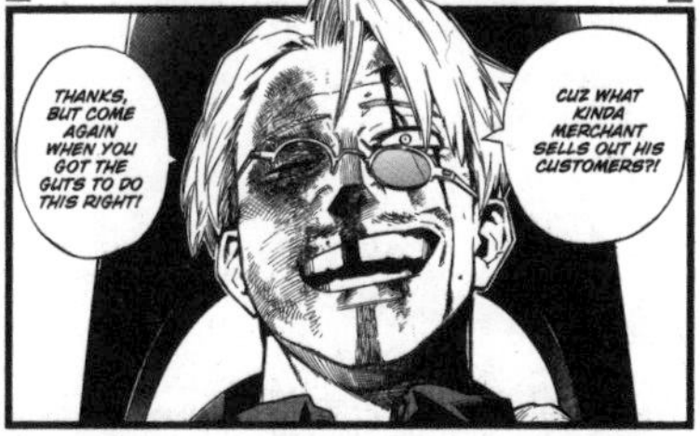

CUZ WHAT KINDA MERCHANT SELLS OUT HIS CUSTOMERS?!
THANKS, BUT COME AGAIN WHEN YOU GOT THE GUTS TO DO THIS RIGHT!

Giran refused to leak any info about the League, so the M.L.A. had to steal it.

**Profile**

Villain name: **Giran**
Real name: **Kagero Okuta**
Quirk: **Muddied**
Affiliation: **League of Villains**
Birthday: **Unknown**
Height: **Unknown**
Blood type: **Unknown**
Personality: **Secretive**

## CONSPIRATOR

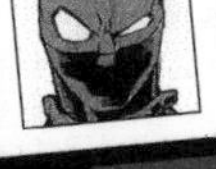

**TWICE**

When Twice was down, Giran introduced him to the League.

**This remodeled monster seeks the strong and continues to evolve.**

# HIGH-END

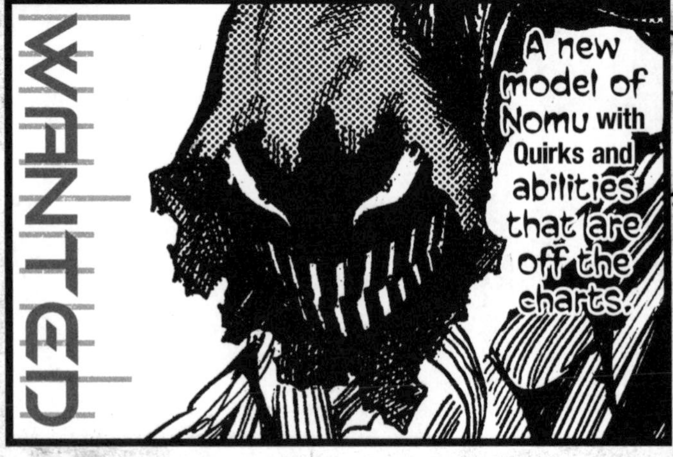
WANTED
A new model of Nomu with Quirks and abilities that are off the charts.

The highest class of Nomu, with more powerful abilities than any other so far. Though this High-End exhibited a bit of the personality and memories of the person it once was, the fight against Endeavor triggered an abnormal reaction.

**QUIRKS》 Various Quirks**

Like other Nomu, this one was given multiple Quirks. It can operate independently to some extent.

**THREAT LEVEL**

**S**

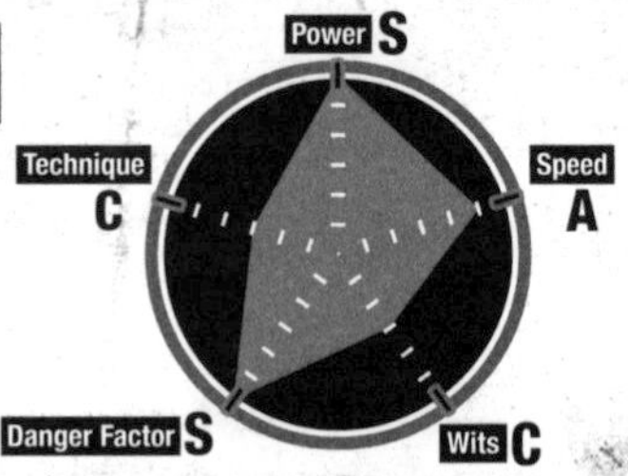
Power S
Speed A
Wits C
Danger Factor S
Technique C

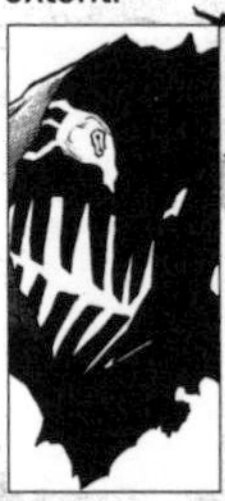

## OFFENSE

**「Perpetrator of the Attack on Fukuoka」**

The High-End known as Hood swooped in from the sky while Hawks and Endeavor were meeting. Its overwhelming power caused untold damage to the city.

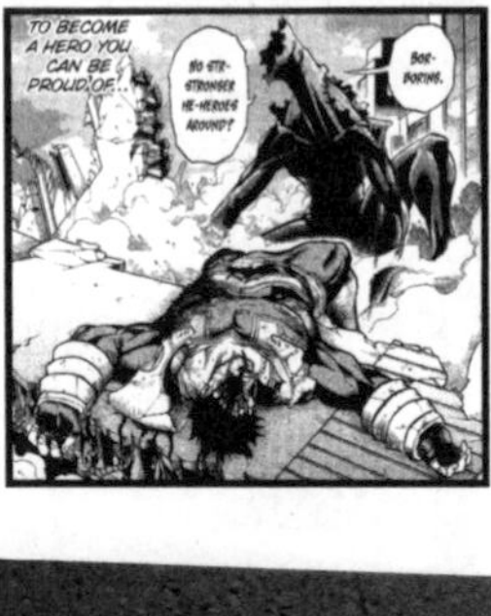
BOR-BORING.
NO STR-STRONGER HE-HEROES AROUND?
TO BECOME A HERO YOU CAN BE PROUD OF...

**Profile**

Villain name: **High-End (Hood)**
Real name: Unknown
Quirk: **Various Quirks**
Affiliation: **League of Villains**
Birthday: **Unknown**
Height: **Unknown**
Blood type: **Unknown**
Personality: **Ambitious and battle crazed**

## CONSPIRATOR

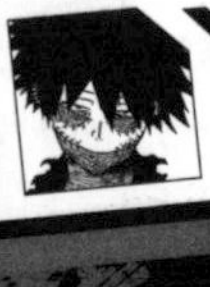

**DABI**

Put in command of various Nomu, including High-End.

**Unstoppable force! The giant brings doom.**

# GIGANTOMACHIA

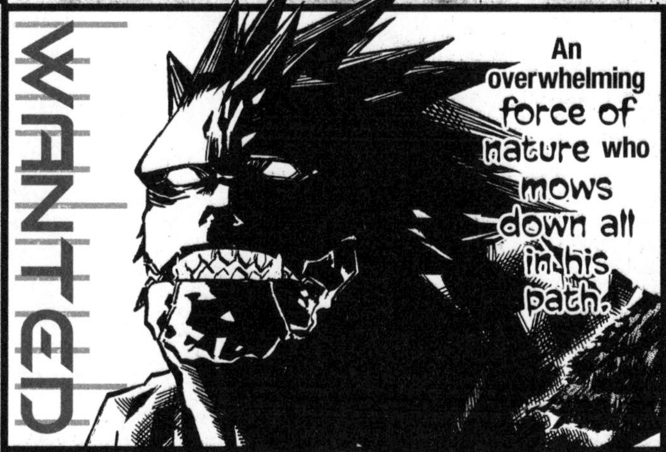
WANTED

An overwhelming force of nature who mows down all in his path.

All For One's loyal servant, equipped with a massive, durable body. When All For One himself was immobilized, Gigantomachia was responsible for going around the country to kidnap heroes and their Quirks for his master.

**QUIRKS 》 Various Quirks**

Details are unclear, but he had the endurance to withstand using multiple Quirks without physical remodeling.

**THREAT LEVEL**

**S**

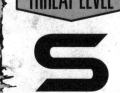

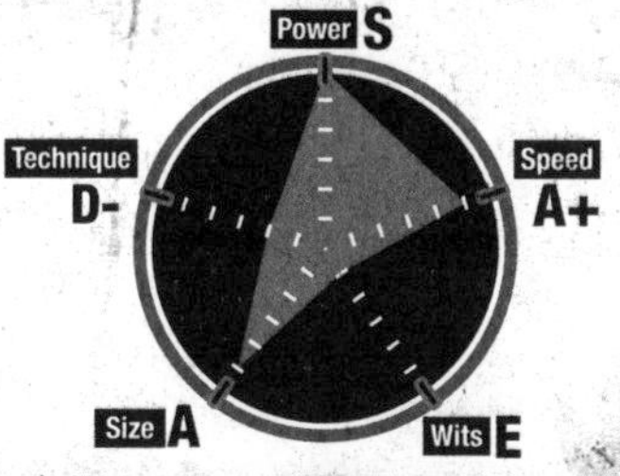
Power S
Speed A+
Wits E
Size A
Technique D-

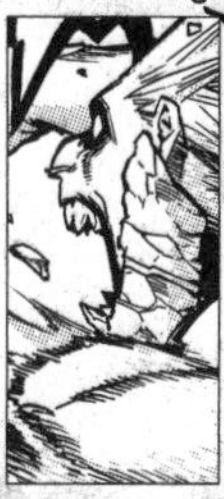

## OFFENSE

**Pledging Loyalty to All For One**

igantomachia iterfered with olice business iring the arrest Kurogiri. After saulting multiple embers of law forcement, fled.

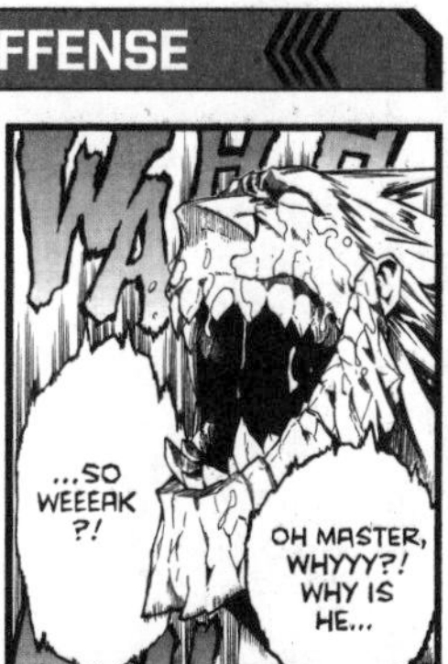
OH MASTER, WHYYY?! WHY IS HE...
...SO WEEEAK?!

**Profile**

Villain name: **Gigantomachia**
Real name: Unknown
Quirk: **Various Quirks**
Affiliation: **League of Villains**
Birthday: **Unknown**
Height: **Unknown**
Blood type: **Unknown**
Personality: **All For One zealot**

## CONSPIRATOR

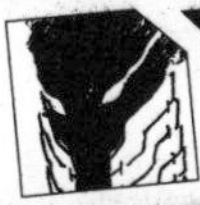

**KUROGIRI**

After Gran Torino beat Kurogiri, Gigantomachia appeared.

# OVERHAUL

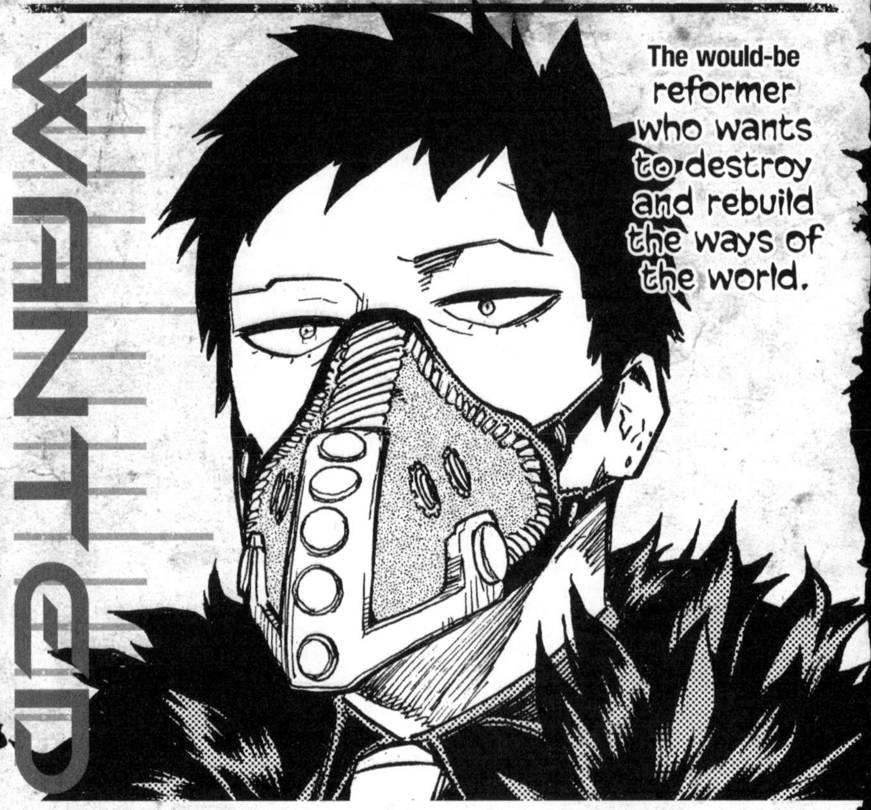
WANTED
The would-be reformer who wants to destroy and rebuild the ways of the world.

**QUIRK** 》 **Overhaul**

**THREAT LEVEL B**

He can break down a target and reconstruct it. He can heal wounds, cure fatigue, and even fuse with others.

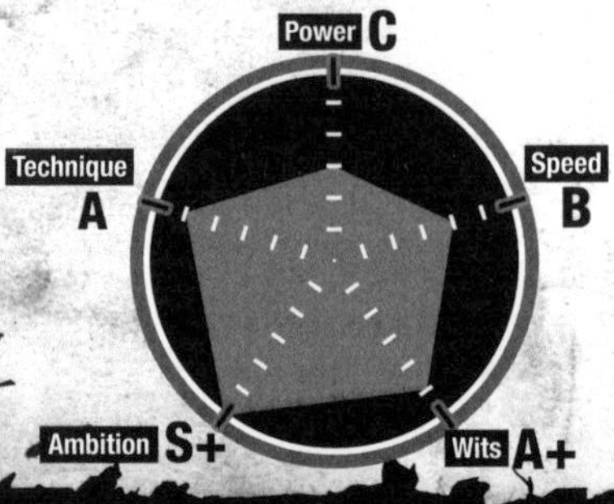
Power C
Speed B
Wits A+
Ambition S+
Technique A

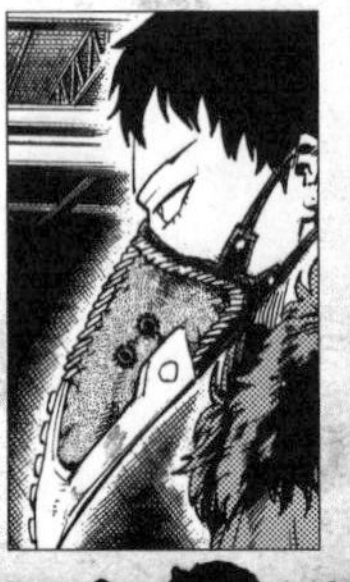

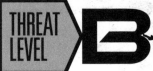

**Profile**

Villain name: **Overhaul**
Real name: **Kai Chisaki**
Quirk: **Overhaul**
Affiliation: **Shie Hassaikai**
Birthday: **Unknown**
Height: **Unknown**
Blood type: **Unknown**
Personality: **Fastidious**

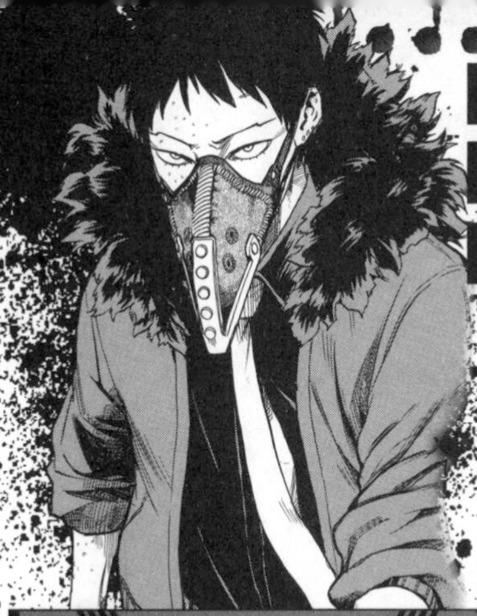

# The ambitious young gangster who vowed to revive Hassaikai.

The young leader of the Shie Hassaikai yakuza gang. Overhaul seized power when the old boss fell ill and sought to rule the underworld. His schemes were unsuccessful, however, and the League of Villains—which he was temporarily allied with—removed his arms. Since then, he's received medical treatment for his wounds, and he's currently imprisoned in Tartarus for his dangerous ideology.

## OFFENSE I

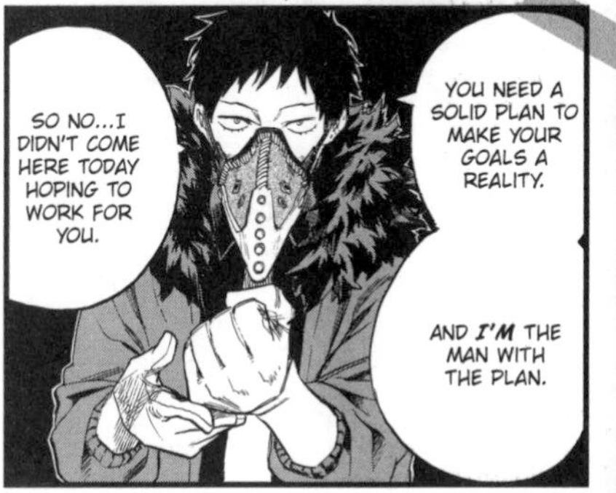
SO NO...I DIDN'T COME HERE TODAY HOPING TO WORK FOR YOU.
YOU NEED A SOLID PLAN TO MAKE YOUR GOALS A REALITY.
AND *I'M* THE MAN WITH THE PLAN.

**Contact with the League of Villains**

In order to secure the funding and personnel to execute his plans, Overhaul reached out to Shigaraki and the League of Villains. He hoped to control the league, but that backfired.

## OFFENSE II

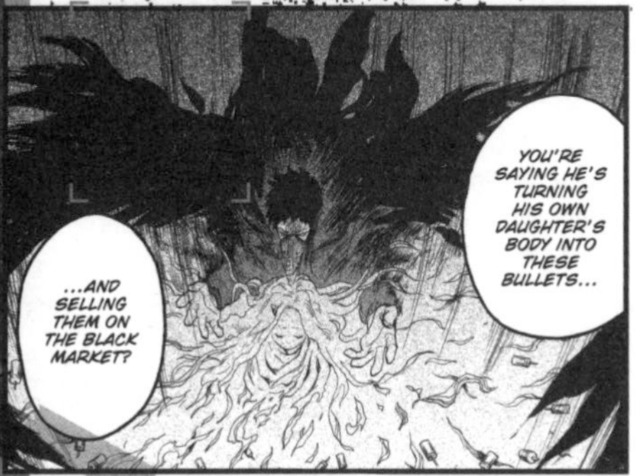
YOU'RE SAYING HE'S TURNING HIS OWN DAUGHTER'S BODY INTO THESE BULLETS...
...AND SELLING THEM ON THE BLACK MARKET?

**Sale of Illegal Drugs**

Overhaul curses heroes as products of diseased thinking and despises the current state of the world. By using Eri's flesh, he succeeded in creating bullets to destroy Quirks.

## CONSPIRATORS

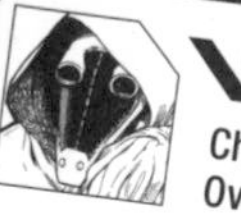

### CHRONOSTASIS

Chronostasis respects Overhau's work ethic. He assisted with the Quirk-killing drug experiments.

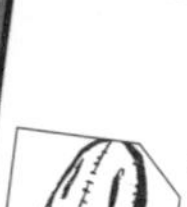

### MIMIC

Shie Hassaikai's HQ director. He used the booster drug and become one with the walls, turning it into a maze.

## Overhaul's Past

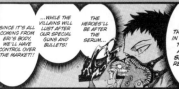

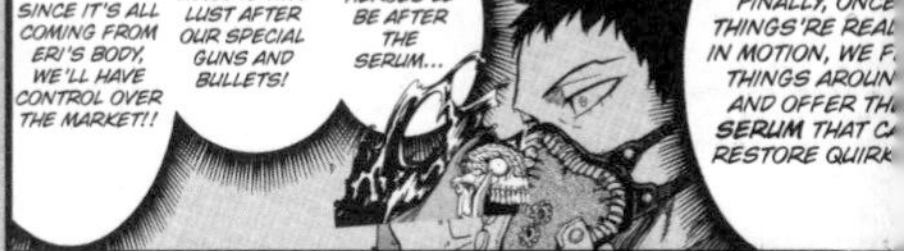
FINALLY, ONCE THINGS'RE REAL IN MOTION, WE F THINGS AROUN AND OFFER TH SERUM THAT C RESTORE QUIRK
THE HEROES'LL BE AFTER THE SERUM...
...WHILE THE VILLAINS WILL LUST AFTER OUR SPECIAL GUNS AND BULLETS!
SINCE IT'S ALL COMING FROM ERI'S BODY, WE'LL HAVE CONTROL OVER THE MARKET!!

⬆The Hassaikai boss scooped up an aimless young Overhaul. To pay him back, Overhaul developed the Quirk-killing drug and antidote, which he planned to use to control the market.

# CHRONOSTASIS

**Overhaul's trusted confidant.**

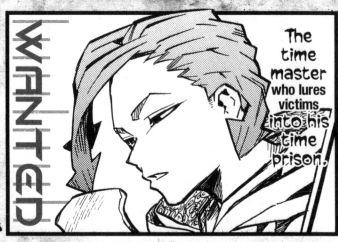

WANTED
The time master who lures victims into his time prison.

A long-serving member of the Shie Hassaikai. Chronostasis has known Overhaul since they were children and is a strong backer of the young boss's plans. He's now locked up in a prison some distance from Tartarus.

**QUIRK » Chronostasis**

After being stabbed with his sharp locks of hair (resembling clock hands), people are slowed or frozen.

**THREAT LEVEL**

# B

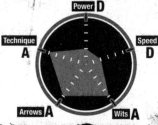

Power D
Speed D
Wits A
Arrows A
Technique A

## OFFENSE

SHE'S REACHED HER LIMIT... HER BODY CAN'T TAKE ANY MORE.
RIGHT... WELL THEN...

**Manufacture of Illegal Drugs**

Involved in the secret, long-running experiments to refine Eri's blood and cells into bullets that destroy Quirks. When Overhaul was defeated, Chronostasis attempted to flee with the bullets and serum but was arrested.

**Profile**

Villain name: **Chronostasis**
Real name: **Hari Kurono**
Quirk: **Chronostasis**
Affiliation: **Shie Hassaikai**
Birthday: **Unknown**
Height: **Unknown**
Blood type: **Unknown**
Personality: **Unflappable**

## CONSPIRATOR

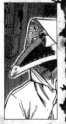

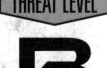

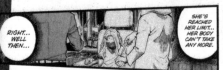

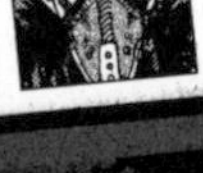

**OVERHAUL**

He feels close enough to Overhaul to call him Kai.

# The audacious and tricky covert operative.

# MIMIC

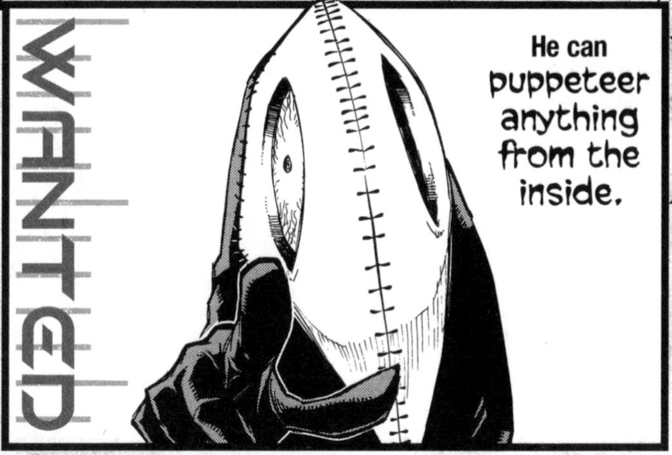
WANTED
He can puppeteer anything from the inside.

A yakuza member given the title of Shie Hassaikai's HQ director. Mimic is easily provoked and petty to a fault, but he gave his all to see Chisaki's ambitions fulfilled, just like Kurono and Katsukame.

**QUIRK ⟫ Mimicry**

He can dive into any object and control it. The bigger the object, the bigger the stamina drain.

**THREAT LEVEL**

**B**

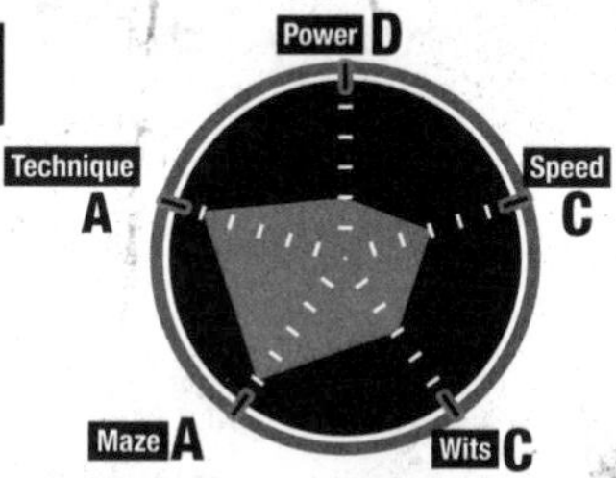
Power D
Speed C
Wits C
Maze A
Technique A

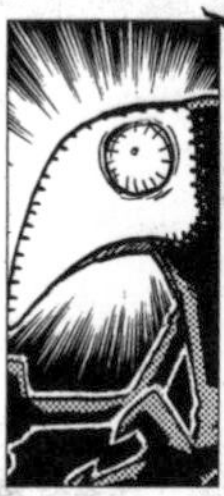

## OFFENSE

**Impeding the Raid on the Shie Hassaikai Compound**

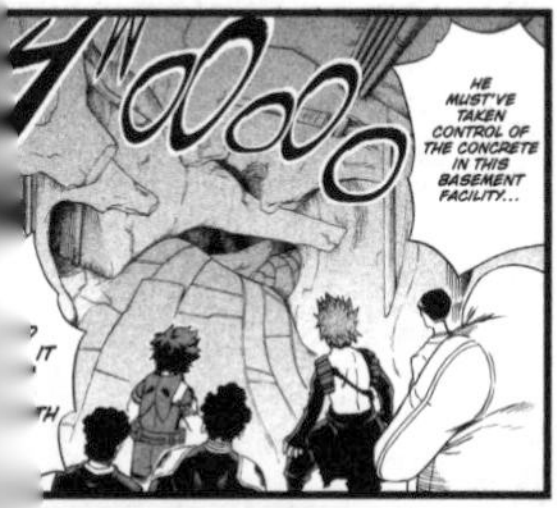
HE MUST'VE TAKEN CONTROL OF THE CONCRETE IN THIS BASEMENT FACILITY...

By melding with the compound's concrete structure, Mimic imprisoned the heroes in an underground maze.

**Profile**

Villain name: **Mimic**
Real name: **Joi Irinaka**
Quirk: **Mimicy**
Affiliation: **Shie Hassaikai**
Birthday: **Unknown**
Height: **Unknown**
Blood type: **Unknown**
Personality: **Short-fused**

## CONSPIRATOR

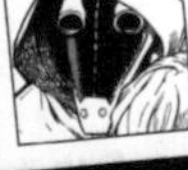

**CHRONOSTASIS**

As Overhaul's aide, he and Mimic ran the HQ.

# TOYA SETSUNO

**Since giving up, he's returned from despair.**

WANTED

Before you know it, this professional thief has robbed you blind.

Setsuno was once betrayed by his sweetheart and saddled with crushing debt. Right when he'd lost sight of a reason to live, Overhaul took him in and showed him the value of being a useful pawn.

## QUIRK >> Larceny

He can cause another person's equipment to warp into his hand. The object has to be visible to him.

### THREAT LEVEL

C

Power **D**

Technique **A**

Speed **D**

Pickpocketry **A**

Wits **C**

---

>>> OFFENSE >>>

**Impeding the Raid on the Shie Hassaikai Compound**

When the raid team stormed the compound, Setsuno attempted to hold them off and buy time. Amajiki brought him down.

KINDA HANDICAPPING YERSELF IF YA WON'T KILL US! WHAT A CHARMED LIFE YA MUST LIVE!

POP

**Profile**

Villain name: **Unknown**
Real name: **Toya Setsuno**
Quirk: **Larceny**
Affiliation: **Shie Hassaikai**

Birthday: **Unknown**
Height: **Unknown**
Blood type: **Unknown**
Personality: **Devious**

## CONSPIRATOR

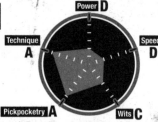

**YU HOJO**
Faced Amajiki with Setsuno and Tabe. Hojo was on offense.

244

# YU HOJO

**There's nothing phony about bonds between allies.**

WANTED
The menacing crystal man with unbreakable pride.


Once used as the tool of a money-grubber who later deemed him worthless trash, Hojo bounced back from his miserable past. He feels indebted to Overhaul and was eager to be exploited as a disposable pawn.

**QUIRK ›› Crystallize**

Crystals grow from his flesh to cover his entire body. Useful for both offense and defense.

**THREAT LEVEL**

**C**

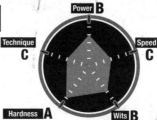

Power B
Speed C
Wits B
Hardness A
Technique C

**Profile**

Villain name: **Unknown**
Real name: **Yu Hojo**
Quirk: **Crystallize**
Affiliation: **Shie Hassaikai**
Birthday: **Unknown**
Height: **Unknown**
Blood type: **Unknown**
Personality: **Calm and collected**

## OFFENSE

A HERO COULD NEVER UNDER-STAND!
PREPARE TO DIE!! YOU WON'T BE SO LUCKY THIS TIME!
SHINK


**Impeding the Raid on the Shie Hassaikai Compound**

epared an ambush for the raid team. He saulted Amajiki with his crystallized body.

## CONSPIRATOR

**SORAMITSU TABE**

Tabe devoured Amajiki's body parts on order from Setsuno.

# SORAMITSU TABE

He can chew, swallow, and digest anything.

From a young age, Tabe's Quirk made it hard for him to get along in society, and he eventually lost his way. Due to persecution, he treasures the friends and allies that he does have. Tabe is currently locked up in the same prison as Hojo and Setsuno.

WANTED

His frightening appetite can never be satisfied.

**QUIRK » Food**

With jaws of steel and an iron stomach, he can chew up and digest vast quantities of anything.

THREAT LEVEL

C

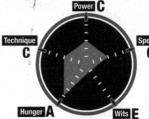

Power C
Speed C
Wits E
Hunger A
Technique C

## OFFENSE

**Impeding the Raid on the Shie Hassaikai Compound**

Tabe was tasked with slowing down the pro heroes. He joined Setsuno and Hojo in attacking Amajiki, who arrived as part of the raid team.

**Profile**

Villain name: **Unknown**
Real name: **Soramitsu Tabe**
Quirk: **Food**
Affiliation: **Shie Hassaikai**
Birthday: **Unknown**
Height: **Unknown**
Blood type: **Unknown**
Personality: **Tricky**

## CONSPIRATOR

**TOYA SETSUNO**

As the trio's leader, Setsuno tried to impede the raid.

# A full-throttle fighter who takes pride in his punches.

# KENDO RAPPA

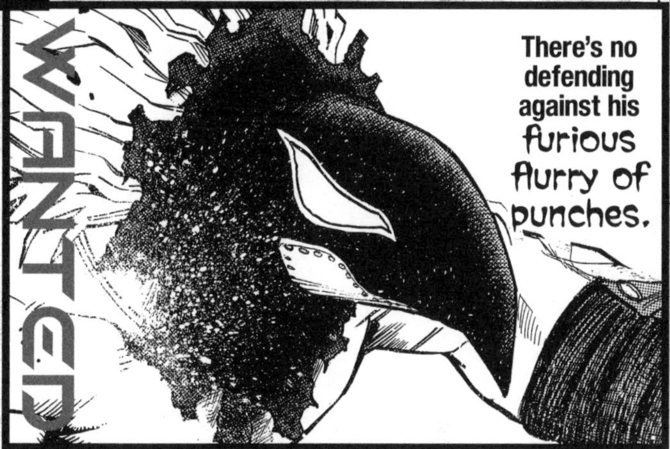
WANTED
There's no defending against his furious flurry of punches.

This Hassai gang member is a street fighter whose Quirk helps him brawl to his heart's content. Tengai was assigned as Rappa's babysitter and partner shortly after the latter joined the gang.

**QUIRK ≫ Strongarm**

His shoulders rotate with incredible efficiency, allowing him to unleash one vicious punch after another.

**THREAT LEVEL**

# B

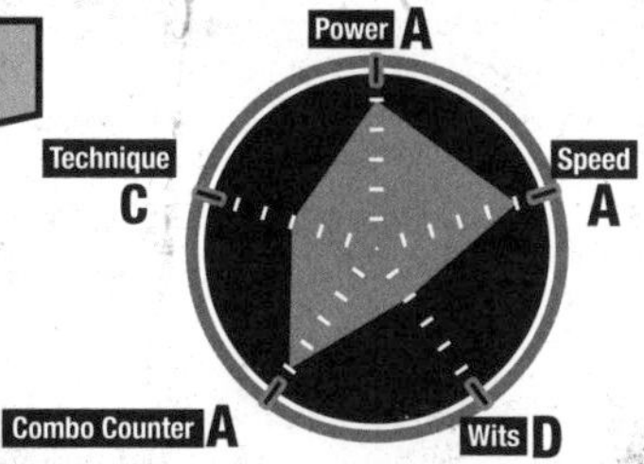
Power A
Speed A
Wits D
Combo Counter A
Technique C

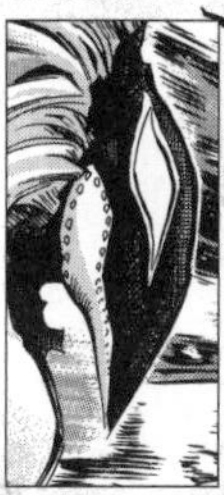

## OFFENSE

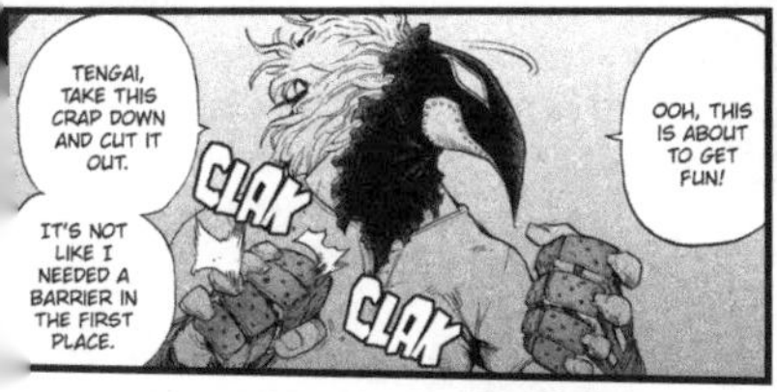
OOH, THIS IS ABOUT TO GET FUN!
TENGAI, TAKE THIS CRAP DOWN AND CUT IT OUT.
CLAK
CLAK
IT'S NOT LIKE I NEEDED A BARRIER IN THE FIRST PLACE.

**Impeding the Raid on the Shie Hassaikai Compound**

ppa fought Fat Gum and Kirishima but lost. Now, wants to challenge Kirishima to a rematch.

**Profile**

Villain name: **Unknown**
Real name: **Kendo Rappa**
Quirk: **Strongarm**
Affiliation: **Shie Hassaikai**
Birthday: **Unknown**
Height: **Unknown**
Blood type: **Unknown**
Personality: **Battle maniac**

## CONSPIRATOR

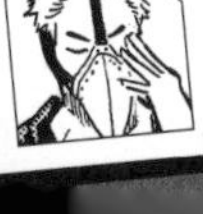

**HEKIJI TENGAI**

As the one on defense, Tengai watches over Rappa.

# HEKIJI TENGAI

**This serene guardian is one of the Eight Bullets.**

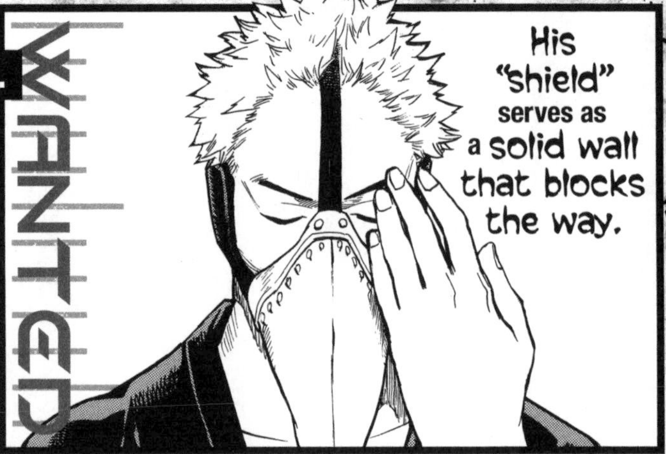
WANTED
His "shield" serves as a solid wall that blocks the way.

As a relatively new member of the Hassai gang, Tengai was brought into the fold to keep Rappa on a leash. Though once a devout Buddhist, he became wholly dedicated to his duties as part of the gang.

**QUIRK » Barrier**

Erects a spherical barrier. He's proud of this iron defense, but those inside can't attack outside.

**THREAT LEVEL**

**C**

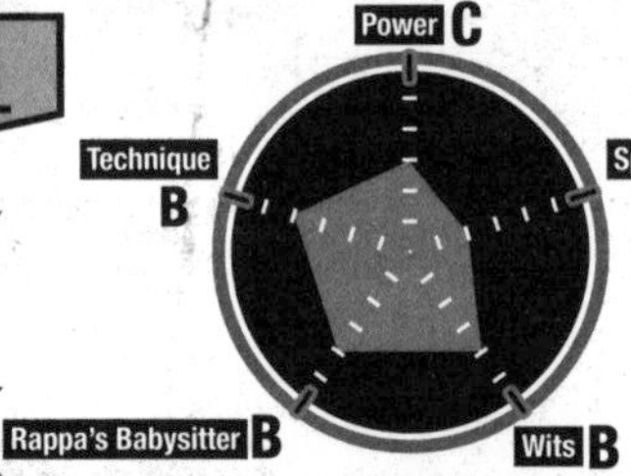
Power C
Speed D
Wits B
Rappa's Babysitter B
Technique B

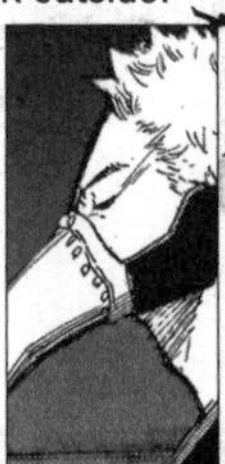

## OFFENSE

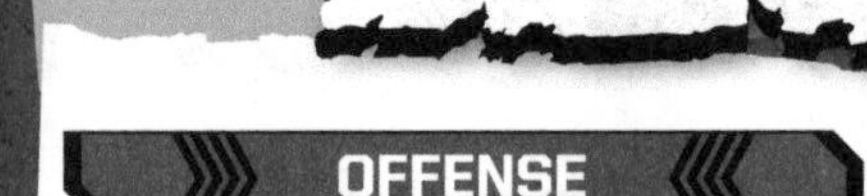
ESPECIALLY SINCE CALLING THE BOY A SHIELD...
...GIVES HIM TOO MUCH CREDIT...

**Impeding the Raid on the Shie Hassaikai Compound**

When Fat Gum and Kirishima found themselves isolated, Tengai and Rappa showed up to bar the way. These two Hassai Bullets had the heroes on the ropes, but Tengai's ultimate defensive barrier was shattered by Fat Gum.

**Profile**

Villain name: **Unknown**
Real name: **Hekiji Tengai**
Quirk: **Barrier**
Affiliation: **Shie Hassaikai**
Birthday: **Unknown**
Height: **Unknown**
Blood type: **Unknown**
Personality: **Sensible**

## CONSPIRATOR

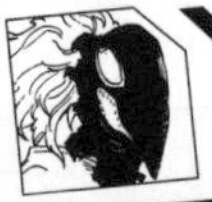

**KENDO RAPPA**

Acted alongside Tengai, his overseer. Not that Rappa agrees.

**A zealot who pledged himself to Overhaul.**

# SHIN NEMOTO

WANTED
This mind melter can expose petty grievances and crush spirits.

A Hassai Bullet, and confidant of Overhaul. Overhaul trusts Nemoto, who desires nothing more than to walk the same path and share in the joy of realizing their goals. Within the Eight Bullets, only Kurono and Irinaka have more seniority than him.

**QUIRK » Confession**

Those questioned by him are forced to speak the truth, sometimes without even realizing it.

**THREAT LEVEL**

# C

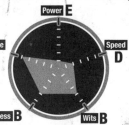

Power E
Speed D
Wits B
Doggedness B
Technique A

## OFFENSE

**Impeding the Raid on the Shie Hassaikai Compound**

Nemoto and Sakaki guarded Overhaul and attempted to impede the raid. Nemoto succeeded in revealing Togata's Quirk and slowed down the young hero.

BLAM
BLAM
I'M NOT LIKE THE REST OF THE PAWNS...
I'M A UNIQUE MEMBER OF THE HASSAIKAI! ONE PERMITTED TO BEAR DIRECT WITNESS TO THE YOUNG MASTER'S AMBITIONS!!

**Profile**

Villain name: **Unknown**
Real name: **Shin Nemoto**
Quirk: **Confession**
Affiliation: **Shie Hassaikai**
Birthday: **Unknown**
Height: **Unknown**
Blood type: **Unknown**
Personality: **Faithful servant**

## CONSPIRATOR

**DEIDORO SAKAKI**

Nemoto and Sakaki unleashed a nasty assault on Togata.

**ets his enemies drunk and enjoys fine liquor.**

One of Overhaul's aides. Since the booze-loving Sakaki is usually drunk, he tends to slur his words and be shaky on his feet. That said, he's skilled with a knife and can hit an opponent's vitals with startling accuracy.

# DEIDORO SAKAKI

WANTED
This drunken killer delivers a boozy shock to the system.

**QUIRK》 Sloshed**

Anyone who approaches him loses their sense of equilibrium and stumbles, as if they were inebriated.

**THREAT LEVEL**

**C**

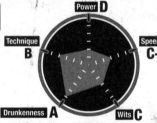

Power D
Speed C-
Wits C
Drunkenness A
Technique B

## OFFENSE

**Impeding the Raid on the Shie Hassaikai Compound**

MISSED EVERY SHOT? YOU SUCK!!
YOU FEELING TIPSY OR WHAT?!
NO, THAT'S YOUR THING.
ME?

Sakaki robbed Togata of equilibrium when the young hero had almost caught up with Overhaul.

**Profile**

Villain name: **Unknown**
Real name: **Deidoro Sakaki**
Quirk: **Sloshed**
Affiliation: **Shie Hassaikai**
Birthday: **Unknown**
Height: **Unknown**
Blood type: **Unknown**
Personality: **Uncouth**

## CONSPIRATOR

**SHIN NEMOTO**

Nemoto worked with Sakaki to keep Togata from Overhaul.

**This anti-raid captain confounds intruders.**

# RIKIYA KATSUKAME

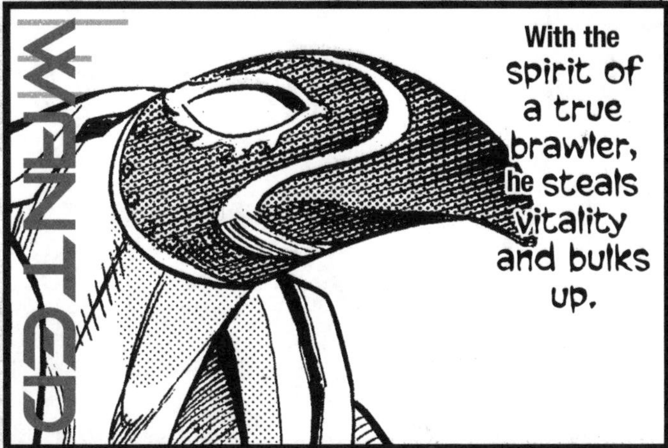
WANTED
With the spirit of a true brawler, he steals vitality and bulks up.

Started out as Overhaul's obedient friend and younger-brother-like figure. Later, Katsukame became one of the Hassai gang's Eight Bullets. The more vitality he steals, the more talkative he gets and the more extreme his attacks become!!

**QUIRK ›› Energy Suck**

By touching someone and breathing in, he steals their vitality, allowing him to grow into a giant.

**THREAT LEVEL**

**C**

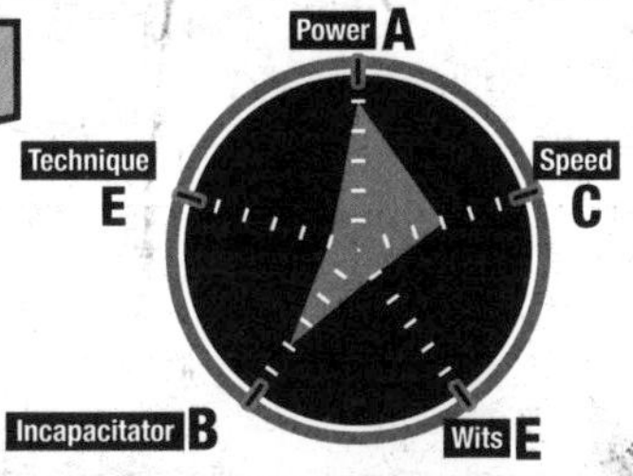
Power A
Speed C
Wits E
Incapacitator B
Technique E

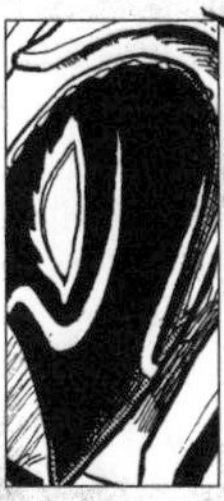

## OFFENSE

**Impeding the Raid on the Shie Hassaikai Compound**

Katsukame greeted the heroes and police at the front gate by stealing their energy.

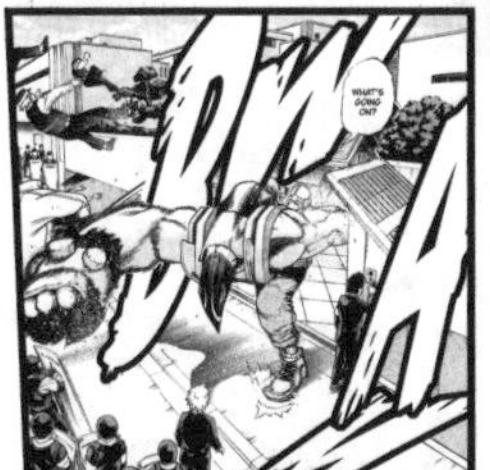
WHAT'S GOING ON?

**Profile**

Villain name: **Unknown**
Real name: **Rikiya Katsukame**
Quirk: **Energy Suck**
Affiliation: **Shie Hassaikai**
Birthday: **Unknown**
Height: **Unknown**
Blood type: **Unknown**
Personality: **One-track mind**

## CONSPIRATOR

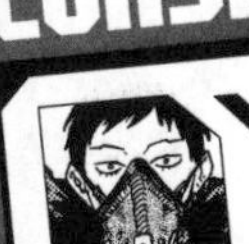

**OVERHAUL**

He disassembled and fused with Katsukame's body.

Elusive outlaw? No! Gentleman thief.

When his hero dreams were dashed, Gentle became a gentleman thief and began committing crimes to record and upload to the internet. He is currently serving time and reflecting on his actions, all while being concerned for La Brava.

# GENTLE CRIMINAL

WANTED
By sharing his crimes with the world, he presents society with another view on justice.

**QUIRK » Elasticity**

One touch lends elasticity to anything, making objects wobbly and bouncy. It even works on air.

THREAT LEVEL

# C

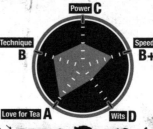

Power C
Speed B+
Wits D
Love for Tea A
Technique B

## OFFENSE

**Multiple Crimes, Uploading Videos of Said Crimes**

Gentle committed a wide range of pranks and minor offenses and uploaded recordings of his capers.

I LOATHE VIOLENCE AS A MEANS OF CONFLICT RESOLUTION!
GENTLY REBOUND
BOING

**Profile**

Villain name: **Gentle Criminal**
Real name: **Danjuro Tobita**
Quirk: **Elasticity**
Affiliation: **Freelancer**
Birthday: **August 29**
Height: **181 cm**
Blood type: **A**
Personality: **Gentlemanly**

## CONSPIRATOR

**LA BRAVA**

Video uploader. Suspected hacker and more.

**This stalker always chases the light of her life.**

# LA BRAVA

WANTED
The hacking pro who lives and breathes for love.

La Brava's tendency to love deeply once backfired. Later on, her love for Gentle motivated her to aid in his criminal escapades. The authorities have since asked her to use her technological skills for good, but she's unwilling to act if it's not for Gentle's sake.

**QUIRK ⟫ Love**

She can provide a strength power-up for her most loved. The stronger the love, the stronger the power-up.

**THREAT LEVEL**

**C**

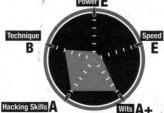

Power E
Speed E
Wits A+
Hacking Skills A
Technique B

## OFFENSE

ALL FOR GENTLE'S SAKE!!
I GOTTA PLAY MY PART IN THIS!!
RUB
RUB

**Hacking**

Brava sympathized with Gentle's ideals and lped produce his videos. It seems she was olved in everything, from planning to editing.

**Profile**

Villain name: **La Brava**
Real name: **Manami Aiba**
Quirk: **Love**
Affiliation: **Freelancer**
Birthday: **February 14**
Height: **111 cm**
Blood type: **B**
Personality: **Obsessed with Gentle**

## CONSPIRATOR

**GENTLE CRIMINAL**

Starred in La Brava's videos. He claims to be the mastermind.

# RE-DESTRO

WANTED

The grand commander of the metahuman liberation movement **seeks to revive Destro's glory.**

## META ABILITY ⟫ Stress

His stress can be converted into strength. The more stress, the bigger and more powerful his body becomes.

**THREAT LEVEL** A

Power **A+**

Technique **A+**

Speed **A**

Command **A**

Wits **A**

**Profile**

Villain name: **Re-Destro**
Real name: **Rikiya Yotsubashi**
Quirk: **Stress**
Affiliation: **Meta Liberation Army**
Birthday: **Unknown**
Height: **Unknown**
Blood type: **Unknown**
Personality: **Very shady**

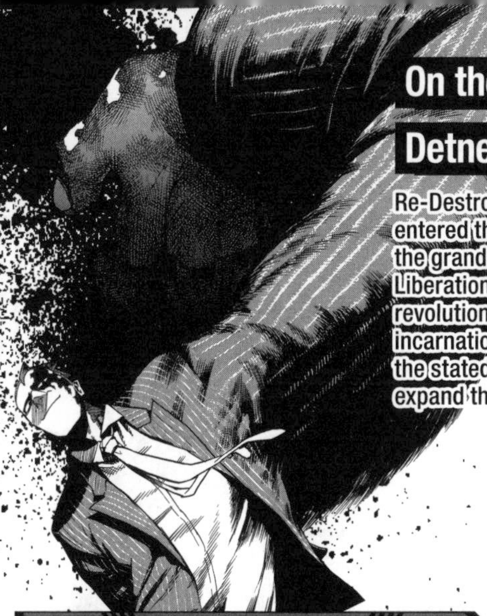

# On the surface, he's CEO of Detnerat, a support company.

Re-Destro is the CEO of a company that's just entered the hero support industry. Secretly he's the grand commander of the Metahuman Liberation Army. A descendant of the revolutionary Destro, he leads the army's current incarnation. Although "metahuman liberation" is the stated goal, Re-Destro actually hopes to expand the scope and scale of the organization.

## OFFENSE I

### Selling on the Black Market

Re-Destro is responsible for filling the black market with Quirk support items. A massive amount of battle data is collected for future application.

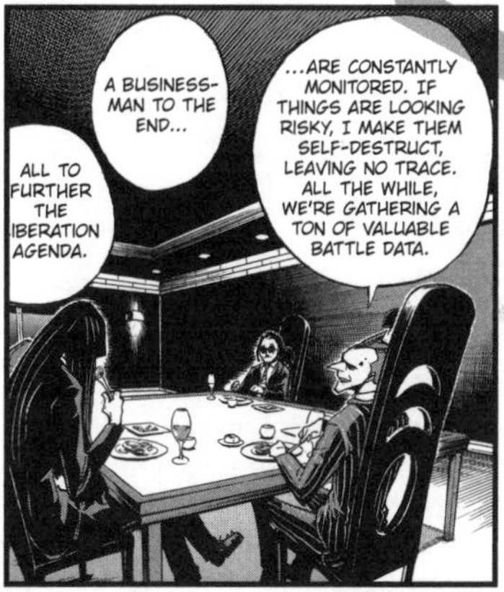
...ARE CONSTANTLY MONITORED. IF THINGS ARE LOOKING RISKY, I MAKE THEM SELF-DESTRUCT, LEAVING NO TRACE. ALL THE WHILE, WE'RE GATHERING A TON OF VALUABLE BATTLE DATA.
A BUSINESS-MAN TO THE END...
ALL TO FURTHER THE IBERATION AGENDA.

## OFFENSE II

### Leading the Metahuman Liberation Army

Re-Destro stands at the top of an organization 116,516 members strong. Ninety percent of them live in Deika City, a giant sleeper cell. Re-Destro is suspected of using the city as a base for the army's "revival party."

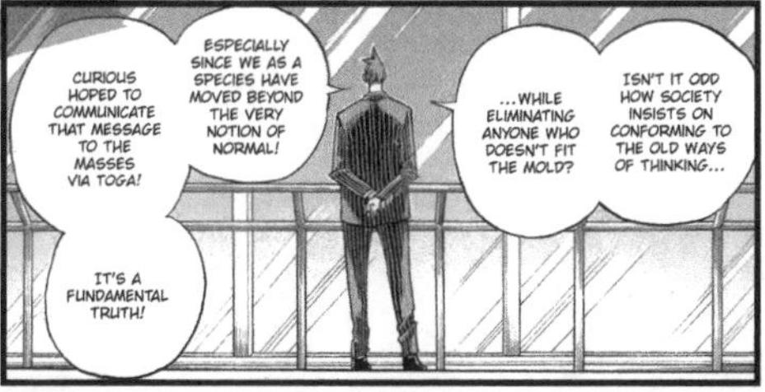
ISN'T IT ODD HOW SOCIETY INSISTS ON CONFORMING TO THE OLD WAYS OF THINKING...
...WHILE ELIMINATING ANYONE WHO DOESN'T FIT THE MOLD?
ESPECIALLY SINCE WE AS A SPECIES HAVE MOVED BEYOND THE VERY NOTION OF NORMAL!
CURIOUS HOPED TO COMMUNICATE THAT MESSAGE TO THE MASSES VIA TOGA!
IT'S A FUNDAMENTAL TRUTH!

## CONSPIRATORS

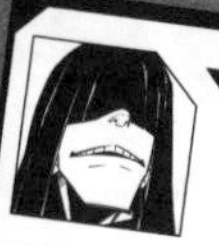

### SKEPTIC

In charge of communications and his anthropomorphs.

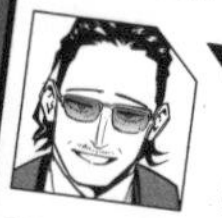

### TRUMPET

He riles up the warriors to send them into battle.

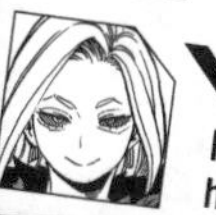

### CURIOUS

Publishing executive. Also handles publicity for the M.L.A.

## Re-Destro's Past

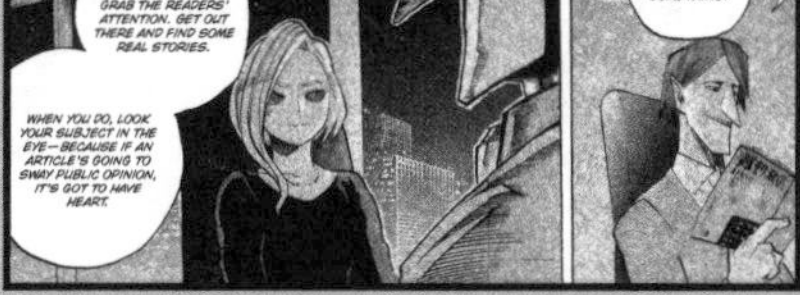
KIZUKI.
THIS WRITING OF YOURS WON'T MOVE PEOPLE. IT'S LACKING SOMETHING.
BEAT REPORTING ON RUMORS WON'T GRAB THE READERS' ATTENTION. GET OUT THERE AND FIND SOME REAL STORIES.
WHEN YOU DO, LOOK YOUR SUBJECT IN THE EYE—BECAUSE IF AN ARTICLE'S GOING TO SWAY PUBLIC OPINION, IT'S GOT TO HAVE HEART.

⬆Re-Destro gave advice to Curious during her earlier days at Shoowaysha. He's always shown an aptitude for leadership.

# CURIOUS

**Propaganda for the Meta Liberation Army.**

A commander in the Meta Liberation Army who began her career as a reporter for a publisher. Kizuki admired Yotsubashi after meeting him in her youth. She attempted to frame Himiko Toga as a tragic heroine, but her inquisitive spirit led to her early death.

**Profile**

Liberation code name: **Curious**
Real name: **Chitose Kizuki**
Meta ability: **Landmine**
Affiliation: **Meta Liberation Army**
Birthday: **Unknown**
Height: **Unknown**
Blood type: **Unknown**
Personality: **Callous**

WANTED
Sets up land mines to corner her prey.

**META ABILITY ›› Landmine**

Anything she touches turns explosive. There's no limit to how many she can transform.

THREAT LEVEL **C**

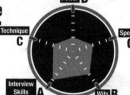

Power D
Speed C
Wits B
Interview Skills A
Technique C

# SKEPTIC

**A businessman with an eerie grin.**

Board member at an I.T. company and a strategist in the Meta Liberation Army who uses accumulated data to concoct elaborate plans. Though Chikazoku's company is now an industry behemoth, the security system he constructed was once hacked.

**Profile**

Liberation code name: **Skeptic**
Real name: **Chikazoku**
Meta ability: **Anthropomorph**
Affiliation: **Meta Liberation Army**
Birthday: **Unknown**
Height: **Unknown**
Blood type: **Unknown**
Personality: **Perfectionist**

WANTED
A puppeteer for the modern age who manipulates shape-shifting homunculi.

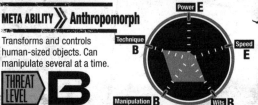

**META ABILITY ›› Anthropomorph**

Transforms and controls human-sized objects. Can manipulate several at a time.

THREAT LEVEL **B**

Power E
Speed E
Wits B
Manipulation B
Technique B

# TRUMPET

**This politician seeks to usher in a new era.**

A commander in the Meta Liberation Army and a political party leader. His skill at public speaking and meta ability make him particularly persuasive, allowing him to recruit a large number of supporters. He favors human-wave tactics and powers up his followers.

A faux preacher who controls his followers **with the electromagnetic waves in his voice.**

**Profile**

Liberation code name:
**Trumpet**
Real name: **Koku Hanabata**
Meta ability: **Incite**
Affiliation: **Meta Liberation Army**
Birthday: **Unknown**
Height: **Unknown**
Blood type: **Unknown**
Personality: **Silver-tongued**

**META ABILITY** 》 **Incite**

The electromagnetic waves in his voice strengthen his chosen followers.

**THREAT LEVEL** 》 **B**

| | Power | E |
| Technique B | | Speed E |
| Rallying Ability A | | Wits B |

---

# GETEN

**A zealot devoted to training his meta ability.**

He never attended school but instead received Yotsubashi's patronage, which he repaid with undying loyalty. Proficient at analysis, Geten has also elevated his meta ability. His powerful ice attacks make him a pillar of the Liberation Army's offense.

This ice user hunts down enemies of the Liberation Army.

**Profile**

Liberation code name: **Geten**
Real name: **Unknown**
Meta ability: **Unknown**
Affiliation: **Meta Liberation Army**
Birthday: **Unknown**
Height: **Unknown**
Blood type: **Unknown**
Personality: **Advocate of rule by the strong**

**META ABILITY** 》 **Unknown**

Can control ice and fine-tune its exact temperature. Further details unknown.

**THREAT LEVEL** 》 **B**

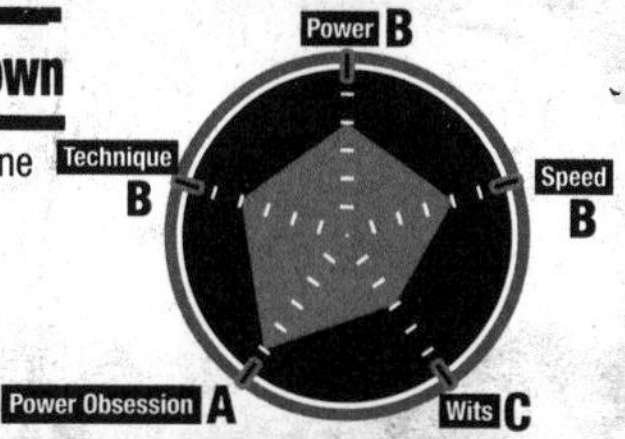

| | Power | B |
| Technique B | | Speed B |
| Power Obsession A | | Wits C |

All For One's ally. A supporter of the league.

A man of mystery who worked on healing All For One, helped form the League of Villains, and has been instrumental in the manufacture of the life-forms known as Nomu. Ujiko owns multiple orphanages and Quirk hospitals, and he's constantly gathering ideal test subjects.

**Profile**

Liberation code name: **Daruma Ujiko (?)**
Real name: **Unknown**
Quirk: **Unknown**
Affiliation: **League of Villains (?)**
Birthday: **Unknown**
Height: **Unknown**
Blood type: **Unknown**
Personality: **True scientist**

# DARUMA UJIKO (?)

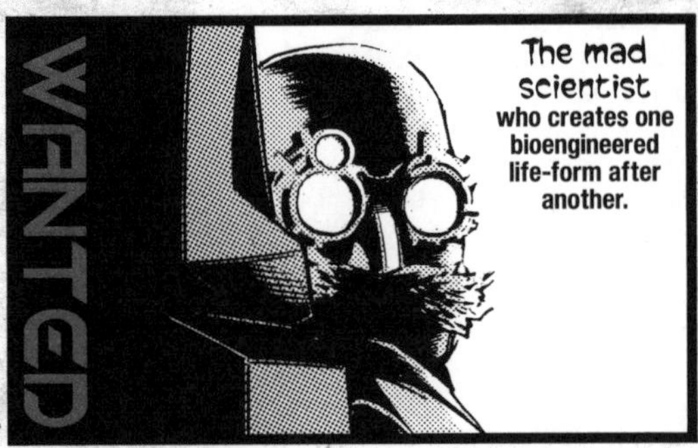
WANTED
The mad scientist
who creates one bioengineered life-form after another.

**QUIRK » Unknown**

Details concerning his Quirk are unknown at this time. Requires further investigation.

THREAT LEVEL **A**

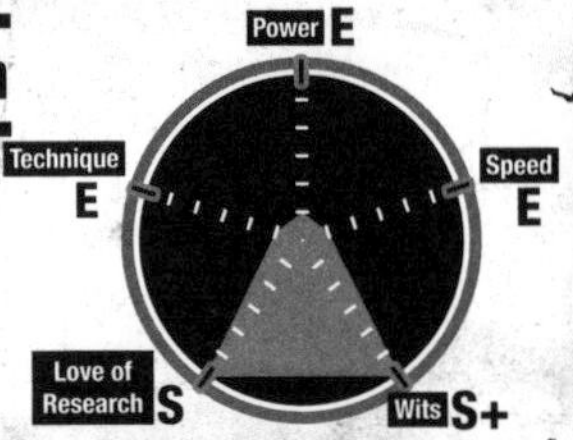
Power E
Speed E
Wits S+
Love of Research S
Technique E

## TRAPEZIUS HEADGEAR

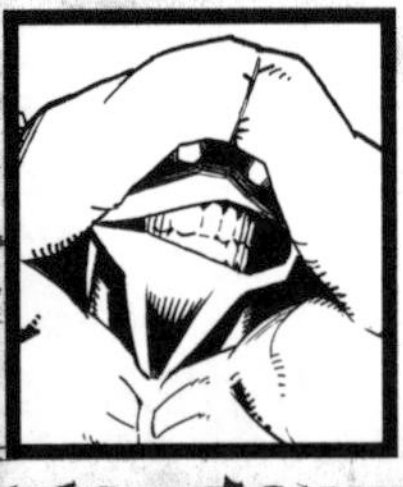

Serial offender with overgrown muscles. More than willing to play dirty. Believes he can defy society.

## GIANT VILLAIN

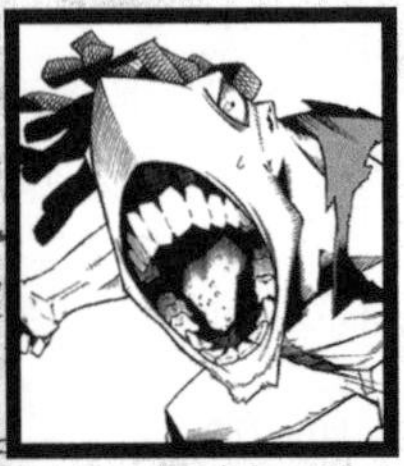

A gigantified villain who got caught snatching purses. He gave the heroes near Tatoin Station trouble but lost to Mt. Lady.

## BYE-BITES

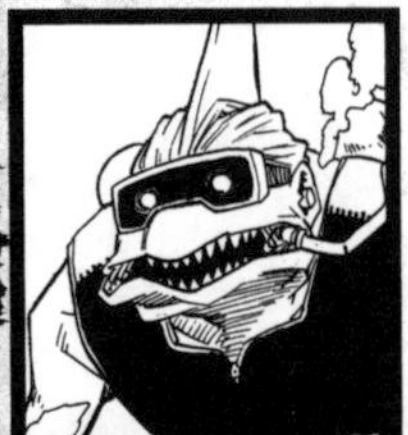

Bye-Bites attempted to chomp down on the submerged Midoriya but was stopped by Asui. His catchphrase is "Say goodbye!"

## SLUDGE VILLAIN

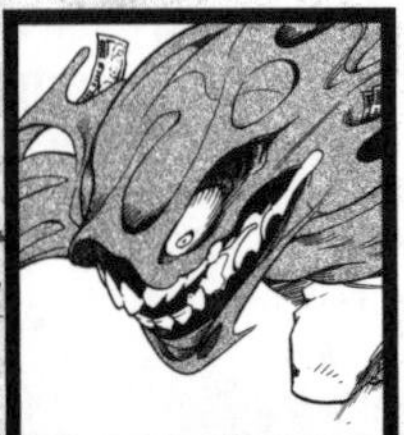

Has a liquefied nature and can hijack other people's bodies. Tried to take over Bakugo, but All Might blasted him to bits.

## OXY-MAN

Can control oxygen and hid in the flood zone for an ambush, but Midoriya beat him before he could do anything.

## DOZAEMON

A calm villain. He cleaved the boat carrying Midoriya and friends. Disturbing name (Dozaemon means "drowned corpse").

## SHIE HASSAIKAI BOSS

Eri's grandfather and Chisaki's father figure. He was opposed to the plot but was unable to stop it and fell into a coma.

## RESERVOIR DOGS

Made trouble to mark All Might's retirement but fell to the Hassaikai, who staged an accident. In prison.

## C.R.C. (CREATURE REJECTION CLAN)

A hate group against heteromorphs. It lost support due to its extremism and dissolved.

## CIDER HOUSE

These thieves had well-laid plans. The leader has a carbonation-related Quirk.

## OJI HARIMA

A bizarrely dressed robber who stole from the rich and shared the wealth. Though a criminal, some praised his actions.

## DESTRO

Created the M.L.A. He fought the government and lost. His ideology faded away, but Re-Destro has inherited Destro's will.

# COLUMN 3

ITEMS PROCURED BY

## UNDERWORLD BROKER GIRAN

Giran the broker has made quite a name for himself on the black market. Here, he and Twice introduce some of the stuff he's rustled up!

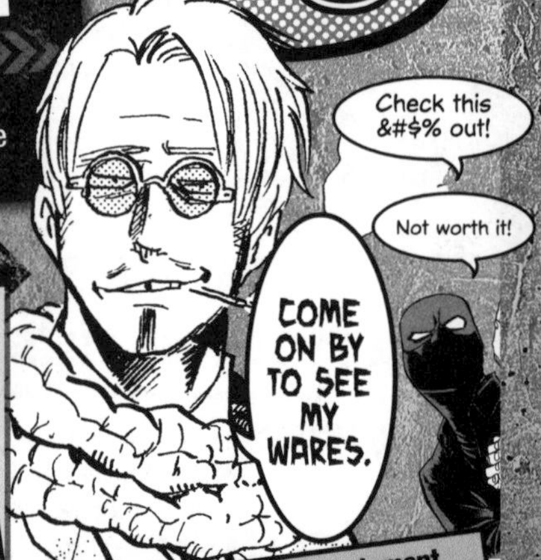
Check this &#$% out!
Not worth it!
COME ON BY TO SEE MY WARES.

### No.1 Twice's Bodysuit and Weapons

The bodysuit is top class (made with highly durable material), and the measuring tapes that extend from each wrist have deadly sharp edges.

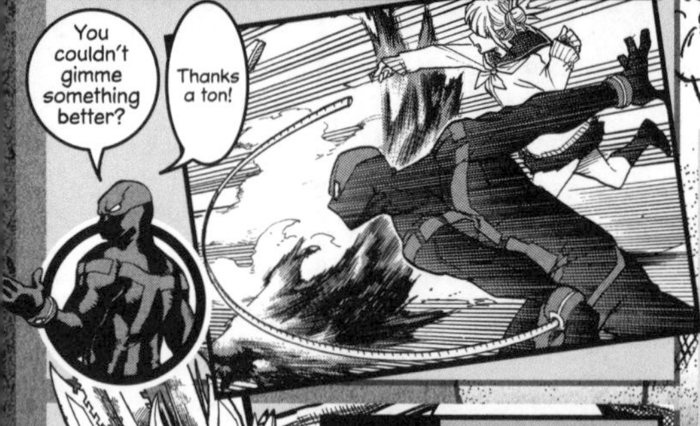
Thanks a ton!
You couldn't gimme something better?

### No.2 Himiko Toga's Equipment

Toga herself wasn't pleased with the design, but this equipment allows her to use her Quirk to its full potential.

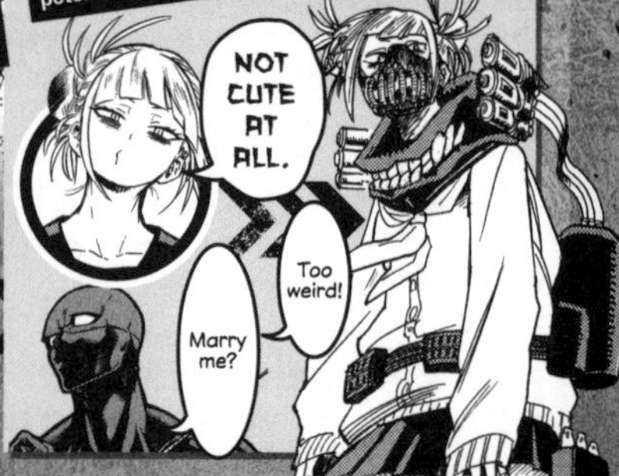
NOT CUTE AT ALL.
Too weird!
Marry me?

### No.3 Super Knife-Knife Sword

Spinner's request was simply "Lotsa blades!" Some of the weapons within have, let's say, interesting stories.

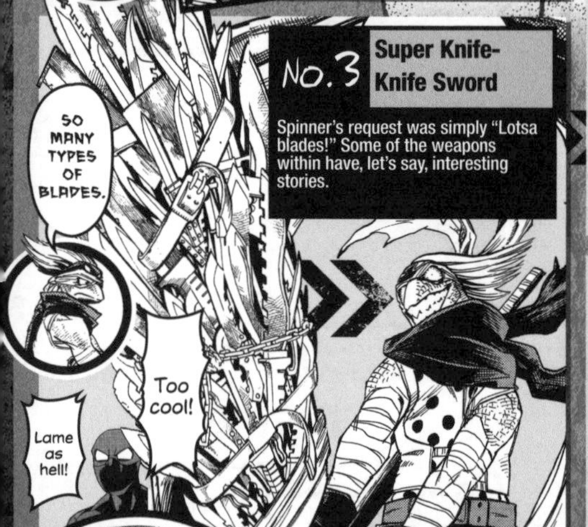
SO MANY TYPES OF BLADES.
Too cool!
Lame as hell!

### No.4 Mr. Compress's Prosthetic Arm

It took a lot of searching to find a quality prosthetic that could re-create Mr. Compress's former dexterity.

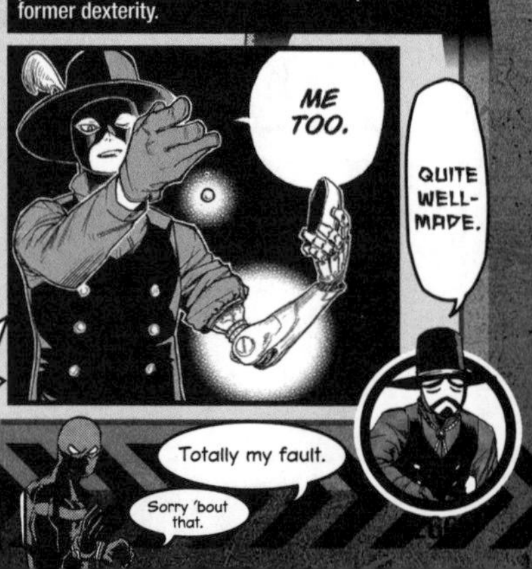
ME TOO.
QUITE WELL-MADE.
Totally my fault.
Sorry 'bout that.

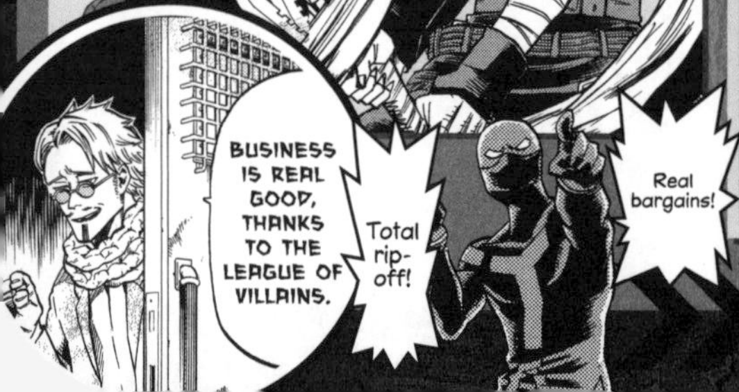
Real bargains!
Total rip-off!
BUSINESS IS REAL GOOD, THANKS TO THE LEAGUE OF VILLAINS.

# EX

## EDITION III

**PLUS EXTRA**

A bevy of Plus Ultra content, including a talk between Kubo Sensei and Horikoshi Sensei, art originally posted on Twitter, and *MHA*'s first-ever glossary of terms!!

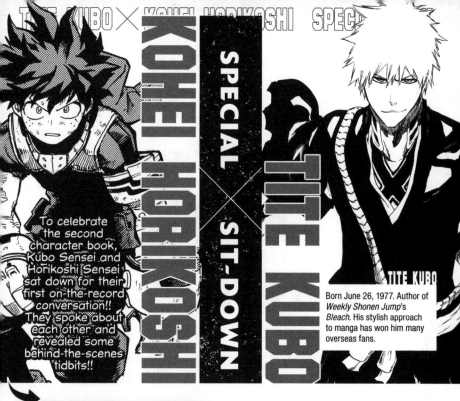

KOHEI HORIKOSHI

SPECIAL × SIT-DOWN

TITE KUBO

To celebrate the second character book, Kubo Sensei and Horikoshi Sensei sat down for their first on-the-record conversation!! They spoke about each other and revealed some behind-the-scenes tidbits!!

**TITE KUBO**

Born June 26, 1977. Author of *Weekly Shonen Jump*'s *Bleach*. His stylish approach to manga has won him many overseas fans.

## Meeting, and Impressions of Each Other's Work

▶ **When did you two first meet?**

**Horikoshi:** I believe I introduced myself at a dinner party, around when my first series ended.

**Kubo:** I don't actually remember that. (laughs) What I do remember was Yusei Matsui doing the honors during a party at your place, I think?

**Horikoshi:** I was so nervous to be surrounded by so many greats, so I pretty much hid in the corner the whole time… Maybe that was when my second series ended?

**Kubo:** You're right—I don't think you said a single word to me then. (laughs) But we did grab a meal together recently. I didn't really read *Jump* when I had my own series going, but I have ever since my

thing ended, and *MHA* grabbed me, which is why I wanted to meet up with you. It was then that we discussed the possibility of this sit-down we're doing right now.

▶ **Could you both talk about your impressions of each other's work?**

**Kubo:** I'm always impressed by the sheer amount of art he manages to cram into a weekly release. The biggest difference between our respective series is the density of our backgrounds.

**Horikoshi:** But your characters can just stand there all on their own and have this striking presence. I don't think my own style is capable of that, so I end up filling every nook and cranny of those backgrounds. Almost like I'm thinking, "I'll compete by making my drawings dense."

**Kubo:** I think *MHA*'s characters can also stand on their own and qualify as art. One part that really left an impression was that abandoned factory area full of pipes during

## I'M THINKING, "I'LL COMPETE BY MAKING MY DRAWINGS DENSE."

—Horikoshi

## THERE'S A PART OF ME THAT ONLY DRAWS SCENES TO GET CERTAIN DIALOGUE IN.

—Kubo

STOP! THEY'RE HERE!!

window dressing like that. I bet the other mangaka feel the same way—like you're this living embodiment of style.

**Kubo:** I think it's like, there's a part of me that only draws scenes to get certain dialogue in, and I only draw manga at all in order to make those scenes happen.

**Horikoshi:** Ahh, that makes sense.

**Kubo:** Sometimes, I create characters and dialogue simultaneously. When I want to use a particular line of dialogue, I think about what sort of character would be the most likely speaker of said line. Then, I create a situation where it makes sense for that character to say that line, and voila—I've got a scene.

**Horikoshi:** Interesting. We take completely different approaches.

**Kubo:** Do you ever have specific lines that you just need someone to say?

**Horikoshi:** Yes. When I think about future plot developments, I know there are some lines that would just be so darn cool to have someone say. So I guess I do often come up with character moments and situations that way.

**Kubo:** Not so different after all, then?

the class-versus-class battles. That was nuts. As I read those chapters, I was thinking, "I could never pull this off..." (laughs)

**Horikoshi:** Every week during that arc, my assistants would come to me and ask, "When is it gonna ennnd?" (laughs) I needed an environment where every character could shine in their own way, so I wound up with that.

**Kubo:** If it were me, I'd 100 percent come up with a solution that involved zero pipes. (laughs)

**Horikoshi:** But I'm jealous of your design sense and the strength of your art, since it means that you don't have to rely on

## Different Approaches to Making Manga

▶ **Horikoshi Sensei, could you speak to your process when creating characters?**

**Horikoshi:** I don't really have a set process. Sometimes I recycle old visual concepts from before the series even started, and sometimes I start with a superpower and work from there. To use Hawks as a recent example, I needed a character who would fill a very specific role within the overarching plot.

**Kubo:** Ah, so he was born because you specifically needed a double agent.

**Horikoshi:** Yes. Incidentally, I didn't even have Hawks's visual design locked down during the drafting phase.

**Kubo:** So you came up with it along the way?

**Horikoshi:** Yeah...

**Kubo:** Trying to nail down the design while drawing can be tough.

**Horikoshi:** I have a bad habit of making my designs overly detailed, because I want that panel where a character first appears to be extra cool and impressive. I guess my mantra is that details and density are the tricks to making a design cool.

**Kubo:** You sure do like those dense, tightly packed designs.

**Horikoshi:** I find that that approach also draws attention away from bad proportions and angles that would otherwise seem weird.

HE DOES THINGS HIS WAY, BUT ALWAYS FIERCELY! WITH UNSTOPPABLE MOMENTUM, HE'S MADE IT TO SECOND PLACE!

NO. 2!

LAYING IT ON THICK, HUH?

WING HERO: HAWKS!

▶ **And you, Kubo Sensei? How do you create characters?**

**Kubo:** When the lines of dialogue and the character come about simultaneously, sometimes it's actually the name that comes first. For example, Rukia started with nothing but a name.

**Horikoshi:** Ooh, I didn't expect to hear that.

## RUKIA STARTED WITH NOTHING BUT A NAME.
### —Kubo

## I'M ALWAYS WRITING DOWN NOTES OR DOODLING WHEN TALKING.
### —Horikoshi

**Kubo:** While I was drawing, I had the TV on in the background and heard something or other about the ancestor of cosmos flowers, which sounded to me like "kuitilutia," so I jotted down that note for later. The components of the word sounded like *kuchiki* (a Japanese surname) plus *lucia* (derived from the Latin word for "light"), which, when combined as Rukia Kuchiki, seemed like a great name for a Soul Reaper. She started out as a Soul Reaper with a scythe, but then her weapons and outfit changed…and that's how that process went.

**Horikoshi:** The story behind her creation already makes her cool… In *MHA*, the only character whose name preceded the design was probably Tsutsutaka Agoyamato. That minor character came about as a result of some doodles during a planning meeting.

**Kubo:** Huh? You like to doodle during meetings?

**Horikoshi:** I'm always writing down notes or doodling when talking. I take it you don't, Kubo Sensei?

**Kubo:** In my meetings, we go over the order of business and then get to chitchatting—that's it. They're over in 30 minutes, so no, I don't take notes. I must be a pain in the ass for the editor in charge. (laughs)

▶ **Did any other characters start with just a name?**

**Kubo:** Bambietta came about because I wanted someone with the nickname "Bambina." Those five Sternritter members all have alliterative initials (like B.B. and G.G.) because I decided on that rule for their naming scheme.

**Horikoshi:** Come to think of it, there is a lot of alliteration in *Bleach* character names. Aaroniero Arruruerie is another cool example. I was going for something similar with Rock Lock, in my story.

**Kubo:** That one dark-skinned hero? Great name.

**Horikoshi:** Ah, I'm so glad you remember! Thank you.

## Did Mirio's Intro Scene Flop?!

▶ **Which characters do you like from each other's series?**

**Horikoshi:** For me, Mayuri is the cream of the crop! When I got Kubo Sensei to sign an autograph board, I requested a drawing of Mayuri. I really love his initial appearance, where you can't quite tell if he's a person or not. That mystery factor was great.

**Kubo:** Mayuri makes quite an impact, huh?

**Horikoshi:** I just had no idea what we'd get with that character. What's he gonna do? Who knows! That really made him stand out.

**Kubo:** Shonen manga has that ironclad rule where the hero's team has to win in the end, no matter how bad things look. I came up with Mayuri because I wanted people to think, "In what crazy way is he gonna win this one?" So I'm thrilled that that was your impression. I didn't conceive of the Thirteen Court Guard Companies as villains—it was more like their moral views led to a clash of ideologies. But I needed readers to see them as villains, so that took a bit of tinkering.

**Horikoshi:** Believe me, I understand.

**Kubo:** Personally, I like Denki Kaminari. He occupies a really nice position in the grand scheme.

TMP
YOU'RE SUCH A PAIN.
OH.
HMPH.

**Horikoshi:** His power is so strong, but he comes off as kind of weak... (laughs)

**Kubo:** That's what's great about him. All the characters in *MHA* are different in their own little ways, so it's hard to choose favorites. Oh, I also like Mirio.

**Horikoshi:** What about him?

**Kubo:** The scene where he protected little Eri all on his own was fantastic.

**Horikoshi:** Actually, when he debuted in the story, I initially thought I'd messed up and that there couldn't be anything interesting about him.

**Kubo:** He comes off as a good-natured big brother type, which is admittedly a tricky position to fill.

**Horikoshi:** Yeah. Also, his initial appearance ended without any sort of emotion, because I was going to rely on the plot to sort of carry him along. But that would've been a disservice to Mirio, and I hoped he'd make a real impression on readers as a character. I put so much work into him because I wanted readers to come away thinking, "Maybe this guy could've been the protagonist?"

**Kubo:** That was definitely the vibe with the scene I'm talking about.

## A "Zero Calorie" Quirk?!

DON'T WORRY !!
I'LL BE YOUR HERO!

**▶ What would you say your own Quirks are? Or, what sort of Quirk would you like to use?**

**Horikoshi:** My existing Quirk is "Sleep," and the Quirk I'd want is "No-Sleep-Necessary." (laughs)

**Kubo:** The Quirk I've got is "I Can Eat Tons of Delicious Stuff and Never Get Sick." I'd want "I Can Eat Tons of Delicious Stuff and It's All Zero Calories."

**Horikoshi:** Let's just call that one "Zero Calorie." (laughs)

**Kubo:** With that one, I could render any opponent immobile.

## [MAYURI'S] MYSTERY FACTOR WAS GREAT.
### —Horikoshi

## [KAMINARI] OCCUPIES A REALLY NICE POSITION IN THE GRAND SCHEME.
### —Kubo

**Horikoshi:** Wait, I thought it would just remove all the calories from whatever you were eating? (laughs) That'd be one powerful Quirk.

**Kubo:** Yes, powerful! I imagine the ladies would love a Quirk that could make anything zero calories. And with that name, I'm picturing a sandwich for some reason. (laughs)

### Kubo Sensei, a Hero?!

▶ **What is a hero, in your opinion? What is evil?**

**Kubo:** I feel like the author of *MHA* has to answer this one by saying, "Read my story to find out."

**Horikoshi:** I'm definitely still searching around for those answers. Hopefully I can provide them in the final scene of the very last chapter.

**Kubo:** Personally, I can't wait.

**Horikoshi:** What were your general ideas about justice and evil while drawing your series, Kubo Sensei?

**Kubo:** I love hero stories myself, but I'm not the type to base my work around a single big theme. So forget that—I want to hear about heroes from your life, Horikoshi.

**Horikoshi:** Right, sure. My heroes would have to be the three pillars who held up

*Jump* when I was getting really fired up about manga. That is to say, Oda Sensei, Kishimoto Sensei, and you, Kubo Sensei. Ah! Please don't think I'm just sucking up to you, though. (laughs)

**Kubo:** Brownnoser says what? (laughs)

**Horikoshi:** The way I see it, that period was the absolute pinnacle of *Jump*!

**Kubo:** I think that's how we felt about *Jump* when *Dragon Ball* was running.

**Horikoshi:** Right, you get it. That's why you three are my heroes!

▶ ***Bleach* started when you were in middle school, Horikoshi Sensei. Were you influenced by it?**

**Horikoshi:** At that point, I still hadn't attempted drawing anything resembling manga. It was more about doodling and imagining worlds and characters. With that stuff, I definitely copied elements of *Bleach*. Plenty of my doodled characters wielded Zanpakuto. (laughs)

**Kubo:** I'd love to see that! So you designed original Zanpakuto for your characters?

**Horikoshi:** Yes. The blades would transform, but they didn't have Bankai forms. (laughs) Anyway, yes—I drew a ton of those.

**Kubo:** I assume none of those drawings survived?

**Horikoshi:** Probably not. They would've been in some old B5 notebooks back home...

**Kubo:** I wish you'd sent some of that in as fan art! I keep all the fan mail I get, so if you had, we'd still have access to it.
**Horikoshi:** I'd also have to say that *Bleach* became my standard regarding the power of words. Not that I have that same sense of style… That's just another aspect where I'm unpolished.
**Kubo:** Let's call it "zeal"?
**Horikoshi:** I guess I can leave an impression on people through sheer overbearingness.
**Kubo:** I was kind of taken aback by how Deku is such a worrywart, but after getting to know you… Well, it makes sense. (laughs)
**Horikoshi:** At first, I thought Deku's plainness was appealing, but looking back, I'm like, "Why'd I make him so gloomy and boring?" (laughs) I think Deku's biggest flaw is that he angsts too much and can't come to quick decisions. Like me, he's constantly thinking, "Is this right? Is this good enough?!" That's how he progresses, but it's difficult.
**Kubo:** But there's something cute about his brand of negativity.
**Horikoshi:** Way before I started drawing *MHA*, an older author at a dinner party said, "When your series starts to really sell, you'll feel invincible." But I haven't felt that shift at all. (laughs) Instead of being happy or satisfied, I've grown anxious about how there are so many others with way more talent than me, so I'd better not let any of this go to my head.
**Kubo:** When we met up last time, you said, "Once you go up, there's nowhere to go but down." (laughs)
**Horikoshi:** That said, I've never forgotten something you once told me, Kubo Sensei. We were in a taxi, and I was getting angsty about not knowing my own strengths. Without hesitation, you said, "It's your art," and I felt like the path ahead was suddenly clear.
**Kubo:** I don't remember the conversation being that angsty… But yes, I'm pretty sure "It's your art" was exactly what I said to you. That sounds right.
**Horikoshi:** I'm glad you remember!!

## Ultimate Names for Ultimate Moves!

**▶ Can you talk about the big, flashy fighting moves in your respective series?**

**Horikoshi:** I love "Tentei Kura" in *Bleach*. It's just a communication move, but the name makes it sound like some almighty technique.
**Kubo:** I thought it was kind of overblown for just a communication move. (laughs) The meaning behind the kanji characters was what mattered.
**Horikoshi:** At the time, I also thought it seemed too cool for what it was. (laughs)
**Kubo:** Seriously, though. (laughs)
**Horikoshi:** Recently, I've started putting much more thought into my ultimate move names, like with Twice's "Sad Man's Parade."
**Kubo:** That's a good one.
**Horikoshi:** I named it that in the hope that kids would want to say it out loud.

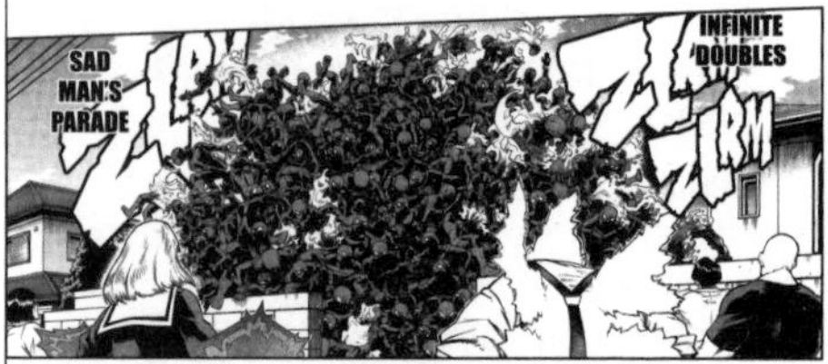
INFINITE DOUBLES
SAD MAN'S PARADE

## Encouragement from Kubo Sensei!

**▶ Finally, Kubo Sensei—what advice would you have for rivals who grew up reading your work?**

**Kubo:** My generation doesn't talk about it a lot, but the feeling that *Jump*'s golden age peaked with *Dragon Ball* and *Slam Dunk* is a fundamental concept that always sticks with us when we're creating art. So all the while, we're thinking, "Are we doing okay? Are we good enough?" Of course, we all tend to think that our own series is the greatest there ever was, but a part of us remembers the sheer intensity of those series from our youth and thinks, "Am I really capable of creating anything even remotely as good as that stuff?" We can't escape that. So it's a big relief to hear Horikoshi say that his generation was reading *Jump* at its peak. By extension, the kids reading today must think the same thing about this period.

**Horikoshi:** You don't know how happy that makes me. And yes, it's a relief for me too.
**Kubo:** When I look at the industry newcomers nowadays, it's abundantly clear from their work how much some of them love *MHA*. So you know the kids out there must love it too.
**Horikoshi:** Right… Maybe I am doing okay? I'll do my best not to fall behind!!
**Horikoshi:** Thanks for doing this today, Kubo Sensei!!
**Kubo:** Right back at you!!

# TITE KUBO × KOHEI HORIKOSHI

After the sit-down, each author contributed to this signing board! Ichigo in a U.A. school uniform makes this an ultrarare piece of art!!

[After hearing your words], I felt like the path ahead was suddenly clear.
—Horikoshi

It's a big relief to hear Horikoshi say that his generation was reading *Jump* at its peak.
—Kubo

## Horikoshi's Gallery

# Twitter collection

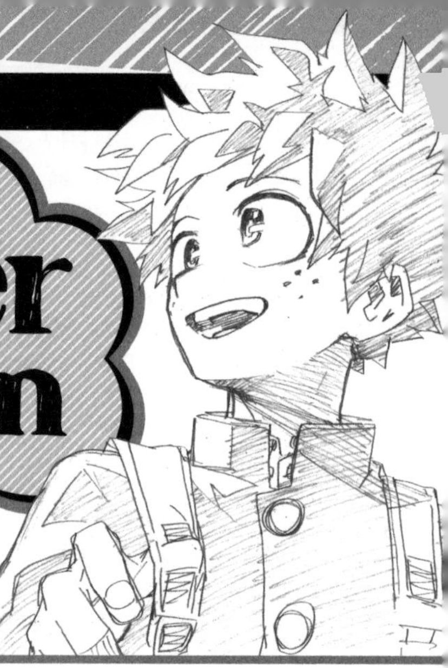

**Posts from April 2016 to August 2019, along with comments from Horikoshi Sensei!!**

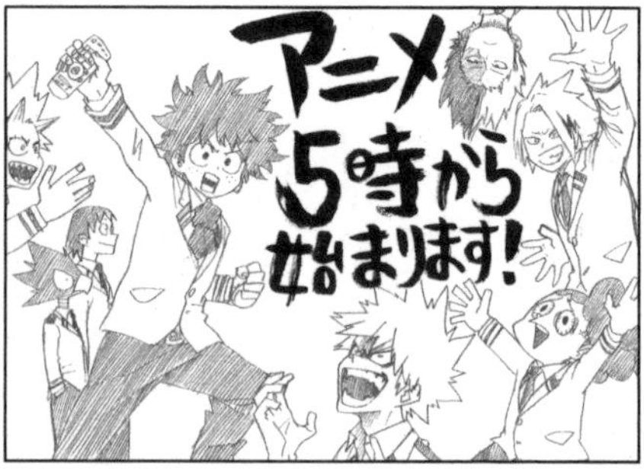
アニメ
5時から
始まります!

April 3, 2016 ⬆ **Season 1, begin!**

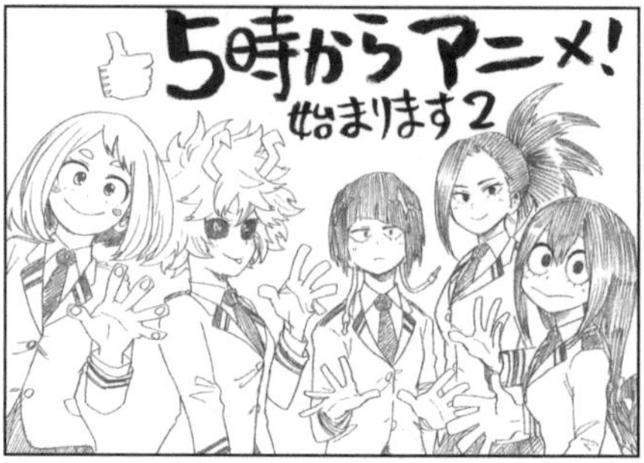
5時からアニメ!
始まります2

April 3, 2016 ⬆ **I was so happy I just kept drawing.**

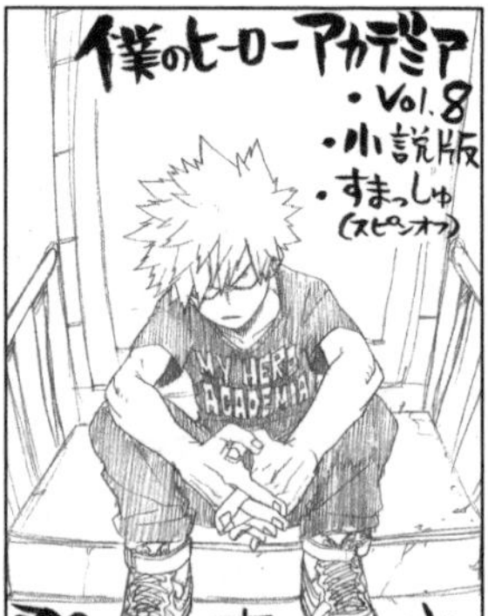
僕のヒーローアカデミア
・Vol.8
・小説版
・すまっしゅ
(スピンオフ)
発売中

April 5, 2016 ⬆ **I just wanted to draw those shoes.**

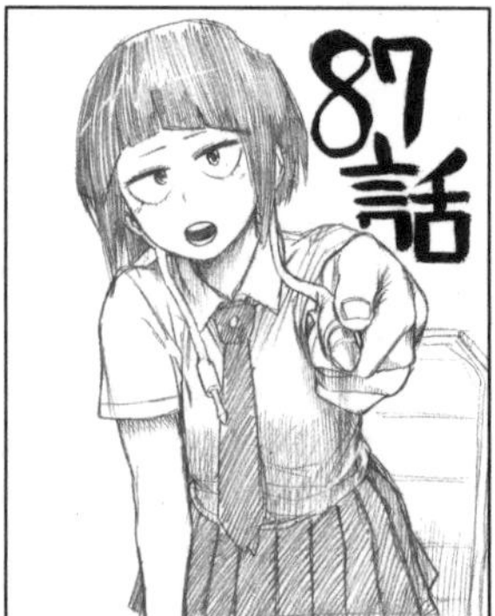
87話

April 18, 2016 ⬆ **Jiro's face is a little odd here.**

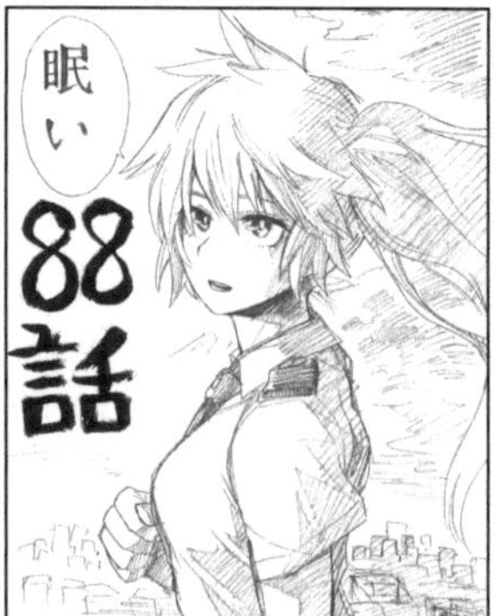
眠い
88話

April 25, 2016 ⬆ **She was supposed to be on a small hill, bathed by the sun's morning glow.**

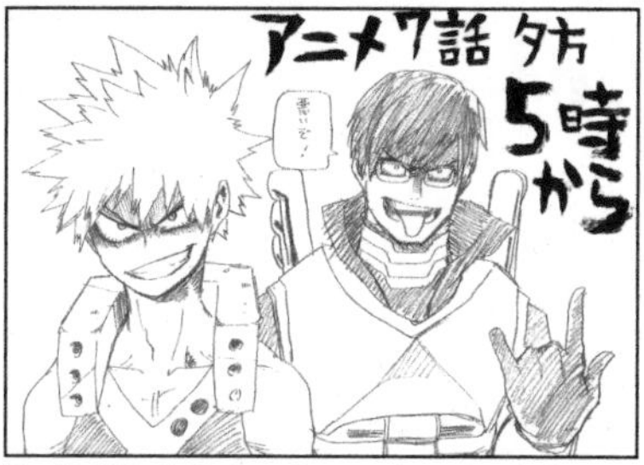
アニメ7話 夕方
5時
から

May 15, 2016 ⬆ **I try to make my anime-related ads somehow tie into the storyline.**

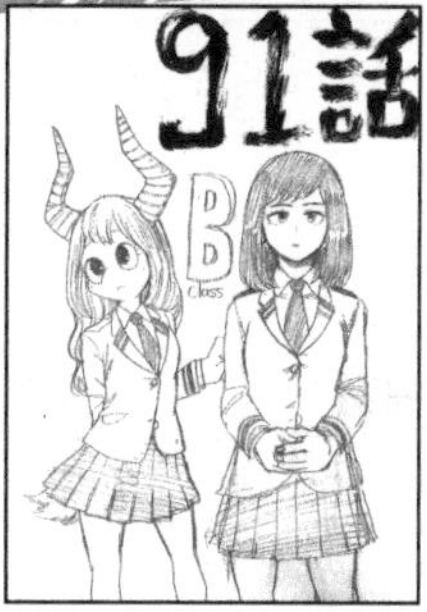
91話

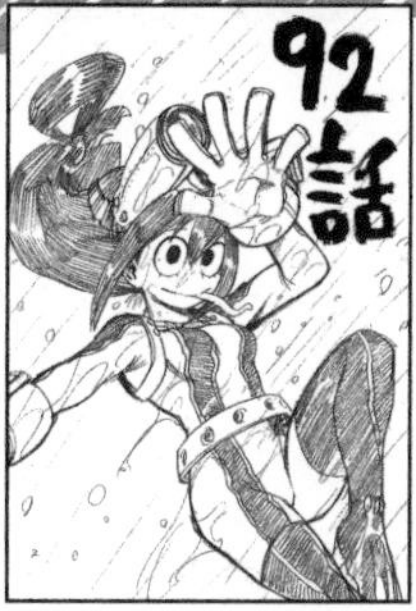
92
話

May 30, 2016 ⬆ **I used to do sketch ads on Jump release days, but not anymore.** ⬆ May 23, 2016

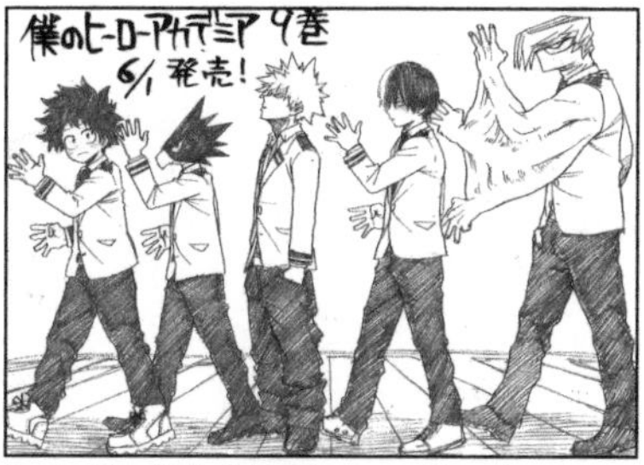
僕のヒーローアカデミア 9巻
6/1 発売!

June 3, 2016 ⬆ **The Bakugo bodyguard brigade.**

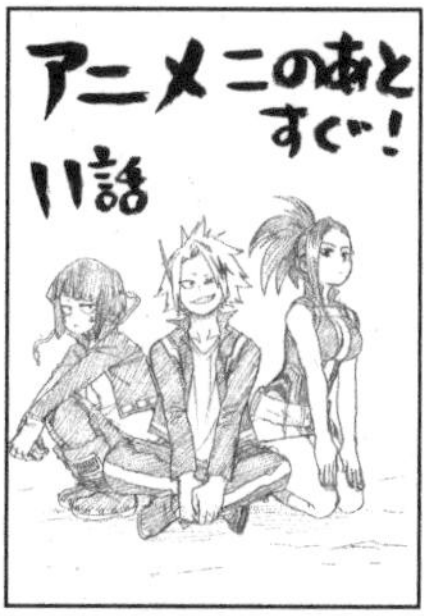
アニメこのあと
すぐ!
11話

June 12, 2016 ⬆ **During the U.S.J. story line.**

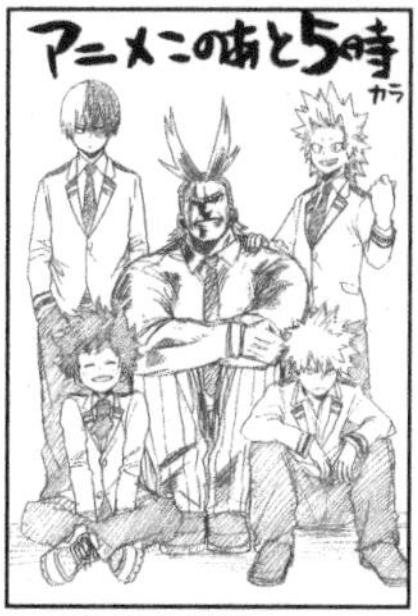
アニメこのあと5時
カラ

June 19, 2016 ⬆ **The group involved in the battle.**

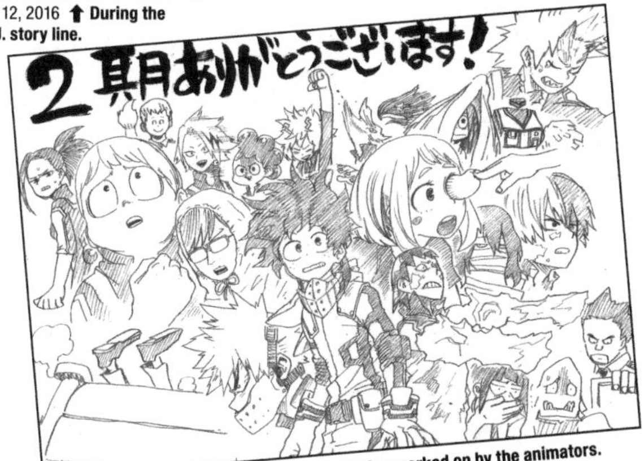
2期ありがとうございます!

April 26, 2016 ⬆ **All of these were scenes being worked on by the animators.**

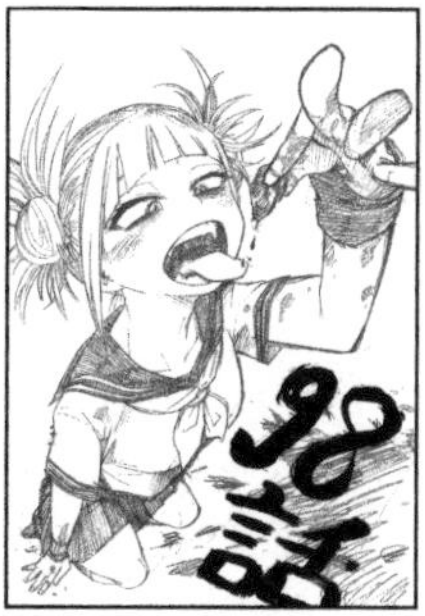
98
話

July 11, 2016 ⬆ **Gross.**

June 28, 2016 ⬇ **I like tousled hair like this.**

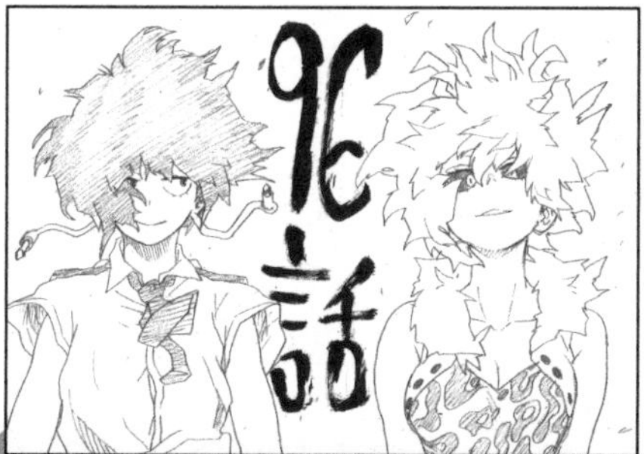
96
話

**ANIME SEASON 2— CONFIRMED!**

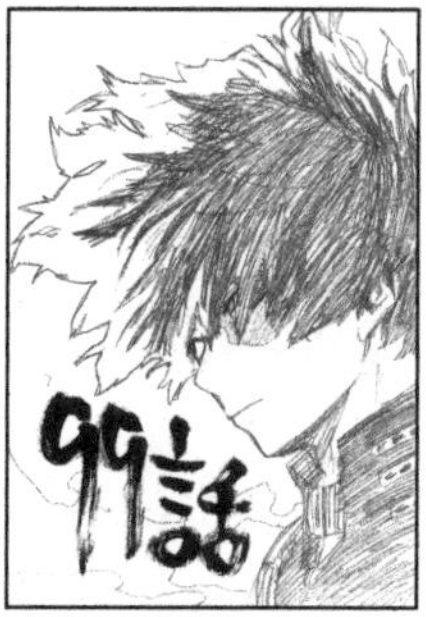
99話

July 16, 2016 ⬆ **More wind-tossed hair.**

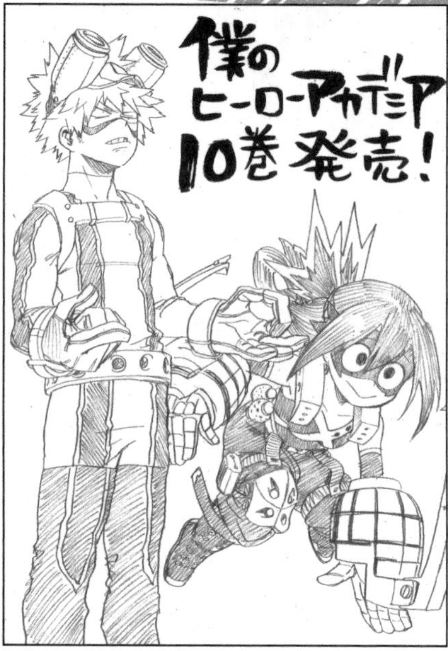
僕のヒーローアカデミア
10巻発売!

September 2, 2016 ⬆ **At this point, I started running out of ideas.**

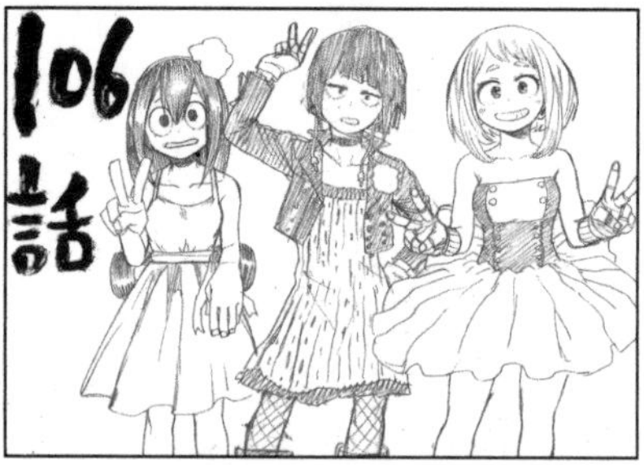
106話

September 13, 2016 ⬆ **I enjoy thinking up new outfits.**

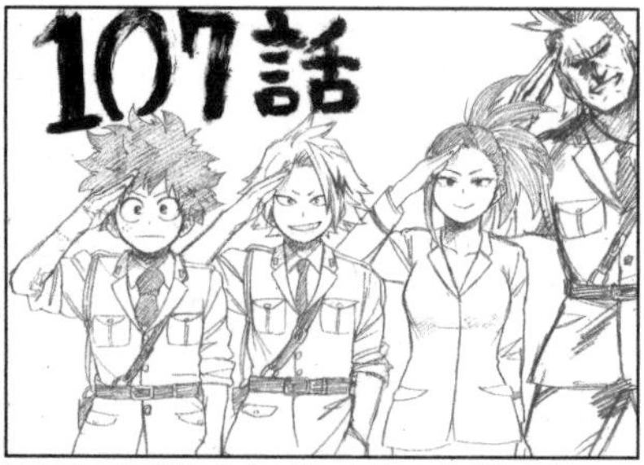
107話

September 17, 2016 ⬆ **To celebrate the end of *KochiKame*. Not sure why Kaminari is dead center.**

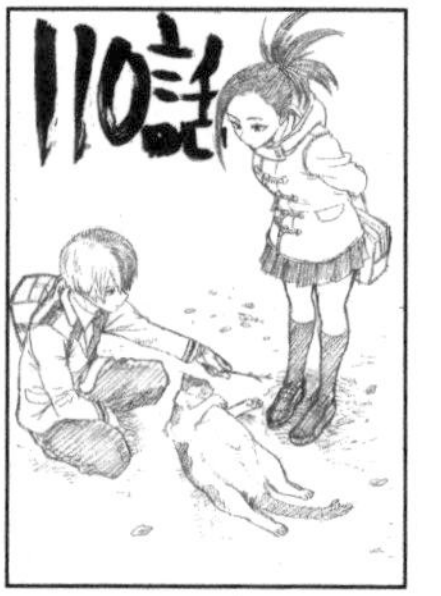
110話

October 11, 2016 ⬆ **That's actually my cat.**

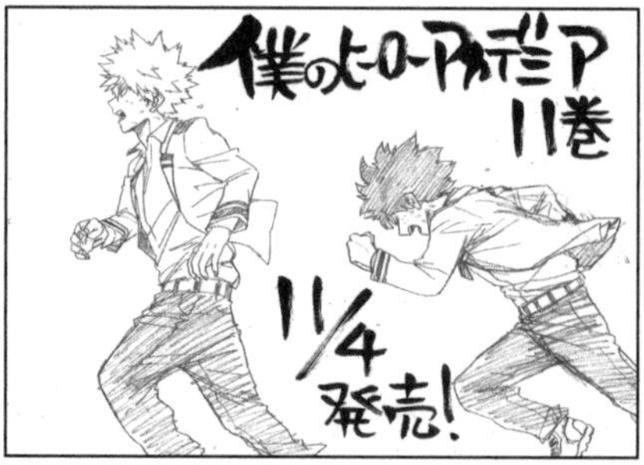
僕のヒーローアカデミア
11巻
11/4
発売!

November 4, 2016 ⬆ **I really like this sketch.**

February 14, 2017 ⬇ **Bubble Girl sure is cute.**

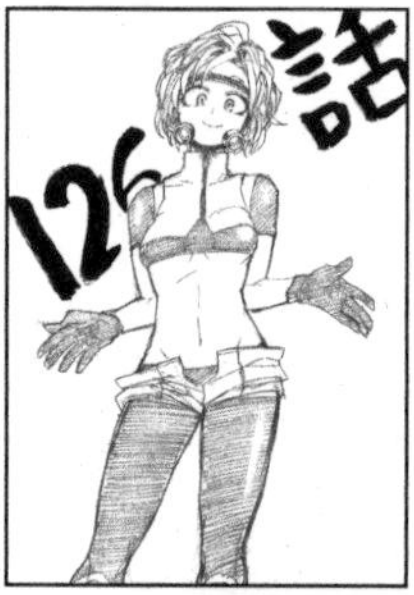
126話

March 25, 2017 ⬇ **I barely had any time to get this one done.**

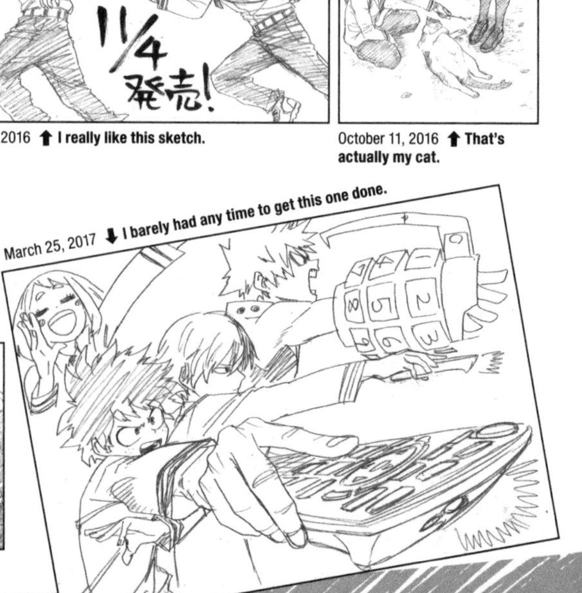

**ON TV!!**

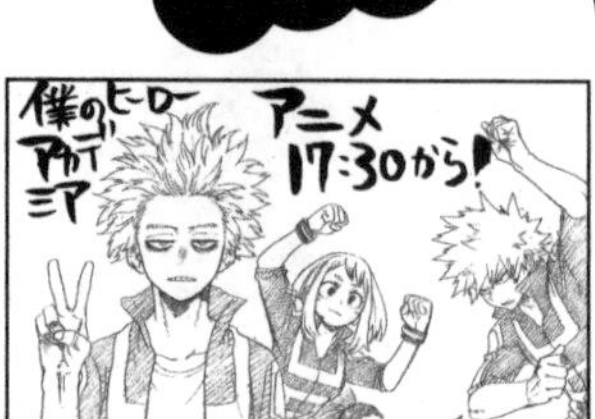
僕のヒーローアカデミア
アニメ
17:30から!

May 13, 2017 ⬆ **This is what you get when I can't think of anything.**

# CELEBRATING THREE WHOLE YEARS!!

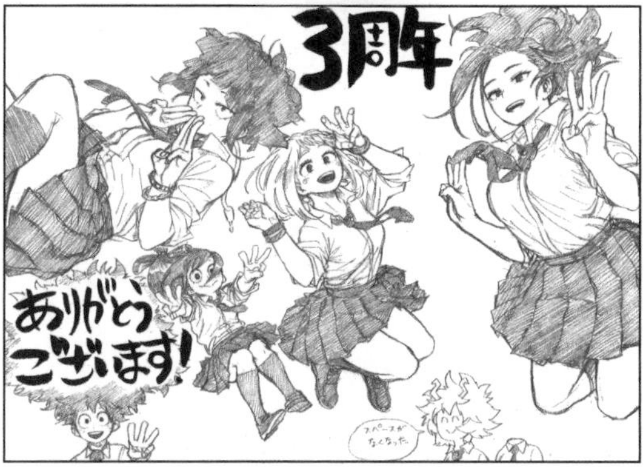
3周年
ありがとうございます!
スペースがなくなった

July 25, 2017 ⬆ **I wanted to draw the girls jumping around.**

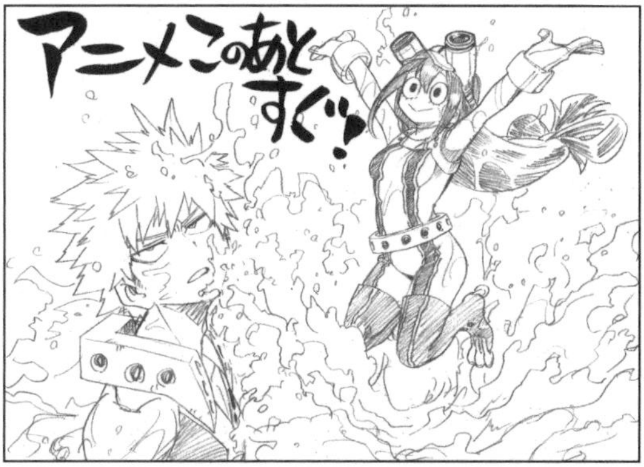
アニメこのあとすぐッ!

August 12, 2017 ⬆ **After drawing Tsuyu like that, I had so much space left over.**

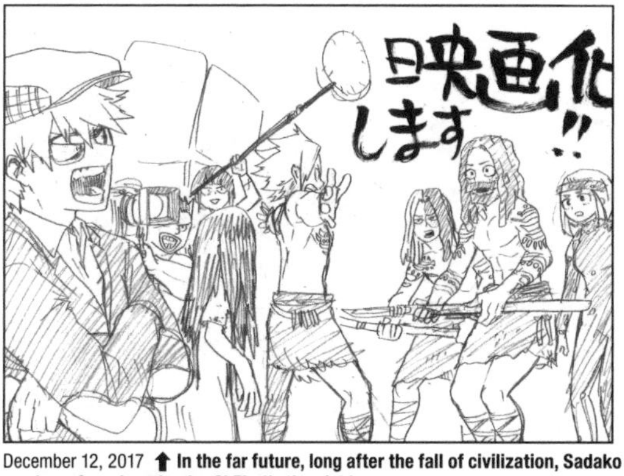
映画化します!!

December 12, 2017 ⬆ **In the far future, long after the fall of civilization, Sadako awakens from her slumber?! That's the plot here.**

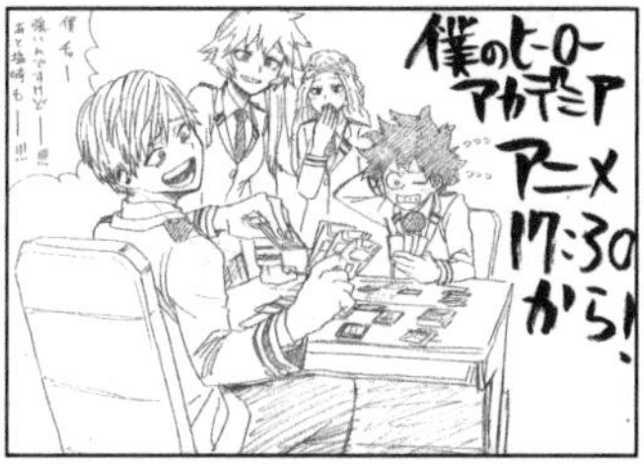
僕のヒーローアカデミア
アニメ
17:30から!

May 20, 2017 ⬆ **A card game. Fun, yeah?**

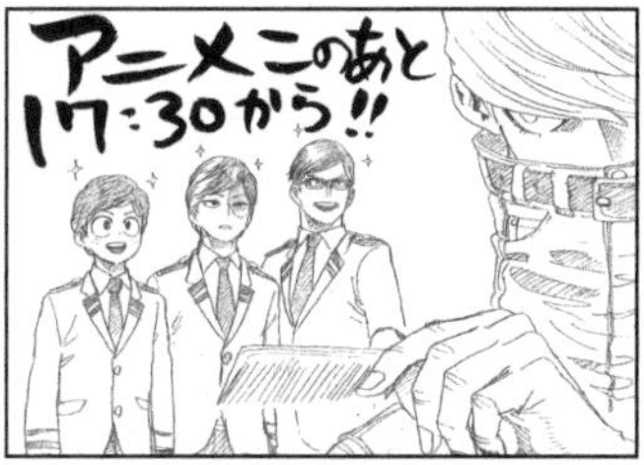
アニメこのあと
17:30から!!

July 22, 2017 ⬆ **I honestly wish I could've drawn the whole class.**

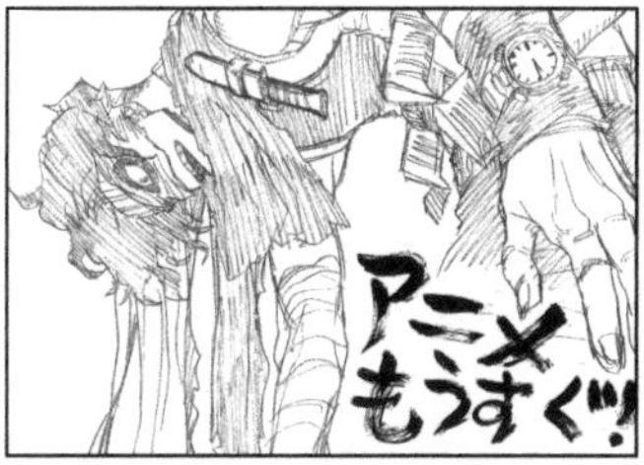
アニメ
もうすぐ!!

July 29, 2017 ⬆ **Honestly, any character would've worked for this composition.**

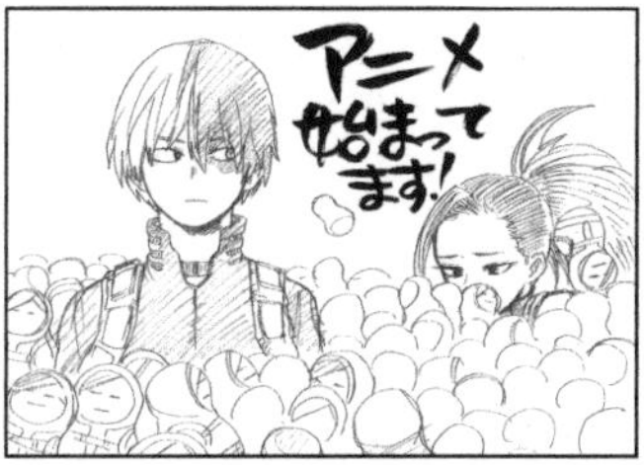
アニメ
始まってます!

September 9, 2017 ⬆ **I drew this one in a hurry.**

## A MOVIE! WOO-HOO!!

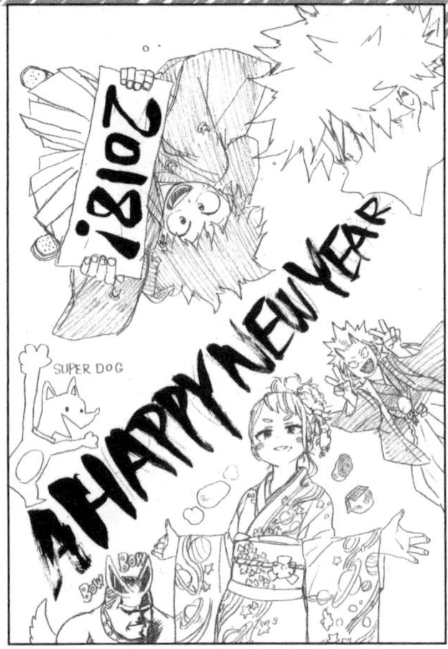
2018!
A HAPPY NEW YEAR
SUPER DOG
BOW
BOW
January 1, 2018 ⬆ **I was desperate to fill in all that blank space.**

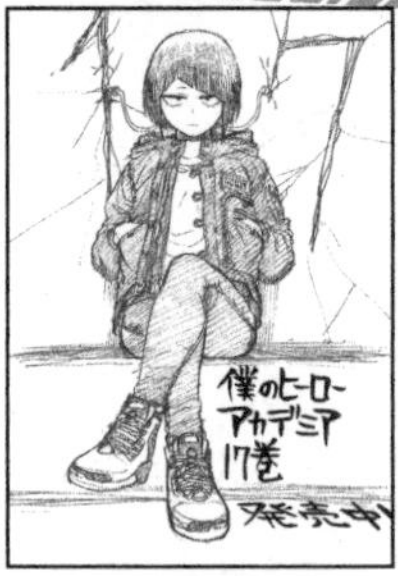
僕のヒーローアカデミア17巻
発売中
February 4, 2018 ⬆ **I wanted to draw shoes.**

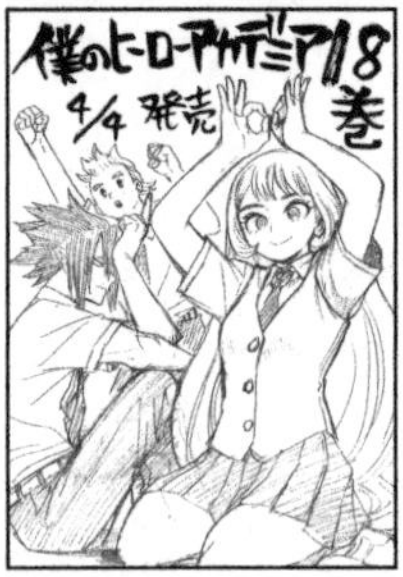
僕のヒーローアカデミア18巻
4/4 発売
April 4, 2018 ⬆ **I drew Nejire too big here.**

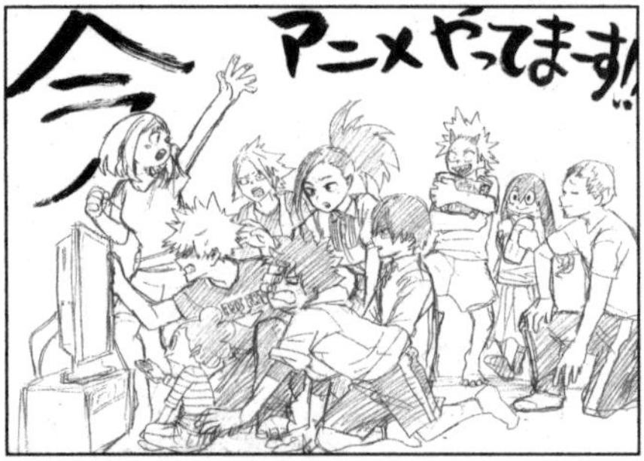
今アニメやってまーす!!
April 7, 2018 ⬆ **What a commotion.**

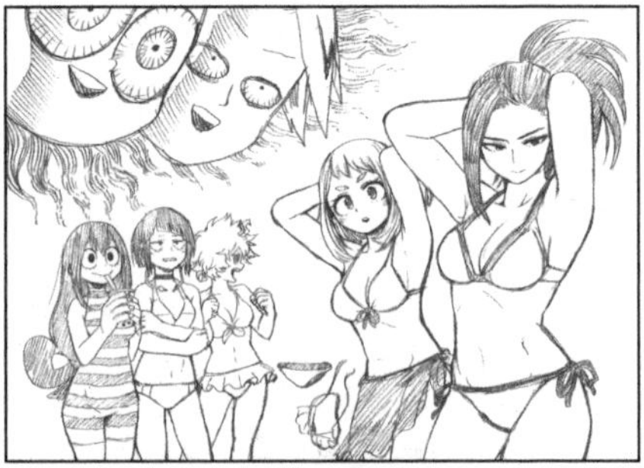
April 9, 2018 ⬆ **The swimsuits in the anime were A++.**

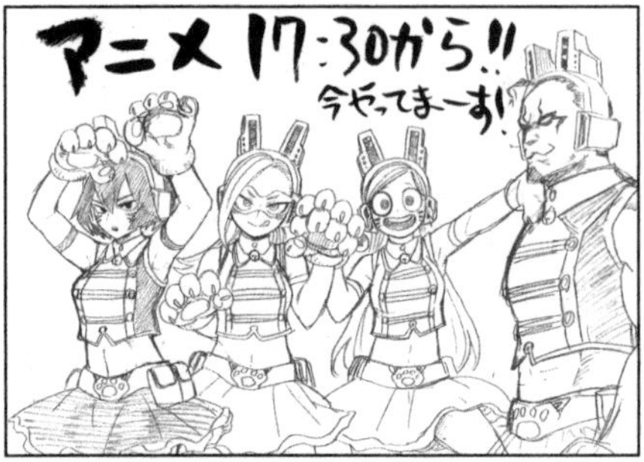
アニメ 17:30から!!
今やってまーす!
April 21, 2018 ⬆ **I like the Pussycats.**

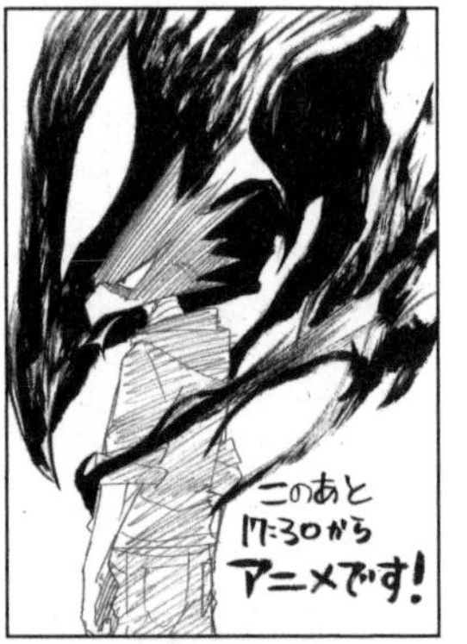
このあと
17:30から
アニメです!
May 12, 2018 ⬆ **Isn't he the coolest? Like, just the best.**

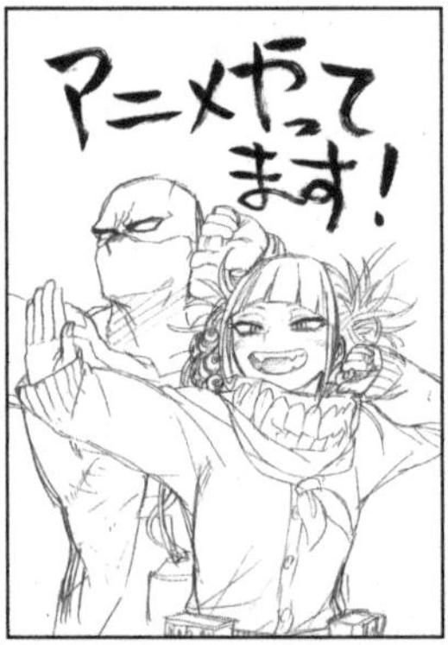
アニメやってます!
June 2, 2018 ⬆ **I didn't finish this before the episode started.**

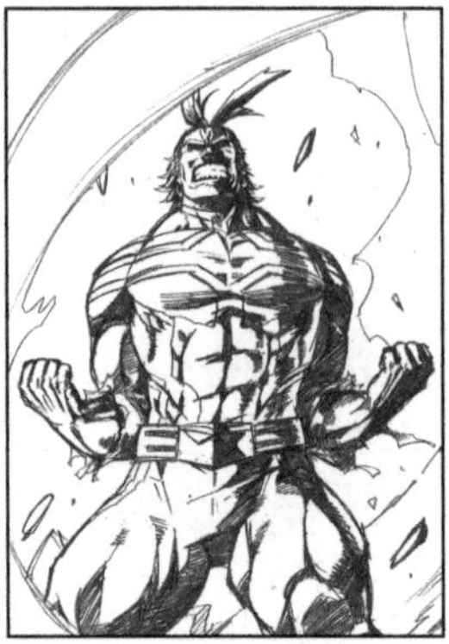
June 10, 2018 ⬆ **All Might is easy to draw with a pencil.**

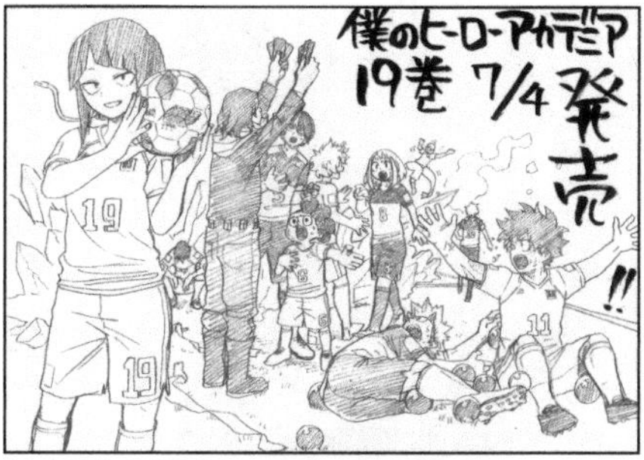
僕のヒーローアカデミア
19巻 7/4発売!!

July 4, 2018 ⬆ **This is because I was watching soccer.**

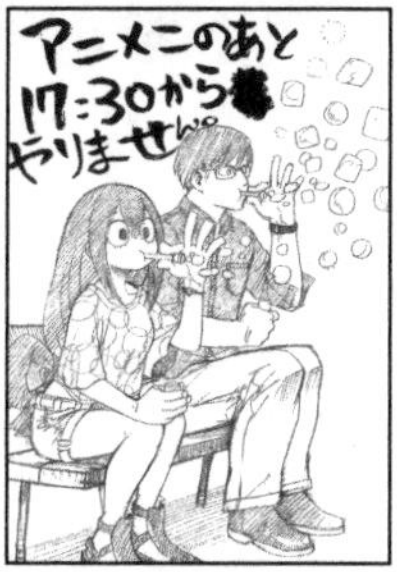
アニメこのあと
17:30から
やりません

July 7, 2018 ⬆ **The anime took a week off.**

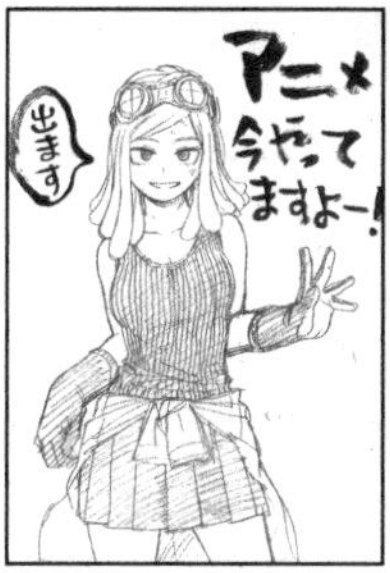
アニメ今やってますよー!
出ます

July 14, 2018 ⬆ **Hatsume.**

**CELEBRATING FOUR YEARS!!**

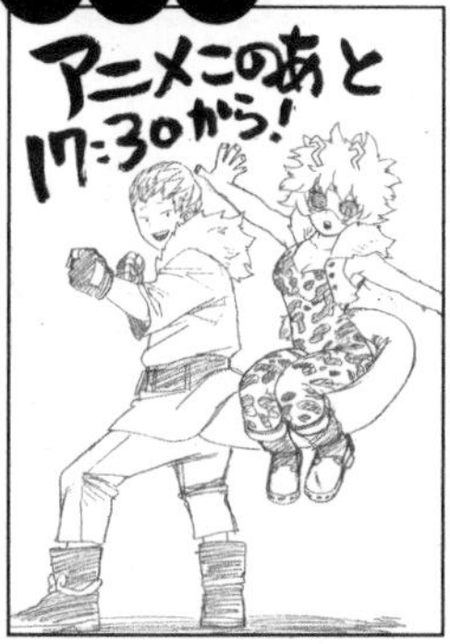
アニメこのあと17:30から!

July 28, 2018 ⬆ **I wanted to draw Ojiro's tail.**

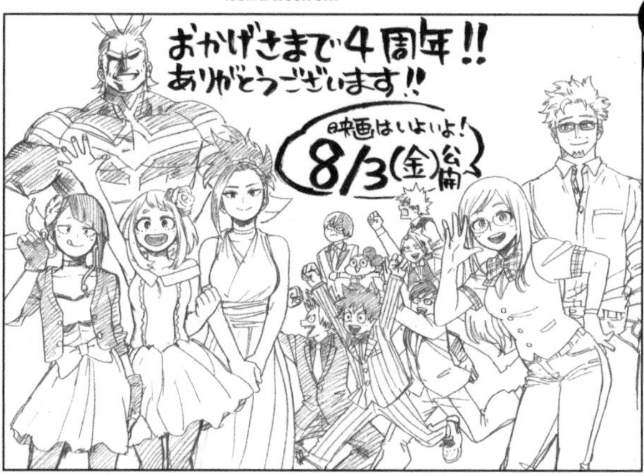
おかげさまで4周年!!
ありがとうございます!!
映画はいよいよ!
8/3(金)公開

July 31, 2018 ⬆ **The idea here was "The movie's coming out soon!"**

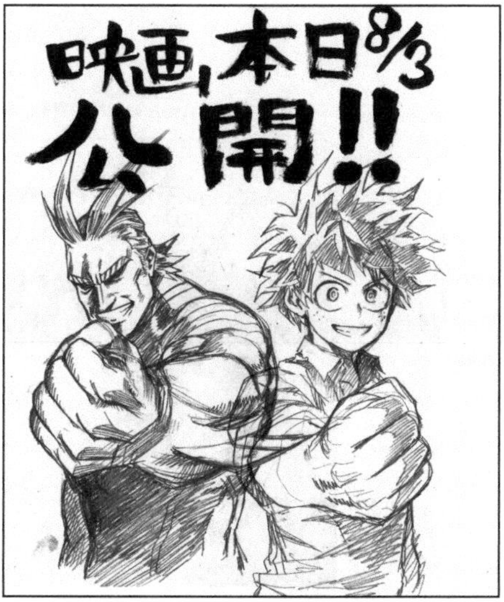
映画、本日8/3
公開!!

August 3, 2018 ⬆ **No messing around in this sketch.**

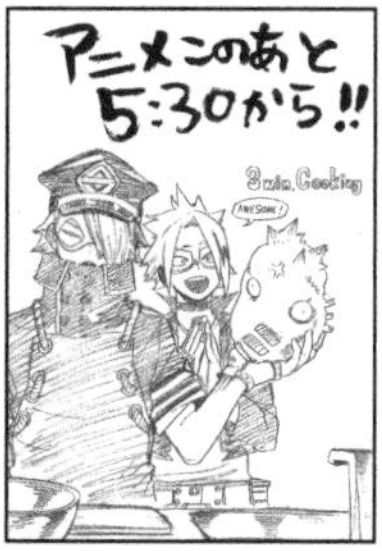
アニメこのあと
5:30から!!
3min. Cooking
AWESOME!

August 11, 2018 ⬆ **Meat senpai!!**

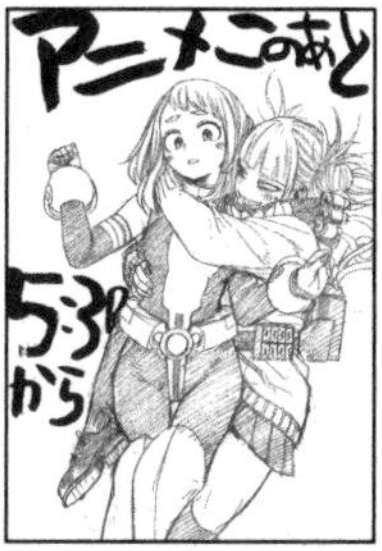
アニメこのあと
5:30から

August 18, 2018 ⬆ **Stuck on you.**

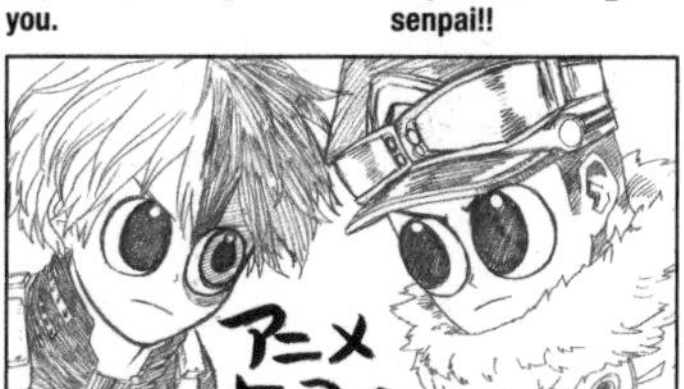
アニメ
5:30
から!!

September 1, 2018 ⬆ **Currently obsessed with this eye thing.**

## DIVING INTO SEASON 4!!

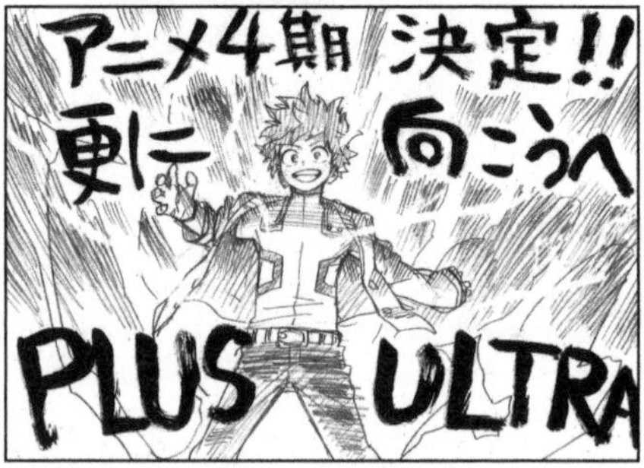
アニメ4期 決定!!
更に 向こうへ
PLUS ULTRA

September 29, 2018 ⬆ **This is just something I found myself wanting to draw.**

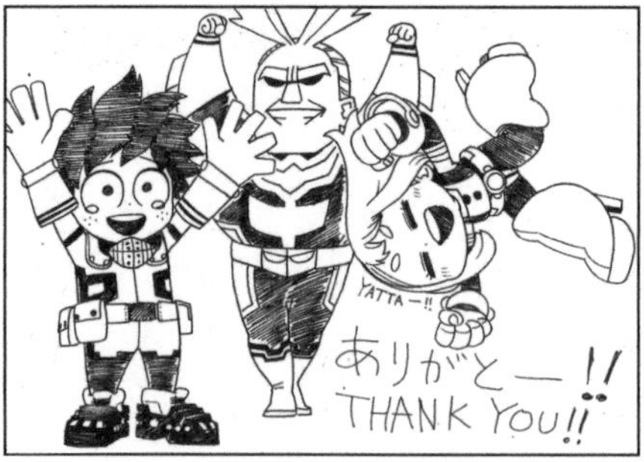
YATTA—!!
ありがとー!!
THANK YOU!!

November 21, 2018 ⬆ **I'm not great at drawing chibi characters.**

## DRAWING FOR NEW YEAR'S!!

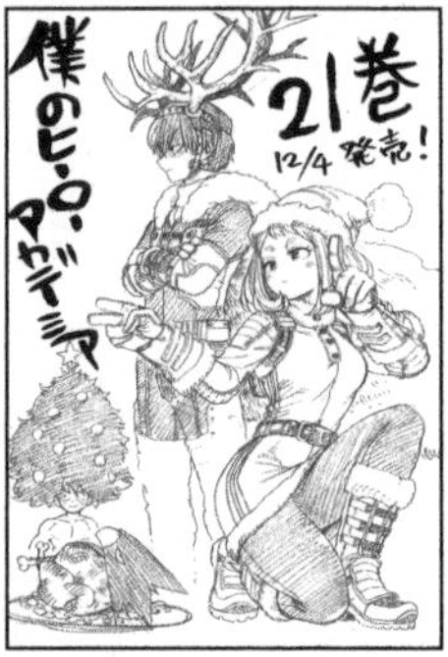
僕のヒーローアカデミア
21巻
12/4 発売!

December 4, 2018 ⬆ **When I have extra space, I draw unnecessary nonsense.**

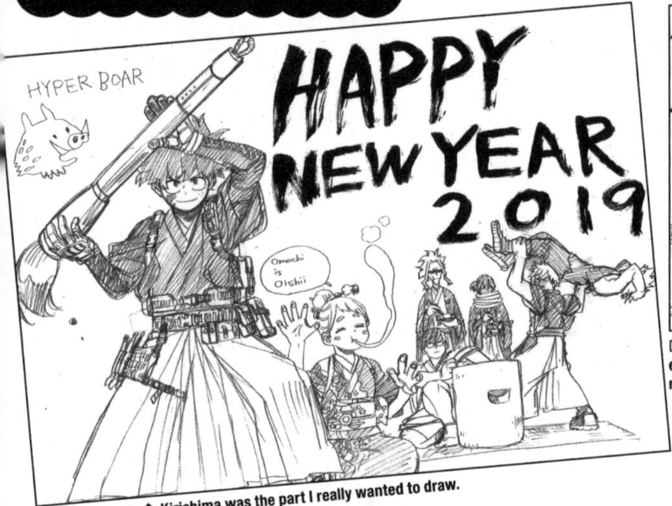
HYPER BOAR
HAPPY NEW YEAR 2019
Omochi is Oishii

January 2, 2019 ⬆ **Kirishima was the part I really wanted to draw.**

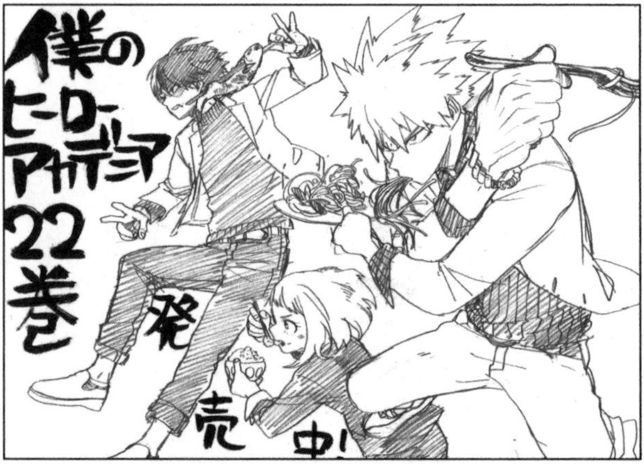
僕のヒーローアカデミア 22巻
発売中!

February 5, 2019 ⬆ **"I want them to be eating." This is how that turned out.**

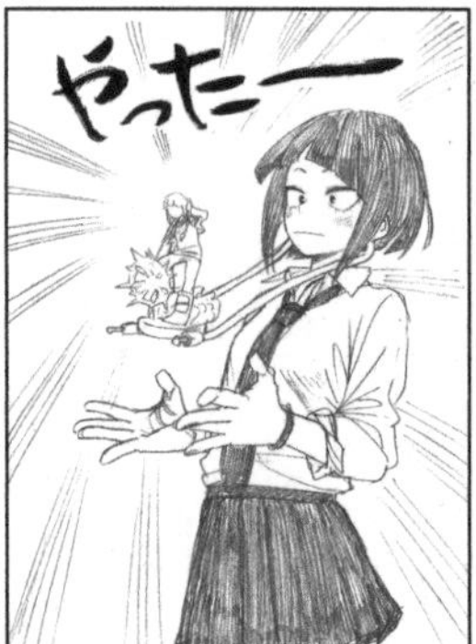
やったー

March 5, 2019 ⬆ **They made a figure of Jiro!**

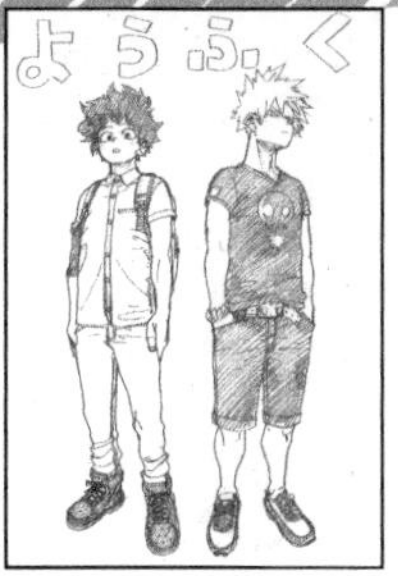

May 10, 2019 ⬆ **I suddenly got the urge to draw this.**

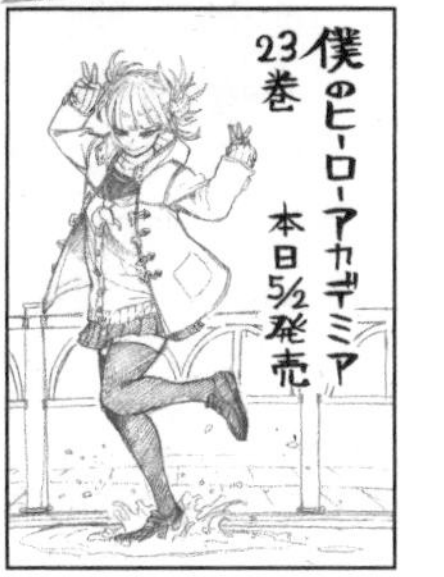
僕のヒーローアカデミア
23巻
本日5/2発売

May 2, 2019 ⬆ **Based on a high schooler hanging at a station.**

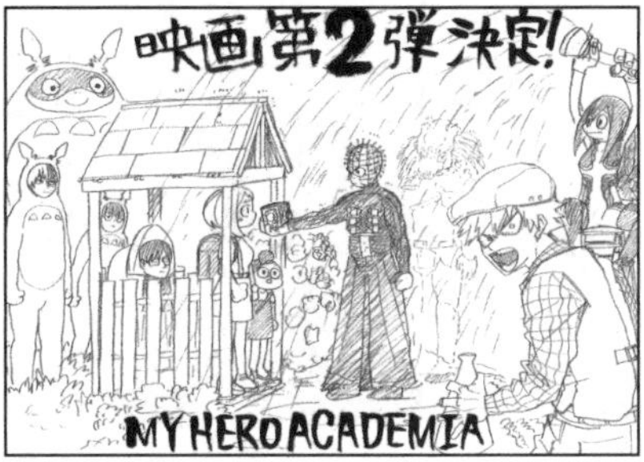
映画第2弾決定!
MY HERO ACADEMIA

March 24, 2019 ⬆ **What a jumbled-up crossover.**

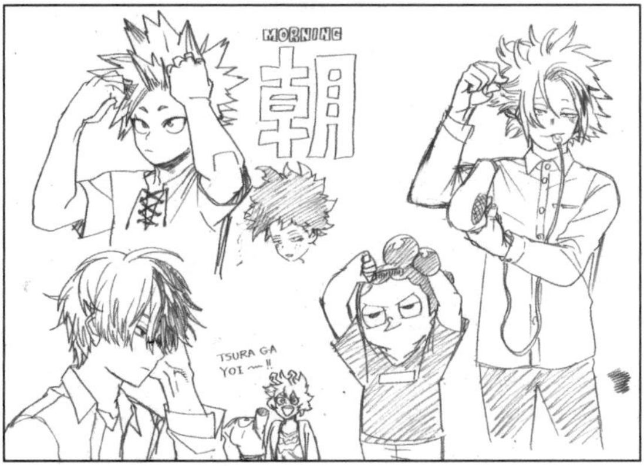
MORNING
朝
TSURA GA YOI~!!

May 10, 2019 ⬆ **Another sudden urge, since at the time I'd been drawing nothing but villains.**

June 10, 2019 ➡ **Rainy season ("Tsuyu" in Japanese) ➡ rain ➡ abandoned puppy ➡ barking ➡ Katsuki. That was the train of thought.**

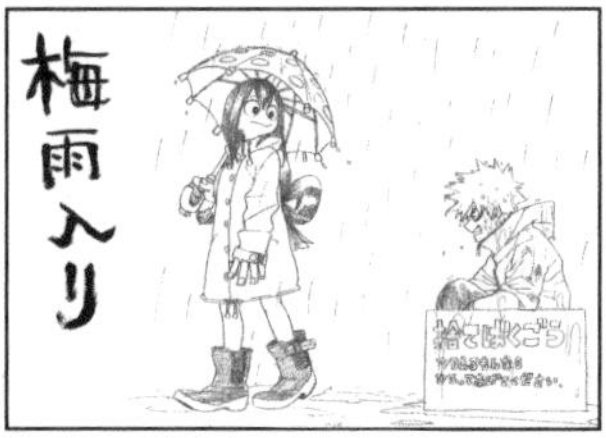
梅雨入り

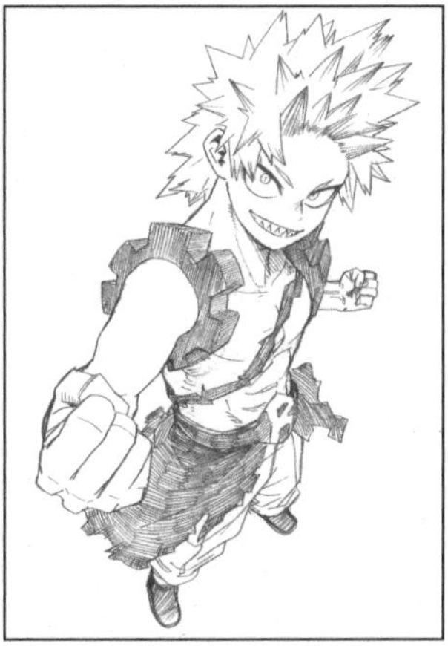

May 23, 2019 ⬆ **Looking slick, Kirishima!**

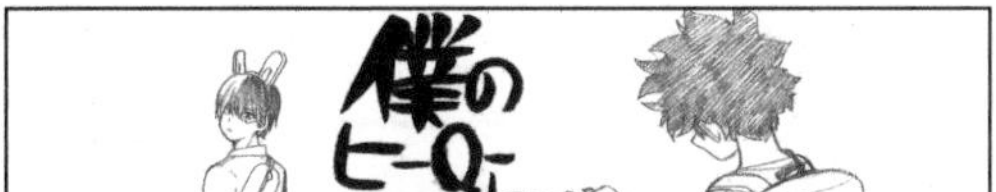
僕のヒーローアカデミア
24巻
8/2発売

August 2, 2019 ⬆ **I wanted to draw Deku in this pose. The other four are just there to fill the space.**

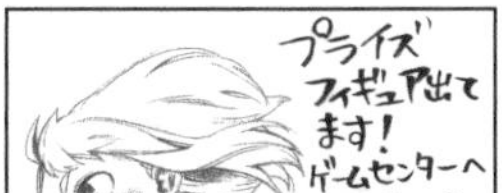
プライズフィギュア出てます!
ゲームセンターへGO!

July 23, 2019 ⬆ **I'd done "Deku reveals his costume under his uniform" before, so I wanted to do the same with a girl.**

# MY HERO ACADEMIA

# Glossary

**Here's a handy breakdown of 68 key terms and phrases that appear in the story. It's *MHA*'s first-ever glossary, to help you go even more Plus Ultra!!**

## A

**Athletic Field Gamma ◆** Training grounds made to resemble a dense industrial area, filled with complex structures and mazelike paths. One of U.A. High School's many facilities.

## B

**babies ◆** What Mei Hatsume calls the support items she invents. In her eyes, every single one is an "ultra super-duper cute baby."

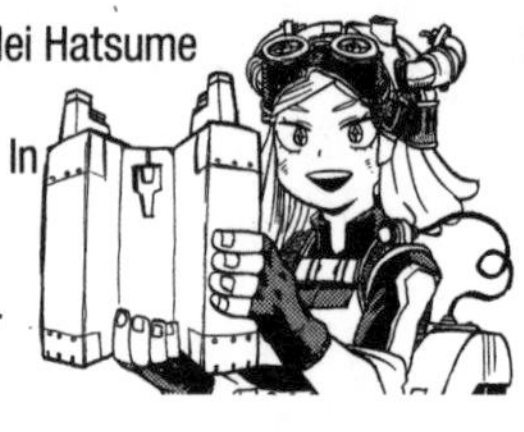

**Big Three ◆** The moniker for the three U.A. students with the highest grades. The title can change hands whenever grades are reevaluated, and students engage in friendly rivalries in pursuit of the throne.

## C

**cement gun ◆** Used by Gang Orca's sidekicks against the students during the provisional license exam. The guns fire quick-acting cement to lock the examinees in place.

**Center Exam ◆** U.A. students who wish to may elect to take this test in the hope of transferring to the Hero Course. However, it's a rigorous trial with an unforgiving rubric.

**costume revisions ◆** The government needs to approve any official revisions made to hero costumes. Minor modifications can be requested from design agencies, but more drastic changes require a lengthier application and order form.

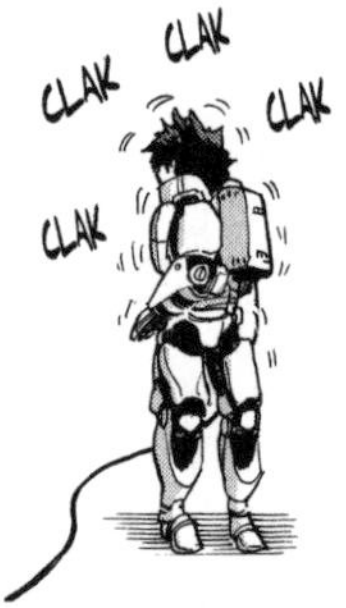
CLAK
CLAK
CLAK
CLAK

**costume subsidy** ◆ Under this fantastic system, students admitted to a Hero Course submit a Quirk registry form and bodily specifications before starting school so that a support company assigned to the school can create tailor-made costumes.

**Creature Rejection Clan** ◆ A cultish hate group that devotes itself to the ideology that those with body-altering Quirks ought to be discriminated against and harmed. Since bias against any given type of Quirk has all but vanished from society, modern-day C.R.C. members are seen as living fossils.

## D

**Deika City** ◆ A city in a rural area of Aichi Prefecture. Ninety percent of the city's population is made up of Liberation Army sleeper agents who support the Hearts and Mind Party and call Deika "the Liberation Sector."

**Detnerat** ◆ A lifestyle support company that rocketed to the top of the industry through its proprietary technologies and systems that meet the demands of an increasingly diverse consumer base. In recent years, the company has entered the hero support item industry in earnest.

**Donki Oote** ◆ Everything's crazy cheap there. This shop is an ally to common folk, as one can find everything from miscellaneous housewares to decorative goods at low, low prices. At Yaoyorozu's suggestion, the students who set out to rescue Bakugo bought disguises at Donki Oote so as to better blend into the nightlife crowd. For some reason, Yaoyorozu was 120 percent more excited about the rescue operation after visiting the store.

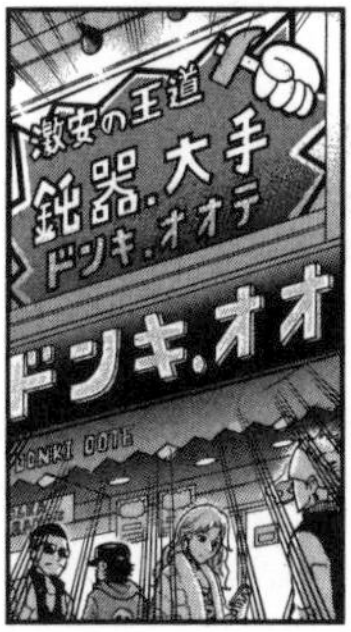
激安の王道
鈍器.大手
ドンキ.オオテ
ドンキ.オオ
DONKI OOTE

**Droid Technical High** ◆ A high school with an infamous reputation and a student body consisting mostly of delinquents. It's located in Kirishima's hometown.

## F

**Feel Good Inc.** ◆ A software developer and distributor that specializes in systems management for businesses. It boasts a considerable share of the market.

**fourth generation** ◆ Refers to the fourth generation since Quirks became the norm in society. All Might and Midoriya's parents are members of this generation.

## H

**"Hero Analysis for My Future" notebooks** ◆ Notes taken since Midoriya was young, meant to be useful for his future career as a hero. As of year three in middle school, he was up to notebook number 13. The sight of him furiously scribbling notes is unsettling to Midoriya's classmates.

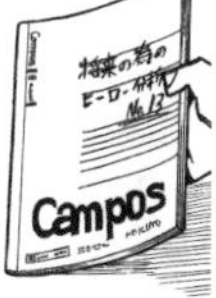
No.13
Campos

**Hero Billboard Chart Japan** ◆ These numbered rankings for active heroes take into account incident resolution rate, societal contributions, and public approval ratings. Revised rankings are announced twice per year, and the public is always heavily invested.

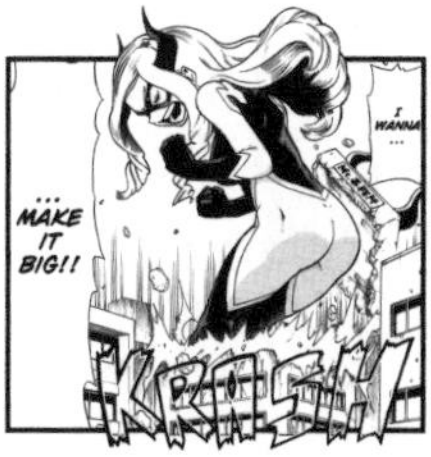
...MAKE IT BIG!!
KRASH!

**hero deduction ◆** An aspect of the tax code that allows heroes to deduct job-related expenses and damages incurred on the job.

**hero name ◆** Also known as a code name, this self-given moniker is meant to symbolize and emphasize a hero's unshakable convictions.

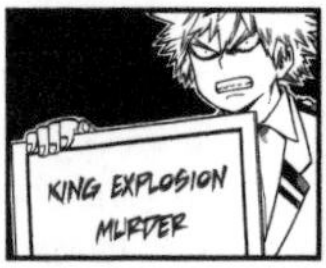
KING EXPLOSION MURDER

**Hero Network ◆** Abbreviated as H.N., this national network allows one to view hero news, check Quirk data, and submit requests for assistance. Only licensed pro heroes can use these services.

**hero-saturated society ◆** Years of hero activity and the presence of the Safety Commission brought about a period of peace that has seen heroism fortified, all while villainy statistics are on a downward trend. The result is a society saturated with heroes, where the general public has come to expect speedy rescues and quick disposal of villains on demand.

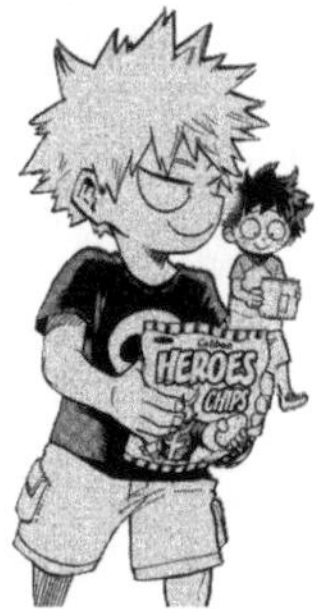
HEROES
CHIPS

**Heroes Chips ◆** Popular with children, this long-standing snack item includes one hero trading card in every bag. Bakugo and Midoriya both received an All Might card at the same time once, and the latter has held on to that treasure ever since.

**Heroes Public Safety Commission ◆** The government agency responsible for managing heroes in a society where peace, law, and order are upheld by said heroes. The commission handles a wide range of administrative functions, such as issuing hero licenses, compiling and presenting the billboard chart rankings, managing public relations, and even conducting intelligence assessments.

**Hosu City ◆** A city located to the west of Tokyo where Stain attacked Ingenium and other heroes in the name of his warped goals.

**H.U.C. ◆** "Help Us Company." This organization of professional "rescuees" offers training exercises. Through practical effects and acting, the rescuees help rescuers perfect the craft. H.U.C. employs people of all ages.

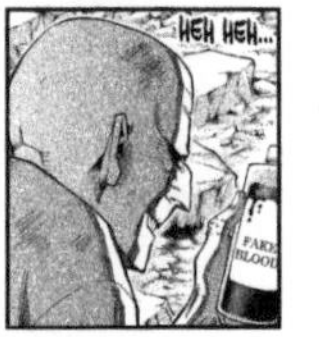
HEH HEH...

## I

***Idiot's Guide to Teaching* ◆** A book purchased by All Might, given his role as a new teacher at U.A. High. It's sure to make him a world-class educator in no time! ...Or maybe not.

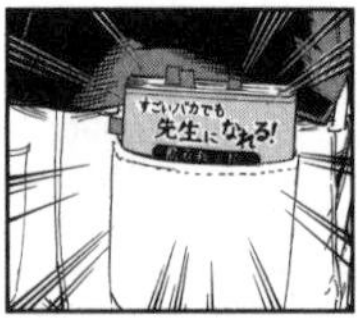
すごいバカでも
先生になれる!

**internship ◆** Training meant to give students the experience of real hero work in the field. Students who receive offers from agencies can choose where to go. Those without offers take into account their strengths and specialties before applying to agencies that have preexisting relationships with the school.

## K

**Kamino Nightmare ◆** All For One and a pack of Nomu foiled a raid on the hideout of the league. Though All For One was arrested, half of Kamino Ward suffered immense damage, many pro heroes were injured, and All Might retired. This night came to be known as the Kamino Nightmare.

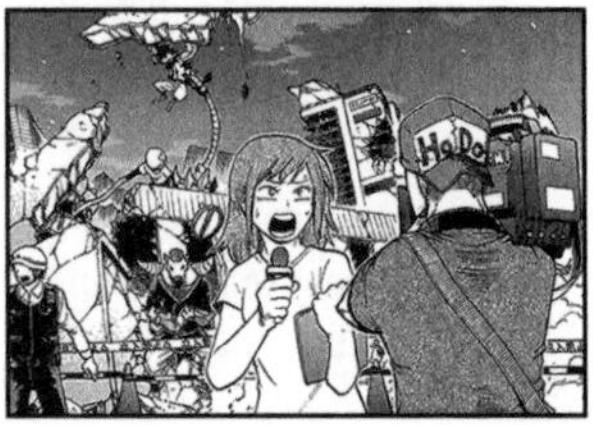

**Kiyashi Ward Shopping Mall** ◆ The mall boasting the greatest number of shops within the prefecture. The wide range of shopping options appeal to everyone from teens to seniors, and the architecture itself is slick, fresh, and cutting-edge.

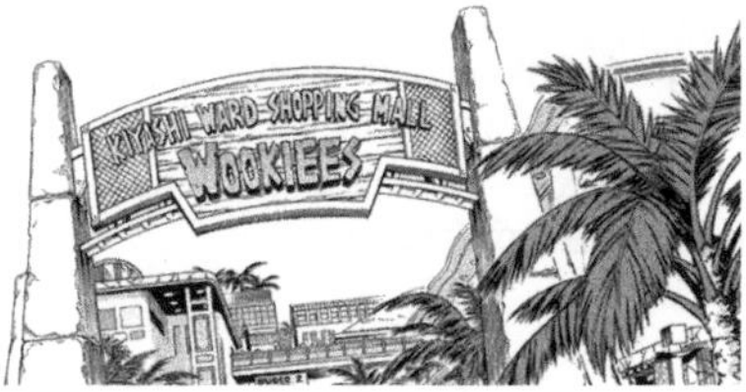
KIYASHI WARD SHOPPING MALL
WOOKIEES

## L

**League of Villains** ◆ A criminal group made up of a few elites (led by Tomura Shigaraki) who seek to destroy order. Responsible for the Kamino Nightmare, the attack in Fukuoka City, and others.

**license** ◆ Before a company can manufacture, modify, or sell support items and costumes designed with specific Quirks in mind, it must hold a special license from the government.

## M

**Masegaki Elementary School** ◆ The school that provided the children whose hearts needed to be won over by Bakugo, Todoroki, and the other provisional license supplement course trainees. That one teacher is cute.

***Meta Liberation War*** ◆ The autobiography of Chikara Yotsubashi, a.k.a. Destro, meant to pass his principles to future generations. Destro sought liberation from suppression and founded the Metahuman Liberation Army to carry out terrorist attacks, but his movement was subjugated and the man himself was put in prison. It was there that he wrote this book.

## N

**National Takoba Arena** ◆ The stadium where Midoriya and the rest of class 1-A tested for their provisional hero licenses. With its various fields, this massive facility can host any number of sporting events and competitions.

**N.H.A.** ◆ A terrestrial basic broadcaster that reaches all of Japan. One of its particularly spirited female reporters (with a tendency to appear live on the scene) has a niche following among viewers.

## O

**Orudera Middle School** ◆ The public middle school attended by Midoriya and Bakugo. It was put in the spotlight when two of its graduates were admitted to the prestigious U.A. High School.

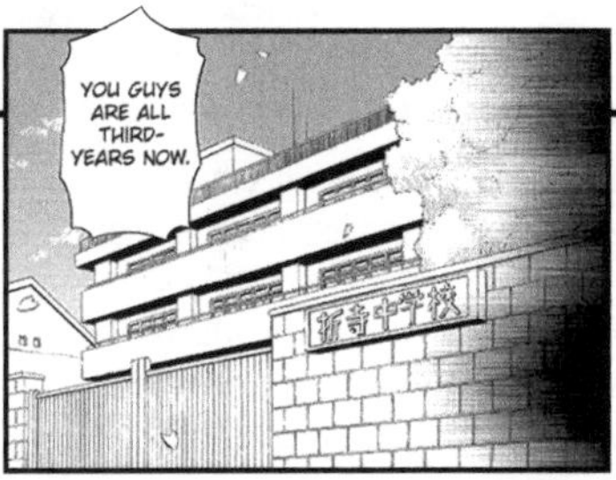
YOU GUYS ARE ALL THIRD-YEARS NOW.
折寺中学校

## P

**Pass the Test, American Dream Plan** ◆ A special training regimen put together by All Might to help Midoriya pass the U.A. Hero Course entrance exam. It was a rough schedule that assigned specific training exercises and meals and even designated a certain number of hours for sleeping.

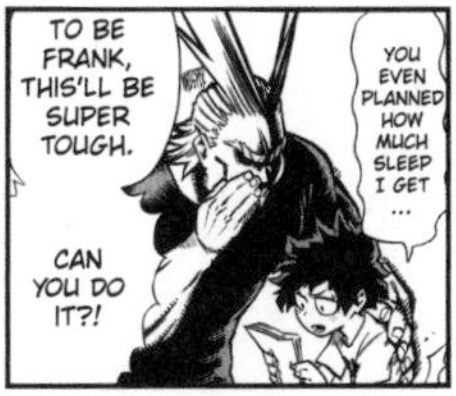
YOU EVEN PLANNED HOW MUCH SLEEP I GET ...
TO BE FRANK, THIS'LL BE SUPER TOUGH.
CAN YOU DO IT?!

**Plus Ultra** ◆ A phrase that literally means "further beyond," and one that expresses the notion that a hero must always be ready to smash through a dire situation and overcome barriers. Also, U.A.'s school motto.

**Pre-Upgrade Roki** ◆ Sero's name for the version of Todoroki from before the Sports Festival, when his heart was still encased in metaphorical ice.

**Prince of Nonsense** ◆ A quip lobbed by All Might (along with a chop to the shoulder) at Midoriya when the latter was acting particularly negative and overly serious. In a similar situation, All Might once said, "There's no one more dedicated to the world of nonsense than you, kid!!"

**pro hero agency** ◆ An office started by a licensed professional hero that can serve as base of operations and point of contact. Agencies can team up with each other, but each is still an independent business.

**provisional hero license** ◆ This limited license authorizes the holder to use their Quirk in a limited capacity during emergencies.

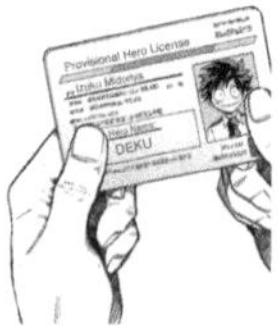

## Q

**Quirk** ◆ The plus-alpha elements within a standard body, or the supernatural phenomenon activated by those elements. "Quirk factors" refer to everything included in those plus-alpha elements.

***Quirks and Us*** ◆ An illustrated children's book published by Shoowaysha that promotes the theme "Let's not judge people by their Quirks." It received a widespread positive response.

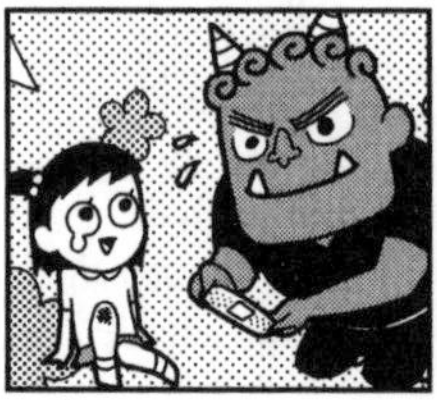

**Quirk aptitude tests** ◆ Unlike standard physical fitness tests, these tests permit students to use their Quirks so as to measure their maximum potential. By discerning what an individual student is capable of, the educator can determine the ideal way to teach said student.

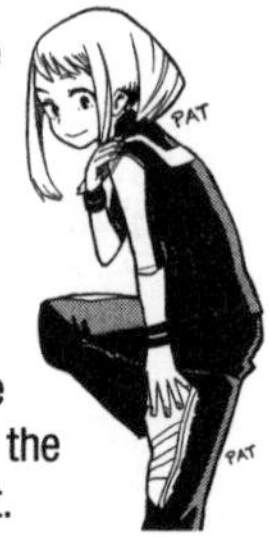
PAT
PAT

**Quirk marriage** ◆ An outdated, unethical practice in which a spouse is chosen and forced to wed for the sole purpose of passing on a strengthened version of one's own Quirk to one's offspring.

**Quirk singularity** ◆ As generations pass, Quirks blend and become more complex. The Quirk singularity is a theorized doomsday point at which Quirks will rampage out of control.

## R

**rational deception** ◆ Eraser Head prioritizes rationality in all things, and if that means inventing a fake rule or two to motivate his students to do their best, so be it.

## S

**scum of society** ◆ Tomura described All Might this way. "A tool for violence, made to keep us down! And violence only breeds more violence."

**Shie Hassaikai** ◆ Once a minor "respectable" yakuza group, this gang grew worse when Chisaki took power. Under him, Shie Hassaikai sought glory and to disrupt society by distributing illegal substances.

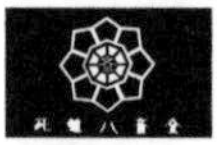

**Shiketsu High School** ◆ "U.A. by east, Shiketsu by west," as the saying goes. More so than U.A., this prestigious school emphasizes discipline in its educational methods. For example, the school administration picks the class presidents.

**Shoowaysha** ◆ A prominent publisher that puts out everything from picture books to dictionaries. The first-ever republishing of *Meta Liberation War* became an instant best seller, with over 100,000 copies sold.

**sidekick** ◆ A hero employed by a pro hero agency meant to broaden the agency's capabilities. The number of employed sidekicks can vary greatly, depending on a given agency's scale and specialties.

**Sludge Incident** ◆ Refers to the time in middle school when Bakugo had his body hijacked by a villain. It isn't a moment he looks back on fondly.

**S.L.E.** ◆ Short for "school-like event," and what class 1-A shouted in unison when Eraser Head announced the School Festival. The students are all too happy to participate in S.L.E.s that aren't just exams.

**Somei Middle School** ◆ The private middle school attended by Tenya Ida. Its students tend to be elites with sound character and conduct beyond reproach. That reputation is known nationwide.

**Symbol of Peace** ◆ The nickname All Might gained after years of using his overwhelming power to defeat villains, thereby reducing overall villainy statistics.

## T

**Takoba Municipal Beach Park** ◆ The location chosen by All Might for Midoriya's initial training. By clearing away the mountains of trash with his own muscles, Midoriya honed his body and became a suitable vessel.

**Tatoin Station** ◆ An NR Railways station in Midoriya's home area. The location made headlines as the spot where Mt. Lady knocked out a gigantified villain with her Canyon Cannon attack during her debut.

**Tartarus** ◆ An inescapable prison meant for the worst. Its prisoners are kept underground, beneath layers of security. The prison was named after the term in Greek mythology that describes both a region of the underworld as well as a primordial god. Stain the Hero Killer is locked up in Tartarus.

**Training Kitchen Lab** ◆ A nickname for Gymnasium Gamma at U.A., because Cementoss can "cook up" the ideal training structures, catered to each student.

## U

**U.A. High School** ◆ A competitive school that produced alums such as All Might and Endeavor. Only 1 in 300 applicants are accepted yearly through the entrance exam, for 36 slots.

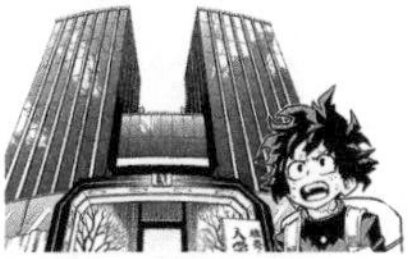

**U.A. Sports Festival** ◆ A massive event in Japan that has effectively taken the place of the Olympics. Notably, pros attend to scout future heroes.

**Unforeseen Simulation Joint** ◆ A facility designed by Thirteen that provides a variety of simulated disaster zones, perfect for mock training exercises.

## V

**Vanguard Action Squad** ◆ This villain squad attacked during the training camp. The powerful fighters accomplished their goal.

**villain insurance** ◆ A form of insurance that covers injuries and property damage caused by a villain or during the capture of one. It's a must-have for pro heroes.

**villain** ◆ Generic term for an individual who uses their Quirk to menace or otherwise damage Society.

**Vinegar Suicide Incident** ◆ All Might once saved a drowning boy whose Quirk turned water into vinegar. His eyes stung, producing a squinty smile. Serious fans tend to love this anecdote.

## W

**work study** ◆ Unlike the standard internship, a work study involves at least one month spent at a pro hero's agency, as well as monetary remuneration. Trainees are regarded as sidekicks and, in many cases, go on to receive full employment at the same agency.

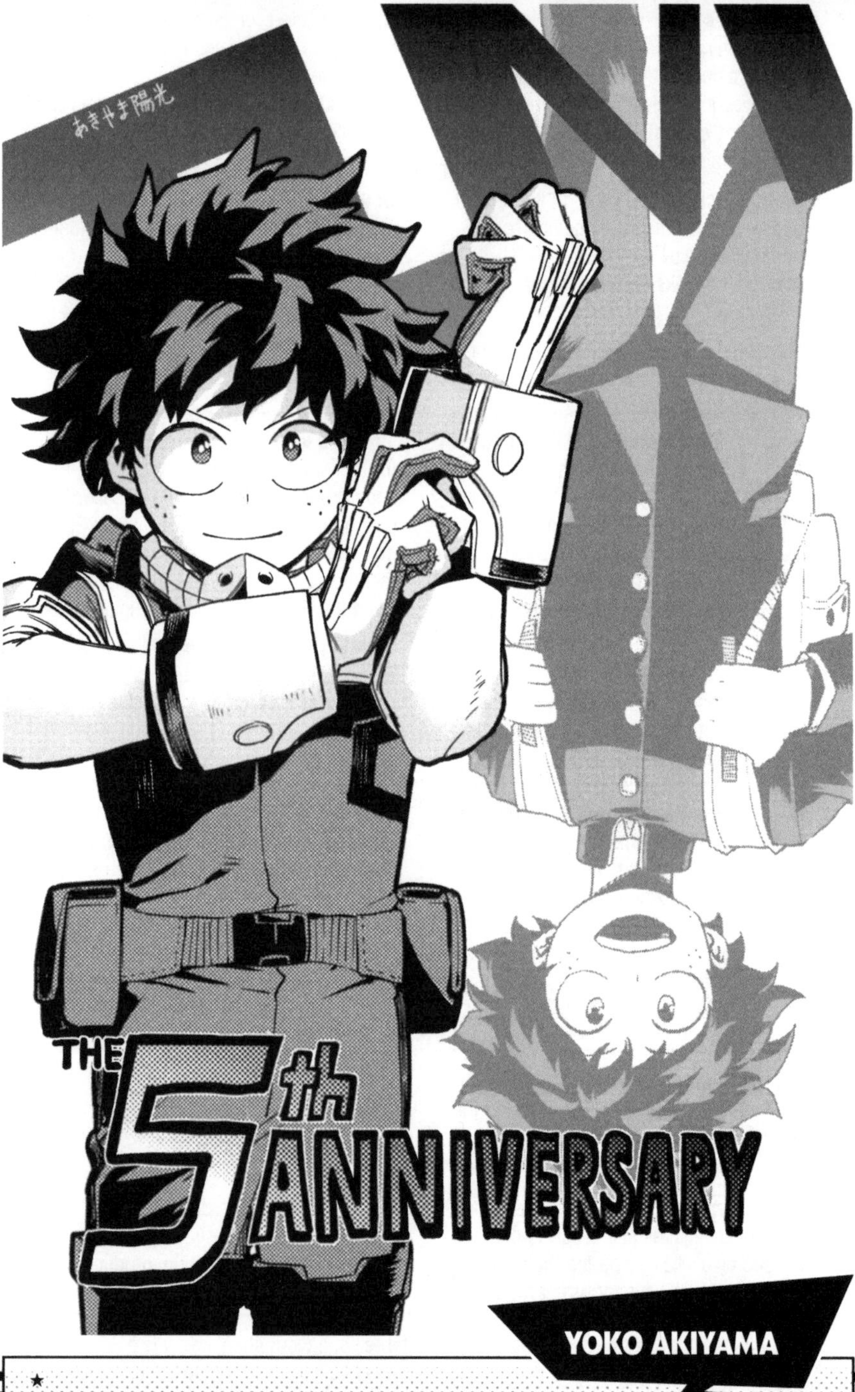
あきやま陽光
THE 5th ANNIVERSARY

YOKO AKIYAMA

★ Author of *My Hero Academia: Team-Up Missions!*

## ★ SPECIAL GUEST ★

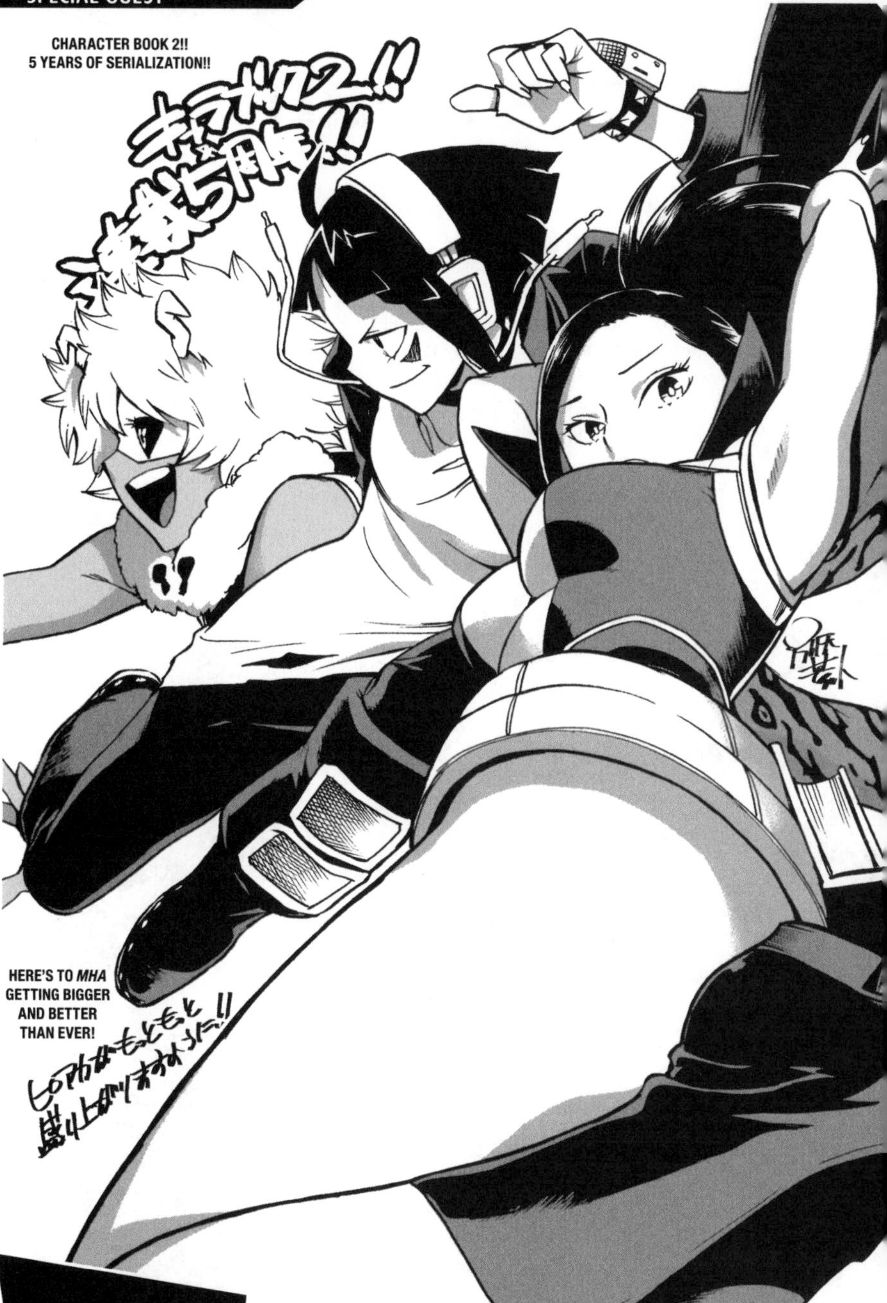
CHARACTER BOOK 2!!
5 YEARS OF SERIALIZATION!!
キャラブック2…!!
連載5周年…!!
HERE'S TO *MHA* GETTING BIGGER AND BETTER THAN EVER!
ヒロアカがもっともっと
盛り上がりますように!!

## BETTEN COURT

Artist of *My Hero Academia: Vigilantes!*

# AFTERWORD

...is what I'm calling this doodle space, I guess. I thought I'd use these two pages to draw something or other, but it grew into this stressful mess. Anyway, how'd you like the second character book? I never imagined I'd get to release two whole books like this one. The energy's gonna keep ramping up until the very end of the main series, so I hope you'll stick around to support Deku and friends!

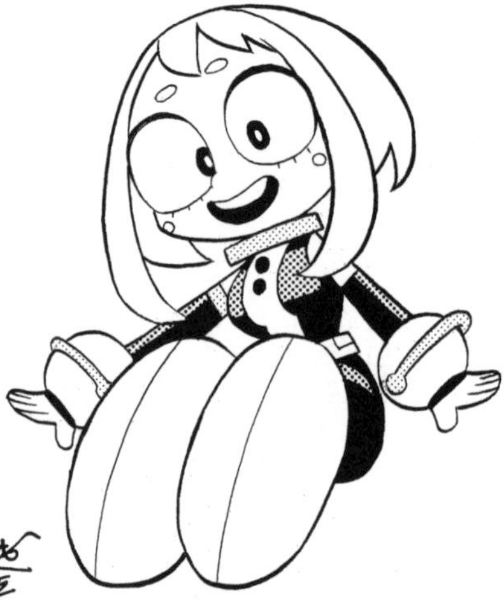

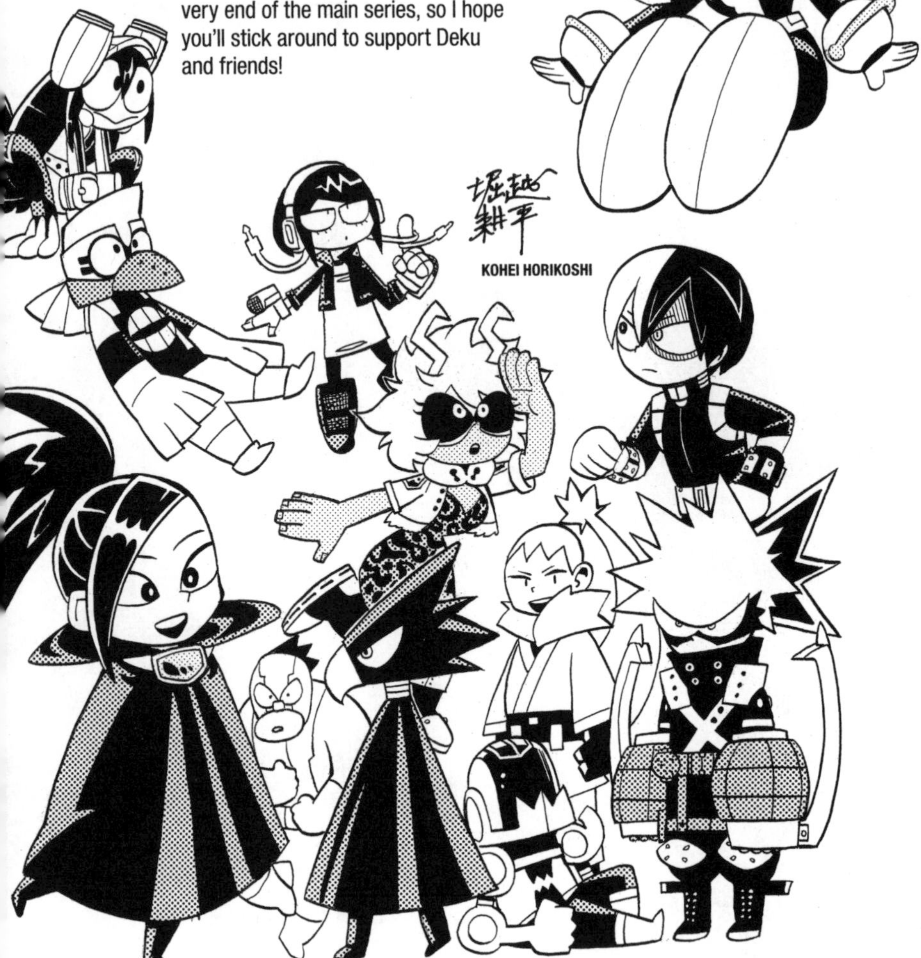

KOHEI HORIKOSHI

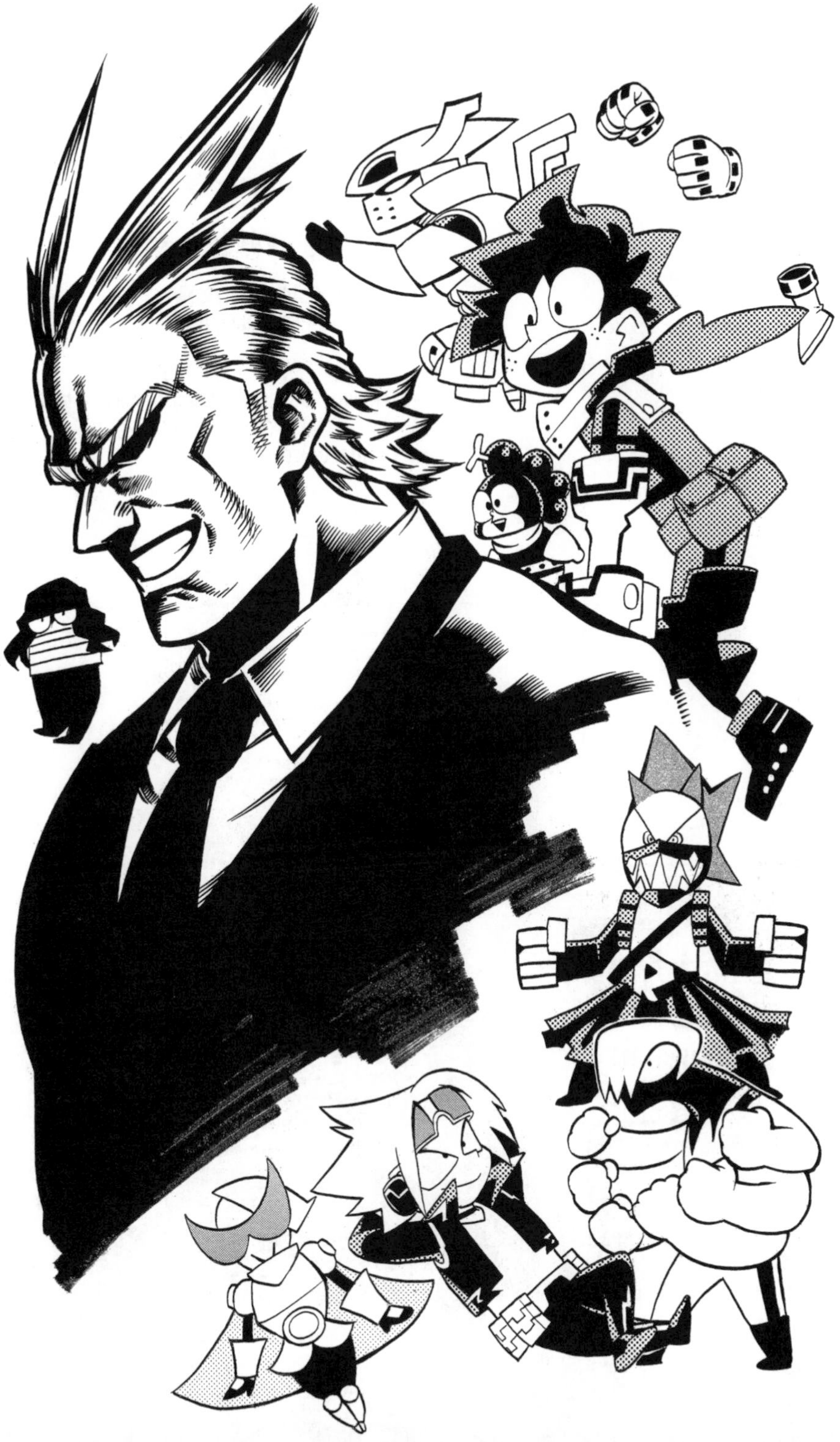

## KOHEI HORIKOSHI

I'm happy to say that the second character book is now available! You're probably thinking, "Dangit, Horikoshi—there are way too many characters to remember now!" If so, it's your lucky day, since this book was made just for you! Enjoy!

## Ultra Analysis

**SHONEN JUMP EDITION**
**BY KOHEI HORIKOSHI**

Translation FREE LANCER (CALEB COOK)
Design SHAZAWN! (SHAWN CARRICO) & KAMEN KAMMO (KAM LI)
Editorial Assistance LUKA BAZOOKA (LUKA M.)
Editor DAVID BANNER (DAVID BROTHERS)

BOKU NO HERO ACADEMIA OFFICIAL CHARACTER BOOK 2
ULTRA ANALYSIS © 2019 by Kohei Horikoshi
All rights reserved.
First published in Japan in 2019 by SHUEISHA Inc., Tokyo.
English translation rights arranged by SHUEISHA Inc.

The stories, characters, and incidents mentioned in this publication are entirely fictional.

No portion of this book may be reproduced or transmitted in any form or by any means without written permission from the copyright holders.

Printed in the U.S.A.

Published by VIZ Media, LLC
P.O. Box 77010
San Francisco, CA 94107

10 9 8 7 6 5 4 3 2 1
First printing, November 2021

viz.com

## ORIGINAL JAPANESE EDITION CREDITS

### DESIGNING HEROES

**Banana Grove Studio Co., Ltd.**
Captain★Aberyo (Ryoji Abe)
Nakato Crawler (Emi Nakano)
Doctor Strantsuji (Tomomi Tsuji)
Mighty Sor (Sota Ichimura)
Makkura Kamen (Mayumi Matsukura)
She Muraka (Kaori Shimura)
Shinty Thor (Shingo Maekawa)

### EDITING HEROES

Ryojhon (Ryosuke Yoritomi)
Best Parkanist (Keiichiro Takahashi)

## EDITORIAL HEROES

**Jump Comic Publishing Editorial Department**
Shinovenom (Shinobu Nakamura)

**Wedge Holdings Co., Ltd.**
Yaspider-Man (Yasutsugu Takahashi)
Deadumi (Chiho Uchiumi)
Green Tarrow (Seitaro Nakamura)
Nick Hory (Shota Horinouchi)
Nandeyanen (Teppei Odagiri)
Rocket & Flute (A & F)

### PRINTING HERO

Tony States (Tetsuro Matsuzawa)